AMERICAN SEA WRITING

A Literary Anthology

American Sea Writing

A Literary Anthology

Peter Neill, editor

Foreword by Nathaniel Philbrick

A SPECIAL PUBLICATION OF
THE LIBRARY OF AMERICA

Endpapers from the journal of William Wells Eldredge, January 1876.
Courtesy The Kendall Whaling Museum, Sharon, Mass.

 See page 667 for acknowledgments.

Published by The Library of America. Distributed to the trade in the United States by Penguin Putnam Inc. and in Canada by Penguin Books Canada, Ltd.

Library of Congress Cataloging-in-Publication Data:
American sea writing : a literary anthology / Peter Neill, editor.
p. cm.
ISBN 1–883011–83–3
1. Ocean—Literary collections. 2. Ocean travel—Literary collections.
3. Seafaring life—Literary collections. 4. American literature.
I. Neill, Peter, 1941–

PS509.S34 A44 2000
810.8′032162—dc21 00–039106

10 9 8 7 6 5 4 3 2 1

American Sea Writing
has been published with support from the
Susan and Elihu Rose Foundation.

Contents

Foreword

AMERICANS have always been fascinated by the notion of a frontier—that wild, often deadly space between them and the promise of a new beginning. We have come to think of the West as that archetypal hinterland, but as this collection of American sea writing vividly demonstrates, it all started with the Atlantic Ocean. Before European settlers or African slaves laid eyes on the New World, they were forced to traverse a storm-wracked wilderness that made the impenetrable forests of the American interior look like a welcoming refuge. "Being thus arived in a good harbor and brought safe to land," William Bradford writes of the Pilgrims' first landfall at Cape Cod, "they fell upon their knees and blessed the God of heaven, who had brought them over the vast and furious ocean, and delivered them from all the periles and miseries therof, againe to set their feete on the firme and stable earth, their proper elemente."

But for many, if not most, new arrivals, this was just the beginning of their engagement with the sea. Since overland travel remained slow and dangerous throughout the eighteenth century, sailing vessels were the preferred mode of transportation in what was still a string of coastal communities. This meant that the sea was what "the road" is today: the place where Americans spent an inordinate amount of time. Not surprisingly, the colonists developed an attitude toward the sea that was markedly different from what prevailed back in Europe. Instead of a chaotic and frightful void, the American sea was part highway, part workplace. In his *Letters from an American Farmer* (1782), Hector St. John Crèvecoeur exuberantly describes the Atlantic as a kind of watery plantation: "a boundless field . . . which will not be fully cultivated in many ages!"

Americans appear to have inherited this optimistic attitude from their native predecessors. Roger Williams has left us with a fascinating record of his experiences with the Narragansett during the first half of the seventeenth century. There are dangers aplenty in the waters surrounding Rhode Island, and yet a cheerful bravado characterizes the Narragansett's relationship with the sea. "It is wonderfull to see how they will venture in those Canoes," Williams writes, "and how (being oft overset as I have my selfe been with them) they will swim a mile, yea two or more safe to Land . . . and when sometimes in great danger I have questioned safety, they have said to me: Feare not, if we be overset I will carry you safe to Land." More than two hundred years later, the "naked Nantucketers" of Herman Melville's *Moby-Dick* (1851) would be animated by this same spirit of boisterous intrepidity: "The Nantucketer, he alone resides and riots on the sea; he alone in Bible language, goes down to it in ships. . . . *There* is his home; *there* lies his business, which a Noah's flood would not interrupt, though it overwhelmed all the millions in China."

By the beginning of the nineteenth century the American enthusiasm for the sea had become a point of national pride. During the War of 1812 the fledgling U.S. Navy won several significant, sometimes stunning victories against a superior English force. In the decades to come, American packet and merchant vessels established standards of performance and reliability with which the fleets of all other countries would be compared. Long before Melville chose to write about them in *Moby-Dick*, the American whalemen had spearheaded the advance into a scarcely charted territory larger than all the earth's land masses combined—the Pacific Ocean.

As critics such as Bert Bender, Thomas Philbrick, and Jonathan Raban have pointed out, the emergence of Romanticism in the early nineteenth century had a pivotal role in determining American attitudes toward the sea. The Romantics' exaltation of nature played to what were already the nation's strengths. America might not be as socially sophisticated as Europe, but it was bordered by the forest and the sea, and American attitudes toward these dual frontiers became almost interchangeable. In *The Pilot* (1824), the novel that first applied lessons learned from Byron and Sir Walter Scott to the maritime scene, James Fenimore Cooper creates the character of the coxswain Long Tom Coffin—a nautical Natty Bumppo equipped with the whaler's harpoon instead of the backwoodsman's rifle. In the climactic scene excerpted in this volume, Coffin demonstrates all the bravery, grace, and unaffected wisdom we have come to expect of a Romantic hero. The sea is ultimately a terrifying destroyer, but it also elicits a religious sense of ecstasy and wonder.

Richard Henry Dana would add an element of realism to the mix in *Two Years Before the Mast* (1840), providing an unvarnished look at the boredom and brutality of shipboard life, as well as an appreciation of its camaraderie. In the meantime, Edgar Allan Poe was moving in the opposite direction, plumbing the sea's depths for insights into the dark, often disturbed workings of the human imagination. However, Poe's creepy vision of an immense ghost ship in "MS. Found in a Bottle" (1833) is no more fantastic than first mate Owen Chase's true account of being attacked by an enraged sperm whale in the farthest reaches of the Pacific. Melville would incorporate Chase's 1821 narrative of the *Essex* disaster into *Moby-Dick*, a novel that draws on the Romantic sublimity of Cooper, the psychological complexity of Poe, and the congenial realism of Dana, among many other influences, to create the supreme masterpiece of American sea writing.

It is an underappreciated fact that Melville was not describing the American whale fishery as it existed at the time of *Moby-Dick*'s publication in 1851 but was looking back more than a decade to an earlier, more glorious era. And with good reason. By the midpoint of the nineteenth century, it was California, gold, and the winning of the West—not the sea—that captured the imagination of the American public. In the years to come the rise of steam power would make the sea a far less glamorous place. Instead of climbing the mast of a graceful square-rigger, a sailor found himself in the bowels of a noisy, smoke-belching metal tub.

These changes were accompanied by shifting intellectual currents as the inherent spirituality of Romanticism gave way to what were popularly interpreted to be the grim and godless theories of Charles Darwin and Herbert Spencer. The sea of Stephen Crane's "The Open Boat" (1898) is utterly indifferent to the noble faith of a Long Tom Coffin. "When it occurs to a man that nature does not regard him as important," Crane writes, "and that she feels she would not maim the universe by disposing of him, he at first wishes to throw bricks at the temple." And yet, even the skeptical reporter in Crane's story takes strength and reassurance from his companions in the lifeboat. Despite the monumental "unconcern of the universe," a sense of brotherhood connects these four castaways.

Instead of going out to sea, increasing numbers of Americans were content to watch the waves from shore. Walt Whitman writes eloquently of his musings on a beach: "that suggesting, dividing line, contact, junction, the solid marrying the liquid—that curious, luring something." Almost a hundred years later Rachel Carson applied a scientist's rigor to this tradition of American sea-gazing. For Carson, as it is for writers as different as Henry David Thoreau, Henry Beston, and Robert Lowell, the edges of the ocean are where the "spectacle of living creatures faced by the cosmic reality of their world is crystal clear."

Many of the writers who go to sea in the twentieth century do so because they want to, not because they have to; and more often than not, they elect to stay within sight of land. Whether it's Jack London discovering the excitement of surfing in Hawaii or John Steinbeck collecting marine specimens in the shallows of the Sea of Cortez, this is a sea for recreation and edification rather than work and transportation. Dangers exist, but the menace has been domesticated to the extent that E. B. White can write, "A small sailing craft is not only beautiful, it is seductive and full of strange promise and the hint of trouble."

For those writers who do venture beyond the safety of coastal harbors and bays—to conduct oceanographic research, fight a war, test their navigational abilities—the sea is still a hazardous wilderness. Humanity may have inflicted countless ecological disasters on the world's oceans, but as any commercial fisherman or tanker captain will tell you, man has not yet learned how to subdue the sea's often devastating power. "To riffle through a stack of the *Mariners*

Weather Log . . . " John McPhee writes in *Looking for a Ship* (1990), "is to develop a stop-action picture of casualties of the sea. . . . You see the Arctic Viking hit an iceberg off Labrador, the Panbali Kamara capsize off Sierra Leone, the Maria Ramos sink off southern Brazil. A ferry with a thousand passengers hits a freighter with a radioactive cargo and sinks her in a Channel fog. A cargo shifts in high winds and the Islamar Tercero goes down with twenty-six, somewhere south of the Canaries." This is just the beginning of an enumeration of modern-day nautical disasters that goes on for four pages.

Unlike the American West, which is now crisscrossed with superhighways and dotted with towns and cities, the oceans that bracket the nation will never be tamed. The storms that afflict the anonymous, largely foreign merchant seamen listed by McPhee are no different from the storm with which this collection begins: "Winds and Seas were as mad," William Strachey writes of the gale that shipwrecked him on Bermuda in 1609, "as fury and rage could make them." The formative power of this violent baptism is something few Americans today fully appreciate even though the sea remains steadfast in its ability to obliterate man's self-made world. Perhaps it is Melville who says it best: "[F]or ever and for ever, to the crack of doom, the sea will insult and murder him, and pulverize the stateliest, stiffest frigate he can make; nevertheless, by the continual repetition of these very impressions, man has lost that sense of the full awfulness of the sea which aboriginally belongs to it."

Anyone interested in reclaiming an appreciation of this ancient and enduring awe—an awe that was once an essential part of the American experience—should read this book.

Nathaniel Philbrick
Egan Institute of Maritime Studies
Nantucket, Massachusetts

Introduction

"By vast odds," wrote Herman Melville in *Moby-Dick*, "the most terrific of all mortal disasters have immemorially and indiscriminately befallen tens and hundreds of thousands of those who have gone upon the waters. . . . Panting and snorting like a mad battle steed that has lost its rider, the masterless ocean overruns the globe." Those harsh and timeless observations are echoed from first to last in the anthology you hold in your hands: from William Strachey's 1609 letter describing the storm in which a ship bearing colonists to the New World was wrecked to John McPhee's catalogue of contemporary catastrophes at sea: "Somewhere, any time, someone is getting it." The peculiar power of sea writing, in any era, has much to do with its unflinching acknowledgment of ultimate human powerlessness. A note of urgency, a keen sense of how provisional any momentary calm can be underlies even the simplest entry in a ship's log.

By the same token, sea writing is immersed in everything we can muster to make up for that powerlessness, from the most intricate technical mastery to sheer endurance. The ever-present dangers of the sea give added zest to other aspects of maritime life that figure in these pages: the pleasures of seagoing camaraderie, the transient beauties of light and weather, the astonishments of exploration both above and below the waves, the meditations spurred by silence and vast unbroken space.

The sea has no national identity, and it is legitimate to ask what American sea writing, as against any other kind, might be. This book answers that question by following American interaction with the sea from voyages of settlement in the early seventeenth century to the opening of new scientific vistas on underwater life at the end of the twentieth. The range of experience covered—the slave trade, voyages of exploration in the Pacific and to Antarctica, the evolution of whaling, naval engagements from the War of 1812 to World War II, the social life on the great ocean liners, the perspectives opened by modern oceanography, the fate of commercial fishing in the face of ecological degradation—demonstrates how central the sea has been to American life.

This is a literary anthology, and many of our greatest writers are represented here, from Cooper, Irving, Dana, and of course Melville, to such latter-day seafarers as Stephen Crane, Jack London, Eugene O'Neill, and Langston Hughes. There is a maritime current in American verse that runs from Longfellow and Whitman to Hart Crane and Elizabeth Bishop, of which we indicate only a few high points. But many of the most memorable voices in this collection are not those of celebrated writers but of people whose lives brought them firsthand impressions of the sea: settlers and sailors, captains and captains' wives, whalers and naval commanders, diplomats and fishermen. There are moments of extraordinary violence and extraordinary beauty. John Ledyard witnesses the violent death of Captain Cook; Owen Chase reports on the moment when the *Essex* gave way to the head-on attack of an enormous whale; Celia Thaxter, a lighthouse keeper's daughter, hauntingly describes the seascape that was her entire childhood world.

No single anthology can do more than suggest the diversity of America's sea writing. Many of the accounts included here form part of longer works that deserve to be read in their entirety. Because of the difficulty of adequately representing novels through excerpts, many significant and enthralling examples of maritime fiction are not represented: to name only a few, James Gould Cozzens' *S.S. San Pedro*, Herman Wouk's *The Caine Mutiny*, John Casey's *Spartina*, Peter Matthiessen's *Far Tortuga*, Robert Stone's *Outerbridge Reach*. It is my hope that what we have chosen to include will whet readers' appetites for this neglected area of American writing, and by extension deepen their curiosity about a crucial aspect of American experience. If we have paid a great deal of attention to the history and legends of the American West, we have tended to underappreciate the *other* wide open spaces that shaped our history.

To read these pieces in sequence is to experience a slow

historic change, the mapping of undiscovered islands, the emergence of America as a commercial and naval power, the inexorable alterations in old technologies and old ways of life. At the same time, there are constants: the rigors of seamanship, the working rhythms and rituals of ships, the brute presence of water and weather. The sea is finally as much a character in these pages as any of the travelers moving upon its surface, and it is the intimate knowledge of the sea—in all its dangers and wonders—that gives this body of writing its unique and enduring fascination.

PETER NEILL

William Strachey

On June 2, 1609, William Strachey (1572–1621)—a member of the minor gentry and sometime poet—set sail on the Sea Venture, *the flagship of a fleet of nine vessels carrying 600 colonists to Jamestown in Virginia. It was almost a year before he reached his destination: blown off course in a storm, the* Sea Venture *was wrecked on one of the islands of Bermuda. A longboat sent ahead to Jamestown for help was lost. Strachey and his party (including Sir Thomas Gates, governor of Jamestown colony 1611–1614), built two new vessels with salvaged timbers and local cedar.*

Strachey's elegant and moving account of his ordeal, addressed to an unknown Lady, soon reached London; among its readers was William Shakespeare, who drew from it in 1611 as he wrote The Tempest.

from *A True Reportory of the Wrack and Redemption of Sir Thomas Gates, Knight*

For four and twenty hours the storm, in a restless tumult, had blown so exceedingly, as we could not apprehend in our imaginations any possibility of greater violence. Yet did wee still find it not only more terrible, but more constant, fury added to fury, and one storm urging a second more outrageous than the former; whether it so wrought upon our fears, or indeed met with new forces. Sometimes strikes in our Ship amongst women, and passengers, not used to such hurly and discomforts, made us look one upon the other with troubled hearts, and panting bosoms. Our clamors drowned in the winds, and the winds in thunder. Prayers might well be in the heart and lips, but drowned in the outcries of the Officers; nothing heard that could give comfort, nothing seen that might encourage hope. It is impossible for me, had I the voice of *Stentor*, and expression of as many tongues as his throat of voices, to express the outcries and miseries, not languishing, but wasting his spirits, and art constant to his own principles, but not prevailing.

Our sails wound up lay without their use, and if at any time we bore but a Hollocke, or half forecourse, to guide her before the Sea, six and sometimes eight men were not enough to hold the whipstaffe in the steerage, and the tiller below in the Gunner room, by which may be imagined the strength of the storm, in which the Sea swelled above the Clouds, and gave battle unto heaven. It could not be said to rain; the waters like whole Rivers did flood in the air. And this I did still observe: that whereas upon the Land, when a storm hath poured itself forth once in drifts of rain, the wind as beaten down, and vanquished therewith, not long after endures; here the glut of water (as if throttling the wind ere while) was no sooner a little emptied and qualified, but instantly the winds (as having gotten their mouths now free, and at liberty) spoke more loud, and grew more tumultuous, and malignant.

What shall I say? Winds and Seas were as mad, as fury and rage could make them. For mine own part, I had been in some storms before, as well upon the coast of *Barbary* and *Algeere*, in the *Levant*, and once more distressful in the *Adriatique* gulf, in a bottom of Candy. So as I may well say, *Ego quid sit ater Adriæ noui sinus, & quid albus Peccet Iapex*. Yet all that I had ever suffered gathered together, might not hold comparison with this. There was not a moment in which the sudden splitting, or instant over-setting of the Ship was not expected.

Howbeit this was not all. It pleased God to bring a greater affliction yet upon us; for in the beginning of the storm we had received likewise a mighty leak. And the Ship in every joint almost, having spewed out her Oakum, before we were aware (a casualty more desperate than any other that a Voyage by Sea draws with it) was grown five foot suddenly deep with water above her ballast, and we almost drowned within, whilst we sat looking when to perish from above. This imparting no less terror than danger, ran through the whole Ship with much fright and amazement, startled and turned the blood, and took down the braves of the most hardy Mariner of them all, insomuch as he that before happily felt not the sorrow of others, now began to sorrow for himself, when he saw such a pond of water so suddenly broken in, and which he knew could not (without present avoiding) but instantly sink him. So as joining (only for his own sake, not yet worth the saving) in the public safety, there might be seen Master, Master's Mate, Boatswain, Quarter Master, Coopers, Carpenters, and who not, with candles in their hands, creeping along the ribs viewing the sides, searching every corner, and listening in every place, if they could hear the water run. Many a weeping leak was this way found, and hastily stopped, and at length one in the Gunner room made up with I know not how many pieces of Beef; but all was to no purpose, the Leak (if it were but one) which drunk in our greatest Seas, and took in our destruction fastest, could not then be found, nor ever was, by any labor, counsel, or search. The waters still increasing, and the Pumps going, which at length choked with bringing up whole and continual Biscuit (and indeed all we had, ten thousand weight) it was conceived, as most likely, that the Leak might be sprung in the Breadroom, whereupon the Carpenter went down, and ripped up all the room, but could not find it so.

I am not able to give unto your Ladyship every man's thought in this perplexity, to which we were now brought. But to me, this Leakage appeared as a wound given to men that were before dead. The Lord knows, I had as little hope, as desire of life in the storm; and in this it went beyond my will, because beyond my reason. Why should we labor to preserve life? Yet we did, either because so dear are a few lingering hours of life in all mankind, or that our *Christian* knowledges taught us how much we owed to the rites of Nature, as bound, not to be false to ourselves, nor to neglect the means of our own preservation; the most despairefull things amongst men, being matters of no wonder nor moment with him who is the rich Fountain and admirable Essence of all mercy.

Our Governor, upon the tuesday morning (at what time, by such who had been below in the hold, the Leak was first discovered) had caused the whole Company, about one hundred and forty, besides women, to be equally divided into three parts, and opening the Ship in three places (under the forecastle, in the waste, and hard by the Bitacke) appointed each man where to attend. And thereunto every man came duly upon his watch, took the Bucket, or Pump for one hour, and rested another. Then men might be seen to labor, I may well say, for life, and the better sort, even our Governor, and Admiral themselves, not refusing their turn, and to spell each the other, to give example to others. The common sort stripped naked, as men in Galleys, the easier both to hold out, and to shrink from under the salt water, which continually leapt in among them, kept their eyes waking, and their thoughts and hands working, with tired bodies, and wasted spirits, three days and four nights destitute of outward comfort, and desperate of any deliverance, testifying how mutually willing they were, yet by labor to keep each other from drowning albeit each one drowned whilst he labored.

William Bradford

The voyage of the Mayflower *and the arrival of the Pilgrims at Plymouth Rock in 1620 have been absorbed into national myth. The actual details of the 65-day crossing—as presented, starkly and unsentimentally, in* History of Plymouth Plantation, *a first-hand account by William Bradford (1590–1657), who later became governor of the colony—are all the more arresting. One incident is startling for its omission: the death of Bradford's first wife, Dorothy, by drowning, at the end of the voyage. His reticence, historians speculate, suggests that she may have committed suicide, unable, as she looked from the ship at the bleak winter dunes of the Cape Cod coast, to contemplate a life in America.*

from *History of Plymouth Plantation*

Of their vioage, and how they passed the sea, and of their safe arrivall at Cape Codd

SEPT[R]: 6. These troubles being blowne over, and now all being compacte togeather in one shipe, they put to sea againe with a prosperus winde, which continued diverce days togeather, which was some incouragmente unto them; yet according to the usuall maner many were afflicted with sea-sicknes. And I may not omite hear a spetiall worke of Gods providence. Ther was a proud and very profane yonge man, one of the sea-men, of a lustie, able body, which made him the more hauty; he would allway be contemning the poore people in their sicknes, and cursing them dayly with greevous execrations, and did not let to tell them, that he hoped to help to cast halfe of them over board before they came to their jurneys end, and to make mery with what they had; and if he were by any gently reproved, he would curse and swear most bitterly. But it pleased God before they came halfe seas over, to smite this young man with a greeveous disease, of which he dyed in a desperate maner, and so was him selfe the first that was throwne overbord. Thus his curses light on his owne head; and it was an astonishmente to all his fellows, for they noted it to be the just hand of God upon him.

After they had injoyed faire winds and weather for a season, they were incountred many times with crosse winds, and mette with many feirce stormes, with which the shipe was shroudly shaken, and her upper works made very leakie; and one of the maine beames in the midd ships was bowed and craked, which put them in some fear that the shipe could not be able to performe the vioage. So some of the cheefe of the company, perceiveing the mariners to feare the suffisiencie of the shipe, as appeared by their mutterings, they entred into serious consulltation with the master and other officers of the ship, to consider in time of the danger; and rather to returne then to cast them selves into a desperate and inevitable perill. And truly ther was great distraction and differance of oppinion amongst the mariners them selves; faine would they doe what could be done for their wages sake, (being now halfe the seas over,) and on the other hand they were loath to hazard their lives too desperatly. But in examening of all oppinions, the master and others affirmed they knew the ship to be stronge and firme underwater; and for the buckling of the maine beame, ther was a great iron scrue the passengers brought out of Holland, which would raise the beame into his place; the which being done, the carpenter and master affirmed that with a post put under it, set firme in the lower deck, and otherways bounde, he would make it sufficiente. And as for the decks and uper workes they would calke them as well as they could, and though with the workeing of the ship they would not longe keepe stanch, yet ther would otherwise be no great danger, if they did not overpress her with sails. So they commited them selves to the will of God, and resolved to proseede. In sundrie of these stormes the winds were so feirce, and the seas so high, as they could not beare a knote of saile, but were forced to hull, for diverce days togither. And in one of them, as they thus lay at hull, in a mighty storme, a lustie yonge man (called John Howland) coming upon some occasion above the grattings, was, with a seele of the shipe throwne into the sea; but it pleased God that he caught hould of the top-saile halliards, which hunge over board, and rane out at length; yet he held his hould (though he was sundrie fadomes under water) till he was hald up by the same rope to the brime of the water, and then with a boathooke and other means got into the shipe againe, and his life saved; and though he was something ill with it, yet he lived many years after, and became a profitable member both in church and commone wealthe. In all this viage ther died but one of the passengers, which was William Butten, a youth, servant to Samuell Fuller, when they drew near the coast. But to omite other things, (that I may be breefe,) after longe beating at sea they fell with that land which is called Cape Cod; the which being made and certainly knowne to be it, they were not a litle joyfull. After some deliberation had amongst them selves and with the master of the ship, they tacked aboute and resolved to stande for the southward (the wind and weather being faire) to finde some place aboute Hudsons river for their habitation. But after they had sailed that course aboute halfe the day, they fell amongst deangerous shoulds and roring breakers, and they were so farr intangled ther with as they conceived them selves in great danger; and the wind shrinking upon them withall, they resolved to bear up againe for the Cape, and thought them selves hapy to gett out of those dangers before night overtooke them, as by Gods good providence they did. And the next day they gott into the Cape-harbor wher they ridd in saftie. A word or too by the way of this cape; it was thus first named by Capten Gosnole and his company, Anno: 1602, and after by Capten Smith was caled Cape James; but it retains the former name amongst seamen. Also that pointe which first shewed those dangerous shoulds unto them, they called Pointe Care, and Tuckers Terrour; but the French and Dutch to this day call it Malabarr, by reason of those perilous shoulds, and the losses they have suffered their.

Being thus arived in a good harbor and brought safe to land, they fell upon their knees and blessed the God of heaven, who had brought them over the vast and furious ocean, and delivered them from all the periles and miseries therof, againe to set their feete on the firme and stable earth, their proper elemente. And no marvell if they were thus joyefull, seeing wise Seneca was so affected with sailing a few miles on the coast of his owne Italy; as he affirmed, that he had rather remaine twentie years on his way by land, then pass by sea to any place in a short time; so tedious and dreadfull was the same unto him.

Roger Williams

Roger Williams (1603–1683), a young clergyman, crossed the Atlantic from Bristol to Boston in the winter of 1630–1631. His passage was uneventful, for the period, but his subsequent career in America would be turbulent in the extreme. Angering Puritan authorities by his religious nonconformism and his defense of the rights of Indians, he was banished from the Massachusetts Bay Colony, and in 1636 founded Providence, the first settlement in Rhode Island.

"Of the Sea" is taken from A Key into the Language of America *(1643). Written as Williams sailed to London to secure a patent for the newly formed settlement, the book is more than a mere lexicon: it offers vital glimpses into the cultural and spiritual lives of the Narragansett Indians, whose canoes were plying the waters of Narragansett Bay before any Englishman arrived in America.*

Of the Sea

Wechêkum, Kítthan.	*The Sea.*
Paumpágussit.	*The Sea-God*, or, that name which they give that Deitie or Godhead which they conceive to be in the Sea.
Mishoòn	*An* Indian *Boat*, or *Canow* made of a Pine or Oake, or Chestnut-tree.

Obs. I have seene a Native goe into the woods with his hatchet, carrying onely a Basket of Corn with him, & stones to strike fire when he had feld his tree (being a *chestnut*) he made him a little House or shed of the bark of it, he puts fire and followes the burning of it with fire, in the midst in many places: his corne he boyles and hath the Brook by him, and sometimes angles for a little fish: but so hee continues burning and hewing untill he hath within ten or twelve dayes (lying there at his worke alone) finished, and (getting hands,) lanched his Boate; with which afterward hee ventures out to fish in the Ocean.

Mishoonémese. *A little Canow.*

Some of them will not well carry above three or foure: but some of them twenty, thirty, forty men.

Wunnauanoûnuck. *A Shallop.*
Wunnauanounuckquèse *A Skiffe.*

Obs. Although themselves have neither, yet they give them such names, which in their Language signifieth carrying Vessells.

Kitônuck. *A Ship.*
Kitônuckquese. *A little ship.*
Mishíttouwand. *A great Canow.*
Peewàsu. *A little one.*
Paugautemissaûnd. *An Oake Canow.*
Kowawwaûnd. *A pine Canow.*
Wompmissaûnd. *A chesnut Canow.*
Ogwhan. *A boat adrift.*
Wuskon-tógwhan. *It will goe adrift.*
Cuttunnamíinnea. *Help me to launch.*
Cuttunnummútta. *Let us launch.*
Cuttúnnamoke. *Launch.*
Cuttánnummous. *I will help you.*
Wútkunck. *A paddle* or *Oare.*
Namacóuhe cómishoon. *Lend me your Boate.*
Paûtousnenótehunck. *Bring hither my paddle.*
Comishóonhom? *Goe you by water?*
Chémosh-chémeck. *Paddle* or *row.*
Maumínikish & Maumanetepweéas. *Pull up,* or *row lustily.*
Sepâkehig. *A Sayle.*
Sepagehommaûta. *Let us saile.*
Wunnâgehan. *We have a faire wind.*

Obs. Their owne reason hath taught them, to pull of a Coat or two and set it up on a small pole, with which they will saile before a wind ten, or twenty mile, &c.

Wauaúpunish.	*Hoyse up.*
Wuttáutnish.	*Pull to you.*
Nókanish.	*Take it downe.*
Pakétenish.	*Let goe* or *let flie.*
Nikkoshkowwaúmen.	*We shall be drown'd.*
Nquawupshâwmen.	*We overset.*
Wussaûme pechepaûsha.	*The Sea comes in too fast upon us.*
Maumaneeteántass.	*Be of good courage.*

Obs. It is wonderfull to see how they will venture in those Canoes, and how (being oft overset as I have my selfe been with them) they will swim a mile, yea two or more safe to Land: I having been necessitated to passe waters diverse times with them, it hath pleased God to make them many times the instruments of my preservation; and when sometimes in great danger I have questioned safety, they have said to me: Feare not, if we be overset I will carry you safe to Land.

Paupaútuckquash.	*Hold water.*
Kínnequass.	*Steere.*
Tiáckomme kínniquass.	*Steere right.*
Kunnósnep.	*A Killick,* or *Anchor.*
Chowwophómmin.	*To cast over-board.*
Chouwóphash.	*Cast over-board.*
Touwopskhómmke.	*Cast anchor.*
Mishittáshin.	*It is a storme.*
Awêpesha.	*It caulmes.*
Awêpu.	*A calme.*
Nanoúwashin.	*A great caulme.*
Tamóccon.	*Floud.*
Nanashowetamóccon.	*Halfe Floud.*
Keesaqúshin.	*High water.*
Taumacoks.	*Upon the Floud.*
Mishittommóckon.	*A great Floud.*
Maúchetan & skàt.	*Ebb.*

Mittâeskat.	*A low Ebb.*
Awánick Paûdhuck?	*Who comes there?*

Obs. I have knowne thirty or forty of their Canowes fill'd with men, and neere as many more of their enemies in a Sea-fight.

Caupaúshess.	*Goe ashoare.*
Caupaushâuta.	*Let us goe ashoare.*
Wusséheposh.	*Heave out of the water.*
Asképunish.	*Make fast the Boat.*
Kspúnsh & Kspúnemoke.	*Tie it fast.*
Maumínikish.	*Tie it hard.*
Neene Cuthómwock.	*Now they goe off.*
Kekuthomwushánnick.	*They are gone already.*

Generall Observations *of the* Sea.

How unsearchable are the depth of the Wisedome and Power of God in separating from *Europe*, *Asia* and *Africa* such a mightie vast continent as *America* is? and that for so many ages? as also, by such a Westerne Ocean of about three thousand of *English* miles breadth in passage over?

More particular:

[1.] *They see Gods wonders that are call'd*
Through dreadfull Seas to passe,
In tearing winds and roaring seas,
And calmes as smooth as glasse.

[2.] *I have in* Europes *ships, oft been*
In King of terrours hand;
When all have cri'd, Now, now we sinck,
Yet God brought safe to land.

[3.] *Alone 'mongst* Indians *in Canoes,*
Sometime o're-turn'd, I have been
Halfe inch from death, in Ocean deepe,
Gods wonders I have seene.

Cotton Mather

Cotton Mather (1663–1728), grandson and namesake of two prominent founders of Puritan Massachusetts, entered Harvard College at age 12, the youngest student ever admitted, and became minister of Boston's Second Church, a prolific author, and the most widely read American of his time. His Magnalia Christi Americana *(1702), or "Works of Christ in America," was intended as an epic celebrating God's special relationship with New England. Published at a time when there was a general sense that the saintliness of the earlier generations was waning, his book attempted to rekindle religious sentiment by describing the settlement of New England, the lives of governors and famous divines, and other aspects of early history. But its most influential section was the record of "remarkable providences," or events in which God showed his favor by directly revealing his power in the colonies. Despite the fact that Mather was a scientist and rationalist, and a member of the Royal Society, he would be best known to later generations for accounts like this one of a ghostly apparitional ship, which inaugurates the supernatural strain in American sea writing.*

from *Magnalia Christi Americana*

Reverend and Dear Sir,

IN Compliance with your Desires, I now give you the Relation of that *Apparition* of a *Ship in the Air*, which I have received from the most Credible, Judicious and Curious Surviving Observers of it.

In the Year 1647, besides much other Lading, a far more Rich Treasure of Passengers, (Five or Six of which were Persons of chief Note and Worth in *New-Haven*) put themselves on Board a *New Ship*, built at *Rhode-Island*, of about 150 Tuns; but so walty, that the Master, (*Lamberton*) often said she would prove their Grave. In the Month of *January*, cutting their way thro' much Ice, on which they were accompanied with the Reverend Mr. *Davenport*, besides many other Friends, with many Fears, as well as Prayers and Tears, they set Sail. Mr. *Davenport* in Prayer with an observable *Emphasis* used these Words, *Lord, if it be thy pleasure to bury these our Friends in the bottom of the Sea, they are thine; save them!* The Spring following no Tidings of these Friends arrived with the Ships from *England*: *New-Haven's* Heart began to fail her: This put the Godly People on much *Prayer*, both Publick and Private, *That the Lord would (if it was his Pleasure) let them hear what he had done with their dear Friends, and prepare them with a suitable Submission to his Holy Will.* In *June* next ensuing, a great *Thunder-storm* arose out of the *North-West*: after which, (the *Hemisphere* being serene) about an Hour before Sunset a SHIP of like Dimensions with the aforesaid, with her Canvas and Colours abroad (tho' the Wind Northernly) appeared in the Air coming up from our Harbour's Mouth, which lyes Southward from the Town, seemingly with her *Sails* filled under a fresh Gale, holding her Course North, and continuing under Observation, Sailing against the Wind for the space of half an Hour. *Many* were drawn to behold this great Work of God; yea, the very *Children* cry'd out, *There's a Brave Ship!* At length, crouding up as far as there is usually *Water* sufficient for such a Vessel, and so near some of the Spectators, as that they imagined a Man might hurl a Stone on Board her, her *Maintop* seem'd to be blown off, but left hanging in the Shrouds; then her *Missen-top*; then all her *Masting* seemed blown away by the Board: Quickly after the *Hull* brought unto a Careen, she overset, and so vanished into a smoaky Cloud, which in some time dissipated, leaving, as everywhere else, a clear Air. The admiring Spectators could distinguish the several Colours of each Part, the Principal Riging, and such Proportions, as caused not only the generality of Persons to say, *This was the Mould of their Ship, and thus was her Tragick End:* But Mr. *Davenport* also in publick declared to this Effect, *That God had condescended, for the quieting of their afflicted Spirits, this Extraordinary Account of his Soveraign*

Disposal of those for whom so many Fervent Prayers were made continually. Thus I am, Sir,

Your Humble Servant,
James Pierpont.

Reader, There being yet living so many Credible Gentlemen, that were Eye-Witnesses of this *Wonderful* Thing, I venture to Publish it for a thing as *undoubted*, as 'tis *wonderful.*

William Walling

In the spring of 1726, a man from Middletown, New Jersey—of whom little record remains other than the narrative that follows—set out on what ought to have been a routine trip home from New York. The circumstances that quickly overtook him, at times only a few hundred yards off the New Jersey coast, seem as harrowing as almost any experienced in the middle of the ocean: an early-18th-century commuter's nightmare.

The Wonderful Providence of God Exemplified in the Preservation of William Walling

I *William Walling* of *Middletown* in *Monmouth* County, in the Province of *New-Jersey*, took Passage with *Abraham Watson* to go to *New-York*, on Thursday the ninth of *March*, 1726 in the Evening, and arrived there safely the next Day; but being hindred by the Weather from doing any Business, I went over to *Gravesend* on *Long-Island*, on Saturday I returned with an Intention to do my Business, in order to go home with *Abraham Watson*. On Monday Morning *Abraham Watson* was ready to go home, and because I had not finished my Business, he was forc'd to go without me. On Tuesday morning I met with one *Tys Deriks*, who was bound to the same Shore, about ten Miles from *Middletown*, and I desiring to be at home took Passage with him. There were also three Women Passengers on Board. We left the City of *New-York* about Noon; and when we came to the Narrows, one *Nathaniel Gardner*, who together with another Man was hired to go in a Boat belonging to this *Tys Dericks*, called to us and came off in a Canoe; when he came on Board he told *Tys Dericks*, That the Boat had lost the great Anchor, and that she had been upon the Rocks and was so leaky that he knew not how to get home with her, for his Companion had left the Boat. Then *Tys Dericks* asked him if he thought that he could get home in her safely? Gardner answered that he thought he could, if one kept pumping continually; thereupon *Tys*

Dericks asked me to go and help him home with the Boat, saying that he would give me over and above my Passage five Shillings. I consented and went on Shore with *Gardner* in the Canoe, and found the Boat aground. Then I repented that I had not gone with *Tys Dericks*, for I began to fear that we should have a tedious Passage. Here we were oblig'd to stay still *Thursday* before the Boat floated, and then it blew so hard that we could not go; but on *Fryday*, the wind being moderate and pretty fair, we ventured to set Sail in Company with another small Boat that was going the same Way. When we were got about half way over to the *Neversink* Shore the Wind dyed away, and it continued stark calm for a little while; Then the Wind sprung up at South and blew very fresh. We turn'd it to windward with great Difficulty for some time, but when we saw the other Boat turn back we followed her, to go round *Statten Island*, and so home by the Way of Amboy: But on the North Side of *Statten-Island* we run a-ground, and did not get off till Saturday Night.

On Sunday Morning we set Sail again, fetch'd all our Provisions and we ate all. We were not satisfied, for I had not brought above two Meals for both of us on Board when we left *Long-Island*: But with the Beginning of the Ebb the Wind dyed away and we drove a stern, so we turn'd about with an Intention to go through the Narrows; but before we got out of the Narrows the Wind Sprung up at South West and blew pretty hard; however we laid it along, the Tyde of Ebb helping us: But when we were got about half Way over to the *Neversinks*, it began to blow so hard that the Boat lay with her Gunel under Water sometimes; we lower'd the Mainsail, and *Gardner* was for turning back again, but I wanting to be at home, would not consent to it; for I told him, if he could but get within the Hook, I could lay her into *Sperma-Caeta-Cove*, then we could walk home on foot, he told me he thought that he could get within the Hook. Thus through an over great desire of being at Home I brought my self into extream great Sufferings. We laid it along, as well as we could, till we came within about three or four Hundred Yards of the Hook, and then he told me that he could not get within the Hook, so I told him to run her aground any where:

But whilst we were talking a very hard Flaw overtook us, which almost overset us, for the Mast just touch'd the Water, I immediately let fly the Main-Hall-Yards, (for I held them in my Hands for more Security) & pulled down the Main-Sail as fast as I could, which helped her to rise again, but the Foresail was pulled in Pieces and blown away. As soon as she was righted we bore away and scudded before the Wind, and by this time she was half full of Water. Now the Fear of Death began to come hard upon me, for I did not expect to live an Hour longer, and my Companion was so affected with seeing himself blown away from shore in a leaky Vessel, half full of Water, that he cryed out with a loud Voice, *We are drowned!* However thinking my self oblig'd to make the best of all Means for our Preservation, I went to Pumping, and encouraged him to mind the Helm; I laboured very hard, both in Body and Mind: For the Tho'ts of being drove out to Sea in a leaky Boat, without a Morsel of any kind of Victuals or a drop of Drink, affected me very sorely. Add to this, that I tho't my self the Author, not only of my own, but another Man's Misfortune's also because I hindred *Gardner* from going back when it was in his Power. I repented very much that I did not let him take his own Course, as being more us'd to the Water than I, and consequently saw the Danger we were in sooner. In short it is impossible to describe the Horrour & anguish of my Mind. My Companion also was very much dejected, And I believe labouring with the same Thoughts. After I had pumpt some time the Pump stopt, so that I could do nothing with it, then I took the Bucket and went to Bailing. The Wind blew so hard that we lost Sight of Land in about two Hours after we had the hard Flaw of Wind. Some time in the Afternoon it began to snow very hard and continued for some time. About Sun-set I began to get the upperhand of the Water, this with the Hopes of striking upon some Part of *Long-Island* was some Comfort to us. Some time in the Night I got the Water out pretty clean, & after that Time I took care to pump or bail before there was too much Water in her.

All this Night the Wind continued, and on *Monday* it was the same, so that we had enough to do to keep the Boat afloat and before the Wind, for she began to be so leaky now, that I think she would have been full in less than 12 Hours Time.

On *Tuesday* some time before Noon the Wind began to Moderate, and in the Afternoon the Weather was so moderate that we could let the Boat drive without steering. My Companion, for want of Sleep, now begun to talk idle, and among other silly Things said, he was sure we were bewitch'd. I told him that I believ'd no such thing, and perswaded him to go to sleep, for we had neither of us slept since Saturday night, and he seemed to want Sleep very much; but before he went down into the Cabin I desired him to show me how to clear the Pump, for I wet my self so much with bailing that I was never dry; and whilst he was doing that there appeared a Vessel in sight, but at so great a Distance that we could not see her when we lay in the Trough of the Sea; we lost sight of her in less than half an Hours Time, then my Companion laid himself down to sleep, and when I Pumpt the water out of the Boat I laid my self down also. After I had slept a little while I heard the Wind blow harder and the Boat tumbled so much that I awaked and got up, and felt my self something refreshed with the little Sleep I had got, but extremely hungry; I guessed that it was about three a Clock then: I freed the Boat of the Water again and then I took the Helm and steer'd before the Wind as well as I could till about five a-Clock, and then there was much Water in her Hold, so I called to *Nathaniel* to take the Helm, for the Wind blew hard, and the Sea was so rough that I was afraid a Sea might break in upon her broad side and sink her if I should let her drive; as soon as I had called him he came up hastily and in a Consternation, telling me that he had seen two Spirits on Board in Shape of Women, and would have me go down into the Hold to see them, I reproved him and told him that he should not give way to such idle Fancies; But he persisted in the Notion that he had seen them, and I could not satisfy him without going down into the Cabin to see them so I went down, (not that I believ'd I should see any thing, but only to satisfy him) when I came up again he asked me whether I had seen them? I answered No, and that I did not believe that he had. Then he said, that they would not let me see them, but as soon as he should come on Shore he would go to a Justice of the Peace and take his Oath that he had seen them. When I had freed the Boat of the Water I took the Helm again, then he pull'd off his Coat and Jacket, and wrapt a Piece of an old Blanket about his Waste and Chest in Fashion of Indian Women; I asked him what he did that for? He answered *The Spirits told me, that all those that wear Petticoats they wont hurt, and all those that do not they will kill, and this is the best Peticoat I have, I hope they will be contented with it.* I told him that these were only Imaginations, and perswaded him to put on his Cloaths, for he shivered very much with the Cold, and about Sun set he put on his Cloaths again. About two hours in the Night I asked him to stand to the Helm again, and I freed her of the Water; then I steer'd till about Midnight, and there being a great deal of Water in her, I called to *Nathaniel* to take the Helm that I might free her, but he was very unwilling to come up again, telling me I might pull out the Tiller and let her drive; I told him that the Wind blew too hard and the Sea run too high to let her drive, for every Wave seemed high enough to run over the Mast, and if a Sea should break in upon her broad side, she would surely be stav'd and sink. Thus I argued with him a long Time before he would come; however at length he came, and then I freed her of the Water again. As soon as I had done Bailing I crept through the Bulk Head into the Cabin to get a Blanket to wrap about me, for I was wet and cold, and the Blankets were wet also; but as soon as he perceived that I was in the Cabin he called me to take the Helm, I desired him to hold it so long that I might get a Blanket, he said that he would let it go if I did not come up presently, whereupon I stept up to him hastily and took the Helm, for I fear'd that the Sea would take her broad side if he should let her go: Then I asked him, why he would neither steer nor pump, nor throw water out of the boat (for he had neither pump'd nor bail'd so long as we were drove away, tho' he had steer'd two Days and two Nights constantly) he answer'd, he wanted to go into the Cabin, so I stood aside that he might go in, for we always stood upon a Plank in the Cabbin Door to Steer. When I had stood there about half an hour, I heard a very unusual strangling noise, which struck me immediately with a fear and concern for him lest he should make Way with himself; and as soon as I had rais'd the Sea that was coming after me, I stoopt down, calling upon him & put my hand back into the Cabbin, so far till I catch'd hold of his hair, & pull'd him right to me, talking to him all the while, but he made me no Answer, neither could he, for I found, upon feeling that he had made a Noose into one Corner of his Handkerchief, and put the other corner thro' it, & drawn it together about his naked neck (for, he had unbutton'd his Coller) that he was past Speaking or Breathing by all that I could perceive. I made all the haste I could to untie the Handkerchief; but before I got it loose our Boat came too and a Sea broke in over her Quarter with such Violence that I expected her to be stove to Pieces and filled and going down, tho' it pleas'd God to order it otherwise. As soon as I had untied the Handkerchief he begun to Cough, & soon after to Vomit, and then to Speak; as soon as he begun to speak I asked him why he went to murder himself thus both Body and Soul & he said, that he wanted to cut his throat just now, but the Knife was so dull that he could not cut with it, but he had cut two Gashes into his Neck. I told him again sharply, *that if he did kill himself, he would expect nothing but Damnation and eternal Misery for his poor Soul, as soon as it Departed from his Body. Why,* said he, *the Devil told me that he would carry me away alive, if I did not kill my self.* Then said I, *the Devil's ends in persuading you to Self-Murder are, that he might have Power over your poor Soul, he well knows Self-Murder to be the worst Murder, for there is no Repentance to the Grave. Ah!* (said he) *do you take a Rope and hang me, then I shall not be guilty of so heinous a Crime.* I answered him, *that in so doing I should be guilty not only of Murdering him, but also of burying his Soul to eternal Destruction, and he could not be guiltless because he desired it.* Then he ask'd me, *What he should do? for the Devil told him, he would carry him away alive, and he was resolved he should not, for he would kill himself first.* But I admonished him to think otherwise and not to give so much way to those Destructive Whiles, but rather to put his Trust in God, and Call upon him for assistance. While I was yet talking to him, he cryed out saying, *Look! how he stands in the Hold of the Vessel, telling me to kill myself or he will carry me away alive; don't you hear him?* Then I asked him where he was? He answered, *In the Hold of the Vessel, don't you see him? No* said I *and how can you see him since it is so very dark? Why,* says he, *he stands all of a light Fire, Laughing and Grinning at me, and are not you afraid? No,* said I, *and if all the Devils in Hell were in the Hold, I should not be afraid, nor entertain the least thought of their hurting me, for I believed that God would preserve and protect me from the Devil.* And herein I was confirmed by the Raging of the Sea, since one Wave was enough to make an end of us, if the Almighty did not preserve us. After some Time he Burst out in Tears and bemoan'd himself sadly, calling very often on the name of the *Lord Jesus Christ*, seeming to be very much Terrified in his mind for Fear the Devil should carry him away, and I believe that he began to Repent of his Sins, for all this Day (*Wednesday*) he Cry'd and Groan'd under the Weight of them very much Confessing and Praying for forgiveness, notwithstanding all this and my Comforting of him as well as I could (for God knows I needed Comfort my Self) he was so very much afraid, that if I went from the Quarter-deck to the Fore-castle he would follow me and hold me fast, and if I went down into the Hold he would lie down upon Deck and look down to keep me in sight. This Day he drank abundance of Salt Water, tho' I spoke against it very much.

On *Thursday* he was taken violently with a Fever and Flux, & about Noon he was Speechless. My Condition now began to be very dismal, for my Strength decay'd & I was no more able to do as I was used to do, my Companion lay as tho' every breath would be his last; yet I trusted in God that he would deliver me, and therefore I did my utmost to keep the Boat afloat. I was now alone, and so spent the most of my Time in Prayer and Meditation.

Friday and *Saturday* nothing particular happened to me, it being good weather.

On *Sunday* Morning I began to pump about the dawning of the Day, and got her clear'd about Sun rising, then I sat my self down on Deck, poor and low in Body, (tho' strong in Spirit, thro' the Grace of God.) After I had sat about two Hours musing on my desperate State, I thought to get up to pump again, but I found my Strength so wasted that I was not able to rise, I made several efforts but to no purpose, for then with much Labour I was got upon my Legs, I was not able to stand, nor is it to be wondered at, for this was the eighth Day that I had had no manner of Sustenance but three black Walnuts, and my own Water, of which I could hardly make enough to wet my Mouth at last, tho' I mixt Salt Water with it. Then I crept down into the Cabbin and laid me down in one of the Cuddies upon the Boards, for there was no Bed in it, and began to compose my self to meet my Fate, which I thought approaching. In this Posture I lay till about Noon and then I was overcome by Sleep, after I had slept some time, how long I know not, I awak'd and saw the Water pouring in at the Cabbin Window, and then I began afresh to recommend my Soul to the Almighty, as expecting no other than to be reliev'd by Death in a short time. I had not been thus employ'd long before I heard a Cock crow, and four or five Men hallowing, this revived me very much and I got up upon Deck as if I was well, tho' I was truly an object of Pity, and saw a Sloop sailing by, I call'd to them in the Name of the Lord *Jesus* to relieve me! and they answered that they could. Then they immediately hoisted out their Boat and fetch'd me and my Companion, whom I had given over for dead, and carried us on board of their Sloop, my poor Companion they laid into a warm Bed, but I being more able to help my self than he, desir'd that I might go down into the Fore-castle where the Mate gave me some dry Cloaths. I had not been long by the Fire before I fainted, so they brought me a little Water and Wine & a little Sugar in it, of which they gave me about a Mouthful, and then they gave me a little Victuals, and put me into the Mates Cabbin, where he began to examine my Feet and found that they were frozen; at first I could not believe him, but he went and warm'd a Stone and put it to my feet, but when they began to be warm, I felt a most exquisite pain in them. The next Day they roasted Turnips and laid on my Feet, this they continued for four or five Days and then their Turnips were spent. As for my Companion, after they had shifted him, & laid him into the Captains Cabbin, (where the Captain like a good charitable Christian tended him himself) they gave him a little Victuals and Drink, which so revived him that he recovered his Senses and Speech and talk'd very sensibly for about three Hours, & then his Speech fail'd again, and the next Day he departed to Eternity. Now altho' this Man was but a Stranger to me, yet it griev'd me sore when he died. The next Day they sow'd him up in a Rug, and Buried him in the Sea.

After all their Turnips were gone, the Mate, who had skill in frozen Feet, made Poultises of Indian Meal and continued that for fourteen Days, and by that time all the skin and Nails came off of my Feet, then he made an Ointment and applied to them which gave me some ease.

Fourteen Days after I was taken up I was brought to *Nantucket*, and two Days after the People hearing of my Misfortunes, gathered together to consult what to do with me, at length they concluded that I should be brought to the House of one *Isaac Coleman*, whose Wife had some skill in frozen Feet, and because they had no Children they tho't that the properst House for me; the next Day I was carried thither in a Calash and staid there six Weeks, and then I began to walk about upon Crutches, but one *Nathaniel Starbuck* told me I should stay there no longer for they must be paid, and if I would come to his House I should be very welcome: He was a good and just Man, and feared God. The next Day several of the principal Men came to me and advised me to ask her what I had to pay, and they would lend me the Money to pay her (tho' their design was to give it, as they told me afterwards) but they knew her to be a Woman of no Conscience, or a very evil one, and therefore made use of that Device to the end that she might not ask me too much. When I asked her what she must have, she told me she would have thirteen Pounds and no less; when I had told my Friends what she Demanded, they told me, I should have nothing to do with her, for they would pay her, which they did, giving her seven Pounds ten shillings. She was a very slanderous Woman, for while I was in her

House she always had something or other to say of every one that came to the House, for this Reason I did not like her, for I tho't she did not do as a Christian ought to do.

I continued here till the second Day of *June*, and when I was going away, I had about five Pounds given me towards defraying the Charges of my going home, by several well disposed People. I went on Board one Capt. *Bush* of *New York*, who gave me my Passage to *New-Port* on *Rhode-Island*, where we arrived in a very short Time. Here I met with Capt. *Watson* and another Neighbour, the seeing of my Neighbours once more on this side of the Grave, perfectly rejoiced me. Capt. *Watson* immediately offered me Assistance, if I wanted either Money or any other Thing that he could help me to, for which I thank'd him, and told him that I wanted to go home with him, to which he replied very affectionately, that he would carry me home thro' the help of God. We left *New-Port* the eleventh of *June* and on the nineteenth I arrived at *Monmouth* County in *New-Jersey*, to the great Joy of all my Friends who had given me over for lost. I was drove out to Sea on a *Sunday*, I was taken up on a *Sunday*, I was brought into *Nantucket* on a *Sunday*, and I arrived at my own home, on a *Sunday*.

Olaudah Equiano

It is estimated that the slave trade brought more than ten million Africans to the western hemisphere, and that more than a million died crossing the Atlantic. One of the most remarkable firsthand accounts of the horrors of the Middle Passage appears in The Interesting Narrative of the Life of Olaudah Equiano, or Gustavus Vassa, the African, Written By Himself, *published in 1789. Born in the southeastern region of present-day Nigeria, Equiano (1745–1797) grew up among the Ibo people before he was kidnapped at the age of 11 and sold into slavery. Sent to Barbados and then to Virginia, he was sold to a lieutenant in the British Navy, who took him to England as a servant. Equiano spent most of his youth aboard ships of the Royal Navy; he was subsequently sold to a West Indian trader and then to a Philadelphia merchant from whom he bought his freedom in 1766. After participating in an Arctic expedition and voyages to Central America and Turkey, Equiano settled in England in 1777. In 1787 he was appointed "commissary of provisions and stores" for a colonization venture in Sierra Leone, but his criticism of the venture's leaders led to his dismissal before he could return to West Africa. After the publication of* The Interesting Narrative, *Equiano traveled extensively in England, Scotland, and Ireland promoting the book and arranging for the publication of eight subsequent editions.*

from *The Interesting Narrative of the Life*

THE first object which saluted my eyes when I arrived on the coast was the sea, and a slave ship, which was then riding at anchor, and waiting for its cargo. These filled me with astonishment, which was soon converted into terror when I was carried on board. I was immediately handled and tossed up to see if I were sound by some of the crew; and I was now persuaded that I had gotten into a world of bad spirits, and that they were going to kill me. Their complexions too differing so much from ours, their long hair, and the language they spoke, (which was very different from any I had ever heard) united to confirm me in this belief. Indeed such were the horrors of my views and fears at the moment, that, if ten thousand worlds had been my own, I would have freely parted with them all to have exchanged my condition with that of the meanest slave in my own country. When I looked round the ship too and saw a large furnace or copper boiling, and a multitude of black people of every description chained together, every one of their countenances expressing dejection and sorrow, I no longer doubted of my fate; and, quite overpowered with horror and anguish, I fell motionless on the deck and fainted. When I recovered a little I found some black people about me, who I believed were some of those who brought me on board, and had been receiving their pay; they talked to me in order to cheer me, but all in vain. I asked them if we were not to be eaten by those white men with horrible looks, red faces, and loose hair. They told me I was not; and one of the crew brought me a small portion of spirituous liquor in a wine glass; but, being afraid of him, I would not take it out of his hand. One of the blacks therefore took it from him and gave it to me, and I took a little down my palate, which, instead of reviving me, as they thought it would, threw me into the greatest consternation at the strange feeling it produced, having never tasted any such liquor before. Soon after this the blacks who brought me on board went off, and left me abandoned to despair. I now saw myself deprived of all chance of returning to my native country, or even the least glimpse of hope of gaining the shore, which I now considered as friendly; and I even wished for my former slavery in preference to my present situation, which was filled with horrors of every kind, still heightened by my ignorance of what I was to undergo. I was not long suffered to indulge my grief; I was soon put down under the decks, and there I received such a salutation in my nostrils as I had never experienced in my life: so that, with the loathsomeness of the stench, and crying together, I became so sick and low that I was not able to eat, nor had I the least desire to taste any thing. I now wished for the last friend, death, to relieve me; but soon, to my grief, two of the white men offered me eatables; and, on my refusing to eat, one of them held me fast by the hands, and laid me across I think the windlass, and tied my feet, while the other flogged me severely. I had never experienced any thing of this kind before; and although, not being used to the water, I naturally feared that element the first time I saw it, yet nevertheless, could I have got over the nettings, I would have jumped over the side, but I could not; and, besides, the crew used to watch us very closely who were not chained down to the decks, lest we should leap into the water: and I have seen some of these poor African prisoners most severely cut for attempting to do so, and hourly whipped for not eating. This indeed was often the case with myself. In a little time after, amongst the poor chained men, I found some of my own nation, which in a small degree gave ease to my mind. I inquired of these what was to be done with us; they gave me to understand we were to be carried to these white people's country to work for them. I then was a little revived, and thought, if it were no worse than working, my situation was not so desperate: but still I feared I should be put to death, the white people looked and acted, as I thought, in so savage a manner; for I had never seen among any people such instances of brutal cruelty; and this not only shewn towards us blacks, but also to some of the whites themselves. One white man in particular I saw, when we were permitted to be on deck, flogged so unmercifully with a large rope near the foremast, that he died in consequence of it; and they tossed him over the side as they would have done a brute. This made me fear these people the more; and I expected nothing less than to be treated in the same manner. I could not help expressing my fears and apprehensions to some of my countrymen: I asked them if these people had no country, but lived in this hollow place (the ship): they told me they did not, but came from a distant one. 'Then,' said I, 'how comes it in all our country we never heard of them?' They told me because they lived so very far off. I then asked where were their women? had they any like themselves? I was told they had: 'and why,' said I, 'do we not see them?' they answered, because they were left behind. I asked how the vessel could go?

they told me they could not tell; but that there were cloths put upon the masts by the help of the ropes I saw, and then the vessel went on; and the white men had some spell or magic they put in the water when they liked in order to stop the vessel. I was exceedingly amazed at this account, and really thought they were spirits. I therefore wished much to be from amongst them, for I expected they would sacrifice me: but my wishes were vain; for we were so quartered that it was impossible for any of us to make our escape. While we stayed on the coast I was mostly on deck; and one day, to my great astonishment, I saw one of these vessels coming in with the sails up. As soon as the whites saw it, they gave a great shout, at which we were amazed; and the more so as the vessel appeared larger by approaching nearer. At last she came to an anchor in my sight, and when the anchor was let go I and my countrymen who saw it were lost in astonishment to observe the vessel stop; and were not convinced it was done by magic. Soon after this the other ship got her boats out, and they came on board of us, and the people of both ships seemed very glad to see each other. Several of the strangers also shook hands with us black people, and made motions with their hands, signifying I suppose we were to go to their country; but we did not understand them. At last, when the ship we were in had got in all her cargo, they made ready with many fearful noises, and we were all put under deck, so that we could not see how they managed the vessel. But this disappointment was the least of my sorrow. The stench of the hold while we were on the coast was so intolerably loathsome, that it was dangerous to remain there for any time, and some of us had been permitted to stay on the deck for the fresh air; but now that the whole ship's cargo were confined together, it became absolutely pestilential. The closeness of the place, and the heat of the climate, added to the number in the ship, which was so crowded that each had scarcely room to turn himself, almost suffocated us. This produced copious perspirations, so that the air soon became unfit for respiration, from a variety of loathsome smells, and brought on a sickness among the slaves, of which many died, thus falling victims to the improvident avarice, as I may call it, of their purchasers. This wretched situation was again aggravated by the galling of the chains, now become insupportable; and the filth of the necessary tubs, into which the children often fell, and were almost suffocated. The shrieks of the women, and the groans of the dying, rendered the whole a scene of horror almost inconceivable. Happily perhaps for myself I was soon reduced so low here that it was thought necessary to keep me almost always on deck; and from my extreme youth I was not put in fetters. In this situation I expected every hour to share the fate of my companions, some of whom were almost daily brought upon deck at the point of death, which I began to hope would soon put an end to my miseries. Often did I think many of the inhabitants of the deep much more happy than myself. I envied them the freedom they enjoyed, and as often wished I could change my condition for theirs. Every circumstance I met with served only to render my state more painful, and heighten my apprehensions, and my opinion of the cruelty of the whites. One day they had taken a number of fishes; and when they had killed and satisfied themselves with as many as they thought fit, to our astonishment who were on the deck, rather than give any of them to us to eat as we expected, they tossed the remaining fish into the sea again, although we begged and prayed for some as well as we could, but in vain; and some of my countrymen, being pressed by hunger, took an opportunity, when they thought no one saw them, of trying to get a little privately; but they were discovered, and the attempt procured them some very severe floggings. One day, when we had a smooth sea and moderate wind, two of my wearied countrymen who were chained together (I was near them at the time), preferring death to such a life of misery, somehow made through the nettings and jumped into the sea: immediately another quite dejected fellow, who, on account of his illness, was suffered to be out of irons, also followed their example; and I believe many more would very soon have done the same if they had not been prevented by the ship's crew, who were instantly alarmed. Those of us that were the most active were in a moment put down under the deck, and there was such a noise and confusion amongst the people of the ship as I never heard before, to stop her, and get the boat out to go after the slaves. However two of the wretches were drowned, but they got the other, and afterwards flogged him unmercifully for thus attempting to prefer death to slavery. In this manner we continued to undergo more hardships than I can now relate, hardships which are inseparable from this accursed trade. Many a time we were near suffocation from the want of fresh air, which we were often without for whole days together. This, and the stench of the necessary tubs, carried off many. During our passage I first saw flying fishes, which surprised me very much: they used frequently to fly across the ship, and many of them fell on the deck. I also now first saw the use of the quadrant; I had often with astonishment seen the mariners make observations with it, and I could not think what it meant. They at last took notice of my surprise; and one of them, willing to increase it, as well as to gratify my curiosity, made me one day look through it. The clouds appeared to me to be land, which disappeared as they passed along. This heightened my wonder; and I was now more persuaded than ever that I was in another world, and that every thing about me was magic. At last we came in sight of the island of Barbadoes, at which the whites on board gave a great shout, and made many signs of joy to us. We did not know what to think of this; but as the vessel drew nearer we plainly saw the harbour, and other ships of different kinds and sizes; and we soon anchored amongst them off Bridge Town. Many merchants and planters now came on board, though it was in the evening. They put us in separate parcels, and examined us attentively. They also made us jump, and pointed to the land, signifying we were to go there. We thought by this we should be eaten by these ugly men, as they appeared to us; and, when soon after we were all put down under the deck again, there was much dread and trembling among us, and nothing but bitter cries to be heard all the night from these apprehensions, insomuch that at last the white people got some old slaves from the land to pacify us. They told us we were not to be eaten, but to work, and were soon to go on land, where we should see many of our country people. This report eased us much; and sure enough, soon after we were landed, there came to us Africans of all languages. We were conducted immediately to the merchant's yard, where we were all pent up together like so many sheep in a fold, without regard to sex or age. As every object was new to me every thing I saw filled me with surprise. What struck me first was that the houses were built with stories, and in every other respect different from those in Africa: but I was still more astonished on seeing people on horseback. I did not know what this could mean; and indeed I thought these people were full of nothing but magical arts. While I was in this astonishment one of my fellow prisoners spoke to a countryman of his about the horses, who said they were the same kind they had in their country. I understood them, though they were from a distant part of Africa, and I thought it odd I had not seen any horses there; but afterwards, when I came to converse with different Africans, I found they had many horses amongst them, and much larger than those I then saw. We were not many days in the merchant's custody before we were sold after their usual manner, which is this:—On a signal given, (as the beat of a drum) the buyers rush at once into the yard where the slaves are confined, and make choice of that parcel they like best. The noise and clamour with which this is attended, and the eagerness visible in the countenances of the buyers, serve not a little to increase the apprehensions of the terrified Africans, who may well be supposed to consider them as the ministers of that destruction to which they think themselves devoted. In this manner, without scruple, are relations and friends separated, most of them never to see each other again. I remember in the vessel in which I was brought over, in the men's apartment, there were several brothers, who, in the sale, were sold in different lots; and it was very moving on this occasion to see and hear their cries at parting. O, ye nominal Christians! might not an African ask you, learned you this from your God, who says unto you, Do unto all men as you would men should do unto you? Is it not enough that we are torn from our country and friends to toil for your luxury and lust of gain? Must every tender feeling be likewise sacrificed to your avarice? Are the dearest friends and relations, now rendered more dear by their separation from their kindred, still to be parted from each other, and thus prevented from cheering the gloom of slavery with the small comfort of being together and mingling their sufferings and sorrows? Why are parents to lose their children, brothers their sisters, or husbands their wives? Surely this is a new refinement in cruelty, which, while it has no advantage to atone for it, thus aggravates distress, and adds fresh horrors even to the wretchedness of slavery.

J. Hector St. John Crèvecoeur

In December 1759, J. Hector St. John Crèvecoeur (1735–1813), an officer in the French Army captured in Quebec, left his ship at New York City and chose to begin a new life in the British colonies. Six years later he became a British subject, and by 1769 he had married an American woman, settled on a farm in Orange County, New York, and begun his classic Letters from an American Farmer *(1782).*

Crèvecoeur traveled widely in his adopted country, with an eye attentive to the distinctively American qualities of the people, places, manners, and institutions he encountered along the way. In Nantucket—that "great nursery" of maritime manpower and skill—he observed the modest beginnings of a culture that Melville would marvel at a century later in Moby-Dick*: "thus have these Nantucketers, these sea hermits, issuing from their ant-hill in the sea, overrun and conquered the watery world like so many Alexanders; parcelling out among them the Atlantic, Pacific, and Indian oceans."*

from *Peculiar Customs at Nantucket*

In order to view the island in its longest direction from the town, I took a ride to the easternmost parts of it, remarkable only for the Pochick Rip, where their best fish are caught. I passed by the Tetoukèmah lots, which are the fields of the community; the fences were made of cedar posts and rails, and looked perfectly straight and neat; the various crops they enclosed were flourishing; thence I descended into Barry's Valley, where the blue and the spear grass looked more abundant than I had seen on any other part of the island; thence to Gib's Pond; and arrived at last at Siasconcet. Several dwellings had been erected on this wild shore for the purpose of sheltering the fishermen in the season of fishing; I found them all empty, except that particular one to which I had been directed. It was like the others, built on the highest part of the shore, in the face of the great ocean; the soil appeared to be composed of no other stratum but sand, covered with a scattered herbage. What rendered this house still more v of notice in my eyes was that it had been built on the ruins of one of the ancient huts erected by the first settlers for observing the appearance of the whales. Here lived a single family without a neighbour; I had never before seen a spot better calculated to cherish contemplative ideas, perfectly unconnected with the great world, and far removed from its perturbations. The ever-raging ocean was all that presented itself to the view of this family; it irresistibly attracted my whole attention: my eyes were involuntarily directed to the horizontal line of that watery surface, which is ever in motion and ever threatening destruction to these shores. My ears were stunned with the roar of its waves rolling one over the other, as if impelled by a superior force to overwhelm the spot on which I stood. My nostrils involuntarily inhaled the saline vapours which arose from the dispersed particles of the foaming billows or from the weeds scattered on the shores. My mind suggested a thousand vague reflections, pleasing in the hour of their spontaneous birth, but now half forgotten, and all indistinct; and who is the landman that can behold without affright so singular an element, which by its impetuosity seems to be the destroyer of this poor planet, yet at particular times accumulates the scattered fragments and produces islands and continents fit for men to dwell on! Who can observe the regular vicissitudes of its waters without astonishment, now swelling themselves in order to penetrate through every river and opening and thereby facilitate navigation, at other times retiring from the shores to permit man to collect that variety of shell-fish which is the support of the poor? Who can see the storms of wind, blowing sometimes with an impetuosity sufficiently strong even to move the earth, without feeling himself affected beyond the sphere of common ideas? Can this wind which but a few days ago refreshed our American fields and cooled us in the shade be the same element which now and then so powerfully convulses the waters of the sea, dismasts vessels, causes so many shipwrecks and such extensive desolations? How diminutive does a man appear to himself when filled with these thoughts, and standing as I did on the verge of the ocean! This family lived entirely by fishing, for the plough has not dared yet to disturb the parched surface of the neighbouring plain; and to what purpose could this operation be performed! Where is it that mankind will not find safety, peace, and abundance, with freedom and civil happiness? Nothing was wanting here to make this a most philosophical retreat but a few ancient trees to shelter contemplation in its beloved solitude. There I saw a numerous family of children of various ages—the blessings of an early marriage; they were ruddy as the cherry, healthy as the fish they lived on, hardy as the pine knots; the eldest were already able to encounter the boisterous waves and shuddered not at their approach, early initiating themselves in the mysteries of that seafaring career, for which they were all intended; the younger, timid as yet, on the edge of a less agitated pool, were teaching themselves with nutshells and pieces of wood, in imitation of boats, how to navigate in a future day the larger vessels of their father through a rougher and deeper ocean. I stayed two days there on purpose to become acquainted with the different branches of their economy and their manner of living in this singular retreat. The clams, the oysters of the shores, with the addition of Indian dumplings, constituted their daily and most substantial food. Larger fish were often caught on the neighbouring rip; these afforded them their greatest dainties; they had likewise plenty of smoked bacon. The noise of the wheels announced the industry of the mother and daughters; one of them had been bred a weaver, and having a loom in the house, found means of clothing the whole family; they were perfectly at ease and seemed to want for nothing.

John Ledyard

In January 1778—about fourteen hundred years after the first inhabitants of Hawaii began to arrive in sailing canoes from Tahiti or the Marquesas—Captain James Cook, aboard H.M.S. Resolution, *became the first European in over 200 years to visit Hawaii. Hailed at first as a demi-divinity, Cook was killed just over a year later in a fight with angry natives on the beach at Kealakekua bay.*

John Ledyard (1751–1789) was uniquely positioned to chronicle the Hawaiians' gradual disillusion with their British visitors. Born in Groton, Connecticut, the son of a sea captain, he had joined Cook's third Pacific expedition after a stint as a common sailor in the Mediterranean. On his return to London, in the midst of the American Revolution, he was confined to barracks for two years for refusing to fight against his countrymen. He later escaped to Hartford, where he wrote his account of what he had seen in the Pacific—an account that reflects the independent and critical spirit of the times. In later years Ledyard became an enthusiastic advocate for opening up the fur trade along America's northwest coast—another legacy of Cook's voyages. He died in Cairo organizing an expedition to find the source of the Niger.

from *A Journal of Captain Cook's Last Voyage*

Our return to this bay was as disagreeable to us as it was to the inhabitants, for we were reciprocally tired of each other. They had been oppressed and were weary of our prostituted alliance, and we were agrieved by the consideration of wanting the provisions and refreshments of the country, which we had every reason to suppose from their behavior antecedent to our departure would now be withheld from us or brought in such small quantities as to be worse than none. What we anticipated was true. When we entered the bay where before we had the shouts of thousands to welcome our arrival, we had the mortification not to see a single canoe, and hardly any inhabitants in the towns. Cook was chagrined and his people were soured. Towards night however the canoes came in, but the provisions both in quantity and quality plainly informed us that times were altered, and what was very remarkable was the exorbitant price they asked; and the particular fancy they all at once took to iron daggers or dirks, which was the only article that was any ways current, with the chiefs at least. It was also equally evident from the looks of the natives as well as every other appearance that our former friendship was at an end, and that we had nothing to do but to hasten our departure to some different island where our vices were not known, and where our extrinsic virtues might gain us another short space of being wondered at, and doing as we pleased, or as our tars expressed it of being happy by the month.

Nor was their passive appearance of disgust all we had to fear, nor did it continue long: before dark a canoe with a number of armed chiefs came along side of us without provisions and indeed without any perceptible design, after staying a short time only they went to the Discovery where they went on board a part of them. Here they affected great friendship, and unfortunately overacting the dissemblance Clerke was jealous & ordered two centinels on the gangways. These men were purposely sent by the chief who had formerly been so very intimate with Clerke, and afterwards so ill treated by him with the charge of stealing his jolly boat. They came with a determination of mischief, and effected it. After they were returned to the canoe all but one they got their paddles and every thing ready for a start. Those in the canoes observing the sentry to be watchful took off his attention by some conversation that they knew would be pleasing to him, and by this means favored the designs of the man on board, who watching his opportunity snatched two pair of tongs, and other iron tools that then lay close by the armourers at work at the forge, and mounting the gangway-rail, with one leap threw himself and his goods into the canoe, that was then upon the movement, and taking up his paddle joined the others and standing directly for the shore, they were out of our reach almost instantaneously; even before a musket could be had from the armed chest to fire at them. The sentries had only hangers.

This was the boldest exploit that had yet been attempted, and had a bad aspect with it. Clerke immediately sent to the commodore who advised to send a boat on shore to endeavor at least to regain the goods if they could not the men who took them, but the errand was illy executed as contrived, and the master of the Discovery was glad to return with a severe drubbing from the very chief who had been so male treated by Clerke: the crew were also pelted with stones and had all their oars broke, and they had not a single weapon in the boat not even a single cutlass to defend themselves. When Cook heard of this he went armed himself in person to the guard on shore, took a file of marines and went through the whole town demanding restitution, and threatening the delinquents and their abettors with the severest punishments, but not being able to effect any thing, came off just at sun-set highly displeased and not a little concerned at the bad appearance of things. But even this was nothing to what followed.

On the 13th at night the Discovery's large cutter which was at her usual moorings at the bower buoy was taken away.

On the 14th the captains met to consult what should be done on this alarming occasion, and the issue of their opinions was that one of the two captains should land with armed boats and a guard of marines at Kiverua, and attempt to persuade Kireeaboo who was then at his house in that town to come on board upon a visit, and that when he was on board he should be kept prisoner until his subjects should release him by a restitution of the cutter, and if it was afterwards thought proper, he or some of the family who might accompany him should be kept as perpetual hostages for the good behavior of the people, during the remaining part of our continuance at Kireekakooa, and this plan was the more approved of by Cook as he had so repeatedly on former occasions to the southward employed it with success.

Clerke was then in a deep decline in his health, and too feeble to undertake the affair though it naturally devolved upon him as a point of duty not well transferable, he therefore beged Cook to oblige him so much as to take that part of the business of the day upon himself in his stead. This Cook agreed to, but previous to his landing made some additional arrangements respecting the possible event of things, though it is certain from the appearance of the subsequent arrangements that he guarded more against the flight of Kireeaboo or those he could wish to see, than from an attack, or even much insult. The disposition of our guards when the movements began were thus: Cook in his pennace with six private marines: a corporal, serjeant and two lieutenants of marines went a head followed by the launch with other marines and seamen on one quarter, and the small cutter on the other with only the crew on board. This part of the guard rowed for Kireekakoa. Our large cutter and two boats from the Discovery had orders to proceed to the mouth of the bay, form at equal distances across, and prevent any communication by water from any other part of the island to the towns within the bay, or from them without. Cook landed at Kiverua about nine o'clock in the morning with the marines in the pennace, and went by a circuitous march to the house of Kireeaboo in order to evade the suspicion of any design. This rout led them through a considerable part of the town which discovered every symptom of mischief, though Cook blinded by some fatal cause could not perceive it, or too self-confident would not regard it.

The town was evacuated by the women and children, who had retired to the circumadjacent hills, and appeared almost destitute of men, but there were at that time 200 chiefs and more than twice that number of other men detached and secreted in different parts of the houses nearest to Kireeaboo exclusive of unknown numbers without the skirts of the town, and those that were seen were dressed many of them in black. When the guard reached Kireeaboo's house, Cook ordered the lieutenant of marines to go in and see if he was at home, and if he was to bring him out; the lieutenant went in and found the old man sitting with two or three old women of distinction, and when he gave Kireeaboo to understand that Cook was without and wanted to see him he discovered the greatest marks of uneasiness, but arose and accompanied the lieutenant out, holding his hand; when he came before Cook he squatted down upon his hams as a mark of humiliation, and Cook took him by the hand from the lieutenant, and conversed with him.

The appearance of our parade both by water and on shore, though conducted with the utmost silence and with as little ostentation as possible, had alarmed the towns on both sides of the bay, but particularly Kiverua, who were in complete order for an onset otherwise it would have been a matter of surprise, that though Cook did not see 20 men in passing through the town, yet before he had conversed 10 minutes with Kireeaboo he was surrounded by three or four hundred people, and above half of them chiefs. Cook grew uneasy when he observed this, and was the more urgent in his persuasions with Kireeaboo to go on board, and actually persuaded the old man to go at length, and led him within a rod or two of the shore, but the just fears and conjectures of the chiefs at last interposed. They held the old man back, and one of the chiefs threatened Cook when he attempted to make them quit Kireeaboo. Some of the crowd now cried out that Cook was going to take their king from them and kill him, and there was one in particular that advanced towards Cook in an attitude that alarmed one of the guard who presented his bayonet and opposed him: Acquainting Cook in the mean time of the danger of his situation, and that the Indians in a few minutes would attack him, that he had overheard the man whom he had just stopped from rushing in upon him say that our boats which were out in the harbour had just killed his brother and he would be revenged. Cook attended to what this man said, and desired him to shew him the Indian that had dared to attempt a combat with him, and as soon as he was pointed out Cook fired at him with a blank. The Indian perceiving he received no damage from the fire rushed from without the croud a second time, and threatened any one that should oppose him. Cook perceiving this fired a ball, which entering the Indian's groin he fell and was drawn off by the rest. Cook perceiving the people determined to oppose his designs, and that he should not succeed without further bloodshed ordered the lieutenant of marines (Mr. Phillips) to withdraw his men and get them into the boats, which were then laying ready to receive them. This was effected by the serjeant, but the instant they began to retreat Cook was hit with a stone, and perceiving the man who hove, shot him dead: The officer in the boats perceiving the guard retreating, and hearing this third discharge ordered the boats to fire, this occasioned the guard to face about and fire, and then the attack became general, Cook and Mr. Phillips were together a few paces in the rear of the guard, and perceiving a general fire without orders quitted Kireeaboo, and ran to the shore to put a stop to it, but not being able to make themselves heard, and being close pressed upon by the chiefs they joined the guard and fired as they retreated. Cook having at length reached the margin of the water between the fire of the boats waved with his hat to cease firing and come in, and while he was doing this a chief from behind stabbed him with one of our iron daggers just under the shoulder-blade, and passed quite through his body. Cook fell with his face in the water and immediately expired. Mr. Phillips not being able any longer to use his fusee drew his sword and engageing the chief who he saw kill Cook soon dispatched him, his guard in the mean time were all killed but two, and they had plunged into the water and were swimming to the boats, he stood thus for some time the butt of all their force, and being as complete in the use of his sword as he was accomplished: his noble atchievments struck the barbarians with awe, but being wounded and growing faint from loss of blood, and excessive action, he plunged into the sea with his sword in his hand and swam to the boats, where however he was scarcely taken on board before somebody saw one of the marines that had swam from the shore laying flat upon the bottom. Phillips hearing this run aft, threw himself in after him and brought him up with him to the surface of the water and both were taken in.

The boats had hitherto kept up a very hot fire, and laying off without the reach of any weapons but stones had received no damage, and being fully at leisure to keep up an unremitted and uniform action made great havoc among the Indians, particularly among the chiefs who stood foremost in the crowd and were most exposed, but whether from their bravery or ignorance of the real cause that deprived so many of them of life, they made such a stand, may be questioned since it is certain that they in general if not universally understood heretofore that it was the fire only of our arms that destroyed them, this seems to be strengthened by the circumstance of the large thick mats they were observed to wear, which were also constantly kept wet, and furthermore the Indian that Cook fired at with a blank discovered no fear when he found his mat unburnt, saying in their language when he showed it to the bystanders that there was no fire had touched it. This may be supposed at least to have had some influence. It is however certain whether from one or both those causes that the numbers who fell made no apparent impression on those who survived, they were immediately taken off and had their places supplied in a constant determined succession.

Lieutenant Gore who commanded as first lieutenant under Cook in the Resolution, which lay opposite the place where this attack was made, perceiving with his glass that the guard on shore was cut off, and that Cook had fell, immediately passed a spring upon one of the cables, and bringing the ship's starboard guns to bear, and fired two round shot over the boats into the middle of the croud and both the thunder of the cannon and the effects of the shot, operated so powerfully, that it produced a most precipitate retreat from the shore to the town. This was done that the boats might land and secure our dead. But the lieutenant who commanded the boats did not chose to improve the hint, though the people in the boats were eager at least to get the bodies of their comrades and their lost commander, if they did no more. Mr. Phillips was so enraged at this palpable instance of apparent pusillanimity, that the altercation he had with this other lieutenant would have ended in the immediate death of one of them had not a signal from the ship that instant hove out put an end to it by orders to return.

When the boats from the shore reached the ships the boats in the mouth of the bay also returned. The conduct of the lieutenant, who commanded the boats at the town, was an object that required an early attention, but from the situation of other matters of more immediate importance it was defered. Our mast that was repairing at Kireekakoa, and our astronomical tents were only protected by a corporal and six marines exclusive of the carpenters at work upon it, and demanded immediate protection: As soon, therefore, as the people were refreshed with some grog and reinforced they were ordered thither. In the mean time the marine who had been taken up by Mr. Phillips discovered returning life and seemed in a way to recover, and we found Mr. Phillips's wound not dangerous, though very bad. We also observed at Kiverua that our dead were drawn off by the Indians, which was a mortifying sight, but after the boats were gone they did it in spite of our cannon, which were firing at them several minutes, but they had no sooner effected this matter than they retired to the hills to avoid our shot. The expedition to Kiverua had taken up about an hour and an half, and we lost besides Cook a corporal and three marines.

Notwithstanding the dispatch that was used in sending a force to Kireekakoa, the small party there were already attacked before their arrival, but by an excellent manœuvre of taking possession of the Morai they defended themselves without any material damage until the succours came. The natives did not attempt to molest the boats in their debarkation of our people, which we much wondered at, and they soon joined the others upon the Morai amounting in the whole to about 60. Mr. Phillips notwithstanding his wound, was present, and in conjunction with lieutenant King carried the chief command. The plan was to act only defensivly until we could get our mast into the water to tow off, and our tents into the boats; and as soon as that was effected to return on board: This we did in about an hours time, but not without killing a number of the natives, who resolutely attacked us and endeavored to mount the walls of the Morai, where they were lowest, but being opposed with our skill in such modes of attack and the great superiority of our arms they were even repulsed with loss, and at length retreated among the houses adjacent to the Morai, which affording a good opportunity to retreat to our boats we embraced it and got off all well. Our mast was taken on the booms and repaired there though to disadvantage.

About two o'clock Capt. Clerke came on board to take command of the Resolution, and the same day Mr. John Gore who had been Cook's first lieutenant, and next in command at Cook's death, went on board to take command of the Discovery. About four o'clock Clerke sent three boats well manned and armed to Kiverua with orders to demand the bodies of our dead, and if refused to return without doing any thing to obtain them by force. Mr. King who was now first lieutenant in the Resolution took the command in the Pennace carrying a white jack in the stern: the boats formed in a line within stones throw of the shore where they remained about a quarter of an hour conversing with the inhabitants, who upon seeing us approach had assembled again, as numerous and as well appointed as ever; nothing material happened during this parley: we demanded the bodies, and they refused them, or what was as bad, they ridiculed us, and when we moved to return hove stones at us, shewed us Cook's hanger all bloody, his hat and the cloaths of the other dead.

The people in the boats who supposed they were going to attack them again were much disappointed and at their return vented their complaints, and somewhat more than asked to be revenged upon their savage insulting foes; but they would have taken perhaps an undue advantage had they attacked them from the boats, even supposing them to have had the fairest claim to justice, in a prosecution of the broil, for they were entirely secure even from being wounded in the contest, and in fact it would have looked too much like sporting with the lives of men, and turning war which is or ought to be one of the most serious circumstances in life into a cruel farce, not to say any thing worse; besides there really at that time was no necessity for it, for the bodies were gone we did not know where, and had we again strewed the shore with their dead, we never should have obtained the bodys unless we had landed and took them. After dark the sentries upon the gangways saw a canoe approaching the ship in a very silent and hasty manner, and when she got within call the officer of the deck hailed her, but the Indians returning no answer the sentry fired at her, and shot one of the Indians through the leg, upon which he bawled out tutee tutee, that is Cook. Clerke was acquainted with the matter and came upon deck and ordered her along side and the Indians on board: there were only three of them, and one had Cook's hat on his head which he gave us to understand he had brought at the hazard of his life: the man that was wounded was taken to the surgeon and had his wound dressed. But we were extremely affected and disgusted when the other Indian produced from a bundle he had under his arm a part of Cook's thigh wrapped up in clean cloth which he said he saw himself cut from the bone in the manner we saw it, and when we enquired what had become of the remaining part of him, he gnashed his teeth and said it was to be eaten that night. As soon as the wound of the Indian that was shot was dressed, they departed with a promise if they could to bring the remainder of Cook's body the next night.

The prospect of recovering Cook's body though by pieces afforded some satisfaction and we therefore suspended the further prosecution of business on shore for the next day. In the evening about the same time he appeared before, we saw the same Indian with other parts of Cook's body, to wit the upper part of his head and both his hands, which he said he had been at infinite pains to procure, and that the other parts could not be obtained, especially the flesh which was mostly eat up: the head was scalped and all the brains taken out: the hands were scored and salted: these fragments of the body of the unfortunate Cook were put into a box and preserved in hopes of getting more of them: the Indians who brought them were well satisfied with presents, and returned again to the shore the same night, and though they assured us they could not procure any more of those remains: we yet waited another day but saw no more of the Indian.

On the 17th the Discovery having the least draught of water was ordered to remove as near the watering place as possible: moore, and with a spring bring her broadside to bear upon it, in order to protect the watering parties in case of insult. As soon as this was done the boats with a small party landed, and made out to set off one turn of water but no more: the natives had assembled to oppose them behind the houses and the stone walls, from whence they discharged whole clouds of stones, and being in some places within 20 yards of our people, wounded several of them very badly: and at length they began to come out upon the beach upon which a signal was made for the boats to return, and the ship fired two cannon which killed three men, and we afterwards heard took off a woman's arm.

As we had hitherto to act only on the defensive part, and finding we could not succeed we were determined to alter our mode of attack: go to sea without water we could not, and as we made no doubt that our endeavors at any of the other islands who had heard of our situation, would be attended with the same difficulties, we were determined to try the contest here where the broil first originated.

On the 18th we took all the force we could spare from both ships and landed at eight in the morning. We were attacked again in the same manner the small party had been yesterday, upon which we formed such of our seamen as were most expert at small arms into two divisions in conjunction with the marines amounting to about twenty-five each division: Of some of the other seamen we composed two scouting parties armed with pistols, cutlasses, hand-grenades and torches: The waterers had arms and were to act as occasion required. Our first manœuvre was to draw them from among the houses on to the beach by stratagem and expose them to the fire of the ship as well as ours; but failing in this we joined the two divisions and advanced through an avenue that led directly into this part of the town in a solid column: The natives seeing this flung themselves into it to oppose our progress and attacked us at close quarters with their short spears, daggers and stones, but they soon gave way when the front of the column pressed upon them with their bayonets and retired to some houses about ten rods off where they again rallied: During this little attack we had several wounded, but none killed; the Indians took off the most of their killed, which were near a hundred: In the mean while our scouting parties improving the opportunity had circumvented that part of the town nearest the watering place and had just set fire to it, and joining us we retreated to the beach pretendedly in great disorder, and the natives seeing their town in flames and supposing we were going off followed us to the water where we again attacked them, and the ship improving the opportunity made such use of her cannon that they soon again run and were pursued many of them into the flames of their own houses, where if they were not instantly killed they were burnt to death. The fire had now spread universally, and the houses consisting of light dry materials, burnt with such rapidity that in half an hour every one north-west of the Morai was leveled, and had this part not been detached from the south-east part, the whole town of Kireekakooa consisting of above a thousand houses, would have been destroyed: thus ended this days business.

WILLIAM CLARK

"Ocian in view! O! the joy!" Thus William Clark (1770–1838) recorded the ecstatic realization—on November 7, 1805, a year and a half after their departure up the lower Missouri—that he and Meriwether Lewis and their party had succeeded in crossing the continent. They had arrived at the confluence of the Columbia River and the Pacific—a region of violent waves and tidal currents that would later become the site of John Jacob Astor's fur-trading outpost Fort Astoria and of dozens of shipwrecks. Short of provisions, and with what little they had soaked by the near-constant rain, they waited for a supply ship Thomas Jefferson had inexplicably failed to send. Two months later, as recounted in the journal excerpt that follows, they made their way along the coast in search of food.

from *The Journals of the Lewis & Clark Expedition*

Wednesday 8th January 1806

THE last night proved fair and Cold wind hard from the S. E. we Set out early and proceeded to the top of the mountain next to the which is much the highest part and that part faceing the Sea is open, from this point I beheld the grandest and most pleasing prospects which my eyes ever surveyed, in my frount a boundless Ocean; to the N. and N. E. the coast as far as my sight Could be extended, the Seas rageing with emence wave and brakeing with great force from the rocks of Cape Disapointment as far as I could See to the N. W. The Clatsops Chinnooks and other villagers on each Side of the Columbia river and in the Praries below me, the meanderings of 3 handsom Streams heading in Small lakes at the foot the high Country; The Columbia River for a Some distance up, with its Bays and Small rivers and on the other Side I have a view of the Coast for an emence distance to the S. E. by S. the nitches and points of high land which forms this Corse for a long ways aded to the inoumerable rocks of emence Sise out at a great distance from the Shore and against which the Seas brak with great force gives this Coast a most romantic appearance. from this point of View my guide pointed to a village at the mouth of a Small river near which place he Said the whale was, he also pointed to 4 other places where the princpal Villages of the *Kil la mox* were Situated, I could plainly See the houses of 2 of those Villeges & the Smoke of a 3rd which was two far of for me to disern with my naked eye— after taking the Courses and computed the Distances in my own mind, I proceeded on down a Steep decent to a Single house the remains of an old *Kil a mox* Town in a nitch imediately on the Sea Coast, at which place great no. of eregular rocks are out and the waves comes in with great force. Near this old Town I observed large Canoes of the neetest kind on the ground Some of which appeared nearly decayed others quit Sound, I examoned those Canoes and found they were the repository of the dead— This Custom of Secureing the Dead differs a little from the Chinnooks. the Kil a mox Secure the dead bodies in an oblong box of Plank, which is placed in an open Canoe resting on the ground, in which is put a paddle and Sundery other articles the property of the disceased. The Coast in the neighbourhood of this old village is slipping from the Sides of the high hills, in emence masses; fifty or a hundred acres at a time give way and a great proportion of an instant precipitated into the Ocean. those hills and mountains are principally composed of a yellow Clay; their Slipping off or Spliting assunder at this time is no doubt Caused by the incessant rains which has fallen within the last two months. the mountans Covered with a verry heavy Croth of pine & furr, also the white Cedar or *arbor vita* and a Small proportion of the black alder, this alder grows to the hight of Sixty or Seventy feet and from 2 to 3 feet in diamiter. Some Species of pine on the top of the Point of View rise to the emmence hight of 210 feet and from 8 to 12 feet in diameter, and are perfectly Sound and Solid. Wind hard from the S. E and See looked [ ] in the after part of the Day breaking with great force against the Scattering rocks at Some distance from Shore, and the ruged rockey points under which we wer obleged to pass and if we had unfortunately made one false Stet we Should eneviateably have fallen into the Sea and dashed against the rocks in an instant, fortunately we passed over 3 of those dismal points and arived on a butifull Sand Shore on which we Continued for 2 miles, Crossed a Creek 80 yards near 5 Cabins, and proceeded to the place the whale had perished, found only the Skelleton of this monster on the Sand between 2 of the villages of the *Kil a mox* nation; the Whale was already pillaged of every valuable part by the Kil a mox Inds. in the vecinity of whose village's it lay on the Strand where the waves and tide had driven up & left it. this Skeleton measured 105 feet. I returned to the village of 5 Cabins on the Creek which I shall call *E co-la* or whale Creek, found the nativs busily engaged boiling the blubber, which they performed in a large Squar wooden trought by means of hot Stones; the oil when extracted was Secured in bladders and the Guts of the whale; the blubber from which the oil was only partially extracted by this process, was laid by in their Cabins in large flickes for use; those flickes they usially expose to the fire on a wooden Spit untill it is prutty well wormed through and then eate it either alone or with roots of the rush, *Shaw na tâk we* or diped in the oil. The *Kil a mox* although they possessed large quantities of this blubber and oil were so prenurious that they disposed of it with great reluctiance and in Small quantities only; insomuch that my utmost exertion aided by the party with the Small Stock of merchindize I had taken with me were not able to precure more blubber than about 300 wt. and a fiew gallons of oil; Small as this Stock is I prise it highly; and thank providence for directing the whale to us; and think him much more kind to us than he was to jonah, having Sent this monster to be *Swallowed by us* in Sted of *Swallowing of us* as jonah's did.

David Porter

In 1812 the United States declared war on Great Britain, the strongest naval power in the world, in large part because of maritime grievances, including British impressment of American seamen and seizures of American ships trading with Napoleonic France. Unable to fight fleet actions because of its small number of ships, the U.S. Navy adopted a strategy of commerce raiding. Late in 1812 the 46-gun frigate Essex *rounded Cape Horn and became the first American warship to sail in the Pacific. Her captain, David Porter (1780–1843), had joined the navy in 1798, fought against the French and the Tripoli pirates, and been given command of the* Essex *in 1811. This excerpt from his* Journal of a Cruise *begins on May 28, 1813, in the Galapagos Islands; the* Barclay *was an American whaling ship, the* Montezuma *and* Policy *British whalers the* Essex *had captured. The* Essex *seized a total of 12 British ships in the Pacific before being trapped off the coast of Chile on March 28, 1814, by the frigate* Phoebe *and sloop* Cherub. *After a battle in which 58 of his men were killed, Porter surrendered his ship.*

from *Journal of a Cruise Made to the Pacific Ocean*

On the afternoon of the 28th, as we were standing to the northward with the Montezuma in tow, the Barclay looking out on our starboard, and the Policy on our larboard quarter, the men on the lookout on board the Essex discovered a sail right ahead, and immediately the Montezuma was cast off, and all sail made in chase. At sunset we could see her plainly from deck, and, as she was standing from us with all the sail she could crowd, I entertained no hopes of coming up with her in the night, as I had no doubt of her altering her course, and thus eluding us. I continued, however, to carry all the sail the ship would bear, in order to near her as much as possible; and being well aware of the prevalence of calms in this quarter, I had strong hopes that, as usual, it would fall calm before morning, and keep us in sight of each other. But as the wind continued fresh, and believing she would change her course as soon as it grew dark, I hove to, at nine o'clock, for the other vessels to come up, when I directed the Montezuma to run northwest (which was his bearing when we last saw him) seven miles, and then heave to, the Barclay to run the same distance to the east, and I intended sending the Policy to the southwest, but she did not come up in time. This arrangement I hoped would enable one or the other of the vessels to get sight of the chase in the morning, and I was not disappointed; for next day the Montezuma made a signal for a sail to the northward, and at the same time we bore away in pursuit of her with all the sail we could carry, but it was not until two hours after we had given chase to her, that we could discover her from our mast-heads. About meridian the wind began to die away; I had now sight of the stranger from deck, and had no doubt of his being an enemy. The Montezuma was still between us and him, and distant from us about six miles. I determined now that he should not again escape us, for I was fully convinced this was the same vessel we had chased the day before. I directed three of the fastest rowing boats to be manned with as many armed men as they could carry, and to proceed, under the command of lieutenant Wilmer, to the Montezuma, with orders to take three of that ship's boats, and before night to proceed to take his station astern of the stranger, so that he could keep sight of him, placing the other in a line astern of him, so that a communication could be had by signal from the headmost boat to the Montezuma, and from thence to the Essex. By this arrangement I hoped to be guided by flashes in my pursuit of the enemy, and prevent the probability of his escaping. I directed lieutenant Wilmer not to make any attack on her, unless it should prove perfectly calm, and then to row up with muffled oars, and board her by surprise. To prevent any other mode of attack being made, I allowed them no other arms than a pistol, cutlass, and boarding-axe each.

After the boats had left us, a breeze sprung up, which enabled us to continue the chase; and, as we soon passed the boats, I made a signal for the Montezuma to heave to and pick them up. As we approached the chase, she hauled close on a wind to the eastward, and shortly afterwards hove about to stand for us. From her warlike appearance, and the signals made by her, I supposed her to be an English sloop of war, as she wore both the English ensign and pendant. I now made such preparations for action as my weak crew would admit of, directing the marines and top-men to lay by their muskets, and, as well as the bracemen and all others on board, to take their stations at the guns. All my officers were away from the ship; but still I could not perceive that the small remains of my men had, in time of need, lost any of their wonted energy and zeal.

We were soon along side of him, when I hoisted English colours, and directed her commander to come on board, which order was soon complied with, when at this instant another strange sail was descried from the mast-head. A few men were taken out of our prize, which proved to be the British letter of marque ship Atlantic, Obadiah Wier master, employed in whaling, and mounting six guns, (eighteen pounders.) As soon as the Montezuma came up, I threw some men on board the Atlantic, with lieutenant M'Knight, and sent her in pursuit of the other stranger to the northwest, while I steered more northerly; for, as the Atlantic was reputed the fastest sailer in those seas, I had no doubt, by this means, of rendering her capture certain. We were soon convinced that the Atlantic deserved her character for sailing, as during the chase we had very little advantage of her, notwithstanding we had all the sail we could carry, and she the whole time without her studding-sails, having none bent. Night was now fast approaching; we were doubtful whether we were near enough to keep sight of our new chase, which our prisoners informed us was another British letter of marque. As it grew dark, we once lost sight of her; but we soon discovered her again by means of our night-glasses, and on her heaving about to elude us, on the supposition that we could no longer see her, we soon got along side of her, and on firing a shot at her, she hove to. I directed her commander to repair on board, which he refused to do until he knew who we were. I now perceived by his lights that he was prepared for action, and fired one shot between his masts to intimidate him, threatening him with a broadside if he did not repair on board immediately. This had the desired effect, as he soon came on board, prepared to meet in us an enemy. This vessel proved to be the British letter of marque ship Greenwich, of ten guns, a prime sailer, employed in the whale-fishery. Her captain had taken in a good stock of Dutch courage, and, from the preparations that were made on board his vessel, there could be no doubt of his intentions to have fired into us, had he not been intimidated by the shot we gave him between his masts. He expressed great regret that the Atlantic and his ship had not joined one another before their capture, as he believed they would then have been more than a match for us. Indeed, considering the then weakened state of the crew, and the absence of every officer, (except the chaplain, the clerk, and the boatswain, from whom I received every assistance in their power,) it seems not unlikely, as they were in every respect well prepared for action, that they would have given us some trouble, and rendered the capture of one of them at least doubtful.

I must here observe, that the captain of the Atlantic, (an American from Nantucket, where he has a wife and family,) on his first coming on board the Essex, expressed his extreme pleasure on finding (as he supposed we were) an English frigate in those seas. He informed me that he had sailed from England under convoy of the Java frigate, and had put into port Praya a few days after the Essex, an American frigate, had left there; that the Java had sailed immediately in pursuit of her, and that it was the general belief the Essex had gone around the Cape of Good Hope. He parted with the Java after crossing the line, and on his arrival at Conception, heard she had been sunk off Bahia by the American frigate Constitution. On enquiry respecting the American vessels in the South Seas, he informed me that about Conception was the best place to cruise for them, for he had left at that place nine of them in an unprotected and defenceless state, and entirely at a loss what to do with themselves; that they were almost daily arriving there, and that he had no doubt, by going off there, we should be enabled to take the most of them. I asked him how he reconciled it to himself to sail from England under the British flag, and in an armed ship, after hostilities had taken place between the two countries. He said he found no difficulty in reconciling it to himself; for, although he was born in America, he was an Englishman at heart. This man appeared the polished gentleman in his manners, but evidently possessed a corrupt heart, and, like all other renegadoes, was desirous of doing his native country all the injury in his power, with the hope of thereby ingratiating himself with his new friends. I permitted him to remain in his error some time, but at length introduced to him the captains of the Montezuma and the Georgiana, who soon undeceived him with respect to our being an English frigate. I had felt great pity for these two last gentlemen, and had made the evils of war bear as light on them as possible, by purchasing of them, for the use of the crew, their private adventures, consisting of slop-clothing, tobacco, and spirits, for which they were sincerely grateful. But towards this man I could not feel the same favourable disposition, nor could I conceal my indignation at his conduct. He endeavoured to do away the impression his conduct had made, by artfully putting the case to myself; and with a view of rendering him easy, as I did not wish to triumph over the wretch, I informed him that I was willing to make some allowances for his conduct.

After the capture of the Greenwich, I informed her commander, John Shuttleworth, as well as Obadiah Wier, of the Atlantic, that I felt every disposition to act generously toward them. Shuttleworth was however so much intoxicated, and his language so insulting, that it was with difficulty I could refrain from turning him out of my cabin. Wier was more reserved during my presence there; but, duty requiring me on deck, he, in the presence of some of the officers, used the most bitter invectives against the government of the United States; and he, as well as Shuttleworth, consoled themselves with the pleasing hope, that British frigates would soon be sent to chastise us for our temerity in venturing so far from home. They were at length, however, shown to the apartment allotted them, where feeling, in some measure, restraint removed, they gave full vent to their anger, and indulged in the most abusive language against our government, the ship and her officers, lavishing on me in particular the most scurrilous epithets, and giving me appellations that would have suited a buccanier. They really appeared to have forgotten they were prisoners and in my power, and that it would be more to their advantage to trust entirely to my generosity, than to irritate me by such unprovoked abuse. However, I determined next day to make them sensible of the impropriety of their conduct, and did so without violating either the principles of humanity or the rules of war. I let them feel that they were dependent entirely on my generosity; and this haughty Englishman, who thought to have terrified us with the name of a Briton, and this renegado, who would have sacrificed the interests of his country, were now so humbled by a sense of their own conduct, and of what they merited, that they would have licked the dust from my feet, had it been required of them to do so.

Washington Irving

Washington Irving (1783–1859) set sail aboard the Mexico *on May 25, 1815, bound for Liverpool. The voyage was apparently not a pleasant one—the weather was rough, and Irving found himself, he complained in a letter to his friend Henry Brevoort, "mewed up together for thirty days in dirty cabins" with his fellow passengers.*

Geoffrey Crayon, the urbane and fanciful narrator of Irving's Sketch Book of Geoffrey Crayon, Gent. *(1819–1820), crosses an Atlantic artfully less uncomfortable than Irving himself had—in a "continual reverie," interrupted only briefly by dramatic, rather than authentically threatening, bad weather. Crayon's experience suggests something of a phenomenon still essentially unknown in Irving's day—the pleasure cruise.*

The Voyage

Ships, ships, I will descrie you
Amidst the main,
I will come and try you
What you are protecting
And projecting,
What's your end and aim.
One goes abroad for merchandize and trading,
Another stays to keep his country from invading,
A third is coming home with rich and wealthy lading.
Hallo my fancie, whither wilt thou go?

Old Poem

To an American visiting Europe the long voyage he has to make is an excellent preparative. The temporary absence of worldly scenes and employments produces a state of mind peculiarly fitted to receive new and vivid impressions. The vast space of waters, that separates the hemispheres is like a blank page in existence. There is no gradual transition by which as in Europe the features and population of one country blend almost imperceptibly with those of another. From the moment you lose sight of the land you have left, all is vacancy until you step on the opposite shore, and are launched at once into the bustle and novelties of another world.

In travelling by land there is a continuity of scene and a connected succession of persons and incidents, that carry on the story of life, and lessen the effect of absence and separation. We drag, it is true, "a lengthening chain" at each remove of our pilgrimage; but the chain is unbroken—we can trace it back link by link; and we feel that the last still grapples us to home. But a wide sea voyage severs us at once.—It makes us conscious of being cast loose from the secure anchorage of settled life and sent adrift upon a doubtful world. It interposes a gulph, not merely imaginary, but real, between us and our homes—a gulph subject to tempest and fear and uncertainty, rendering distance palpable and return precarious.

Such at least was the case with myself. As I saw the last blue line of my native land fade away like a cloud in the horizon, it seemed as if I had closed one volume of the world and its concerns, and had time for meditation before I opened another. That land too, now vanishing from my view; which contained all that was most dear to me in life; what vicissitudes might occur in it—what changes might take place in me, before I should visit it again.—Who can tell when he sets forth to wander, whither he may be driven by the uncertain currents of existence; or when he may return; or whether it may ever be his lot to revisit the scenes of his childhood?

I said that at sea all is vacancy—I should correct the expression. To one given to day dreaming and fond of losing himself in reveries, a sea voyage is full of subjects for meditation: but then they are the wonders of the deep and of the air, and rather tend to abstract the mind from worldly themes. I delighted to loll over the quarter railing or climb to the main top of a calm day, and muse for hours together, on the tranquil bosom of a summer's sea. To gaze upon the piles of golden clouds just peering above the horizon; fancy them some fairy realms and people them with a creation of my own. To watch the gently undulating billows, rolling their silver volumes as if to die away on those happy shores.

There was a delicious sensation of mingled security and awe with which I looked down from my giddy height on the monsters of the deep at their uncouth gambols. Shoals of porpoises tumbling about the bow of the ship; the grampus slowly heaving his huge form above the surface, or the ravenous shark darting like a spectre through the blue waters. My imagination would conjure up all that I had heard or read of the watery world beneath me. Of the finny herds that roam its fathomless valleys; of the shapeless monsters that lurk among the very foundations of the earth and of those wild phantasms that swell the tales of fishermen and sailors.

Sometimes a distant sail, gliding along the edge of the ocean would be another theme of idle speculation. How interesting this fragment of a world, hastening to rejoin the great mass of existence. What a glorious monument of human invention; which has in a manner triumphed over wind and wave; has brought the ends of the earth into communion; has established an interchange of blessings,—pouring into the sterile regions of the north all the luxuries of the south; has diffused the light of knowledge and the charities of cultivated life, and has thus bound together those scattered portions of the human race, between which nature seemed to have thrown an insurmountable barrier.

We one day described some shapeless object drifting at a distance. At sea every thing that breaks the monotony of the surrounding expanse attracts attention. It proved to be the mast of a ship that must have been completely wrecked; for there were the remains of handkerchiefs, by which some of the crew had fastened themselves to this spar to prevent their being washed off by the waves. There was no trace by which the name of the ship could be ascertained. The wreck had evidently drifted about for many monsths: clusters of shell fish had fastened about it; and long sea weeds flaunted at its sides.

But where, thought I, is the crew!—Their struggle has long been over—they have gone down amidst the roar of the tempest—their bones lie whitening among the caverns of the deep. Silence—oblivion, like the waves, have closed over them, and no one can tell the story of their end. What sighs have been wafted after that ship; what prayers offered up at the deserted fireside of home. How often has the mistress, the wife, the mother pored over the daily news to catch some casual intelligence of this rover of the deep. How has expectation darkened into anxiety—anxiety into dread and dread into despair. Alas! not one memento may ever return for love to cherish. All that may ever be known is, that she sailed from her port, "and was never heard of more!"

The sight of this wreck, as usual, gave rise to many dismal anecdotes. This was particularly the case in the evening when the weather, which had hitherto been fair began to look wild and threatening, and gave indications of one of those sudden storms which will sometimes break in upon the serenity of a summer voyage. As we sat round the dull light of a lamp in the cabin, that made the gloom more ghastly, every one had his tale of shipwreck and disaster. I was peculiarly struck with a short one related by the captain.

"As I was once sailing," said he, "in a fine stout ship across the banks of Newfoundland, one of those heavy fogs which prevail in those parts rendered it impossible for us to see far ahead even in the day time; but at night the weather was so thick that we could not distinguish any object at twice the length of the ship. I kept lights at the mast head and a constant watch forward to look out for fishing smacks, which are accustomed to lie at anchor on the banks. The wind was blowing a smacking breeze and we were going at a great rate through the water. Suddenly the watch gave the alarm of 'a sail ahead!'—it was scarcely uttered before we were upon her. She was a small schooner at anchor, with the broad side toward us. The crew were all asleep and had neglected to hoist a light. We struck her just a mid-ships. The force, the size and weight of our vessel bore her down below the waves—we passed over her and were hurried on our course. As the crashing wreck was sinking beneath us I had a glimpse of two or three half-naked wretches, rushing from her cabin—they just started from their beds to be swallowed shrieking by the waves. I heard their drowning cry mingling with the wind. The blast that bore it to our ears swept us out of all further hearing—I shall never forget that cry!—It was some time before we could put the ship about; she was under such headway. We returned as nearly as we could guess to the place where the smack had anchored. We cruised about for several hours in the dense fog. We fired signal guns and listened if we might hear the halloo of any survivors; but all was silent—we never saw or heard any thing of them more!—"

I confess these stories for a time put an end to all my fine fancies. The storm encreased with the night. The sea was lashed up into tremendous confusion. There was a fearful sullen sound of rushing waves and broken surges. Deep called unto deep. At times the black volume of clouds over head seemed rent asunder by flashes of lightning which quivered along the foaming billows, and made the succeeding darkness doubly terrible. The thunders bellowed over the wild waste of waters and were echoed and prolonged by the mountain waves. As I saw the ship staggering and plunging among these roaring caverns, it seemed miraculous that she regained her balance or preserved her buoyancy. Her yards would dip into the water; her bow was almost buried beneath the waves. Sometimes an impending surge appeared ready to overwhelm her, and nothing but a dextrous movement of the helm preserved her from the shock.

When I retired to my cabin the awful scene still followed me. The whistling of the wind through the rigging sounded like funereal wailings. The creaking of the masts; the straining and groaning of bulk heads as the ship laboured in the weltering sea were frightful. As I heard the waves rushing along the side of the ship and roaring in my very ear, it seemed as if death were raging round this floating prison, seeking for his prey—the mere starting of a nail—the yawning of a seam might give him entrance.

A fine day, however, with a tranquil sea and favouring breeze soon put all these dismal reflections to flight. It is impossible to resist the gladdening influence of fine weather and fair wind at sea. When the ship is decked out in all her canvass, every sail swelled, and careering gaily over the curling waves, how lofty, how gallant she appears—how she seems to lord it over the deep!

I might fill a volume with the reveries of a sea voyage, for with me it is almost a continual reverie—but it is time to get to shore.

It was a fine sunny morning when the thrilling cry of Land! was given from the mast head. None but those who have experienced it can form an idea of the delicious throng of sensations which rush into an American's bosom, when he first comes in sight of Europe. There is a volume of associations with the very name. It is the land of promise, teeming with every thing of which his childhood has heard, or on which his studious years have pondered.

From that time until the moment of arrival it was all feverish excitement. The ships of war that prowled like guardian giants along the coast—the headlands of Ireland stretching out into the channel—the Welsh mountains towering into the clouds, all were objects of intense interest. As we sailed up the Mersey I reconnoitered the shores with a telescope. My eye dwelt with delight on neat cottages with their trim shrubberies and green grass plots. I saw the mouldering ruin of an abbey over run with ivy, and the taper spire of a village church rising from the brow of a neighbouring hill—all were characteristic of England.

The tide and wind were so favourable that the ship was enabled to come at once to the pier. It was thronged with people; some idle lookers-on, others eager expectants of friends or relatives. I could distinguish the merchant to whom the ship was consigned. I knew him by his calculating brow and restless air. His hands were thrust into his pockets; he was whistling thoughtfully and walking to and fro, a small space having been accorded him by the crowd in deference to his temporary importance. There were repeated cheerings and salutations interchanged between the shore and the ship, as friends happened to recognize each other. I particularly noticed one young woman of humble dress, but interesting demeanour. She was leaning forward from among the crowd; her eye hurried over the ship as it neared the shore, to catch some wished for countenance. She seemed disappointed and agitated; when I heard a faint voice call her name. It was from a poor sailor who had been ill all the voyage and had excited the sympathy of every one on board. When the weather was fine his messmates had spread a mattress for him on deck in the shade, but of late his illness had so encreased, that he had taken to his hammock, and only breathed a wish that he might see his wife before he died. He had been helped on deck as we came up the river, and was now leaning against the shrouds, with a countenance so wasted, so pale, so ghastly that it was no wonder even the eye of affection did not recognize him. But at the sound of his voice her eye darted on his features—it read at once a whole volume of sorrow—she clasped her hands; uttered a faint shriek and stood wringing them in silent agony.

All now was hurry and bustle. The meetings of acquaintances—the greetings of friends—the consultations of men of business. I alone was solitary and idle. I had no friend to meet, no cheering to receive. I stepped upon the land of my forefathers—but felt that I was a stranger in the land.

Amasa Delano

Born in Duxbury, Massachusetts, Amasa Delano (1763–1823) made his first long voyage at 16, on board the privateer Mars *during the Revolutionary War. He sailed again two years later in a merchant ship bound for the West Indies. By the time he published his* Narrative of Voyages and Travels *(1817)—parts of which inspired Melville's story "Benito Cereno"—Delano had had almost 30 years of experience on merchant vessels, experience he shares in this excerpt.*

from *A Narrative of Voyages and Travels in the Northern and Southern Hemispheres*

My brother and myself built a small ship of two hundred tons and more, with the plan that I should take a voyage in her to the Pacific Ocean. She was launched and fitted; the company for the voyage was formed; and she was manned and armed for the South Pacific, and for the north west coast of America. A suitable cargo for this coast was put on board; eleven six pound guns were mounted; a crew of thirty men was shipped; and every thing was prepared for a double voyage.

From my experience I offer a few remarks on fitting ships for this trade. The vessel ought to be new, good, and strong, or at least nearly new, and always sound. On no account, and under no circumstances, ought an old decayed ship to be employed for this voyage. The common expression, "I believe she will perform the voyage *well enough*," is a disgrace to the judgment and feelings of him who uses it; it shows a feeble, inefficient mind, and a spirit of self-defeating economy. There should never be a doubt as to the fitness of a ship for such a long voyage. She ought not merely to be able to perform it with something like a luck which partakes of the miraculous, but should be qualified, in the judgment of an honest and decided man, for the hazard, without an *if* or a *but* remaining. The fair conclusion should be "I know that she will perform the voyage, if any ship can." She should be at least two hundred tons, and never four hundred, as so large a ship is never required. She should be always coppered, and the metal should be fresh. Except when whales, or seals, are the object of the voyage, and the ship is to return immediately to America, she should be armed, and that according to the tenor of the voyage. If she goes to China, with what is necessary for that market, she should have from six to ten guns, some of them long to reach objects at long shots. Every part of the armament should be of a good quality that he who commands may always know on what to depend. The difference is a trifle between the best and that which is mean, a difference which none but a halting mind would regard. The guns ought all to be of one calibre to prevent the mistakes that are usually made without this, in taking cartridges, shots, ladles, sponges, and rammers, in the time of action. Let every article of the rigging be good, and let every ship have a large surplus of all kinds, as well of canvass, blocks, and twine, as of ropes. The provision should be of good quality, and put up in such good order as to be unquestionable. Put the bread in new casks, or in those which have been filled with brandy, and are well dried, any other liquor tending to give the bread a bad taste. They must be air tight, or the bread will surely spoil. Butter, lard, and pickles should be put into double casks, the outside one filled with salt or brine. The beef and pork for such a voyage ought to be packed with peculiar care, and the cheap kind as it comes into the market should not be purchased. I have had beef put up by Samuel Greggs, which I have carried round the world in a three years voyage, half the time between the tropics, and out of nearly an hundred barrels I never opened one in which the beef was not as sweet and good as when it was first put up. I brought some of it home to Boston again, which was cooked, and considered as corned beef. As a contrast to this, I have known beef, which was put up in this place, spoil in six months, and be thrown over board. This is no small or unimportant difference; and it is an article demanding much more attention than it commonly receives. There should be a large stock of beans, peas, dried apples and whortleberries, pickled cabbage, pigs and cattles feet and ears, tripe, and pickles of various kinds. Take plenty of live stock, and a great abundance of water. To crown the whole, keep the stores in the best order. Let the hold, and all parts of the ship, be thoroughly and constantly aired; keep the hatches off in good weather; employ wind sails freely to force the air below; and remember the necessity of this to preserve the provisions, or a perishable cargo. Have frequent examinations or overhaulings. See if the casks are out of order; inspect the powder; and have it turned over once in every two months. Mark one side of the barrels with an X; stow that side up; and in two months put it down. One half of the powder in the casks will be spoiled without this precaution.

In voyages for seals, you must have men who understand the business, and not raw hands, who will certainly make it a losing enterprize. Out of twenty, which should be the least number for a crew, the captain and six others at least ought to be able to teach the rest their business with skill. Such a set of men will do more and better than twice the number of those who are untaught. Let every man depend on his share of the seals for the voyage. In no other way will the men do well. Including what has been previously received, half the voyage may be computed and paid at Canton, as a fair principle. The shares to prime seamen, or sealers, should be one per cent. or a hundredth part of the voyage, where there are thirty men belonging to the ship including the captain and officers. The money is to be divided after the expense of the boats for carrying the skins to Canton from the ship is deducted.—No other expenses are to come from the skins. The perquisite of the captain should be ten per cent. on all that can be realized from the cargo in the return of the ship. The cargo for the north west coast should consist of coarse cutlery, iron hollow ware, tin, iron, hard ware, blue cloth, blankets, bread, molasses, honey, sugar, and different kinds of arms. But no man should attempt to fit a ship for that voyage except one who has been concerned in the trade. At least, a ship should always be fitted under the direction of a man who has had this experience.

These remarks upon the mode of fitting out ships for such long voyages as those to the North West Coast, I hope may be regarded more than I fear they will be. The difference of expense between doing this well, and doing it ill, is small; but the difference of character, implied in the two modes, is immense. One is humane, honorable, magnanimous, and the source of a pure and manly pleasure; while the other is mean, selfish, inhuman, pusillanimous, and the source of nothing but self reproach, where apathy has not taken entire possession of the heart.

I now come to the close of a chapter, which is also the close of a series of voyages in foreign countries, some fortunate and happy, and others disastrous and afflictive. My recollections of the time, spent with commodore McClure and his officers, are full of interest and pleasure, mingled indeed with regret that such feelings, as I then enjoyed, should not be longer in continuance, and able to bear a greater variety of vicissitudes. At that period, my mind was elastic, and ready to draw agreeable emotion from every companion, every object, and every event. But the trials and depressions, which I have since met and endured, have taken away this elasticity of the faculties and the affections, and have left me with that kind of tranquillity which always succeeds the permanent disappointment of our high hopes, and which is some compensation for their loss. Chastised expectations, a sort of contentment with ordinary comforts, diminished activity, and the small still pleasures of a life of peace, without much responsibility remain.

In the voyage of survey and discovery among the oriental islands, I had an opportunity to learn much of the human character in various circumstances, and under various institutions. Virtue and vice, happiness and misery, are much more equally distributed to nations than those are permitted to suppose who have never been from home, and who believe, like the Chinese, that their residence is in the center of the world, of light, of privilege, and of enjoyment. National prejudices, to a certain extent, may be very useful, and possibly necessary; but they are always attended by considerable evils in the narrow and intolerant spirit which they perpetuate, and in the contentions which they produce. The more enlarged a mind becomes in its views of men and the world, the less it will be disposed to denounce the varieties of opinion and pursuit, and the more it will enjoy the benevolent results to which wisdom and philosophy point. A narrow mind chafes itself by its own prejudices; but a man, who is accustomed to generalise his observations, principles, and feelings, and to subdue his prejudices by a practical philanthropy, acquires an habitual superiority to the inequalities and provocations of society, and has learned the divine art of extracting good from evil.

Owen Chase

As he cruised toward the Pacific whaling grounds on board the Acushnet *in the early 1840s, Herman Melville first heard the "wondrous story" of the* Essex, *sunk nearby by a whale some 20 years earlier, on November 20, 1820. Later during the same voyage, the* Acushnet *gammed with a ship on which Melville met Owen Chase's teenage son, who loaned him a copy of Chase's* Narrative*—parts of which, including the chapter that follows, helped inspire the climactic final scene of* Moby-Dick. *(Edgar Allan Poe also borrowed from Chase when he wrote his* Narrative of Arthur Gordon Pym.*)*

Of the 20 seamen who escaped the wreck recounted here, only eight survived. Afraid of encountering the cannibals rumored to inhabit the nearby Marquesas Islands, the whalemen of the Essex *headed instead to the distant coast of South America—so distant that, for want of food and water, they were themselves eventually forced into cannibalism. (The two survivors on one boat were found "sucking the bones of their dead mess mates, which they were loath to part with.")*

Chase was rescued by the British brig Indian *after almost three months at sea and returned to Nantucket, where he told his tale. He was soon back at sea, the master of a whaler, and made a number of profitable voyages.*

from *Narrative of the Most Extraordinary and Distressing Shipwreck of the Whale-Ship Essex, of Nantucket*

I HAVE not been able to recur to the scenes which are now to become the subject of description, although a considerable time has elapsed, without feeling a mingled emotion of horror and astonishment at the almost incredible destiny that has preserved me and my surviving companions from a terrible death. Frequently, in my reflections on the subject, even after this lapse of time, I find myself shedding tears of gratitude for our deliverance, and blessing God, by whose divine aid and protection we were conducted through a series of unparalleled suffering and distress, and restored to the bosoms of our families and friends. There is no knowing what a stretch of pain and misery the human mind is capable of contemplating, when it is wrought upon by the anxieties of preservation; nor what pangs and weaknesses the body is able to endure, until they are visited upon it; and when at last deliverance comes, when the dream of hope is realized, unspeakable gratitude takes possession of the soul, and tears of joy choke the utterance. We require to be taught in the school of some signal suffering, privation, and despair, the great lessons of constant dependence upon an almighty forbearance and mercy. In the midst of the wide ocean, at night, when the sight of the heavens was shut out, and the dark tempest came upon us; then it was, that we felt ourselves ready to exclaim, "Heaven have mercy upon us, for nought but that can save us now." But I proceed to the recital.—On the 20th of November, (cruising in latitude 0°40′ S. longitude 119°0′ W.) a shoal of whales was discovered off the lee-bow. The weather at this time was extremely fine and clear, and it was about 8 o'clock in the morning, that the man at the mast-head gave the usual cry of, "there she blows." The ship was immediately put away, and we ran down in the direction for them. When we had got within half a mile of the place where they were observed, all our boats were lowered down, manned, and we started in pursuit of them. The ship, in the mean time, was brought to the wind, and the main-top-sail hove aback, to wait for us. I had the harpoon in the second boat; the captain preceded me in the first. When I arrived at the spot where we calculated they were, nothing was at first to be seen. We lay on our oars in anxious expectation of discovering them come up somewhere near us. Presently one rose, and spouted a short distance ahead of my boat; I made all speed towards it, came up with, and struck it; feeling the harpoon in him, he threw himself, in an agony, over towards the boat, (which at that time was up alongside of him,) and giving a severe blow with his tail, struck the boat near the edge of the water, amidships, and stove a hole in her. I immediately took up the boat hatchet, and cut the line, to disengage the boat from the whale, which by this time was running off with great velocity. I succeeded in getting clear of him, with the loss of the harpoon and line; and finding the water to pour fast in the boat, I hastily stuffed three or four of our jackets in the hole, ordered one man to keep constantly bailing, and the rest to pull immediately for the ship; we succeeded in keeping the boat free, and shortly gained the ship. The captain and the second mate, in the other two boats, kept up the pursuit, and soon struck another whale. They being at this time a considerable distance to leeward, I went forward, braced around the mainyard, and put the ship off in a direction for them; the boat which had been stove was immediately hoisted in, and after examining the hole, I found that I could, by nailing a piece of canvass over it, get her ready to join in a fresh pursuit, sooner than by lowering down the other remaining boat which belonged to the ship. I accordingly turned her over upon the quarter, and was in the act of nailing on the canvass, when I observed a very large spermaceti whale, as well as I could judge, about eighty-five feet in length; he broke water about twenty rods off our weather-bow, and was lying quietly, with his head in a direction for the ship. He spouted two or three times, and then disappeared. In less than two or three seconds he came up again, about the length of the ship off, and made directly for us, at the rate of about three knots. The ship was then going with about the same velocity. His appearance and attitude gave us at first no alarm; but while I stood watching his movements, and observing him but a ship's length off, coming down for us with great celerity, I involuntarily ordered the boy at the helm to put it hard up; intending to sheer off and avoid him. The words were scarcely out of my mouth, before he came down upon us with full speed, and struck the ship with his head, just forward of the fore-chains; he gave us such an appalling and tremendous jar, as nearly threw us all on our faces. The ship brought up as suddenly and violently as if she had struck a rock, and trembled for a few seconds like a leaf. We looked at each other with perfect amazement, deprived almost of the power of speech. Many minutes elapsed before we were able to realize the dreadful accident; during which time he passed under the ship, grazing her keel as he went along, came up alongside of her to leeward, & lay on the top of the water, (apparently stunned with the violence of the blow,) for the space of a minute; he then suddenly started off, in a direction to leeward. After a few moments' reflection, and recovering, in some measure, from the sudden consternation that had seized us, I of course concluded that he had stove a hole in the ship, and that it would be necessary to set the pumps going. Accordingly they were rigged, but had not been in operation more than one minute, before I perceived the head of the ship to be gradually settling down in the water; I then ordered the signal to be set for the other boats, which, scarcely had I despatched, before I again discovered the whale, apparently in convulsions, on the top of the water, about one hundred rods to leeward. He was enveloped in the foam of the sea, that his continual and violent thrashing about in the water had created around him, and I could distinctly see him smite his jaws together, as if distracted with rage and fury. He remained a short time in this situation, and then started off with great velocity, across the bows of the ship, to windward. By this time the ship had settled down a considerable distance in the water, and I gave her up as lost. I however, ordered the pumps to be kept constantly going, and endeavoured to collect my thoughts for the occasion. I turned to the boats, two of which we then had with the ship, with an intention of clearing them away, and getting all things ready to embark in them, if there should be no other resource left; and while my attention was thus engaged for a moment, I was aroused with the cry of a man at the hatchway, "here he is—he is making for us again." I turned around, & saw him about one hundred rods directly ahead of us, coming down apparently with twice his ordinary speed, and to me at that moment, it appeared with tenfold fury and vengeance in his aspect. The surf flew in all directions about him, and his course towards us was marked by a white foam of a rod in width, which he made with the continual violent thrashing of his tail; his head was about half out of water, and in that way he came upon, and again struck the ship. I was in hopes when I descried him making for us, that by a dexterous movement of putting the ship away immediately, I should be able to cross the line of his approach, before he could get up to us, and thus avoid, what I knew, if he should strike us again, would prove our inevitable destruction. I bawled out to the helmsman, "hard up!" but she had not fallen off more than a point, before we took the second shock. I should judge the speed of the ship to have been at this time about three knots, and that of the whale about six. He struck her to windward, directly under the cat-head, and completely stove in her bows. He passed under the ship again, went off to leeward, and we saw no more of him. Our situation at this juncture can be more readily imagined than described. The shock to our feelings was such, as I am sure none can have an adequate conception of, that were not there: the misfortune befel us at a moment when we least dreamt of any accident; and from the pleasing anticipations we had formed, of realizing the certain profits of our labour, we were dejected by a sudden, most mysterious, and overwhelming calamity. Not a moment, however, was to be lost in endeavouring to provide for the extremity to which it was now certain we were reduced. We were more than a thousand miles from the nearest land, and with nothing but a light open boat, as the resource of safety for myself and companions. I ordered the men to cease pumping, and every one to provide for himself; seizing a hatchet at the same time, I cut away the lashings of the spare boat, which lay bottom up, across two spars directly over the quarter deck, and cried out to those near me, to take her as she came down. They did so accordingly, and bore her on their shoulders as far as the waist of the ship. The steward had in the mean time gone down into the cabin twice, and saved two quadrants, two practical navigators, and the captain's trunk and mine; all which were hastily thrown into the boat, as she lay on the deck, with the two compasses which I snatched from the binnacle. He attempted to descend again; but the water by this time had rushed in, and he returned without being able to effect his purpose. By the time we had got the boat to the waist, the ship had filled with water, and was going down on her beam-ends: we shoved our boat as quickly as possible from the plank-shear into the water, all hands jumping in her at the same time, and launched off clear of the ship. We were scarcely two boat's lengths distant from her, when she fell over to windward, and settled down in the water.

Amazement and despair now wholly took possession of us. We contemplated the frightful situation the ship lay in, and thought with horror upon the sudden and dreadful calamity that had overtaken us. We looked upon each other, as if to gather some consolatory sensation from an interchange of sentiments, but every countenance was marked with the paleness of despair. Not a word was spoken for several minutes by any of us; all appeared to be bound in a spell of stupid consternation; and from the time we were first attacked by the whale, to the period of the fall of the ship, and of our leaving her in the boat, more than ten minutes could not certainly have elapsed! God only knows in what way, or by what means, we were enabled to accomplish in that short time what we did; the cutting away and transporting the boat from where she was deposited would of itself, in ordinary circumstances, have consumed as much time as that, if the whole ship's crew had been employed in it. My companions had not saved a single article but what they had on their backs; but to me it was a source of infinite satisfaction, if any such could be gathered from the horrors of our gloomy situation, that we had been fortunate enough to have preserved our compasses, navigators, and quadrants. After the first shock of my feelings was over, I enthusiastically contemplated them as the probable instruments of our salvation; without them all would have been dark and hopeless. Gracious God! what a picture of distress and suffering now presented itself to my imagination. The crew of the ship were saved, consisting of twenty human souls. All that remained to conduct these twenty beings through the stormy terrors of the ocean, perhaps many thousand miles, were three open light boats. The prospect of obtaining any provisions or water from the ship, to subsist upon during the time, was at least now doubtful. How many long and watchful nights, thought I, are to be passed? How many tedious days of partial starvation are to be endured, before the least relief or mitigation of our sufferings can be reasonably anticipated? We lay at this time in our boat, about two ships' lengths off from the wreck, in perfect silence, calmly contemplating her situation, and absorbed in our own melancholy reflections, when the other boats were discovered rowing up to us. They had but shortly before discovered that some accident had befallen us, but of the nature of which they were entirely ignorant. The sudden & mysterious disappearance of the ship was first discovered by the boat-steerer in the captain's boat, and with a horror-struck countenance and voice, he suddenly exclaimed, "Oh, my God! where is the ship?" Their operations upon this were instantly suspended, and a general cry of horror and despair burst from the lips of every man, as their looks were directed for her, in vain, over every part of the ocean. They immediately made all haste towards us. The captain's boat was the first that reached us. He stopped about a boat's length off, but had no power to utter a single syllable: he was so completely overpowered with the spectacle before him, that he sat down in his boat, pale and speechless. I could scarcely recognise his countenance, he appeared to be so much altered, awed, and overcome, with the oppression of his feelings, and the dreadful reality that lay before him. He was in a short time however enabled to address the inquiry to me, "My God, Mr. Chase, what is the matter?" I answered, "We have been stove by a whale." I then briefly told him the story. After a few moments' reflection he observed, that we must cut away her masts, and endeavour to get something out of her to eat. Our thoughts were now all accordingly bent on endeavours to save from the wreck whatever we might possibly want, and for this purpose we rowed up and got on to her. Search was made for every means of gaining access to her hold; and for this purpose the lanyards were cut loose, and with our hatchets we commenced to cut away the masts, that she might right up again, and enable us to scuttle her decks. In doing which we were occupied about three quarters of an hour, owing to our having no axes, nor indeed any other instruments, but the small hatchets belonging to the boats. After her masts were gone she came up about two-thirds of the way upon an even keel. While we were employed about the masts the captain took his quadrant, shoved off from the ship, and got an observation. We found ourselves in latitude 0°40′ S. longitude 119° W. We now commenced to cut a hole through the planks, directly above two large casks of bread, which most fortunately were between decks, in the waist of the ship, and which being in the upper side, when she upset, we had strong hopes was not wet. It turned out according to our wishes, and from these casks we obtained six hundred pounds of hard bread. Other parts of the deck were then scuttled, and we got without difficulty as much fresh water as we dared to take in the boats, so that each was supplied with about sixty-five gallons; we got also from one of the lockers a musket, a small canister of powder, a couple of files, two rasps, about two pounds of boat nails, and a few turtle. In the afternoon the wind came on to blow a strong breeze; and having obtained every thing that occurred to us could then be got out, we began to make arrangements for our safety during the night. A boat's line was made fast to the ship, and to the other end of it one of the boats was moored, at about fifty fathoms to leeward; another boat was then attached to the first one, about eight fathoms astern; and the third boat, the like distance astern of her. Night came on just as we had finished our operations; and such a night as it was to us! so full of feverish and distracting inquietude, that we were deprived entirely of rest. The wreck was constantly before my eyes. I could not, by any effort, chase away the horrors of the preceding day from my mind: they haunted me the live-long night. My companions—some of them were like sick women; they had no idea of the extent of their deplorable situation. One or two slept unconcernedly, while others wasted the night in unavailing murmurs. I now had full leisure to examine, with some degree of coolness, the dreadful circumstances of our disaster. The scenes of yesterday passed in such quick succession in my mind that it was not until after many hours of severe reflection that I was able to discard the idea of the catastrophe as a dream. Alas! it was one from which there was no awaking; it was too certainly true, that but yesterday we had existed as it were, and in one short moment had been cut off from all the hopes and prospects of the living! I have no language to paint out the horrors of our situation. To shed tears was indeed altogether unavailing, and withal unmanly; yet I was not able to deny myself the relief they served to afford me. After several hours of idle sorrow and repining I began to reflect upon the accident, and endeavoured to realize by what unaccountable destiny or design, (which I could not at first determine,) this sudden and most deadly attack had been made upon us: by an animal, too, never before suspected of premeditated violence, and proverbial for its insensibility and inoffensiveness. Every fact seemed to warrant me in concluding that it was any thing but chance which directed his operations; he made two several attacks upon the ship, at a short interval between them, both of which, according to their direction, were calculated to do us the most injury, by being made ahead, and thereby combining the speed of the two objects for the shock; to effect which, the exact manœuvres which he made were necessary. His aspect was most horrible, and such as indicated resentment and fury. He came directly from the shoal which we had just before entered, and in which we had struck three of his companions, as if fired with revenge for their sufferings. But to this it may be observed, that the mode of fighting which they always adopt is either with repeated strokes of their tails, or snapping of their jaws together; and that a case, precisely similar to this one, has never been heard of amongst the oldest and most experienced whalers. To this I would answer, that the structure and strength of the whale's head is admirably designed for this mode of attack; the most prominent part of which is almost as hard and as tough as iron; indeed, I can compare it to nothing else but the inside of a horse's hoof, upon which a lance or harpoon would not make the slightest impression. The eyes and ears are removed nearly one-third the length of the whole fish, from the front part of the head, and are not in the least degree endangered in this mode of attack. At all events, the whole circumstances taken together, all happening before my own eyes, and producing, at the time, impressions in my mind of decided, calculating mischief, on the part of the whale, (many of which impressions I cannot now recall,) induce me to be satisfied that I am correct in my opinion. It is certainly, in all its bearings, a hitherto unheard of circumstance, and constitutes, perhaps, the most extraordinary one in the annals of the fishery.

William Lay and Cyrus M. Hussey

The mutiny that broke out on board the Globe *on the night of January 25, 1824, was the bloodiest in the history of American whaling. Its leader, the harpooner Samuel Comstock, was the 20-year-old son of a Quaker schoolmaster on Nantucket; its cause remains unclear, although another survivor testified that on the day of the mutiny Captain Thomas Worth had flogged one of the crew for insubordination. Within days of the mutiny its perpetrators fell out among themselves. On January 28 Samuel Comstock had William Humphries hanged for allegedly plotting to kill him and Silas Payne. The* Globe *reached Mili Atoll in the Marshall Islands of the central Pacific on February 14. Three days later Payne and John Oliver killed Samuel Comstock. That night George Comstock and five other sailors escaped on the* Globe, *reaching Chile nearly four months later. Meanwhile, Payne began to flog and chain the Marshall Islanders who displeased him; they retaliated on February 21 by killing all of the remaining crew members except Cyrus Hussey (c. 1805–1829) and William Lay (c. 1805–?). Rescued by the U.S. Navy in November 1825, Hussey and Lay returned to the United States in the spring of 1827 and published their* Narrative of the Mutiny.

from *A Narrative of the Mutiny On Board the Ship Globe*

On the 15th day of December, we sailed from Edgartown, on a whaling voyage, to the Pacific Ocean, but in working out, having carried away the crossjack-yard, we returned to port, and after having refitted and sent aloft another, we sailed again on the 19th and on the same day anchored in Holmes Hole. On the following day a favourable opportunity offering to proceed to sea, we got under way, and after having cleared the land, discharged the pilot, made sail, and performed the necessary duties of stowing the anchors, unbending and coiling away the cables, etc. On the 1st of January 1823, we experienced a heavy gale from N. W. which was but the first in the catalogue of difficulties we were fated to encounter. As this was our first trial of a seaman's life, the scene presented to our view, "mid the howling storm," was one of terrific grandeur, as well as of real danger. But as the ship scudded well, and the wind was fair, she was kept before it, under a close reefed main-top-sail and fore-sail, although during the gale, which lasted forty-eight hours, the sea frequently threatened to board us, which was prevented by the skillful management of the helm. On the 9th of January we made the Cape Verde Islands, bearing S. W. twenty-five miles distant, and on the 17th, crossed the Equator. On the 29th of the same month we saw sperm whales, lowered our boats, and succeeded in taking one; the blubber of which, when boiled out, yielded us seventy-five barrels of oil. Pursuing our voyage, on the twenty-third of February we passed the Falkland Islands, and about the 5th of March, doubled the great promontory of South America, Cape Horn, and stood to the northward.

We saw whales once only before we reached the Sandwich Islands, which we made on the first of May early in the morning. When drawing in with the Island of Hawaii about four in the afternoon, the man at the mast head gave notice that he saw a shoal of black fish on the lee bow; which we soon found to be canoes on their way to meet us. It falling calm at this time prevented their getting along side until night fall, which they did, at a distance of more than three leagues from the land. We received from them a very welcome supply of potatoes, sugar cane, yams, coconuts, bananas, fish, etc., for which we gave them in return pieces of iron hoop, nails, and similar articles. We stood off and on during the next day, and after obtaining a sufficient supply of vegetables and fruit, we shaped our course for Oahu, at which place we arrived on the following day, and, after lying there twenty hours, sailed for the coast of Japan, in company with the whaling ship *Palladium* of Boston, and *Pocahontas* of Falmouth; from which ships we parted company when two days out. After cruising in the Japan seas several months, and obtaining five hundred and fifty barrels of oil, we again shaped our course for the Sandwich Islands, to obtain a supply of vegetables, etc.

While lying at Oahu, six of the men deserted in the night; two of them having been re-taken were put in irons, but one of them having found means to divest himself of his irons set the other at liberty, and both escaped.

To supply their places, we shipped the following persons, viz: Silas Payne, John Oliver, Anthony Hanson, a native of Oahu, Wm. Humphries, a black man, and steward, and Thomas Lilliston. Having accommodated ourselves with as many vegetables and much fruit as could be preserved, we again put to sea, fondly anticipating a successful cruise, and a speedy and happy meeting with our friends. After leaving Oahu we ran to the south of the equator, and after cruising a short time for whales without much success, we steered for Fanning Island, which lies in lat. 3°49′ N. and long. 158°29′ W. While cruising off this Island an event occurred which, whether we consider the want of motives, or the cold blooded and obstinate cruelty with which it was perpetrated, has not often been equalled. We speak of the want of motives because, although some occurrences which we shall mention had given the crew some ground for dissatisfaction, there had been no abuse or severity which could in the least degree excuse or palliate so barbarous a mode of redress and revenge. During our cruise to Japan the season before, many complaints were uttered by the crew among themselves with respect to the manner and quantity in which they received their *meat*, the quantity sometimes being more than sufficient for the number of men, and at others not enough to supply the ship's company; and it is fair to presume that the most dissatisfied deserted the ship at Oahu.

But the reader will no doubt consider it superfluous for us to attempt an unrequired vindication of the conduct of the officers of the *Globe* whose aim was to maintain a correct discipline, which should result in the furtherance of the voyage and be a benefit to all concerned, more especially when he is informed that part of the men shipped at Oahu, in the room of the deserters, were abandoned wretches, who frequently were the cause of severe reprimands from the officers, and in one instance one of them received a severe flogging. The reader will also please to bear in mind that Samuel B. Comstock, the ringleader of the mutiny, was an officer (being a boat-steerer) and as is customary, ate in the cabin. The conduct and deportment of the Captain towards this individual was always decorous and gentlemanly, a proof of intentions long premeditated to destroy the ship. Some of the crew were determined to leave the ship provided she touched at Fanning Island, and we believe had concerted a plan of escape, but of which the perpetration of a deed chilling to humanity precluded the necessity. We were at this time in company with the ship *Lyra*, of New Bedford, the Captain of which had been on board the *Globe* during the most of the day, but had returned in the evening to his own ship. An agreement had been made by him with the Captain of the *Globe* to set a light at midnight as a signal for tacking. It may not be amiss to acquaint the reader of the manner in which whalemen keep watch during the night. They generally carry three boats, though some carry four, five, and sometimes six; the *Globe*, however, being of the class carrying three. The Captain, mate, and second mate stand no watch except there is *blubber* to be boiled; the boat-steerers taking charge of the watch and managing the ship with their respective boat's crews, and in this instance dividing the night into three parts, each taking a third. It so happened that Smith, after keeping the first watch, was relieved by Comstock (whom we shall call by his sir name in contradistinction to his brother George) and the *waist boat's crew*, and the former watch retired below to their berths and hammocks. George Comstock took the helm, during his *trick*, received orders from his brother to "keep the ship a good full," swearing that the ship was too nigh the wind. When his time at the helm had expired he took the *rattle* (an instrument used by whalemen to announce the expiration of the hour, the watch, etc.) and began to shake it, when Comstock came to him, and, in the most peremptory manner, ordered him to desist, saying "If you make the least damn bit of noise, I'll send you to hell!" He then lighted a lamp and went into the steerage. George, becoming alarmed at this conduct of his unnatural brother, again took the *rattle* for the purpose of alarming some one; Comstock arrived in time to prevent him, and, with threatenings dark and diabolical, so congealed the blood of his trembling brother, that even had he possessed the power of alarming the unconscious and fated victims below, his life would have been the forfeit of his temerity!

Comstock now laid something heavy upon a small work bench near the cabin gangway, which was afterwards found to be a boarding knife. It is an instrument used by whalers to cut the *blubber* when hoisting it in, is about four feet in length, two or three inches wide, and necessarily kept very sharp, and, for greater convenience when in use, is two edged.

In giving a detail of this chilling transaction, we shall be guided by the description given of it by the younger Comstock, who, as has been observed, was upon deck at the time, and afterwards learned several particulars from his brother, to whom alone they could have been known. Comstock went down into the cabin, accompanied by Silas Payne or Paine, of Sag Harbour, John Oliver, of Shields, Eng., William Humphries, the steward of Philadelphia, and Thomas Lilliston; the latter, however, went no farther than the cabin gangway, and then ran forward and *turned in*. According to his own story he did not think they would attempt to put their designs in execution, until he saw them actually descending into the cabin, having gone so far, to use his own expression, to show himself as brave as any of them. But we believe he had not the smallest idea of assisting the villains. Comstock entered the cabin so silently as not to be perceived by the man at the helm, who was first apprised of his having begun the work of death by the sound of a heavy blow with an axe, which he distinctly heard.

The Captain was asleep in a hammock, suspended in the cabin, his state room being uncomfortably warm; Comstock approaching him with the axe, struck him a blow upon the head, which was nearly severed in two by the first stroke! After repeating the blow, he ran to Payne, who it seems was stationed with the before mentioned boarding knife, to attack the mate, as soon as the Captain was killed. At this instant, Payne making a thrust at the mate, he awoke, and terrified, exclaimed, "What! what! what!" "Is this— Oh! Payne! Oh! Comstock!" "Don't kill me, don't." "Have I not always—." Here Comstock interrupted him saying, "Yes! you have always been a d—d rascal; you tell lies of me out of the ship will you? It's a d—d good time to beg now, but you're too late." Here the mate sprang, and grasped him by the throat. In the scuffle, the light which Comstock held in his hand was knocked out and the axe fell from his hand; but the grasp of Mr. Beetle upon his throat did not prevent him from making Payne understand that his weapon was lost, who felt about until he found it, and, having given it to Comstock, he managed to strike him a blow upon the head, which fractured his skull; when he fell into the pantry where he lay groaning until dispatched by Comstock! The steward held a light at this time, while Oliver put in a blow as often as possible!

The second and third mates, fastened in their state rooms, lay in their berths listening, fearing to speak, and being ignorant of the numerical strength of the mutineers, and unarmed, thought it best to wait the dreadful issue, hoping that their lives might yet be spared.

Comstock, leaving a watch at the second mate's door, went upon deck to light another lamp at the binnacle, it having been again accidentally extinguished. He was there asked by his terrified brother, whose agony of mind we will not attempt to portray, if he intended to hurt Smith, the other boat-steerer. He replied that he did; and inquired where he was. George, fearing that Smith would be *immediately* pursued, said he had not seen him. Comstock then perceiving his brother to be shedding tears asked sternly, "What are you crying about?" "I am afraid," replied George, "that they will hurt me!" "I *will* hurt you," said he, "if you talk in that manner!"

But the work of death was not yet finished. Comstock took his light into the cabin, and made preparations for attacking the second and third mates, Mr. Fisher, and Mr. Lumbert. After loading two muskets, he fired one through the door, in the direction as near as he could judge of the officers, and then inquired if either was shot! Fisher replied, "Yes, I am shot in the mouth!" Previous to his shooting Fisher, Lumbert asked if he was going to kill him? To which he answered with apparent unconcern, "Oh no, I guess not."

They now opened the door, and Comstock, making a pass at Mr. Lumbert, missed him, and fell into the state room. Mr. Lumbert collared him, but he escaped from his hands. Mr. Fisher had got the gun, and actually presented the bayonet to the monster's heart! But Comstock assuring him that his life should be spared if he gave it up, he did so; when Comstock immediately ran Mr. Lumbert through the body several times!

He then turned to Mr. Fisher, and told him there was no hope for *him*! ! "You have got to die," said he, "remember the scrape you got me into, when in company with the *Enterprise* of Nantucket." The "scrape" alluded to was as follows. Comstock came up to Mr. Fisher to wrestle with him. Fisher being the most athletic of the two, handled him with so much ease, that Comstock in a fit of passion *struck* him. At this Fisher seized him, and laid him upon deck several times in a pretty rough manner.

Comstock then made some violent threats, which Fisher paid no attention to, but which now fell upon his soul with all the horrors of reality. Finding his cruel enemy deaf to his remonstrances, and entreaties, he said, "If there is no hope, I will at least die like a man!" and having, by order of Comstock, turned back too, said in a firm voice, *"I am ready!!"*

Comstock then put the muzzle of the gun to his head, and fired, which instantly put an end to his existence! Mr. Lumbert, during this time, was begging for life, although no doubt mortally wounded. Comstock, turned to him and said, "I am a bloody man! I have a bloody hand and *will* be avenged!" and *again* run him through the body with a bayonet! He then begged for a little water; "I'll give you water," said he, and once more plunging the weapon in his body, left him for dead!

Thus it appears that this more than demon, murdered with his own hand, the whole! Gladly would we wash from "memory's waste" all remembrance of that bloody night. The compassionate reader, however, whose heart sickens within him at the perusal, as does ours at the recital, of this tale of woe, will not, we hope, disapprove our publishing these melancholy facts to the world. As, through the boundless mercy of Providence we have been restored to the bosom of our families and homes, we deemed it a duty we owe to the world to record our "unvarnished tale."

JAMES FENIMORE COOPER

"It was Cooper," wrote his contemporary William Cullen Bryant, "who first gave us the poetry of a seaman's life, extracted a dramatic interest from the log book, and suspended the hopes and fears of his plot upon the maneuvering of a vessel." After dropping out of Yale at age 16, Cooper (1789–1851) went to sea as a sailor on the merchant ship Stirling. *Subsequently he joined the navy, serving as a midshipman from 1808 to 1810. This nautical experience would provide the basis for a series of novels—*The Pilot *(1824),* The Red Rover *(1827),* The Water-Witch *(1830),* The Two Admirals *(1842),* Wing-and-Wing *(1842),* Ned Myers *(1843),* Afloat and Ashore *(1844),* Miles Wallingford *(1844), and* The Sea Lions *(1849)—that opened up seagoing life and naval warfare as themes for fiction. However melodramatic Cooper's plot contrivance and however stilted his dialogue, the vigor of his maritime episodes, with their blend of technical detail and sweeping imagery, remains undiminished.*

In this climactic episode from The Pilot, *the American schooner* Ariel, *on a mission to raid the coast of England during the American Revolution, is driven onto the rocks. The characters brought to the fore here include the* Ariel*'s commander, Lieutenant Richard Barnstable; his prisoner Christopher Dillon, who has sought to betray the raiders; and the coxswain Long Tom Coffin, who set the mold for a long fictional line of stoic, weathered seamen.*

from *The Pilot*

THE Ariel continued to struggle against the winds and ocean for several hours longer, before the day broke on the tempestuous scene, and the anxious mariners were enabled to form a more accurate estimate of their real danger. As the violence of the gale increased, the canvas of the schooner had been gradually reduced, until she was unable to show more than was absolutely necessary to prevent her driving helplessly on the land. Barnstable watched the appearance of the weather, as the light slowly opened upon them, with an intense anxiety, which denoted that the presentiments of the cockswain were no longer deemed idle. On looking to windward, he beheld the green masses of water that were rolling in towards the land, with a violence that seemed irresistible, crowned with ridges of foam; and there were moments when the air appeared filled with sparkling gems, as the rays of the rising sun fell upon the spray that was swept from wave to wave. Towards the land the view was still more appalling. The cliffs, but a short half-league under the lee of the schooner, were, at all times, nearly hid from the eye by the pyramids of water, which the furious element, so suddenly restrained in its violence, cast high into the air, as if seeking to overleap the boundaries that nature had fixed to its dominion. The whole coast, from the distant headland at the south to the well-known shoals that stretched far beyond their course in the opposite direction, displayed a broad belt of foam, into which it would have been certain destruction for the proudest ship that ever swam to enter. Still the Ariel floated on the billows, lightly and in safety, though yielding to the impulses of the waters, and, at times, appearing to be engulfed in the yawning chasm which apparently opened beneath her to receive the little fabric. The low rumor of acknowledged danger had found its way through the schooner, and the seamen, after fastening their hopeless looks on the small spot of canvas that they were still able to show to the tempest, would turn to view the dreary line of coast, that seemed to offer so gloomy an alternative. Even Dillon, to whom the report of their danger had found its way, crept from his place of concealment in the cabin, and moved about the decks unheeded, devouring, with greedy ears, such opinions as fell from the lips of the sullen mariners.

At this moment of appalling apprehension, the cockswain exhibited the calmest resignation. He knew all had been done that lay in the power of man, to urge their little vessel from the land, and it was now too evident to his experienced eyes that it had been done in vain; but, considering himself as a sort of fixture in the schooner, he was quite prepared to abide her fate, be it for better or for worse. The settled look of gloom that gathered around the frank brow of Barnstable was in no degree connected with any considerations of himself; but proceeded from that sort of parental responsibility, from which the sea-commander is never exempt. The discipline of the crew, however, still continued perfect and unyielding. There had, it is true, been a slight movement made by one or two of the older seamen, which indicated an intention to drown the apprehensions of death in ebriety; but Barnstable had called for his pistols, in a tone that checked the procedure instantly, and, although the fatal weapons were, untouched by him, left to lie exposed on the capstan, where they had been placed by his servant, not another symptom of insubordination appeared among the devoted crew. There was even what to a landsman might seem an appalling affectation of attention to the most trifling duties of the vessel; and the men who, it should seem, ought to be devoting the brief moments of their existence to the mighty business of the hour, were constantly called to attend to the most trivial details of their profession. Ropes were coiled, and the slightest damages occasioned by the waves, which, at short intervals, swept across the low decks of the Ariel, were repaired, with the same precision and order as if she yet lay embayed in the haven from which she had just been driven. In this manner the arm of authority was kept extended over the silent crew, not with the vain desire to preserve a lingering though useless exercise of power, but with a view to maintain that unity of action that now could alone afford them even a ray of hope.

"She can make no head against this sea, under that rag of canvas," said Barnstable, gloomily, addressing the cockswain, who, with folded arms and an air of cool resignation, was balancing his body on the verge of the quarter-deck, while the schooner was plunging madly into waves that nearly buried her in their bosom: "the poor little thing trembles like a frightened child, as she meets the water."

Tom sighed heavily, and shook his head, before he answered:

"If we could have kept the head of the mainmast an hour longer, we might have got an offing, and fetched to windward of the shoals; but as it is, sir, mortal man can't drive a craft to windward—she sets bodily in to land, and will be in the breakers in less than an hour, unless God wills that the wind shall cease to blow."

"We have no hope left us, but to anchor; our ground tackle may yet bring her up."

Tom turned to his commander, and replied, solemnly, and with that assurance of manner that long experience only can give a man in moments of great danger:

"If our sheet-cable was bent to our heaviest anchor, this sea would bring it home, though nothing but her launch was riding by it. A northeaster in the German Ocean must and will blow itself out; nor shall we get the crown of the gale until the sun falls over the land. Then, indeed, it may lull; for the winds do often seem to reverence the glory of the heavens too much to blow their might in its very face!"

"We must do our duty to ourselves and the country," returned Barnstable. "Go, get the two bowers spliced, and have a kedge bent to a hawser: we'll back our two anchors together, and veer to the better end of two hundred and forty fathoms; it may yet bring her up. See all clear there for anchoring and cutting away the mast! we'll leave the wind nothing but a naked hull to whistle over."

"Ay, if there was nothing but the wind, we might yet live to see the sun sink behind them hills," said the cockswain; "but what hemp can stand the strain of a craft that is buried, half the time, to her foremast in the water?"

The order was, however, executed by the crew, with a sort of desperate submission to the will of their commander; and when the preparations were completed, the anchors and kedge were dropped to the bottom, and the instant that the Ariel tended to the wind, the axe was applied to the little that was left of her long, raking masts. The crash of the falling spars, as they came, in succession, across the decks of the vessel, appeared to produce no sensation amid that scene of complicated danger; but the seamen proceeded in silence to their hopeless duty of clearing the wrecks. Every eye followed the floating timbers, as the waves swept them away from the vessel, with a sort of feverish curiosity, to witness the effect produced by their collision with those rocks that lay so fearfully near them; but long before the spars entered the wide border of foam, they were hid from view by the furious element in which they floated. It was now felt by the whole crew of the Ariel, that their last means of safety had been adopted; and, at each desperate and headlong plunge the vessel took into the bosom of the seas that rolled upon her forecastle, the anxious seamen thought that they could perceive the yielding of the iron that yet clung to the bottom, or could hear the violent surge of the parting strands of the cable, that still held them to their anchors. While the minds of the sailors were agitated with the faint hopes that had been excited by the movements of their schooner, Dillon had been permitted to wander about the deck unnoticed: his rolling eyes, hard breathing, and clenched hands excited no observation among the men, whose thoughts were yet dwelling on the means of safety. But now, when, with a sort of frenzied desperation, he would follow the retiring waters along the decks, and venture his person nigh the group that had collected around and on the gun of the cockswain, glances of fierce or of sullen vengeance were cast at him, that conveyed threats of a nature that he was too much agitated to understand.

"If ye are tired of this world, though your time, like my own, is probably but short in it," said Tom to him, as he passed the cockswain in one of his turns, "you can go forward among the men; but if ye have need of the moments to foot up the reck'ning of your doings among men, afore ye're brought to face your Maker, and hear the log-book of Heaven, I would advise you to keep as nigh as possible to Captain Barnstable or myself."

"Will you promise to save me if the vessel is wrecked?" exclaimed Dillon, catching at the first sounds of friendly interest that had reached his ears since he had been recaptured; "Oh! if you will, I can secure your future ease, yes, wealth, for the remainder of your days!"

"Your promises have been too ill kept afore this, for the peace of your soul," returned the cockswain, without bitterness, though sternly; "but it is not in me to strike even a whale that is already spouting blood."

The intercessions of Dillon were interrupted by a dreadful cry, that arose among the men forward, and which sounded with increased horror, amid the roarings of the tempest. The schooner rose on the breast of a wave at the same instant, and, falling off with her broadside to the sea, she drove in towards the cliffs, like a bubble on the rapids of a cataract.

"Our ground-tackle has parted," said Tom, with his resigned patience of manner undisturbed; "she shall die as easy as man can make her!"—While he yet spoke, he seized the tiller, and gave to the vessel such a direction as would be most likely to cause her to strike the rocks with her bows foremost.

There was, for one moment, an expression of exquisite anguish betrayed in the dark countenance of Barnstable; but, at the next, it passed away, and he spoke cheerfully to his men:

"Be steady, my lads, be calm; there is yet a hope of life for *you*—our light draught will let us run in close to the cliffs, and it is still falling water—see your boats clear, and be steady."

The crew of the whale-boat, aroused by this speech from a sort of stupor, sprang into their light vessel, which was quickly lowered into the sea, and kept riding on the foam, free from the sides of the schooner, by the powerful exertions of the men. The cry for the cockswain was earnest and repeated, but Tom shook his head, without replying, still grasping the tiller, and keeping his eyes steadily bent on the chaos of waters into which they were driving. The launch, the largest boat of the two, was cut loose from the "gripes," and the bustle and exertion of the moment rendered the crew insensible to the horror of the scene that surrounded them. But the loud hoarse call of the cockswain, to "look out—secure yourselves!" suspended even their efforts, and at that instant the Ariel settled on a wave that melted from under her, heavily on the rocks. The shock was so violent, as to throw all who disregarded the warning cry from their feet, and the universal quiver that pervaded the vessel was like the last shudder of animated nature.

For a time long enough to breathe, the least experienced among the men supposed the danger to be past; but a wave of great height followed the one that had deserted them, and raising the vessel again, threw her roughly still farther on the bed of rocks, and at the same time its crest broke over her quarter, sweeping the length of her decks with a fury that was almost resistless. The shuddering seamen beheld their loosened boat driven from their grasp, and dashed against the base of the cliffs, where no fragment of her wreck could be traced, at the receding of the waters. But the passing billow had thrown the vessel into a position which, in some measure, protected her decks from the violence of those that succeeded it.

"Go, my boys, go," said Barnstable, as the moment of dreadful uncertainty passed; "you have still the whale-boat, and she, at least, will take you nigh the shore. Go into her, my boys. God bless you, God bless you all! You have been faithful and honest fellows, and I believe he will not yet desert you; go, my friends, while there is a lull."

The seamen threw themselves, in a mass, into the light vessel, which nearly sank under the unusual burden; but when they looked around them, Barnstable and Merry, Dillon and the cockswain, were yet to be seen on the decks of the Ariel. The former was pacing, in deep and perhaps bitter melancholy, the wet planks of the schooner, while the boy hung, unheeded, on his arm, uttering disregarded petitions to his commander to desert the wreck. Dillon approached the side where the boat lay, again and again, but the threatening countenances of the seamen as often drove him back in despair. Tom had seated himself on the heel of the bowsprit, where he continued, in an attitude of quiet resignation, returning no other answers to the loud and repeated calls of his shipmates, than by waving his hand towards the shore.

"Now hear me," said the boy, urging his request, to tears; "if not for my sake, or for your own sake, Mr. Barnstable, or for the hope of God's mercy, go into the boat, for the love of my cousin Katherine."

The young lieutenant paused in his troubled walk, and for a moment he cast a glance of hesitation at the cliffs; but, at the next instant, his eyes fell on the ruin of his vessel, and he answered:

"Never, boy, never; if my hour has come, I will not shrink from my fate."

"Listen to the men, dear sir; the boat will be swamped, alongside the wreck, and their cry is, that without you they will not let her go."

Barnstable motioned to the boat, to bid the boy enter it, and turned away in silence.

"Well," said Merry, with firmness, "if it be right that a lieutenant shall stay by the wreck, it must also be right for a midshipman; shove off; neither Mr. Barnstable nor myself will quit the vessel."

"Boy, your life has been intrusted to my keeping, and at my hands will it be required," said his commander, lifting the struggling youth, and tossing him into the arms of the seamen. "Away with ye, and God be with you; there is more weight in you now than can go safe to land."

Still the seamen hesitated, for they perceived the cockswain moving, with a steady tread, along the deck, and they hoped he had relented, and would yet persuade the lieutenant to join his crew. But Tom, imitating the example of his commander, seized the latter suddenly in his powerful grasp, and threw him over the bulwarks with an irresistible force. At the same moment he cast the fast of the boat from the pin that held it, and, lifting his broad hands high into the air, his voice was heard in the tempest:

"God's will be done with me," he cried. "I saw the first timber of the Ariel laid, and shall live just long enough to see it turn out of her bottom; after which I wish to live no longer."

But his shipmates were swept far beyond the sounds of his voice, before half these words were uttered. All command of the boat was rendered impossible, by the numbers it contained, as well as the raging of the surf; and, as it rose on the white crest of a wave, Tom saw his beloved little craft for the last time. It fell into a trough of the sea, and in a few moments more its fragments were ground into splinters on the adjacent rocks. The cockswain still remained where he had cast off the rope, and beheld the numerous heads and arms that appeared rising, at short intervals, on the waves; some making powerful and well-directed efforts to gain the sands, that were becoming visible as the tide fell, and others wildly tossed in the frantic movements of helpless despair. The honest old seaman gave a cry of joy, as he saw Barnstable issue from the surf, bearing the form of Merry in safety to the sands, where, one by one, several seamen soon appeared also, dripping and exhausted. Many others of the crew were carried, in a similar manner, to places of safety; though, as Tom returned to his seat on the bowsprit, he could not conceal from his reluctant eyes the lifeless forms that were, in other spots, driven against the rocks with a fury that soon left them but few of the outward vestiges of humanity.

Dillon and the cockswain were now the sole occupants of their dreadful station. The former stood in a kind of stupid despair, a witness of the scene we have related; but as his curdled blood began again to flow more warmly through his heart, he crept close to the side of Tom, with that sort of selfish feeling that makes even hopeless misery more tolerable, when endured in participation with another.

"When the tide falls," he said, in a voice that betrayed the agony of fear, though his words expressed the renewal of hope, "we shall be able to walk to land."

"There was One and only One to whose feet the waters were the same as a dry dock," returned the cockswain; "and none but such as have his power will ever be able to walk from these rocks to the sands." The old seaman paused, and turning his eyes, which exhibited a mingled expression of disgust and compassion, on his companion, he added, with reverence: "Had you thought more of Him in fair weather, your case would be less to be pitied in this tempest."

"Do you still think there is much danger?" asked Dillon.

"To them that have reason to fear death. Listen! do you hear that hollow noise beneath ye?"

" 'Tis the wind driving by the vessel!"

" 'Tis the poor thing herself," said the affected cockswain, "giving her last groans. The water is breaking up her decks, and, in a few minutes more, the handsomest model that ever cut a wave will be like the chips that fell from her timbers in framing!"

"Why then did you remain here!" cried Dillon, wildly.

"To die in my coffin, if it should be the will of God," returned Tom. "These waves, to me, are what the land is to you; I was born on them, and I have always meant that they should be my grave."

"But I—I," shrieked Dillon, "I am not ready to die!—I cannot die!—I will not die!"

"Poor wretch!" muttered his companion; "you must go, like the rest of us; when the death-watch is called, none can skulk from the muster."

"I can swim," Dillon continued, rushing with frantic eagerness to the side of the wreck. "Is there no billet of wood, no rope, that I can take with me?"

"None; everything has been cut away, or carried off by the sea. If ye are about to strive for your life, take with ye a stout heart and a clean conscience, and trust the rest to God!"

"God!" echoed Dillon, in the madness of his frenzy; "I know no God! there is no God that knows me!"

"Peace!" said the deep tones of the cockswain, in a voice that seemed to speak in the elements; "blasphemer, peace!"

The heavy groaning, produced by the water in the timbers of the Ariel, at that moment added its impulse to the raging feelings of Dillon, and he cast himself headlong into the sea.

The water, thrown by the rolling of the surf on the beach, was necessarily returned to the ocean, in eddies, in different places favorable to such an action of the element. Into the edge of one of these countercurrents, that was produced by the very rocks on which the schooner lay, and which the watermen call the "undertow," Dillon had, unknowingly, thrown his person; and when the waves had driven him a short distance from the wreck, he was met by a stream that his most desperate efforts could not overcome. He was a light and powerful swimmer, and the struggle was hard and protracted. With the shore immediately before his eyes, and at no great distance, he was led, as by a false phantom, to continue his efforts, although they did not advance him a foot. The old seaman, who at first had watched his motions with careless indifference, understood the danger of his situation at a glance; and, forgetful of his own fate, he shouted aloud, in a voice that was driven over the struggling victim to the ears of his shipmates on the sands:

"Sheer to port, and clear the undertow! Sheer to the southward!"

Dillon heard the sounds, but his faculties were too much obscured by terror to distinguish their object; he, however, blindly yielded to the call, and gradually changed his direction, until his face was once more turned towards the vessel. The current swept him diagonally by the rocks, and he was forced into an eddy, where he had nothing to contend against but the waves, whose violence was much broken by the wreck. In this state, he continued still to struggle, but with a force that was too much weakened to overcome the resistance he met. Tom looked around him for a rope, but all had gone over with the spars, or been swept away by the waves. At this moment of disappointment, his eyes met those of the desperate Dillon. Calm and inured to horrors as was the veteran seaman, he involuntarily passed his hand before his brow, to exclude the look of despair he encountered; and when, a moment afterwards, he removed the rigid member, he beheld the sinking form of the victim as it gradually settled in the ocean, still struggling, with regular but impotent strokes of the arms and feet, to gain the wreck, and to preserve an existence that had been so much abused in its hour of allotted probation.

"He will soon know his God, and learn that his God knows him!" murmured the cockswain to himself. As he yet spoke, the wreck of the Ariel yielded to an overwhelming sea, and, after an universal shudder, her timbers and planks gave way, and were swept towards the cliffs, bearing the body of the simple-hearted cockswain among the ruins.

OLIVER WENDELL HOLMES

The frigate Constitution *earned her nickname "Old Ironsides" when a cannonball bounced off her hull during an August 19, 1812, engagement with the H.M.S.* Guerriere*; she later captured three British frigates in separate engagements during the War of 1812. Oliver Wendell Holmes (1809–1894)—author of fiction, poetry, drama, and the celebrated "Breakfast-Table" series of essays—wrote this poem in response to a report that the Navy Department planned to scrap the venerable ship. First published in the Boston* Daily Advertiser *on September 16, 1830, Holmes' poem was soon widely reprinted. Its popularity inspired a successful effort to preserve the vessel; in 1997, she sailed from Boston Harbor for the first time in over a century after a major restoration.*

Old Ironsides

Ay, tear her tattered ensign down!
    Long has it waved on high,
And many an eye has danced to see
    That banner in the sky;
Beneath it rung the battle shout,
    And burst the cannon's roar;—
The meteor of the ocean air
    Shall sweep the clouds no more!

Her deck, once red with heroes' blood
    Where knelt the vanquished foe,
When winds were hurrying o'er the flood
    And waves were white below,
No more shall feel the victor's tread,
    Or know the conquered knee;—
The harpies of the shore shall pluck
    The eagle of the sea!

O better that her shattered hulk
Should sink beneath the wave;
Her thunders shook the mighty deep,
And there should be her grave;
Nail to the mast her holy flag,
Set every thread-bare sail,
And give her to the god of storms,—
The lightning and the gale!

FANNY KEMBLE

The actress Fanny Kemble (1809–1893) sailed for New York with her father on August 1, 1832, in the hope of reviving the family's fortunes with a two-year American theatrical tour. Despite the homesickness Kemble felt during the crossing, she did not return to England until 1840. She received an enthusiastic reception from American audiences—"we have never seen her equal," wrote the New Yorker Philip Hone—and at the end of her tour met Pierce Butler, her first husband. Kemble's account of her voyage and subsequent American adventures was published in 1835 as Journal of a Young Actress. *She was also the author, among other books, of* A Year of Consolation *(1847),* Journal of a Residence on a Georgian Plantation, 1838–39 *(1863), and* Records of a Girlhood *(1878).*

from *Journal of a Young Actress*

Wednesday, August 1st, 1832

ANOTHER break in my journal and here I am on board the *Pacific*, bound for America, having left home and all the world behind—Well! We reached the quay just as the ship was being pushed and pulled and levered to the entrance of the dock. The quays were lined with people among whom were several known faces, who came on board to take my letters and bid us goodbye.

I had a bunch of carnations in my hand, which I had snatched from our drawing-room chimney—English flowers! dear English flowers! they will be withered long before I see land again, but I will keep them until I once more stand upon the soil on which they grew.

The sky had become clouded and the wind blew cold. Came down and put our narrow room to rights. Worked at my Bible cover till dinner time. We dined at half past three. The table was excellent, cold dinner because it was the first day—but everything was good—champagne and dessert and every luxury imaginable, rendered it as little like a ship-dinner as maybe. The man who sat by me was an American, very good-natured and talkative. Our passengers are all men, with the exception of three; a nice pretty-looking girl who is going out with her brother, a fat old woman and a fat young one. I cried almost the whole of dinner time.

After dinner the ladies adjourned to their own cabin, and the gentlemen began to debate about regulating the meal hours. They adopted the debating society tone, called my dear father to the chair, and presently I heard—oh horror! (what I had not thought to hear again for six weeks) the clapping of hands. They sent him in to consult us about dinner hour, and we having decided four o'clock, the debate continued with considerable merriment. Presently my father, Colonel Sibell and Mr. Hodgkinson came into our cabin, and the former read us Washington Irving's speech at the New York dinner. Some of it is very beautiful, all of it is in good feeling—it made me cry. Oh my home, my land, my England, glorious little England! I sat working till the gentlemen left us, and then wrote my journal. I am weary and sad, and will try to go to sleep—it rains, I cannot see the moon.

Thursday, August 2nd

It rained all night and in the morning the wind had died away, and we lay rocking becalmed on the waveless waters. At eight o'clock they brought us some breakfast, after which I got up. While dressing I could not help being amused at hearing the cocks crowing, the cows lowing and ducks gabbling, as though we were in the midst of a farm-yard. Having finished my toilet, I emerged, and Miss Hodgkinson and I walked upon the deck. The sea lay grey and still, a sheet of lead, the sky was the same dull colour and the deck was wet and comfortless. The whole was melancholy and sadder than all, sat a poor woman dressed in mourning in a corner of the deck. She was a steerage passenger, and I never saw so much sorrow in any face. Poor thing, her heart was aching for home and kindred left behind her, and it made mine ache to look at her.

Miss Hodgkinson and I walked up and down for an hour. I like my companion well; she is a nice quiet young thing, just come from a country home. Came down and began getting out books for my German lesson, but turning rather awful, left my learning on the floor, and betook myself to my birth. Slept till nearly dinner time—took my place at table, but presently the misery returned, and getting up while I had sufficient steadiness left to walk becomingly down the room, I came to my cabin. My dinner followed me thither, and lying on my back, I very comfortably discussed it. Later I got up, devoured some raspberry tart and grapes, and being altogether delightful again, sat working and singing till tea-time.

Friday, August 3rd

Dressed and came on deck. The day was lovely, the sea one deep, dark sapphire, the sky bright and cloudless, the wind mild and soft, too mild to fill our sails, which hung lazily against the masts. Walked on deck with Miss Hodgkinson and Captain Whaite. The latter is a very good-natured, intelligent person, rough and bluff and only seven and twenty, which makes him having command of the ship rather an awful consideration. Presently we were summoned by the sound of a bell and oyez!—oyez!—oyez!—and a society was established for the good demeanour and sociability of the passengers. My father was in the chair. Mr. James Bell was voted secretary. A badge was established, rules and regulations laid down, a code framed, and much laughter and merriment ensued. After dinner, went on deck again, and took a brisk walk with Captain Whaite.

Wednesday, August 15th

Somebody asked me if I had any of Mrs. Siddons' hair, so I sent for my dressing box, and forthwith it was overhauled by half the company, whom a rainy day had reduced to a state worse than usual want of occupation. The rain continued all day, and we ladies dined in the round house, where the Captain and Colonel Sibell joined us, and began drinking champagne and induced us to do the same. Afterwards they fell to singing and while they did so, the sky darkened; the rain came pelting down, the black sea swelled and rose, and broke upon the ship's sides into boiling furrows of foam, that fled like ghosts along the inky face of the ocean. The ship scudded before the blast and we managed to keep ourselves warm by singing.

Thursday, August 16th

Rose at about half past eight, and as soon as our tent was spread after breakfast, went on deck and took a longish walk with Mr. Hodgkinson—I like him very much. Gossiped till lunch-time and then took up *Childe Harold*. I thought of dear Harriet. She admires Byron more than I do, and yet how wildly I did, how deeply I do still worship his might, majesty and loveliness. After dinner, I and Mr. Bell took a long walk on deck, talking flimsy morality and philosophy. The day was bright and bitter cold, the sea blue and transparent with a lining of pearly foam and glittering spray that enchanted me.

Friday, August 17th

On my back all day—the ship reeled about like a drunken thing. I lay down and began reading Byron's life. Had he been less of an egoist would he have been so great a poet? I question it. I wonder Byron was moved by criticism. I should have thought him at once too highly armed and too self-wrapped to care for it. Ate nothing but figs and raisins. In the evening some of our gentlemen came into our cabin and sat with us. I in very desperation and sea-sickness began embroidering one of my nightcaps, wherein I persevered till sleep overtook me.

Saturday, August 18th

Rose about half past eight, dawdled about as usual, and read a few more pages of Byron's life. After breakfast got Colonel Sibell to read *Quentin Durward* to us as we sat working under our canvas pavilion. Our company consists chiefly of traders in cloth and hardware, clerks and counting-house men. Most of them have crossed this trifling ditch half a dozen times in the course of their various avocations. Mr. Hodgkinson read to us after lunch, and we sat happily under our awning till the rain drove us in. Our main-top gallant mast had been split in one of our late blows, and I went out in the rain to see them restore the spar. Towards evening the wind freshened and our gentlemen's spirits rose, and soon, in spite of the rain, they were dancing and singing and romping like mad things. Mr. Bell and I sang through the whole volume of Moore's melodies, and at ten o'clock we adjourned to the gentlemen's cabin to drink to "sweethearts and wives" according to sailors' approved practice.

Sunday, August 19th

Dressed and came on deck—the morning was brilliant. I amused myself with finding the lessons and collects and psalms for the whole ship's company. After lunch, they spread our tent, a chair was placed for my father, and a little bell being rung, we collected in our rude church. It affected me much, this praying on the lonely sea, in words that at the same hour were being uttered by millions of kindred tongues in our dear home. Oh how I felt all this as we spoke aloud that touching invocation—"Almighty God, who hast promised that when two or three are gathered together in Thy name"—etc. The bright cloudless sky and glorious sea seemed to respond in their silent magnificence to our Te Deum—'twas good—oh! very, very good!

Monday, August 20th

Calm, utter calm—a roasting August sun, a waveless sea, the sails flapping idly against our mast. Wrote my journal, walked about and in the evening danced merrily, quadrilles and country dances. Fairly danced myself tired and came to bed. But oh! not to sleep—mercy what a night! The wind blowing like mad, the ship pitching, bouncing, shuddering, creaking and groaning, till ten o'clock, when I got up and was going to see how near drowning we were, when Dall, who was lying awake too, implored me to lie down again. Lay till daylight, the gale was increasing furiously, boxes, chairs, beds and their contents rolling about in glorious confusion.

Wednesday, August 22nd

A fair wind, a fair day—though very very cold and damp. The only one of our crew I cotton on to fairly are the

Hodgkinsons and that good-natured lad, Mr. Staley. Though the former rather distress me by their abundant admiration, and the latter by his inveterate Yorkshire, and never opening his mouth when he sings, which, as he has a very sweet voice, is a cruel piece of selfishness, keeping half his tones and all his words for his own private satisfaction.

Thursday, August 23rd

A fine day, walked about, wrote journal, read some of it to the Hodgkinsons, who seemed much gratified by my doing so. I go on with Byron's life. He is too much of an egoist. I think I never read anything professing to be a person's undisguised feelings and opinions with so much heartlessness, so little goodness in it. Dined at table again. They abound in toasts, and among others, gave "the friends we have left and those we are going to!" My heart sank. I am going to no friend, and the "stranger" with which the Americans salute wayfarers through their land, is the only title I can claim. After dinner, danced and saw the sun sink in a bed of gorgeous stormy clouds.

Friday, August 24th

Rose late after a fair night's sleep, and after breakfast read a canto of Dante, when—"A sail! a sail!" was cried from all quarters. Remembering my promise to dear Harriet, I got together my writing materials and scrawled her a few lines. The vessel bore down rapidly upon us, but as there was no prospect of either her or us lying to, Mr. Hodgkinson tied my missive, together with one he had just scribbled, to a lump of lead, and presently we all rushed on deck to see the ship pass us. She was an English packet, from Valparaiso, bound for London, and as she passed us, Mr. Hodgkinson got up into a boat to have a better chance of throwing. I saw him fling powerfully, the little packet whizzed through the air, but the distance was impossible. The dark waters received it within twenty feet of the ship, which sailed rapidly on and soon left us far behind. I believe I screamed as the black sea closed over my poor letter. Came down to my cabin and cried like a wretch. After dinner had a sick headache, and walked on deck. The wind and the sea were both rising, the sky had grown mirk as midnight, and the wind that came rushing over the sea was hot from the south. At tea, the crazy old ship in one of her headlong bounces, flung my whole supper in my lap. The wind and water were riotous and the whole ship plunged and shuddered.

Wednesday, August 28th

A miserable day spent between heart-ache and side-ache. The Captain today brought me a land-swallow, which having flown out so far, came hovering over the ship and suffered itself to be caught. Poor little creature! I felt sad for its weary little wings and frightened heart which beat against my hand. I made a cage in a basket for it and gave it some seed, which it will not eat, carniverous little wretch!—I must catch some flies for it.

Thursday, August 29th

My poor little bird is dead. Poor little creature! I wish it had not died—I would have borne it tenderly and carefully to shore, and given it back to the air again.

Friday, August 30th

A fog and calm. Sky yellow, sea grey, dripping, dark, damp, and very disagreeable. Sat working, reading and talking in our cabin all day. Its too hard to be becalmed within thirty hours of our destination.

Saturday, August 31st

Becalmed again till about two o'clock, when a fair wind sprang up and we set to rolling before it like mad. Got very sick and lay on the ground till dinner time. Went to table but withdrew while it was still in my power to do so gracefully. It suddenly occurred to me that it was our last Saturday night on board. Last—last—what is there in that word? I don't know one of the ship's company, don't care for some of them—I have led a loathsome life in it for the past month, and yet the *last* Saturday night seemed sad to me. Came to bed at about half past twelve, and while undressing, I heard the Captain announce that we were clear of Nantucket shoal, and within one hundred and fifty miles of New York, which intelligence was received with three cheers.

September 1st, Sunday

Rose at half past six, went on deck, the sun was shining brilliantly. The morning was glorious, the sun had risen two hours ago, the sea was cut by a strong breeze, and curled into ridges that came like emerald banks crowned with golden spray round our ship. After breakfast put my things to rights and while doing so, the joyful sound—"Land! land!" was heard aloft. I rushed on deck and between the blue waveless sea and the bright unclouded sky, lay the wished-for line of a darker element. 'Twas Long Island. Hail, strange land! my heart greets you coldly and sadly! The day was heavenly, though intensely hot, the sky utterly cloudless. They tell me that this is their American weather almost till Christmas—that's nice, for those who like frying. Commend me to dear England's soft, rich, harmonious skies and foliage, commend me to the misty curtain of silver vapour that hangs over her September woods at morning, and shrouds them at night—in short—I am homesick before touching land.

We were talking today to one of our steerage passengers, a Huddersfield manufacturer, going out in quest of a living, with five children of his own to take care of, and two nephews. The father of the latter, said our Yorkshireman, having married a second time, and these poor children being as it were, thrust into the world—"why, I just took care of them". Verily, verily, he will have his reward—these tender mercies of the poor to one another are beautiful and most touching.

September 2nd, Monday

I had desired the mate to call me by sunrise, and accordingly in the midst of a very sound sleep, Mr. Curtis shook me roughly by the arm, informing me that the sun was just about to rise. I called Harriet, and we remained on deck watching the clouds like visions of brightness and beauty, at every moment assuming more fantastic shapes and gorgeous tints. Oh, it was surpassing! We were becalmed, however, which rather damped all our spirits, and made the Captain swear. Towards midday we had to thank heaven for an incident. A brig had been standing aft against the horizon for some hours past, and we presently descried a boat rowing towards us from her. The distance was some five miles, they rowed stoutly and in due time boarded us. She was an English brig from Bristol, had been out eleven weeks, distressed by contrary winds and was in want of provisions. Our dear Captain supplied them with everything they wanted, and the poor steerage passengers sent their mite to the distressed crews in the shape of the sack of potatoes. After this the whole day was one of continual excitement. At about four o'clock, a schooner came alongside with a news collector—he was half devoured with questions, news of the cholera, reports of the tariff and bank questions were loudly demanded. Poor people, how anxiously they looked for replies to the first. Mr. Hodgkinson turned as pale as death while asking how it had visited Boston.

Poor fellow! poor people! my heart ached for their anxiety. As the evening darkened, the horizon became studded with sails. At about eight o'clock we discovered the Highlands of Neversink, the entrance to New York harbour, and presently the twin lights of Sandy Hook glimmered against the sky. We were all in high spirits, a fresh breeze had sprung up, and the Captain alone seemed anxious, eagerly looking out for the pilot. Some had gathered at the ship's side, to watch the progress of Colonel Sibell, who had left us to go into the newsboat, which was dancing by the side of our dark vessel. Cheering resounded on all sides, rockets were fired from the ship's stern, we were all dancing, when suddenly a cry echoed round—"A pilot! a pilot!", and close under the ship's side a light graceful little schooner shot like an arrow through the dim twilight. She tacked and lay to, but proved to be only another newsboat. While we were all gathered round, the pilot-boat came alongside, with the pilot on board. The Captain gave up the cares and glories of command and we danced an interminable country dance. All was excitement and joyous confusion. Poor Mr. Bell alone seemed smitten with sudden anxiety. The cholera reports had filled him with alarm, lest his agent should have died, and his affairs on arrival be in confusion and ruin—poor fellow, I was very sorry for him. We went down to supper at ten, and were very merry, in spite of the ship's bumping once or twice upon the sands. Came up and saw them cast anchor, away went the chain, down dropped the heavy stay, the fair ship swung round, and there lay New York before us, with its clustered lights shining like a distant constellation against the dark land. Our cradle rocks no longer, but lies on the still waters. We have reached our destination—thank God! I did so with all my soul.

NATHANIEL PARKER WILLIS

When the poet, essayist, and editor Nathaniel Parker Willis (1806–1867) sailed to Europe as foreign correspondent for the New-York Mirror *in 1831, he was one of America's most successful writers. Described by Oliver Wendell Holmes as "something between a remembrance of Count D'Orsay and an anticipation of Oscar Wilde," Willis delighted in the glamour of fashionable places, and had a gift for conveying vivid, immediate impressions in his seemingly effortless prose. He remained in Europe for five years, sending breezy accounts of his travels to the* Mirror *at the rate of one essay per week. In his description of his 1832 voyage, later published as* A Summer Cruise in the Mediterranean, *a ball on board the* Constellation, *even when interrupted by a storm, is rendered with all the enchantment and bustle of light opera.*

from *A Summer Cruise in the Mediterranean*

I HAD come from Florence to join the "United States," at the polite invitation of the officers of the ward-room, on a cruise up the Mediterranean. My cot was swung immediately on my arrival, but we lay three days longer than was expected in the harbor, riding out a gale of wind, which broke the chain cables of both ships, and drove several merchant vessels on the rocks. We got under way on the third of June, and the next morning were off Elba, with Corsica on our quarter, and the little island of Capreja just ahead.

The firing of guns took me just now to the deck. Three Sardinian gun-boats had saluted the commodore's flag in passing, and it was returned with twelve guns. They were coming home from the affair at Tunis. It is a fresh, charming morning, and we are beating up against a light head-wind, all the officers on deck, looking at the island with their glasses, and discussing the character of the great man to whom this little barren spot was a temporary empire. A bold fortification just appears on the point, with the Tuscan flag flying from the staff. The sides of the hills are dotted with desolate looking buildings, among which are one or two monasteries, and in rounding the side of the island, we have passed two or three small villages, perched below and above on the rocks. Off to the east, we can just distinguish Piombino, the nearest town of the Italian shore, and very beautiful it looks, rising from the edge of the water like Venice, with a range of cloudy hills relieving it in the rear.

Our anchor is dropped in the bay of Porto Ferrajo. As we ran lightly in upon the last tack, the walls of the fort appeared crowded with people, the whole town apparently assembled to see the unusual spectacle of two ships-of-war entering their now quiet waters. A small curving bay opened to us, and as we rounded directly under the walls of the fort, the tops of the houses in the town behind appeared crowded with women, whose features we could easily distinguish with a glass. By the constant exclamations of the midshipmen, who were gazing intently from the quarter deck, there was among them a fair proportion of beauty, or what looked like it in the distance. Just below the summit of the fort, upon a terrace commanding a view of the sea, stood a handsome house, with low windows shut with Venetian blinds and shaded with acacias, which the pilot pointed out to us as the town residence of Napoleon. As the ship lost her way, we came in sight of a gentle amphitheatre of hills rising away from the cove, in a woody ravine of which stood a handsome building, with eight windows, built by the exile as a country-house. Twenty or thirty, as good or better, spot the hills around, ornamented with avenues and orchards of low olive-trees. It is altogether a rural scene, and disappoints us agreeably after the barren promise of the outer sides of the isle.

The Constellation came slowly in after us, with every sail set, and her tops crowded with men; and as she fell under the stern of the commodore's ship, the word was given, and her vast quantity of sail was furled with that wonderful alacrity which so astonishes a landsman. I have been continually surprised in the few days that I have been on board, with the wonders of sea discipline; but for a spectacle, I have seen nothing more imposing than the entrance of these two beautiful frigates into the little port of Elba, and their magical management. The anchors were dropped, the yards came down by the run, the sails disappeared, the living swarm upon the rigging slid below, all in a moment, and then struck up the delightful band on our quarter deck, and the sailors leaned on the guns, the officers on the quarter railing, and boats from the shore, filled with ladies, lay off at different distances, the whole scene as full of repose and enjoyment, as if we had lain idle for a month in these glassy waters. How beautiful are the results of order!

* * *

The ships have been thronged with visitors during the two or three days we have lain at Naples, among whom have been the prime minister and his family. Orders are given to admit every one on board that wishes to come, and the decks, morning and evening, present the most motley scene imaginable. Cameo and lava sellers expose their wares on the gun-carriages, surrounded by the midshipmen—Jews and fruit-sellers hail the sailors through the ports—boats full of chickens and pigs, all in loud outcry, are held up to view with a recommendation in broken English—contadini in their best dresses walk up and down, smiling on the officers, and wondering at the cleanliness of the decks, and the elegance of the captain's cabin—Punch plays his tricks under the gun-deck ports—bands of wandering musicians sing and hold out their hats, as they row around, and all is harmony and amusement. In the evening, it is pleasanter still, for the band is playing, and the better class of people come off from the shore, and boats filled with these pretty, dark-eyed Neapolitans, row round and round the ship, eying the officers as they lean over the bulwarks, and ready with but half a nod to make acquaintance and come up the gangway. I have had a private pride of my own in showing the frigate as American to many of my foreign friends. One's nationality becomes nervously sensitive abroad, and in the beauty and order of the ships, the manly elegance of the officers, and the general air of superiority and decision throughout, I have found food for some of the highest feelings of gratification of which I am capable.

* * *

Trieste.—A ball on board the United States. The guns were run out of the ports; the main and mizen-masts were wound with red and white bunting; the capstan was railed with arms and wreathed with flowers; the wheel was tied with nosegays; the American eagle stood against the mainmast, with a star of midshipmen's swords glittering above it; festoons of evergreens were laced through the rigging; the companion-way was arched with hoops of green leaves and roses; the decks were tastefully chalked; the commodore's skylight was piled with cushions and covered with red damask for an ottoman; seats were laid along from one carronade to the other; and the whole was enclosed with a temporary tent lined throughout with showy flags, and studded all over with bouquets of all the flowers of Illyria. Chandeliers made of bayonets, battle-lanterns, and candles in any quantity, were disposed all over the hall. A splendid supper was set out on the gun-deck below, draped in with flags. Our own and the Constellation's boats were to be at the pier at nine o'clock to bring off the ladies, and at noon every thing promised of the brightest.

First, about four in the afternoon, came up a saucy looking cloud from the westernmost peak of the Friuli. Then followed from every point toward the north, an extending edge of a broad solid black sheet which rose with the regularity of a curtain, and began to send down a wind upon us which made us look anxiously to our ball-room bowlines. The midshipmen were all forward, watching it from the forecastle. The lieutenants were in the gangway, watching it from the ladder. The commodore looked seriously out of the larboard cabin port. It was as grave a ship's company as ever looked out for a shipwreck.

The country about Trieste is shaped like a bellows, and the city and harbor lie in the nose. They have a wind that comes down through the valley, called the "bora," which several times in the year is strong enough to lift people from their feet.

We could see, by the clouds of dust on the mountain roads, that it was coming. At six o'clock the shrouds began to creak; the white tops flew from the waves in showers of spray, and the roof of our sea palace began to shiver in the wind. There was no more hope. We had waited even too long. All hands were called to take down the chandeliers, sword-stars, and ottomans, and before it was half done, the storm was upon us; the bunting was flying and flapping, the nicely chalked decks were swashed with rain, and strown with leaves of flowers, and the whole structure, the taste and labor of the ship's company for two days, was a watery wreck.

Lieutenant C——, who had had the direction of the whole, was the officer of the deck. He sent for his pea-jacket, and leaving him to pace out his watch among the ruins of his imagination, we went below to get early to bed, and forgot our disappoint in sleep.

The next morning the sun rose without a veil. The "blue Friuli" looked clear and fresh; the southwest wind came over softly from the shore of Italy, and we commenced retrieving our disaster with elastic spirit. Nothing had suffered seriously except the flowers, and boats were despatched ashore for fresh supplies; while the awnings were lifted higher and wider than before, the bright-colored flags replaced, the arms polished and arranged in improved order, and the decks re-chalked with new devices. At six in the evening everything was swept up, and the ball-room astonished even ourselves. It was the prettiest place for a dance in the world.

The ship has an admirable band of twenty Italians, collected from Naples and other ports, and a fanciful orchestra was raised for them on the larboard side of the mainmast. They struck up a march as the first boatful of ladies stepped upon the deck, and in the course of half an hour the waltzing commenced with at least two hundred couples, while the ottoman and seats under the hammock-cloths were filled with spectators. The frigate has a lofty poop, and there was room enough upon it for two quadrilles after it had served as a reception-room. It was edged with a temporary balustrade, wreathed with flowers and studded with lights, and the cabin beneath (on a level with the main ball-room), was set out with card-tables. From the gangway entrance, the scene was like a brilliant theatrical *ballet*.

An amusing part of it was the sailors' imitation on the forward decks. They had taken the waste, shrubbery and evergreens, of which there was a great quantity, and had formed a sort of grove, extending all round. It was arched with festoons of leaves, with quantities of fruit tied among them; and over the entrance was suspended a rough picture of a frigate with the inscription, "*Free trade and sailors' rights*." The forecastle was ornamented with cutlasses, and one or two nautical transparencies, with pistols and miniature ships interspersed, and the whole lit up handsomely. The men were dressed in their white duck trowsers and blue jackets, and sat round on the guns playing at draughts, or listening to the music, or gazing at the ladies constantly promenading fore and aft, and to me this was one of the most interesting parts of the spectacle. Five hundred weather-beaten and manly faces are a fine sight anywhere.

The dance went gaily on. The reigning belle was an American, but we had lovely women of all nations among our guests. There are several wealthy Jewish families in Trieste, and their dark-eyed daughters, we may say at this distance, are full of the thoughtful loveliness peculiar to the race. Then we had Illyrians and Germans, and—Terpsichore be witness—how they danced! My travelling companion, the Count of Friuli, was there; and his little Viennese wife, though she spoke no Christian language, danced as featly as a fairy. Of strangers passing through Trieste, we had several of distinction. Among them was a fascinating Milanese marchioness, a relative of Manzoni's, the novelist (and as enthusiastic and eloquent a lover of her countruy as I ever listened to on the subject of oppressed Italy), and two handsome young men, the count Neipperg, sons-in-law to Maria Louisa, who amused themselves as if they had seen nothing better in the little duchy of Parma.

We went below at midnight, to supper, and the ladies came up with renewed spirit to the dance. It was a brilliant scene indeed. The officers of both ships, in full uniform, the gentlemen from the shore, mostly military, in full dress, the gayety of the bright red bunting, laced with white and blue, and studded, wherever they would stand, with flowers, and the really uncommon number of beautiful women, with the foreign features and complexions so rich and captivating to our eyes, produced altogether an effect unsurpassed by any thing I have ever seen even at the court *fêtes* of Europe. The daylight gun fired at the close of a *galopado*, and the crowded boats pulled ashore with their lovely freight by the broad light of morning.

Ralph Waldo Emerson

In December 1832, two months after resigning as pastor of Boston's Second Church, Ralph Waldo Emerson (1803–1882) traveled for the first time to Europe, where he would meet William Wordsworth, Samuel Taylor Coleridge, John Stuart Mill, and Thomas Carlyle. He had planned to spend the winter with his brother Edward in Puerto Rico, but gave in to "a purpureal vision of Naples & Italy" after hearing that the Jasper, *a 236-ton cargo ship, was to sail from Boston to Malta in early December. His passage was nearly refused by the* Jasper'*s captain, Cornelius Ellis, who worried that Emerson, then in poor health, might not survive the arduous midwinter voyage. At first, Captain Ellis's caution seemed prescient: after languishing for three weeks in Boston harbor, the* Jasper *sailed on Christmas Day and encountered stormy seas the next morning. Unable to eat, read, or write in his journal, Emerson spent the first week at sea holed up with the* Jasper'*s four other passengers in a single cabin below decks, fearing for his life. After this terrifying beginning, the rest of the six-week voyage was uneventful and even restored Emerson's health, despite the irritations of forced sociability for a man who prized solitude.*

from *Journals*

At Sea. Jan. 2, 1833. Sailed from Boston for Malta Dec. 25, 1832 in Brig Jasper, Capt Ellis, 236 tons laden with logwood, mahogany, tobacco, sugar, coffee, beeswax, cheese, &c.Dec.

A long storm from the second morn of our departure consigned all the five passengers to the irremediable chagrins of the stateroom, to wit, nausea, darkness, unrest, uncleanness, harpy appetite & harpy feeding, the ugly sound of water in mine ears, anticipations of going to the bottom, & the treasures of the memory. I remembered up nearly the whole of Lycidas, clause by clause, here a verse & there a word, as Isis in the fable the broken body of Osiris.

Out occasionally crawled we from our several holes, but hope & fair weather would not, so there was nothing for it but to wriggle again into the crooks of the transom. Then it seemed strange that the first man who came to sea did not turn round & go straight back again. Strange that because one of my neighbors had some trumpery logs & notions which would sell for a few cents more here than there he should thrust forth this company of his poor countrymen to the tender mercies of the northwest wind.

We study the sailor, the man of his hands, man of all work; all eye, all finger, muscle, skill, & endurance; a tailor, a carpenter, cooper, stevedore, & clerk & astronomer besides. He is a great saver, and a great quiddle by the necessity of his situation.

The Captain believes in the superiority of the American to every other countryman. "You will see, he says, when you get out here how they manage in Europe; they do everything by main strength & ignorance. Four truckmen & four stevedores at Long Wharf will load my brig quicker than 100 men at any port in the Mediterranean." It seems the Sicilians have tried once or twice to bring their fruit to America in their own bottoms, & made the passage, he says, in 120 days.

* * *

Thursday 3 Jan. N. lat 37.53. Dr Johnson rightly defends conversation upon the weather. With more reason we at sea beat that topic thin. We are pensioners of the wind. The weather cock is the wisest man. All our prosperity, enterprize, temper come & go with the fickle air. If the wind should forget to blow we must eat our masts. Sea farmers must make hay when the sun shines. The gale collects plenty of work for the calm. Now are we all awaiting a smoother sea to stand at our toilette. A headwind makes grinning Esaus of us. Happy that there is a time for all things under the moon, so that no man need give a dinner party in a brig's cabin, nor shave himself by the gulf lightning.

Sat. Eve. 5 Jan. I like the latitude of 37° better than my bitter native 42°. We have sauntered all this calm day at one or two knots the hour & nobody on board well pleased but I.

And why should I be pleased? I have nothing to record. I have read little. I have done nothing. What then? Need we be such barren scoundrels that the whole beauty of heaven, the main, & man cannot entertain us unless we too must needs hold a candle & daub God's world with a smutch of our own insignificance? Not I, for one. I will be pleased though I do not deserve it. I will act in all up to my conceit of last week when I exulted in the power & art with which we rode tilting over this January ocean, albeit to speak truth, our individual valours lay very sick the while, lodged each in the waistcoat pocket of the brave brig's transom. So that each passenger's particular share in the glory was much the same as the sutler's or grocer's who turns his penny in the army of Leonidas or Washington. The southing latitude does not yet make early mornings. The steward's lanthorn & trumpery matutinal preparations are to me for the rosy ray, the silver cloud, or chaunt of earliest bird. But days will come.

* * *

Sunday 6 Jan. lat 37 23. long. 39 59 w. Last ev'g fair wind & full moon suddenly lost in squall & rain. There are no attractions in the sailor's life. Its best things are only alleviations. "A prison with the chance of being drowned." It is even so and yet they do not run blind into unmeasured danger as seems to the landsman; those chances are all counted & weighed & experience has begotten this confidence in the proportioned strength of spars & rigging to the ordinary forces of wind & water which by being habitual constitutes the essence of a sailor's fearlessness. Suppose a student confined to a ship, I see not why he might not trim his lamp to as good purpose as in college attic. Why should he be less efficient in his vocation than the poor steward who ingloriously deals ever in pork & beans, let the quadrant or the chart or the monsoon say what they will? The caboose is his Rome.

* * *

Storm, storm; ah we! the sea to us is but a lasting storm. We have had no fine weather to last an hour. Yet I must thank the sea & rough weather for a truckman's health & stomach,—how connected with celestial gifts!

The wind is the sole performer in these parts of nature & the royal Aeolus understands his work well, &, to give him his due, shifts the scene & varies the accompaniment as featly & as often as the audience can desire. Certainly he rings his few chimes with wondrous skill of permutation. Sometimes we his pets are cross & say 'tis nought but salt & squalls & sometimes we are ourselves & admit that it is divine Architecture.

7 Jan. w long 36.11. n. lat. 37.4. Sailors are the best dressed of mankind. Convenience is studied from head to heel, & they have a change for every emergency. It seems to me they get more work out of the sailor than out of any other craftsman. His obedience is prompt as a soldier's & willing as a child's, & reconciles me to some dim remembrances of authority I wondered at. Thin skins do not believe in thick. Jack never looks an inch beyond his orders. "Brace the yards," quoth the master; "Ay Ay, sir," answers Jack, and never looks over the side at the squall or the sea that cometh as if it were no more to him than to the capstan.

But though I do not find much attraction in the seaman yet I can discern that the naval hero is a hero. It takes all the thousand thousand European voyages that have been made to stablish our faith in the practicability of this our hodiurnal voyage. But to be Columbus, to steer WEST steadily day after day, week after week, for the first time, and wholly alone in his opinion, shows a mind as solitary & self-subsistent as any that ever lived.

I am learning the use of the quadrant. Another voyage would make an astronomer of me. How delicately come out these stars at sea. The constellations show smaller & a ship though with the disadvantage of motion is a fine observatory. But I am ashamed of myself for a dull scholar. Every day I display a more astounding ignorance. The whole world is a mill stone to me. The experiment of the philosopher is but a separation to bring within his optics the comprehension of a fact which is done masterly & in harmony in God's laboratory of the world.

* * *

13 Jan. We have but 14 degrees of longitude to make to reach the rock of Gibraltar but the fickle wind may make these

fourteen longer measure than all we have meted. A gale day before yesterday; yesterday a heavy sea & a cold head wind today. Yet still we hope & drift along. In the Ocean the vessel gains a large commission on every mile sailed even with a wind dead ahead. In a narrow sea much less. A sea voyage at the best is yet such a bundle of perils & inconveniences that no person as much a lover of the present moment as I am would be swift to pay that price for any commodity which any thing else would buy. Yet if our horses are somewhat wild & the road uneven & lonely & without inns yet experience shows us that the coward eye magnifies the dangers.

* * *

I comfort the mate by assuring him that the sea life is excellent preparation for life ashore. No man well knows how many fingers he has got nor what are the faculties of a knife & a needle or the capabilities of a pine board until he has seen the expedients, & the ambidexterous invincibility of Jack Tar. Then he may buy an orchard or retreat to his paternal acres with a stock of thrifty science that will make him independent of all the village carpenters, masons, & wheelwrights & add withal an enchanting beauty to the waving of his yellow corn & sweetness to his shagbarks in his chimney corner. No squally Twelve o'clock Call the Watch shall break his dreams.

* * *

Wednesday, 16 Jan. W. long. 11.30 North latitude 30

16 Jan. I rose betimes & saw every fold of the banner of the morning unrolled from starlight to full day. We are as poor as we are rich. We brag of our memory but in the lonely night watch it will not always befriend us but leaves the scholar's brain as barren as the steward's. But that I sat in the confessional last night I should parade my rags again. The good Captain rejoices much in my ignorance. He confounded me the other day about the book in the Bible where God was not mentioned & last night upon St Paul's shipwreck. Yet I comforted myself at midnight with Lycidas. What marble beauty in that classic Pastoral. I should like well to see an analysis of the pleasure it gives. That were criticism for the gods.

The inconvenience of living in a cabin is that people become all eye. 'Tis a great part of wellbeing to ignorize a good deal of your fellowman's history & not count his warts nor expect the hour when he shall wash his teeth.

17 JAN. n. lat 36 29 w long 9.48 Another day as beautiful as ever shines on the monotonous sea but a wind so soft will not fill our sails & we lie like a log so near our haven too. Ατρυγετη θαλασση—the sea is a blank & all the minstrelsy of nature rings but a few changes on the instrument. The more it should send us to the inner Music; but that is a capricious shell which sometimes vibrates wildly with multitudinous impulses & sometimes is mute as wood. The inner shell is like its marine archetype which murmurs only where there is already noise.

Friday 18 Jan. lat 36 36 long 8 20 w.

Well thou navigating Muse of mine 'tis now the hour of Chinese inspiration, the post-tea-cup-time, the epical creative moment to all thinking heads of the modern world & what print have the ethereal footsteps of Night & Morn left upon your tablets? Another day, another profusion of the divine munificence yet taken & spent by us as by the oysters. The boar feeds under the tree & never looks up to see who shakes down the mast & I glide in leisure & safety & health & fulness over this liquid Sahara & the Invisible Leader so venerable is seldom worshipped & much a stranger in the bosom of his child. We feel sometimes as if the sweet & awful melodies we have once heard would never return. As if we were deaf and fear we shall not again aspire to the glory of a moral life, of a will as punctual as the little needle in the binnacle over my head. The sea tosses on the horns of its waves the framework of habits so slight & epicurean as mine & I make the voyage one long holiday which like all holidays is dull.

Sat. 19 Jan. Mem. No trust to be put in a seaman's eye. He can see land wherever he wishes to see it & always has a cloud & "the stuff" ready to cover up a mistake. No word suits the sea but I hope. Every sign fails.

20 Jan. Straits of Gibraltar. Last evening they saw land from the mast-head & this morning broke over the bold & picturesque mountains of Africa behind Cape Spartel & Tangiers. On the left was Cape Trafalgar & Spain. The passengers greeted each other & mused each in his own way on this animating vision. But now as Tarifa light opened upon us we have encountered an adverse current, a thing unknown in the books or to the sailors in these waters where they say the current always sets from the Ocean into the Mediterranean. Meantime all the other craft great & small are flying by us & we seem anchored in the middle of the stream. What is this to me beyond my fellowfeeling for the master? Shall not I be content to look at the near coast of Andalusia & Morocco? I have seen this morn the smokes of Moorish fishers or mountaineers on one side & of Spanish on the other. We could not quite open Tangier Bay enow to see that Mauritanian town, but the watch towers & the cultivated enclosures & the farm houses of the Spaniard are very discernible. Not many weeks ago I should scarce have been convinced that I should so soon look on these objects, yet what is their poetry or what is it not? Is not a hut in America a point that concentrates as much life & sentiment as a hut in Europe or on the ragged side of Mount Atlas? Ah! it is all in the Anointed eye. Yet will not I refine overmuch on the love of the remote & the renowned, nor affirm them both to be only a mixture of colors upon the retina of the eye, nor say of a man he is mammiferous & of beauty it is but gelatine & oxygen.

21 Jan. A squall with copious rain helped us out of our Straits & last evening I saw the lights of the barracks at Gibraltar on one side & at Ceuta on the other. The summit of the hill at Gibraltar is 1500 feet high.

This day we sail bravely 5, 6, & 7 knots. Sunrise was charming; the pillars of Hercules astern; the Barbary Coast on the lee quarter; & the mountains of Grenada covered with snow, having white villages half way up their sides on the left hand. A grand show they make. The Sierra Nevada is the name of the range, & the easternmost summit which we saw is the highest in Spain & except the Alps in Europe to wit 11,690 ft. We glided by Malaga the country of the finest grape but were too far seaward to spy the town. Twenty one sail were in sight at sunrise.

* * *

25 Jan. N. Lat. 37° 31 E. long. 1° 20′ Head winds are sore vexations & the more passengers the sorer. Yesterday the Captain killed a porpoise & I witnessed the cutting up of my mammiferous fellow creature.

When men & women sit mum by the hour & week, shall I doubt the doctrine that every natural character is interesting? By no means; there is always sweet music in the pipe but it needs a skilful player to draw it out, else month by month we may be packed in the same closet, & shall be all only so much ash & ebony.

If the sea teaches any lesson it thunders this through the throat of all its winds "That there is no knowledge that is not valuable." How I envied my fellow passenger who yesterday had knowledge & nerve enough to prescribe for the sailor's sore throat & this morning to bleed him. In this little balloon of ours, so far from the human family and their sages & colleges & manufactories every accomplishment, every natural or acquired talent, every piece of information is some time in request. And a short voyage will show the difference between the man & the apprentice as surely as it will show the superior value of beef & bread to lemons & sugar-plums. Honour evermore aboard ship to the man of action,—to the brain in the hand. Here is our stout master worth a thousand philosophers—a man who can strike a porpoise, & make oil out of his blubber, & steak out of his meat; who can thump a mutineer into obedience in two minutes; who can bleed his sick sailor, & mend the box of his pump; who can ride out the roughest storm on the American coast, &, more than all, with the sun & a three cornered bit of wood, & a chart, can find his way from Boston across 3000 miles of stormy water into a little gut of inland sea 9 miles wide with as much precision as if led by a clue.

2 Feb. Made St Elmo's light at 1 o'clock this morning; lay to in a gale till daylight & then sailed into St Paul's bay. The pilot boat was quickly followed by a procession of boats who after a short loud wrangling with the unflinching captain came into his terms & took the rope & brought us in. So here we are in Malta, in the renowned harbor of Marsa Muscette the Quarantine roads for a fortnight, imprisoned for poor dear Europe's health lest it should suffer prejudice from the unclean sands & mountains of America. The truth is it is all pro forma on the part of the English government, this quarantine being enforced in accordance with the rules of Naples & Trieste merely that vessels quarantined here may be admitted to full pratique in those ports.

We were presently visited by the Harbor-master, then by the boats of the grocer & ship chandler presenting their cards at the end of a pole to us leprous men, then the clamorous *Spenditori* to offer their services, then by the merchant signor Paul Eynaud.

This P.M. I visited the Parlatorio where those in quarantine converse with those out across barriers. It looked to me like the wildest masquerade. There jabbered Turks, Moors, Sicilians, Germans, Greeks, English, Maltese, with friars & guards & maimed & beggars. And such grotesque faces! It resembled more some brave antique picture than a congregation of flesh & blood. The human family can seldom see their own differences of color & form so sharply contrasted as in this house. I noticed however that all the curiosity manifested was on our part. Our cousins of Asia & Europe did not pay us the compliment of a second glance.

In Quarantine, our acquaintance has been confined chiefly to the Maltese boatmen, a great multitude of poor, swarthy, goodnatured people, who speak their own tongue, not much differing from the Arabic, & most of them know very few words of Italian & less of English.

* * *

21 Feb. At 8 o'clock P.M. we embarked for Syracuse in a Sicilian brigantine "Il Santissimo Ecce Homo," and a most ridiculous scene our ship's company offered, they to us & we to

them. The little brig was manned with 14 men who were all on a perfect level with each other. The steersman sat down at the helm & when they brought him his supper the captain affectionately took his post whilst he ate. The boy was employed in sitting down by the steersman & watching the hour glass so that he might turn it when it ran out. But the whole interest of master & men was concentrated on us his five passengers. We had hired for $30 the whole cabin, so they put all their heads into the scuttle & companionway to behold all that we did, the which seemed to amuse them mightily. When any thing was to be done to sails or spars they did it who had a mind to it & the captain got such obedience as he could. In the morning the mate brought up his gazetteer to find Boston the account of which he read aloud, and all the crew gathered round him whilst he read. They laughed heartily at the captain & passed jokes upon him & when the little boy did something amiss every body gave him a knock. A cask of blood red wine was on tap, from which every body drank when it pleased him in a quart measure. Their food was a boiled fish called *purpo* (which looks like an eel & tastes like lobster) with bread & green onions eaten raw. Their little vessel sailed fast & in 16 hours we saw the ancient city of Syracuse. Abundance of fuss & vexation did the Sanita & the Dogana give us before we were suffered to land our baggage but our Captain & mate helped us all they could, & our money opened all the gates at last.

* * *

What is a passenger? He is a much enduring man who bends under the load of his leisure. He fawns upon the Captain, reveres the mate, but his eye follows the Steward; scans accurately as symptomatic, all the motions of that respectable officer.

The species is contemplative, given to imitation, viciously inquisitive, immensely capable of sleep, large eaters, swift digesters, their thoughts ever running on men & things ashore & their eye usually squinting over the bulwark, to estimate the speed of the bubbles.

Edgar Allan Poe

The terrors of the sea, both natural and supernatural, are an indispensable component of the Gothic sublime, from Coleridge's Ancient Mariner to Wagner's Flying Dutchman. "MS. Found in a Bottle," first published in 1833, is Poe's distinctive variant of the Flying Dutchman legend, richly overlaid with exotic detail and narrated by a protagonist who characteristically amuses himself by detecting errors in the works of German moralists. The descriptions of the ghost ship, with its ancient crew and obsolete instruments, sustain a mood of lucid dread right up to the final catastrophe. Here as elsewhere—in "A Descent into the Maelström" and The Narrative of Arthur Gordon Pym*—Poe finds in the sea an apt element for invoking his direst fantasies of ultimate engulfment.*

MS. Found in a Bottle

Qui n'a plus qu'un moment à vivre
N'a plus rien à dissimuler.

Quinault—Atys

Of my country and of my family I have little to say. Ill usage and length of years have driven me from the one, and estranged me from the other. Hereditary wealth afforded me an education of no common order, and a contemplative turn of mind enabled me to methodise the stores which early study very diligently garnered up. Beyond all things, the works of the German moralists gave me great delight; not from any ill-advised admiration of their eloquent madness, but from the ease with which my habits of rigid thought enabled me to detect their falsities. I have often been reproached with the aridity of my genius; a deficiency of imagination has been imputed to me as a crime; and the Pyrrhonism of my opinions has at all times rendered me notorious. Indeed, a strong relish for physical philosophy has, I fear, tinctured my mind with a very common error of this age—I mean the habit of referring occurrences, even the least susceptible of such reference, to the principles of that science. Upon the whole, no person could be less liable than myself to be led away from the severe precincts of truth by the *ignes fatui* of superstition. I have thought proper to premise thus much, lest the incredible tale I have to tell should be considered rather the raving of a crude imagination, than the positive experience of a mind to which the reveries of fancy have been a dead letter and a nullity.

After many years spent in foreign travel, I sailed in the year 18—, from the port of Batavia, in the rich and populous island of Java, on a voyage to the Archipelago of the Sunda islands. I went as passenger—having no other inducement than a kind of nervous restlessness which haunted me as a fiend.

Our vessel was a beautiful ship of about four hundred tons, copper-fastened, and built at Bombay of Malabar teak. She was freighted with cotton-wool and oil, from the Lachadive islands. We had also on board coir, jaggeree, ghee, cocoanuts, and a few cases of opium. The stowage was clumsily done, and the vessel consequently crank.

We got under way with a mere breath of wind, and for many days stood along the eastern coast of Java, without any other incident to beguile the monotony of our course than the occasional meeting with some of the small grabs of the Archipelago to which we were bound.

One evening, leaning over the taffrail, I observed a very singular, isolated cloud, to the N. W. It was remarkable, as well for its color, as from its being the first we had seen since our departure from Batavia. I watched it attentively until sunset, when it spread all at once to the eastward and westward, girting in the horizon with a narrow strip of vapor, and looking like a long line of low beach. My notice was soon afterwards attracted by the dusky-red appearance of the moon, and the peculiar character of the sea. The latter was undergoing a rapid change, and the water seemed more than usually transparent. Although I could distinctly see the bottom, yet, heaving the lead, I found the ship in fifteen fathoms. The air now became intolerably hot, and was loaded with spiral exhalations similar to those arising from heated iron. As night came on, every breath of wind died away, and a more entire calm it is impossible to conceive. The flame of a candle burned upon the poop without the least perceptible motion, and a long hair, held between the finger and thumb, hung without the possibility of detecting a vibration. However, as the captain said he could perceive no indication of danger, and as we were drifting in bodily to shore, he ordered the sails to be furled, and the anchor let go. No watch was set, and the crew, consisting principally of Malays, stretched themselves deliberately upon deck. I went below—not without a full presentiment of evil. Indeed, every appearance warranted me in apprehending a Simoon. I told the captain my fears; but he paid no attention to what I said, and left me without deigning to give a reply. My uneasiness, however, prevented me from sleeping, and about midnight I went upon deck. As I placed my foot upon the upper step of the companion-ladder, I was startled by a loud, humming noise, like that occasioned by the rapid revolution of a mill-wheel, and before I could ascertain its meaning, I found the ship quivering to its centre. In the next instant, a wilderness of foam hurled us upon our beam-ends, and, rushing over us fore and aft, swept the entire decks from stem to stern.

The extreme fury of the blast proved, in a great measure, the salvation of the ship. Although completely water-logged, yet, as her masts had gone by the board, she rose, after a minute, heavily from the sea, and, staggering awhile beneath the immense pressure of the tempest, finally righted.

By what miracle I escaped destruction, it is impossible to say. Stunned by the shock of the water, I found myself, upon recovery, jammed in between the stern-post and rudder. With great difficulty I gained my feet, and looking dizzily around, was at first struck with the idea of our being among breakers; so terrific, beyond the wildest imagination, was the whirlpool of mountainous and foaming ocean within which we were ingulfed. After a while, I heard the voice of an old Swede, who had shipped with us at the moment of our leaving port. I hallooed to him with all my strength, and presently he came reeling aft. We soon discovered that we were the sole survivors of the accident. All on deck, with the exception of ourselves, had been swept overboard; the captain and mates must have perished as they slept, for the cabins were deluged with water. Without assistance, we could expect to do little for the security of the ship, and our exertions were at first paralyzed by the momentary expectation of going down. Our cable had, of course, parted like pack-thread, at the first breath of the hurricane, or we should have been instantaneously overwhelmed. We scudded with frightful velocity before the sea, and the water made clear breaches over us. The frame-work of our stern was shattered excessively, and, in almost every respect, we had received considerable injury; but to our extreme joy we found the pumps unchoked, and that we had made no great shifting of our ballast. The main fury of the blast had already blown over, and we apprehended little danger from the violence of the wind; but we looked forward to its total cessation with dismay; well believing, that in our shattered condition, we should inevitably perish in the tremendous swell which would ensue. But this very just apprehension seemed by no means likely to be soon verified. For five entire days and nights—during which our only subsistence was a small quantity of jaggeree, procured with great difficulty from the forecastle—the hulk flew at a rate defying computation, before rapidly succeeding flaws of wind, which, without equalling the first violence of the Simoon, were still more terrific than any tempest I had before encountered. Our course for the first four days was, with trifling variations, S. E. and by S.; and we must have run down the coast of New Holland. On the fifth day the cold became extreme, although the wind had hauled round a point more to the northward. The sun arose with a sickly yellow lustre, and clambered a very few degrees above the horizon—emitting no decisive light. There were no clouds apparent, yet the wind was upon the increase, and blew with a fitful and unsteady fury. About noon, as nearly as we could guess, our attention was again arrested by the appearance of the sun. It gave out no light, properly so called, but a dull and sullen glow without reflection, as if all its rays were polarized. Just before sinking within the turgid sea, its central fires suddenly went out, as if hurriedly extinguished by some unaccountable power. It was a dim, silver-like rim, alone, as it rushed down the unfathomable ocean.

We waited in vain for the arrival of the sixth day—that day to me has not arrived—to the Swede, never did arrive. Thenceforward we were enshrouded in pitchy darkness, so that we could not have seen an object at twenty paces from the ship. Eternal night continued to envelop us, all unrelieved by the phosphoric sea-brilliancy to which we had been accustomed in the tropics. We observed too, that, although the tempest continued to rage with unabated violence, there was no longer to be discovered the usual appearance of surf, or foam, which had hitherto attended us. All around were horror, and thick gloom, and a black sweltering desert of ebony. Superstitious terror crept by degrees into the spirit of the old Swede, and my own soul was wrapped up in silent wonder. We neglected all care of the ship, as worse than useless, and securing ourselves, as well as possible, to the stump of the mizen-mast, looked out bitterly into the world of ocean. We had no means of calculating time, nor could we form any guess of our situation. We were, however, well aware of having made farther to the southward than any previous navigators, and felt great amazement at not meeting with the usual impediments of ice. In the meantime every moment threatened to be our last—every mountainous billow hurried to overwhelm us. The swell surpassed anything I had imagined possible, and that we were not instantly buried is a miracle. My companion spoke of the lightness of our cargo, and reminded me of the excellent qualities of our ship; but I could not help feeling the utter hopelessness of hope itself, and prepared myself gloomily for that death which I thought nothing could defer beyond an hour, as, with every knot of way the ship made, the swelling of the black stupendous seas became more dismally appalling. At times we gasped for breath at an elevation beyond the albatross—at times became dizzy with the velocity of our descent into some watery hell, where the air grew stagnant, and no sound disturbed the slumbers of the kraken.

We were at the bottom of one of these abysses, when a quick scream from my companion broke fearfully upon the night. "See! see!" cried he, shrieking in my ears, "Almighty God! see! see!" As he spoke, I became aware of a dull, sullen glare of red light which streamed down the sides of the vast chasm where we lay, and threw a fitful brilliancy upon our deck. Casting my eyes upwards, I beheld a spectacle which froze the current of my blood. At a terrific height directly above us, and upon the very verge of the precipitous descent, hovered a gigantic ship, of perhaps four thousand tons. Although upreared upon the summit of a wave more than a hundred times her own altitude, her apparent size still exceeded that of any ship of the line or East Indiaman in existence. Her huge hull was of a deep dingy black, unrelieved by any of the customary carvings of a ship. A single row of brass cannon protruded from her open ports, and dashed from their polished surfaces the fires of innumerable battle-lanterns, which swung to and fro about her rigging. But what mainly inspired us with horror and astonishment, was that she bore up under a press of sail in the very teeth of that supernatural sea, and of that ungovernable hurricane. When we first discovered her, her bows were alone to be seen, as she rose slowly from the dim and horrible gulf beyond her. For a moment of intense terror she paused upon the giddy pinnacle, as if in contemplation of her own sublimity, then trembled and tottered, and—came down.

At this instant, I know not what sudden self-possession came over my spirit. Staggering as far aft as I could, I awaited fearlessly the ruin that was to overwhelm. Our own vessel was at length ceasing from her struggles, and sinking with her head to the sea. The shock of the descending mass struck her, consequently, in that portion of her frame which was already under water, and the inevitable result was to hurl me, with irresistible violence, upon the rigging of the stranger.

As I fell, the ship hove in stays, and went about; and to the confusion ensuing I attributed my escape from the notice of the crew. With little difficulty I made my way, unperceived, to the main hatchway, which was partially open, and soon found an opportunity of secreting myself in the hold. Why I did so I can hardly tell. An indefinite sense of awe, which at first sight of the navigators of the ship had taken hold of my mind, was perhaps the principle of my concealment. I was unwilling to trust myself with a race of people who had offered, to the cursory glance I had taken, so many points of vague novelty, doubt, and apprehension. I therefore thought proper to contrive a hiding-place in the hold. This I did by removing a small portion of the shifting-boards, in such a manner as to afford me a convenient retreat between the huge timbers of the ship.

I had scarcely completed my work, when a footstep in the hold forced me to make use of it. A man passed by my place of concealment with a feeble and unsteady gait. I could not see his face, but had an opportunity of observing his general appearance. There was about it an evidence of great age and infirmity. His knees tottered beneath a load of years, and his entire frame quivered under the burthen. He muttered to himself, in a low broken tone, some words of a language which I could not understand, and groped in a corner among a pile of singular-looking instruments, and decayed charts of navigation. His manner was a wild mixture of the peevishness of second childhood and the solemn dignity of a God. He at length went on deck, and I saw him no more.

A feeling, for which I have no name, has taken possession of my soul—a sensation which will admit of no analysis, to which the lessons of by-gone time are inadequate, and for which I fear futurity itself will offer me no key. To a mind constituted like my own, the latter consideration is an evil. I shall never—I know that I shall never—be satisfied with regard to the nature of my conceptions. Yet it is not wonderful that these conceptions are indefinite, since they have their origin in sources so utterly novel. A new sense—a new entity is added to my soul.

It is long since I first trod the deck of this terrible ship, and the rays of my destiny are, I think, gathering to a focus. Incomprehensible men! Wrapped up in meditations of a kind which I cannot divine, they pass me by unnoticed. Concealment is utter folly on my part, for the people *will not* see. It was but just now that I passed directly before the eyes of the mate; it was no long while ago that I ventured into the captain's own private cabin, and took thence the materials with which I write, and have written. I shall from time to time continue this journal. It is true that I may not find an opportunity of transmitting it to the world, but I will not fail to make the endeavor. At the last moment I will enclose the MS. in a bottle, and cast it within the sea.

An incident has occurred which has given me new room for meditation. Are such things the operation of ungoverned chance? I had ventured upon deck and thrown myself down, without attracting any notice, among a pile of ratlin-stuff and old sails, in the bottom of the yawl. While musing upon the singularity of my fate, I unwittingly daubed with a tar-brush the edges of a neatly-folded studding-sail which lay near me on a barrel. The studding-sail is now bent upon the ship, and the thoughtless touches of the brush are spread out into the word DISCOVERY.

I have made many observations lately upon the structure of the vessel. Although well armed, she is not, I think, a ship of war. Her rigging, build, and general equipment, all negative a supposition of this kind. What she *is not*, I can easily perceive; what she *is*, I fear it is impossible to say. I know not how it is, but in scrutinizing her strange model and singular cast of spars, her huge size and overgrown suits of canvass, her severely simple bow and antiquated stern, there will occasionally flash across my mind a sensation of familiar things, and there is always mixed up with such indistinct shadows of recollection, an unaccountable memory of old foreign chronicles and ages long ago. * * *

I have been looking at the timbers of the ship. She is built of a material to which I am a stranger. There is a peculiar character about the wood which strikes me as rendering it unfit for the purpose to which it has been applied. I mean its extreme *porousness*, considered independently of the worm-eaten condition which is a consequence of navigation in these seas, and apart from the rottenness attendant upon age. It will appear perhaps an observation somewhat over-curious, but this wood would have every characteristic of Spanish oak, if Spanish oak were distended by any unnatural means.

In reading the above sentence, a curious apothegm of an old weather-beaten Dutch navigator comes full upon my recollection. "It is as sure," he was wont to say, when any doubt was entertained of his veracity, "as sure as there is a sea where the ship itself will grow in bulk like the living body of the seaman." * * *

About an hour ago, I made bold to thrust myself among a group of the crew. They paid me no manner of attention, and, although I stood in the very midst of them all, seemed utterly unconscious of my presence. Like the one I had at first seen in the hold, they all bore about them the marks of a hoary old age. Their knees trembled with infirmity; their shoulders were bent double with decrepitude; their shrivelled skins rattled in the wind; their voices were low, tremulous, and broken; their eyes glistened with the rheum of years; and their gray hairs streamed terribly in the tempest. Around them, on every part of the deck, lay scattered mathematical instruments of the most quaint and obsolete construction.

I mentioned, some time ago, the bending of a studding-sail. From that period, the ship, being thrown dead off the wind, has continued her terrific course due south, with every rag of canvass packed upon her, from her trucks to her lower studding-sail booms, and rolling every moment her top-gallant yard-arms into the most appalling hell of water which it can enter into the mind of man to imagine. I have just left the deck, where I find it impossible to maintain a footing, although the crew seem to experience little inconvenience. It appears to me a miracle of miracles that our enormous bulk is not swallowed up at once and for ever. We are surely doomed to hover continually upon the brink of eternity, without taking a final plunge into the abyss. From billows a thousand times more stupendous than any I have ever seen, we glide away with the facility of the arrowy sea-gull; and the colossal waters rear their heads above us like demons of the deep, but like demons confined to simple threats, and forbidden to destroy. I am led to attribute these frequent escapes to the only natural cause which can account for such effect. I must suppose the ship to be within the influence of some strong current, or impetuous under-tow. * * *

I have seen the captain face to face, and in his own cabin—but, as I expected, he paid me no attention. Although in his appearance there is, to a casual observer, nothing which might bespeak him more or less than man, still, a feeling of irrepressible reverence and awe mingled with the sensation of wonder with which I regarded him. In stature, he is nearly my own height; that is, about five feet eight inches. He is of a well-knit and compact frame of body, neither robust nor remarkably otherwise. But it is the singularity of the expression which reigns upon the face—it is the intense, the wonderful, the thrilling evidence of old age, so utter, so extreme, which excites within my spirit a sense—a sentiment ineffable. His forehead, although little wrinkled, seems to bear upon it the stamp of a myriad of years. His gray hairs are records of the past, and his grayer eyes are sybils of the future. The cabin floor was thickly strewn with strange, iron-clasped folios, and mouldering instruments of science, and obsolete long-forgotten charts. His head was bowed down upon his hands, and he pored, with a fiery, unquiet eye, over a paper which I took to be a commission, and which, at all events, bore the signature of a monarch. He muttered to himself—as did the first seaman whom I saw in the hold—some low peevish syllables of a foreign tongue; and although the speaker was close at my elbow, his voice seemed to reach my ears from the distance of a mile. * * *

The ship and all in it are imbued with the spirit of Eld. The crew glide to and fro like the ghosts of buried centuries; their eyes have an eager and uneasy meaning; and when their figures fall athwart my path in the wild glare of the battle-lanterns, I feel as I have never felt before, although I have been all my life a dealer in antiquities, and have imbibed the shadows of fallen columns at Balbec, and Tadmor, and Persepolis, until my very soul has become a ruin. * * *

When I look around me, I feel ashamed of my former apprehensions. If I trembled at the blast which has hitherto attended us, shall I not stand aghast at a warring of wind and ocean, to convey any idea of which, the words tornado and simoon are trivial and ineffective? All in the immediate vicinity of the ship, is the blackness of eternal night, and a chaos of foamless water; but, about a league on either side of us, may be seen, indistinctly and at intervals, stupendous ramparts of ice, towering away into the desolate sky, and looking like the walls of the universe. * * *

As I imagined, the ship proves to be in a current—if that appellation can properly be given to a tide which, howling and shrieking by the white ice, thunders on to the southward with a velocity like the headlong dashing of a cataract.

To conceive the horror of my sensations is, I presume, utterly impossible; yet a curiosity to penetrate the mysteries of these awful regions, predominates even over my despair, and will reconcile me to the most hideous aspect of death. It is evident that we are hurrying onwards to some exciting knowledge—some never-to-be-imparted secret, whose attainment is destruction. Perhaps this current leads us to the southern pole itself. It must be confessed that a supposition apparently so wild has every probability in its favor.

The crew pace the deck with unquiet and tremulous step; but there is upon their countenances an expression more of the eagerness of hope than of the apathy of despair.

In the meantime the wind is still in our poop, and, as we carry a crowd of canvass, the ship is at times lifted bodily from out the sea! Oh, horror upon horror!—the ice opens suddenly to the right, and to the left, and we are whirling dizzily, in immense concentric circles, round and round the borders of a gigantic amphitheatre, the summit of whose walls is lost in the darkness and the distance. But little time will be left me to ponder upon my destiny! The circles rapidly grow small—we are plunging madly within the grasp of the whirlpool—and amid a roaring, and bellowing, and thundering of ocean and of tempest, the ship is quivering—oh God! and—going down!

Note.—The "MS. Found in a Bottle," was originally published in 1831; and it was not until many years afterwards that I became acquainted with the maps of Mercator, in which the ocean is represented as rushing, by four mouths, into the (northern) Polar Gulf, to be absorbed into the bowels of the earth; the Pole itself being represented by a black rock, towering to a prodigious height.

Richard Henry Dana Jr.

For 19th-century readers, the great American sea book was not Moby-Dick *but Richard Henry Dana Jr.'s* Two Years Before the Mast. *Dana (1815–1882), a 19-year-old Harvard student and scion of a distinguished Boston family, found a berth as an ordinary seaman on the merchant brig* Pilgrim, *by his own account as a cure for eye problems resulting from an attack of measles. From his voyage to California, his sojourn there devoted largely to the lowly work of gathering and curing hides for shipment, and his return voyage on the* Alert, *Dana fashioned a book that conveys as no other the real life of an ordinary seaman. Its most famous episodes—the flogging, the death on shipboard—take their place among chapters devoted largely to a meticulous and compassionate account of daily backbreaking labor under circumstances of danger and deprivation. A tremendous bestseller when it was published anonymously in 1840 and for many decades thereafter,* Two Years Before the Mast *remains endlessly fascinating for the immediacy and unflinching realism of its observation.*

from *Two Years Before the Mast*

Monday, November 19th. This was a black day in our calendar. At seven o'clock in the morning, it being our watch below, we were aroused from a sound sleep by the cry of "All hands ahoy! A man overboard!" This unwonted cry sent a thrill through the heart of everyone, and, hurrying on deck, we found the vessel hove flat aback, with all her studding sails set; for, the boy who was at the helm leaving it to throw something overboard, the carpenter, who was an old sailor, knowing that the wind was light, put the helm down and hove her aback. The watch on deck were lowering away the quarter boat, and I got on deck just in time to fling myself into her as she was leaving the side; but it was not until out upon the wide Pacific, in our little boat, that I knew whom we had lost. It was George Ballmer, the young English sailor, whom I have before spoken of as the life of the crew. He was prized by the officers as an active and willing seaman, and by the men as a lively, hearty fellow, and a good shipmate. He was going aloft to fit a strap round the maintop masthead, for ringtail halyards, and had the strap and block, a coil of halyards, and a marlinespike about his neck. He fell from the starboard futtock shrouds, and, not knowing how to swim, and being heavily dressed, with all those things round his neck, he probably sank immediately. We pulled astern, in the direction in which he fell, and though we knew that there was no hope of saving him, yet no one wished to speak of returning, and we rowed about for nearly an hour, without an idea of doing anything, but unwilling to acknowledge to ourselves that we must give him up. At length we turned the boat's head and made toward the brig.

Death is at all times solemn, but never so much so as at sea. A man dies on shore; his body remains with his friends, and "the mourners go about the streets"; but when a man falls overboard at sea and is lost, there is a suddenness in the event, and a difficulty in realizing it, which give to it an air of awful mystery. A man dies on shore—you follow his body to the grave, and a stone marks the spot. You are often prepared for the event. There is always something which helps you to realize it when it happens, and to recall it when it has passed. A man is shot down by your side in battle, and the mangled body remains an object, and a real evidence; but at sea, the man is near you—at your side—you hear his voice, and in an instant he is gone, and nothing but a vacancy shows his loss. Then, too, at sea—to use a homely but expressive phrase—you *miss* a man so much. A dozen men are shut up together in a little bark upon the wide, wide sea, and for months and months see no forms and hear no voices but their own, and one is taken suddenly from among them, and they miss him at every turn. It is like losing a limb. There are no new faces or new scenes to fill up the gap. There is always an empty berth in the forecastle, and one man wanting when the small night watch is mustered. There is one less to take the wheel, and one less to lay out with you upon the yard. You miss his form, and the sound of his voice, for habit had made them almost necessary to you, and each of your senses feels the loss.

All these things make such a death peculiarly solemn, and the effect of it remains upon the crew for some time. There is more kindness shown by the officers to the crew, and by the crew to one another. There is more quietness and seriousness. The oath and the loud laugh are gone. The officers are more watchful, and the crew go more carefully aloft. The lost man is seldom mentioned, or is dismissed with a sailor's rude eulogy—"Well, poor George is gone! His cruise is up soon! He knew his work, and did his duty, and was a good shipmate." Then usually follows some allusion to another world, for sailors are almost all believers, in their way, though their notions and opinions are unfixed and at loose ends. They say, "God won't be hard upon the poor fellow," and seldom get beyond the common phrase which seems to imply that their sufferings and hard treatment here will be passed to their credit in the books of the Great Captain hereafter—*"To work hard, live hard, die hard, and go to hell after all would be hard indeed!"* Our cook, a simplehearted old African, who had been through a good deal in his day, and was rather seriously inclined, always going to church twice a day when on shore, and reading his Bible on a Sunday in the galley, talked to the crew about spending the Lord's Days badly, and told them that they might go as suddenly as George had, and be as little prepared.

Yet a sailor's life is at best but a mixture of a little good with much evil, and a little pleasure with much pain. The beautiful is linked with the revolting, the sublime with the commonplace, and the solemn with the ludicrous.

Not long after we had returned on board with our sad report, an auction was held of the poor man's effects. The captain had first, however, called all hands aft and asked them if they were satisfied that everything had been done to save the man, and if they thought there was any use in remaining there longer. The crew all said that it was in vain, for the man did not know how to swim, and was very heavily dressed. So we then filled away and kept the brig off to her course.

The laws regulating navigation make the captain answerable for the effects of a sailor who dies during the voyage, and it is either a law or a custom, established for convenience, that the captain should soon hold an auction of his things, in which they are bid off by the sailors, and the sums which they give are deducted from their wages at the end of the voyage. In this way the trouble and risk of keeping his things through the voyage are avoided, and the clothes are usually sold for more than they would be worth on shore. Accordingly, we had no sooner got the ship before the wind, than his chest was brought up upon the forecastle, and the sale began. The jackets and trousers in which we had seen him dressed so lately were exposed and bid off while the life was hardly out of his body, and his chest was taken aft and used as a store chest, so that there was nothing left which could be called *his*. Sailors have an unwillingness to wear a dead man's clothes during the same voyage, and they seldom do so, unless they are in absolute want.

As is usual after a death, many stories were told about George. Some had heard him say that he repented never having learned to swim, and that he knew that he should meet his death by drowning. Another said that he never knew any good to come of a voyage made against the will, and the deceased man shipped and spent his advance, and was afterward very unwilling to go, but, not being able to refund, was obliged to sail with us. A boy, too, who had become quite attached to him, said that George talked to him, during most of the watch on the night before, about his mother and family at home, and this was the first time that he had mentioned the subject during the voyage.

The night after this event, when I went to the galley to get a light, I found the cook inclined to be talkative, so I sat down on the spars, and gave him an opportunity to hold a yarn. I was the more inclined to do so, as I found that he was full of the superstitions once more common among seamen, and which the recent death had waked up in his mind. He talked about George's having spoken of his friends, and said he believed few men died without having a warning of it, which he supported by a great many stories of dreams, and of unusual behavior of men before death. From this he went on to other superstitions, the Flying Dutchman, &c., and talked rather mysteriously, having something evidently on his mind. At length he put his head out of the galley and looked carefully about to see if anyone was within hearing, and, being satisfied on that point, asked me in a low tone:

"I say! You know what countryman 'e carpenter be?"

"Yes," said I, "he's a German."

"What kind of a German!" said the cook.

"He belongs to Bremen," said I.

"Are you sure o' dat?" said he.

I satisfied him on that point by saying that he could speak no language but the German and English.

"I'm plaguy glad o' dat," said the cook. "I was mighty 'fraid he was a Finn. I tell you what, I been plaguy civil to that man all the voyage."

I asked him the reason of this, and found that he was fully possessed with the notion that Finns are wizards, and especially have power over winds and storms. I tried to reason with him about it, but he had the best of all arguments, that from experience, at hand, and was not to be moved. He had been to the Sandwich Islands in a vessel in which the sailmaker was a Finn, and could do anything he was of a mind to. This sailmaker kept a junk bottle in his berth, which was always just half full of rum, though he got drunk upon it nearly every day. He had seen him sit for hours together, talking to this bottle, which he stood up before him on the table. The same man cut his throat in his berth, and everybody said he was possessed.

He had heard of ships, too, beating up the Gulf of Finland against a head wind, and having a ship heave in sight astern, overhaul and pass them, with as fair a wind as could blow, and all studding sails out, and find she was from Finland.

"Oh, no!" said he. "I've seen too much o' dem men to want to see 'em 'board a ship. If dey can't have dare own way, they'll play the d——l with you."

As I still doubted, he said he would leave it to John, who was the oldest seaman aboard, and would know, if anybody did. John, to be sure, was the oldest, and at the same time the most ignorant, man in the ship; but I consented to have him called. The cook stated the matter to him, and John, as I anticipated, sided with the cook, and said that he himself had been in a ship where they had a head wind for a fortnight, and the captain found out at last that one of the men, with whom he had had some hard words a short time before, was a Finn, and immediately told him if he didn't stop the head wind he would shut him down in the forepeak. The Finn would not give in, and the captain shut him down in the forepeak, and would not give him anything to eat. The Finn held out for a day and a half, when he could not stand it any longer, and did something or other which brought the wind round again, and they let him up.

"Dar," said the cook, "what you tink o' dat?"

I told him I had no doubt it was true, and that it would have been odd if the wind had not changed in fifteen days, Finn or no Finn.

"Oh," says he, "go 'way! You tink, 'cause you been to college, you know better dan anybody. You know better dan dem as 'as seen it wid der own eyes. You wait till you've been to sea as long as I have, and den you'll know."

* * *

For several days the captain seemed very much out of humor. Nothing went right, or fast enough for him. He quarreled with the cook, and threatened to flog him for throwing wood on deck, and had a dispute with the mate about reeving a Spanish burton; the mate saying that he was right, and had been taught how to do it by a man *who was a sailor!* This the captain took in dudgeon, and they were at swords' points at once. But his displeasure was chiefly turned against a large, heavy-molded fellow from the Middle States, who was called Sam. This man hesitated in his speech, was rather slow in his motions, and was only a tolerably good sailor, but usually seemed to do his best; yet the captain took a dislike to him, thought he was surly and lazy, and "if you once give a dog a bad name," as the sailor phrase is, "he may as well jump overboard." The captain found fault with everything this man did, and hazed him for dropping a marlinespike from the main yard, where he was at work. This, of course, was an accident, but it was set down against him. The captain was on board all day Friday, and everything went on hard and disagreeably. "The more you drive a man, the less he will do" was as true with us as with any other people. We worked late Friday night, and were turned to early Saturday morning. About ten o'clock the captain ordered our new officer, Russell, who by this time had become thoroughly disliked by all the crew, to get the gig ready to take him ashore. John, the Swede, was sitting in the boat alongside, and Mr. Russell and I were standing by the main hatchway, waiting for the captain, who was down in the hold, where the crew were at work, when we heard his voice raised in violent dispute with somebody, whether it was with the mate or one of the crew I could not tell, and then came blows and scuffling. I ran to the side and beckoned to John, who came aboard, and we leaned down the hatchway, and though we could see no one, yet we knew that the captain had the advantage, for his voice was loud and clear:

"You see your condition! You see your condition! Will you ever give me any more of your 'jaw'?" No answer; and then came wrestling and heaving, as though the man was trying to turn him. "You may as well keep still, for I have got you," said the captain. Then came the question, "Will you ever give me any more of your jaw?"

"I never gave you any, sir," said Sam; for it was his voice that we heard, though low and half choked.

"That's not what I ask you. Will you ever be impudent to me again?"

"I never have been, sir," said Sam.

"Answer my question, or I'll make a spread eagle of you! I'll flog you, by G—d."

"I'm no Negro slave," said Sam.

"Then I'll make you one," said the captain; and he came to the hatchway, and sprang on deck, threw off his coat, and, rolling up his sleeves, called out to the mate, "Seize that man up, Mr. Amerzene! Seize him up! Make a spread eagle of him! I'll teach you all who is master aboard!"

The crew and officers followed the captain up the hatchway; but it was not until after repeated orders that the mate laid hold of Sam, who made no resistance, and carried him to the gangway.

"What are you going to flog that man for, sir?" said John, the Swede, to the captain.

Upon hearing this, the captain turned upon John; but, knowing him to be quick and resolute, he ordered the steward to bring the irons, and, calling upon Russell to help him, went up to John.

"Let me alone," said John. "I'm willing to be put in irons. You need not use any force"; and, putting out his hands, the captain slipped the irons on, and sent him aft to the quarter-deck. Sam, by this time, was "seized up," as it is called, that is, placed against the shrouds, with his wrists made fast to them, his jacket off, and his back exposed. The captain stood on the break of the deck, a few feet from him, and a little raised, so as to have a good swing at him, and held in his hand the end of a thick, strong rope. The officers stood round, and the crew grouped together in the waist. All these preparations made me feel sick and almost faint, angry and excited as I was. A man—a human being, made in God's likeness—fastened up and flogged like a beast! A man, too, whom I had lived with, eaten with, and stood watch with for months, and knew so well! If a thought of resistance crossed the minds of any of the men, what was to be done? Their time for it had gone by. Two men were fast, and there were left only two men besides Stimson and myself, and a small boy of ten or twelve years of age; and Stimson and I would not have joined the men in a mutiny, as they knew. And then, on the other side, there were (beside the captain) three officers, steward, agent, and clerk, and the cabin supplied with weapons. But beside the numbers, what is there for sailors to do? If they resist, it is mutiny; and if they succeed, and take the vessel, it is piracy. If they ever yield again, their punishment must come; and if they do not yield, what are they to be for the rest of their lives? If a sailor resist his commander, he resists the law, and piracy or submission is his only alternative. Bad as it was, they saw it must be borne. It is what a sailor ships for. Swinging the rope over his head, and bending his body so as to give it full force, the captain brought it down upon the poor fellow's back. Once, twice—six times. "Will you ever give me any more of your jaw?" The man writhed with pain, but said not a word. Three times more. This was too much, and he muttered something which I could not hear; this brought as many more as the man could stand, when the captain ordered him to be cut down, and to go forward.

"Now for you," said the captain, making up to John, and taking his irons off. As soon as John was loose, he ran forward to the forecastle. "Bring that man aft!" shouted the captain. The second mate, who had been in the forecastle with these men the early part of the voyage, stood still in the waist, and the mate walked slowly forward; but our third officer, anxious to show his zeal, sprang forward over the windlass, and laid hold of John; but John soon threw him from him. The captain stood on the quarterdeck, bareheaded, his eyes flashing with rage, and his face as red as blood, swinging the rope, and calling out to his officers, "Drag him aft! Lay hold of him! I'll 'sweeten' him!" &c., &c. The mate now went forward, and told John quietly to go aft; and he, seeing resistance vain, threw the blackguard third mate from him, said he would go aft of himself, that they should not drag him, and went up to the gangway and held out his hands; but as soon as the captain began to make him fast, the indignity was too much, and he struggled; but, the mate and Russell holding him, he was soon seized up. When he was made fast, he turned to the captain, who stood rolling up his sleeves and getting ready for the blow, and asked him what he was to be flogged for. "Have I ever refused my duty, sir? Have you ever known me to hang back, or to be insolent, or not to know my work?"

"No," said the captain, "it is not that that I flog you for; I flog you for your interference, for asking questions."

"Can't a man ask a question here without being flogged?"

"No," shouted the captain. "Nobody shall open his mouth aboard this vessel but myself," and began laying the blows upon his back, swinging half round between each blow, to give it full effect. As he went on, his passion increased, and he danced about the deck, calling out, as he swung the rope, "If you want to know what I flog you for, I'll tell you. It's because I like to do it—because I like to do it! It suits me! That's what I do it for!"

The man writhed under the pain until he could endure it no longer, when he called out, with an exclamation more common among foreigners than with us: "O Jesus Christ! O Jesus Christ!"

"Don't call on Jesus Christ," shouted the captain. "*He can't help you. Call on Frank Thompson!* He's the man! He can help you! Jesus Christ can't help you now!"

At these words, which I never shall forget, my blood ran cold. I could look on no longer. Disgusted, sick, I turned away, and leaned over the rail, and looked down into the water. A few rapid thoughts, I don't know what—our situation, a resolution to see the captain punished when we got home—crossed my mind; but the falling of the blows and the cries of the man called me back once more. At length they ceased, and, turning round, I found that the mate, at a signal from the captain, had cast him loose. Almost doubled up with pain, the man walked slowly forward, and went down into the forecastle. Everyone else stood still at his post, while the captain, swelling with rage, and with the importance of his achievement, walked the quarterdeck, and at each turn, as he came forward, calling out to us: "You see your condition! You see where I've got you all, and you know what to expect! . . . You've been mistaken in me; you didn't know what I was! Now you know what I am! . . . I'll make you toe the mark, every soul of you, or I'll flog you all, fore and aft, from the boy up! . . . You've got a driver over you! Yes, a *slave driver—a nigger driver!* I'll see who'll tell me he isn't a nigger slave!" With this and the like matter, equally calculated to quiet us, and to allay any apprehensions of future trouble, he entertained us for about ten minutes, when he went below. Soon after, John came aft, with his bare back covered with stripes and wales in every direction, and dreadfully swollen, and asked the steward to ask the captain to let him have some salve, or balsam, to put upon it. "No," said the captain, who heard him from below. "Tell him to put his shirt on; that's the best thing for him, and pull me ashore in the boat. Nobody is going to lay up on board this vessel." He then called to Mr. Russell to take those two men and two others in the boat, and pull him ashore. I went for one. The two men could hardly bend their backs, and the captain called to them to "give way . . . give way!" but, finding they did their best, he let them alone. The agent was in the stern sheets, but during the whole pull—a league or more—not a word was spoken. We landed; the captain, agent, and officer went up to the house, and left us with the boat. I, and the man with me, stayed near the boat, while John and Sam walked slowly away, and sat down on the rocks. They talked some time together, but at length separated, each sitting alone. I had some fears of John. He was a foreigner, and violently tempered, and under suffering; and he had his knife with him, and the captain was to come down alone to the boat. But nothing happened; and we went quietly on board. The captain was probably armed, and if either of them had lifted a hand against him, they would have had nothing before them but flight, and starvation in the woods of California, or capture by the soldiers and Indians, whom the offer of twenty dollars would have set upon them.

After the day's work was done, we went down into the forecastle, and ate our plain supper; but not a word was spoken. It was Saturday night; but there was no song, no "sweethearts and wives." A gloom was over everything. The two men lay in their berths, groaning with pain, and we all turned in, but, for myself, not to sleep. A sound coming now and then from the berths of the two men showed that they were awake, as awake they must have been, for they could hardly lie in one posture long; the dim, swinging lamp shed its light over the dark hole in which we lived, and many and various reflections and purposes coursed through my mind. I had no apprehension that the captain would try to lay a hand on me; but I thought of our situation, living under a tyranny, with an ungoverned, swaggering fellow administering it; of the character of the country we were in; the length of the voyage; the uncertainty attending our return to America; and then, if we should return, the prospect of obtaining justice and satisfaction for these poor men; and I vowed that, if God should ever give me the means, I would do something to redress the grievances and relieve the sufferings of that class of beings with whom my lot had so long been cast.

* * *

Santa Barbara looked very much as it did when I left it five months before: the long sand beach, with the heavy rollers, breaking upon it in a continual roar, and the little town, embedded on the plain, girt by its amphitheater of mountains. Day after day the sun shone clear and bright upon the wide bay and the red roofs of the houses, everything being as still as death, the people hardly seeming to earn their sunlight. Daylight was thrown away upon them. We had a few visitors, and collected about a hundred hides, and every night, at sundown, the gig was sent ashore to wait for the captain, who spent his evenings in the town. We always took our monkey jackets with us, and flint and steel, and made a fire on the beach with the driftwood and the bushes which we pulled from the neighboring thickets, and lay down by it, on the sand. Sometimes we would stray up to the town, if the captain was likely to stay late, and pass the time at some of the houses, in which we were almost always well received by the inhabitants. Sometimes earlier and sometimes later, the captain came down; when, after a good drenching in the surf, we went aboard, changed our clothes, and turned in for the night—yet not for all the night, for there was the anchor watch to stand.

This leads me to speak of my watchmate for nine months—and, taking him all in all, the most remarkable man I had ever seen—Tom Harris. An hour, every night, while lying in port, Harris and I had the deck to ourselves, and walking fore and aft, night after night, for months, I learned his character and history, and more about foreign nations, the habits of different people, and especially the secrets of sailors' lives and hardships, and also of practical seamanship, in which he was abundantly capable of instructing me, than I could ever have learned elsewhere. His memory was perfect, seeming to form a regular chain, reaching from his earliest childhood up to the time I knew him, without a link wanting. His power of calculation, too, was extraordinary. I called myself pretty quick at figures, and had been through a course of mathematical studies; but, working by my head, I was unable to keep within sight of this man, who had never been beyond his arithmetic. He carried in his head, not only a logbook of the voyage, which was complete and accurate, and from which no one thought of appealing, but also an accurate registry of the cargo, knowing where each thing was stowed, and how many hides we took in at each port.

One night he made a rough calculation of the number of hides that could be stowed in the lower hold, between the fore- and mainmasts, taking the depth of hold and breadth of beam (for he knew the dimensions of every part of a ship before he had been long on board), and the average area and thickness of a hide; and he came surprisingly near the number, as it afterward turned out. The mate frequently came to him to know the capacity of different parts of the vessel, and he could tell the sailmaker very nearly the amount of canvas he would want for each sail in the ship; for he knew the hoist of every mast, and spread of each sail, on the head and foot, in feet and inches. When we were at sea, he kept a running account, in his head, of the ship's way—the number of knots and the courses—and, if the courses did not vary much during the twenty-four hours, by taking the whole progress and allowing so many eighths southing or northing, to so many easting or westing, he would make up his reckoning just before the captain took the sun at noon, and often came very near the mark. He had, in his chest, several volumes giving accounts of inventions in mechanics, which he read with great pleasure, and made himself master of. I doubt if he forgot anything that he read. The only thing in the way of poetry that he ever read was Falconer's "Shipwreck," which he was charmed with, and pages of which he could repeat. He said he could recall the name of every sailor that had ever been his shipmate, and also of every vessel, captain, and officer, and the principal dates of each voyage; and a sailor whom we afterward fell in with, who had been in a ship with Harris nearly twelve years before, was much surprised at having Harris tell him things about himself which he had entirely forgotten. His facts, whether dates or events, no one thought of disputing; and his opinions few of the sailors dared to oppose, for, right or wrong, he always had the best of the argument with them. His reasoning powers were striking. I have had harder work maintaining an argument with him in a watch, even when I knew myself to be right, and he was only doubting, than I ever had before, not from his obstinacy, but from his acuteness. Give him only a little knowledge of his subject, and, among all the young men of my acquaintance at college, there is not one whom I had not rather meet in an argument than this man. I never answered a question from him, or advanced an opinion to him, without thinking more than once. With an iron memory, he seemed to have your whole past conversation at command, and if you said a thing now which ill agreed with something you had said months before, he was sure to have you on the hip. In fact, I felt, when with him, that I was with no common man. I had a positive respect for his powers of mind, and thought, often, that if half the pains had been spent upon his education which are thrown away yearly in our colleges, he would have made his mark. Like many self-taught men of real merit, he overrated the value of a regular education; and this I often told him, though I had profited by his error; for he always treated me with respect, and often unnecessarily gave way to me, from an overestimate of my knowledge. For the intellectual capacities of all the rest of the crew—captain and all—he had a sovereign contempt. He was a far better sailor, and probably a better navigator, than the captain, and had more brains than all the after part of the ship put together. The sailors said, "Tom's got a head as long as the bowsprit," and if anyone fell into an argument with him, they would call out, "Ah, Jack! You had better drop that as you would a hot potato, for Tom will turn you inside out before you know it!"

I recollect his posing me once on the subject of the Corn Laws. I was called to stand my watch, and, coming on deck, found him there before me; and we began, as usual, to walk fore and aft, in the waist. He talked about the Corn Laws; asked me my opinion about them, which I gave him, and my reasons, my small stock of which I set forth to the best advantage, supposing his knowledge on the subject must be less than mine, if, indeed, he had any at all. When I had got through, he took the liberty of differing from me, and brought arguments and facts which were new to me, and to which I was unable to reply. I confessed that I knew almost nothing of the subject, and expressed my surprise at the extent of his information. He said that, a number of years before, while at a boardinghouse in Liverpool, he had fallen in with a pamphlet on the subject, and, as it contained calculations, had read it very carefully, and had ever since wished to find someone who could add to his stock of knowledge on the question. Although it was many years since he had seen the book, and it was a subject with which he had had no previous acquaintance, yet he had the chain of reasoning, founded upon principles of political economy, fully in his memory; and his facts, so far as I could judge, were correct; at least, he stated them with precision. The principles of the steam engine, too, he was familiar with, having been several months on board a steamboat, and made himself master of its secrets. He knew every lunar star in both hemispheres, and was a master of the quadrant and sextant. The men said he could take a meridian altitude of the sun from a tar bucket. Such was the man, who, at forty, was still a dog before the mast, at twelve dollars a month. The reason of this was to be found in his past life, as I had it, at different times, from himself.

He was an Englishman, a native of Ilfracombe, in Devonshire. His father was skipper of a small coaster from Bristol, and, dying, left him, when quite young, to the care of his mother, by whose exertions he received a common-school education, passing his winters at school and his summers in the coasting trade until his seventeenth year, when he left home to go upon foreign voyages. Of this mother he spoke with the greatest respect, and said that she was a woman of a strong mind, and had an excellent system of education, which had made respectable men of his three brothers, and failed in him only from his own indomitable obstinacy. One thing he mentioned, in which he said his mother differed from all other mothers that he had ever seen disciplining their children; that was, that when he was out of humor and refused to eat, instead of putting his plate away, saying that his hunger would bring him to it in time, she would stand over him and oblige him to eat it—every mouthful of it. It was no fault of hers that he was what I saw him; and so great was his sense of gratitude for her efforts, though unsuccessful, that he determined, when the voyage should end, to embark for home with all the wages he should get, to spend with and for his mother, if perchance he should find her alive.

After leaving home, he had spent nearly twenty years sailing upon all sorts of voyages, generally out of the ports of New York and Boston. Twenty years of vice! Every sin that a sailor knows, he had gone to the bottom of. Several times he had been hauled up in the hospitals, and as often the great strength of his constitution had brought him out again in health. Several times, too, from his acknowledged capacity, he had been promoted to the office of chief mate, and as often his conduct when in port, especially his drunkenness, which neither fear nor ambition could induce him to abandon, put him back into the forecastle. One night, when giving me an account of his life, and lamenting the years of manhood he had thrown away, "There," said he, "in the forecastle, at the foot of those steps, a chest of old clothes, is the result of twenty-two years of hard labor and exposure—worked like a horse, and treated like a dog." As he had grown older, he began to feel the necessity of some provision for his later years, and came gradually to the conviction that rum had been his worst enemy. One night, in Havana, a young shipmate of his was brought aboard drunk, with a dangerous gash in his head, and his money and new clothes stripped from him. Harris had been in hundreds of such scenes as these, but in his then state of mind it fixed his determination, and he resolved never to taste a drop of strong drink of any kind. He signed no pledge, and made no vow, but relied on his own strength of purpose. The first thing with him was a reason, and then a resolution, and the thing was done. The date of his resolution he knew, of course, to the very hour. It was three years before I became acquainted with him, and during all that time nothing stronger than cider or coffee had passed his lips. The sailors never thought of enticing Tom to take a glass, any more than they would of talking to the ship's compass. He was now a temperate man for life, and capable of filling any berth in a ship, and many a high station there is on shore which is held by a meaner man.

He understood the management of a ship upon scientific principles, and could give the reason for hauling every rope; and a long experience, added to careful observation at the time, gave him a knowledge of the expedients and resorts for times of hazard, for which I became much indebted to him, as he took the greatest pleasure in opening his stores of information to me, in return for what I was enabled to do for him. Stories of tyranny and hardship which had driven men to piracy; of the incredible ignorance of masters and mates, and of horrid brutality to the sick, dead, and dying; as well as of the secret knavery and impositions practiced upon seamen by connivance of the owners, landlords, and officers—all these he had, and I could not but believe them; for he made the impression of an exact man, to whom exaggeration was falsehood; and his statements were always credited. I remember, among other things, his speaking of a captain whom I had known by report, who never handed a thing to a sailor, but put it on deck and kicked it to him; and of another, who was highly connected in Boston, who absolutely murdered a lad from Boston who went out with him before the mast to Sumatra, by keeping him hard at work while ill of the coast fever, and obliging him to sleep in the close steerage. (The same captain has since died of the same fever on the same coast.)

In fact, taking together all that I learned from him of seamanship, of the history of sailors' lives, of practical wisdom, and of human nature under new circumstances and strange forms of life—a great history from which many are shut out—I would not part with the hours I spent in the watch with that man for the gift of many hours to be passed in study and intercourse with even the best of society.

* * *

We had been below but a short time, before we had the usual premonitions of a coming gale—seas washing over the whole forward part of the vessel, and her bows beating against them with a force and sound like the driving of piles. The watch, too, seemed very busy trampling about decks, and singing out at the ropes. A sailor can tell, by the sound, what sail is coming in; and, in a short time, we heard the topgallant sails come in, one after another, and then the flying jib. This seemed to ease her a good deal, and we were fast going off to the land of Nod, when, *bang, bang, bang* on the scuttle, and "All hands, reef topsails, ahoy!" started us out of our berths; and, it not being very cold weather, we had nothing extra to put on, and were soon on deck. I shall never forget the fineness of the sight. It was a clear, and rather a chilly night; the stars were twinkling with an intense brightness, and as far as the eye could reach there was not a cloud to be seen. The horizon met the sea in a defined line. A painter could not have painted so clear a sky. There was not a speck upon it. Yet it was blowing great guns from the northwest. When you can see a cloud to windward, you feel that there is a place for the wind to come from; but here it seemed to come from nowhere. No person could have told from the heavens, by their eyesight alone, that it was not a still summer's night. One reef after another, we took in the topsails, and before we could get them hoisted up we heard a sound like a short, quick rattling of thunder, and the jib was blown to atoms out of the boltrope. We got the topsails set, and the fragments of the jib stowed away, and the fore-topmast staysail set in its place, when the great mainsail gaped open, and the sail ripped from head to foot. "Lay up on that main yard and furl the sail, before it blows to tatters!" shouted the captain; and in a moment we were up, gathering the remains of it upon the yard. We got it wrapped round the yard, and passed gaskets over it as snugly as possible, and were just on deck again, when, with another loud rent, which was heard throughout the ship, the fore-topsail, which had been double-reefed, split in two athwartships, just below the reef band, from earing to earing. Here again it was: down yard, haul out reef tackles, and lay out upon the yard for reefing. By hauling the reef tackles chockablock we took the strain from the other earings, and passing the close-reef earing, and knotting the points carefully, we succeeded in setting the sail, close-reefed.

We had but just got the rigging coiled up, and were waiting to hear, "Go below, the watch!" when the main royal worked loose from the gaskets, and blew directly out to leeward, flapping, and shaking the mast like a wand. Here was a job for somebody. The royal must come in or be cut adrift, or the mast would be snapped short off. All the light hands in the starboard watch were sent up one after another, but they could do nothing with it. At length, John, the tall Frenchman, the head of the starboard watch (and a better sailor never stepped upon a deck), sprang aloft, and, by the help of his long arms and legs, succeeded, after a hard struggle—the sail blowing over the yardarm to leeward, and the skysail adrift directly over his head—in smothering it and frapping it with long pieces of sennit. He came very near being blown or shaken from the yard several times, but he was a true sailor, every finger a fish hook. Having made the sail snug, he prepared to send the yard down, which was a long and difficult job; for, frequently, he was obliged to stop, and hold on with all his might for several minutes, the ship pitching so as to make it impossible to do anything else at that height. The yard at length came down safe, and, after it, the fore and mizzen royal yards were sent down. All hands were then sent aloft, and for an hour or two we were hard at work, making the booms well fast, unreeving the studdingsail and royal and skysail gear, getting rolling ropes on the yard, setting up the weather breast backstays, and making other preparations for a storm. It was a fine night for a gale; just cool and bracing enough for quick work, without being cold, and as bright as day. It was sport to have a gale in such weather as this. Yet it blew like a hurricane. The wind seemed to come with a spite, an edge to it, which threatened to scrape us off the yards. The force of the wind was greater than I had ever felt it before; but darkness, cold, and wet are the worst parts of a storm, to a sailor.

Having got on deck again, we looked round to see what time of night it was, and whose watch. In a few minutes the man at the wheel struck four bells, and we found that the other watch was out, and our own half out. Accordingly, the starboard watch went below, and left the ship to us for a couple of hours, yet with orders to stand by for a call.

Hardly had they got below, before away went the fore-topmast staysail, blown to ribands. This was a small sail, which we could manage in the watch, so that we were not obliged to call up the other watch. We laid out upon the bowsprit, where we were under water half the time, and took in the fragments of the sail, and, as she must have some headsail on her, prepared to bend another staysail. We got the new one out into the nettings; seized on the tack, sheets, and halyards, and the hanks; manned the halyards, cut adrift the frapping lines, and hoisted away; but before it was halfway up the stay it was blown all to pieces. When we belayed the halyards, there was nothing left but the boltrope. Now large eyes began to show themselves in the foresail, and, knowing that it must soon go, the mate ordered us upon the yard to furl it. Being unwilling to call up the watch who had been on deck all night, he roused out the carpenter, sailmaker, cook, and steward, and with their help we manned the foreyard, and, after nearly half an hour's struggle mastered the sail, and got it well furled round the yard. The force of the wind had never been greater than at this moment. In going up the rigging, it seemed absolutely to pin us down to the shrouds; and, on the yard, there was no such thing as turning a face to windward. Yet here was no driving sleet, and darkness, and wet, and cold, as off Cape Horn; and instead of stiff oilcloth suits, southwester caps, and thick boots, we had on hats, round jackets, duck trousers, light shoes, and everything light and easy. These things make a great difference to a sailor. When we got on deck, the man at the wheel struck eight bells (four o'clock in the morning), and "All Starbowlines, ahoy!" brought the other watch up, but there was no going below for us. The gale was now at its height, "blowing like scissors and thumbscrews"; the captain was on deck; the ship, which was light, rolling and pitching as though she would shake the long sticks out of her, and the sails were gaping open and splitting in every direction. The mizzen topsail, which was a comparatively new sail, and close-reefed, split from head to foot, in the bunt; the fore-topsail went, in one rent, from clew to earing, and was blowing to tatters; one of the chain bobstays parted; the spritsail yard sprung in the slings; the martingale had slued away off to leeward; and, owing to the long dry weather, the lee rigging hung in large bights at every lurch. One of the main-topgallant shrouds had parted; and, to crown all, the galley had got adrift, and gone over to leeward, and the anchor on the lee bow had worked loose, and was thumping the side. Here was work enough for all hands for half a day. Our gang laid out on the mizzen-topsail yard, and after more than half an hour's hard work, furled the sail, though it bellied out over our heads, and again, by a slat of the wind, blew in under the yard with a fearful jerk, and almost threw us off from the footropes.

Double gaskets were passed round the yards, rolling tackles and other gear boused taut, and everything made as secure as it could be. Coming down, we found the rest of the crew just coming down the forerigging, having furled the tattered topsail, or, rather, swathed it round the yard, which looked like a broken limb, bandaged. There was no sail now on the ship but the spanker and the close-reefed main topsail, which still held good. But this was too much after sail, and order was given to furl the spanker. The brails were hauled up, and all the light hands in the starboard watch sent out on the gaff to pass the gaskets; but they could do nothing with it. The second mate swore at them for a parcel of "sogers," and sent up a couple of the best men; but they could do no better, and the gaff was lowered down. All hands were now employed in setting up the lee rigging, fishing the spritsail yard, lashing the galley, and getting tackles upon the martingale, to bouse it to windward. Being in the larboard watch, my duty was forward, to assist in setting up the martingale. Three of us were out on the martingale guys and backropes for more than half an hour, carrying out, hooking and unhooking the tackles, several times buried in the seas, until the mate ordered us in, from fear of our being washed off. The anchors were then to be taken up on the rail, which kept all hands on the forecastle for an hour, though every now and then the seas broke over it, washing the rigging off to leeward, filling the lee scuppers breast-high, and washing chock aft to the taffrail.

Having got everything secure again, we were promising ourselves some breakfast, for it was now nearly nine o'clock in the forenoon, when the main topsail showed evident signs of giving way. Some sail must be kept on the ship, and the captain ordered the fore and main spencer gaffs to be lowered down, and the two spencers (which were storm sails, brand-new, small, and made of the strongest canvas) to be got up and bent; leaving the main topsail to blow away, with a blessing on it, if it would only last until we could set the spencers. These we bent on very carefully, with strong robands and seizings, and, making tackles fast to the clews, boused them down to the waterways. By this time the main topsail was among the things that have been, and we went aloft to stow away the remnant of the last sail of all those which were on the ship twenty-four hours before. The spencers were now the only whole sails on the ship, and, being strong and small, and near the deck, presenting but little surface to the wind above the rail, promised to hold out well. Hove to under these, and eased by having no sail above the tops, the ship rose and fell, and drifted off to leeward like a line-of-battle ship.

It was now eleven o'clock, and the watch was sent below to get breakfast, and at eight bells (noon), as everything was snug, although the gale had not in the least abated, the watch was set, and the other watch and idlers sent below. For three days and three nights the gale continued with unabated fury, and with singular regularity. There were no lulls, and very little variation in its fierceness. Our ship, being light, rolled so as almost to send the fore yardarm under water, and drifted off bodily to leeward. All this time there was not a cloud to be seen in the sky, day or night; no, not so large as a man's hand. Every morning the sun rose cloudless from the sea, and set again at night in the sea, in a flood of light. The stars, too, came out of the blue one after another, night after night, unobscured, and twinkled as clear as on a still, frosty night at home, until the day came upon them. All this time the sea was rolling in immense surges, white with foam, as far as the eye could reach, on every side, for we were now leagues and leagues from shore.

The between decks being empty, several of us slept there in hammocks, which are the best things in the world to sleep in during a storm; it not being true of them, as it is of another kind of bed, "when the wind blows the cradle will rock"; for it is the ship that rocks, while they hang vertically from the beams. During these seventy-two hours we had nothing to do but to turn in and out, four hours on deck, and four below, eat, sleep, and keep watch. The watches were only varied by taking the helm in turn, and now and then by one of the sails, which were furled, blowing out of the gaskets, and getting adrift, which sent us up on the yards, and by getting tackles on different parts of the rigging, which were slack. Once the wheel rope parted, which might have been fatal to us, had not the chief mate sprung instantly with a relieving tackle to windward, and kept the tiller up, till a new rope could be rove. On the morning of the twentieth, at daybreak, the gale had evidently done its worst, and had somewhat abated; so much so that all hands were called to bend new sails, although it was still blowing as hard as two common gales. One at a time, and with great difficulty and labor, the old sails were unbent and sent down by the buntlines, and three new topsails, made for the homeward passage round Cape Horn, which had never been bent, were got up from the sail room, and, under the care of the sailmaker, were fitted for bending, and sent up by the halyards into the tops, and, with stops and frapping lines, were bent to the yards, close-reefed, sheeted home, and hoisted. These were bent one at a time, and with the greatest care and difficulty. Two spare courses were then got up and bent in the same manner and furled, and a storm jib, with the bonnet off, bent and furled to the boom. It was twelve o'clock before we got through, and five hours of more exhausting labor I never experienced; and no one of that ship's crew, I will venture to say, will ever desire again to unbend and bend five large sails in the teeth of a tremendous northwester. Toward night a few clouds appeared in the horizon, and, as the gale moderated, the usual appearance of driving clouds relieved the face of the sky. The fifth day after the commencement of the storm, we shook a reef out of each topsail, and set the reefed foresail, jib, and spanker, but it was not until after eight days of reefed topsails that we had a whole sail on the ship, and then it was quite soon enough, for the captain was anxious to make up for leeway, the gale having blown us half the distance to the Sandwich Islands.

Inch by inch, as fast as the gale would permit, we made sail on the ship, for the wind still continued ahead, and we had many days' sailing to get back to the longitude we were in when the storm took us. For eight days more we beat to windward under a stiff topgallant breeze, when the wind shifted and became variable. A light southeaster, to which we could carry a reefed topmast studding sail, did wonders for our dead reckoning.

NATHANIEL HAWTHORNE

Nathaniel Hawthorne (1804–1864), who grew up near the bustling wharves of Salem and lived close to the sea for much of his life, was descended from ship captains. His grandfather was fatally wounded in the Revolutionary War while commanding the True American*; the heroism of "bold Hathorne" was celebrated in a ballad composed by the ship's surgeon. His father died of yellow fever on a voyage to Surinam when Hawthorne was four years old, an experience that provided the background for the story "The Wives of the Dead." As a boy Hawthorne dreamed of going to sea, and as late as 1837 he attempted to obtain a position as historian with the U.S. South Seas Exploring Expedition. In 1845 he edited an account of his friend Horatio Bridge's travels, titled* Journal of an African Cruiser.

"Foot-prints on the Sea-shore," first published in 1838 and collected in the enlarged edition of Twice-told Tales *(1842), describes the attraction of the sea from the vantage of a leisurely wanderer on the beach who lets his fancy take him where it will. Characteristically for Hawthorne, the tale blurs the line between the actual and the unreal, evoking the charm of the seaside as a place for childlike discoveries and imaginative diversion.*

Foot-prints on the Sea-shore

IT MUST be a spirit much unlike my own, which can keep itself in health and vigor without sometimes stealing from the sultry sunshine of the world, to plunge into the cool bath of solitude. At intervals, and not infrequent ones, the forest and the ocean summon me—one with the roar of its waves, the other with the murmur of its boughs—forth from the haunts of men. But I must wander many a mile, ere I could stand beneath the shadow of even one primeval tree, much less be lost among the multitude of hoary trunks, and hidden from earth and sky by the mystery of darksome foliage. Nothing is within my daily reach more like a forest than the acre or two of woodland near some suburban farm-house. When, therefore, the yearning for seclusion becomes a necessity within me, I am drawn to the sea-shore, which extends its line of rude rocks and seldom-trodden sands, for leagues around our bay. Setting forth, at my last ramble, on a September morning, I bound myself with a hermit's vow, to interchange no thoughts with man or woman, to share no social pleasure, but to derive all that day's enjoyment from shore, and sea, and sky,—from my soul's communion with these, and from fantasies, and recollections, or anticipated realities. Surely here is enough to feed a human spirit for a single day. Farewell, then, busy world! Till your evening lights shall shine along the street—till they gleam upon my sea-flushed face, as I tread homeward—free me from your ties, and let me be a peaceful outlaw.

Highways and cross-paths are hastily traversed; and, clambering down a crag, I find myself at the extremity of a long beach. How gladly does the spirit leap forth, and suddenly enlarge its sense of being to the full extent of the broad, blue, sunny deep! A greeting and a homage to the Sea! I descend over its margin, and dip my hand into the wave that meets me, and bathe my brow. That far-resounding roar is Ocean's voice of welcome. His salt breath brings a blessing along with it. Now let us pace together—the reader's fancy arm in arm with mine—this noble beach, which extends a mile or more from that craggy promontory to yonder rampart of broken rocks. In front, the sea; in the rear, a precipitous bank, the grassy verge of which is breaking away, year after year, and flings down its tufts of verdure upon the barrenness below. The beach itself is a broad space of sand, brown and sparkling, with hardly any pebbles intermixed. Near the water's edge there is a wet margin, which glistens brightly in the sunshine, and reflects objects like a mirror; and as we tread along the glistening border, a dry spot flashes around each footstep, but grows moist again, as we lift our feet. In some spots, the sand receives a complete impression of the sole—square toe and all; elsewhere, it is of such marble firmness, that we must stamp heavily to leave a print even of the iron-shod heel. Along the whole of this extensive beach gambols the surf-wave; now it makes a feint of dashing onward in a fury, yet dies away with a meek murmur, and does but kiss the strand; now, after many such abortive efforts, it rears itself up in an unbroken line, heightening as it advances, without a speck of foam on its green crest. With how fierce a roar it flings itself forward, and rushes far up the beach!

As I threw my eyes along the edge of the surf, I remember that I was startled, as Robinson Crusoe might have been, by the sense that human life was within the magic circle of my solitude. Afar off in the remote distance of the beach, appearing like sea-nymphs, or some airier things, such as might tread upon the feathery spray, was a group of girls. Hardly had I beheld them, when they passed into the shadow of the rocks and vanished. To comfort myself—for truly I would fain have gazed a while longer—I made acquaintance with a flock of beach-birds. These little citizens of the sea and air preceded me by about a stone's-throw along the strand, seeking, I suppose, for food upon its margin. Yet, with a philosophy which mankind would do well to imitate, they drew a continual pleasure from their toil for a subsistence. The sea was each little bird's great playmate. They chased it downward as it swept back, and again ran up swiftly before the impending wave, which sometimes overtook them and bore them off their feet. But they floated as lightly as one of their own feathers on the breaking crest. In their airy flutterings, they seemed to rest on the evanescent spray. Their images,—long-legged little figures, with grey backs and snowy bosoms,—were seen as distinctly as the realities in the mirror of the glistening strand. As I advanced, they flew a score or two of yards, and, again alighting, recommenced their dalliance with the surf-wave; and thus they bore me company along the beach, the types of pleasant fantasies, till, at its extremity, they took wing over the ocean, and were gone. After forming a friendship with these small surf-spirits, it is really worth a sigh, to find no memorial of them save their multitudinous little tracks in the sand.

When we have paced the length of the beach, it is pleasant, and not unprofitable, to retrace our steps, and recall the whole mood and occupation of the mind during the former passage.

Our tracks, being all discernible, will guide us with an observing consciousness through every unconscious wandering of thought and fancy. Here we followed the surf in its reflux, to pick up a shell which the sea seemed loth to relinquish. Here we found a sea-weed, with an immense brown leaf, and trailed it behind us by its long snake-like stalk. Here we seized a live horse-shoe by the tail, and counted the many claws of that queer monster. Here we dug into the sand for pebbles, and skipped them upon the surface of the water. Here we wet our feet while examining a jelly-fish, which the waves, having just tossed it up, now sought to snatch away again. Here we trod along the brink of a fresh-water brooklet, which flows across the beach, becoming shallower and more shallow, till at last it sinks into the sand, and perishes in the effort to bear its little tribute to the main. Here some vagary appears to have bewildered us; for our tracks go round and round, and are confusedly intermingled, as if we had found a labyrinth upon the level beach. And here, amid our idle pastime, we sat down upon almost the only stone that breaks the surface of the sand, and were lost in an unlooked-for and overpowering conception of the majesty and awfulness of the great deep. Thus, by tracking our foot-prints in the sand, we track our own nature in its wayward course, and steal a glance upon it, when it never dreams of being so observed. Such glances always make us wiser.

This extensive beach affords room for another pleasant pastime. With your staff, your may write verses—love-verses, if they please you best—and consecrate them with a woman's name. Here, too, may be inscribed thoughts, feelings, desires, warm outgushings from the heart's secret places, which you would not pour upon the sand without the certainty that, almost ere the sky has looked upon them, the sea will wash them out. Stir not hence, till the record be effaced. Now—for there is room enough on your canvass—draw huge faces—huge as that of the Sphynx on Egyptian sands—and fit them with bodies of corresponding immensity, and legs which might stride half-way to yonder island. Child's play becomes magnificent on so grand a scale. But, after all, the most fascinating employment is simply to write your name in the sand. Draw the letters gigantic, so that two strides may barely measure them, and three for the long strokes! Cut deep, that the record may be permanent! Statesmen, and warriors, and poets, have spent their strength in no better cause than this. Is it accomplished? Return, then, in an hour or two, and seek for this mighty record of a name. The sea will have swept over it, even as time rolls its effacing waves over the names of statesmen, and warriors, and poets. Hark, the surf-wave laughs at you!

Passing from the beach, I begin to clamber over the crags, making my difficult way among the ruins of a rampart, shattered and broken by the assaults of a fierce enemy. The rocks rise in every variety of attitude; some of them have their feet in the foam, and are shagged half-way upward with sea-weed; some have been hollowed almost into caverns by the unwearied toil of the sea, which can afford to spend centuries in wearing away a rock, or even polishing a pebble. One huge rock ascends in monumental shape, with a face like a giant's tombstone, on which the veins resemble inscriptions, but in an unknown tongue. We will fancy them the forgotten characters of an antediluvian race; or else that nature's own hand has here recorded a mystery, which, could I read her language, would make mankind the wiser and the happier. How many a thing has troubled me with that same idea! Pass on, and leave it unexplained. Here is a narrow avenue, which might seem to have been hewn through the very heart of an enormous crag, affording passage for the rising sea to thunder back and forth, filling it with tumultuous foam, and then leaving its floor of black pebbles bare and glistening. In this chasm there was once an intersecting vein of softer stone, which the waves have gnawed away piecemeal, while the granite walls remain entire on either side. How sharply, and with what harsh clamor, does the sea rake back the pebbles, as it momentarily withdraws into its own depths! At intervals, the floor of the chasm is left nearly dry; but anon, at the outlet, two or three great waves are seen struggling to get in at once; two hit the walls athwart, while one rushes straight through, and all three thunder, as if with rage and triumph. They heap the chasm with a snow-drift of foam and spray. While watching this scene, I can never rid myself of the idea, that a monster, endowed with life and fierce energy, is striving to burst his way through the narrow pass. And what a contrast, to look through the stormy chasm, and catch a glimpse of the calm bright sea beyond!

Many interesting discoveries may be made among these broken cliffs. Once, for example, I found a dead seal, which a recent tempest had tossed into a nook of the rocks, where his shaggy carcass lay rolled in a heap of eel-grass, as if the sea-monster sought to hide himself from my eye. Another time, a shark seemed on the point of leaping from the surf to swallow me; nor did I, wholly without dread, approach near enough to ascertain that the man-eater had already met his own death from some fisherman in the bay. In the same ramble, I encountered a bird—a large grey bird—but whether a loon, or a wild goose, or the identical albatross of the Ancient Mariner, was beyond my ornithology to decide. It reposed so naturally on a bed of dry sea-weed, with its head beside its wing, that I almost fancied it alive, and trod softly lest it should suddenly spread its wings skyward. But the sea-bird would soar among the clouds no more, nor ride upon its native waves; so I drew near, and pulled out one of its mottled tail-feathers for a remembrance. Another day, I discovered an immense bone, wedged into a chasm of the rocks; it was at least ten feet long, curved like a scimetar, bejewelled with barnacles and small shell-fish, and partly covered with a growth of sea-weed. Some leviathan of former ages had used this ponderous mass as a jaw-bone. Curiosities of a minuter order may be observed in a deep reservoir, which is replenished with water at every tide, but becomes a lake among the crags, save when the sea is at its height. At the bottom of this rocky basin grow marine plants, some of which tower high beneath the water, and cast a shadow in the sunshine. Small fishes dart to and fro, and hide themselves among the sea-weed; there is also a solitary crab, who appears to lead the life of a hermit, communing with none of the other denizens of the place; and likewise several five-fingers—for I know no other name than that which children give them. If your imagination be at all accustomed to such freaks, you may look down into the depths of this pool, and fancy it the mysterious depth of ocean. But where are the hulks and scattered timbers of sunken ships?—where the treasures that old Ocean hoards?—where the corroded cannon?—where the corpses and skeletons of seamen, who went down in storm and battle?

On the day of my last ramble, (it was a September day, yet as warm as summer,) what should I behold as I approached the above described basin but three girls sitting on its margin, and—yes, it is veritably so—laving their snowy feet in the sunny water! These, these are the warm realities of those three visionary shapes that flitted from me on the beach. Hark! their merry voices, as they toss up the water with their feet! They have not seen me. I must shrink behind this rock, and steal away again.

In honest truth, vowed to solitude as I am, there is something in the encounter that makes the heart flutter with a strangely pleasant sensation. I know these girls to be realities of flesh and blood, yet, glancing at them so briefly, they mingle like kindred creatures with the ideal beings of my mind. It is pleasant, likewise, to gaze down from some high crag, and watch a group of children, gathering pebbles and pearly shells, and playing with the surf, as with old Ocean's hoary beard. Nor does it infringe upon my seclusion, to see yonder boat at anchor off the shore, swinging dreamily to and fro, and rising and sinking with the alternate swell; while the crew—four gentlemen in round-about jackets—are busy with their fishing-lines. But, with an inward antipathy and a headlong flight, do I eschew the presence of any meditative stroller like myself, known by his pilgrim staff, his sauntering step, his shy demeanour, his observant yet abstracted eye. From such a man, as if another self had scared me, I scramble hastily over the rocks and take refuge in a nook which many a secret hour has given me a right to call my own. I would do battle for it even with the churl that should produce the title-deeds. Have not my musings melted into its rocky walls and sandy floor, and made them a portion of myself?

It is a recess in the line of cliffs, walled round by a rough, high precipice, which almost encircles and shuts in a little space of sand. In front, the sea appears as between the pillars of a portal. In the rear, the precipice is broken and intermixed with earth, which gives nourishment not only to clinging and twining shrubs, but to trees, that gripe the rock with their naked roots, and seem to struggle hard for footing and for soil enough to live upon. These are fir trees; but oaks hang their heavy branches from above, and throw down acorns on the beach, and shed their withering foliage upon the waves. At this autumnal season, the precipice is decked with variegated splendor; trailing wreaths of scarlet flaunt from the summit downward; tufts of yellow-flowering shrubs, and rose bushes, with their reddened leaves and glossy seed-berries, sprout from each crevice; at every glance, I detect some new light or shade of beauty, all contrasting with the stern, grey rock. A rill of water trickles down the cliff and fills a little cistern near the base. I drain it at a draught, and find it fresh and pure. This recess shall be my dining-hall. And what the feast? A few biscuits, made savory by soaking them in sea-water, a tuft of samphire gathered from the beach, and an apple for the dessert. By this time, the little rill has filled its reservoir again; and, as I quaff it, I thank God more heartily than for a civic banquet, that He gives me the healthful appetite to make a feast of bread and water.

Dinner being over, I throw myself at length upon the sand, and basking in the sunshine, let my mind disport itself at will. The walls of this my hermitage have no tongue to tell my follies, though I sometimes fancy that they have ears to hear them, and a soul to sympathize. There is a magic in this spot. Dreams haunt its precincts, and flit around me in broad sunlight, nor require that sleep shall blindfold me to real objects, ere these be visible. Here can I frame a story of two lovers, and make their shadows live before me, and be mirrored in the tranquil water, as they tread along the sand, leaving no foot-prints. Here, should I will it, I can summon up a single shade, and be myself her lover. Yes, dreamer,—but your lonely heart will be the colder for such fancies. Sometimes, too, the Past comes back, and finds me here, and in her train come faces which were gladsome, when I knew them, yet seem not gladsome now. Would that my hiding place were lonelier, so that the Past might not find me! Get ye all gone, old friends, and let me listen to the murmur of the sea,—a melancholy voice, but less sad than yours. Of what mysteries is it telling? Of sunken ships, and whereabouts they lie? Of islands afar and undiscovered, whose tawny children are unconscious of other islands and of continents, and deem the stars of heaven their nearest neighbours? Nothing of all this. What then? Has it talked for so many ages, and meant nothing all the while? No; for those ages find utterance in the sea's unchanging voice, and warn the listener to withdraw his interest from mortal vicissitudes, and let the infinite idea of eternity pervade his soul. This is wisdom; and, therefore, will I spend the next half-hour in shaping little boats of drift-wood, and launching them on voyages across the cove, with the feather of a sea-gull for a sail. If the voice of ages tell me true, this is as wise an occupation as to build ships of five hundred tons, and launch them forth upon the main, bound to 'far Cathay.' Yet, how would the merchant sneer at me!

And, after all, can such philosophy be true? Methinks I could find a thousand arguments against it. Well, then, let yonder shaggy rock, mid-deep in the surf—see! he is somewhat wrathful,—he rages and roars and foams—let that tall rock be my antagonist, and let me exercise my oratory like him of Athens, who bandied words with an angry sea and got the victory. My maiden speech is a triumphant one; for the gentleman in sea-weed has nothing to offer in reply, save an immitigable roaring. His voice, indeed, will be heard a long while after mine is hushed. Once more I shout, and the cliffs reverberate the sound. Oh, what joy for a shy man to feel himself so solitary, that he may lift his voice to its highest pitch without hazard of a listener! But, hush!—be silent, my good friend!—whence comes that stifled laughter? It was musical,—but how should there be such music in my solitude?

Looking upwards, I catch a glimpse of three faces, peeping from the summit of the cliff, like angels between me and their native sky. Ah, fair girls, you may make yourselves merry at my eloquence,—but it was my turn to smile when I saw your white feet in the pool! Let us keep each other's secrets.

The sunshine has now passed from my hermitage, except a gleam upon the sand just where it meets the sea. A crowd of gloomy fantasies will come and haunt me, if I tarry longer here, in the darkening twilight of these grey rocks. This is a dismal place in some moods of the mind. Climb we, therefore, the precipice, and pause a moment on the brink, gazing down into that hollow chamber by the deep, where we have been, what few can be, sufficient to our own pastime—yes, say the word outright!—self-sufficient to our own happiness. How lonesome looks the recess now, and dreary too,—like all other spots where happiness has been! There lies my shadow in the departing sunshine with its head upon the sea. I will pelt it with pebbles. A hit! a hit! I clap my hands in triumph, and see my shadow clapping its unreal hands, and claiming the triumph for itself. What a simpleton must I have been all day, since my own shadow makes a mock of my fooleries!

Homeward! homeward! It is time to hasten home. It is time; it is time; for as the sun sinks over the western wave, the sea grows melancholy, and the surf has a saddened tone. The distant sails appear astray, and not of earth, in their remoteness amid the desolate waste. My spirit wanders forth afar, but finds no resting place, and comes shivering back. It is time that I were hence. But grudge me not the day that has been spent in seclusion, which yet was not solitude, since the great sea has been my companion, and the little sea-birds my friends, and the wind has told me his secrets, and airy shapes have flitted around me in my hermitage. Such companionship works an effect upon a man's character, as if he had been admitted to the society of creatures that are not mortal. And when, at noontide, I tread the crowded streets, the influence of this day will still be felt; so that I shall walk among men kindly and as a brother, with affection and sympathy, but yet shall not melt into the indistinguishable mass of human kind. I shall think my own thoughts, and feel my own emotions, and possess my individuality unviolated.

But it is good, at the eve of such a day, to feel and know that there are men and women in the world. That feeling and that knowledge are mine, at this moment; for, on the shore, far below me, the fishing-party have landed from their skiff, and are cooking their scaly prey by a fire of drift-wood, kindled in the angle of two rude rocks. The three visionary girls are likewise there. In the deepening twilight, while the surf is dashing near their hearth, the ruddy gleam of the fire throws a strange air of comfort over the wild cove, bestrewn as it is with pebbles and sea-weed, and exposed to the 'melancholy main.' Moreover, as the smoke climbs up the precipice, it brings with it a savory smell from a pan of fried fish, and a black kettle of chowder, and reminds me that my dinner was nothing but bread and water, and a tuft of samphire, and an apple. Methinks the party might find room for another guest, at that flat rock which serves them for a table; and if spoons be scarce, I could pick up a clam-shell on the beach. They see me now; and—the blessing of a hungry man upon him!—one of them sends up a hospitable shout—halloo, Sir Solitary! come down and sup with us! The ladies wave their handkerchiefs. Can I decline? No; and be it owned, after all my solitary joys, that this is the sweetest moment of a Day by the Sea-Shore.

Henry Wadsworth Longfellow

Longfellow (1807–1882) was not only the most popular 19th-century American poet, he was also among the most erudite. His perennially popular "The Wreck of the Hesperus" (1841), memorializing a tragedy that had occurred in the seas off Gloucester, Massachusetts, is a pitch-perfect pastiche of medieval Scottish balladry. The theme had a natural appeal for Longfellow: for all the aura of geniality that surrounds his poetry, it has at its heart a northern chill, at home in the roughest Atlantic waters.

The Wreck of the Hesperus

It was the schooner Hesperus,
That sailed the wintry sea;
And the skipper had taken his little daughter,
To bear him company.

Blue were her eyes as the fairy-flax,
Her cheeks like the dawn of day,
And her bosom white as the hawthorn buds,
That ope in the month of May.

The skipper he stood beside the helm,
His pipe was in his mouth,
And he watched how the veering flaw did blow
The smoke now West, now South.

Then up and spake an old Sailòr,
Had sailed the Spanish Main,
"I pray thee, put into yonder port,
For I fear a hurricane.

"Last night, the moon had a golden ring,
And to-night no moon we see!"
The skipper, he blew a whiff from his pipe,
And a scornful laugh laughed he.

Colder and louder blew the wind,
    A gale from the Northeast;
The snow fell hissing in the brine,
    And the billows frothed like yeast.

Down came the storm, and smote amain,
    The vessel in its strength;
She shuddered and paused, like a frighted steed,
    Then leaped her cable's length.

"Come hither! come hither! my little daughtèr,
    And do not tremble so;
For I can weather the roughest gale,
    That ever wind did blow."

He wrapped her warm in his seaman's coat
    Against the stinging blast;
He cut a rope from a broken spar,
    And bound her to the mast.

"O father! I hear the church-bells ring,
    O say, what may it be?"
"'T is a fog-bell on a rock-bound coast!"—
    And he steered for the open sea.

"O father! I hear the sound of guns,
    O say, what may it be?"
"Some ship in distress, that cannot live
    In such an angry sea!"

"O father! I see a gleaming light,
    O say, what may it be?"
But the father answered never a word,
    A frozen corpse was he.

Lashed to the helm, all stiff and stark,
    With his face turned to the skies,

The lantern gleamed through the gleaming snow
 On his fixed and glassy eyes.

Then the maiden clasped her hands and prayed
 That savèd she might be;
And she thought of Christ, who stilled the wave
 On the Lake of Galilee.

And fast through the midnight dark and drear,
 Through the whistling sleet and snow,
Like a sheeted ghost, the vessel swept
 Towards the reef of Norman's Woe.

And ever the fitful gusts between
 A sound came from the land;
It was the sound of the trampling surf,
 On the rocks and the hard sea-sand.

The breakers were right beneath her bows,
 She drifted a dreary wreck,
And a whooping billow swept the crew
 Like icicles from her deck.

She struck where the white and fleecy waves
 Looked soft as carded wool,
But the cruel rocks, they gored her side
 Like the horns of an angry bull.

Her rattling shrouds, all sheathed in ice,
 With the masts went by the board;
Like a vessel of glass, she stove and sank,
 Ho! ho! the breakers roared!

At daybreak, on the bleak sea-beach,
 A fisherman stood aghast,
To see the form of a maiden fair,
 Lashed close to a drifting mast.

The salt-sea was frozen on her breast,
    The salt tears in her eyes;
And he saw her hair, like the brown sea-weed,
    On the billows fall and rise.

Such was the wreck of the Hesperus,
    In the midnight and the snow!
Christ save us all from a death like this,
    On the reef of Norman's Woe!

William Reynolds

William Reynolds (1815–1880) entered the U.S. Navy as a midshipman in 1831 and sailed from Norfolk in 1838 as a member of the U.S. South Seas Exploring Expedition, often known as the Wilkes Expedition after its commander, Lieutenant Charles Wilkes. The expedition had as one of its main goals the exploration of Antarctica. Although American seal hunters had made sightings and landings along the Antarctic coast in 1820–21, it was still uncertain whether the land discovered in the south polar region was part of a seventh continent or merely a chain of islands. The expedition's first voyage into Antarctic waters early in 1839 ended in disaster when one of its six ships, the sloop Sea Gull, *disappeared. In January 1840 the sloop* Peacock *and three other ships returned to the Antarctic and eventually surveyed over 1,000 miles of coastline, definitively establishing the existence of a southern polar continent. The expedition returned to the U.S. in 1842, after traversing over 87,000 nautical miles, surveying 280 islands, collecting extensive geological, botanical, and zoological specimens, and mapping 800 miles of the Oregon coast, where the* Peacock *was lost on a sandbar off the Columbia River. Reynolds served as a supply officer during the Civil War and retired from the navy in 1877 with the rank of rear admiral.*

from *Voyage to the Southern Ocean*

U.S. Ship Peacock
Sydney, March 4th 1840

My dear Mother,

A few days ago I sent you a very short letter by way of New Zealand merely mentioning that we were obliged to return here to repair damages received among the Ice, etc. etc. I think it likely you may get this first and as I have now a little leisure, I will endeavour to spin you the whole yarn.

We left Sydney the day after Christmas and after rather a rough time for more than two weeks, we reached the barrier of Ice, having made *Maquarie Island* on our way. *Ice bergs* we met with in Lat. 61° S. and passed them daily until we arrived at the *field of Ice*, which prevented our farther progress South and sent us along its edge to the Westward. We separated from the Squadron while in the clear sea, but fell in with the Vincennes and Brigs soon after we made the *barrier*. We did not continue together, however, but parted, each to do our best, alone.

When we crossed the 60th degree of Latitude, we seemed to leave the stormy region behind us entirely. The weather was fair and mild and the Sea smooth; fog and sleet disappeared, and we had sunshine instead, which was gladly welcomed. Our hopes were high; appearances were so flattering, that we were sanguine of penetrating to a high parrelel without encountering danger or obstruction, confident that we should have the fame and the honor of finding *Land* where none had ever sought for it before; full of joy that we should accomplish this and so gain a name for us and for our country.

On, on we sailed for days with a fair breeze over almost a summer Sea and meeting with no signs of a *barrier* to cloud our fair expectations. At 12 o'clock on the 16th January, there *was not a particle of Ice to be seen from the mast head* and *we were nearly as far South as the Ship had gone last year*: the weather was quite clear and the excitement on board was intense. We were confident that we should eclipse all former navigators and leave but little for those who would come after us. Antartic Stock was high! We were so elated at the prospect of such easy success that we could not restrain our feelings and we became quite extravagant, and almost wild.

We had no night—'twas broad daylight through the whole twenty four hours. We used no candles. The Sun *set in the East* about 10½ P.M. and rose again, close by where he disappeared, before 2 A.M. We shot birds at all hours and the *men read Pickwick* in the middle watch; the Doctor brought *his wife's bible* on deck every night at 12 o'clock and *read a chapter*.

But at 4 o'clock on the 16th we fell in with the Porpoise and the barrier of Ice together, and our course was at once arrested and our hopes dampened for the time. The Brig had sailed along the Ice for some days without finding any opening, and all we had to do was to proceed to the Westward and if there should be any break in the Ice, enter it, if practicable—but this would be tedious and was uncertain; our glorious hopes were most cruelly destroyed.

A few days after turning to the Westward, we came to an opening in the Ice, which we entered though we scarcely thought it extended far to the Southward: we sailed along 30 miles ere we came to the head of it and were then enclosed on all sides, save the one small passage to the North, by immense fields of Ice. The long swell of the Ocean was shut off altogether, the water was smooth and motionless as an Inland Lake and lay like a vast mirror in its frosted frame. It was as a Bay making far into the Land, but the boundaries *were not the green of Earth*. As we approached the end of the Bay, we fell in with innumerable pieces of floating Ice, broken off from the mass and drifting out into the Sea. Though the temperature was 21°, I spent more than one hour at the mast head for the sight from thence was grand, wild, strange beyond description: far as the eye could see, the Icy plains extended until they met the sky; the slightness of their elevation above the water, relieved in many places by towering Ice bergs of every form and hue and by immense Islands that arose like mountains from amidst the Desert of Ice; the whiteness of all this was dazzling and intense; unbroken, save by the glistening sheet of water where the Ship floated, idle, quiet and at rest.

I was alone on my airy perch; the hum of voices from the deck did not reach my ear for the tones of all were subdued and there was naught to disturb the solemn and almost awful stillness that hung over the frozen plains: the Ship ceased her groaning and the very sea birds had gone from us; all that there was of life in the picture was beneath my feet, and *that* I heeded not. I thought there was no one but God near me and as I looked upon the mighty scene around which was neither Earth nor Sea, I was more impressed with the idea of His creative power and of the insignificance of man, than by any prospect that ever Earth afforded, or Sea assumed. *My feelings were new* and I enjoyed the hour far more than I can tell.

Once we thought we saw Land and as it happened I had been the first to discern the appearance, from the mast head: we neared it, and its high and broken sides and summit confirmed our conjectures. We were sure it was a portion of the Southern Continent and were elated beyond measure. We gave names to Points and Peaks and I stipulated for two, which were to be *Lancaster* and *Cornwall*, besides a *Cape Reynolds*. Alas! we could not land upon it but it seemed to be an Island 1000 feet high or more. So it was frequently, though we were more than once deceived. Many circumstances prevented a close approach and the snowy mantle deceived us and kept us long in doubt and suspense.

On Thursday evening January 24th we were in another Bay and were strongly impressed with the belief that we were near Land and that some ridges that we saw were not all Ice, but Earth beneath. Two boats were sent away from the Ship for different purposes and the Lead line was put over the side. It was watched going down by eager eyes and when it brought up suddenly, there was almost a scream of delight: we had found the bottom at 350 fathoms—*mud* and *pebbles* came up on the lead and line and *then* we got a first sight of the Southern Land. Great was the joy and excitement throughout the Ship, for this was a certain indication that our belief was correct *this time*. We had "terra firma" in our grasp, as we thought, and the prize would be our own, poor, short sighted fools that we were! The boats were returning about this time and the crew were sent into the rigging to give three cheers for our luck; they did this with such a hearty good will that the old Ice rang out with the sound.

All was bustle about the decks; below, some were playing shuffle board; on the Gun deck, we were *rolling nine pins* (the Ship was so perfectly at rest) and on the Spar deck, the men were running away cheerily with the lead line to the music of the fiddle, occasionally bursting into the songs and hurrahs common among them when at any exciting work. When this was finished, all hands were called *to splice the main brace* and we were a merry Ship. Little did any one think of the change that a few short hours would bring about! I shall never give way to high wrought hopes again! When I have done so, disappointment was sure to come with a mountain's weight!

One of the Boats brought on board a mammoth penguin. A beautiful and kingly bird he was, but it was a bad day for him that the Peacock came to his haunts; he was cruelly put to death that his skin might be preserved for the satisfaction of those who are content to see the curious things of the world second hand.

The Sun set at 10 with all the splendor of a warmer clime, leaving a ruddy glow in the Horizon which vanished not, but chamelion like changed its hues from bright to brighter. 'Twas my middle watch and when I came on deck at 12, there was a deep peace all around; but a breath of air was stirring and the Ship was quiet and motionless as she would have been in *Speedwell dam*. The Moon was bright in the Heavens, but she threw no light abroad: this eternal day puts her to shame and blots out the Stars altogether. The East was illuminated with those soft and blended tints that form the glory of an Italian sky at Eve and the reflection of these colours upon the Ice produced an effect, splendid, dazzling, grand beyond conception; the eye quailed at the sight and the imagination was utterly confounded. I felt that I was looking upon the painting of God! To heighten the scene, in the North and West the clouds were black and hung in gloomy contrast over the stainless field of Ice beneath them. Tell me no more of Earth! I have seen its fairest portions, but never have I looked upon so much vast, sublime and wondrous beauty as this rising and setting of the Sun presented in the midst of the Icy Sea.

The Captain came on deck in the greatest glee—35 large pebbles had been taken from the maw of the Penguin, another sympton that there was *Land* about. Poor man! he was nearly beside himself with joy.

At 4 o'clock I turned in, dreading no evil and confident that we would succeed in finding the desired Land ere we were many days older—true! even in a few hours we came near to finding it, *but at the bottom of the Sea!*

At 8 o'clock, I found the Ship entered among the pieces of drift Ice; the Captain was trying to get near the barrier to determine whether the appearances of Land were real or false. At 8.40 it was evident we could go no farther with safety and that we had best get back into the clear water as speedily as possible. We were entirely surrounded by loose Ice; some pieces were much larger than the Ship and they were packed so closely together that we had no room to proceed or to manoeuvre in. Here and there small clear patches occurred, but these filled up and changed continually. In endeavouring to tack, the Ship got Sternboard and went Stern on to a huge lump of ice, splitting the rudder head and carrying away the wheel ropes. This shock sent her ahead, against all her sails, and it brought all hands on deck; but in another moment she gathered sternway once more and this time coming in contact with the same mass, the rudder was shattered and the head of it carried away entirely.

This was a terrible disaster alone: the Ship, with all her spars standing, her hull entire, her crew safe, was helpless as an infant—her *guiding power* was gone—but this was *merely* the *commencement* of our troubles. Our situation was evident at a glance; we must get clear of the Ice at once, *if we could?* repair the rudder, *if we could?* and get back to Sydney, *if we could?* All, or either of which, was problematical in the highest degree. We failed in the first attempt, *to get out!* Our own efforts could not succeed and we were most reluctantly obliged to run her farther into the Ice to reach a clear place that we noticed near a large Island of Ice.

We were obliged to steer the Ship by the Sails and of course her movements were awkward and slow: we could not avoid the Ice in our way and thumped heavily many times, carrying away part of the Fore foot and doing other damage. This was becoming too serious, the Ship could *not bear such shocks long*. It was really terrible to see her bearing down upon these masses and then feel her bring up, arrested at once by the mighty obstacles in her way; her whole frame quivered and shook and the poor craft groaned in her distress. *How* we watched her as she freed herself and more than once we thought spars and all would come down about our heads: *the danger was thickening fast*.

We now lowered the Boats and carried out Ice Anchors to the largest pieces, hoping to ride by them until we could hoist in the rudder: the sails were furled, but, vain hopes, the anchors would not hold; the wind freshened a little and, notwithstanding the exertions of the men to keep the Iron flues in their bed, we broke adrift and ere we could raise a hand to save ourselves, the Ship *went on to the Ice Island with a tremendous crash*. This Island was many miles in extent: from the mast head, I could see over its flat top a long, long distance, but could not discern its termination. It rose from the Water, bluff as the sides of a house, the upper edge projecting like the eaves and when we were under it, it towered above the mast head. It was the weakest part of the Ship's frame that came in contact with this mass, and the shock and crash and splintering of the riven spars and upper works was any thing but agreeable.

For *an instant, I thought that* the whole stern frame *must* be stove in and that a few moments would send us to the bottom. I thought any struggle for life would be in vain: to reach a piece of Ice would only be to linger in agony and suffer a more horrible death, and I settled in my mind with startling quickness *that it would be best to go down with the Ship*. With this thought came neither terror nor dismay, though it was the thought of going to my eternal sleep. (One does not know what the mind is capable of bearing in such situations until experience has learned us; I was astonished to find myself *reasoning* in such a moment as this.) An hour before we had been in safety: *now* we were a wreck at the mercy of the elements and the Ice. I may safely say I felt neither fear nor dread, though there was that quickening rush of blood towards the heart and those creeping thrilling sensations, indescribable, but such as must come over every one at the startling approach of sudden death. Of course no one felt at ease, but there were no shrieks, no exhibitions of bewilderment; and from what I know of my own feelings and from what others have told me of theirs, I verily believe that *had* the old Ship *settled* in the water, she would have gone down to her grave with three as hearty cheers as ever came from an hundred throats. God knows what it is that should prompt a man to send out his last breath in a hurrah! I do not! I thought my feelings strange and perhaps unnatural, but I was mistaken: the burst would have been spontaneous and universal, curious as it may seem. I know now as well as I know that I am sitting here, I can *see* the very *one* who would have been the first to say, *"let's give her a cheer my lads as she goes!"* and it would have been done!

The action was prompt, there was no time to lose, and sail was made with as much celerity and steadiness as if we were leaving a Harbour. The Ship moved, her head paid off from the danger, slowly but surely she reached ahead and *we were clear of the Island*, where to have struck again would have ensured our destruction. *Scarcely* had we got from under the pile, when *down came the overhanging ledge of snow*, flinging the foam it raised in the Sea upon our decks. *Mercy! a moment longer and it had crushed us*. I cannot tell you *how* I looked upon that Island as we were leaving it, by inches; there were the marks of the Ship's form and paint, and there, at its foot, were the tumbled heaps of snow that had so nearly overwhelmed us.

I had been almost immediately relieved from the apprehension of the Ship's sinking. The destruction had been great, but it was *only* the *upper* part of the Ship's frame, that was carried away, and *she was saved!* I shall never forget the look of the old craft as she lay beneath that ridge of Ice, trembling from the blow, and Ice, Ice piled around her, so that we could see nothing else from the deck. The dark figures of the men and boats were the only relief to the dreary whiteness.

Now that we were freed from this peril, it was determined to struggle again for the clear Sea: 'twas about 11 A.M. We thumped, thumped until 3 in the afternoon, making but little progress and drifting to leeward all the while, with the Ice and the distance between us and the open Sea increased every moment from the quantity of floating pieces brought down by the wind. The men were kept incessantly at work, but all our efforts to get into places where the Ice was thinnest were of no avail; we were so jammed and the Ship so unmanageable that we missed every chance and became more and more involved.

An hundred times we thought we should *surely succeed*, but the Ice crowded upon us the more and the Ship continued to strike as if she would knock herself to pieces. Labour was not slackened, however unfavorable appearances were: all the resources that ingenuity suggested were tried and the men did their duty, as sailors always do when working for their lives: calm, obedient and untiring, they pursued their exertions with a steadiness that could not be overthrown.

At 3 the wind died away and it came up *thick* and *blinding with snow*. We made fast again with Ice anchors and hoisted the rudder in. All of us were relieved to see *it* inboard, for oh! *how much depended on its being repaired!* The Carpenters went immediately to work upon it. Soon after, the breeze sprang up again, the anchors would not hold, and we made sail once more to try and force her out. It was the same thing over, with the same ill success; we became more and more shut in and the chances for *getting out* seemed more remote than ever. To dwell at all upon our situation, while in a measure free from instant risk, afforded but little consolation: the Ship was so helpless without her rudder and it seemed as if we were striving against fate and would *never get clear*: allowing that we did escape the Ice, until we could get command of the Ship once more we could not choose our course; and after that *would* be accomplished, in the imperfect manner that was alone practicable, we had a long tract of stormy Sea to pass over ere we could reach our port. I did not allow these anticipations to occupy my mind, but I could not help their intruding at times: how wearily the time wore by and how vexatious, killing, torturing it was to miss chance after chance for escape, when we had struggled for dear life to obtain them. *You good people* in your *quiet Home* can know but little of men's feelings in situations such as this and sure am I that I can tell you mine but very faintly.

We toiled, toiled on: "*never say die*" was the word. Even the Boys worked with all the ardour of Hercules, if not with his strength. Officers and all, there was no one idle, no one thought of rest. We used the Boats to plant the anchors for warping by and when we could use them no longer, the men went upon the Ice and crossing from piece to piece by planks laid over the chasms, transported the anchors to different positions; we had spars over the bows also, pushing with might and main. In this way, by 6 o'clock our exertions had brought us to within 100 yards of the open Sea, but we were wedged immoveable: we could neither advance nor recede and we had the cruel mortification of seeing the place of *comparative safety* so close at hand, and yet be in as much and more peril than we had experienced through the day. We *could all have walked* to the edge of the Ice, but the masses surrounding the Ship were so huge that all our thumping only did *her* injury, while it did not budge them an inch. *Now* was the time when the anxiety became *almost terrible!* Hitherto the weather, though thick, had not threatened. The wind had been moderate and there was but little swell; consequently the Ice had but little motion, not sufficient to throw *it* with any force against us: the *Ship* had been forced upon *it*! Now it seemed the tables were to be turned: Black clouds were gathering in the West; they were rolled and curled together in windy looking wreaths and they had all the appearance of *a coming storm.* I went up aloft and I fixed my gaze upon that portentous sky; I watched until I *saw its shadow coming over the water* and then I thought in sad earnest, *our time has come at last!*

While I was in the rigging descending to the deck, when as I thought the last grand scene in the drama of Life was so soon to be enacted, there was *something spoke at my heart* and with a few words I recommended my Soul to the mercy and keeping of God! *I gave up all hope of Life!* The approach of the squall seemed so evident and certain that I saw no prospect of escape and I thought that in less than an hour there would not be a vestige left of the Peacock or her crew! I know of no feelings more terrible than those that are likely to be called up in moments such as these: here were *two hundred of us* in the full vigour of health and strength and in a few moments *not one* would be left to tell the tale of our destruction: *all must go*, without *even the hope of a struggle for life*: there could be *no resistance*; when the crash came, *we* should be swept away like the spars and timbers of the Ship!

Every one was watching those clouds: men and boys knew that in their shape hung our fate and *they were coming on like the angel of death*. Every rag was taken in and now, as we could do no more, we *silently awaited our chance*. The little breeze which had been blowing from another quarter died away entirely and that sort of breathless calm succeeded which is generally ominous of the wrath and tempest about to follow. *Now* you might see eye turn to eye, seeking for Hope or a glance of consolation; but even during this dreadful crisis, which thank God! was brief, there was no feeling *betrayed* that any one should be ashamed of. *With nothing to do*, you could read anxiety in many a face; you could tell of the trouble within by the quivering lips and the unsettled eye, but there was neither the voice of murmur or of fright; there was naught that could cast a stigma upon the manhood of the crew. Those who were timid kept their fears to themselves; if they needed the example of restraint and composure, it was set to them by the many who were made of firmer stuff.

I am not going to say that while we were in this harrowing suspense, I or any one else felt unconcerned or at ease. On the contrary, my feelings were *almost* overpowering in their force: the sense of the dreadful fate impending over us was suffocating and all the tumult of thoughts likely to crowd upon a man with *such a death* before his eyes pressed with a *stunning* weight upon my poor heart. So it was with others, so *they* tell *me since*.

Nearer and nearer came the funeral cloud; but suddenly its appearance changed! It spread wide and broke away! It lost its stormy aspect; the windy looking wreaths were dissolved in mist and thick snow! With *that change*, our sense of *present* danger passed away. We were relieved from the *fear of instant destruction!* It was evident to the eyes that had watched the progress of that cloud with so much anxiety that there need no longer be any apprehension of a storm. With the keenness of judgement common to seamen, every one knew *that the crisis had gone by* and that we might once more deem ourselves in comparative safety. The spell was broken! we breathed freely! the deep and joyful feelings of *that moment cannot be told!*

Heavens! What a hideous death we escaped: the poor old Ship was lying with her whole broadside exposed to the Ice, pressed, strained, groaning in every part of her frame. Her strong build alone enabled her to hold together; the Vincennes could not have borne it so long. The least increase of either breeze or swell would have brought the Ice down upon us in a thousand *avalanches*! We could not fly, we could not stay the advancing Ice; Ship and men would have gone down beneath the frozen piles and our fate would have been forever sealed in the mystery which enshrouds the Polar Sea!

Cold and weary, some of us went below to solace ourselves with some hot compound and something more substantial. We enjoyed the lunch with a keen relish and returned on deck to participate in the toil that was renewed.

Instead of a storm of wind from the cloud, we had a thick snow squall that almost blinded us and shut both Ice and Sea from our view. Presently a light breeze sprang up and sail was made once more. The Ice still came drifting down and, as before, when we had got the Ship nearly in a channel, it would close up and we had to try another and be again disappointed. In this way the time wore heavily and wearily away.

At 1 in the morning, we had all been up 17 hours hard at work and as it was *labour in vain*, one watch's hammocks were piped down and the officers and crew, save the watch on deck, went below to sleep—if they could. I turned into my cot at once to make the best of a short *three* hours, for I had the morning watch to keep. I suffered horrible tortures during my troubled Sleep; all the feelings I had mastered during the day haunted me in dreams. I died an hundred deaths, I was buried crushed under the Ice and the whole terrible catastrophe of a wreck, from the first moment of the Ice striking the Ship to the last drowning gasp, occurred with a vividness that I shall never forget. God keep me from ever feeling so, when awake! At every jar of the Ship or when any one touched my cot, I started up in agony with the idea that we were sinking and with the suffocating sense of strangling in my throat (a cold in the head was nearly choking me from the accumulation of phlegm). Those 3 hours in my cot were worse a thousand times than all the time on deck with real danger to look upon. I was glad when they were passed and got up very willingly to renew my watch. Just at this time, aided by a light breeze and a fortunate opening of the Ice, the Ship of her own accord slid into the clear water, free from the rough and cold embrace that had held her so long.

The weather was thick and chill and the wind light, but we managed to steer our disabled craft tolerably well, and without further accident reached the middle of the Bay we had entered with so much confidence and where our hopes had been raised so high. Towards 8 the mist cleared and all around as far as we could see the Icy barrier extended, save one little corner left for us to creep out of.

My eyes were red and smarting from the loss of rest and I was fairly done over, half dead from anxiety and exertion. The Carpenters had worked all night upon the rudder and at 10 A.M. it was ready to be shipped. This was too important an operation not to be witnessed by every one on board and so, foregoing the chance for sleep, we all assembled to see it completed. The precarious manoeuvre was accomplished with a seaman's ready skill and by 11 we were once more on our way, heading for the only passage that lead to the ocean.

I lay me down until dinner time, but it was not until after this meal that I could get any refreshing rest. But from 3 to 6, I slept like one of the dead and when I had to rise to my watch again, I felt fresh as ever: the change was blessed indeed.

The evening was clear and mild, the sky rosy, the Ice no longer dangerous but reflecting a thousand tints, the Ship was manageable once more, and *all was different* from the same hour of the previous night.

Henry David Thoreau

The wreck of the St. John *near Cohasset, Massachussetts, on October 7, 1849, claimed more than 100 lives. Henry David Thoreau (1817–1862) described the gruesome aftermath of the shipwreck in the opening chapter of* Cape Cod *(1865), an expanded version of essays published in* Putnam's Monthly Magazine *in 1855. Thoreau's excursion to Cohasset was not his only encounter with a shipwreck. In July 1850, the* Elizabeth *sank off the coast of Fire Island. Among its passengers was Margaret Fuller, returning from Italy with her husband and young son. At Emerson's request, Thoreau went to Fire Island in an unsuccessful attempt to recover Fuller's body and any of her personal effects; he arrived five days later, to discover that much of the recovered wreckage had been looted.*

When Thoreau returned to the beach at Cohasset in July 1852 he found no trace of the St. John *catastrophe. He wrote in his journal: "Not a vestige of a wreck left. It was not grand and sublime now, but beautiful. The water held in the little hollows of the rocks, on the receding of the tide, is so crystal-pure that you cannot believe it salt, but wish to drink it."*

from *Cape Cod*

We left Concord, Massachusetts, on Tuesday, October 9th, 1849. On reaching Boston, we found that the Provincetown steamer, which should have got in the day before, had not yet arrived, on account of a violent storm; and, as we noticed in the streets a handbill headed, "Death! one hundred and forty-five lives lost at Cohasset," we decided to go by way of Cohasset. We found many Irish in the cars, going to identify bodies and to sympathize with the survivors, and also to attend the funeral which was to take place in the afternoon;—and when we arrived at Cohasset, it appeared that nearly all the passengers were bound for the beach, which was about a mile distant, and many other persons were flocking in from the neighboring country. There were several hundreds of them streaming off over Cohasset common in that direction, some on foot and some in wagons,—and among them were some sportsmen in their hunting-jackets, with their guns, and game-bags, and dogs. As we passed the graveyard we saw a large hole, like a cellar, freshly dug there, and, just before reaching the shore, by a pleasantly winding and rocky road, we met several hay-riggings and farm-wagons coming away toward the meeting-house, each loaded with three large, rough deal boxes. We did not need to ask what was in them. The owners of the wagons were made the undertakers. Many horses in carriages were fastened to the fences near the shore, and, for a mile or more, up and down, the beach was covered with people looking out for bodies, and examining the fragments of the wreck. There was a small island called Brook Island, with a hut on it, lying just off the shore. This is said to be the rockiest shore in Massachusetts, from Nantasket to Scituate,—hard sienitic rocks, which the waves have laid bare, but have not been able to crumble. It has been the scene of many a shipwreck.

The brig St. John, from Galway, Ireland, laden with emigrants, was wrecked on Sunday morning; it was now Tuesday morning, and the sea was still breaking violently on the rocks. There were eighteen or twenty of the same large boxes that I have mentioned, lying on a green hill-side, a few rods from the water, and surrounded by a crowd. The bodies which had been recovered, twenty-seven or eight in all, had been collected there. Some were rapidly nailing down the lids, others were carting the boxes away, and others were lifting the lids, which were yet loose, and peeping under the cloths, for each body, with such rags as still adhered to it, was covered loosely with a white sheet. I witnessed no signs of grief, but there was a sober despatch of business which was affecting. One man was seeking to identify a particular body, and one undertaker or carpenter was calling to another to know in what box a certain child was put. I saw many marble feet and matted heads as the cloths were raised, and one livid, swollen, and mangled body of a drowned girl,—who probably had intended to go out to service in some American family,—to which some rags still adhered, with a string, half concealed by the flesh, about its swollen neck; the coiled-up wreck of a human hulk, gashed by the rocks or fishes, so that the bone and muscle were exposed, but quite bloodless,—merely red and white,—with wide-open and staring eyes, yet lustreless, dead-lights; or like the cabin windows of a stranded vessel, filled with sand. Sometimes there were two or more children, or a parent and child, in the same box, and on the lid would perhaps be written with red chalk, "Bridget such-a-one, and sister's child." The surrounding sward was covered with bits of sails and clothing. I have since heard, from one who lives by this beach, that a woman who had come over before, but had left her infant behind for her sister to bring, came and looked into these boxes, and saw in one,—probably the same whose superscription I have quoted,—her child in her sister's arms, as if the sister had meant to be found thus; and within three days after, the mother died from the effect of that sight.

We turned from this and walked along the rocky shore. In the first cove were strewn what seemed the fragments of a vessel, in small pieces mixed with sand and sea-weed, and great quantities of feathers; but it looked so old and rusty, that I at first took it to be some old wreck which had lain there many years. I even thought of Captain Kidd, and that the feathers were those which sea-fowl had cast there; and perhaps there might be some tradition about it in the neighborhood. I asked a sailor if that was the St. John. He said it was. I asked him where she struck. He pointed to a rock in front of us, a mile from the shore, called the Grampus Rock, and added:—

"You can see a part of her now sticking up; it looks like a small boat."

I saw it. It was thought to be held by the chain-cables and the anchors. I asked if the bodies which I saw were all that were drowned.

"Not a quarter of them," said he.

"Where are the rest?"

"Most of them right underneath that piece you see."

It appeared to us that there was enough rubbish to make the wreck of a large vessel in this cove alone, and that it would take many days to cart it off. It was several feet deep, and here and there was a bonnet or a jacket on it. In the very midst of the crowd about this wreck, there were men with carts busily collecting the sea-weed which the storm had cast up, and conveying it beyond the reach of the tide, though they were often obliged to separate fragments of clothing from it, and they might at any moment have found a human body under it. Drown who might, they did not forget that this weed was a valuable manure. This shipwreck had not produced a visible vibration in the fabric of society.

About a mile south we could see, rising above the rocks, the masts of the British brig which the St. John had endeavored to follow, which had slipped her cables, and, by good luck, run into the mouth of Cohasset Harbor. A little further along the shore we saw a man's clothes on a rock; further, a woman's scarf, a gown, a straw bonnet, the brig's caboose, and one of her masts high and dry, broken into several pieces. In another rocky cove, several rods from the water, and behind rocks twenty feet high, lay a part of one side of the vessel, still hanging together. It was, perhaps, forty feet long, by fourteen wide. I was even more surprised at the power of the waves, exhibited on this shattered fragment, than I had been at the sight of the smaller fragments before. The largest timbers and iron braces were broken superfluously, and I saw that no material could withstand the power of the waves; that iron must go to pieces in such a case, and an iron vessel would be cracked up like an egg-shell on the rocks. Some of these timbers, however, were so rotten that I could almost thrust my umbrella through them. They told us that some were saved on this piece, and also showed where the sea had heaved it into this cove, which was now dry. When I saw where it had come in, and in what condition, I wondered that any had been saved on it. A little further on a crowd of men was collected around the mate of the St. John, who was telling his story. He was a slim-looking youth, who spoke of the captain as the master, and seemed a little excited. He was saying that when they jumped into the boat, she filled, and, the vessel lurching, the weight of the water in the boat caused the painter to break, and so they were separated. Whereat one man came away, saying:—

"Well, I don't see but he tells a straight story enough. You see, the weight of the water in the boat broke the painter. A boat full of water is very heavy,"—and so on, in a loud and impertinently earnest tone, as if he had a bet depending on it, but had no humane interest in the matter.

Another, a large man, stood near by upon a rock, gazing into the sea, and chewing large quids of tobacco, as if that habit were forever confirmed with him.

"Come," says another to his companion, "let's be off. We've seen the whole of it. It's no use to stay to the funeral."

Further, we saw one standing upon a rock, who, we were told, was one that was saved. He was a sober-looking man, dressed in a jacket and gray pantaloons, with his hands in the pockets. I asked him a few questions, which he answered; but he seemed unwilling to talk about it, and soon walked away. By his side stood one of the life-boat men, in an oil-cloth jacket, who told us how they went to the relief of the British brig, thinking that the boat of the St. John, which they passed on the way, held all her crew,—for the waves prevented their seeing those who were on the vessel, though they might have saved some had they known there were any there. A little further was the flag of the St. John spread on a rock to dry, and held down by stones at the corners. This frail, but essential and significant portion of the vessel, which had so long been the sport of the winds, was sure to reach the shore. There were one or two houses visible from these rocks, in which were some of the survivors recovering from the shock which their bodies and minds had sustained. One was not expected to live.

We kept on down the shore as far as a promontory called Whitehead, that we might see more of the Cohasset Rocks. In a little cove, within half a mile, there were an old man and his son collecting, with their team, the sea-weed which that fatal storm had cast up, as serenely employed as if there had never been a wreck in the world, though they were within sight of the Grampus Rock, on which the St. John had struck. The old man had heard that there was a wreck, and knew most of the particulars, but he said that he had not been up there since it happened. It was the wrecked weed that concerned him most, rock-weed, kelp, and sea-weed, as he named them, which he carted to his barn-yard; and those bodies were to him but other weeds which the tide cast up, but which were of no use to him. We afterwards came to the life-boat in its harbor, waiting for another emergency,—and in the afternoon we saw the funeral procession at a distance, at the head of which walked the captain with the other survivors.

On the whole, it was not so impressive a scene as I might have expected. If I had found one body cast upon the beach in some lonely place, it would have affected me more. I sympathized rather with the winds and waves, as if to toss and mangle these poor human bodies was the order of the day. If this was the law of Nature, why waste any time in awe or pity? If the last day were come, we should not think so much about the separation of friends or the blighted prospects of individuals. I saw that corpses might be multiplied, as on the field of battle, till they no longer affected us in any degree, as exceptions to the common lot of humanity. Take all the grave-yards together, they are always the majority. It is the individual and private that demands our sympathy. A man can attend but one funeral in the course of his life, can behold but one corpse. Yet I saw that the inhabitants of the shore would be not a little affected by this event. They would watch there many days and nights for the sea to give up its dead, and their imaginations and sympathies would supply the place of mourners far away, who as yet knew not of the wreck. Many days after this, something white was seen floating on the water by one who was sauntering on the beach. It was approached in a boat, and found to be the body of a woman, which had risen in an upright position, whose white cap was blown back with the wind. I saw that the beauty of the shore itself was wrecked for many a lonely walker there, until he could perceive, at last, how its beauty was enhanced by wrecks like this, and it acquired thus a rarer and sublimer beauty still.

Why care for these dead bodies? They really have no friends but the worms or fishes. Their owners were coming to the New World, as Columbus and the Pilgrims did,—they were within a mile of its shores; but, before they could reach it, they emigrated to a newer world than ever Columbus dreamed of, yet one of whose existence we believe that there is far more universal and convincing evidence—though it has not yet been discovered by science—than Columbus had of this; not merely mariners' tales and some paltry drift-wood and sea-weed, but a continual drift and instinct to all our shores. I saw their empty hulks that came to land; but they themselves, meanwhile, were cast upon some shore yet further west, toward which we are all tending, and which we shall reach at last, it may be through storm and darkness, as they did. No doubt, we have reason to thank God that they have not been "shipwrecked into life again." The mariner who makes the safest port in Heaven, perchance, seems to his friends on earth to be shipwrecked, for they deem Boston Harbor the better place; though perhaps invisible to them, a skilful pilot comes to meet him, and the fairest and balmiest gales blow off that coast, his good ship makes the land in halcyon days, and he kisses the shore in rapture there, while his old hulk tosses in the surf here. It is hard to part with one's body, but, no doubt, it is easy enough to do without it when once it is gone. All their plans and hopes burst like a bubble! Infants by the score dashed on the rocks by the enraged Atlantic Ocean! No, no! If the St. John did not make her port here, she has been telegraphed there. The strongest wind cannot stagger a Spirit; it is a Spirit's breath. A just man's purpose cannot be split on any Grampus or material rock, but itself will split rocks till it succeeds.

HERMAN MELVILLE

The very notion of a distinctly American sea writing is inextricably connected to the works of Herman Melville (1819–1891). From the happenstance of a merchant's son abandoning an incipient teaching career to go to sea came a body of writing that transformed American literature, even if its full impact was not felt until years after the author's death. Melville's sea experience was intensive and varied. His first voyage was from New York to Liverpool on the St. Lawrence, *June–October 1839. In January 1841 he sailed from New Bedford on the* Acushnet, *jumping ship in the Marquesas to spend a month among the natives of Nuku Hiva; transported to Tahiti and confined as a mutineer, he escaped and ultimately sailed on the Nantucket whaler* Charles and Henry *on a voyage that took him to Honolulu in May 1843. There he joined the U.S. Navy, returning home in October 1844. The use that Melville made of all these experiences was more unpredictable and extraordinary than the experiences themselves: from his early books—*Typee *(1846),* Omoo *(1847),* Mardi *(1849),* Redburn *(1849),* White-Jacket *(1850), culminating in the masterpiece* Moby-Dick *(1851)—to such later works as* The Piazza Tales *(1856), the poetry collection* John Marr and Other Sailors *(1888), and the novella* Billy Budd, *unpublished in his lifetime. The selections included here offer no more than a sampling of his work's unparalleled range and richness.*

from *Mardi*

A Calm

NEXT DAY there was a calm, which added not a little to my impatience of the ship. And, furthermore, by certain nameless associations revived in me my old impressions upon first witnessing as a landsman this phenomenon of the sea. Those impressions may merit a page.

To a landsman a calm is no joke. It not only revolutionizes his abdomen, but unsettles his mind; tempts him to recant his belief in the eternal fitness of things; in short, almost makes an infidel of him.

At first he is taken by surprise, never having dreamt of a state of existence where existence itself seems suspended. He shakes himself in his coat, to see whether it be empty or no. He closes his eyes, to test the reality of the glassy expanse. He fetches a deep breath, by way of experiment, and for the sake of witnessing the effect. If a reader of books, Priestley on Necessity occurs to him; and he believes in that old Sir Anthony Absolute to the very last chapter. His faith in Malte Brun, however, begins to fail; for the geography, which from boyhood he had implicitly confided in, always assured him, that though expatiating all over the globe, the sea was at least margined by land. That over against America, for example, was Asia. But it is a calm, and he grows madly skeptical.

To his alarmed fancy, parallels and meridians become emphatically what they are merely designated as being: imaginary lines drawn round the earth's surface.

The log assures him that he is in such a place; but the log is a liar; for no place, nor any thing possessed of a local angularity, is to be lighted upon in the watery waste.

At length horrible doubts overtake him as to the captain's competency to navigate his ship. The ignoramus must have lost his way, and drifted into the outer confines of creation, the region of the everlasting lull, introductory to a positive vacuity.

Thoughts of eternity thicken. He begins to feel anxious concerning his soul.

The stillness of the calm is awful. His voice begins to grow strange and portentous. He feels it in him like something swallowed too big for the esophagus. It keeps up a sort of involuntary interior humming in him, like a live beetle. His cranium is a dome full of reverberations. The hollows of his very bones are as whispering galleries. He is afraid to speak loud, lest he be stunned; like the man in the bass drum.

But more than all else is the consciousness of his utter helplessness. Succor or sympathy there is none. Penitence for embarking avails not. The final satisfaction of despairing may not be his with a relish. Vain the idea of idling out the calm. He may sleep if he can, or purposely delude himself into a crazy fancy, that he is merely at leisure. All this he may compass; but he may not lounge; for to lounge is to be idle; to be idle implies an absence of any thing to do; whereas there is a calm to be endured: enough to attend to, Heaven knows.

His physical organization, obviously intended for locomotion, becomes a fixture; for where the calm leaves him, there he remains. Even his undoubted vested rights, comprised in his glorious liberty of volition, become as naught. For of what use? He wills to go: to get away from the calm: as ashore he would avoid the plague. But he can not; and how foolish to revolve expedients. It is more hopeless than a bad marriage in a land where there is no Doctors' Commons. He has taken the ship to wife, for better or for worse, for calm or for gale; and she is not to be shuffled off. With yards akimbo, she says unto him scornfully, as the old beldam said to the little dwarf:—"Help yourself."

And all this, and more than this, is a calm.

from *White-Jacket*

The last of the Jacket

ALREADY has White-Jacket chronicled the mishaps and inconveniences, troubles and tribulations of all sorts brought upon him by that unfortunate but indispensable garment of his. But now it befalls him to record how this jacket, for the second and last time, came near proving his shroud.

Of a pleasant midnight, our good frigate, now somewhere off the Capes of Virginia, was running on bravely, when the breeze, gradually dying, left us slowly gliding toward our still invisible port.

Headed by Jack Chase, the quarter-watch were reclining in the top, talking about the shore delights into which they intended to plunge, while our captain often broke in with allusions to similar conversations when he was on board the English line-of-battle ship, the Asia, drawing nigh to Portsmouth, in England, after the battle of Navarino.

Suddenly an order was given to set the main-top-gallant-stun'-sail, and the halyards not being rove, Jack Chase assigned to me that duty. Now this reeving of the halyards of a main-top-gallant-stun'-sail is a business that eminently demands sharpsightedness, skill, and celerity.

Consider that the end of a line, some two hundred feet long, is to be carried aloft, in your teeth, if you please, and dragged far out on the giddiest of yards, and after being wormed and twisted about through all sorts of intricacies—turning abrupt corners at the abruptest of angles—is to be dropped, clear of all obstructions, in a straight plumb-line right down to the deck. In the course of this business, there is a multitude of sheeve-holes and blocks, through which you must pass it; often the rope is a very tight fit, so as to make it like threading a fine cambric needle with rather coarse thread. Indeed, it is a thing only deftly to be done, even by day. Judge, then, what it must be to be threading cambric needles by night, and at sea, upward of a hundred feet aloft in the air.

With the end of the line in one hand, I was mounting the top-mast shrouds, when our Captain of the Top told me that I had better off jacket; but though it was not a very cold night, I had been reclining so long in the top, that I had become somewhat chilly, so I thought best not to comply with the hint.

Having reeved the line through all the inferior blocks, I went out with it to the end of the weather-top-gallant-yard-arm, and was in the act of leaning over and passing it through the suspended jewel-block there, when the ship gave a plunge in the sudden swells of the calm sea, and pitching me still further over the yard, threw the heavy skirts of my jacket right over my head, completely muffling me. Somehow I thought it was the sail that had flapped, and, under that impression, threw up my hands to drag it from my head, relying upon the sail itself to support me meanwhile. Just then the ship gave another sudden jerk, and, head foremost, I pitched from the yard. I knew where I was, from the rush of the air by my ears, but all else was a nightmare. A bloody film was before my eyes, through which, ghost-like, passed and repassed my father, mother, and sisters. An unutterable nausea oppressed me; I was conscious of gasping; there seemed no breath in my body. It was over one hundred feet that I fell—down, down, with lungs collapsed as in death. Ten thousand pounds of shot seemed tied to my head, as the irresistible law of gravitation dragged me, head foremost and straight as a die, toward the infallible centre of this terraqueous globe. All I had seen, and read, and heard, and all I had thought and felt in my life, seemed intensified in one fixed idea in my soul. But dense as this idea was, it was made up of atoms. Having fallen from the projecting yard-arm end, I was conscious of a collected satisfaction in feeling, that I should not be dashed on the deck, but would sink into the speechless profound of the sea.

With the bloody, blind film before my eyes, there was a still stranger hum in my head, as if a hornet were there; and I thought to myself, Great God! this is Death! Yet these thoughts were unmixed with alarm. Like frost-work that flashes and shifts its scared hues in the sun, all my braided, blended emotions were in themselves icy cold and calm.

So protracted did my fall seem, that I can even now recall the feeling of wondering how much longer it would be, ere all was over and I struck. Time seemed to stand still, and all the worlds seemed poised on their poles, as I fell, soul-becalmed, through the eddying whirl and swirl of the Maelstrom air.

At first, as I have said, I must have been precipitated head foremost; but I was conscious, at length, of a swift, flinging motion of my limbs, which involuntarily threw themselves out, so that at last I must have fallen in a heap. This is more likely, from the circumstance, that when I struck the sea, I felt as if some one had smote me slantingly across the shoulder and along part of my right side.

As I gushed into the sea, a thunder-boom sounded in my ear; my soul seemed flying from my mouth. The feeling of death flooded over me with the billows. The blow from the sea must have turned me, so that I sank almost feet foremost through a soft, seething, foamy lull. Some current seemed hurrying me away; in a trance I yielded, and sank deeper down with a glide. Purple and pathless was the deep calm now around me, flecked by summer lightnings in an azure afar. The horrible nausea was gone; the bloody, blind film turned a pale green; I wondered whether I was yet dead, or still dying. But of a sudden some fashionless form brushed my side—some inert, coiled fish of the sea; the thrill of being alive again tingled in my nerves, and the strong shunning of death shocked me through.

For one instant an agonizing revulsion came over me as I found myself utterly sinking. Next moment the force of my fall was expended; and there I hung, vibrating in the mid-deep. What wild sounds then rang in my ear! One was a soft moaning, as of low waves on the beach; the other wild and heartlessly jubilant, as of the sea in the height of a tempest. Oh soul! thou then heardest life and death: as he who stands upon the Corinthian shore hears both the Ionian and the Ægean waves. The life-and-death poise soon passed; and then I found myself slowly ascending, and caught a dim glimmering of light.

Quicker and quicker I mounted; till at last I bounded up like a buoy, and my whole head was bathed in the blessed air.

I had fallen in a line with the main-mast; I now found myself nearly abreast of the mizzen-mast, the frigate slowly gliding by like a black world in the water. Her vast hull loomed out of the night, showing hundreds of seamen in the hammock-nettings, some tossing over ropes, others madly flinging overboard the hammocks; but I was too far out from them immediately to reach what they threw. I essayed to swim toward the ship; but instantly I was conscious of a feeling like being pinioned in a feather-bed, and, moving my hands, felt my jacket puffed out above my tight girdle with water. I strove to tear it off; but it was looped together here and there, and the strings were not then to be sundered by hand. I whipped out my knife, that was tucked at my belt, and ripped my jacket straight up and down, as if I were ripping open myself. With a violent struggle I then burst out of it, and was free. Heavily soaked, it slowly sank before my eyes.

Sink! sink! oh shroud! thought I; sink forever! accursed jacket that thou art!

"See that white shark!" cried a horrified voice from the taffrail; "he'll have that man down his hatchway! Quick! the *grains*! the *grains*!"

The next instant that barbed bunch of harpoons pierced through and through the unfortunate jacket, and swiftly sped down with it out of sight.

Being now astern of the frigate, I struck out boldly toward the elevated pole of one of the life-buoys which had been cut away. Soon after, one of the cutters picked me up. As they dragged me out of the water into the air, the sudden transition of elements made my every limb feel like lead, and I helplessly sunk into the bottom of the boat.

Ten minutes after, I was safe on board, and, springing aloft, was ordered to reeve anew the stun'-sail-halyards, which, slipping through the blocks when I had let go the end, had unrove and fallen to the deck.

The sail was soon set; and, as if purposely to salute it, a gentle breeze soon came, and the Neversink once more glided over the water, a soft ripple at her bows, and leaving a tranquil wake behind.

from *Moby-Dick*

Midnight, Forecastle

HARPOONERS AND SAILORS.

(*Foresail rises and discovers the watch standing, lounging, leaning, and lying in various attitudes, all singing in chorus.*)

Farewell and adieu to you, Spanish ladies!
Farewell and adieu to you, ladies of Spain!
Our captain's commanded—

1ST NANTUCKET SAILOR.

Oh, boys, don't be sentimental; it's bad for the digestion! Take a tonic, follow me!

(*Sings, and all follow.*)

Our captain stood upon the deck,
A spy-glass in his hand,
A viewing of those gallant whales
That blew at every strand.
Oh, your tubs in your boats, my boys,
And by your braces stand,
And we'll have one of those fine whales,
Hand, boys, over hand!
So, be cheery, my lads! may your hearts never fail!
While the bold harpooneer is striking the whale!

MATE'S VOICE FROM THE QUARTER-DECK.

Eight bells there, forward!

2D NANTUCKET SAILOR.

Avast the chorus! Eight bells there! d'ye hear, bell-boy? Strike the bell eight, thou Pip! thou blackling! and let me call the watch. I've the sort of mouth for that—the hogshead mouth. So, so, (*thrusts his head down the scuttle,*) Star—bo-l-e-e-n-s, a-h-o-y! Eight bells there below! Tumble up!

DUTCH SAILOR.

Grand snoozing to-night, maty; fat night for that. I mark this in our old Mogul's wine; it's quite as deadening to some as filliping to others. We sing; they sleep—aye, lie down there, like ground-tier butts. At 'em again! There, take this copper-pump, and hail 'em through it. Tell 'em to avast dreaming of their lasses. Tell 'em it's the resurrection; they must kiss their last, and come to judgment. That's the way—*that's* it; thy throat ain't spoiled with eating Amsterdam butter.

FRENCH SAILOR.

Hist, boys! let's have a jig or two before we ride to anchor in Blanket Bay. What say ye? There comes the other watch. Stand by all legs! Pip! little Pip! hurrah with your tambourine!

PIP.

(*Sulky and sleepy.*)

Don't know where it is.

FRENCH SAILOR.

Beat thy belly, then, and wag thy ears. Jig it, men, I say; merry's the word; hurrah! Damn me, won't you dance? Form, now, Indian-file, and gallop into the double-shuffle? Throw yourselves! Legs! Legs!

ICELAND SAILOR.

I don't like your floor, maty; it's too springy to my taste. I'm used to ice-floors. I'm sorry to throw cold water on the subject; but excuse me.

MALTESE SAILOR.

Me too; where's your girls? Who but a fool would take his left hand by his right, and say to himself, how d'ye do? Partners! I must have partners!

SICILIAN SAILOR.

Aye; girls and a green!—then I'll hop with ye; yea, turn grasshopper!

LONG-ISLAND SAILOR.

Well, well, ye sulkies, there's plenty more of us. Hoe corn when you may, say I. All legs go to harvest soon. Ah! here comes the music; now for it!

AZORES SAILOR.

(*Ascending, and pitching the tambourine up the scuttle.*)

Here you are, Pip; and there's the windlass-bitts; up you mount! Now, boys!

(*The half of them dance to the tambourine; some go below; some sleep or lie among the coils of rigging. Oaths a-plenty.*)

AZORES SAILOR.

(*Dancing.*)

Go it, Pip! Bang it, bell-boy! Rig it, dig it, stig it, quig it, bell-boy! Make fire-flies; break the jinglers!

PIP.

Jinglers, you say?—there goes another, dropped off; I pound it so.

CHINA SAILOR.

Rattle thy teeth, then, and pound away; make a pagoda of thyself.

FRENCH SAILOR.

Merry-mad! Hold up thy hoop, Pip, till I jump through it! Split jibs! tear yourselves!

TASHTEGO.

(*Quietly smoking.*)

That's a white man; he calls that fun: humph! I save my sweat.

OLD MANX SAILOR.

I wonder whether those jolly lads bethink them of what they are dancing over. I'll dance over your grave, I will—that's the bitterest threat of your night-women, that beat head-winds round corners. O Christ! to think of the green navies and the green-skulled crews! Well, well; belike the whole world's one ball, as your scholars have it; and so 'tis right to make one ball-room of it. Dance on, lads, you're young; I was once.

3D NANTUCKET SAILOR.

Spell oh!—whew! this is worse than pulling after whales in a calm—give us a whiff, Tash.

(*They cease dancing, and gather in clusters.*
Meantime the sky darkens—the wind rises.)

LASCAR SAILOR.

By Brahma! boys, it'll be douse sail soon. The sky-born, high-tide Ganges turned to wind! Thou showest thy black brow, Seeva!

MALTESE SAILOR.

(*Reclining and shaking his cap.*)

It's the waves'—the snow-caps' turn to jig it now. They'll shake their tassels soon. Now would all the waves were women, then I'd go drown, and chassee with them evermore! There's naught so sweet on earth—heaven may not match it!—as those swift glances of warm, wild bosoms in the dance, when the over-arboring arms hide such ripe, bursting grapes.

SICILIAN SAILOR.

(*Reclining.*)

Tell me not of it! Hark ye, lad—fleet interlacings of the limbs—lithe swayings—coyings—flutterings! lip! heart! hip!

all graze: unceasing touch and go! not taste, observe ye, else come satiety. Eh, Pagan? (*Nudging.*)

TAHITIAN SAILOR.

(*Reclining on a mat.*)

Hail, holy nakedness of our dancing girls!—the Heeva-Heeva! Ah! low valed, high palmed Tahiti! I still rest me on thy mat, but the soft soil has slid! I saw thee woven in the wood, my mat! green the first clay I brought ye thence; now worn and wilted quite. Ah me!—not thou nor I can bear the change! How then, if so be transplanted to yon sky? Hear I the roaring streams from Pirohitee's peak of spears, when they leap down the crags and drown the villages?—The blast! the blast! Up, spine, and meet it! (*Leaps to his feet.*)

PORTUGUESE SAILOR.

How the sea rolls swashing 'gainst the side! Stand by for reefing, hearties! the winds are just crossing swords, pell-mell they'll go lunging presently.

DANISH SAILOR.

Crack, crack, old ship! so long as thou crackest, thou holdest! Well done! The mate there holds ye to it stiffly. He's no more afraid than the isle fort at Cattegat, put there to fight the Baltic with storm-lashed guns, on which the sea-salt cakes!

4TH NANTUCKET SAILOR.

He has his orders, mind ye that. I heard old Ahab tell him he must always kill a squall, something as they burst a waterspout with a pistol—fire your ship right into it!

ENGLISH SAILOR.

Blood! but that old man's a grand old cove! We are the lads to hunt him up his whale!

ALL.

Aye! aye!

OLD MANX SAILOR.

How the three pines shake! Pines are the hardest sort of tree to live when shifted to any other soil, and here there's none but the crew's cursed clay. Steady, helmsman! steady. This is the sort of weather when brave hearts snap ashore, and keeled hulls split at sea. Our captain has his birth-mark; look yonder, boys, there's another in the sky—lurid-like, ye see, all else pitch black.

DAGGOO.

What of that? Who's afraid of black's afraid of me! I'm quarried out of it!

SPANISH SAILOR.

(*Aside.*) He wants to bully, ah!—the old grudge makes me touchy. (*Advancing.*) Aye, harpooneer, thy race is the undeniable dark side of mankind—devilish dark at that. No offence.

DAGGOO.

(*Grimly.*)

None.

ST. JAGO'S SAILOR.

That Spaniard's mad or drunk. But that can't be, or else in his one case our old Mogul's fire-waters are somewhat long in working.

5TH NANTUCKET SAILOR.

What's that I saw—lightning? Yes.

SPANISH SAILOR.

No; Daggoo showing his teeth.

DAGGOO.

(*Springing.*)

Swallow thine, mannikin! White skin, white liver!

SPANISH SAILOR.

(*Meeting him.*)

Knife thee heartily! big frame, small spirit!

ALL.

A row! a row! a row!

TASHTEGO.

(*With a whiff.*)

A row a'low, and a row aloft—Gods and men—both brawlers! Humph!

BELFAST SAILOR.

A row! arrah a row! The Virgin be blessed, a row! Plunge in with ye!

ENGLISH SAILOR.

Fair play! Snatch the Spaniard's knife! A ring, a ring!

OLD MANX SAILOR.

Ready formed. There! the ringed horizon. In that ring Cain struck Abel. Sweet work, right work! No? Why then, God, mad'st thou the ring?

MATE'S VOICE FROM THE QUARTER DECK.

Hands by the halyards! in top-gallant sails! Stand by to reef topsails!

ALL.

The squall! the squall! jump, my jollies! (*They scatter.*)

PIP.

(*Shrinking under the windlass.*)

Jollies? Lord help such jollies! Crish, crash! there goes the jib-stay! Blang-whang! God! Duck lower, Pip, here comes the royal yard! It's worse than being in the whirled woods, the last day of the year! Who'd go climbing after chestnuts now? But there they go, all cursing, and here I don't. Fine prospects to 'em; they're on the road to heaven. Hold on hard! Jimmini, what a squall! But those chaps there are worse yet—they are your white squalls, they. White squalls? white whale, shirr! shirr! Here have I heard all their chat just now, and the white whale—shirr! shirr!—but spoken of once! and only this evening—it makes me jingle all over like my tambourine—that anaconda of an old man swore 'em in to hunt him! Oh, thou big white God aloft there somewhere in yon darkness, have mercy on this small black boy down here; preserve him from all men that have no bowels to feel fear!

* * *

Brit

STEERING north-eastward from the Crozetts, we fell in with vast meadows of brit, the minute, yellow substance, upon which the Right Whale largely feeds. For leagues and leagues it undulated round us, so that we seemed to be sailing through boundless fields of ripe and golden wheat.

On the second day, numbers of Right Whales were seen, who, secure from the attack of a Sperm Whaler like the Pequod, with open jaws sluggishly swam through the brit, which, adhering to the fringing fibres of that wondrous Venetian blind in their mouths, was in that manner separated from the water that escaped at the lip.

As morning mowers, who side by side slowly and seethingly advance their scythes through the long wet grass of marshy meads; even so these monsters swam, making a strange, grassy, cutting sound; and leaving behind them endless swaths of blue upon the yellow sea.*

But it was only the sound they made as they parted the brit which at all reminded one of mowers. Seen from the mast-heads, especially when they paused and were stationary for a while, their vast black forms looked more like lifeless masses of rock than anything else. And as in the great hunting countries of India, the stranger at a distance will sometimes pass on the plains recumbent elephants without knowing them to be such, taking them for bare, blackened elevations of the soil; even so, often, with him, who for the first time beholds this species of the leviathans of the sea. And even when recognised at last, their immense magnitude renders it very hard really to believe that such bulky masses of overgrowth can possibly be instinct, in all parts, with the same sort of life that lives in a dog or a horse.

Indeed, in other respects, you can hardly regard any creatures of the deep with the same feelings that you do those of the shore. For though some old naturalists have maintained that all creatures of the land are of their kind in the sea; and though taking a broad general view of the thing, this may very well be; yet coming to specialities, where, for example, does the ocean furnish any fish that in disposition answers to the sagacious kindness of the dog? The accursed shark alone

*That part of the sea known among whalemen as the "Brazil Banks" does not bear that name as the Banks of Newfoundland do, because of there being shallows and soundings there, but because of this remarkable meadow-like appearance, caused by the vast drifts of brit continually floating in those latitudes, where the Right Whale is often chased.

can in any generic respect be said to bear comparative analogy to him.

But though, to landsmen in general, the native inhabitants of the seas have ever been regarded with emotions unspeakably unsocial and repelling; though we know the sea to be an everlasting terra incognita, so that Columbus sailed over numberless unknown worlds to discover his one superficial western one; though, by vast odds, the most terrific of all mortal disasters have immemorially and indiscriminately befallen tens and hundreds of thousands of those who have gone upon the waters; though but a moment's consideration will teach, that however baby man may brag of his science and skill, and however much, in a flattering future, that science and skill may augment; yet for ever and for ever, to the crack of doom, the sea will insult and murder him, and pulverize the stateliest, stiffest frigate he can make; nevertheless, by the continual repetition of these very impressions, man has lost that sense of the full awfulness of the sea which aboriginally belongs to it.

The first boat we read of, floated on an ocean, that with Portuguese vengeance had whelmed a whole world without leaving so much as a widow. That same ocean rolls now; that same ocean destroyed the wrecked ships of last year. Yea, foolish mortals, Noah's flood is not yet subsided; two thirds of the fair world it yet covers.

Wherein differ the sea and the land, that a miracle upon one is not a miracle upon the other? Preternatural terrors rested upon the Hebrews, when under the feet of Korah and his company the live ground opened and swallowed them up for ever; yet not a modern sun ever sets, but in precisely the same manner the live sea swallows up ships and crews.

But not only is the sea such a foe to man who is an alien to it, but it is also a fiend to its own offspring; worse than the Persian host who murdered his own guests; sparing not the creatures which itself hath spawned. Like a savage tigress that tossing in the jungle overlays her own cubs, so the sea dashes even the mightiest whales against the rocks, and leaves them there side by side with the split wrecks of ships. No mercy, no power but its own controls it. Panting and snorting like a mad battle steed that has lost its rider, the masterless ocean overruns the globe.

Consider the subtleness of the sea; how its most dreaded creatures glide under water, unapparent for the most part, and treacherously hidden beneath the loveliest tints of azure. Consider also the devilish brilliance and beauty of many of its most remorseless tribes, as the dainty embellished shape of many species of sharks. Consider, once more, the universal cannibalism of the sea; all whose creatures prey upon each other, carrying on eternal war since the world began.

Consider all this; and then turn to this green, gentle, and most docile earth; consider them both, the sea and the land; and do you not find a strange analogy to something in yourself? For as this appalling ocean surrounds the verdant land, so in the soul of man there lies one insular Tahiti, full of peace and joy, but encompassed by all the horrors of the half known life. God keep thee! Push not off from that isle, thou canst never return!

* * *

The Grand Armada

THE long and narrow peninsula of Malacca, extending south-eastward from the territories of Birmah, forms the most southerly point of all Asia. In a continuous line from that peninsula stretch the long islands of Sumatra, Java, Bally, and Timor; which, with many others, form a vast mole, or rampart, lengthwise connecting Asia with Australia, and dividing the long unbroken Indian ocean from the thickly studded oriental archipelagoes. This rampart is pierced by several sally-ports for the convenience of ships and whales; conspicuous among which are the straits of Sunda and Malacca. By the straits of Sunda, chiefly, vessels bound to China from the west, emerge into the China seas.

Those narrow straits of Sunda divide Sumatra from Java; and standing midway in that vast rampart of islands, buttressed by that bold green promontory, known to seamen as Java Head; they not a little correspond to the central gateway opening into some vast walled empire: and considering the inexhaustible wealth of spices, and silks, and jewels, and gold, and ivory, with which the thousand islands of that oriental sea are enriched, it seems a significant provision of nature, that such treasures, by the very formation of the land, should at least bear the appearance, however ineffectual, of being guarded from the all-grasping western world. The shores of the Straits of Sunda are unsupplied with those domineering fortresses which guard the entrances to the Mediterranean, the Baltic, and the Propontis. Unlike the Danes, these Orientals do not demand the obsequious homage of lowered top-sails from the endless procession of ships before the wind, which for centuries past, by night and by day, have passed between the islands of Sumatra and Java, freighted with the costliest cargoes of the east. But while they freely waive a ceremonial like this, they do by no means renounce their claim to more solid tribute.

Time out of mind the piratical proas of the Malays, lurking among the low shaded coves and islets of Sumatra, have sallied out upon the vessels sailing through the straits, fiercely demanding tribute at the point of their spears. Though by the repeated bloody chastisements they have received at the hands of European cruisers, the audacity of these corsairs has of late been somewhat repressed; yet, even at the present day, we occasionally hear of English and American vessels, which, in those waters, have been remorselessly boarded and pillaged.

With a fair, fresh wind, the Pequod was now drawing nigh to these straits; Ahab purposing to pass through them into the Javan sea, and thence, cruising northwards, over waters known to be frequented here and there by the Sperm Whale, sweep inshore by the Philippine Islands, and gain the far coast of Japan, in time for the great whaling season there. By these means, the circumnavigating Pequod would sweep almost all the known Sperm Whale cruising grounds of the world, previous to descending upon the Line in the Pacific; where Ahab, though everywhere else foiled in his pursuit, firmly counted upon giving battle to Moby Dick, in the sea he was most known to frequent; and at a season when he might most reasonably be presumed to be haunting it.

But how now? in this zoned quest, does Ahab touch no land? does his crew drink air? Surely, he will stop for water. Nay. For a long time, now, the circus-running sun has raced within his fiery ring, and needs no sustenance but what's in himself. So Ahab. Mark this, too, in the whaler. While other hulls are loaded down with alien stuff, to be transferred to foreign wharves; the world-wandering whale-ship carries no cargo but herself and crew, their weapons and their wants. She has a whole lake's contents bottled in her ample hold. She is ballasted with utilities; not altogether with unusable pig-lead and kentledge. She carries years' water in her. Clear old prime Nantucket water; which, when three years afloat, the Nantucketer, in the Pacific, prefers to drink before the brackish fluid, but yesterday rafted off in casks, from the Peruvian or Indian streams. Hence it is, that, while other ships may have gone to China from New York, and back again, touching at a score of ports, the whale-ship, in all that interval, may not have sighted one grain of soil; her crew having seen no man but floating seamen like themselves. So that did you carry them the news that another flood had come; they would only answer—"Well, boys, here's the ark!"

Now, as many Sperm Whales had been captured off the western coast of Java, in the near vicinity of the Straits of Sunda; indeed, as most of the ground, roundabout, was generally recognised by the fishermen as an excellent spot for cruising; therefore, as the Pequod gained more and more upon Java Head, the look-outs were repeatedly hailed, and admonished to keep wide awake. But though the green palmy cliffs of the land soon loomed on the starboard bow, and with delighted nostrils the fresh cinnamon was snuffed in the air, yet not a single jet was descried. Almost renouncing all thought of falling in with any game hereabouts, the ship had well nigh entered the straits, when the customary cheering cry was heard from aloft, and ere long a spectacle of singular magnificence saluted us.

But here be it premised, that owing to the unwearied activity with which of late they have been hunted over all four oceans, the Sperm Whales, instead of almost invariably sailing in small detached companies, as in former times, are now frequently met with in extensive herds, sometimes embracing so great a multitude, that it would almost seem as if numerous nations of them had sworn solemn league and covenant for mutual assistance and protection. To this aggregation of the Sperm Whale into such immense caravans, may be imputed the circumstance that even in the best cruising grounds, you may now sometimes sail for weeks and months together, without being greeted by a single spout; and then be suddenly saluted by what sometimes seems thousands on thousands.

Broad on both bows, at the distance of some two or three miles, and forming a great semicircle, embracing one half of the level horizon, a continuous chain of whale-jets were up-playing and sparkling in the noon-day air. Unlike the straight perpendicular twin-jets of the Right Whale, which, dividing at top, fall over in two branches, like the cleft drooping boughs of a willow, the single forward-slanting spout of the Sperm Whale presents a thick curled bush of white mist, continually rising and falling away to leeward.

Seen from the Pequod's deck, then, as she would rise on a high hill of the sea, this host of vapory spouts, individually curling up into the air, and beheld through a blending atmosphere of bluish haze, showed like the thousand cheerful chimneys of some dense metropolis, descried of a balmy autumnal morning, by some horseman on a height.

As marching armies approaching an unfriendly defile in the mountains, accelerate their march, all eagerness to place that perilous passage in their rear, and once more expand in comparative security upon the plain; even so did this vast fleet of whales now seem hurrying forward through the straits; gradually contracting the wings of their semicircle, and swimming on, in one solid, but still crescentic centre.

Crowding all sail the Pequod pressed after them; the harpooneers handling their weapons, and loudly cheering from the heads of their yet suspended boats. If the wind only held, little doubt had they, that chased through these Straits of Sunda, the vast host would only deploy into the Oriental seas to witness the capture of not a few of their number. And who could tell whether, in that congregated caravan, Moby Dick himself might not temporarily be swimming, like the worshipped white-elephant in the coronation procession of the Siamese! So with stun-sail piled on stun-sail, we sailed along, driving these leviathans before us; when, of a sudden, the voice of Tashtego was heard, loudly directing attention to something in our wake.

Corresponding to the crescent in our van, we beheld another in our rear. It seemed formed of detached white vapors, rising and falling something like the spouts of the whales; only they did not so completely come and go; for they constantly hovered, without finally disappearing. Levelling his glass at this sight, Ahab quickly revolved in his pivot-hole, crying, "Aloft there, and rig whips and buckets to wet the sails;—Malays, sir, and after us!"

As if too long lurking behind the headlands, till the Pequod should fairly have entered the straits, these rascally Asiatics were now in hot pursuit, to make up for their over-cautious delay. But when the swift Pequod, with a fresh leading wind, was herself in hot chase; how very kind of these tawny philanthropists to assist in speeding her on to her own chosen pursuit,—mere riding-whips and rowels to her, that they were. As with glass under arm, Ahab to-and-fro paced the deck; in his forward turn beholding the monsters he chased, and in the after one the bloodthirsty pirates chasing *him*; some such fancy as the above seemed his. And when he glanced upon the green walls of the watery defile in which the ship was then sailing, and bethought him that through that gate lay the route to his vengeance, and beheld, how that through that same gate he was now both chasing and being chased to his deadly end; and not only that, but a herd of remorseless wild pirates and inhuman atheistical devils were infernally cheering him on with their curses;—when all these conceits had passed through his brain, Ahab's brow was left gaunt and ribbed, like the black sand beach after some stormy tide has been gnawing it, without being able to drag the firm thing from its place.

But thoughts like these troubled very few of the reckless crew; and when, after steadily dropping and dropping the pirates astern, the Pequod at last shot by the vivid green Cockatoo Point on the Sumatra side, emerging at last upon the broad waters beyond; then, the harpooneers seemed more to grieve that the swift whales had been gaining upon the ship, than to rejoice that the ship had so victoriously gained upon the Malays. But still driving on in the wake of the whales, at length they seemed abating their speed; gradually the ship neared them; and the wind now dying away, word was passed to spring to the boats. But no sooner did the herd, by some presumed wonderful instinct of the Sperm Whale, become notified of the three keels that were after them,—though as yet a mile in their rear,—than they rallied again, and forming in close ranks and battalions, so that their spouts all looked like flashing lines of stacked bayonets, moved on with redoubled velocity.

Stripped to our shirts and drawers, we sprang to the white-ash, and after several hours' pulling were almost disposed to renounce the chase, when a general pausing commotion among the whales gave animating token that they were now at last under the influence of that strange perplexity of inert irresolution, which, when the fishermen perceive it in the whale, they say he is *gallied*.* The compact martial columns in which they had been hitherto rapidly and steadily swimming, were now broken up in one measureless rout; and like King Porus' elephants in the Indian battle with Alexander, they

*To *gally*, or *gallow*, is to frighten excessively,—to confound with fright. It is an old Saxon word. It occurs once in Shakspere:—

"The wrathful skies
Gallow the very wanderers of the dark,
And make them keep their caves."
Lear, Act III. sc. ii.

To common land usages, the word is now completely obsolete. When the polite landsman first hears it from the gaunt Nantucketer, he is apt to set it down as one of the whaleman's self-derived savageries. Much the same is it with many other sinewy Saxonisms of this sort, which emigrated to the New-England rocks with the noble brawn of the old English emigrants in the time of the Commonwealth. Thus, some of the best and furthest-descended English words—the etymological Howards and Percys—are now democratised, nay, plebeianised—so to speak—in the New World.

seemed going mad with consternation. In all directions expanding in vast irregular circles, and aimlessly swimming hither and thither, by their short thick spoutings, they plainly betrayed their distraction of panic. This was still more strangely evinced by those of their number, who, completely paralysed as it were, helplessly floated like water-logged dismantled ships on the sea. Had these leviathans been but a flock of simple sheep, pursued over the pasture by three fierce wolves, they could not possibly have evinced such excessive dismay. But this occasional timidity is characteristic of almost all herding creatures. Though banding together in tens of thousands, the lion-maned buffaloes of the West have fled before a solitary horseman. Witness, too, all human beings, how when herded together in the sheepfold of a theatre's pit, they will, at the slightest alarm of fire, rush helter-skelter for the outlets, crowding, trampling, jamming, and remorselessly dashing each other to death. Best, therefore, withhold any amazement at the strangely gallied whales before us, for there is no folly of the beasts of the earth which is not infinitely outdone by the madness of men.

Though many of the whales, as has been said, were in violent motion, yet it is to be observed that as a whole the herd neither advanced nor retreated, but collectively remained in one place. As is customary in those cases, the boats at once separated, each making for some one lone whale on the outskirts of the shoal. In about three minutes' time, Queequeg's harpoon was flung; the stricken fish darted blinding spray in our faces, and then running away with us like light, steered straight for the heart of the herd. Though such a movement on the part of the whale struck under such circumstances, is in no wise unprecedented; and indeed is almost always more or less anticipated; yet does it present one of the more perilous vicissitudes of the fishery. For as the swift monster drags you deeper and deeper into the frantic shoal, you bid adieu to circumspect life and only exist in a delirious throb.

As, blind and deaf, the whale plunged forward, as if by sheer power of speed to rid himself of the iron leech that had fastened to him; as we thus tore a white gash in the sea, on all sides menaced as we flew, by the crazed creatures to and fro rushing about us; our beset boat was like a ship mobbed by ice-isles in a tempest, and striving to steer through their complicated channels and straits, knowing not at what moment it may be locked in and crushed.

But not a bit daunted, Queequeg steered us manfully; now sheering off from this monster directly across our route in advance; now edging away from that, whose colossal flukes were suspended overhead, while all the time, Starbuck stood up in the bows, lance in hand, pricking out of our way whatever whales he could reach by short darts, for there was no time to make long ones. Nor were the oarsmen quite idle, though their wonted duty was now altogether dispensed with. They chiefly attended to the shouting part of the business. "Out of the way, Commodore!" cried one, to a great dromedary that of a sudden rose bodily to the surface, and for an instant threatened to swamp us. "Hard down with your tail, there!" cried a second to another, which, close to our gunwale, seemed calmly cooling himself with his own fan-like extremity.

All whaleboats carry certain curious contrivances, originally invented by the Nantucket Indians, called druggs. Two thick squares of wood of equal size are stoutly clenched together, so that they cross each other's grain at right angles; a line of considerable length is then attached to the middle of this block, and the other end of the line being looped, it can in a moment be fastened to a harpoon. It is chiefly among gallied whales that this drugg is used. For then, more whales are close round you than you can possibly chase at one time. But sperm whales are not every day encountered; while you may, then, you must kill all you can. And if you cannot kill them all at once, you must wing them, so that they can be afterwards killed at your leisure. Hence it is, that at times like these the drugg comes into requisition. Our boat was furnished with three of them. The first and second were successfully darted, and we saw the whales staggeringly running off, fettered by the enormous sidelong resistance of the towing drugg. They were cramped like malefactors with the chain and ball. But upon flinging the third, in the act of tossing overboard the clumsy wooden block, it caught under one of the seats of the boat, and in an instant tore it out and carried it away, dropping the oarsman in the boat's bottom as the seat slid from under him. On both sides the sea came in at the wounded planks, but we stuffed two or three drawers and shirts in, and so stopped the leaks for the time.

It had been next to impossible to dart these drugged-harpoons, were it not that as we advanced into the herd, our whale's way greatly diminished; moreover, that as we went still further and further from the circumference of commotion, the direful disorders seemed waning. So that when at last the jerking harpoon drew out, and the towing whale sideways vanished; then, with the tapering force of his parting momentum, we glided between two whales into the innermost heart of the shoal, as if from some mountain torrent we had slid into a serene valley lake. Here the storms in the roaring glens between the outermost whales, were heard but not felt. In this central expanse the sea presented that smooth satin-like surface, called a sleek, produced by the subtle moisture thrown off by the whale in his more quiet moods. Yes, we were now in that enchanted calm which they say lurks at the heart of every commotion. And still in the distracted distance we beheld the tumults of the outer concentric circles, and saw successive pods of whales, eight or ten in each, swiftly going round and round, like multiplied spans of horses in a ring; and so closely shoulder to shoulder, that a Titanic circus-rider might easily have overarched the middle ones, and so have gone round on their backs. Owing to the density of the crowd of reposing whales, more immediately surrounding the embayed axis of the herd, no possible chance of escape was at present afforded us. We must watch for a breach in the living wall that hemmed us in; the wall that had only admitted us in order to shut us up. Keeping at the centre of the lake, we were occasionally visited by small tame cows and calves; the women and children of this routed host.

Now, inclusive of the occasional wide intervals between the revolving outer circles, and inclusive of the spaces between the various pods in any one of those circles, the entire area at this juncture, embraced by the whole multitude, must have contained at least two or three square miles. At any rate—though indeed such a test at such a time might be deceptive—spoutings might be discovered from our low boat that seemed playing up almost from the rim of the horizon. I mention this circumstance, because, as if the cows and calves had been purposely locked up in this innermost fold; and as if the wide extent of the herd had hitherto prevented them from learning the precise cause of its stopping; or, possibly, being so young, unsophisticated, and every way innocent and inexperienced; however it may have been, these smaller whales—now and then visiting our becalmed boat from the margin of the lake—evinced a wondrous fearlessness and confidence, or else a still, becharmed panic which it was impossible not to marvel at. Like household dogs they came snuffling round us, right up to our gunwales, and touching them; till it almost seemed that some spell had suddenly domesticated them. Queequeg patted their foreheads; Starbuck scratched their backs with his lance; but fearful of the consequences, for the time refrained from darting it.

But far beneath this wondrous world upon the surface, another and still stranger world met our eyes as we gazed over the side. For, suspended in those watery vaults, floated the forms of the nursing mothers of the whales, and those that by their enormous girth seemed shortly to become mothers. The lake, as I have hinted, was to a considerable depth exceedingly transparent; and as human infants while suckling will calmly and fixedly gaze away from the breast, as if leading two different lives at the time; and while yet drawing mortal nourishment, be still spiritually feasting upon some unearthly reminiscence;—even so did the young of these whales seem looking up towards us, but not at us, as if we were but a bit of Gulf-weed in their new-born sight. Floating on their sides, the mothers also seemed quietly eyeing us. One of these little infants, that from certain queer tokens seemed hardly a day old, might have measured some fourteen feet in length, and some six feet in girth. He was a little frisky; though as yet his body seemed scarce yet recovered from that irksome position it had so lately occupied in the maternal reticule; where, tail to head, and all ready for the final spring, the unborn whale lies bent like a Tartar's bow. The delicate side-fins, and the palms of his flukes, still freshly retained the plaited crumpled appearance of a baby's ears newly arrived from foreign parts.

"Line! line!" cried Queequeg, looking over the gunwale; "him fast! him fast!—Who line him! Who struck?—Two whale; one big, one little!"

"What ails ye, man?" cried Starbuck.

"Look-e here," said Queequeg pointing down.

As when the stricken whale, that from the tub has reeled out hundreds of fathoms of rope; as, after deep sounding, he floats up again, and shows the slackened curling line buoyantly rising and spiralling towards the air; so now, Starbuck saw long coils of the umbilical cord of Madame Leviathan, by which the young cub seemed still tethered to its dam. Not seldom in the rapid vicissitudes of the chase, this natural line, with the maternal end loose, becomes entangled with the hempen one, so that the cub is thereby trapped. Some of the subtlest secrets of the seas seemed divulged to us in this enchanted pond. We saw young Leviathan amours in the deep.*

And thus, though surrounded by circle upon circle of consternations and affrights, did these inscrutable creatures at the centre freely and fearlessly indulge in all peaceful concernments; yea, serenely revelled in dalliance and delight. But even so, amid the tornadoed Atlantic of my being, do I myself still for ever centrally disport in mute calm; and while ponderous planets of unwaning woe revolve round me, deep down and deep inland there I still bathe me in eternal mildness of joy.

*The sperm whale, as with all other species of the Leviathan, but unlike most other fish, breeds indifferently at all seasons; after a gestation which may probably be set down at nine months, producing but one at a time; though in some few known instances giving birth to an Esau and Jacob:—a contingency provided for in suckling by two teats, curiously situated, one on each side of the anus; but the breasts themselves extend upwards from that. When by chance these precious parts in a nursing whale are cut by the hunter's lance, the mother's pouring milk and blood rivallingly discolor the sea for rods. The milk is very sweet and rich; it has been tasted by man; it might do well with strawberries. When overflowing with mutual esteem, the whales salute *more hominum*.

Meanwhile, as we thus lay entranced, the occasional sudden frantic spectacles in the distance evinced the activity of the other boats, still engaged in drugging the whales on the frontier of the host; or possibly carrying on the war within the first circle, where abundance of room and some convenient retreats were afforded them. But the sight of the enraged drugged whales now and then blindly darting to and fro across the circles, was nothing to what at last met our eyes. It is sometimes the custom when fast to a whale more than commonly powerful and alert, to seek to hamstring him, as it were, by sundering or maiming his gigantic tail-tendon. It is done by darting a short-handled cutting-spade, to which is attached a rope for hauling it back again. A whale wounded (as we afterwards learned) in this part, but not effectually, as it seemed, had broken away from the boat, carrying along with him half of the harpoon line; and in the extraordinary agony of the wound, he was now dashing among the revolving circles like the lone mounted desperado Arnold, at the battle of Saratoga, carrying dismay wherever he went.

But agonizing as was the wound of this whale, and an appalling spectacle enough, any way; yet the peculiar horror with which he seemed to inspire the rest of the herd, was owing to a cause which at first the intervening distance obscured from us. But at length we perceived that by one of the unimaginable accidents of the fishery, this whale had become entangled in the harpoon-line that he towed; he had also run away with the cutting spade in him; and while the free end of the rope attached to that weapon, had permanently caught in the coils of the harpoon-line round his tail, the cutting-spade itself had worked loose from his flesh. So that tormented to madness, he was now churning through the water, violently flailing with his flexible tail, and tossing the keen spade about him, wounding and murdering his own comrades.

This terrific object seemed to recall the whole herd from their stationary fright. First, the whales forming the margin of our lake began to crowd a little, and tumble against each other, as if lifted by half spent billows from afar; then the lake itself began faintly to heave and swell; the submarine bridal-chambers and nurseries vanished; in more and more contracting orbits the whales in the more central circles began to swim in thickening clusters. Yes, the long calm was departing. A low advancing hum was soon heard; and then like to the tumultuous masses of block-ice when the great river Hudson breaks up in Spring, the entire host of whales came tumbling upon their inner centre, as if to pile themselves up in one common mountain. Instantly Starbuck and Queequeg changed places; Starbuck taking the stern.

"Oars! Oars!" he intensely whispered, seizing the helm—"gripe your oars, and clutch your souls, now! My God, men, stand by! Shove him off, you Queequeg—the whale there!—prick him!—hit him! Stand up—stand up, and stay so! Spring, men—pull, men; never mind their backs—scrape them!—scrape away!"

The boat was now all but jammed between two vast black bulks, leaving a narrow Dardanelles between their long lengths. But by desperate endeavor we at last shot into a temporary opening; then giving way rapidly, and at the same time earnestly watching for another outlet. After many similar hair-breadth escapes, we at last swiftly glided into what had just been one of the outer circles, but now crossed by random whales, all violently making for one centre. This lucky salvation was cheaply purchased by the loss of Queequeg's hat, who, while standing in the bows to prick the fugitive whales, had his hat taken clean from his head by the air-eddy made by the sudden tossing of a pair of broad flukes close by.

Riotous and disordered as the universal commotion now was, it soon resolved itself into what seemed a systematic movement; for having clumped together at last in one dense body, they then renewed their onward flight with augmented fleetness. Further pursuit was useless; but the boats still lingered in their wake to pick up what drugged whales might be dropped astern, and likewise to secure one which Flask had killed and waifed. The waif is a pennoned pole, two or three of which are carried by every boat; and which, when additional game is at hand, are inserted upright into the floating body of a dead whale, both to mark its place on the sea, and also as token of prior possession, should the boats of any other ship draw near.

The result of this lowering was somewhat illustrative of that sagacious saying in the Fishery,—the more whales the less fish. Of all the drugged whales only one was captured. The rest contrived to escape for the time, but only to be taken, as will hereafter be seen, by some other craft than the Pequod.

from *Israel Potter*

They Fight the Serapis

THE battle between the Bon Homme Richard and the Serapis stands in history as the first signal collision on the sea between the Englishman and the American. For obstinacy, mutual hatred, and courage, it is without precedent or subsequent in the story of ocean. The strife long hung undetermined, but the English flag struck in the end.

There would seem to be something singularly indicatory in this engagement. It may involve at once a type, a parallel, and a prophecy. Sharing the same blood with England, and yet her proved foe in two wars; not wholly inclined at bottom to forget an old grudge: intrepid, unprincipled, reckless, predatory, with boundless ambition, civilized in externals but a savage at heart, America is, or may yet be, the Paul Jones of nations.

Regarded in this indicatory light, the battle between the Bon Homme Richard and the Serapis—in itself so curious—may well enlist our interest.

Never was there a fight so snarled. The intricacy of those incidents which defy the narrator's extrication, is not ill figured in that bewildering intertanglement of all the yards and anchors of the two ships, which confounded them for the time in one chaos of devastation.

Elsewhere than here the reader must go who seeks an elaborate version of the fight, or, indeed, much of any regular account of it whatever. The writer is but brought to mention the battle, because he must needs follow, in all events, the fortunes of the humble adventurer whose life he records. Yet this necessarily involves some general view of each conspicuous incident in which he shares.

Several circumstances of the place and time served to invest the fight with a certain scenic atmosphere, casting a light almost poetic over the wild gloom of its tragic results. The battle was fought between the hours of seven and ten at night; the height of it was under a full harvest moon, in view of thousands of distant spectators crowding the high cliffs of Yorkshire.

From the Tees to the Humber, the eastern coast of Britain, for the most part, wears a savage, melancholy, and Calabrian aspect. It is in course of incessant decay. Every year the isle which repulses nearly all other foes, succumbs to the Attila assaults of the deep. Here and there the base of the cliffs is strewn with masses of rock, undermined by the waves, and tumbled headlong below; where, sometimes, the water completely surrounds them, showing in shattered confusion detached rocks, pyramids, and obelisks, rising half-revealed from the surf,—the Tadmores of the wasteful desert of the sea. Nowhere is this desolation more marked than for those fifty miles of coast between Flamborough Head and the Spurn.

Weathering out the gale which had driven them from Leith, Paul's ships, for a few days, were employed in giving chase to various merchantmen and colliers; capturing some, sinking others, and putting the rest to flight. Off the mouth of the Humber they ineffectually manœuvered with a view of drawing out a king's frigate, reported to be lying at anchor within. At another time a large fleet was encountered, under convoy of some ships of force. But their panic caused the fleet to hug the edge of perilous shoals very nigh the land, where, by reason of his having no competent pilot, Paul durst not approach to molest them. The same night he saw two strangers further out at sea, and chased them until three in the morning; when, getting pretty nigh, he surmised that they must needs be vessels of his own squadron, which, previous to his entering the Firth of Forth, had separated from his command. Daylight proved this supposition correct. Five vessels of the original squadron were now once more in company. About noon, a fleet of forty merchantmen appeared coming round Flamborough Head, protected by two English men-of-war, the Serapis and Countess of Scarborough. Descrying the five cruisers sailing down, the forty sail, like forty chickens, fluttered in a panic under the wing of the shore. Their armed protectors bravely steered from the land, making the disposition for battle. Promptly accepting the challenge, Paul, giving the signal to his consorts, earnestly pressed forward. But, earnest as he was, it was seven in the evening ere the encounter began. Meantime his comrades, heedless of his signals, sailed independently along. Dismissing them from present consideration, we confine ourselves, for a while to the Richard and the Serapis, the grand duellists of the fight.

The Richard carried a motley crew, to keep whom in order one hundred and thirty-five soldiers—themselves a hybrid band—had been put on board, commanded by French officers of inferior rank. Her armament was similarly heterogeneous; guns of all sorts and calibres; but about equal on the whole to those of a thirty-two gun frigate. The spirit of baneful intermixture pervaded this craft throughout.

The Serapis was a frigate of fifty guns, more than half of which individually exceeded in calibre any one gun of the Richard. She had a crew of some three hundred and twenty trained man-of-war's men.

There is something in a naval engagement which radically distinguishes it from one on the land. The ocean, at times, has what is called its *sea* and its *trough of the sea*; but it has neither rivers, woods, banks, towns, nor mountains. In mild weather, it is one hammered plain. Stratagems,—like those of disciplined armies, ambuscades—like those of Indians, are impossible. All is clear, open, fluent. The very element which sustains the combatants, yields at the stroke of a feather. One wind and one tide at one time operate upon all who here engage. This simplicity renders a battle between two men-of-war, with their huge white wings, more akin to the Miltonic contests of archangels than to *the comparatively squalid* tussels of earth.

As the ships neared, a hazy darkness overspread the water. The moon was not yet risen. Objects were perceived with difficulty. Borne by a soft moist breeze over gentle waves, they came within pistol-shot. Owing to the obscurity, and the known neighborhood of other vessels, the Serapis was uncertain who the Richard was. Through the dim mist each ship loomed forth to the other vast, but indistinct, as the ghost of Morven. Sounds of the trampling of resolute men echoed from either hull, whose tight decks dully resounded like drum-heads in a funeral march.

The Serapis hailed. She was answered by a broadside. For half an hour the combatants deliberately manœuvered, continually changing their position, but always within shot fire. The Serapis—the better sailer of the two—kept critically circling the Richard, making lounging advances now and then, and as suddenly steering off; hate causing her to act not unlike a wheeling cock about a hen, when stirred by the contrary passion. Meantime, though within easy speaking distance, no further syllable was exchanged; but an incessant cannonade was kept up.

At this point, a third party, the Scarborough, drew near, seemingly desirous of giving assistance to her consort. But thick smoke was now added to the night's natural obscurity. The Scarborough imperfectly discerned two ships, and plainly saw the common fire they made; but which was which, she could not tell. Eager to befriend the Serapis, she durst not fire a gun, lest she might unwittingly act the part of a foe. As when a hawk and a crow are clawing and beaking high in the air, a second crow flying near, will seek to join the battle, but finding no fair chance to engage, at last flies away to the woods; just so did the Scarborough now. Prudence dictated the step. Because several chance shot—from which of the combatants could not be known—had already struck the Scarborough. So, unwilling uselessly to expose herself, off went for the present this baffled and ineffectual friend.

Not long after, an invisible hand came and set down a great yellow lamp in the east. The hand reached up unseen from below the horizon, and set the lamp down right on the rim of the horizon, as on a threshold; as much as to say, Gentlemen warriors, permit me a little to light up this rather gloomy looking subject. The lamp was the round harvest moon; the one solitary foot-light of the scene. But scarcely did the rays from the lamp pierce that languid haze. Objects before perceived with difficulty, now glimmered ambiguously. Bedded in strange vapors, the great foot-light cast a dubious half demoniac glare across the waters, like the phantasmagoric stream sent athwart a London flagging in a night-rain from an apothecary's blue and green window. Through this sardonical mist, the face of the Man-in-the-Moon—looking right towards the combatants, as if he were standing in a trap-door of the sea, leaning forward leisurely with his arms complacently folded over upon the edge of the horizon,—this queer face wore a serious, apishly self-satisfied leer, as if the Man-in-the-Moon had somehow secretly put up the ships to their contest, and in the depths of his malignant old soul was not unpleased to see how well his charms worked. There stood the grinning Man-in-the-Moon, his head just dodging into view over the rim of the sea:—Mephistopheles prompter of the stage.

Aided now a little by the planet, one of the consorts of the Richard, the Pallas, hovering far outside the fight, dimly discerned the suspicious form of a lonely vessel unknown to her. She resolved to engage it, if it proved a foe. But ere they joined, the unknown ship—which proved to be the Scarborough—received a broadside at long gun's distance from another consort of the Richard, the Alliance. The shot whizzed across the broad interval like shuttlecocks across a great hall. Presently the battledores of both batteries were at work, and rapid compliments of shuttlecocks were very promptly exchanged. The adverse consorts of the two main belligerents fought with all the rage of those fiery seconds who in some desperate duels, make their principal's quarrel their own. Diverted from the Richard and the Serapis by this little by-play, the Man-in-the-Moon, all eager to see what it was, somewhat raised himself from his trap-door with an added grin on his face. By this time, off sneaked the Alliance, and down swept the Pallas, at close quarters engaging the Scarborough; an encounter destined in less than an hour to end in the latter ship's striking her flag.

Compared to the Serapis and the Richard, the Pallas and the Scarborough were as two pages to two knights. In their immature way they showed the same traits as their fully developed superiors.

The Man-in-the-Moon now raised himself still higher to obtain a better view of affairs.

But the Man-in-the-Moon was not the only spectator. From the high cliffs of the shore, and especially from the great promontory of Flamborough Head, the scene was witnessed by crowds of the islanders. Any rustic might be pardoned his curiosity in view of the spectacle presented. Far in the indistinct distance fleets of frightened merchantmen filled the lower air with their sails, as flakes of snow in a snow-storm by night. Hovering undeterminedly, in another direction, were several of the scattered consorts of Paul, taking no part in the fray. Nearer, was an isolated mist, investing the Pallas and Scarborough—a mist slowly adrift on the sea, like a floating isle, and at intervals irradiated with sparkles of fire and resonant with the boom of cannon. Further away, in the deeper water, was a lurid cloud, incessantly torn in shreds of lightning, then fusing together again, once more to be rent. As yet this lurid cloud was neither stationary nor slowly adrift, like the first mentioned one; but, instinct with chaotic vitality, shifted hither and thither, foaming with fire, like a valiant water-spout careering off the coast of Malabar.

To get some idea of the events enacting in that cloud, it will be necessary to enter it; to go and possess it, as a ghost may rush into a body, or the devils into the swine, which running down the steep place perished in the sea; just as the Richard is yet to do.

Thus far the Serapis and the Richard had been manœuvering and chasseing to each other like partners in a cotillon, all the time indulging in rapid repartee.

But finding at last that the superior managableness of the enemy's ship enabled him to get the better of the clumsy old Indiaman, the Richard, in taking position; Paul, with his wonted resolution, at once sought to neutralize this, by hugging him close. But the attempt to lay the Richard right across the head of the Serapis ended quite otherwise, in sending the enemy's jib-boom just over the Richard's great tower of Pisa, where Israel was stationed; who catching it eagerly, stood for an instant holding to the slack of the sail, like one grasping a horse by the mane prior to vaulting into the saddle.

"Aye, hold hard, lad," cried Paul, springing to his side with a coil of rigging. With a few rapid turns he knitted himself to his foe. The wind now acting on the sails of the Serapis forced her, heel and point, her entire length, check by jowl, alongside the Richard. The projecting cannon scraped; the yards interlocked; but the hulls did not touch. A long lane of darkling water lay wedged between, like that narrow canal in Venice which dozes between two shadowy piles, and high in air is secretly crossed by the Bridge of Sighs. But where the six yard-arms reciprocally arched overhead, three bridges of sighs were both seen and heard, as the moon and wind kept rising.

Into that Lethean canal,—pond-like in its smoothness as compared with the sea without—fell many a poor soul that night;—fell, for ever forgotten.

As some heaving rent coinciding with a disputed frontier on a volcanic plain, that boundary abyss was the jaws of death to both sides. So contracted was it, that in many cases the gun-rammers had to be thrust into the opposite ports, in order to enter to muzzles of their own cannon. It seemed more an intestine feud, than a fight between strangers. Or, rather, it was as if the Siamese Twins, oblivious of their fraternal bond, should rage in unnatural fight.

Ere long, a horrible explosion was heard, drowning for the instant the cannonade. Two of the old eighteen-pounders—before spoken of, as having been hurriedly set up below the main deck of the Richard—burst all to pieces, killing the sailors who worked them, and shattering all that part of the hull, as if two exploded steam-boilers had shot out of its opposite sides. The effect was like the fall of the walls of a house. Little now upheld the great tower of Pisa but a few naked crow stanchions. Thenceforth, not a few balls from the

Serapis must have passed straight through the Richard without grazing her. It was like firing buck-shot through the ribs of a skeleton.

But, further forward, so deadly was the broadside from the heavy batteries of the Serapis,—levelled point-blank, and right down the throat and bowels, as it were, of the Richard—that it cleared everything before it. The men on the Richard's covered gun-deck ran above, like miners from the fire-damp. Collecting on the forecastle, they continued to fight with grenades and muskets. The soldiers also were in the lofty tops, whence they kept up incessant volleys, cascading their fire down as pouring lava from cliffs.

The position of the men in the two ships was now exactly reversed. For while the Serapis was tearing the Richard all to pieces below deck, and had swept that covered part almost of the last man; the Richard's crowd of musketry had complete control of the upper deck of the Serapis, where it was almost impossible for a man to remain unless as a corpse. Though in the beginning, the tops of the Serapis had not been unsupplied with marksmen, yet they had long since been cleared by the overmastering musketry of the Richard. Several, with leg or arm broken by a ball, had been seen going dimly downward from their giddy perch, like falling pigeons shot on the wing.

As busy swallows about barn-eaves and ridge-poles, some of the Richard's marksmen quitting their tops, now went far out on their yard-arms, where they overhung the Serapis. From thence they dropped hand-grenades upon her decks, like apples, which growing in one field fall over the fence into another. Others of their band flung the same sour fruit into the open ports of the Serapis. A hail-storm of aerial combustion descended and slanted on the Serapis, while horizontal thunder-bolts rolled crosswise through the subterranean vaults of the Richard. The belligerents were no longer, in the ordinary sense of things, an English ship, and an American ship. It was a co-partnership and joint-stock combustion-company of both ships; yet divided, even in participation. The two vessels were as two houses, through whose party-wall doors have been cut; one family (the Guelphs) occupying the whole lower story; another family (the Ghibelines) the whole upper story.

Meanwhile determined Paul flew hither and thither like the meteoric corposant-ball, which shiftingly dances on the tips and verges of ships' rigging in storms. Wherever he went, he seemed to cast a pale light on all faces. Blacked and burnt, his Scotch bonnet was compressed to a gun-wad on his head. His Parisian coat, with its gold-laced sleeve laid aside, disclosed to the full the blue tatooing on his arm, which sometimes in fierce gestures streamed in the haze of the cannonade, cabalistically terrific as the charmed standard of Satan. Yet his frenzied manner was less a testimony of his internal commotion than intended to inspirit and madden his men, some of whom seeing him, in transports of intrepidity stripped themselves to their trowsers, exposing their naked bodies to the as naked shot. The same was done on the Serapis, where several guns were seen surrounded by their buff crews as by fauns and satyrs.

At the beginning of the fray, before the ships interlocked, in the intervals of smoke which swept over the ships as mist over mountain-tops, affording open rents here and there—the gun-deck of the Serapis, at certain points, showed, congealed for the instant in all attitudes of dauntlessness, a gallery of marble statues—fighting gladiators.

Stooping low and intent, with one braced leg thrust behind, and one arm thrust forward, curling round towards the muzzle of the gun:—there was seen the *loader*, performing his allotted part; on the other side of the carriage, in the same stooping posture, but with both hands holding his long black pole, pike-wise, ready for instant use—stood the eager *rammer and sponger*; while at the breech, crouched the wary *captain of the gun*, his keen eye, like the watching leopard's, burning along the range; and behind, all tall and erect, the Egyptian symbol of death, stood the *matchman*, immovable for the moment, his long-handled match reversed. Up to their two long death-dealing batteries, the trained men of the Serapis stood and toiled in mechanical magic of discipline. They tended those rows of guns, as Lowell girls the rows of looms in a cotton factory. The Parcæ were not more methodical;

Atropos not more fatal; the automaton chess-player not more irresponsible.

"Look, lad; I want a grenade, now, thrown down their main hatch-way. I saw long piles of cartridges there. The powder monkeys have brought them up faster than they can be used. Take a bucket of combustibles, and let's hear from you presently."

These words were spoken by Paul to Israel. Israel did as ordered. In a few minutes, bucket in hand, begrimed with powder, sixty-feet in air, he hung like Apollyon from the extreme tip of the yard over the fated abyss of the hatchway. As he looked down between the eddies of smoke into that slaughterous pit, it was like looking from the verge of a cataract down into the yeasty pool at its base. Watching his chance, he dropped one grenade with such faultless precision, that, striking its mark, an explosion rent the Serapis like a volcano. The long row of heaped cartridges was ignited. The fire ran horizontally, like an express on a railway. More than twenty men were instantly killed: nearly forty wounded. This blow restored the chances of battle, before in favor of the Serapis.

But the drooping spirits of the English were suddenly revived, by an event which crowned the scene by an act on the part of one of the consorts of the Richard, the incredible atrocity of which, has induced all humane minds to impute it rather to some incomprehensible mistake, than to the malignant madness of the perpetrator.

The cautious approach and retreat of a consort of the Serapis, the Scarborough, before the moon rose, has already been mentioned. It is now to be related how that, when the moon was more than an hour high, a consort of the Richard, the Alliance, likewise approached and retreated. This ship, commanded by a Frenchman, infamous in his own navy, and obnoxious in the service to which he at present belonged; this ship, foremost in insurgency to Paul hitherto, and which, for the most part had crept like a poltroon from the fray; the Alliance now was at hand. Seeing her, Paul deemed the battle at an end. But to his horror, the Alliance threw a broadside full into the stern of the Richard, without touching the Serapis.

Paul called to her, for God's sake to forbear destroying the Richard. The reply was, a second, a third, a fourth broadside; striking the Richard ahead, astern, and amidships. One of the volleys killed several men and one officer. Meantime, like carpenters' augurs, and the sea-worm called remora, the guns of the Serapis were drilling away at the same doomed hull. After performing her nameless exploit, the Alliance sailed away, and did no more. She was like the great fire of London, breaking out on the heel of the great Plague. By this time, the Richard had received so many shot-holes low down in her hull, that like a sieve she began to settle.

"Do you strike?" cried the English captain.

"I have not yet begun to fight," howled sinking Paul.

This summons and response were whirled on eddies of smoke and flame. Both vessels were now on fire. The men of either knew hardly which to do; strive to destroy the enemy, or save themselves. In the midst of this, one hundred human beings, hitherto invisible strangers, were suddenly added to the rest. Five score English prisoners, till now confined in the Richard's hold, liberated in his consternation, by the master at arms, burst up the hatchways. One of them, the captain of a letter of marque, captured by Paul, off the Scottish coast, crawled through a port, as a burglar through a window, from the one ship to the other, and reported affairs to the English captain.

While Paul and his lieutenants were confronting these prisoners, the gunner, running up from below, and not perceiving his official superiors, and deeming them dead; believing himself now left sole surviving officer, ran to the tower of Pisa to haul down the colors. But they were already shot down and trailing in the water astern, like a sailor's towing shirt. Seeing the gunner there, groping about in the smoke, Israel asked what he wanted.

At this moment, the gunner, rushing to the rail, shouted "quarter! quarter!" to the Serapis.

"I'll quarter ye," yelled Israel, smiting the gunner with the flat of his cutlass.

"Do you strike?" now came from the Serapis.

"Aye, aye, aye!" involuntarily cried Israel, fetching the gunner a shower of blows.

"Do you strike?" again was repeated from the Serapis; whose captain, judging from the augmented confusion on board the Richard, owing to the escape of the prisoners, and also influenced by the report made to him by his late guest of the port-hole, doubted not that the enemy must needs be about surrendering.

"Do you strike?"

"Aye!—I strike *back*," roared Paul, for the first time now hearing the summons.

But judging this frantic response to come, like the others, from some unauthorized source, the English captain directed his boarders to be called; some of whom presently leaped on the Richard's rail; but, throwing out his tatooed arm at them with a sabre at the end of it, Paul showed them how boarders repelled boarders. The English retreated; but not before they had been thinned out again, like spring radishes, by the unfaltering fire from the Richard's tops.

An officer of the Richard, seeing the mass of prisoners delirious with sudden liberty and fright, pricked them with his sword to the pumps; thus keeping the ship afloat by the very blunder which had promised to have been fatal. The vessels now blazed so in the rigging, that both parties desisted from hostilities to subdue the common foe.

When some faint order was again restored upon the Richard, her chances of victory increased, while those of the English, driven under cover, proportionably waned. Early in the contest, Paul, with his own hand, had brought one of his largest guns to bear against the enemy's main-mast. That shot had hit. The mast now plainly tottered. Nevertheless, it seemed as if, in this fight, neither party could be victor. Mutual obliteration from the face of the waters seemed the only natural sequel to hostilities like these. It is, therefore, honor to him as a man, and not reproach to him as an officer, that, to stay such carnage, Captain Pearson, of the Serapis, with his own hands hauled down his colors. But just as an officer from the Richard swung himself on board the Serapis, and accosted the English captain, the first lieutenant of the Serapis came up from below inquiring whether the Richard had struck, since her fire had ceased.

So equal was the conflict that, even after the surrender, it could be, and was, a question to one of the warriors engaged (who had not happened to see the English flag hauled down) whether the Serapis had struck to the Richard, or the Richard to the Serapis. Nay, while the Richard's officer was still amicably conversing with the English captain, a midshipman of the Richard, in act of following his superior on board the surrendered vessel, was run through the thigh by a pike in the hand of an ignorant boarder of the Serapis. While equally ignorant, the cannons below deck were still thundering away at the nominal conqueror from the batteries of the nominally conquered ship.

But though the Serapis had submitted, there were two misanthropical foes on board the Richard which would not so easily succumb,—fire and water. All night the victors were engaged in suppressing the flames. Not until daylight were the flames got under; but though the pumps were kept continually going, the water in the hold still gained. A few hours after sunrise the Richard was deserted for the Serapis and the other vessels of the squadron of Paul. About ten o'clock, the Richard, gorged with slaughter, wallowed heavily, gave a long roll, and blasted by tornadoes of sulphur, slowly sunk, like Gomorrah, out of sight.

The loss of life in the two ships was about equal; one-half of the total number of those engaged being either killed or wounded.

In view of this battle one may well ask—What separates the enlightened man from the savage? Is civilization a thing distinct, or is it an advanced stage of barbarism?

The Tuft of Kelp

All dripping in tangles green,
  Cast up by a lonely sea,
If purer for that, O Weed,
  Bitterer, too, are ye?

George Henry Preble

The opening of Japan to friendly relations with the United States after a century and a half of isolation required the display of as much pomp, circumstance, and force as the U.S. Navy could muster. When Commodore Matthew Perry arrived in Japanese waters in May 1853, it was with an imposing ten-ship squadron—"black ships of evil mien," as the Japanese described them.

One member of Perry's crew—George Henry Preble (1816–1885), a lieutenant aboard the U.S.S. Macedonian *and later the author of books of maritime history—disobeyed Perry's order that journals and notebooks kept by members of the expedition be surrendered to the government. Under the guise of correspondence with his wife, he kept a diary quite unlike the official report of Perry's mission (*Narrative of the Expedition of an American Squadron to the China Seas and Japan, *1856). In part souvenir book, with sketches of waterspouts, rubbings of Japanese coins, and lithographs of pagodas interspersed between pages of prose, the diary offers a uniquely intimate view of the epic encounter between nations—one of the major diplomatic achievements of the 19th century.*

from *The Opening of Japan*

Treaty Bay, Monday March 27, 1854

THOUGH it has been blowing a stiff and cold N.W. gale it has been a gala day in the squadron. Undeterred by the weather the three Japanese princes visited our ship, and partook of an entertainment to which they were invited by the Commodore, on board the *Powhatan*. They first came to our ship, and as they reached the deck the *Mississippi*'s guns thundered a salute of seventeen guns, which they with childlike eagerness rushed forward on our forecastle to see, the *Miss.* laying ahead of us. They were then shown all over our ship, and inquisitively examined every part of her, an artist of their numerous suite, taking numerous drawings of such things as they particularly admired. After they had seen the ship the drum beat to general quarters, and we amused them with an exercise of our Great Guns, and small arms, showing them how we boarded an enemy, and how we repulsed one attempting to board, and sent axemen into the rigging to chop it away when requisite. Then rang the Fire bell and exercised at fire quarters, drawing water in buckets and throwing it and streams from our force pumps upon the imaginary conflagration. When they witnessed all we had to show them, they left our ship, and went to the *Powhatan*, under a salute of seventeen guns from our eight inch guns. We were to have manned yards always a pretty sight, but the weather was too boisterous. On reaching the *Powhatan*, a flag bearing the Emperor's arms was hoisted at her foremast head, and kept flying while they remained on board and another flag with the arms of the 1st Prince Commissioner, was hoisted at her mast. The Commodore's blue broad pennant kept its usual place at the main mast. Our glorious stars and stripes waved from the peak, and the Union Jack decorated the bowsprit. All of us having received invitations from the Commodore to join in and assist at the entertainment on the *Powhatan*, as many as could be spared from duty, and I was one, hastened on board. After being shown that noble steamer's massive machinery in motion, the three Princes, with their more immediate suite were taken into the Commodores Cabin, and seated at a feast he had spread for them, and Capts and Commanders of our squadron and his suite, as many as the Cabin could conveniently hold about twenty seven in all. On the Quarter Deck another table was spread and ample provisions made for their more numerous and lesser satellites. Our part being to make them eat and drink as much as possible, hoping in accordance with the old adage, if they eat hearty they would give us a good name and eating and drinking seem to be important feature in all the diplomatic meetings we have held with them.

Doing my duty, therefore, in obedience to orders, I plied the Japs in my neighborhood well, and when clean work had been made of Champagne, Madeira, Cherry Cordial, punch and whiskey, I resorted to the Castors and gave them a mixture of catsup and vinegar which they seemed to relish with equal gusto. Following the customs of the country I encouraged them to pocket the remnants of the feast. I saw one fellow walk off with a whole chicken done up in paper under his jacket. Altogether it was an amusing and animated scene. I have not enjoyed such a hearty laugh since we left the U.S. The Commodore wanted to put them in a good humor, as he said the success of his treaty depended upon the success of the entertainment, so we did our best and I am sure it could not have gone off more to his or their satisfaction. They were highly amused when we toasted "The Emperor of Japan," "The President of the U.S.," "The Commodore," "The High Commissioners," and "The Japanese ladies." When the band commenced playing, several commenced shuffling and dancing—and to encourage them some of our greyest and gravest officers danced with them. A funny sight to behold—these bald-pated bundles of clothes—and Doctors, Pursers, Lieuts and Capts. all jumping up and down to the music.

Yesterday several of the guests before the feast sent their fans on board, to have mottos written on them, and then returned to them at the feast: that being one of the polite customs of the country. Several gave me their fans at the feast for the same purpose and I wrote, "Commerce and Agriculture tend to unite America and Japan," "California and Japan are now neighbors; it is to be hoped that they will pass many social evenings together," etc. By the way they have heard probably from the Dutch all about California and the gold discovery, and it is thought the secret of our success lies in their hope to benefit from a trade with California.

When the Commissioners had been sufficiently mellowed in the Cabin, they were brought on deck to witness a performance by the Ethiopian Band of the *Powhatan*, who style themselves "Japanese Minstrels." Then enjoyed the imitations of the negro, and laughed very heartily. In his delight one of the Commissioners went so far as to put his arms around the Commodore's neck and embrace him. Some one remarking to the Commodore, that he did not think he would stand that,

Oh, said old Perry—if he will only sign the Treaty he may kiss me. After the Exhibition they left the ship and returned to shore, as they came, in their own boats, and under a salute of seventeen guns from the *Saratoga*. The object in firing the salutes from different ships being to show the power of their batteries.

The Court Artist, a Doctor, who had cunning humbug depicted in his own face, made quite an accurate sketch of the negro minstrels and their instruments, perhaps to be shown to the Emperor. A most laughable scene was seeing one of our officers toasting the Japs, who looked like two bundles of clothes, skewered by two swords. On top of the cabins, where they could have a better view of the performance. Following the Princes we called our boat, and returned to our own ship to tea.

* * *

Treaty Bay, Friday March 31, 1854

Eureka! It is finished! The great agony is over! In vulgar parlance the egg has hatched its chicken today. The Treaty of Amity and Friendship between Japan and the United States was signed today to the satisfaction of everybody. Even Old Bruin (i.e. the Commodore) would smile if he only knew how to smile.

After the Treaty was signed and had been given to the Commodore, he expressed to the Commissioners (this was an overheard conversation) his intention of taking his squadron as near to Jedo as he could get them to it. The Japanese stoutly objected saying their law was against it. The Commodore said in reply he was aware of that and every other objection, as their laws had been his study for a year past. They had another law which prohibited ships from passing Uraga, but he had come up to this anchorage and done them no damage. On the contrary a treaty of amity and friendship was the consequence. He had even remained on board ship, and respected their laws so far as the land was concerned, though he did think it somewhat uncivil that they had not invited him and his officers on shore. The Emperor and his people had a right to make laws for the land but the sea was free to everybody. The Commissioners then urged that his boats would come to survey, and they did not want the Harbor surveyed. The Commodore told them that was a matter of indifference to him, he had charts enough and survey enough to take him as far as he proposed going, and all he wished was to place his Squadron off Jedo, where the Emperor could see it, and receive a salute. This at once the Commissioners said could not be allowed, but the Commodore finding them obdurate told them his orders were positive to take the ships as near Jedo as possible, and where his Master the President of the U.S. said they must go, there he must take them, and that was the end of it.

A grand reception it is said will be given him at Hakodadi in the straits of Matame, a part that the Treaty provides shall be opened to our Whalemen. We are to go there to survey the Bay before we leave Japanese waters. It is not thought we will remain here a week now that we have opened "the Oyster." Our mess is now so hard up we drink our tea *á la* Japanese and Chinese *sans* sugar or milk; our coffee is 'done and give out' entirely and a few hams and some cans of pickled oyster, so salt we cannot eat them are all we have in our store room save a little strong batter and some flour. These and the ship's ration are now our sole dependence; but for the timely supply of those 'old cocks' we would be hard pushed for something to eat. The last of these we tried we thought must have exercised his juvenile crowing about the commencement of the Christian era. Every succeeding one seems tougher than its predecessor. We know Japan to be a very ancient country, and certainly the one we tried our teeth on today, must have walked out of the Ark before Noah. By boiling them all day, and then working them over in a stew with gravy, rice pepper and other condiments, they are made tolerably palatable and are an improvement on Salt Horse.

I wonder that Job was not sent to sea, and deprived of all knowledge of his home and family for a twelve month as I am like to be. It would have been a greater trial for his patience than any he was made to endure, and he would have cursed and swore sooner than I did I am sure. The laborer, who sees his little ones snuggly in bed, and meets his family every night at sun down, and spends the sweet sabbath with them is far more blessed in his lot than a wanderer like me laboring on ocean.

WALT WHITMAN

Although the oceanic scope of his poetry—from the mate standing "braced in the whaleboat" in the 1855 Leaves of Grass *to the vision in "Passage to India" of the soul's "circumnavigation of the world"—might suggest otherwise, Walt Whitman (1819–1892) never made a deep-sea voyage. Yet, beginning with the summers he spent as a youth on the beaches of "fish-shaped Paumanok" (as he affectionately referred to Long Island), the sea exerted a persistent "invisible influence" on his writing. The range of that influence can be traced in the pieces that follow, from the anguished "As I Ebb'd with the Ocean of Life" (1860) to the calmly observed late prose piece "A Winter Day on the Sea-Beach" (1882).*

As I Ebb'd with the Ocean of Life

1

As I ebb'd with the ocean of life,
As I wended the shores I know,
As I walk'd where the ripples continually wash you
Paumanok,
Where they rustle up hoarse and sibilant,
Where the fierce old mother endlessly cries for her
castaways,
I musing late in the autumn day, gazing off southward,
Held by this electric self out of the pride of which I utter
poems,
Was seiz'd by the spirit that trails in the lines underfoot,
The rim, the sediment that stands for all the water and all the
land of the globe.

Fascinated, my eyes reverting from the south, dropt, to
follow those slender windrows,
Chaff, straw, splinters of wood, weeds, and the sea-gluten,
Scum, scales from shining rocks, leaves of salt-lettuce, left by
the tide,

Miles walking, the sound of breaking waves the other side of me,
Paumanok there and then as I thought the old thought of likenesses,
These you presented to me you fish-shaped island,
As I wended the shores I know,
As I walk'd with that electric self seeking types.

2

As I wend to the shores I know not,
As I list to the dirge, the voices of men and women wreck'd,
As I inhale the impalpable breezes that set in upon me,
As the ocean so mysterious rolls toward me closer and closer,
I too but signify at the utmost a little wash'd-up drift,
A few sands and dead leaves to gather,
Gather, and merge myself as part of the sands and drift.

O baffled, balk'd, bent to the very earth,
Oppress'd with myself that I have dared to open my mouth,
Aware now that amid all that blab whose echoes recoil upon me I have not once had the least idea who or what I am,
But that before all my arrogant poems the real Me stands yet untouch'd, untold, altogether unreach'd,
Withdrawn far, mocking me with mock-congratulatory signs and bows,
With peals of distant ironical laughter at every word I have written,
Pointing in silence to these songs, and then to the sand beneath.

I perceive I have not really understood any thing, not a single object, and that no man ever can,
Nature here in sight of the sea taking advantage of me to dart upon me and sting me,
Because I have dared to open my mouth to sing at all.

3

You oceans both, I close with you,
We murmur alike reproachfully rolling sands and drift,
        knowing not why,
These little shreds indeed standing for you and me and all.

You friable shore with trails of debris,
You fish-shaped island, I take what is underfoot,
What is yours is mine my father.

I too Paumanok,
I too have bubbled up, floated the measureless float, and been
        wash'd on your shores,
I too am but a trail of drift and debris,
I too leave little wrecks upon you, you fish-shaped island.

I throw myself upon your breast my father,
I cling to you so that you cannot unloose me,
I hold you so firm till you answer me something.

Kiss me my father,
Touch me with your lips as I touch those I love,
Breathe to me while I hold you close the secret of the
        murmuring I envy.

4

Ebb, ocean of life, (the flow will return,)
Cease not your moaning you fierce old mother,
Endlessly cry for your castaways, but fear not, deny not me,
Rustle not up so hoarse and angry against my feet as I touch
        you or gather from you.

I mean tenderly by you and all,
I gather for myself and for this phantom looking down where
        we lead, and following me and mine.

Me and mine, loose windrows, little corpses,
Froth, snowy white, and bubbles,

(See, from my dead lips the ooze exuding at last,
See, the prismatic colors glistening and rolling,)
Tufts of straw, sands, fragments,
Buoy'd hither from many moods, one contradicting another,
From the storm, the long calm, the darkness, the swell,
Musing, pondering, a breath, a briny tear, a dab of liquid or soil,
Up just as much out of fathomless workings fermented and thrown,
A limp blossom or two, torn, just as much over waves floating, drifted at random,
Just as much for us that sobbing dirge of Nature,
Just as much whence we come that blare of the cloud-trumpets,
We, capricious, brought hither we know not whence, spread out before you,
You up there walking or sitting,
Whoever you are, we too lie in drifts at your feet.

The World below the Brine

THE world below the brine,
Forests at the bottom of the sea, the branches and leaves,
Sea-lettuce, vast lichens, strange flowers and seeds, the thick tangle, openings, and pink turf,
Different colors, pale gray and green, purple, white, and gold, the play of light through the water,
Dumb swimmers there among the rocks, coral, gluten, grass, rushes, and the aliment of the swimmers,
Sluggish existences grazing there suspended, or slowly crawling close to the bottom,
The sperm-whale at the surface blowing air and spray, or disporting with his flukes,
The leaden-eyed shark, the walrus, the turtle, the hairy sea-leopard, and the sting-ray,

Passions there, wars, pursuits, tribes, sight in those ocean-depths, breathing that thick-breathing air, as so many do,
The change thence to the sight here, and to the subtle air breathed by beings like us who walk this sphere,
The change onward from ours to that of beings who walk other spheres.

A Paumanok Picture

Two boats with nets lying off the sea-beach, quite still,
Ten fishermen waiting—they discover a thick school of mossbonkers—they drop the join'd seine-ends in the water,
The boats separate and row off, each on its rounding course to the beach, enclosing the mossbonkers,
The net is drawn in by a windlass by those who stop ashore,
Some of the fishermen lounge in their boats, others stand ankle-deep in the water, pois'd on strong legs,
The boats partly drawn up, the water slapping against them,
Strew'd on the sand in heaps and windrows, well out from the water, the green-back'd spotted mossbonkers.

A Winter Day on the Sea-Beach

One bright December mid-day lately I spent down on the New Jersey sea-shore, reaching it by a little more than an hour's railroad trip over the old Camden and Atlantic. I had started betimes, fortified by nice strong coffee and a good breakfast (cook'd by the hands I love, my dear sister Lou's—how much better it makes the victuals taste, and then assimilate, strengthen you, perhaps make the whole day comfortable afterwards.) Five or six miles at the last, our track enter'd a broad region of salt grass meadows, intersected by lagoons, and cut up everywhere by watery runs. The sedgy perfume, delightful to my nostrils, reminded me of "the mash" and south bay of my native island. I could have journey'd contentedly till night through these flat and odorous sea-prairies. From half-past 11 till 2 I was nearly all the time along the beach, or in sight of the ocean, listening to its hoarse murmur, and inhaling the bracing and welcome breezes. First, a rapid five-mile drive over the hard sand—our carriage wheels hardly made dents in it. Then after dinner (as there were nearly two hours to spare) I walk'd off in another direction, (hardly met or saw a person,) and taking possession of what appear'd to have been the reception-room of an old bath-house range, had a broad expanse of view all to myself—quaint, refreshing, unimpeded—a dry area of sedge and Indian grass immediately before and around me—space, simple, unornamented space. Distant vessels, and the far-off, just visible trailing smoke of an inward bound steamer; more plainly, ships, brigs, schooners, in sight, most of them with every sail set to the firm and steady wind.

The attractions, fascinations there are in sea and shore! How one dwells on their simplicity, even vacuity! What is it in us, arous'd by those indirections and directions? That spread of waves and gray-white beach, salt, monotonous, senseless—such an entire absence of art, books, talk, elegance—so indescribably comforting, even this winter day—grim, yet so delicate-looking, so spiritual—striking emotional, impalpable depths, subtler than all the poems, paintings, music, I have ever read, seen, heard. (Yet let me be fair, perhaps it is because I have read those poems and heard that music.)

Sea-Shore Fancies

EVEN as a boy, I had the fancy, the wish, to write a piece, perhaps a poem, about the sea-shore—that suggesting, dividing line, contact, junction, the solid marrying the liquid—that curious, lurking something, (as doubtless every objective form finally becomes to the subjective spirit,) which means far more than its mere first sight, grand as that is—blending the real and ideal, and each made portion of the other. Hours, days, in my Long Island youth and early manhood, I haunted the shores of Rockaway or Coney island, or away east to the Hamptons or Montauk. Once, at the latter place, (by the old lighthouse, nothing but sea-tossings in sight in every direction as far as the eye could reach,) I remember well, I felt that I must one day write a book expressing this liquid, mystic theme. Afterward, I recollect, how it came to me that instead of any special lyrical or epical or literary attempt, the sea-shore should be an invisible *influence*, a pervading gauge and tally for me, in my composition. (Let me give a hint here to young writers. I am not sure but I have unwittingly follow'd out the same rule with other powers besides sea and shores—avoiding them, in the way of any dead set at poetizing them, as too big for formal handling—quite satisfied if I could indirectly show that we have met and fused, even if only once, but enough—that we have really absorb'd each other and understand each other.)

There is a dream, a picture, that for years at intervals, (sometimes quite long ones, but surely again, in time,) has come noiselessly up before me, and I really believe, fiction as it is, has enter'd largely into my practical life—certainly into my writings, and shaped and color'd them. It is nothing more or less than a stretch of interminable white-brown sand, hard and smooth and broad, with the ocean perpetually, grandly, rolling in upon it, with slow-measured sweep, with rustle and hiss and foam, and many a thump as of low bass drums. This scene, this picture, I say, has risen before me at times for years. Sometimes I wake at night and can hear and see it plainly.

Mary Rowland

"Seafaring," writes Joan Druett in her pioneering study Hen Frigates: Passion and Peril, Nineteenth-Century Women at Sea, *"was an extraordinary proposition for a nineteenth-century lady"—an observation that helps to explain why so much of the literature of the American maritime experience, at least before the 20th century, was written by men. A remarkable exception can be found in the journals of Mary Rowland, of Setauket, Long Island, who accompanied her husband to sea on increasingly distant voyages throughout their 24-year marriage. Here, in excerpts from the journal Rowland kept on her fourth sea voyage begun in October 1855 with her husband and two small daughters and taking her to ports throughout the world, we are given a fresh perspective on shipboard life, by turns melancholy, salty, and lyrical.*

from *Remarks on Board Brig Thomas W. Rowland*

Monday 18th. This day wind still blowing a gale from the Westward and thick hazy weather.

The Sea runs high and the vessel rolls into it most dreadfully and pitching also—household implements are in much confusion here below and on deck. I heard the roaring of the wind and Sea and H. giving Orders, all are busy attending to the vessel.

My Help—if such she can be termed—is very seasick and of course stowed away more dead than alive, I doctor her as best I can, knowing by experience seasickness is no desireable thing—especially at Sea.

Wednesday 20th. Weather rather better. The reefs were shook out this morning as the wind moderated but this evening have been put in again.

The wind seems determined to blow from the wrong quarter whichever way the Vessel turns her head and we are allways blessed with a head wind.

I have just been out on deck to look around and take the air as I have not been out before in the day on account of the rough weather and I seldom remain below three days at a time for I like well to be out. A Steamer has passed us this evening showing three bright lights and we have ours burning in case we want to show a light but now she has passed on up on the passage and left us behind her with her black smoke. I do not like those animals to approach us in the night beyond a certain proximity. I do not like to travel by steam either myself.

The moon has just risen and I will bid the welcome friend good night and retire, thinking I shall sleep soundly to make up for lost time, but it is an uncertain thing, sleep at sea. It is all rest or none.

At 4 O'clock PM saw the Island of Minorca.

* * *

Saturday 27th. Light winds from NE and fine pleasant weather. I have finished a shirt &c. And the children have had the priviledge of being on deck all the afternoon, where they enjoy themselves much better than in the Cabin. This morning we passed a famous large turtle, and he would have made a good mess for all hands, could we have caught him.

As I was looking around to see if I could discover any thing, I saw something which we thought might be a boat, but as we came up to it, it proved to be only a great log as large as a vessel's mast.

A large gull was perched upon it and around it was a large shoal of fine fish. And they looked very tempting. The Mate threw the grains amongst them and away they went then back again for their old lurking place.

So drifting an object as a log is hardly worth noticing, but when everything is still and nothing new comes along we are even glad to have an old log heave in sight that takes up one's attention for a while.

Lat by Obs 30°25′ N. Lon 18°02′

* * *

Monday 6th Still Calm and very hot. Thermometer stands on 91 down in the Cabin but the steam that arises from the cargo makes it much warmer than it otherwise would be. It is most impossible to sleep, and I sleep but very little nowadays. And we are tormented with vermin, more so than ever before, roaches come by thousands, not only in the pantry where one would suppose them to be, but they take up their abode in my trunks of clothing mostly, and in very little cracks and corners. I do not see what they subsist on, they never do any injury to my clothing, but when I move an article they run out at times by dozens, and hide as quickly as possible in the folds of other garments. The Capt's writing desk is swarming with them and there they are more troublesome as they soil the papers.

If driven hence they fly for refuge somewhere else and it is impossible to scald them, they move so quick. The flies have nearly all left us as we get further out at sea, but we have some more troublesome visitors of late, Musketoes have taken up their abode on board by dozens and whence they came I know not, they must be a tribe of Ocean wanderers. Oh dear how they bite, I cannot get any peace from these troublesome little Devils.

What else are they but a curse sent upon us wretched humanity for our wickedness. I do not know what other purpose the Great giver has placed them on the sea as well as on the dry land.

> And they haunt me still where'er I roam
> In far off Climes or when at home

And now besides these plagues we have still other ones on board, white crawling worms about an inch long come out of the cargo of figs and raisins and large numbers make their appearance in the Cabin and more particularly in my room. They keep hid during the day time and like the Cockroaches & musketoes make their Debut at night, they crawl up on the ceiling overhead and then fall down in a short time but Oh dear they like to hide in my mattress best of all places and although I watch for and destroy all that I can find before I retire, often I am awakened during the night by them as they drop down upon me and then commence to crawl over me occasionaly taking a nip as their appetites suits them. It is disgusting to even think of these reptiles crawling over one's flesh while we are alive, but they are harmless and in a few days there will not be one to be seen—they soon die. They are always present when the Cargo consists of dried fruit. But enough of this, I'll write no more about it. All sail is set. All hands are well and can eat their allowance. The children have not been well till now since I left Malaga. And now I hope to let the medicine chest rest a while.

Lat by Obs. 22°55′ N. Lon by Chro 37°40′

* * *

Tuesday 7th. Still calm but very hot and also clear and pleasant. Lat by Obs 22°35′ Lon by Chro 38°50′ West. This afternoon we have been fishing, it being very still and quiet on board as usual in calm weather, and not a ripple disturbed the surface of the mighty Ocean. We were all tired of ourselves hardly knowing what to do to pass away the time. I had taken my sewing and found a comfortable seat on deck in the shade of the sails and H. had seated himself nearby intent on reading, Rose was taking care of the children, and they were enjoying themselves by being on deck, one watch was below and the other busy. As for the man at the wheel, he had nothing to do.

Some one says, just look at the fish, and one hardly thinks of looking at every fish that comes along, but sure enough all around the vessel the water was alive with fish of several kinds, great baracotas and Dolphin and small black fish and other kinds. Now for a chance— It really appeared as if they were sent to us but we were rather scant for fishing tackle, but soon all hands were out of cabin and forecastle, and fishing for dear life, but not one of the large fish could we get, not having any propper lines and bait. We caught some of the small kinds and the Capt. took several with the grains, so we had a nice dish for our suppers.

Those in the water were still playing around us at dark and I hope they will be here again tomorrow, but had rather have a breeze soon. We proceed but slowly on our passage. This morning we fell in company with Bark Huron of Newport, 27 days out and bound to West Indies. We have had just wind enough today to gain her some distance, now she is out of sight astern and it is doubtful if I ever see her again, and it matters not to me so long as all goes well.

In my travels I have made many acquaintances and in port I have found agreeable friends, and hope I meet with them again—some I may, and many not. In all probability I shall never see most of my companions, being those like myself who had followed their husbands to sea, and when we meet in foreign ports it is very natural and easy for us to become acquainted after the first introduction and the usual compliments passed, which are generally how do you like the sea, and is this your first voyage, are you troubled with seasickness, &c &c.—

and then if we are inclined to be sociable we are bound to keep each other's company as much as convenience will allow of, we being dependent upon our Husbands' time and good nature to attend to us, for we cannot get from our homes on board without some attention.

As for the shopping, that must be attended to and I believe most all men are apt to dislike the business. They willingly afford us any reasonable amount of pocket change to make our purchases with, but they can never have the patience to stand in a store and parley with the knights of the tape and scissors about the quality of such an article, as they think it is of no consequence at all. So when we Sailors' wives find company from home we find it very agreeable and sometimes club together and take a walk on Terra together and thus make our necesary purchases what are wanted for the voyage and I for one endeavor to make as little trouble as possible.

But this evening I shall remain where I am for allthough the weather is fine and pleasant there is many a mile twixt me and some in whom I found kind friends.

Oct. 14th 1856. For the last seven days we have had a combination of light winds and Calm attended with rain squalls, but have not been able to catch much water for washing, and that is a great priviledge, especially where there is little ones that is fond of getting into the dirt and my taulking is in vain when I tell them not to get into the dirt as I have no water to wash with.

It is a lovely night but not one calculated to speed us on our journey—

but still I desire fine weather, although retarded on our way a little while, for it will make no difference to us an hundred years from now.

It was one year ago yesterday since I left home and on the 16 came to sea. I have heard but very little from there since I left, and have written many times but the answers have been few and far between. I know it is not always convenient for me to get an answer in all places, and perhaps there is still a better cause. I may have been forgotten, but I've not so soon forgotten home or friends I left behind me.

No, for I often visit them in fancy, and hope e'er long to greet familiar faces in reality. A year seems quite an age to one unused to leaving home but I am at home here and there and everywhere and in fact am very contented and as happy at sea as anywhere else, so long as my husband and children are with me and all goes well—

let us go where we will, we find there is no lasting happiness here below and find

> This world is all a fleeting show
> To vain illusions given

It would indeed be a gratification for to spend an hour or two at home and have a social chat with those there, but Alass I cannot, for there is too great a space 'twixt me and Long Island, and a mighty Ocean rolls between.

So I will be content for a while where I am—

Consult the Barometer about the state of the weather, take a look at the Sky—

And then go to rest beside my babies, darling pets, heaven bless and protect them from harm, they know not yet no sin or guile   Lat 23°13′ Lon 55°02′ West.

Monday Oct. 20th. This day light winds from the eastward. During the past week we have been favored with a good breeze—in one 24 hours made the distance of 254 miles—a few days work like that would soon shorten up the long distance. Saturday we sailed 220 miles and that is doing very well. So many times we have a dead Calm (to use a sea phrase) then up springs a breeze and pushes us onward, of which we are very glad.

And occasionaly a squall is seen rising, and sometimes comes up very suddenly and blows furiously a few minutes, causing sail to be taken in in a great hurry.

Then again there is every appearance of a heavy squall and it passes over and does not send wind enough to blow away a feather. This morning just as day was breaking in the east we heard heavy thunder for the first time this passage and there was every appearance of a heavy rain squall—the black Clouds came up and hung directly over us and threatened us both wind and rain. The latter I was in hopes to see, but a few drops was all that fell and it passed over leaving us in safety, not so much as giving the men an occasion to put on their Oil Jackets.

Last monday evening there was a total Eclipse of the moon visible to us although the Almanac did not so much as note the fact. It rose at seven O'clock and was nearly obscured at the time and in a short time was totally eclipsed and remained hid two hours, then peeped out from behind her sable covering and showed her full clean face in all her splendor—for she fulled at the same time of the eclipse, which fact the astronomers had not forgot to mention.

We are now only three hundred miles from land and daily see harbingers of it, the water is full of gulfweed and flocks of small land birds are seen hovering around the vessel. And one pretty little fellow having strayed from his companions took shelter on board, to rest its fragile limbs which were tired out with its long flight, but poor mistaken thing it soon became an easy prisoner and was put in the Cage with the Canary, but instead of being happy in its new home it continually thrashed its little body against the wires and tried to get away, so it was again set at liberty, but death will soon set the prisoner free, for he will never be able to reach the land again and e'er now the little sailor Bird is in the mighty Ocean and too small a speck to be seen upon the great roling waves that rests for no one or slumbers not, till the still small voice says "peace, be still, and rebukes the waves."

The weather is uncomfortably warm and it is useless to think of sleeping here in the Cabin, if I was a man I too could sleep on deck in the cool shade. The thermometer stands at 92 deg. And now the breeze has all gone and as there is some swell the vessel is roling and slatting her sails as if she too is impatient for the wind to favor us, but this weather helps to make business for the Sail maker, for this great shaking must wear them more than a breeze of wind.

I will go out a while and see if it is not more comfortable there and keep my husband's company a while, for he does not seem inclined to remain below.

Lat by Obs 26°56′ N. Lon by Chro 71°41¼′ West

Monday Nov 3rd New Orleans

This morning, the wind being favorable, we proceeded on up the river. The scenery being now quite interesting as we get up into the country amongst the plantations. In the fields of sugar cane are flocks of slaves, men and women at work with their hoes and farming implements, some of them now and then leaning upon their hoe handle to gaze at us as we pass swiftly by. We soon came up to the English turn, and a crooked turn it is indeed. First we sail in one direction perhaps a mile, then in another, first north then nearly south, till we come in view of the tall steeples and masts of the ships at New Orleans. And at ten A.M. we were fairly up, and anchored a little below the shipping. At 4 a tow boat came alongside and took us to the Levee No. 23 and in the picayune tier opposite the market.

Most of the sailor men have gone on shore, and probably some or all are by this time carrying a "brick in their hats," and thus find it rather difficult to navigate on the land. Foolish creatures, why will they treat themselves in the manner they do? It takes but a few days for them to rid themselves of their hard-earned money. Their first object generally is to go to some clothing store, and there get a whole new fit-out, then get drunk as soon as possible. Sometimes some of them find their way back on board the vessel by the next day, after their wages, and others not yet, as they do not like to be seen with such a black eye and disfigured face as is apt to be the Case here in N O with them after they have been on the land a few hours. I believe there is plenty of bad company for them here, so report says but enough of this.

Dec 21st. Sunday evening Stormy weather and unpleasant and has been so since yesterday when it was very clear and fine. The sky became suddenly overcast with black clouds Sail was immediately taken in and then the wind blew fresh but was fair for a short time then shifted and came ahead and the rain came down and has been squally ever since and at times blowing a gale then dying out to renew its fury. The water casks have all been filled up. The wind has been blowing from NW to NE but at present the sky looks more favorable although the Barometer denotes no good weather yet awhile. At dark saw a vessel near stearing SW and as we were stearing SE the Course was altered in time to keep a propper distance and we both passed on our way in safty amid the roaring of the wind and Sea. It is nine o'clock and my little Ones are sweetly sleeping heedless of care or trouble yet but there is time enough yet for that.

If they be spared to lengthened years.
To travel through this Vale of tears

Now I retire and try to get some sleep and perhaps I shall in my dreams visit old familiar places and youthful scenes and greet the young smiling happy faces at home and then I must awake to find that I am far away and the Mighty Ocean rolls between us. Just as I had the happiness to find myself asleep for the first time at three o'clock this morning, the Capt who had also just committed himself to morpheus' arms tired and weary enough to wish nothing. Then came the Mate to say that the Sick Man in the forecastle was in great distress and wanted to see the Capt who then turns out and makes him a visit but that is the way with a doctor's life and it seems necessary for a Capt to understand the profession that is if they are all as unfortunate as H is in having sick men and their sickness is generally brought on through some imprudence on their part.

In this latitude at this season the days are short and the nights long so I while away some of these long tedious evenings trying to write a little about this and that and the little events that happen in our life on the Sea. But it is most impossible to sit still enough to write legible. The sea runs mountains high and the vivid lightening is flashing above and around us. Overhead the black clouds hang in heavy masses and filled with rain. Every now and then a copious shower descends and then occasionally out shines a bright star struggling through the mist and fog to make the dismal gloom less cheerless by its presence. Welcome bright messenger Oh bring fair weather, disperse these threatening clouds and tame the maddened elements again to quietness. It is a fearful night to look upon and not a pleasant one to spend at sea. The vessel rolls into the waves heavily and now and then a wave gets astray and the top of it breaks acrost the deck, perchance over the corner of the top of the cabin house and making noise enough to appear below like ten times more than it is

> But our Brig is strong and new
> Heaven grant it she'll live through
> This furious storm of wind and rain
> And pleasant weather find again.

* * *

Wednesday 31st. New Year Eve and it is a fine pleasant night so far clear and the sky spangled o'er with stars. There is a strong breeze and not exactly fair. The Brig heads her Course along and is going through the water at the rate of ten miles per hour and as we push through the white foam In the night it appears as if we were sailing much faster than we really are. This afternoon saw a brig and passed within a short distance. When 1857 is ushered in we shall be 40 miles from here providence permitting. So ends this day. So ends this year.

Jan 3rd 1857. Another year has passed never to return. Alass how swiftly time flies especially at Sea. Days and weeks pass away e'er one is aware of it but time appears longer in bad weather to me. five weeks have passed since we left the Balise and yet we have a distance of 2000 miles to sail before we find our port of Discharge. Today is Saturday. I have been quite busy making mince pies and finished a dress for myself also one for Rose and cut out to small dresses for my little ones to be made when convenient. Lat 13°14′ N Long 31°16′ West

Monday 5th 1857. During these 24 hours attended with rain squalls the wind blowing first from one way then from another and the rain pouring. Now it is perfectly calm and not wind enough to keep steerage way on the vessel. It is quite still now above and below except when the great mainsail gives itself a shake as if impatient for a gentle breeze now it is held in confinement by a reef or two. But I say keep quiet mainsail a little while, have patience. These black clouds will disappear e'er long

Then Jack and Bill with Tom and Harry
Will loose and hoist you with a song right merry
But you must wait so pray be still
Let tired sailors sleep that will
Excepting the deck watch that's stationed on duty
And I believe now 'tis the Black man whose name
they call Beauty.

Samuel Dana Greene

When the U.S. Navy abandoned its shipyard in Norfolk, Virginia, in April 1861, the 40-gun steam frigate Merrimac *was burned and scuttled. The Confederates raised the hull and in July began converting it into a 10-gun ironclad warship. News of this attempt to achieve a decisive technological advantage over the numerically superior Union fleet soon reached the North, and the U.S. Navy authorized the construction of an even more revolutionary vessel. Designed by the Swedish-American engineer John Ericsson, the* Monitor *had a low, flat deck and a single armored turret containing two 11-inch guns. On March 8, 1862, the* Virginia *(the Confederate name for the reworked* Merrimac*) sailed from Norfolk and attacked the Union squadron at Hampton Roads. Protected by four inches of wrought-iron armor laid over its sloping wooden superstructure, the* Virginia *sank the wooden sailing ships* Cumberland *and* Congress, *forced the steam frigate* Minnesota *to run aground, and killed more than 240 men, inflicting the worst defeat suffered by the U.S. Navy until the Japanese attack on Pearl Harbor in 1941. The next day the recently commissioned* Monitor *fought the* Virginia *in the first encounter of ironclad ships in history. Samuel Dana Greene (1840–1884), the executive officer of the* Monitor, *described the battle in an article written for* The Century Magazine *in 1884. The fundamental design of the* Monitor*—an armored steamship with turret-mounted heavy guns—would dominate naval warfare until the ascendancy of the aircraft carrier some 80 years later.*

from *In the Monitor's Turret*

So hurried was the preparation of the *Monitor* that the mechanics worked upon her day and night up to the hour of her departure, and little opportunity was offered to drill the crew at the guns, to work the turret, and to become familiar with the other unusual features of the vessel. The crew was, in fact, composed of volunteers. Lieutenant Worden, having been authorized by the Navy Department to select his men from any ship-of-war in New York harbor, addressed the crews of the *North Carolina* and *Sabine*, stating fully to them the probable dangers of the passage to Hampton Roads and the certainty of having important service to perform after arriving. The sailors responded enthusiastically, many more volunteering than were required. Of the crew Captain Worden said, in his official report of the battle, "A better one no naval commander ever had the honor to command."

We left New York in tow of the tug-boat *Seth Low* at 11 A.M. of Thursday, the 6th of March. On the following day a moderate breeze was encountered, and it was at once evident that the *Monitor* was unfit as a sea-going craft. Nothing but the subsidence of the wind prevented her from being shipwrecked before she reached Hampton Roads. The berth-deck hatch leaked in spite of all we could do, and the water came down under the turret like a waterfall. It would strike the pilot-house and go over the turret in beautiful curves, and it came through the narrow eye-holes in the pilot-house with such force as to knock the helmsman completely round from the wheel. The waves also broke over the blower-pipes, and the water came down through them in such quantities that the belts of the blower-engines slipped, and the engines consequently stopped for lack of artificial draught, without which, in such a confined place, the fires could not get air for combustion. Newton and Stimers, followed by the engineer's force, gallantly rushed into the engine-room and fire-room to remedy the evil, but they were unable to check the inflowing water, and were nearly suffocated with escaping gas. They were dragged out more dead than alive, and carried to the top of the turret, where the fresh air gradually revived them. The water continued to pour through the hawse-hole, and over and down the smoke-stacks and blower-pipes, in such quantities that there was imminent danger that the ship would founder. The steam-pumps could not be operated because the fires had been nearly extinguished, and the engine-room was uninhabitable on account of the suffocating gas with which it was filled. The hand-pumps were then rigged and worked, but they had not enough force to throw the water out through the top of the turret,—the only opening,—and it was useless to bail, as we had to pass the buckets up through the turret, which made it a very long operation. Fortunately, toward evening the wind and the sea subsided, and, being again in smooth water, the engine was put in operation. But at midnight, in passing over a shoal, rough water was again encountered, and our troubles were renewed, complicated this time with the jamming of the wheel-ropes, so that the safety of the ship depended entirely on the strength of the hawser which connected her with the tug-boat. The hawser, being new, held fast; but during the greater part of the night we were constantly engaged in fighting the leaks, until we reached smooth water again, just before daylight.

It was at the close of this dispiriting trial trip, in which all hands had been exhausted in their efforts to keep the novel craft afloat, that the *Monitor* passed Cape Henry at 4 P.M. on Saturday, March 8th. At this point was heard the distant booming of heavy guns, which our captain rightly judged to be an engagement with the *Merrimac*, twenty miles away. He at once ordered the vessel stripped of her sea-rig, the turret keyed up, and every preparation made for battle. As we approached Hampton Roads we could see the fine old *Congress* burning brightly, and soon a pilot came on board and told of the arrival of the *Merrimac*, the disaster to the *Cumberland* and the *Congress*, and the dismay of the Union forces. The *Monitor* was pushed with all haste, and reached the *Roanoke* (Captain Marston), anchored in the Roads, at 9 P.M. Worden immediately reported his arrival to Captain Marston, who suggested that he should go to the assistance of the *Minnesota*, then aground off Newport News. As no pilot was available, Captain Worden accepted the volunteer services of Acting Master Samuel Howard, who earnestly sought the duty. An atmosphere of gloom pervaded the fleet, and the pygmy aspect of the new-comer did not inspire confidence among those who had witnessed the destruction of the day before. Skillfully piloted by Howard, we proceeded on our way, our path illumined by the blaze of the *Congress*. Reaching the *Minnesota*, hard and fast aground, near midnight, we anchored, and Worden reported to Captain Van Brunt. Between 1 and 2 A.M. the *Congress* blew up,—not instantaneously, but successively. Her powder-tanks seemed to explode, each shower of sparks rivaling the other in its height, until they appeared to reach the zenith,—a grand but mournful sight. Near us, too, at the bottom of the river, lay the *Cumberland*, with her silent crew of brave men, who died while fighting their guns to the water's edge, and whose colors were still flying at the peak.

The dreary night dragged slowly on; the officers and crew were up and alert, to be ready for any emergency. At daylight on Sunday the *Merrimac* and her consorts were discovered at anchor near Sewell's Point. At about half-past 7 o'clock the enemy's vessels got under way and steered in the direction of the *Minnesota*. At the same time the *Monitor* got under way, and her officers and crew took their stations for battle. Captain Van Brunt, of the *Minnesota*, officially reports, "I made signal to the *Monitor* to attack the enemy," but the signal was not seen by us; other work was in hand, and Commander Worden required no signal.

The pilot-house of the *Monitor* was situated well forward, near the bow; it was a wrought-iron structure, built of logs of iron nine inches thick, bolted through the corners, and covered with an iron plate two inches thick, which was not fastened down, but was kept in place merely by its weight. The sight-holes or slits were made by inserting quarter-inch plates at the corners between the upper set of logs and the next below. The structure projected four feet above the deck, and was barely large enough inside to hold three men standing. It presented a flat surface on all sides and on top. The steering-wheel was secured to one of the logs on the front side. The position and shape of this structure should be carefully borne in mind.

Worden took his station in the pilot-house, and by his side were Howard, the pilot, and Peter Williams, quartermaster, who steered the vessel throughout the engagement. My place was in the turret, to work and fight the guns with me were Stodder and Stimers and sixteen brawny men, eight to each gun. John Stocking, boatswain's mate, and Thomas Lochrane, seaman, were gun-captains. Newton and his assistants were in the engine and fire rooms to manipulate the boilers and engines, and most admirably did they perform this important service from the beginning to the close of the action. Webber had charge of the powder division on the berth-deck, and Joseph Crown gunner's-mate, rendered valuable service in connection with this duty.

The physical condition of the officers and men of the two ships at this time was in striking contrast. The *Merrimac* had passed the night quietly near Sewell's Point, her people enjoying rest and sleep, elated by thoughts of the victory they had achieved that day, and cheered by the prospects of another easy victory on the morrow. The *Monitor* had barely escaped shipwreck twice within the last thirty-six hours, and since Friday morning, forty-eight hours before, few if any of those on board had closed their eyes in sleep or had anything to eat but hard bread, as cooking was impossible. She was surrounded by wrecks and disaster, and her efficiency in action had yet to be proved.

Worden lost no time in bringing it to test. Getting his ship under way, he steered direct for the enemy's vessels, in order to meet and engage them as far as possible from the *Minnesota*. As he approached, the wooden vessels quickly turned and left. Our captain, to the "astonishment" of Captain Van Brunt (as he states in his official report), made straight for the *Merrimac*, which had already commenced firing; and when he came within short range, he changed his course so as to come alongside of her, stopped the engine, and gave the order, "Commence firing!" I triced up the port, ran out the gun, and, taking deliberate aim, pulled the lockstring. The *Merrimac* was quick to reply, returning a rattling broadside (for she had ten guns to our two), and the battle fairly began. The turrets and other parts of the ship were heavily struck, but the shots did not penetrate; the tower was intact, and it continued to revolve. A look of confidence passed over the men's faces, and we believed the *Merrimac* would not repeat the work she had accomplished the day before.

The fight continued with the exchange of broadsides as fast as the guns could be served and at very short range, the distance between the vessels frequently being not more than a few yards. Worden skillfully manœuvred his quick-turning vessel, trying to find some vulnerable point in his adversary. Once he made a dash at her stern, hoping to disable her screw, which he thinks he missed by not more than two feet. Our shots ripped the iron of the *Merrimac*, while the reverberation of her shots against the tower caused anything but a pleasant sensation. While Stodder, who was stationed at the machine which controlled the revolving motion of the turret, was incautiously leaning against the side of the tower, a large shot struck in the vicinity and disabled him. He left the turret and went below, and Stimers, who had assisted him, continued to do the work.

The drawbacks to the position of the pilot-house were soon realized. We could not fire ahead nor within several points of the bow, since the blast from our own guns would have injured the people in the pilot-house, only a few yards off. Keeler and Toffey passed the captain's orders and messages to me, and my inquiries and answers to him, the speaking-tube from the pilot-house to the turret having been broken early in the action. They performed their work with zeal and alacrity, but, both being landsmen, our technical communications sometimes miscarried. The situation was novel: a vessel of war was engaged in desperate combat with a powerful foe; the captain, commanding and guiding, was inclosed in one place, and the executive officer, working and fighting the guns, was shut up in another, and communication between them was difficult and uncertain. It was this experience which caused Isaac Newton, immediately after the engagement, to suggest the clever plan of putting the pilot-house on top of the turret, and making it cylindrical instead of square; and his suggestions were subsequently adopted in this type of vessel.

As the engagement continued, the working of the turret was not altogether satisfactory. It was difficult to start it revolving, or, when once started, to stop it, on account of the imperfections of the novel machinery, which was now undergoing its first trial. Stimers was an active, muscular man, and did his utmost to control the motion of the turret; but, in spite of his efforts, it was difficult, if not impossible, to secure accurate firing. The conditions were very different from those of an ordinary broadside gun, under which we had been trained on wooden ships. My only view of the world outside of the tower was over the muzzles of the guns, which cleared the ports by only a few inches. When the guns were run in, the port-holes were covered by heavy iron pendulums, pierced with small holes to allow the iron rammer and sponge handles to protrude while they were in use. To hoist these pendulums required the entire gun's crew and vastly increased the work inside the turret.

The effect upon one shut up in a revolving drum is perplexing, and it is not a simple matter to keep the bearings. White marks had been placed upon the stationary deck immediately below the turret to indicate the direction of the starboard and port sides, and the bow and stern; but these marks were obliterated early in the action. I would continually ask the captain, "How does the *Merrimac* bear?" He replied, "On the starboard-beam," or "On the port-quarter," as the case might be. Then the difficulty was to determine the direction of the starboard-beam, or port-quarter, or any other bearing. It finally resulted, that when a gun was ready for firing, the turret would be started on its revolving journey in search of the target, and when found it was taken "on the fly," because the turret could not be accurately controlled. Once the *Merrimac* tried to ram us; but Worden avoided the direct impact by the skillful use of the helm, and she struck a glancing blow, which did no damage. At the instant of collision I planted a solid 180-pound shot fair and square upon the forward part of her casemate. Had the gun been loaded with thirty pounds of powder, which was the charge subsequently used with similar guns, it is probable that this shot would have penetrated her armor; but the charge being limited to fifteen pounds, in accordance with peremptory orders to that effect from the Navy Department, the shot rebounded without doing any more damage than possibly to start some of the beams of her armor-backing.

It is stated by Colonel Wood, of the *Merrimac*, that when that vessel rammed the *Cumberland* her ram, or beak, was broken off and left in that vessel. In a letter to me, about two years since, he described this ram as "of castiron, wedge-shaped, about 1500 pounds in weight, 2 feet under water, and projecting 2½ feet from the stem." A ram of this description, had it been intact, would have struck the *Monitor* at that part of the upper hull where the armor and backing were thickest. It is very doubtful if, under any headway that the *Merrimac* could have acquired at such short range, this ram could have done any injury to this part of the vessel. That it could by no possibility have reached the thin lower hull is evident from a glance at the drawing of the *Monitor*, the overhang or upper hull being constructed for the express purpose of protecting the vital part of the vessel.

The battle continued at close quarters without apparent damage to either side. After a time, the supply of shot in the turret being exhausted, Worden hauled off for about fifteen minutes to replenish. The serving of the cartridges, weighing but fifteen pounds, was a matter of no difficulty; but the hoisting of the heavy shot was a slow and tedious operation, it being necessary that the turret should remain stationary, in order that the two scuttles, one in the deck and the other in the floor of the turret, should be in line. Worden took advantage of the lull, and passed through the port-hole upon the deck outside to get a better view of the situation. He soon renewed the attack, and the contest continued as before.

Two important points were constantly kept in mind: first, to prevent the enemy's projectiles from entering the turret through the port-holes,—for the explosion of a shell inside, by disabling the men at the guns, would have ended the fight, as there was no relief gun's crew on board; second, not to fire into our own pilot-house. A careless or impatient hand, during the confusion arising from the whirligig motion of the tower, might let slip one of our big shot against the pilot-house. For this and other reasons I fired every gun while I remained in the turret.

Soon after noon a shell from the enemy's gun, the muzzle not ten yards distant, struck the forward side of the pilot-house directly in the sight-hole, or slit, and exploded, cracking the second iron log and partly lifting the top, leaving an opening. Worden was standing immediately behind this spot, and received in his face the force of the blow, which partly stunned him, and, filling his eyes with powder, utterly blinded him. The injury was known only to those in the pilot-house and its immediate vicinity. The flood of light rushing through the top of the pilot-house, now partly open, caused Worden, blind as he was, to believe that the pilot-house was seriously injured, if not destroyed; he therefore gave orders to put the helm to starboard and "sheer off." Thus the *Monitor* retired temporarily from the action, in order to ascertain the extent of the injuries she had received. At the same time Worden sent for me, and leaving Stimers the only officer in the turret, I went forward at once, and found him standing at the foot of the ladder leading to the pilot-house.

He was a ghastly sight, with his eyes closed and the blood apparently rushing from every pore in the upper part of his face. He told me that he was seriously wounded, and directed me to take command. I assisted in leading him to a sofa in his cabin, where he was tenderly cared for by Doctor Logue, and then I assumed command. Blind and suffering as he was, Worden's fortitude never forsook him; he frequently asked from his bed of pain of the progress of affairs, and when told that the *Minnesota* was saved, he said, "Then I can die happy."

When I reached my station in the pilot-house, I found that the iron log was fractured and the top partly open; but the steering gear was still intact, and the pilot-house was not totally destroyed, as had been feared. In the confusion of the moment resulting from so serious an injury to the commanding officer, the *Monitor* had been moving without direction. Exactly how much time elapsed from the moment that Worden was wounded until I had reached the pilot-house and completed the examination of the injury at that point, and determined what course to pursue in the damaged condition of the vessel, it is impossible to state; but it could hardly have exceeded twenty minutes at the utmost. During this time the *Merrimac*, which was leaking badly, had started in the direction of the Elizabeth River; and, on taking my station in the pilot-house and turning the vessel's head in the direction of the *Merrimac*, I saw that she was already in retreat. A few shots were fired at the retiring vessel, and she continued on to Norfolk. I returned with the *Monitor* to the side of the *Minnesota*, where preparations were being made to abandon the ship, which was still aground. Shortly afterward Worden was transferred to a tug, and that night he was carried to Washington.

The fight was over. We of the *Monitor* thought, and still think, that we had gained a great victory. This the Confederates have denied. But it has never been denied that the object of the *Merrimac* on the 9th of March was to complete the destruction of the Union fleet in Hampton Roads, and that she was completely foiled and driven off by the *Monitor*; nor has it been denied that at the close of the engagement the *Merrimac* retreated to Norfolk, leaving the *Monitor* in possession of the field.

Raphael Semmes

Raphael Semmes (1809–1877) was born in Maryland and entered the U.S. Navy as a midshipman in 1826. From 1845 on Semmes made his home in Alabama, and in February 1861 he resigned from the navy and entered the Confederate service. In June 1861, Semmes sailed from New Orleans in command of the commerce raider Sumter *and captured or burned 18 American ships before being blockaded in Gibraltar by the Union navy in February 1862. Unable to repair his ship, Semmes left the* Sumter *at dock and made his way to England, where the commerce raider* Alabama *was being built in Liverpool under contract to the Confederacy. Semmes commissioned the ship in international waters off the Azores in August 1862 and resumed his attacks on American merchantmen, eventually capturing or burning 64 ships while cruising in the Atlantic, Caribbean, Gulf of Mexico, and Indian Ocean. On June 19, 1864, the* Alabama *was sunk off Cherbourg, France, by the U.S.S.* Kearsage *in a battle witnessed by 15,000 spectators. Semmes was rescued by an English yacht and eventually returned to the Confederacy. After the war he practiced law and wrote* Memoirs of Service Afloat. *This excerpt describes the international crew of the* Alabama, *which Semmes had recruited with the promise of generous prize money.*

from *Memoirs of Service Afloat During the War Between the States*

On week days we mustered the crew at their quarters twice a day—at nine A.M., and at sunset, and when the weather was suitable, one division, or about one fourth of the crew, was exercised, either at the battery, or with small arms. This not only gave them efficiency in the use of their weapons, but kept them employed—the constant employment of my men being a fundamental article of my philosophy. I found the old adage, that "Idleness is the parent of vice," as true upon the sea as upon the land. My crew were never so happy as when they had plenty to do, and but little to think about. Indeed, as to the thinking, I allowed them to do very little of that. Whenever I found I had a sea-lawyer among them, I got rid of him as soon as possible—giving him a chance to desert. I reserved the *quids*, and *quos*, and *pros* and *cons*, exclusively for myself.

But though I took good care to see that my men had plenty of employment, it was not all work with them. They had their pastimes and pleasures, as well as labors. After the duties of the day were over, they would generally assemble on the forecastle, and, with violin, and tambourine—and I always kept them supplied with these and other musical instruments—they would extemporize a ball-room, by moving the shot-racks, coils of rope, and other impediments, out of the way, and, with handkerchiefs tied around the waists of some of them, to indicate who were to be the ladies of the party, they would get up a dance with all due form and ceremony; the ladies, in particular, endeavoring to imitate all the airs and graces of the sex—the only drawback being a little hoarseness of the voice, and now and then the use of an expletive, which would escape them when something went wrong in the dance, and they forgot they had the aprons on. The favorite dancing-tunes were those of Wapping and Wide Water Street, and when I speak of the airs and graces, I must be understood to mean those rather demonstrative airs and graces, of which Poll and Peggy would be likely to be mistresses of. On these occasions, the discipline of the ship was wont to be purposely relaxed, and roars of laughter, and other evidences of the rapid flight of the jocund hours, at other times entirely inadmissible, would come resounding aft on the quarter-deck.

Sometimes the recreation of the dance would be varied, and songs and story-telling would be the amusements of the evening. The sea is a wide net, which catches all kinds of fish, and in a man-of-war's crew a great many odd characters are always to be found. Broken-down gentlemen, who have spent all the money they have been able to raise, upon their own credit, or that of their friends; defaulting clerks and cashiers; actors who have been playing to empty houses; third-class musicians and poets, are all not unfrequently found in the same ship's company. These gentlemen play a very unimportant *role* in seamanship, but they take a high rank among the crew, when fun and frolic, and not seamanship, are the order of the day—or rather night. In the *Alabama*, we had a capital Falstaff, though Jack's capacious pouch was not often with "fat capon lined;" and as for "sherry-sack," if he now and then got a good glass of "red-eye" instead, he was quite content. We had several Hals, who had defied their harsh old papas, and given them the slip, to keep Falstaff company; and as for *raconteurs*, we had them by the score. Some of these latter were equal to the Italian *lazzaroni*, and could extemporize yarns by the hour; and there is nothing of which a sailor is half so fond as a yarn.

It was my custom, on these occasions, to go forward on the bridge—a light structure spanning the deck, near amidships—which, in the twilight hours, was a sort of lounging-place for the officers, and smoke my single cigar, and listen to whatever might be going on, almost as much amused as the sailors themselves. So rigid is the discipline of a ship of war, that the captain is necessarily much isolated from his officers. He messes alone, walks the quarter-deck alone, and rarely, during the hours of duty, exchanges, even with his first lieutenant, or officer of the deck, other conversation than such as relates to the ship, or the service she is upon. I felt exceedingly the irksomeness of my position, and was always glad of an opportunity to escape from it. On the "bridge," I could lay aside the "captain," gather my young officers around me, and indulge in some of the pleasures of social intercourse; taking care to tighten the reins, gently, again, the next morning. When song was the order of the evening, after the more ambitious of the *amateurs* had delivered themselves of their *solos* and *cantatas*, the entertainment generally wound up with *Dixie*, when the whole ship would be in an uproar of enthusiasm, sometimes as many as a hundred voices joining in the chorus; the unenthusiastic Englishman, the stolid Dutchman, the mercurial Frenchman, the grave Spaniard, and even the serious Malayan, all joining in the inspiring refrain,—

"We'll live and die in Dixie!"

and astonishing old Neptune by the fervor and novelty of their music.

Eight o'clock was the hour at which the night-watches were set, when, of course, all merriment came to an end. When the officer of the deck reported this hour to the captain, and was told by the latter, to "make it so," he put the trumpet to his mouth, and sang out in a loud voice, "Strike the bell eight—call the watch!" In an instant, the most profound silence fell upon the late uproarious scene. The witches did not disappear more magically, in that famous revel of Tam O'Shanter, when Tam sang out, "Weel dune, Cutty Sark!" than the sailors dispersed at this ominous voice of authority. The violinist was arrested with half-drawn bow; the *raconteur* suddenly ceased his yarn in the most interesting part of his story, and even the inspiring chorus of "Dixie" died a premature death, upon the lips of the singers. The shrill call of the boatswain's whistle, followed by his hoarse voice, calling "All the starboard watch!" or "All the port watch!" as the case might be, would now be heard, and pretty soon, the watch, which was off duty, would "tumble" below to their hammocks, and the midshipman would be seen coming forward from the quarter-deck, with lantern and watch-bill in hand, to muster the watch whose turn it was to be on deck. The most profound stillness now reigned on board during the remainder of the night, only broken by the necessary orders and movements, in making or taking in sail, or it may be, by the whistling of the gale, and the surging of the sea, or the cry of the look-outs at their posts, every half hour.

CHARLES WARREN STODDARD

Charles Warren Stoddard (1843–1909) made his first Pacific voyage, in 1864, on doctor's orders—for his nerves. He returned to the South Pacific as often as he could in subsequent years, living alternately in San Francisco and the islands of the South Seas, eking out a living as a freelance journalist. The sketches he sent back to the mainland—"the lightest, sweetest, wildest, freshest things that ever were written about the life of that summer ocean," as William Dean Howells put it—eventually made up Stoddard's first book, South Sea Idyls *(1874), from which this excerpt is taken. He later published* A Cruise under the Crescent, *about his travels around the Mediterranean.*

Pearl-Hunting in the Pomotous

THE Great Western ducked in the heavy swell, shipping her regular deck-load of salt-water every six minutes. Now, the Great Western was nothing more nor less than a seventeen-ton schooner, two hours out from Tahiti. She was built like an old shoe, and shovelled in a head-sea as though it was her business.

It was something like sea life, wading along her submerged deck from morning till night, with a piece of raw junk on one hand and a briny biscuit in the other; we never *could* keep a fire in *that* galley, and as for hard tack, the sooner it got soaked through the sooner it was off our minds, for we knew to this complexion it must shortly come.

Two hours out from Tahiti we settled our course, wafting a theatrical kiss or two toward the gloriously green pyramid we were turning our backs on, as it slowly vanished in the blue desert of the sea.

A thousand palm-crowned and foam-girdled reefs spangled the ocean to the north and east of Tahiti. This train of lovely satellites is known as the Dangerous Archipelago, or, more commonly in that latitude, the Pomotou Islands. It's the very hot-bed of cocoanut-oil, pearls, half-famished Kanakas, shells, and shipwrecks. The currents are rapid and variable; the winds short, sharp, and equally unreliable. If you would have adventure, the real article and plenty of it, make your will, bid farewell to home and friends, and embark for the Pomotous. I started on this principle, and repented knee-deep in the deck-breakers, as we butted our way through the billows, bound for one of the Pomotous on a pearl hunt.

Three days I sat in sackcloth and salt water. Three nights I swashed in my greasy bunk, like a solitary sardine in a box with the side knocked out. In my heart of hearts I prayed for deliverance: you see there is no backing out of a schooner, unless you crave death in fifty fathoms of phosphorescent liquor and a grave in a shark's maw. Therefore I prayed for more wind from the right quarter, for a sea like a boundless mill-pond; in short, for speedy deliverance on the easiest terms possible. Notwithstanding my prayers, we continued to bang away at the great waves that crooked their backs under us and hissed frightfully as they enveloped the Great Western with spray until the fourth night out, when the moon gladdened us and promised much while we held our breath in anxiety.

We were looking for land. We'd been looking for three hours, scarcely speaking all that time. It's a serious matter raising a Pomotou by moonlight.

"Land!" squeaked a weak voice about six feet above us. A lank fellow, with his legs corkscrewed around the shrouds, and his long neck stretched to windward, where it veered like a weather-cock in a nor'wester, chuckled as he sang out "Land!" and felt himself a little lower than Christopher Columbus thereafter. "Where away?" bellowed our chunky little captain, as important as if he were commanding a grown-up ship. "Two points on the weather-bow!" piped the lookout, with the voice of one soaring in space, but unhappily choked in the last word by a sudden lurch of the schooner that brought him speedily to the deck, where he lost his identity and became a proper noun, second person, singular, for the rest of the cruise.

Now, "two points" is an indefinite term that embraces any obstacle ahead of anything; but the "weather-bow" has been the salvation of many a craft in her distress; so we gave three cheers for the "weather-bow," and proceeded to sweep the horizon with unwinking gaze. We could scarcely tell how near the land might lie; fancied we could already hear the roar of surf-beaten reefs, and every wave that reared before us seemed the rounded outline of an island. Of course we shortened sail, not knowing at what moment we might find ourselves close upon some low sea-garden nestling under the rim of breakers that fenced it in, and being morally averse to running it down without warning.

It was scarcely midnight; the moon was radiant; we were silently watching, wrapped in the deep mystery that hung over the weather-bow.

The wind suddenly abated; it was as though it sifted through trees and came to us subdued with a whisper of fluttering leaves and a breath of spice. We knew what it meant, and our hearts leaped within us as over the bow loomed the wave-like outline of shadow that sank not again like the other waves, neither floated off cloud-like, but seemed to be bearing steadily down upon us—a great whale hungry for a modern Jonah.

What a night it was! We heard the howl of waters now; saw the palm-boughs glisten in the moonlight, and the glitter and the flash of foam that fringed the edges of the half-drowned islet.

It looked for all the world like a grove of cocoa-trees that had waded out of sight of land, and didn't know which way to turn next. This was the Ultima Thule of the Great Western's voyage, and she seemed to know it, for she behaved splendidly at last, laying off and on till morning in fine style, evidently as proud as a ship-of-the-line.

I went below and dozed, with the low roar of the reef quite audible: a fellow gets used to such dream-music, and sleeps well to its accompaniment.

At daybreak we began beating up against wind and tide, hoping to work into smooth water by sunrise, which we did easily enough, shaking hands all around over a cup of thick coffee and molasses as three fathoms of chain whizzed overboard after a tough little anchor that buried itself in a dim wilderness of corals and sea-grass.

Then and there I looked about me with delighted eyes. The Great Western rode at anchor in a shallow lake, whose crystal depths seemed never to have been agitated by any harsher breath than at that moment kissed without ruffling its surface. Around us swept an amphitheatre of hills, covered with a dense growth of tropical foliage and cushioned to the hem of the beach with thick sod of exquisite tint and freshness. The narrow rim of beach that sloped suddenly to the tideless margin of the lake was littered with numberless slender canoes drawn out of the water like so many fish, as though they would navigate themselves in their natural element, and they were, therefore, not to be trusted alone too near it. Around the shore, across the hills, and along the higher ridges waved innumerable cocoa-palms, planted like a legion of lances about the encampment of some barbaric prince.

As for the very blue sky and the very white scud that shot across it, they looked windy enough; moreover we could all hear the incoherent booming of the sea upon the reef that encircled our nest. But we forgot the wind and the waves in the inexpressible repose of that armful of tropical seclusion. It was a drop of water in a tuft of moss, on a very big scale; that's just what it was.

In a few moments, as with one impulse, the canoes took to water with a savage or two in each, all gravitating to the schooner, which was for the time being the head-centre of their local commerce; and for an hour or more we did a big business in the exchange of fish-hooks and fresh fruit.

The proportion of canoes at Motu Hilo (Crescent Island) to the natives of said fragment of Eden was as one to several; but the canoeless could not resist the superior attraction of a foreign invader, therefore the rest of the inhabitants went head-first into the lake, and struck out for the middle, where we peacefully swung at anchor.

The place was sharky, but a heavy dirk full twenty inches tall was held between the teeth of the swimmers; and if the smoke-colored dorsal of any devil of a shark had dared to cut the placid surface of the water that morning, he would speedily have had more blades in him than a farrier's knife. A few vigorous strokes of the arms and legs in the neighborhood, a fatal lunge or two, a vermilion cloud in a sea churned to a cream, and a dance over the gaping corpse of some monster who has sucked human blood more than once, probably, does the business in that country.

It was a sensation for unaccustomed eyes, that inland sea covered, littered, I might say, with woolly heads, as though a cargo of cocoanuts had been thrown overboard in a stress of weather. They gathered about as thick as flies at a honey-pot, all talking, laughing, and spouting mouthfuls of water into the air like those impossible creatures that do that sort of thing by the half-dozen in all high-toned and classical fountains.

Out of this amphibious mob one gigantic youth, big enough to eat half our ship's crew, threw up an arm like Jove's, clinched the deck-rail with lithe fingers, and took a rest, swinging there with the utmost satisfaction.

I asked him aboard, but he scorned to forsake his natural element; water *is* as natural as air to those natives. Probably he would have suffered financially had he attempted boarding us, for his thick black hair was netted with a kind of spacious nest and filled with eggs on sale. It was quite astonishing to see the ease with which he navigated under his heavy deck-load.

This colossal youth having observed that I was an amateur humanitarian, virtue received its instant reward (which it doesn't in all climates), for he at once offered me three of his eggs in a very winning and patronizing manner.

I took the eggs because I like eggs, and then I was anxious to get his head above water if possible; therefore I unhesitatingly took the eggs, offering him in return a fish-hook, a tenpenny nail, and a dilapidated key-ring.

These tempting *curios* he spurned, at the same moment reaching me another handful of eggs. His generosity both pleased and alarmed me. I saw with joy that his chin was quite out of water in consequence of his charity, even when he dropped back into the sea, floating for a few moments so as to let the blood circulate in his arm again; but whether this was his magnanimous gift, or merely a trap to involve me in hopeless debt, I was quite at a loss to know, and I paused with my hands full of eggs, saying to myself, There is an end to fish-hooks in the South Pacific and dilapidated key-rings are not my staple product!

In the midst of my alarm he began making vows of eternal friendship. This was by no means disagreeable to me. He was big enough to whip any two of his fellows, and one likes to be on the best side of the stronger party in a strange land.

I reciprocated!

I leaned over the stern-rail of the Great Western in the attitude of Juliet in the balcony scene, assuring that egg-boy that my heart was his if he was willing to take it at second-hand.

He liked my sentiments, and proposed touching noses at once (a barbarous greeting still observed in the most civilized countries with even greater license, since with Christians it is allowable to touch mouths).

We touched noses, though I was in danger of sliding headlong into the sea. After this ceremonial he consented to board the Great Western, which having accomplished with my help, he deposited his eggs at my feet, offered me his nose once more, and communicated to me his name, asking in the same breath for mine.

He was known as Hua Manu, or Bird's Egg. Every native in the South Sea gets named by accident. I knew a fellow whose name was "Cockeye;" he was a standing advertisement of his physical deformity. A fellow that knew me rejoiced in the singular cognomen of "Thrown-from-a-horse." Fortunately he doesn't spell it with so many letters in his tongue. His christening happened in this wise: A bosom friend of his mother was thrown from a horse and killed the day of his birth. Therefore the bereaved mother reared that child, an animated memorial, who in after years clove to me, and was as jolly as though his earthly mission wasn't simply to keep green the memory of his mother's bosom friend sailing through the air with a dislocated neck.

I turned to my new-found friend. "Hua Manu," said I, "for my sake you have made a bird's-nest of your back hair. You have freely given me your young affection and your eggs. Receive the sincere thanks of yours truly, together with these fish-hooks, these tenpenny nails, this key-ring." Hua Manu smiled and accepted, burying the fish-hooks in his matted forelock, and inserting a tenpenny nail and a key-ring in either ear, thereby making himself the envy of the entire population of Motu Hilo, and feeling himself as grand as the best chief in the archipelago.

So we sat together on the deck of the Great Western, quite dry for a wonder, exchanging sheep's-eyes and confidences, mutually happy in each other's society. Meanwhile the captain was arranging his plans for an immediate purchase of such pearls as he might find in possession of the natives, and for a fresh search for pearl oysters at the earliest possible hour. There were no pearls on hand. What are pearls to a man who has as many wives, children, and cocoanuts as he can dispose of? Pearls are small and colorless. Give him a handful of gorgeous glass beads, a stick of sealing-wax, or some spotted beans, and keep your pale sea-tears, milky and frozen and apt to grow sickly yellow and die if they are not cared for.

Motu Hilo is independent. No man has squatted there to levy tax or toll. We were each one of us privileged to hunt for pearls and keep our stores separate. I said to Hua Manu, "Let's invest in a canoe, explore the lagoon for fresh oyster-beds, and fill innumerable cocoanut shells with these little white seeds. It will be both pleasant and profitable, particularly for me." We were scarcely five minutes bargaining for our outfit, and we embarked at once, having agreed to return in a couple of days for news concerning the success of the Great Western and her probable date of sailing.

Seizing a paddle, Hua Manu propelled our canoe with incredible rapidity out of the noisy fleet in the centre of the lake, toward a green point that bounded it, one of the horns of the crescent. He knew a spot where the oyster yawned in profusion, a secret cave for shelter, a forest garden of fruits, a never-failing spring, etc. Thither we would fly and domesticate ourselves. The long, curved point of land soon hid the inner waters from view. We rose and sank on the swell between the great reef and the outer rim of the island, while the sun glowed fiercely overhead and the reef howled in our ears. Still on we skimmed, the water hissing along the smooth sides of the canoe, that trembled at every fierce stroke of Hua Manu's industrious paddle. No chart, no compass, no rudder, no exchange of references, no letter of introduction, yet I trusted that wild Hercules who was hurrying me away, I knew not whither, with an earnestness that forced the sweat from his naked body in living streams.

At last we turned our prow and shot through a low arch in a cliff, so low we both ducked our heads instinctively, letting the vines and parasites trail over our shoulders and down our backs.

It was a dark passage into an inner cave lit from below—a cave filled with an eternal and sunless twilight that was very soothing to our eyes as we came in from the glare of sea and sky.

"Look!" said Hua Manu. Overhead rose a compressed dome of earth, a thick matting of roots, coil within coil. At the side innumerable ledges, shelves, and seams lined with nests, and never a nest without its egg, often two or more together. Below us, in two fathoms of crystal, sunlit and luminous bowers of coral, and many an oyster asleep with its mouth open, and many a prismatic fish poising itself with palpitating gills, and gauzy fins fanning the water incessantly.

"Hua Manu!" I exclaimed in rapture, "permit me to congratulate you. In you I behold a regular South Sea Monte Cristo, and no less magnificent title can do you justice." Thereat Hua Manu laughed immoderately, which laugh having run out we both sat in our canoe and silently sucked eggs for some moments.

A canoe-length from where we floated, a clear rill stole noiselessly from above, mingling its sweet waters with the sea; on the roof of our cavern fruits flourished, and we were wholly satisfied. After such a lunch as ours it behooved us to cease idling and dive for pearls. So Hua Manu knotted his long hair tightly about his forehead, cautiously transferred himself from the canoe to the water, floated a moment, inhaling a wonderfully long breath, and plunged under. How he struggled to get down to the gaping oysters, literally climbing down head first! I saw his dark form wrestling with the elements that strove to force him back to the surface, crowding him out into the air again. He seized one of the shells, but it shut immediately, and he tugged and jerked and wrenched at it like a young demon till it gave way, when he struck out and up for the air. All this seemed an age to me. I took full twenty breaths while he was down. Reaching the canoe, he dropped the great, ugly-looking thing into it, and hung over the outrigger gasping for breath like a man half hanged. He was pale about the mouth, his eyes were suffused with blood, blood oozed from his ears and nostrils; his limbs, gashed with the sharp corals, bled also. The veins of his forehead looked ready to burst, and as he tightened the cords of hair across them it seemed his only salvation.

I urged him to desist, seeing his condition and fearing a repetition of his first experience; but he would go once more; perhaps there was no pearl in that shell; he wanted to get me a pearl. He sank again and renewed his efforts at the bottom of the sea. I scarcely dared to count the minutes now, nor the bubbles that came up to me like little balloons with a death-message in each. Suppose he were to send his last breath in one of those transparent globes, and I look down and see his body snared in the antlers of coral, stained with his blood? Well, he came up all right, and I postponed the rest of my emotion for a later experience.

Some divers remain three minutes under water, but two or three descents are as many as they can make in a day. The ravages of such a life are something frightful.

No more pearl-hunting after the second dive that day; nor the next, because we went out into the air for a stroll on shore to gather fruit and stretch our legs. There was a high wind and a heavy sea that looked threatening enough, and we were glad to return after an hour's tramp. The next day was darker, and the next after that, when a gale came down upon us that seemed likely to swamp Motu Hilo. A swell rolled over the windward reef and made our quarters in the grotto by no means safe or agreeable. It was advisable for us to think of embarking upon that tempestuous sea, or get brained against the roof of our retreat.

Hua Manu looked troubled, and my heart sank. I wished the pearl oysters at the bottom of the sea, the Great Western back at Tahiti, and I loafing under the green groves of Papeete, never more to be deluded abroad.

I observed no visible changes in the weather after I had been wishing for an hour and a half. The swell rather increased; our frail canoe was tossed from side to side in imminent danger of upsetting.

Now and then a heavy roller entirely filled the mouth of our cavern, quite blinding us with spray; having spent its fury it subsided with a concussion that nearly deafened us, and dragged us with fearful velocity toward the narrow mouth of the cave, where we saved ourselves from being swept into the sea by grasping the roots overhead and within reach.

"Could I swim?" asked Hua Manu. Alas, no! That we must seek new shelter at any risk was but too evident. "Let us go on the next wave," said Hua, as he seized a large shell and began clearing the canoe of the water that had accumulated. Then he bound his long hair in a knot to keep it from his eyes, and gave me some hasty directions as to my deportment in the emergency.

The great wave came. We were again momentarily corked up in an air-tight compartment. I wonder the roof was not burst open with the intense pressure that nearly forced the eyes out of my head and made me faint and giddy. Recovering from the shock, with a cry of warning from Hua, and a prayer scarcely articulated, we shot like a bomb from a mortar into the very teeth of a frightful gale.

Nothing more was said, nothing seen. The air was black with flying spray, the roar of the elements more awful than anything I had ever heard before. Sheets of water swept over us with such velocity that they hummed like circular saws in motion.

We were crouched as low as possible in the canoe, yet now and then one of these, the very *blade* of the wave, struck us on the head or shoulders, cutting us like knives. I could scarcely distinguish Hua's outline, the spray was so dense, and as for him, what could he do? Nothing, indeed, but send up a sort of death-wail, a few notes of which tinkled in my ear from time to time, assuring me how utterly without hope we were.

One of those big rollers must have lifted us clean over the reef, for we crossed it and were blown into the open sea, where the canoe spun for a second in the trough of the waves, and was cut into slivers by an avalanche of water that carried us all down into the depths.

I suppose I filled at once, but came up in spite of it (almost everyone has that privilege), when I was clutched by Hua Manu and made fast to his utilitarian back hair. I had the usual round of experiences allotted to all half-drowned people: a panoramic view of my poor life crammed with sin and sorrow and regret; a complete biography written and read through inside of ten seconds. I was half strangled, call it two-thirds, for that comes nearer the truth; heard the water singing in my ears, which was *not* sweeter than symphonies, nor beguiling, nor in the least agreeable. I deny it! In the face of every corpse that ever was drowned I emphatically deny it!

Hua had nearly stripped me with one or two tugs at my thin clothing, because he didn't think that worth towing off to some other island, and he was willing to float me for a day or two, and run the risk of saving me.

When I began to realize anything, I congratulated myself that the gale was over. The sky was clear, the white caps scarce, but the swell still sufficient to make me dizzy as we climbed one big, green hill, and slid off the top of it into a deep and bubbling abyss.

I found Hua leisurely feeling his way through the water, perfectly self-possessed and apparently unconscious that he had a deck passenger nearly as big as himself. My hands were twisted into his hair in such a way that I could rest my chin upon my arms, and thus easily keep my mouth above water most of the time.

My emotions were peculiar. I wasn't accustomed to travelling in that fashion. I knew it had been done before. Even there I thought with infinite satisfaction of the Hawaiian woman who swam for forty hours in such a sea, with an aged and helpless husband upon her back. Reaching land at last she tenderly drew her burden to shore and found him—dead! The fact is historical, and but one of several equally marvellous.

We floated on and on, cheering each other hour after hour; the wind continuing, the sea falling, and anon night coming like an ill omen—night, that buried us alive in darkness and despair.

I think I must have dozed, or fainted, or died several times during the night, for it began to grow light long before I dared to look for it, and then came sunrise—a sort of intermittent sunrise that gilded Hua's shoulder whenever we got to the top of a high wave, and went out again as soon as we settled into the hollows.

Hua Manu's eyes were much better than mine; he seemed to see with all his five senses, and the five told him that *there was land not far off!* I wouldn't believe him; I think I was excusable for questioning his infallibility then and there. The minute he cried out "Land!" I gave up and went to sleep, or to death, for I thought he was daft, and it was a discouraging business, and I wished I could die for good. Hua Manu, what a good egg you were, though it's the bad that usually keep atop of the water, they tell me!

Hua Manu was right. He walked out of the sea an hour later and stood on a mound of coarse sand in the middle of the ocean, with my miserable, water-logged body lying in a heap at his feet.

The place was as smooth and shiny and desolate as anybody's bald head. That's a nice spot to be merry in, isn't it? Yet he tried to make me open my eyes and be glad.

He said he knew the Great Western would be coming down that way shortly; she'd pick us off the shoal, and water and feed us.

Perhaps she might! Meantime we hungered and thirsted as many a poor castaway had before us. That was a good hour for Christian fortitude: beached in the middle of the ocean; shelterless under a sun that blistered Hua's tough skin; eyes blinded with the glare of sun and sea; the sand glowing like brass and burning into flesh already irritated with salt water; a tongue of leather cleaving to the roof of the mouth, and no food within reach, nor so much as a drop of fresh water for Christ's sake!

Down went my face into the burning sand that made the very air *hop* above it. . . . Another night, cool and grateful; a bird or two flapped wearily overhead, looking like spirits in the moonlight. Hua scanned earnestly our narrow horizon, noting every inflection in the voices of the wind and waves—voices audible to him, but worse than dumb to me—mocking monotones reiterated through an agonizing eternity.

A wise monitor was Hua Manu, shaming me to silence in our cursed banishment. Toward the morning after our arrival at the shoal, an owl fluttered out of the sky and fell at our feet quite exhausted. It might have been blown from Motu Hilo, and seemed ominous of something, I scarcely knew what. When it had recovered from its fatigue, it sat regarding us curiously. I wanted to wring its short, thick neck, and eat it, feathers and all. Hua objected; there was a superstition that gave that bland bird its life. It might continue to ogle us with one eye as long as it liked. How the lopsided thing smirked! how that stupid owl-face, like a rosette with three buttons in it, haunted me! It was enough to craze anyone; and, having duly cursed him and his race, I went stark mad and hoped I was dying forever. . . .

There are plenty of stars in this narrative. Stars, and plenty of them, cannot account for the oblivious intervals, suspended animation, or whatever it was, that came to my relief from time to time. I cannot account for them myself. Perhaps Hua Manu might; he seemed always awake, always on the lookout, and ever so patient and faithful. A dream came to me after that owl had stared me into stone—a dream of an island in a sea of glass; soft ripples lapping on the silver shores; sweet airs sighing in a starlit grove; someone gathering me in his arms, hugging me close with infinite tenderness; I was consumed with thirst, speechless with hunger; like an infant I lay in the embrace of my deliverer, who moistened my parched lips and burning throat with delicious and copious draughts. It was an elixir of life; I drank health and strength in every drop; sweeter than mother's milk flowed the warm tide unchecked, till I was satisfied and sank into a deep and dreamless sleep.

The Great Western was plunging in her old style, and I swashed in my bunk as of yore. The captain sat by me with a bottle in his hand and anxiety in his countenance.

"Where are we?" I asked.

"Two hours out from Tahiti, inward bound."

"How! What! When!" etc.; and my mind ran up and down the record of the last fortnight, finding many blots and some blanks.

"As soon as I got into my right mind I could hear all about it;" and the captain shook his bottle, and held on to the side of my bunk to save himself from total wreck in the lee-corners of the cabin.

"Why, wasn't I right-minded? I could tell a hawk from a hernshaw; and, speaking of hawks, where was that cursed owl?"

The captain concluded I was bettering, and put the physic into the locker, so as to give his whole attention to keeping right side up. Well, this is how it happened, as I afterward learned: The Great Western suffered somewhat from the gale at Motu Hilo, though she was comparatively sheltered in that inner sea. Having repaired, and given me up as a deserter, she sailed for Tahiti. The first day out, in a light breeze, they all saw a man apparently wading up to his middle in the sea. The fellow hailed the Great Western, but as she could hardly stand up against the rapid current in so light a wind, the captain let her drift past the man in the sea, who suddenly disappeared. A consultation of officers followed. Evidently someone was cast away and ought to be looked after; resolved to beat up to the rock, big turtle, or whatever it might be that kept that fellow afloat, provided the wind freshened sufficiently; wind immediately freshened; Great Western put about and made for the spot where Hua Manu had been seen hailing the schooner. But when that schooner passed he threw himself upon the sand beside me and gave up hoping at last, and was seen no more.

What did he then? I must have asked for drink. He gave it me from an artery in his wrist, severed by the finest teeth you ever saw. That's what saved me. On came the little schooner, beating up against the wind and tide, while I had my lips sealed to that fountain of life.

The skipper kept banging away with an old blunderbuss that had been left over in his bargains with the savages, and one of these explosions caught the ears of Hua. He tore my lips from his wrist, staggered to his feet, and found help close at hand. Too late they gathered us up out of the deep and strove to renew our strength. They transported us to the little cabin of the schooner, Hua Manu, myself, and that mincing owl, and swung off into the old course. Probably the Great Western never did better sailing since she came from the stocks than that hour or two of beating that brought her up to the shoal. She seemed to be emulating it in the home run, for we went bellowing through the sea in a stiff breeze and the usual flood tide on deck.

I lived to tell the tale. I should think it mighty mean of me not to live after such a sacrifice. Hua Manu sank rapidly. I must have nearly drained his veins, but I don't believe he regretted it. The captain said when he was dying, his faithful eyes were fixed on me. Unconsciously I moved a little; he smiled, and the soul went out of him in that smile, perfectly satisfied. At that moment the owl fled from the cabin, passed through the hatchway, and disappeared.

Hua Manu lay on the deck, stretched under a sail, while I heard this. I wondered if a whole cargo of pearls could make me indifferent to his loss. I wondered if there were many truer and braver than he in Christian lands. They call him a heathen. It *was* heathenish to offer up his life vicariously. He might have taken mine so easily, and perhaps have breasted the waves back to his own people, and been fêted and sung of as the hero he truly was.

Well, if he is a heathen, out of my heart I would make a parable, its rubric bright with his sacrificial blood, its theme this glowing text: "Greater love hath no man than this, that a man lay down his life for a friend."

Celia Thaxter

The peculiar intimacy with which Celia Thaxter (1835–1894) describes the moods of sea and shore has everything to do with the circumstances of her upbringing. Her father was a successful merchant and New Hampshire legislator who, foiled in his ambition to become governor of the state, obtained for himself instead the position of lighthouse keeper on the virtually uninhabited Isles of Shoals, and resolved never to return to the mainland. Celia and her brothers spent their childhood in a seclusion interrupted only by occasional visitors and tutors (one of whom she eventually married). When Thaxter's father opened a hotel on Appledore Island in 1848, it became a favored haunt of writers and artists including Henry David Thoreau, James Russell Lowell, John Greenleaf Whittier, William Morris Hunt, and Childe Hassam. Best known in her lifetime as a poet, Thaxter created in Among the Isles of Shoals *(1873) a neglected classic of descriptive prose, imbued with the atmospheric shifts of her unique early environment.*

from *Among the Isles of Shoals*

THERE are no beaches of any considerable size along the circle of these shores, and except in two narrow fissures, one on Malaga and one on Star, only a few feet wide at their widest, there is no fine, clean sand, such as lies sparkling on the coast at Rye, opposite, and shows, faintly glimmering, white in the far distance. The dock at Smutty-nose is filled with coarse sand and mud, like the little basin of the "Upper Cove" on Appledore; and the largest beach on Star, of the same character, is covered with a stratum of fish-bones several feet deep,—by no means a pleasantly fragrant pavement. Roughly rounded pebbles, not beautiful with warmth of color like those on the Cohasset beaches, but a cold, hard combination of gray granite and dark trap, are heaped in the coves. Indian arrowheads of jasper and flint have been found among them. Now and then a smoother bit consists of a coarse gravel, which, if you examine, you will find to be principally composed of shells ground fine by the waves, a fascinating mixture of blue and purple mussels, lined with the rainbow tints of mother-of-pearl, and fragments of golden and ruddy snail-shells, and striped and colored cockles; with here and there a piece of transparent quartz, white or rosy, or of opaque felspar, faintly straw-colored, or of dull-purple porphyry stone, all clean and moist with the odorous brine. Upon Appledore and the little islets undevastated by civilization these tiny coves are the most delightful places in the world, lovely with their fringe of weeds, thistles, and mullein-stalks drawn clearly against the sky at the upper edge of the slope, and below, their mosaic of stone and shell and sea-wrack, tangles of kelp and driftwood,—a mass of warm neutral tints,—with brown, green, and crimson mosses, and a few golden snail-shells lying on the many-tinted gravel, where the indolent ripples lapse in delicious murmurs. There are few shells more delicate than the variegated snails and cockles and stout whelks that sparsely strew the beaches, but these few are exceedingly beautiful, and more precious from their rarity. Two kinds of pure white spiral shells, not quite an inch long, are occasionally found, and cause one to wonder how they can be rolled together with the heavy pebbles by the breakers and not be annihilated.

After the dark blue mussel-shells have lain long on shore in sun and rain, they take a curious satin sheen, lovely to behold, and the larger kind, shedding their coat of brown varnish, are colored like the eastern sky in clear winter sunsets, a rosy purple, with pearly linings streaked with iridescent hues. The driftwood is always full of suggestions:—a broken oar; a bit of spar with a ragged end of rope-yarn attached; a section of a mast hurriedly chopped, telling of a tragedy too well known on the awful sea; a water-worn buoy, or flakes of rich brown bark, which have been peacefully floated down the rivers of Maine and out on the wide sea, to land at last here and gladden firesides so remote from the deep green wood where they grew; pine-cones, with their spicy fragrance yet lingering about them; apples, green spruce twigs, a shingle, with some carpenter's half-obliterated calculations pencilled upon it; a child's roughly carved boat; drowned butterflies, beetles, birds; dead boughs of ragged fir-trees completely draped with the long, shining ribbon-grass that grows in brackish water near river mouths. The last, after lying awhile in the wind and sun, present a weird appearance, for the narrow ribbons are dried and bleached as white as chalk, and shiver and shudder with every wind that blows. It used to be a great delight to hold such a bough aloft, and watch all the long, delicate pennons and streamers fly trembling out on the breeze. Beyond high-water mark all things in the course of time take a uniform gray color from the weather; wood, shells, stones, deposited by some great tide or storm, and left undisturbed for months, chocolate-colored bark and yellow shingle and gray stone are not to be distinguished one from another, except by their shape. Of course all white things grow whiter, and shells already colorless become as pure as snow. Sometimes the slabs and blocks of wood that float ashore have drifted so long that they are water-logged, and covered with a rich growth of mosses, barnacles, and wondrous sea-creatures. Sometimes they are completely riddled by the pholas, and the hardest shells are pierced smoothly through and through by these soft worms.

* * *

To see a *bona fide* Shoaler "sail a boat" (when the craft is a real boat and no tub) is an experience. The vessel obeys his hand at the rudder as a trained horse a touch on the rein, and seems to bow at the flash of his eye, turning on her heel and running up into the wind, "luffing" to lean again on the other tack,—obedient, graceful, perfectly beautiful, yielding to breeze and to billow, yet swayed throughout by a stronger and more imperative law. The men become strongly attached to their boats, which seem to have a sort of human interest for them,—and no wonder. They lead a life of the greatest hardship and exposure, during the winter especially, setting their trawls fifteen or twenty miles to the eastward of the islands, drawing them next day if the stormy winds and waves will permit, and taking the fish to Portsmouth to sell. It is desperately hard work, trawling at this season, with the bitter wind blowing in their teeth, and the flying spray freezing upon everything it touches,—boats, masts, sails, decks, clothes completely cased in ice, and fish frozen solid as soon as taken from the water. The inborn politeness of these fishermen to stranger-women is something delightful to witness. I remember once landing in Portsmouth, and being obliged to cross three or four schooners just in (with their freight of frozen fish lying open-mouthed in a solid mass on deck) to reach the wharf. No courtly gentlemen could have displayed more beautiful behavior than did these rough fellows, all pressing forward, with real grace,—because the feeling which prompted them was a true and lofty feeling,—to help me over the tangle of ropes and sails and anchors to a safe footing on shore. There is a ledge forty-five miles east of the islands, called Jeffrey's Ledge, where the Shoalers go for spring fishing. During a northeast storm in May, part of the little fleet came reeling in before the gale; and, not daring to trust themselves to beat up into the harbor (a poor shelter at best), round the rocky reefs and ledges, the fishermen anchored under the lee of Appledore, and there rode out the storm. They were in continual peril; for, had their cables chafed apart with the shock and strain of the billows among which they plunged, or had their anchors dragged (which might have been expected, the bottom of the sea between the islands and the mainland being composed of mud, while all outside is rough and rocky), they would have inevitably been driven to their destruction on the opposite coast. It was not pleasant to watch them as the early twilight shut down over the vast, weltering desolation of the sea, to see the slender masts waving helplessly from one side to another,—sometimes almost horizontal, as the hulls turned heavily this way and that, and the long breakers rolled in endless succession against them. They saw the lights in our windows a half-mile away; and we, in the warm, bright, quiet room, sitting by a fire that danced and shone, fed with bits of wreck such as they might scatter on Rye Beach before morning, could hardly think of anything else than the misery of those poor fellows, wet, cold, hungry, sleepless, full of anxiety till the morning should break and the wind should lull. No boat could reach them through the terrible commotion of waves. But they rode through the night in safety, and the morning brought relief. One brave little schooner "toughed it out" on the distant ledge, and her captain told me that no one could stand on board of her; the pressure of the wind down on her decks was so great that she shuddered from stem to stern, and he feared she would shake to pieces, for she was old and not very seaworthy. Some of the men had wives and children watching them from lighted windows at Star. What a fearful night for them! They could not tell from hour to hour, through the thick darkness, if yet the cables held; they could not see till daybreak whether the sea had swallowed up their treasures. I wonder the wives were not white-haired when the sun rose, and showed them those little specks yet rolling in the breakers! The women are excessively timid about the water, more so than landswomen. Having the terror and might of the ocean continually encircling them, they become more impressed with it and distrust it, knowing it so well. Very few accidents happen, however: the islanders are a cautious people. Years ago, when the white sails of their little fleet of whaleboats used to flutter out of the sheltered bight and stand out to the fishing-grounds in the bay, how many eyes followed them in the early light, and watched them in the distance through the day, till, toward sunset, they spread their wings to fly back with the evening wind! How pathetic the gathering of women on the headlands, when out of the sky swept the squall that sent the small boats staggering before it, and blinded the eyes, already drowned in tears, with sudden rain that hid sky and sea and boats from their eager gaze! What wringing of hands, what despairing cries, which the wild wind bore away while it caught and fluttered the homely draperies and unfastened the locks of maid and mother, to blow them about their pale faces and anxious eyes! Now no longer the little fleet goes forth; for the greater part of the islanders have stout schooners, and go trawling with profit, if not with pleasure. A few solitaries fish in small dories and earn a slender livelihood thereby.

The sea helps these poor people by bringing fuel to their very doors; the waves continually deposit driftwood in every fissure of the rocks. But sad, anxious lives they have led, especially the women, many of whom have grown old before their time with hard work and bitter cares, with hewing of wood and drawing of water, turning of fish on the flakes to dry in the sun, endless household work, and the cares of maternity, while their lords lounged about the rocks in their scarlet shirts in the sun, or "held up the walls of the meeting-house," as one expressed it, with their brawny shoulders. I never saw such wrecks of humanity as some of the old women of Star Island, who have long since gone to their rest. In my childhood I caught glimpses of them occasionally, their lean brown shapes crouching over the fire, with black pipes in their sunken mouths, and hollow eyes, "of no use now but to gather brine," and rough, gray, straggling locks: despoiled and hopeless visions, it seemed as if youth and joy could never have been theirs.

* * *

For the last ten years fish have been caught about the Shoals by trawl and seine in such quantities that they are thinning fast, and the trade bids fair to be much less lucrative before many years have elapsed. The process of drawing the trawl is very picturesque and interesting, watched from the rocks or from the boat itself. The buoy being drawn in, then follow the baited hooks one after another. First, perhaps, a rockling shows his bright head above water; a pull, and in he comes flapping, with brilliant red fins distended, gaping mouth, indigo-colored eyes, and richly mottled skin: a few futile somersets, and he subsides into slimy dejection. Next, perhaps, a big whelk is tossed into the boat; then a leaden-gray haddock, with its dark stripe of color on each side; then, perhaps, follow a few bare hooks; then a hake, with horrid, cavernous mouth; then a large purple star-fish, or a clattering crab; then a ling,—a yellow-brown, wide-mouthed piece of ugliness never eaten here, but highly esteemed on the coast of Scotland; then more cod or haddock, or perhaps a lobster, bristling with indignation at the novel situation in which he finds himself; then a cusk, long, smooth, compact, and dark; then a catfish. Of all fiends commend me to the catfish as the most fiendish! Black as night, with thick and hideous skin, which looks a dull, mouldy green beneath the water, a head shaped as much like a cat's as a fish's head can be, in which the devil's own eyes seem to glow with a dull, malicious gleam,—and such a mouth! What terrible expressions these cold creatures carry to and fro in the vast, dim spaces of the sea! All fish have a more or less imbecile and wobegone aspect; but this one looks absolutely evil, and Schiller might well say of him that he "grins through the grate of his spiky teeth," and sharp and deadly are they; every man looks out for his boots when a catfish comes tumbling in, for they bite through leather, flesh, and bones. They seize a ballast-stone between their jaws, and their teeth snap and fly in all directions. I have seen them bite the long blade of a sharp knife so fiercely, that, when it was lifted and held aloft, they kept their furious grip, and dangled, flapping all their clumsy weight, hanging by their teeth to the blade. Sculpins abound, and are a nuisance on the trawls. Ugly and grotesque as are the full-grown fish, there is nothing among the finny tribe more dainty, more quaint and delicate, than the baby sculpin. Sometimes in a pool of crystal water one comes upon him unawares,—a fairy creature, the color of a blush-rose, striped and freaked and pied with silver and gleaming green, hanging in the almost invisible water as a bird in air, with broad, transparent fins suffused with a faint pink color, stretched wide like wings to upbear the supple form. The curious head is only strange, not hideous as yet, and one gazes marvelling at all the beauty lavished on a thing of so little worth.

Wolf-fish, first cousins to the catfish, are found also on the trawls; and dog-fish, with pointed snouts and sand-paper skins, abound to such an extent as to drive away everything else sometimes. Sand-dabs, a kind of flounder, fasten their sluggish bodies to the hooks, and a few beautiful red fish, called bream, are occasionally found; also a few blue-fish and sharks; frequently halibut,—though these latter are generally caught on trawls which are made especially for them. Sometimes is caught on a trawl a monstrous creature of horrible aspect, called the nurse-fish,—an immense fish weighing twelve hundred pounds, with a skin like a nutmeg-grater, and no teeth,—a kind of sucker, hence its name. I asked a Shoaler what the nurse-fish looked like, and he answered promptly, "Like the Devil!" One weighing twelve hundred pounds has "two barrels of liver," as the natives phrase it, which is very valuable for the oil it contains. One of the fishermen described a creature which they call mud-eel,—a foot and a half long, with a mouth like a rat, and two teeth. The bite of this water-snake is poisonous, the islanders aver, and tell a story of a man bitten by one at Mount Desert last year, "who did not live long enough to get to the doctor." They bite at the hooks on the trawl, and are drawn up in a lump of mud, and the men cut the ropes and mangle their lines to get rid of them. Huge sunfish are sometimes harpooned, lying on the top of the water,—a lump of flesh like cocoanut meat encased in a skin like rubber cloth, with a most dim and abject hint of a face, absurdly disproportionate to the size of the body, roughly outlined on the edge. Sword-fish are also harpooned, weighing eight hundred pounds and upward; they are very delicate food. A sword-fish swimming leaves a wake a mile long on a calm day, and bewilders the imagination into a belief in sea-serpents. There's a legend that a torpedo was caught here once upon a time; and the thrasher, fox-shark, or sea-fox occasionally alarms the fisherman with his tremendous flexible tail, that reaches "from the gunnel to the mainmast-top" when the creature comes to the surface. Also they tell of skip-jacks that sprang on board their boats at night when they were hake-fishing,—"little things about as large as mice, long and slender, with beaks like birds." Sometimes a huge horse-mackerel flounders in and drives ashore on a ledge, for the gulls to scream over for weeks. Mackerel, herring, porgies, and shiners used to abound before the seines so thinned them. Bonito and blue-fish and dog-fish help drive away the more valuable varieties. It is a lovely sight to see a herring-net drawn in, especially by moonlight, when every fish hangs like a long silver drop from the close-set meshes. Perch are found in inexhaustible quantities about the rocks, and lump or butter fish are sometimes caught; pollock are very plentiful,—smooth, graceful, slender creatures! It is fascinating to watch them turning somersets in the water close to the shore in full tides, or following a boat at sunset, and breaking the molten gold of the sea's surface with silver-sparkling fin and tail. The rudder-fish is sometimes found, and alewives and menhaden. Whales are more or less plentiful in summer, "spouting their foam-fountains in the sea." Beautiful is the sparkling column of water rising suddenly afar off and falling noiselessly back again. Not long ago a whale twisted his tail in the cable of the schooner Vesper, lying to the eastward of the Shoals, and towed the vessel several miles, at the rate of twenty knots an hour, with the water boiling all over her from stem to stern!

Last winter some of the Shoalers were drawing a trawl between the Shoals and Boone Island, fifteen miles to the eastward. As they drew in the line and relieved each hook of its burden, lo! a horror was lifted half above the surface,—part of a human body, which dropped off the hooks and was gone, while they shuddered, and stared at each other, aghast at the hideous sight.

Porpoises are seen at all seasons. I never saw one near enough to gain a knowledge of its expression, but it always seemed to me that these fish led a more hilarious life than the greater part of their race, and I think they must carry less dejected countenances than most of the inhabitants of the sea. They frisk so delightfully on the surface, and ponderously plunge over and over with such apparent gayety and satisfaction! I remember being out one moonless summer night beyond the lighthouse island, in a little boat filled with gay young people. The sea was like oil, the air was thick and warm, no star broke the upper darkness, only now and then the lighthouse threw its jewelled track along the water, and through the dense air its long rays stretched above, turning solemnly, like the luminous spokes of a gigantic wheel, as the lamps slowly revolved. There had been much talk and song and laughter, much playing with the warm waves (or rather smooth undulations of the sea, for there wasn't a breath of wind to make a ripple), which broke at a touch into pale-green, phosphorescent fire. Beautiful arms, made bare to the shoulder, thrust down into the liquid darkness, shone flaming silver and gold; from the fingers playing beneath, fire seemed to stream; emerald sparks clung to the damp draperies; and a splashing oar-blade half revealed sweet faces and bright young eyes. Suddenly a pause came in talk and song and laughter, and in the unaccustomed silence we seemed to be waiting for something. At once out of the darkness came a slow, tremendous sigh that made us shiver in the soft air, as if all the woe and terror of the sea were condensed in that immense and awful breath; and we took our oars and pulled homeward, with the weird fires flashing from our bows and oar-blades. "Only a porpoise blowing," said the initiated, when we told our tale. It may have been "only a porpoise blowing"; but the leviathan himself could hardly have made a more prodigious sound.

* * *

All through the day the ominous quiet lasts; in the afternoon, while yet the sea is glassy, a curious undertone of mournful sound can be perceived,—not fitful,—a steady moan such as the wind makes over the mouth of an empty jar. Then the islanders say, "Do you hear Hog Island crying? Now look out for a storm!" No one knows how that low moaning is produced, or why Appledore, of all the islands, should alone lament before the tempest. Through its gorges, perhaps, some current of wind sighs with that hollow cry. Yet the sea could hardly keep its unruffled surface were a wind abroad sufficient to draw out the boding sound. Such a calm preceded the storm which destroyed the Minot's Ledge Lighthouse in 1849. I never knew such silence. Though the sun blazed without a cloud, the sky and sea were utterly wan and colorless, and before sunset the mysterious tone began to vibrate in the breezeless air. "Hog Island's crying!" said the islanders. One could but think of the Ancient Mariner, as the angry sun went down in a brassy glare, and still no ripple broke the calm. But with the twilight gathered the waiting wind, slowly and steadily; and before morning the shock of the breakers was like the incessant thundering of heavy guns; the solid rock perceptibly trembled; windows shook, and glass and china rattled in the house. It is impossible to describe the confusion, the tumult, the rush and roar and thunder of waves and wind overwhelming those rocks,—the whole Atlantic rushing headlong to cast itself upon them. It was very exciting: the most timid among us lost all sense of fear. Before the next night the sea had made a breach through the valley on Appledore, in which the houses stand,—a thing that never had happened within the memory of the oldest inhabitant. The waves piled in from the eastward (where Old Harry was tossing the breakers sky-high),—a maddened troop of giants, sweeping everything before them,—and followed one another, white as milk, through the valley from east to west, strewing the space with boulders from a solid wall six feet high and as many thick, which ran across the top of the beach, and which one tremendous wave toppled over like a child's fence of blocks. Kelp and seaweed were piled in banks high up along the shore, and strewed the doorsteps; and thousands of the hideous creatures known among the Shoalers as sea-mice, a holothurian (a livid, shapeless mass of torpid life), were scattered in all directions. While the storm was at its height, it was impossible to do anything but watch it through windows beaten by the blinding spray which burst in flying clouds all over the island, drenching every inch of the soil in foaming brine. In the coves the "yeasty surges" were churned into yellow masses of foam, that blew across in trembling flakes, and clung wherever they lit, leaving a hoary scum of salt when dry, which remained till sweet, fair water dropped out of the clouds to wash it all away. It was long before the sea went down; and, days after the sun began to shine, the fringe of spray still leaped skyward from the eastern shore, and Shag and Mingo Rocks at Duck Island tossed their distant clouds of snow against the blue.

After the wind subsided, it was curious to examine the effects of the breakers on the eastern shore, where huge masses of rock were struck off from the cliffs, and flung among the wild heaps of scattered boulders, to add to the already hopeless confusion of the gorges. The eastern aspects of the islands change somewhat every year or two from this cause; and, indeed, over all their surfaces continual change goes on from the action of the weather. Under the hammer and chisel of frost and heat, masses of stone are detached and fall from the edges of cliffs, whole ledges become disintegrated, the rock cracks in smooth, thin sheets, and, once loosened, the whole mass can be pulled out, sheet by sheet. Twenty years ago those subtle, irresistible tools of the weather had cracked off a large mass of rock from a ledge on the slope of a gentle declivity. I could just lay my hand in the space then: now three men can walk abreast between the ledge and the detached mass; and nothing has touched it save heat and cold. The whole aspect of the rocks is infinitely aged. I never can see the beautiful salutation of sunrise upon their hoary fronts, without thinking how many millions of times they have answered to that delicate touch. On Boone Island,—a low, dangerous rock fifteen miles east of the Shoals,—the sea has even greater opportunities of destruction, the island is so low. Once, after a stormy night, the lighthouse-keeper told me the family found a great stone, weighing half a ton, in the back entry, which Father Neptune had deposited there,—his card, with his compliments!

Often tremendous breakers encompass the islands when the surface of the sea is perfectly calm and the weather serene and still,—the results of great storms far out at sea. A "long swell" swings indolently, and the ponderous waves roll in as if tired and half asleep, to burst into clouds of splendor against the cliffs. Very different is their hurried, eager breaking when the shoulder of a gale compels them. There is no sound more gentle, more slumberous, than the distant roll of these billows,—

"The rolling sea resounding soft,"

as Spenser has it. The rush of a fully alive and closely pursued breaker is, at a distance, precisely like that which a rocket makes, sweeping headlong upward through the air; but the other is a long and peaceful sigh, a dreamy, lulling, beautiful sound, which produces a Lethean forgetfulness of care and pain, makes all earthly ill seem unreal, and it is as if one wandered

> "In dreamful wastes, where footless fancies dwell."

It requires a strong effort to emerge from this lotus-eating state of mind. O, lovely it is, on sunny afternoons to sit high up in a crevice of the rock and look down on the living magnificence of breakers such as made music about us after the Minot's Ledge storm,—to watch them gather, one after another,

> "Cliffs of emerald topped with snow,
> That lift and lift, and then let go
> A great white avalanche of thunder,"

which makes the solid earth tremble, and you, clinging to the moist rock, feel like a little cockle-shell! If you are out of the reach of the heavy fall of spray, the fine salt mist will still stream about you, and salute your cheek with the healthful freshness of the brine, make your hair damp, and encrust your eyebrows with salt. While you sit watching the shifting splendor, uprises at once a higher cloud than usual; and across it springs a sudden rainbow, like a beautiful thought beyond the reach of human expression. High over your head the white gulls soar, gathering the sunshine in the snowy hollows of their wings. As you look up to them floating in the fathomless blue, there is something awful in the purity of that arch beneath their wings, in light or shade, as the broad pinions move with stately grace. There is no bird so white,—nor swan, nor dove, nor mystic ibis: about the ocean-marges there is no dust to soil their perfect snow, and no stormy wind can ruffle their delicate plumes,—the beautiful, happy creatures! One never tires of watching them. Again and again appears the rainbow with lovely colors melting into each other and vanishing, to appear again at the next upspringing of the spray. On the horizon the white sails shine; and far and wide spreads the blue of the sea, with nothing between you and the eastern continent across its vast, calm plain.

JAMES H. WILLIAMS

At age 11, James H. Williams (1864–1927) left his home in Fall River, Massachusetts, for the life of a common sailor. (His father, the son of slaves, had also gone to sea at an early age, and worked as a pilot in Long Island Sound.) After 21 years spent almost continuously under sail, or living along the waterfronts of deep-water ports in North America and Asia, Williams began, as he put it, to "scribble vagrant yarns, and bring them down into a barroom or any other place wherein sailors were wont to foregather, and read them aloud as a sort of light diversion." These casual productions soon took on a more serious purpose: Williams joined the Atlantic Coast Seamen's Union and began to write with a reformer's zeal. "Betrayed," published in The Independent *in 1908, exposes some of the abuses of which Williams had been both witness and victim. Along with his other articles it helped lead to the passage in 1915 of the La Follette Seaman's Act.*

Betrayed

I APPROACH the narration of the following events—for my story is merely a plain, unvarnished statement of facts—with a degree of personal diffidence which few men can appreciate, because few, I think, would care to proclaim themselves self-confest murderers and boast of their crimes in public print.

Yet, for my own part, I feel not the slightest remorse, nor have I ever suffered any qualms of conscience in consequence.

As a truthful chronicler of past events in the old merchant marine, however, I feel it incumbent on me to tell the tale, which can be easily verified and vouched for even now, for public enlightenment as to a subject which is little known and less believed, because of the desperate and successful efforts of the shipowners and their trusty allies to suppress or belie the facts and discredit the testimony of the injured seamen; and further because of the utter inability of the courts to accommodate the ancient and obsolete piratical laws of the sixteenth and seventeenth centuries to modern requirements. I refer to *brutality at sea.*

While I naturally shrink from the recital, therefore, I approach it as a duty to be performed on behalf of the long suffering but humble class of men for whom I am entitled to speak in part, *the seamen*, and to confound some of the oft-quoted misstatements of their persecutors and detractors.

I shall make the recital as brief and direct as possible, avoiding the infusion of all extraneous matter, for such a yarn requires no embellishment to make it *real.*

In the year 188– I was discharged from a New Bedford whaler at Honolulu, H. I. We had just come down from the Arctic, and the ship was so old and decrepit, as the result of sixty years' constant service, battling with ice and storms, that she was no longer considered seaworthy. So, after an extensive survey, she was officially condemned and placed permanently out of commission.

But we had been quite successful in our quest for sperm, and had on board a hold-full and a deckload of oil, 4,000 pounds of bone and a quantity of other by-products, the accumulated results of a two years' cruise.

So we were paid off and legally discharged, a performance which none of us regretted. My share was the "90th" lay, and I received $180 in gold. Of course, I was entitled to more, but that doesn't matter. A sailor's wages are always what he gets, not what he earns.

According to maritime usage under the circumstances, we were entitled to a passage home at the ship's expense. But what's the use of going home when you can go anywhere else? I was less than twenty years old and anxious to see more of the world.

So I carefully sewed up my money in a canvas belt, strapped it securely around my waist next to my skin, and went in search of a ship. I finally secured a berth in a Nova Scotia bark, the "Redwood," which was "cleared for Guam," that is to say, she was free to go to any part of the world in ballast where she might secure a charter.

After a rather tiresome and aimless quest we brought up at Kobe, where I paid myself off with the jib downhaul and went to board with Mrs. Otome, at Kita Nagasi Dori Chicome, No. 18.

A day or two later the bark sailed and I was left a free agent again in consequence. So I crawled out of my erstwhile place of concealment behind the "big rock" and boldly surveyed the town.

There were a number of sailing ships lying in Kobe Bay at the time and I elected to ship in one of them, the "Inquisition." I preferred her to the others because she had just been chartered to trade on the Asiatic coast for three years, and I thought it would afford me a fine opportunity to visit all the various ports in China, Japan, etc., and broaden my sphere of experience; and so it did, greatly to my ultimate sorrow and regret.

From Kobe we went to Nagasaki and loaded coal for Ilo-Ilo, in the Philippine Islands, and from thence we went to Hong-Kong in ballast for orders. That short voyage was a drill to be remembered. I had already been to sea about eight years, but it opened my eyes to the real character of the "bucko" mates and tyrannical skippers and Yankee "hell ships" of which I heard so often and so much. I have no language strong enough to adequately depict the outrageous abuses which I witnessed on that short voyage, nor should I make the attempt if I had, for no one would dare print it if I did. Anyway, it is not a part of this story. I will only say in passing that, thruout the passage, we were hazed and hounded like wild beasts, driven like dumb cattle, beaten like mules and worked like galley slaves. We were never allowed even to speak, to pass even the most casual remark to each other, while at work. We were deprived of our watch below, kept on our bare whack of food, on a coast where everything was both cheap and abundant, reviled and curst from morning to night, and constantly and closely watched over by a half dozen burly, brutal, unprincipled, irresponsible, lynx-eyed bull-drivers who called themselves *officers*! The slightest inadvertence on the part of any member of the crew—to drop a spot of paint or tar on deck or ask a neighbor for a chew of tobacco—

was considered an infraction of the rules, and the unfortunate offender would be promptly attacked with a perfect shower of kicks or blows delivered with any article of hardware which might come to hand, accompanied by the vilest of epithets and the most blasphemous of curses.

Why did we meekly submit to such inhuman treatment? Because even passive resentment—the least word of protest or sign of self-defense—was *insubordination*, punishable by "tricing up," chaining down or imprisonment in the lazarette on hard bread and water, as the master might direct.

Open self-defense was *mutiny*, punishable by years of imprisonment in the penitentiary. Combined self-defense was *piracy*, and, if successful, was punishable by *death*!

To beat, or wound, or starve, or overwork a seaman was not cruelty, nor even a crime in the eye of the then existing medieval maritime law; *it was only discipline!*

Such was the substance of the law; resistance was out of the question without incurring the above penalties.

From Hong-Kong we were ordered to Saigon, in French Cochin China, to load teakwood timber. This valuable timber was brought down to Hong-Kong in large quantities by coasting vessels and afterward trans-shipped by other vessels to Europe.

The "Inquisition" was a large, stately clipper: a perfect specimen of that most graceful, elegant and beautiful of all sailing craft, the American merchant ship.

In every detail of her construction she showed, in its highest development, the subtle cunning and wondrous skill of the shipbuilder's art. Light, lofty, tapering, elegant masts and spars, towering majestically on high above her snow-white decks, erect in stays, symmetrical in design, correct in rake and alignment, perfect in general proportion and complete in artistic finish; beautiful yielding sheer, high, graceful bows, with gilded scroll-work on her classically carved "fiddle head," broad and beautiful overhanging stern, and neatly molded run! What a pity that such an inspiring marvel of elegant perfection, delicate grace, strength and usefulness should be made a floating slaughter-house, a "blood packet," a beautiful, innocent shelter for human suffering, grief and despair, and inhuman, fiendish cruelty, and wanton, unrestrained atrocity.

Our skipper's name was Gammon, and no man in the American merchant marine was ever more widely known, more sincerely hated or more thoroly detested by honest seamen the world over than he. He was a spare, wiry, little man, about fifty years of age, with thin, iron-gray hair, cold, cunning, heartless ferret-like eyes, a flaming brandy knob on the end of his nose, and a face so sharp you could have split kindling wood with it.

He had a shrill, squeaking, dissatisfied voice, entirely in keeping with his features, a most irascible, peevish temper, a strong liking for "three star" brandy and the word *honor* was not in his vocabulary. His proud and frequent boast was that he had "never paid off a son of a —— of a sailor yet, and he'd be damned if he ever would."

The chief mate, Mr. Roarer, was a big, raw-boned, iron-faced giant, with a voice like a young lion, arms like capstan bars, and fingers like belaying pins. He was a Canadian, quite as unprincipled as the captain in his way, and could always be depended upon to do the latter's dirty work without question.

His chief claim to distinction was that he had "never yet seen a —— —— sailor he couldn't lick."

The second mate, whose name was Prettyman, was a tall, squint-eyed, brockey-faced, loose-jointed Nova Scotia-man, nearly as large as his superior, but not so well and strongly set up. His features were not in his favor, for besides the squint eyes just alluded to he had a low, beetling forehead, surmounted by a crop of bristling red hair, a broken nose and a badly scarred face, as tho he'd had the smallpox once in a while.

This incomparable gentleman was noted for his truculent, overbearing disposition, his incessant flow of naval profanity, the dexterity and accuracy with which he could hurl iron belaying pins about, and his wonderful ability to kick with both feet. All these useful and highly professional accomplishments endeared him to the heart of the hatchet-faced little skipper, so that he really was considered *somebody* on board, in spite of his repulsive features and ungainly build. There was also a third mate, a bo'sun and carpenter, and some other inferior petty officers, but they are not worth mentioning at length. Suffice to say that none of them were any good, in our estimation. All were would-be bullies, bull-drivers and brutes, selected by the old man for their willingness to fight rather than for their ability to work.

Our crew was composed of the usual mixt and motley crowd of vagrant unfortunates, among which nearly every human race, nationality and tribe outside of an Esquimau was represented.

Only two among us were Americans—a young Gloucester fisherman, named Staples, who had been enticed into a crimping den while on a spree in Boston and shanghaied for one year's service leaving $40 advance behind him, and myself. All the crew which came out in the ship except Staples had deserted to a man as soon as she reached the coast, and our present crew had been recruited, as I had been, at the different ports she had touched at since.

While lying at Saigon we were never allowed a moment's respite from hard, bone-racking labor. It was long days in midsummer and the weather was terribly hot, yet we were turned to every morning with lamps in the hold and knocked off by lamplight at night. The only distinction made in favor of the Sabbath was that we were not turned to until 8 a. m. and knocked off at 6 p. m. We were usually allowed half an hour for meals and ten minutes for our early coffee.

After the coal dirt had been cleaned from our hold we had to set to work and wash it out as clean as a housewife's kitchen. Then came the painful job of dry holystoning the 'tween decks, a job as unnecessary and useless as it was difficult and excruciating. For two solid weeks we were kept constantly at work with those damnable "holystones" and "prayerbooks" from 4 a. m. to 9 p. m., until the flesh on our knees was worn clean to the bones and all of us were practically cripples.

Then came the timber—great, heavy, square sticks of teak. After that four men were told off every day to stow cargo below, and the rest of us were kept at work on deck or aloft or elsewhere about the ship.

The hold gang was changed every morning, so that by turns we all got a hack at the delicate operation of stowing timber under the gentle objurgations and persuasive caresses of Mr. Prettyman, who was highcockalorum of the lower hold.

We lay in the stream and, of course, the timber had to be lightered off to us. When the hold began to fill up so as to make it necessary to jamb the top tiers under the deck beams we found it impossible for four men to stow the timber as fast as a horde of howling coolies could heave it thru the side ports. Therefore it was decided one morning at breakfast time to ask for more help in the hold. The hold gang for that day consisted of an old Irishman, more than sixty years old, named Dent, a young Swede named Lars, a Dane whom we had nicknamed "Dutchy," and my special chum, Dutton Adams, an Englishman.

No sooner had we bolted our frugal breakfast of lobscouse and hardtack, washed it down with patent marine coffee, sweetened with "long lick," and got a hasty five minutes' session with our pipes, than we heard our ever alert bo'sun, Jack Bender, roaring at the top of his stentorian voice. "Turn to, there, for'rard; look alive there, now!" And then, before the echo of the bo'sun's voice had ceased to reverberate among the yards, the second mate thrust his hideous features thru the forecastle door and bellowed out: "Come on here, now you ——— ——— ——— ——— ———s; comin' out like men, er yer want ter be dragged out like dogs? Come, shake her up, now er I'll come in thar 'n' help some o' yer over the ——— ——— stopwater!"

In response to these gentle summonses we all scrambled hastily on deck and resumed our appointed tasks. Mr. Prettyman went down the hatch, as usual, to superintend the hold gang. It had been previously agreed by the rest of the hold gang, and acceded to by Dent himself that he, being the oldest man, should act as spokesman in asking for more help. Accordingly, as soon as the second mate arrived, old Dent, addressing him with all possible civility, said: "Mr. Prettyman, she's gittin' that full beneath the bames now we can't stow the logs as fasht as the nagurs be's stevin' 'em in, and we nades more help down here to kape up wid 'em."

"More help yer want, is it, yer —— —— lazy old stiff; I'll give ye more help plenty of it!" And he struck poor old Dent a terrific blow between the eyes, knocking him prostrate. But the old man, tho hurt and dazed, was still game, and as soon as he could regain his feet he immediately tried to retaliate on the second mate. 'Twas then the brute's real, cowardly instinct became apparent, for, instead of trying to repel the old man's attack in the natural way, which he could easily have done, he whipped out a huge, murderous-looking knife from his belt and tried to stab him. But the instant the second mate drew the knife and before he had time to use it, Dutton Adams, who stood directly behind him, struck him a powerful blow on top of the head with a slice bar and knocked him senseless. Then the four men, maddened by months of constant hazing and unmerited abuse, all leapt upon the body of the prostrate mate and kicked and beat him unmercifully. They left him for dead, and Adams told me afterward it was their *bona fide* determination to kill him, and that, had they suspected that there still remained a single vestige of the spark of life in his carcass, they would never have desisted until it had been stamped out and extinguished.

The noise of the fracas had attracted the ever-vigilant attention of the second mate's fellow bull-drivers on deck, and they soon came swarming into the hold, closely followed by our wizened-faced skipper, all armed to the teeth with shooting-irons and various kinds of cutlery. The four men were soon secured and brought up on deck. There they were triced up to the forward boat skids with spun yarn sized tightly around their thumbs. We had a Chinese cook named Me-Chow, the only good Chinaman I ever knew. Shortly after the men had been strung up, Me-Chow, unable to bear their screams of anguish, ran out of the galley with a carving knife, with the evident intention of cutting them down. But he was quickly detected by the alert third mate and bo'sun, who were mounted on guard for the express purpose of preventing just such a move being made by any members of the crew. Divining his purpose, the two ruffians promptly pounced upon the poor Chinaman, and in a jiffy the unfortunate Mongolian was hanging by his pigtail beside the four seamen. So the five unfortunate men were allowed to hang in the broiling sun, with the tips of their toes just touching the deck, from 9 o'clock in the morning until 2 in the afternoon. Their shrieks could be heard all over the harbor, but there was none to succor them. At frequent intervals they became unconscious; then they would be lowered down for a time until they revived, on the principle that an unconscious man is insensible to pain, and then, the moment they came to they would be strung up again. Their prayers for mercy were as unheeded as their supplications for water.

While in a paroxysm of delirious anguish Adams began to call down all manner of insane curses upon the captain and all the officers in the ship. Whereupon the bo'sun seized an oaken heaver from a gypsy winch and struck the suspended man a terrible blow in the mouth, knocking out all his front teeth. Such was one phase of disciplinary punishment as practised on some of our stately clippers in the palmy days of our glorious merchant marine. I would rather see men crucified; they would die easier!

But let us draw the curtain on this horrible scene. Why prolong the mental anguish of gentle-hearted, sensitive-minded readers by describing the details of such a hellish orgy?

After this frightful incident every precaution was taken by the after guards to prevent any tidings of it getting ashore.

No one was allowed to leave the ship under any pretext whatsoever. No sampans were allowed alongside except the one regularly employed by the skipper on his daily trips to and from the town. Every evening Captain Gammon and his group of officers would sit for hours on the poop, shooting at the "jolly boat" sampans to keep them at a distance from the vessel; and every night, as soon as we had quit work, we were all locked in the stifling forecastle for the night, lest any of us should try to escape.

It was the most horrible experience I ever endured. When we returned to Hong-Kong a few weeks later the tortured men were still unable to work. Their hands and arms were still black and horribly swollen, and the cook's scalp had been nearly torn from his pate by the long spell of suspension.

Yet none of them received any medical attention or any other attention from aft. At Hong-Kong, as at Saigon, no one was allowed ashore. The only difference in our treatment was that we were not locked in at night, for Hong-Kong is a British port, and the laws governing ships and protecting seamen are more strict and better observed there than in other parts of China.

While we lay in Hong-Kong young Staples's time expired and he demanded to be paid off and discharged. This demand the captain wrathfully refused, telling Staples that he *might* get paid off when the ship returned to the United States, if she ever did and he lived to see it.

That night Staples slacked himself quietly over the side and swam ashore.

He hung around the waterfront until morning and then went to the American consul's office, reported his own situation, prest his demand for his discharge, and told him of the *crucifixion* at Saigon.

The consul at Hong-Kong at that time was a Southerner, an ex-Confederate officer, and notoriously unfavorable toward seamen, however meritorious their cause, but doubly so if they were *Northerners*.

He could not very well overlook Staple's claim for wages, but he *could* shirk his duty toward the injured seamen on the technical plea of *lack of jurisdiction*. And that was precisely what he did.

Later in the day the captain arrived at the consulate and was closeted with that dignitary for some time.

When they came out they suavely persuaded young Staples to take a sampan and go off to the ship for his pay, as, it was explained to him, this arrangement would be much more convenient for him, as the captain had all his money and papers locked up in his cabin. Young sailor-like, young Staples foolishly agreed to this plan, went off to the ship, packed up his bag and waited for the captain's return.

As soon as the old man came on board Staples was called aft to receive his pay. He found the captain seated at the table, with the ship's papers and a bag of money before him.

The young fellow had $90 in gold coming to him, which the old man counted out on the table with rare good humor, Staples thought. He turned the articles and a prepared receipt for $90 and pointed out to Staples where to sign "clear" and sign "off." The moment Staples had affixed his signature to both papers the old man sprang up, covered the little pile of gold pieces with one hand, prest a loaded revolver against his head with the other, and yelled:

"Now, you —— —— —— —— —— ——, git out of my cabin and git over the side quicker 'n greased lightning! I'll teach you, you —— skunk, to sneak up to the consul's and make complaints agin *me* and *my* ship!"

So the poor boy was chased up the companion way at the point of the captain's gun without a cent, and hurried over the side into the waiting sampan by two of the mates, where he found his clothes bag had already preceded him.

"There ye are," sneered the captain, leaning over the rail as the sampan left the side and waving the articles derisively at the poor, hoodwinked lad. "There ye are; you've got yer pay, fer makin' complaints, an' I've got yer receipt fer ther money! Now yer kin go ashore an' complain an' be damned: that's how I pay all my men! *Me* old Cap'n Gammon! Ter hell with yer!"

The next day the *crucified* men were taken ashore and granted a mock hearing. But, as I have already intimated, the case was set aside on the convenient point of maritime *jurisdiction*. All the afterguards, including the steward and excluding the third mate, who was left in charge of the ship, were taken ashore as witnesses for the captain, but not one of the crew was taken to testify for the injured men.

What occurred at that hearing I only know, of course, from hearsay, but I have every reason to believe that my information is correct.

As soon as the captain had made his statement, to the effect that these four men had mutinied, made an *unprovoked* attack on the second mate, with intent to murder him, and that they had afterward *run amuck* in an effort to induce all the crew to mutiny and take charge of the ship, until they had finally, and at a *great hazard* to their captors, been overpowered and *restrained*, etc., etc., etc., the consul formally dismissed the complaint against the captain and officers, and ordered the four men to return on board, without even hearing a word of their testimony. When the poor fellows held up their still helpless and distorted hands, and Dutton Adams pointed to his battered mouth and broken teeth and mumbled an almost unintelligible plea for justice, the only reply he got from the "dignified" United States representative was: "Tut! tut! say another word and I'll give you six months! Go back to your ship and do your duty like men, and the captain *may* feel disposed to forgive you. I've no jurisdiction in this matter. If I had I'd send you all to jail for mutiny and attempted piracy. Go on board and do your duty."

As a matter of fact and of justice, and in accordance with the established and accepted principles of admiralty law the world over, he DID have jurisdiction, for the men were arbitrarily denied the right of recourse to the local consul or port authorities at Saigon.

This is a fair sample of consular justice in the early '80s.

I had now been nearly four months on board this notorious blood packet, and I had long been heartsick, sore and sorry for my foolish venture at Kobe. I heartily wished myself back in the "Redwood" or even in that round-bellied, slab-sided, old blubber hunter which I had left at Honolulu. I, therefore, determined to seize the first opportunity to desert at whatever cost, hazard or loss.

I still had my cherished money belt securely strapped around my waist, a fact which no one on board ever suspected, because I had prudently kept its existence a profound secret.

After the affair at the consul's office we were granted a little more freedom and treated with a little more leniency by the after guards. This was a matter of policy, of course, on the skipper's part, but we accepted it for what it was worth and made the most of it, like the true philosophers we were.

One fine morning, just after breakfast, we were all astounded by the sudden announcement that the port watch was ordered aft to receive their liberty money and go ashore for the day. We naturally thought that such welcome news was too good to be true, so we all started aft with palpitating hearts to investigate.

But, sure enough, there stood the old man at the companion way, where he doled out five Mexican dollars to each of us, telling us all to go ashore and be good, and be sure and return on board before turn-to time next morning. He also added that we should have free sampan fare both ways if we were on time. Then, with the generous, forgiving dispositions of deep-water sailors, we promptly forgot all our recent sufferings and sorrows and tribulations in our exuberant, overwhelming gratitude for one day's respite from our hardship and toil. So we left the ship's side as light-hearted and jubilant as schoolboys released for recess, with three ringing cheers for the "Inquisition," as tho she were the best ship afloat.

The little diversions we enjoyed that day are not a part of our story, but one little incident of my own experience is significant of what follows after. In Typhooshang I met a quartermaster belonging to an English steamer lying at one of the docks in front of the city. During the time we were conversing together I told him of what had occurred on board the "Inquisition" and of my present anxiety to leave her.

There is a sort of tacit freemasonry among deep-water sailors which always bids them help each other in distress, and which does not take race, nationality or color into account. The young Englishman promptly understood my meaning, and offered to assist me or any of my shipmates who could manage to reach his steamer after midnight, when he went on watch, to the extent of stowing us away until they reached the next port. On that particular night, he explained, he would not be on board, as he was on twenty-four hours' leave. The steamer's name, he told me, was the "Sandon," of

Sunderland; that, like our own ship, she was chartered for a term of years on the coast, and that she was scheduled to lay at Hong-Kong three days longer. We parted late that evening with many expressions of friendship, and I went directly on board and turned in.

Next morning all of our boys showed up punctually at turn-to time with the exception of one or two laggards, who were brought off later in the police boat and charged three dollars apiece for their ride.

That day the starboard watch went ashore and all went smoothly.

The idea of deserting grew upon me with the passing hours, and the more I thought about it the more determined I became to put it into effect. Of course, I might have slipped over the side unobserved in the darkness and swam ashore, but where was I going to stow away? The captain would undoubtedly offer a reward for my apprehension and return. For the same reason I considered it unwise to swim to the "Sandon" and take my friendly quartermaster at his word to stow me away, for once the reward was offered and the hue and cry was raised, every policeman and coolie in Hong-Kong would be on the alert for my recapture, and every ship in port would be thoroly searched.

Moreover, I had a splendid outfit of clothes, the result of eight years' gathering, and worth at least $100 in American money, which I hated to leave behind.

I had long since decided that the "Inquisition" was no place for me. I felt sure that the sudden show of kindness exhibited toward us by Captain Gammon was only the merest pretense, a temporary truce which would be declared off and the old *régime* of "turn to, knock down and drag out" resumed, more rigorously than ever, as soon as we left Hong-Kong and got out of earshot of the port authorities.

The more I became possest with the idea of desertion, the more determined I was to put it into execution at all hazards.

According to the universal custom in Far Eastern ports, Captain Gammon assigned a "bum boat" to the ship, to supply us with such articles as we needed or wanted, such as clothes, small stores, tobacco, food and even cash, instead of giving us the money to supply our own requirements.

The "bum boat" man, of course, took full advantage of the situation and charged the sailors three prices for his wares, and paid the captain 50 per cent. commission for the privilege of robbing his crew.

Our "bum boat" man was an oily-mouthed, smooth-spoken, two-faced Mongolian whom everybody detested but with whom everybody was obliged to deal, nevertheless. This "bum boat" man was known among the sailors frequenting the port by the somewhat opprobrious cognomen of "Cummshaw," which is pigeon English for *commission*. Like all of his class he was artful and cunning, utterly unscrupulous, cruel and treacherous, and as avaricious as old Shylock himself.

When "Cummshaw" came on board that particular morning I invested much more liberally in his wares than usual, and, craftily, induced some of my unsuspicious shipmates to do the same.

"Cummshaw" was so highly pleased with my unwonted interest in his behalf that he gave me a fine camphorwood box and a couple of small curios by way of "backsheesh."

Having thus gotten into the good graces of the crafty "Cummshaw," I took him aside and offered him ten Mexican dollars to set me ashore with my belongings that night, after midnight, at the same time exhibiting the money as an evidence of good faith. I could tell by the greedy twinkle of "Cummshaw's" wicked little almond eyes that it was a bargain; he simply could not resist the sight of money; it really was his god and high Joss.

So it was agreed between us that he should come after me that night at "two 'clock mornin' time" and take me "shore side." With this understanding we parted; "Cummshaw" sculled ashore and I went about my day's work as usual, with a head and a heart full of plans for the impending adventure.

Punctual to the minute, "Cummshaw" sculled his sampan silently under our bows at 2 a. m., while I sat on the knightheads with my bag ready packed and slung to the end of the jib downhaul, ready for immediate departure.

I was soon in the boat, dun and dunnage, and we sculled away into the darkness silently, propelled by the long, half rotary sweeps of "Cummshaw's" oar.

"Cummshaw" sculled directly up to a small jetty or boat landing confronting the native settlement on the extreme outskirts of the town.

Making his sampan fast, he shouldered my heavy bag and piloted me thru a mystic maze of narrow, crooked, filthy, dark streets until he came to a small but neat native house, with two hideous-looking wooden images standing in front of the doorway, the diabolical grimaces which distorted their frozen features being accentuated and rendered more intensely horrible by the shaft of light which fell athwart them with unwonted brilliancy thru the glazed paper window.

Here "Cummshaw" dropt my bag, and, instead of knocking, gave a low call. The door was promptly opened by an aged Chinawoman, and we walked in. We were evidently expected, for the woman seemed in nowise surprised by our arrival, even at such an unearthly hour.

The ground floor of the house appeared to be divided into two rooms, and overhead was a loft which was reached by a ladder extending from the floor of the living room below to a scuttle in the floor of the attic room above.

The interior of the house was perfectly neat and clean, and all its internal arrangements showed constant attention, as well as care, and thrift and simple good taste. The furniture was a sort of compromise between the European and Chinese designs, evidently intended to suit all comers. For instance, there were European tables and chairs for the accommodation of white, and low tables and squat mats for the convenience of native guests. And so on thruout the whole household arrangements. A Yankee clock, made in Connecticut, ornamented a small shelf in one corner of the room, and a large American lamp with an enameled bowl stood upon an ordinary drop-leaf table and shed a brilliant light over the whole scene by the illuminating properties of Standard oil. The walls were decorated in the usual Chinese fashion, with painted paper flowers, fans, birds, dragons, etc., and further ornamented with hand-painted pictures of the familiar Chinese conception.

On the whole, the house was anything but forbidding.

After a brief conversation with the old woman who had admitted us, the exact import of which I could not understand, tho, of course, I inferred that it referred to myself, "Cummshaw" turned to me and said shortly, pointing toward the woman by way of introduction: "This my old mama; velly good 'ooman; s'pose you give two dollar, you can stop two day, three day, four day; mama give plenty chow—velly good chow. By'mby, morning time, my sister come; my sister go C'listian school, speak plenty Englese, you by'mby make plenty chin-chin. By'mby, s'ip go 'way, me come tell you, you take 'nother s'ip homeside gallow. Savvy?"

I savvied and paid "Cummshaw" the promised ten dollars and gave "old mama" three more for chow; then "Cummshaw" departed and I retired to rest on a bamboo couch in the loft aforementioned.

Next morning "old mama" called me to breakfast, and when I came down the ladder I saw a young Chinese girl, who might have been anywhere from ten to thirteen years old, seated demurely on a bamboo settee. This was the "sister" "Cummshaw" had referred to the night before. "Old mama" brought me clean water in an earthen basin, a ball of soap and a large towel. After a washup I sat down to breakfast, at which repast the little girl and "old mama" bashfully refused to join me. A good breakfast it was, too, and I did ample justice to it. It consisted of rice, boiled as only a Chinese *can* boil it, with every grain a separate, tempting factor of the meal; small fishes deliciously cooked in oil, fresh duck eggs, watercresses, vegetables, fresh wheat bread and excellent tea.

After breakfast "old mama" presented me with a package of cigarros and I proceeded to smoke and while away the time in an effort to draw the little girl into conversation. She was very timid and shy at first, but by degrees her reserve melted, so that at the end of an hour or two we were on the most familiar terms.

She spoke excellent English, and with a very slight accent, and seemed to be in all respects entirely natural and childish. She said she had been attending one of the mission schools almost from infancy, and that she was anxious to learn to teach. She told me also that she was not "Cummshaw's" sister (I had suspected as much), but she *was* his niece, and that "old mama" was her grandmother and "Cummshaw's" aunt, and not his mother, as he had intimated.

It was rather irksome sitting in the house all day with nothing to do, and I was in hopes that "Cummshaw" would drop in in the evening and bring me some tidings about the ship. I dared not go out for fear of being observed, and information travels fast among the Mongolians, especially when you don't want it to.

After dinner the little girl returned to her school duties and left me more lonesome than ever, for "old mama" could neither utter nor understand a syllable of English. After a hearty supper I got a book out of my bag and sat down to read until 10 o'clock. Then I went aloft and turned in and was soon sound asleep.

I had not slept long, however, when I was suddenly awakened by the glare of a bull's-eye lantern shining full in my face, a rough hand shaking me by the shoulder, and a loud voice commanding me in good, vigorous Anglo-Saxon to "get up and dress."

I started up in bed and my astonished gaze fell upon two English officers in uniform, and "Cummshaw's" snakelike almond eyes peering at me exultantly in the background. Then the whole situation dawned upon me like a flash. "Cummshaw" had betrayed me and I was under arrest and would be sentenced without trial to three years in purgatory, on board the "Inquisition."

I got out of bed mechanically and began slowly and absentmindedly to dress.

"What is the meaning of this, officer?" I asked, as tho I didn't know.

"It means that you are under arrest," replied one of them, drawing a Queen's warrant about a fathom long from his breast pocket, "on a charge of desertion from the American ship 'Inquisition,' and we are under orders to convey you back to the ship and deliver you to the master. Do you want to hear the warrant read?"

"Yes," I said; "you might as well do everything in regular order." I was not at all anxious to hear the warrant, but I wanted to gain time to collect my thoughts.

So I let him wade thru the long rigmarole of legal dogmatisms while in the meantime I fumbled into my clothes. As soon as the officer had concluded the perusal of the warrant, of which I had heard not a word, I announced myself ready to go. While he was replacing the document in his breast pocket and buttoning up his coat, I asked how they came to know where I was.

"Why," said the officer, "as soon as you were missed the captain posted a reward of twenty dollars with the American consul for your apprehension, and this Chink here," indicating "Cummshaw," went up and split on you to claim the reward; not often these beggars see twenty dollars in gold, you know."

"How came you to leave the ship?" asked the other officer, who until now had remained silent.

"Because she was a living hell," I answered, "like too many of our American and Nova Scotia blood packets."

Then I mentioned briefly some of the horrors which had occurred on board, and how poor Staples had been paid off at Hong-Kong.

"It's a bloody h'outrage," said the first officer, feelingly, "an' h'I don't min' tellin' yer, pore chap, as we don't 'arf like this y'ere job; but duty is duty, you know, an' we must h'obey h'orders."

"I understand your position in the matter perfectly, gentlemen," I said, "and I sincerely thank you for your sympathy; so I'll go aboard with you without delay and face whatever is coming to me. I suppose you want to shackle me," I added, extending my hands toward them in token of humility.

"Naw!" exclaimed one officer, disdainfully. "We ain't got no darbies with us an' I wouldn't put 'em on you if we had.

You don't look like a troublesome chap and you're a good lad, anyhow."

We descended the ladder and went out into the night. A drizzling rain was falling, a sort of "Scotch mist," and there was not a breath of wind.

I walked silently along between the two policemen, "Cummshaw" preceding us with my bag on his shoulder thru the maze of narrow streets leading by devious routes toward the Quay.

"Cummshaw's" sampan was moored to the same little jetty where I had landed the previous night. The surface of the water was as placid as a mill pond and the night was as dark as night ever was.

Without a word of ceremony we entered the sampan and cast off. My bag was placed in the bows, the two officers seated themselves together in the stern sheets, while I took my place on a thwart just in front of them. "Cummshaw" took up his position just forward of me, shipped his long, curved and jointed sculling oar on the little knob which held it to the gunwale, and gave way with long, regular sweeps back and forth in the regular Chinese style.

So we started up stream, our way illumined only by the faint glow from the little Colza oil lamp burning dimly at our bows.

Such a tumult of passionate thoughts as assailed my mind as I sat in that sampan I have never experienced before nor since. I knew that to return to the ship meant three years of actual slavery, constant drudgery, torture, humiliation and abuse. I knew the character of the men with whom I would have to deal, and I knew that for three years to come I would be entirely at their fiendish mercy without hope of succor, escape or redress, and without any assurance of being rewarded for my labor in the end. I would be triced up, shackled down, kicked, cuffed, beaten, maimed or starved, just according to the whim of Captain Gammon and his horde of "buckos." At every port we came to I would be chained to a ringbolt at night or locked down in the lazarette to prevent me from escaping again.

Such, in brief, was the prospect I conjured up in my mind concerning my future treatment if I returned on board, and from what I knew of American ships in general and the "Inquisition" in particular, I felt that in my mental picture I had not exaggerated my probable fate in the least.

These thoughts, in conjunction with my helpless, hopeless situation in the swaying sampan, almost maddened me, and I began to cast about wildly for some means of escape. To leap overboard and try to get away by swimming would be useless; to attack the two big, well-armed policemen would be equally futile and even more foolhardy.

But at length, as we wended our way through the assembled merchant fleet riding at anchor, I could discern the outlines of the "Inquisition" swinging lazily at her cable less than half a mile away. I could tell her even in the almost impenetrable darkness—partly by her position, perhaps, but mainly by long familiarity with her long, low, sneaking hull, the graceful outline of her bows, and the exact rake and slender, tapering symmetry of her lofty spars—so different from any other ship in the harbor, and distinguishable even in the darkness.

Yes, I saw her, a black, infernal specter, silhouetted against the night, and the sight aroused me to desperation.

Then my gaze rested for a moment on the dim figure of the Chinese traitor laboring strongly at his oar, as unconcerned about my future as tho I had been a mad dog.

And then my blood boiled with ungovernable rage and hatred toward this man who had accepted my bribe and then deliberately betrayed me, and who now would sell me into slavery for money earned with the wringing of my own heart's blood. And then as I regarded the swaying figure at the oar a desperate thought entered my brain and took full possession of my whole being: "If I could get rid of him and that infernal oar," I thought, "I would have just one chance."

Lying across the thwarts in the sampan was a short piece of a small English oar with the blade sawed off, leaving about six feet of the shaft. I had noticed it several times in the sampan before I left the ship, but had never been inquisitive enough to ask "Cummshaw" where he got it. I presume, however, that he had picked it up among the flotsam and jetsam of the stream.

This oar shaft was now within easy reach, and I clutched one end of it firmly with my left hand. Then, for a brief space, having made sure of my weapon, I watched the dim figure swaying back and forth in the murky darkness with rhythmical precision, and the long queue waving with pendulumlike regularity with each stroke.

Behind me I could hear the two officers conversing in low tones, apparently satisfied that their task was to be an easy one and that it was about over.

I realized that any chance of possible success must be dependent upon my own quickness and sureness of aim, but I was young, strong and nimble, as well as desperate, and, therefore, ready to take a chance. So, watching my opportunity, just as "Cummshaw" started on an outward stroke, I suddenly arose and struck him on the back of the head with that oar shaft, exerting all the force I could muster in delivering the blow.

The Chinaman fairly flew over the edge of the sampan, taking the oar, which he still blindly clutched in a deathlike grip, along with him. Then, before the astonished officers could realize what had happened, I dived over the other side and swam away.

The sampan, impelled by her own momentum, continued up stream for a while until her momentum was spent, and then she went with the tide. There is a very strong current in Hong-Kong harbor, and since the officers had nothing with which to propel or control their craft they were entirely at the mercy of the elements.

As for me, I swam under water as long as possible to make a good offing from the sampan. When I came up to blow I could hear the officers shouting and shooting into the darkness, but I don't think they hit anything but the air and water. I am sure they didn't hit me.

As soon as I arose to the surface I made a tangent for the shore. I could tell the direction by the thousands of lights gleaming thickly along the water front and more thinly scattered up the slopes of the great hills overlooking the city.

As I swam toward the shore I could still hear the shouting and the shooting of the forsaken officers adrift in the sampan growing fainter and fainter as they drifted rapidly down stream. My only fear was that the racket they made might alarm some of the harbor police and that I might be pursued and recaptured before I could reach a place of refuge.

But, anyway, the darkness shielded me from view as well as from bullets, and whatever else happened in Hong-Kong harbor that I know not, but they did not get me.

As soon as I got near enough inshore to locate the "Sandon" I swam directly down to her and climbed up her gangway dripping like a drowned rat.

As I had surmised, it was past midnight and my new chum, the quartermaster, was on watch.

"Good God, man!" he exclaimed, as I stood wet and dripping in the glare of the gangway lantern, "is that you? How did you get off her?"

I briefly related my late experiences.

"Come down for'ard, lad," he said, "but be quiet. We'll gi' you a passage down to the Straits, and you'se 'll be clear o' the blame Yankee 'hell hooker.' "

Fifteen minutes later I was clad in a dry suit of clothes, and my wet ones were hung in the fiddley to dry. I was also supplied with food, a pipe and tobacco, and given a good, comfortable bunk.

Next morning at sunrise the "Sandon" cast off her shore fasts and steamed out of Hong-Kong en route for Singapore, 1,450 miles further down the coast.

And, dear reader, that is how I got out of the "Inquisition."

P. S.—I expect to be severely criticised, if not utterly condemned in some quarters, for telling such a yarn as this.

But "judge not, that ye be not judged." I could tell others still more horrible and equally true if I chose and no man could contradict them.

I was young and very reckless in those days; so, too, were the brutal mates who hazed and hounded me to desperation; so was the Chinaman who first accepted my bribe and afterward betrayed me, and so were the kind-hearted policemen who brought the warrant but forgot the handcuffs. But it is all ancient history now. The Chinaman is dead, the policemen have resigned, the ship is lost, and the warrant is outlawed. So I say again, *pax nobis*.

Lafcadio Hearn

The wandering life of Lafcadio Hearn (1850–1904) took him from the Ionian islands of Greece, where he was born to a British military surgeon and a local woman, to Ireland and England, where he endured an unhappy upbringing by relatives, and finally to the United States, where he began a career in journalism. In New Orleans, where he had gone to recuperate after a breakdown, he discovered the tropical landscapes and Creole culture that suffuse his early stories and sketches. In his first novel, Chita *(1889), set in the Gulf islands off the coast of Louisiana, he evokes, in lush fin-de-siècle prose, the tidal wave that swept over L'Île Dernière (now the multiple Iles Dernieres) in 1856. A residence in Martinique inspired* Two Years in the French West Indies *(1890) and the novel* Youma *(1890). In 1890 Hearn settled in Japan, eventually becoming a Japanese subject. His many books on Japanese folklore and history include* Kokoro *(1896),* In Ghostly Japan *(1899), and* Kwaidan *(1904).*

from *Chita: A Memory of Last Island*

On the Gulf side of these islands you may observe that the trees—when there are any trees—all bend away from the sea; and, even of bright, hot days when the wind sleeps, there is something grotesquely pathetic in their look of agonized terror. A group of oaks at Grande Isle I remember as especially suggestive: five stooping silhouettes in line against the horizon, like fleeing women with streaming garments and wind-blown hair,—bowing grievously and thrusting out arms desperately northward as to save themselves from falling. And they are being pursued indeed;—for the sea is devouring the land. Many and many a mile of ground has yielded to the tireless charging of Ocean's cavalry: far out you can see, through a good glass, the porpoises at play where of old the sugar-cane shook out its million bannerets; and shark-fins now seam deep water above a site where pigeons used to coo. Men build dikes; but the besieging tides bring up their battering-rams—whole forests of drift—huge trunks of water-oak and weighty cypress. Forever the yellow Mississippi strives to build; forever the sea struggles to destroy;—and amid their eternal strife the islands and the promontories change shape, more slowly, but not less fantastically, than the clouds of heaven.

And worthy of study are those wan battle-grounds where the woods made their last brave stand against the irresistible invasion,—usually at some long point of sea-marsh, widely fringed with billowing sand. Just where the waves curl beyond such a point you may discern a multitude of blackened, snaggy shapes protruding above the water,—some high enough to resemble ruined chimneys, others bearing a startling likeness to enormous skeleton-feet and skeleton-hands,—with crustaceous white growths clinging to them here and there like remnants of integument. These are bodies and limbs of drowned oaks,—so long drowned that the shell-scurf is inch-thick upon parts of them. Farther in upon the beach immense trunks lie overthrown. Some look like vast broken columns; some suggest colossal torsos imbedded, and seem to reach out mutilated stumps in despair from their deepening graves;—and beside these are others which have kept their feet with astounding obstinacy, although the barbarian tides have been charging them for twenty years, and gradually torn away the soil above and beneath their roots. The sand around,—soft beneath and thinly crusted upon the surface,—is everywhere pierced with holes made by a beautifully mottled and semi-diaphanous crab, with hairy legs, big staring eyes, and milk-white claws;—while in the green sedges beyond there is a perpetual rustling, as of some strong wind beating among reeds: a marvellous creeping of "fiddlers," which the inexperienced visitor might at first mistake for so many peculiar beetles, as they run about sideways, each with his huge single claw folded upon his body like a wing-case. Year by year that rustling strip of green land grows narrower; the sand spreads and sinks, shuddering and wrinkling like a living brown skin; and the last standing corpses of the oaks, ever clinging with naked, dead feet to the sliding beach, lean more and more out of the perpendicular. As the sands subside, the stumps appear to creep; their intertwisted masses of snakish roots seem to crawl, to writhe,—like the reaching arms of cephalopods. . . .

. . . Grande Terre is going: the sea mines her fort, and will before many years carry the ramparts by storm. Grande Isle is going,—slowly but surely: the Gulf has eaten three miles into her meadowed land. Last Island has gone! How it went I first heard from the lips of a veteran pilot, while we sat one evening together on the trunk of a drifted cypress which some high tide had pressed deeply into the Grande Isle beach. The day had been tropically warm; we had sought the shore for a breath of living air. Sunset came, and with it the ponderous heat lifted,—a sudden breeze blew,—lightnings flickered in the darkening horizon,—wind and water began to strive together,—and soon all the low coast boomed. Then my companion began his story; perhaps the coming of the storm inspired him to speak! And as I listened to him, listening also to the clamoring of the coast, there flashed back to me recollection of a singular Breton fancy: that the Voice of the Sea is never one voice, but a tumult of many voices—voices of drowned men,—the muttering of multitudinous dead,—the moaning of innumerable ghosts, all rising, to rage against the living, at the great Witch-call of storms. . . .

The charm of a single summer day on these island shores is something impossible to express, never to be forgotten. Rarely, in the paler zones, do earth and heaven take such luminosity: those will best understand me who have seen the splendor of a West Indian sky. And yet there is a tenderness of tint, a caress of color, in these Gulf-days which is not of the Antilles,—a spirituality, as of eternal tropical spring. It must have been to even such a sky that Xenophanes lifted up his eyes of old when he vowed the Infinite Blue was God;—it was indeed under such a sky that De Soto named the vastest and grandest of Southern havens Espiritu Santo,—the Bay of the Holy Ghost. There is a something unutterable in this bright Gulf-air that compels awe,—something vital, something holy, something pantheistic: and reverentially the mind asks itself if what the eye beholds is not the Πνεῦμα indeed, the Infinite Breath, the Divine Ghost, the great Blue Soul of the Unknown. All, all is blue in the calm,—save the low land under your feet, which you almost forget, since it seems only as a tiny green flake afloat in the liquid eternity of day. Then slowly, caressingly, irresistibly, the witchery of the Infinite grows upon you: out of Time and Space you begin to dream with open eyes,—to drift into delicious oblivion of facts,—to forget the past, the present, the substantial,—to comprehend nothing but the existence of that infinite Blue Ghost as something into which you would wish to melt utterly away forever. . . .

And this day-magic of azure endures sometimes for months together. Cloudlessly the dawn reddens up through a violet east: there is no speck upon the blossoming of its Mystical Rose,—unless it be the silhouette of some passing gull, whirling his sickle-wings against the crimsoning. Ever, as the sun floats higher, the flood shifts its color. Sometimes smooth and gray, yet flickering with the morning gold, it is the vision of John,—the apocalyptic Sea of Glass mixed with fire;—again, with the growing breeze, it takes that incredible purple tint familiar mostly to painters of West Indian scenery;—once more, under the blaze of noon, it changes to a waste of broken emerald. With evening, the horizon assumes tints of inexpressible sweetness,—pearl-lights, opaline colors of milk and fire; and in the west are topaz-glowings and wondrous flushings as of nacre. Then, if the sea sleeps, it dreams of all these,—faintly, weirdly,—shadowing them even to the verge of heaven.

Beautiful, too, are those white phantasmagoria which, at the approach of equinoctial days, mark the coming of the winds. Over the rim of the sea a bright cloud gently pushes up its head. It rises; and others rise with it, to right and left—slowly at first; then more swiftly. All are brilliantly white and flocculent, like loose new cotton. Gradually they mount in enormous line high above the Gulf, rolling and wreathing into an arch that expands and advances,—bending from horizon to horizon. A clear, cold breath accompanies its coming. Reaching the zenith, it seems there to hang poised awhile,—a ghostly bridge arching the empyrean,—upreaching its measureless span from either underside of the world. Then the colossal phantom begins to turn, as on a pivot of air,—always preserving its curvilinear symmetry, but moving its unseen ends beyond and below the sky-circle. And at last it floats away unbroken beyond the blue sweep of the world, with a wind following after. Day after day, almost at the same hour, the white arc rises, wheels, and passes. . . .

. . . Never a glimpse of rock on these low shores;—only long sloping beaches and bars of smooth tawny sand. Sand and sea teem with vitality;—over all the dunes there is a constant susurration, a blattering and swarming of crustacea;—through all the sea there is a ceaseless play of silver lightning,—flashing of myriad fish. Sometimes the shallows are thickened with minute, transparent, crablike organisms,—all colorless as gelatine. There are days also when countless medusæ drift in—beautiful veined creatures that throb like hearts, with perpetual systole and diastole of their diaphanous envelops: some, of translucent azure or rose, seem in the flood the shadows or ghosts of huge campanulate flowers;—others have the semblance of strange living vegetables,—great milky tubers, just beginning to sprout. But woe to the human skin grazed by those shadowy sproutings and spectral stamens!—the touch of glowing iron is not more painful. . . . Within an hour or two after their appearance all these tremulous jellies vanish mysteriously as they came.

Perhaps, if a bold swimmer, you may venture out alone a long way—once! Not twice!—even in company. As the water deepens beneath you, and you feel those ascending wave-currents of coldness arising which bespeak profundity, you will also begin to feel innumerable touches, as of groping fingers—touches of the bodies of fish, innumerable fish, fleeing towards shore. The farther you advance, the more thickly you will feel them come; and above you and around you, to right and left, others will leap and fall so swiftly as to daze the sight, like intercrossing fountain-jets of fluid silver. The gulls fly lower about you, circling with sinister squeaking cries; —perhaps for an instant your feet touch in the deep something heavy, swift, lithe, that rushes past with a swirling shock. Then the fear of the Abyss, the vast and voiceless Nightmare of the Sea, will come upon you; the silent panic of all those opaline millions that flee glimmering by will enter into you also. . . .

From what do they flee thus perpetually? Is it from the giant sawfish or the ravening shark?—from the herds of the porpoises, or from the *grande-écaille*,—that splendid monster whom no net may hold,—all helmed and armored in argent plate-mail?—or from the hideous devilfish of the Gulf,—gigantic, flat-bodied, black, with immense side-fins ever outspread like the pinions of a bat,—the terror of luggermen, the uprooter of anchors? From all these, perhaps, and from other monsters likewise—goblin shapes evolved by Nature as destroyers, as equilibrists, as counterchecks to that prodigious fecundity, which, unhindered, would thicken the deep into one measureless and waveless ferment of being. . . . But when there are many bathers these perils are forgotten,—numbers give courage,—one can abandon one's self, without fear of the invisible, to the long, quivering, electrical caresses of the sea. . . .

MARK TWAIN

The tireless traveler Samuel Clemens (1835–1910) made numerous ocean crossings, including the voyage around the world described in his 1897 travel book Following the Equator. *"About All Kinds of Ships," written on board the* Havel *and first published in 1893, ended a dry spell for the usually prolific writer. The two excerpts included here register Mark Twain's alertness to the swift transformations of the Gilded Age. In "The Modern Steamer and the Obsolete Steamer," Twain catalogs the "beautiful ingenuities" of the* Havel *that make conditions on board the* Batavia, *on which Clemens sailed from England to America in 1872, seem hopelessly retrograde. Twain's enthusiasm for the opulent comforts of the modern steamer was tempered by nostalgia; "A Vanished Sentiment" records his wistful recollections of his first voyage and the lost "romance of the sea."*

from *About All Kinds of Ships*

The Modern Steamer and the Obsolete Steamer.

WE are victims of one common superstition—the superstition that we realize the changes that are daily taking place in the world because we read about them and know what they are. I should not have supposed that the modern ship could be a surprise to me, but it is. It seems to be as much of a surprise to me as it could have been if I had never read anything about it. I walk about this great vessel, the "Havel," as she plows her way through the Atlantic, and every detail that comes under my eye brings up the miniature counterpart of it as it existed in the little ships I crossed the ocean in, fourteen, seventeen, eighteen, and twenty years ago.

In the "Havel" one can be in several respects more comfortable than he can be in the best hotels on the continent of Europe. For instance, she has several bath rooms, and they are as convenient and as nicely equipped as the bath rooms in a fine private house in America; whereas in the hotels of the continent one bath room is considered sufficient, and it is generally shabby and located in some out of the way corner of the house; moreover, you need to give notice so long beforehand that you get over wanting a bath by the time you get it. In the hotels there are a good many different kinds of noises, and they spoil sleep; in my room in the ship I hear no sounds. In the hotels they usually shut off the electric light at midnight; in the ship one may burn it in one's room all night.

In the steamer "Batavia," twenty years ago, one candle, set in the bulkhead between two state-rooms, was there to light both rooms, but did not light either of them. It was extinguished at 11 at night, and so were all the saloon lamps except one or two, which were left burning to help the passenger see how to break his neck trying to get around in the dark. The passengers sat at table on long benches made of the hardest kind of wood; in the "Havel" one sits on a swivel chair with a cushioned back to it. In those old times the dinner bill of fare was always the same: a pint of some simple, homely soup or other, boiled codfish and potatoes, slab of boiled beef, stewed prunes for dessert—on Sundays "dog in a blanket," on Thursdays "plum duff." In the modern ship the menu is choice and elaborate, and is changed daily. In the old times dinner was a sad occasion; in our day a concealed orchestra enlivens it with charming music. In the old days the decks were always wet, in our day they are usually dry, for the promenade-deck is roofed over, and a sea seldom comes aboard. In a moderately disturbed sea, in the old days, a landsman could hardly keep his legs, but in such a sea in our day, the decks are as level as a table. In the old days the inside of a ship was the plainest and barrenest thing, and the most dismal and uncomfortable that ingenuity could devise; the modern ship is a marvel of rich and costly decoration and sumptuous appointment, and is equipped with every comfort and convenience that money can buy. The old ships had no place of assembly but the dining-room, the new ones have several spacious and beautiful drawing-rooms. The old ships offered the passenger no chance to smoke except in the place that was called the "fiddle." It was a repulsive den made of rough boards (full of cracks) and its office was to protect the main hatch. It was grimy and dirty; there were no seats; the only light was a lamp of the rancid-oil-and-rag kind; the place was very cold, and never dry, for the seas broke in through the cracks every little while and drenched the cavern thoroughly. In the modern ship there are three or four large smoking-rooms, and they have card tables and cushioned sofas, and are heated by steam and lighted by electricity. There are few European hotels with such smoking-rooms.

The former ships were built of wood, and had two or three water-tight compartments in the hold with doors in them which were often left open, particularly when the ship was going to hit a rock. The modern leviathan is built of steel, and the water-tight bulkheads have no doors in them; they divide the ship into nine or ten water-tight compartments and endow her with as many lives as a cat. Their complete efficiency was established by the happy results following the memorable accident to the City of Paris a year or two ago.

One curious thing which is at once noticeable in the great modern ship is the absence of hubbub, clatter, rush of feet, roaring of orders. That is all gone by. The elaborate manœuvres necessary in working the vessel into her dock are conducted without sound; one sees nothing of the processes, hears no commands. A Sabbath stillness and solemnity reign, in place of the turmoil and racket of the earlier days. The modern ship has a spacious bridge fenced chin-high with sail-cloth, and floored with wooden gratings; and this bridge, with its fenced fore-and-aft annexes, could accommodate a seated audience of a hundred and fifty men. There are three steering equipments, each competent if the others should break. From the bridge the ship is steered, and also handled. The handling is not done by shout or whistle, but by signaling with patent automatic gongs. There are three tell-tales, with plainly lettered dials—for steering, handling the engines, and for communicating orders to the invisible mates who are conducting the landing of the ship or casting off. The officer who is astern is out of sight and too far away to hear trumpet calls; but the gongs near him tell him to haul in, pay out, make fast, let go, and so on; he hears, but the passengers do not, and so the ship seems to land herself without human help.

This great bridge is thirty or forty feet above the water, but the sea climbs up there sometimes; so there is another bridge twelve or fifteen feet higher still, for use in these emergencies. The force of water is a strange thing. It slips between one's fingers like air, but upon occasion it acts like a solid body and will bend a thin iron rod. In the "Havel" it has splintered a heavy oaken rail into broom-straws instead of merely breaking it in two as would have been the seemingly natural thing for it to do. At the time of the awful Johnstown disaster, according to the testimony of several witnesses, rocks were carried some distance on the surface of the stupendous torrent; and at St. Helena, many years ago, a vast sea-wave carried a battery of cannon forty feet up a steep slope and deposited the guns there in a row. But the water has done a still stranger thing, and it is one which is credibly vouched for. A marlinspike is an implement about a foot long which tapers from its butt to the other extremity and ends in a sharp point. It is made of iron and is heavy. A wave came aboard a ship in a storm and raged aft, breast high, carrying a marlinspike point-first with it, and with such lightning-like swiftness and force as to drive it three or four inches into a sailor's body and kill him.

In all ways the ocean greyhound of to-day is imposing and impressive to one who carries in his head no ship-pictures of a recent date. In bulk she comes near to rivaling the Ark; yet this monstrous mass of steel is driven five hundred miles through the waves in twenty-four hours. I remember the brag run of a steamer which I traveled in once on the Pacific—it was two hundred and nine miles in twenty-four hours; a year or so later I was a passenger in the excursion-tub "Quaker City," and on one occasion in a level and glassy sea, it was claimed that she reeled off two hundred and eleven miles between noon and noon, but it was probably a campaign lie. That little steamer had seventy passengers, and a crew of forty men, and seemed a good deal of a bee-hive. But in this present ship we are living in a sort of solitude, these soft summer days, with sometimes a hundred passengers scattered about the spacious distances, and sometimes nobody in sight at all; yet, hidden somewhere in the vessel's bulk, there are (including crew,) near eleven hundred people.

The stateliest lines in the literature of the sea are these:

"Britannia needs no bulwark, no towers along the steep—
Her march is o'er the mountain wave, her home is on the
deep!"

There it is. In those old times the little ships climbed over the waves and wallowed down into the trough on the other side; the giant ship of our day does not climb over the waves, but crushes her way through them. Her formidable weight and mass and impetus give her mastery over any but extraordinary storm-waves.

The ingenuity of man! I mean in this passing generation. To-day I found in the chart-room a frame of removable wooden slats on the wall, and on the slats was painted uninforming information like this:

Trim-Tank.	Empty
Double-Bottom No. 1	Full
Double-Bottom No. 2	Full
Double-Bottom No. 3	Full
Double-Bottom No. 4	Full

While I was trying to think out what kind of a game this might be and how a stranger might best go to work to beat it, a sailor came in and pulled out the "Empty" end of the first slat and put it back with its reverse side to the front, marked "Full." He made some other change, I did not notice what. The slat-frame was soon explained. Its function was to indicate how the ballast in the ship was distributed. The striking thing was, that that ballast was water. I did not know that a ship had ever been ballasted with water. I had merely read, some time or other, that such an experiment was to be tried. But that is the modern way: between the experimental trial of a new thing and its adoption, there is no wasted time, if the trial proves its value.

On the wall, near the slat-frame, there was an outline drawing of the ship, and this betrayed the fact that this vessel has twenty-two considerable lakes of water in her. These lakes are in her bottom; they are imprisoned between her real bottom and a false bottom. They are separated from each other, thwartships, by water-tight bulkheads, and separated down the middle by a bulkhead running from the bow four-fifths of the way to the stern. It is a chain of lakes four hundred feet long and from five to seven feet deep. Fourteen of the lakes contain fresh water brought from shore, and the aggregate weight of it is four hundred tons. The rest of the lakes contain salt water—six hundred and eighteen tons. Upwards of a thousand tons of water, altogether.

Think how handy this ballast is. The ship leaves port with the lakes all full. As she lightens forward through consumption of coal, she loses trim—her head rises, her stern sinks down. Then they spill one of the sternward lakes into the sea, and the trim is restored. This can be repeated right along as occasion may require. Also, a lake at one end of the ship can be moved to the other end by pipes and steam pumps. When the sailor changed the slat-frame to-day, he was posting a transference of that kind. The seas had been increasing, and the vessel's head needed more weighting, to keep it from rising on the waves instead of plowing through them; therefore, twenty-five tons of water had been transferred to the bow from a lake situated well toward the stern.

A water compartment is kept either full or empty. The body of water must be compact, so that it cannot slosh around. A shifting ballast would not do, of course.

The modern ship is full of beautiful ingenuities, but it seems to me that this one is the king. I would rather be the originator of that idea than of any of the others. Perhaps the trim of a ship was never perfectly ordered and preserved until now. A vessel out of trim will not steer, her speed is maimed, she strains and labors in the seas. Poor creature, for six thousand years she has had no comfort until these latest days. For six thousand years she swam through the best and cheapest ballast in the world, the only perfect ballast, but she couldn't tell her master and he had not the wit to find it out for himself. It is odd to reflect that there is nearly as much water inside of this ship as there is outside, and yet there is no danger.

* * *

A Vanished Sentiment.

One thing is gone, to return no more forever—the romance of the sea. Soft sentimentality about the sea has retired from the activities of this life, and is but a memory of the past, already remote and much faded. But within the recollection of men still living, it was in the breast of every individual; and the further any individual lived from salt water the more of it he kept in stock. It was as pervasive, as universal, as the atmosphere itself. The mere mention of the sea, the romantic sea, would make any company of people sentimental and mawkish at once. The great majority of the songs that were sung by the young people of the back settlements had the melancholy wanderer for subject and his mouthings about the sea for refrain. Picnic parties paddling down a creek in a canoe when the twilight shadows were gathering, always sang

Homeward bound, homeward bound
From a foreign shore;

and this was also a favorite in the West with the passengers on sternwheel steamboats. There was another—

My boat is by the shore
And my bark is on the sea,
But before I go, Tom Moore,
Here's a double health to thee.

And this one, also—

O, pilot, 'tis a fearful night,
There's danger on the deep.

And this—

A life on the ocean wave
And a home on the rolling deep,

Where the scattered waters rave
And the winds their revels keep!

And this—

A wet sheet and a flowing sea,
And a wind that follows fair.

And this—

My foot is on my gallant deck,
Once more the rover is free!

And the "Larboard Watch"—the person referred to below is at the masthead, or somewhere up there—

O, who can tell what joy he feels,
As o'er the foam his vessel reels,
And his tired eyelids slumb'ring fall,
He rouses at the welcome call
Of "Larboard watch—ahoy!"

Yes, and there was forever and always some jackass-voiced person braying out—

Rocked in the cradle of the deep,
I lay me down in peace to sleep!

Other favorites had these suggestive titles: "The Storm at Sea;" "The Bird at Sea;" "The Sailor Boy's Dream;" "The Captive Pirate's Lament;" "We are far from Home on the Stormy Main"—and so on, and so on, the list is endless. Everybody on a farm lived chiefly amid the dangers of the deep on those days, in fancy.

But all that is gone, now. Not a vestige of it is left. The iron-clad, with her unsentimental aspect and frigid attention to business, banished romance from the war-marine, and the unsentimental steamer has banished it from the commercial marine. The dangers and uncertainties which made sea life romantic have disappeared and carried the poetic element along with them. In our day the passengers never sing sea-songs on board a ship, and the band never plays them. Pathetic songs about the wanderer in strange lands far from home, once so popular and contributing such fire and color to the imagination by reason of the rarity of that kind of wanderer, have lost their charm and fallen silent, because everybody is a wanderer in the far lands now, and the interest in that detail is dead. Nobody is worried about the wanderer; there are no perils of the sea for him, there are no uncertainties. He is safer in the ship than he would probably be at home, for there he is always liable to have to attend some friend's funeral and stand over the grave in the sleet, bareheaded—and that means pneumonia for him, if he gets his deserts; and the uncertainties of his voyage are reduced to whether he will arrive on the other side in the appointed afternoon, or have to wait till morning.

The first ship I was ever in was a sailing vessel. She was twenty-eight days going from San Francisco to the Sandwich Islands. But the main reason for this particularly slow passage was, that she got becalmed and lay in one spot fourteen days in the centre of the Pacific two thousand miles from land. I hear no sea-songs in this present vessel, but I heard the entire layout in that one. There were a dozen young people—they are pretty old now, I reckon—and they used to group themselves on the stern, in the starlight or the moonlight, every evening, and sing sea-songs till after midnight, in that hot, silent, motionless calm. They had no sense of humor, and they always sang "Homeward Bound," without reflecting that that was practically ridiculous, since they were standing still and not proceeding in any direction at all; and they often followed that song with "Are we almost there, are we almost there, said the dying girl as she drew near home?"

It was a very pleasant company of young people, and I wonder where they are now. Gone, oh, none knows whither; and the bloom and grace and beauty of their youth, where is that? Among them was a liar; all tried to reform him, but none could do it. And so, gradually, he was left to himself, none of us would associate with him. Many a time since, I have seen in fancy that forsaken figure, leaning forlorn against the taffrail, and have reflected that perhaps if we had tried harder, and been more patient, we might have won him from his fault and persuaded him to relinquish it. But it is hard to tell; with him the vice was extreme, and was probably incurable. I like to think—and indeed I do think—that I did the best that in me lay to lead him to higher and better ways.

There was a singular circumstance. The ship lay becalmed that entire fortnight in exactly the same spot. Then a handsome breeze came fanning over the sea, and we spread our white wings for flight. But the vessel did not budge. The sails bellied out, the gale strained at the ropes, but the vessel moved not a hair's breadth from her place. The captain was surprised. It was some hours before we found out what the cause of the detention was. It was barnacles. They collect very fast in that part of the Pacific. They had fastened themselves to the ship's bottom; then others had fastened themselves to the first bunch, others to these, and so on, down and down and down, and the last bunch had glued the column hard and fast to the bottom of the sea, which is five miles deep at that point. So the ship was simply become the handle of a walking cane five miles long—yes, and no more movable by wind and sail than a continent is. It was regarded by every one as remarkable.

Well, the next week—however, Sandy Hook is in sight.

Stephen Crane

In late December 1896, Stephen Crane (1871–1900) sailed from Jacksonville, Florida, as a reporter on the steamer Commodore, *heading toward Cuba with a cargo of arms for the rebel forces. On January 2 the ship foundered and sank; what ensued provided the material for what is perhaps the most famous of all stories of survival at sea. The story was written soon after the event; those interested in the full circumstances of the catastrophe can read his newspaper account, "Stephen Crane's Own Story," which was published in the* New York Press *on January 7, while Crane was recuperating from the effects of his ordeal. In Cuba in 1898 Crane suffered from fever and, for the remaining two years of his life, flare-ups of the tuberculosis that eventually killed him.*

The Open Boat

A tale intended to be after the fact. Being the experience of four men from the sunk steamer Commodore

I

None of them knew the color of the sky. Their eyes glanced level, and were fastened upon the waves that swept toward them. These waves were of the hue of slate, save for the tops, which were of foaming white, and all of the men knew the colors of the sea. The horizon narrowed and widened, and dipped and rose, and at all times its edge was jagged with waves that seemed thrust up in points like rocks.

Many a man ought to have a bath-tub larger than the boat which here rode upon the sea. These waves were most wrongfully and barbarously abrupt and tall, and each froth-top was a problem in small boat navigation.

The cook squatted in the bottom and looked with both eyes at the six inches of gunwale which separated him from the ocean. His sleeves were rolled over his fat forearms, and the two flaps of his unbuttoned vest dangled as he bent to bail out the boat. Often he said: "Gawd! That was a narrow clip." As he remarked it he invariably gazed eastward over the broken sea.

The oiler, steering with one of the two oars in the boat, sometimes raised himself suddenly to keep clear of water that swirled in over the stern. It was a thin little oar and it seemed often ready to snap.

The correspondent, pulling at the other oar, watched the waves and wondered why he was there.

The injured captain, lying in the bow, was at this time buried in that profound dejection and indifference which comes, temporarily at least, to even the bravest and most enduring when, willy nilly, the firm fails, the army loses, the ship goes down. The mind of the master of a vessel is rooted deep in the timbers of her, though he command for a day or a decade, and this captain had on him the stern impression of a scene in the grays of dawn of seven turned faces, and later a stump of a top-mast with a white ball on it that slashed to and fro at the waves, went low and lower, and down. Thereafter there was something strange in his voice. Although steady, it was deep with mourning, and of a quality beyond oration or tears.

"Keep'er a little more south, Billie," said he.

" 'A little more south,' sir," said the oiler in the stern.

A seat in this boat was not unlike a seat upon a bucking broncho, and, by the same token, a broncho is not much smaller. The craft pranced and reared, and plunged like an animal. As each wave came, and she rose for it, she seemed like a horse making at a fence outrageously high. The manner of her scramble over these walls of water is a mystic thing, and, moreover, at the top of them were ordinarily these problems in white water, the foam racing down from the summit of each wave, requiring a new leap, and a leap from the air. Then, after scornfully bumping a crest, she would slide, and race, and splash down a long incline and arrive bobbing and nodding in front of the next menace.

A singular disadvantage of the sea lies in the fact that after successfully surmounting one wave you discover that there is another behind it just as important and just as nervously anxious to do something effective in the way of swamping boats. In a ten-foot dingey one can get an idea of the resources of the sea in the line of waves that is not probable to the average experience, which is never at sea in a dingey. As each slaty wall of water approached, it shut all else from the view of the men in the boat, and it was not difficult to imagine that this particular wave was the final outburst of the ocean, the last effort of the grim water. There was a terrible grace in the move of the waves, and they came in silence, save for the snarling of the crests.

In the wan light, the faces of the men must have been gray. Their eyes must have glinted in strange ways as they gazed steadily astern. Viewed from a balcony, the whole thing would doubtlessly have been weirdly picturesque. But the men in the boat had no time to see it, and if they had had leisure there were other things to occupy their minds. The sun swung steadily up the sky, and they knew it was broad day because the color of the sea changed from slate to emerald-green, streaked with amber lights, and the foam was like tumbling snow. The process of the breaking day was unknown to them. They were aware only of this effect upon the color of the waves that rolled toward them.

In disjointed sentences the cook and the correspondent argued as to the difference between a life-saving station and a house of refuge. The cook had said: "There's a house of refuge just north of the Mosquito Inlet Light, and as soon as they see us, they'll come off in their boat and pick us up."

"As soon as who see us?" said the correspondent.

"The crew," said the cook.

"Houses of refuge don't have crews," said the correspondent. "As I understand them, they are only places where clothes and grub are stored for the benefit of shipwrecked people. They don't carry crews."

"Oh, yes, they do," said the cook.

"No, they don't," said the correspondent.

"Well, we're not there yet, anyhow," said the oiler, in the stern.

"Well," said the cook, "perhaps it's not a house of refuge that I'm thinking of as being near Mosquito Inlet Light. Perhaps it's a life-saving station."

"We're not there yet," said the oiler, in the stern.

II

As the boat bounced from the top of each wave, the wind tore through the hair of the hatless men, and as the craft plopped her stern down again the spray slashed past them. The crest of each of these waves was a hill, from the top of which the men surveyed, for a moment, a broad tumultuous expanse, shining and wind-riven. It was probably splendid. It was probably glorious, this play of the free sea, wild with lights of emerald and white and amber.

"Bully good thing it's an on-shore wind," said the cook. "If not, where would we be? Wouldn't have a show."

"That's right," said the correspondent.

The busy oiler nodded his assent.

Then the captain, in the bow, chuckled in a way that expressed humor, contempt, tragedy, all in one. "Do you think we've got much of a show, now, boys?" said he.

Whereupon the three were silent, save for a trifle of hemming and hawing. To express any particular optimism at this time they felt to be childish and stupid, but they all doubtless possessed this sense of the situation in their mind. A young man thinks doggedly at such times. On the other hand, the ethics of their condition was decidedly against any open suggestion of hopelessness. So they were silent.

"Oh, well," said the captain, soothing his children, "we'll get ashore all right."

But there was that in his tone which made them think, so the oiler quoth: "Yes! If this wind holds!"

The cook was bailing. "Yes! If we don't catch hell in the surf."

Canton flannel gulls flew near and far. Sometimes they sat down on the sea, near patches of brown sea-weed that rolled over the waves with a movement like carpets on a line in a gale. The birds sat comfortably in groups, and they were envied by some in the dingey, for the wrath of the sea was no more to them than it was to a covey of prairie chickens a thousand miles inland. Often they came very close and stared at the men with black bead-like eyes. At these times they were uncanny and sinister in their unblinking scrutiny, and the men hooted angrily at them, telling them to be gone. One came, and evidently decided to alight on the top of the captain's head. The bird flew parallel to the boat and did not circle, but made short sidelong jumps in the air in chicken-fashion. His black eyes were wistfully fixed upon the captain's head. "Ugly brute," said the oiler to the bird. "You look as if you were made with a jack-knife." The cook and the correspondent swore darkly at the creature. The captain naturally wished to knock it away with the end of the heavy painter, but he did not dare do it, because anything resembling an emphatic gesture would have capsized this freighted boat, and so with his open hand, the captain gently and carefully waved the gull away. After it had been discouraged from the pursuit the captain breathed easier on account of his hair, and others breathed easier because the bird struck their minds at this time as being somehow grewsome and ominous.

In the meantime the oiler and the correspondent rowed. And also they rowed.

They sat together in the same seat, and each rowed an oar. Then the oiler took both oars; then the correspondent took both oars; then the oiler; then the correspondent. They rowed and they rowed. The very ticklish part of the business was when the time came for the reclining one in the stern to take his turn at the oars. By the very last star of truth, it is easier to steal eggs from under a hen than it was to change seats in the dingey. First the man in the stern slid his hand along the thwart and moved with care, as if he were of Sèvres. Then the man in the rowing seat slid his hand along the other thwart. It was all done with the most extraordinary care. As the two sidled past each other, the whole party kept watchful eyes on the coming wave, and the captain cried: "Look out now! Steady there!"

The brown mats of sea-weed that appeared from time to time were like islands, bits of earth. They were travelling, apparently, neither one way nor the other. They were, to all intents, stationary. They informed the men in the boat that it was making progress slowly toward the land.

The captain, rearing cautiously in the bow, after the dingey soared on a great swell, said that he had seen the light-house at Mosquito Inlet. Presently the cook remarked that he had seen it. The correspondent was at the oars, then, and for some reason he too wished to look at the light-house, but his back was toward the far shore and the waves were important, and for some time he could not seize an opportunity to turn his head. But at last there came a wave more gentle than the others, and when at the crest of it he swiftly scoured the western horizon.

"See it?" said the captain.

"No," said the correspondent, slowly, "I didn't see anything."

"Look again," said the captain. He pointed. "It's exactly in that direction."

At the top of another wave, the correspondent did as he was bid, and this time his eyes chanced on a small still thing on the edge of the swaying horizon. It was precisely like the point of a pin. It took an anxious eye to find a light-house so tiny.

"Think we'll make it, Captain?"

"If this wind holds and the boat don't swamp, we can't do much else," said the captain.

The little boat, lifted by each towering sea, and splashed viciously by the crests, made progress that in the absence of seaweed was not apparent to those in her. She seemed just a wee thing wallowing, miraculously, top-up, at the mercy of five oceans. Occasionally, a great spread of water, like white flames, swarmed into her.

"Bail her, cook," said the captain, serenely.

"All right, Captain," said the cheerful cook.

III

It would be difficult to describe the subtle brotherhood of men that was here established on the seas. No one said that it was so. No one mentioned it. But it dwelt in the boat, and each man felt it warm him. They were a captain, an oiler, a cook, and a correspondent, and they were friends, friends in a more curiously iron-bound degree than may be common. The hurt captain, lying against the water-jar in the bow, spoke always in a low voice and calmly, but he could never command a more ready and swiftly obedient crew than the motley three of the dingey. It was more than a mere recognition of what was best for the common safety. There was surely in it a quality that was personal and heartfelt. And after this devotion to the commander of the boat there was this comradeship that the correspondent, for instance, who had been taught to be cynical of men, knew even at the time was the best experience of his life. But no one said that it was so. No one mentioned it.

"I wish we had a sail," remarked the captain. "We might try my overcoat on the end of an oar and give you two boys a chance to rest." So the cook and the correspondent held the mast and spread wide the overcoat. The oiler steered, and the little boat made good way with her new rig. Sometimes the oiler had to scull sharply to keep a sea from breaking into the boat, but otherwise sailing was a success.

Meanwhile the light-house had been growing slowly larger. It had now almost assumed color, and appeared like a little gray shadow on the sky. The man at the oars could not be prevented from turning his head rather often to try for a glimpse of this little gray shadow.

At last, from the top of each wave the men in the tossing boat could see land. Even as the light-house was an upright shadow on the sky, this land seemed but a long black shadow on the sea. It certainly was thinner than paper. "We must be about opposite New Smyrna," said the cook, who had coasted this shore often in schooners. "Captain, by the way, I believe they abandoned that life-saving station there about a year ago."

"Did they?" said the captain.

The wind slowly died away. The cook and the correspondent were not now obliged to slave in order to hold high the oar. But the waves continued their old impetuous swooping at the dingey, and the little craft, no longer under way, struggled woundily over them. The oiler or the correspondent took the oars again.

Shipwrecks are *apropos* of nothing. If men could only train for them and have them occur when the men had reached pink condition, there would be less drowning at sea. Of the four in the dingey none had slept any time worth mentioning for two days and two nights previous to embarking in the dingey, and in the excitement of clambering about the deck of a foundering ship they had also forgotten to eat heartily.

For these reasons, and for others, neither the oiler nor the correspondent was fond of rowing at this time. The correspondent wondered ingenuously how in the name of all that was sane could there be people who thought it amusing to row a boat. It was not an amusement; it was a diabolical punishment, and even a genius of mental aberrations could never conclude that it was anything but a horror to the muscles and a crime against the back. He mentioned to the boat in general how the amusement of rowing struck him, and the weary-faced oiler smiled in full sympathy. Previously to the foundering, by the way, the oiler had worked double-watch in the engine-room of the ship.

"Take her easy, now, boys," said the captain. "Don't spend yourselves. If we have to run a surf you'll need all your strength, because we'll sure have to swim for it. Take your time."

Slowly the land arose from the sea. From a black line it became a line of black and a line of white—trees and sand. Finally, the captain said that he could make out a house on the shore. "That's the house of refuge, sure," said the cook. "They'll see us before long, and come out after us."

The distant light-house reared high. "The keeper ought to be able to make us out now, if he's looking through a glass," said the captain. "He'll notify the life-saving people."

"None of those other boats could have got ashore to give word of the wreck," said the oiler, in a low voice. "Else the life-boat would be out hunting us."

Slowly and beautifully the land loomed out of the sea. The wind came again. It had veered from the northeast to the southeast. Finally, a new sound struck the ears of the men in the boat. It was the low thunder of the surf on the shore.

"We'll never be able to make the light-house now," said the captain. "Swing her head a little more north, Billie."

" 'A little more north,' sir," said the oiler.

Whereupon the little boat turned her nose once more down the wind, and all but the oarsman watched the shore grow. Under the influence of this expansion doubt and direful apprehension was leaving the minds of the men. The management of the boat was still most absorbing, but it could not prevent a quiet cheerfulness. In an hour, perhaps, they would be ashore.

Their back-bones had become thoroughly used to balancing in the boat and they now rode this wild colt of a dingey like circus men. The correspondent thought that he had been drenched to the skin, but happening to feel in the top pocket of his coat, he found therein eight cigars. Four of them were soaked with sea-water; four were perfectly scatheless. After a search, somebody produced three dry matches, and thereupon the four waifs rode impudently in their little boat, and with an assurance of an impending rescue shining in their eyes, puffed at the big cigars and judged well and ill of all men. Everybody took a drink of water.

IV

"Cook," remarked the captain, "there don't seem to be any signs of life about your house of refuge."

"No," replied the cook. "Funny they don't see us!"

A broad stretch of lowly coast lay before the eyes of the men. It was of dunes topped with dark vegetation. The roar of the surf was plain, and sometimes they could see the white lip of a wave as it spun up the beach. A tiny house was blocked out black upon the sky. Southward, the slim light-house lifted its little gray length.

Tide, wind, and waves were swinging the dingey northward. "Funny they don't see us," said the men.

The surf's roar was here dulled, but its tone was, nevertheless, thunderous and mighty. As the boat swam over the great rollers, the men sat listening to this roar. "We'll swamp sure," said everybody.

It is fair to say here that there was not a life-saving station within twenty miles in either direction, but the men did not know this fact and in consequence they made dark and opprobrious remarks concerning the eyesight of the nation's life-savers. Four scowling men sat in the dingey and surpassed records in the invention of epithets.

"Funny they don't see us."

The light-heartedness of a former time had completely faded. To their sharpened minds it was easy to conjure pictures of all kinds of incompetency and blindness and, indeed, cowardice. There was the shore of the populous land, and it was bitter and bitter to them that from it came no sign.

"Well," said the captain, ultimately, "I suppose we'll have to make a try for ourselves. If we stay out here too long, we'll none of us have strength left to swim after the boat swamps."

And so the oiler, who was at the oars, turned the boat straight for the shore. There was a sudden tightening of muscles. There was some thinking.

"If we don't all get ashore—" said the captain. "If we don't all get ashore, I suppose you fellows know where to send news of my finish?"

They then briefly exchanged some addresses and admonitions. As for the reflections of the men, there was a great deal of rage in them. Perchance they might be formulated thus: "If I am going to be drowned—if I am going to be drowned—if I am going to be drowned, why, in the name of the seven mad gods who rule the sea, was I allowed to come thus far and contemplate sand and trees? Was I brought here merely to have my nose dragged away as I was about to nibble the sacred cheese of life? It is preposterous. If this old ninny-woman, Fate, cannot do better than this, she should be deprived of the management of men's fortunes. She is an old hen who knows not her intention. If she has decided to drown me, why did she not do it in the beginning and save me all this trouble. The whole affair is absurd. . . . But, no, she cannot mean to drown me. She dare not drown me. She cannot drown me. Not after all this work." Afterward the man might have had an impulse to shake his fist at the clouds. "Just you drown me, now, and then hear what I call you!"

The billows that came at this time were more formidable. They seemed always just about to break and roll over the little boat in a turmoil of foam. There was a preparatory and long growl in the speech of them. No mind unused to the sea would have concluded that the dingey could ascend these sheer heights in time. The shore was still afar. The oiler was a wily surfman. "Boys," he said, swiftly, "she won't live three minutes more and we're too far out to swim. Shall I take her to sea again, Captain?"

"Yes! Go ahead!" said the captain.

This oiler, by a series of quick miracles, and fast and steady oarsmanship, turned the boat in the middle of the surf and took her safely to sea again.

There was a considerable silence as the boat bumped over the furrowed sea to deeper water. Then somebody in gloom spoke. "Well, anyhow, they must have seen us from the shore by now."

The gulls went in slanting flight up the wind toward the gray desolate cast. A squall, marked by dingy clouds, and clouds brick-red, like smoke from a burning building, appeared from the southeast.

"What do you think of those life-saving people? Ain't they peaches?"

"Funny they haven't seen us."

"Maybe they think we're out here for sport! Maybe they think we're fishin'. Maybe they think we're damned fools."

It was a long afternoon. A changed tide tried to force them southward, but wind and wave said northward. Far ahead, where coast-line, sea, and sky formed their mighty angle, there were little dots which seemed to indicate a city on the shore.

"St. Augustine?"

The captain shook his head. "Too near Mosquito Inlet."

And the oiler rowed, and then the correspondent rowed. Then the oiler rowed. It was a weary business. The human back can become the seat of more aches and pains than are registered in books for the composite anatomy of a regiment. It is a limited area, but it can become the theatre of innumerable muscular conflicts, tangles, wrenches, knots, and other comforts.

"Did you ever like to row, Billie?" asked the correspondent.

"No," said the oiler. "Hang it."

When one exchanged the rowing-seat for a place in the bottom of the boat, he suffered a bodily depression that caused him to be careless of everything save an obligation to wiggle one finger. There was cold sea-water swashing to and fro in the boat, and he lay in it. His head, pillowed on a thwart, was within an inch of the swirl of a wave crest, and sometimes a particularly obstreperous sea came in-board and drenched him once more. But these matters did not annoy him. It is almost certain that if the boat had capsized he would have tumbled comfortably out upon the ocean as if he felt sure that it was a great soft mattress.

"Look! There's a man on the shore!"

"Where?"

"There! See 'im? See 'im?"

"Yes, sure! He's walking along."

"Now he's stopped. Look! He's facing us!"

"He's waving at us!"

"So he is! By thunder!"

"Ah, now, we're all right! Now we're all right! There'll be a boat out here for us in half an hour."

"He's going on. He's running. He's going up to that house there."

The remote beach seemed lower than the sea, and it required a searching glance to discern the little black figure. The captain saw a floating stick and they rowed to it. A bath-towel was by some weird chance in the boat, and, tying this on the stick, the captain waved it. The oarsman did not dare turn his head, so he was obliged to ask questions.

"What's he doing now?"

"He's standing still again. He's looking, I think. . . . There he goes again. Toward the house. . . . Now he's stopped again."

"Is he waving at us?"

"No, not now! he was, though."

"Look! There comes another man!"

"He's running."

"Look at him go, would you."

"Why, he's on a bicycle. Now he's met the other man. They're both waving at us. Look!"

"There comes something up the beach."

"What the devil is that thing?"

"Why, it looks like a boat."

"Why, certainly it's a boat."

"No, it's on wheels."

"Yes, so it is. Well, that must be the life-boat. They drag them along shore on a wagon."

"That's the life-boat, sure."

"No, by——, it's—it's an omnibus."

"I tell you it's a life-boat."

"It is not! It's an omnibus. I can see it plain. See? One of those big hotel omnibuses."

"By thunder, you're right. It's an omnibus, sure as fate. What do you suppose they are doing with an omnibus? Maybe they are going around collecting the life-crew, hey?"

"That's it, likely. Look! There's a fellow waving a little black flag. He's standing on the steps of the omnibus. There come those other two fellows. Now they're all talking together. Look at the fellow with the flag. Maybe he ain't waving it!"

"That ain't a flag, is it? That's his coat. Why, certainly, that's his coat."

"So it is. It's his coat. He's taken it off and is waving it around his head. But would you look at him swing it!"

"Oh, say, there isn't any life-saving station there. That's just a winter resort hotel omnibus that has brought over some of the boarders to see us drown."

"What's that idiot with the coat mean? What's he signaling, anyhow?"

"It looks as if he were trying to tell us to go north. There must be a life-saving station up there."

"No! He thinks we're fishing. Just giving us a merry hand. See? Ah, there, Willie."

"Well, I wish I could make something out of those signals. What do you suppose he means?"

"He don't mean anything. He's just playing."

"Well, if he'd just signal us to try the surf again, or to go to sea and wait, or go north, or go south, or go to hell—there would be some reason in it. But look at him. He just stands there and keeps his coat revolving like a wheel. The ass!"

"There come more people."

"Now there's quite a mob. Look! Isn't that a boat?"

"Where? Oh, I see where you mean. No, that's no boat."

"That fellow is still waving his coat."

"He must think we like to see him do that. Why don't he quit it. It don't mean anything."

"I don't know. I think he is trying to make us go north. It must be that there's a life-saving station there somewhere."

"Say, he ain't tired yet. Look at 'im wave."

"Wonder how long he can keep that up. He's been revolving his coat ever since he caught sight of us. He's an idiot. Why aren't they getting men to bring a boat out. A fishing boat—one of those big yawls—could come out here all right. Why don't he do something?"

"Oh, it's all right, now."

"They'll have a boat out here for us in less than no time, now that they've seen us."

A faint yellow tone came into the sky over the low land. The shadows on the sea slowly deepened. The wind bore coldness with it, and the men began to shiver.

"Holy smoke!" said one, allowing his voice to express his impious mood, "if we keep on monkeying out here! If we've got to flounder out here all night!"

"Oh, we'll never have to stay here all night! Don't you worry. They've seen us now, and it won't be long before they'll come chasing out after us."

The shore grew dusky. The man waving a coat blended gradually into this gloom, and it swallowed in the same manner the omnibus and the group of people. The spray, when it dashed uproariously over the side, made the voyagers shrink and swear like men who were being branded.

"I'd like to catch the chump who waved the coat. I feel like soaking him one, just for luck."

"Why? What did he do?"

"Oh, nothing, but then he seemed so damned cheerful."

In the meantime the oiler rowed, and then the correspondent rowed, and then the oiler rowed. Gray-faced and bowed forward, they mechanically, turn by turn, plied the leaden oars. The form of the light-house had vanished from the southern horizon, but finally a pale star appeared, just lifting from the sea. The streaked saffron in the west passed before the all-merging darkness, and the sea to the east was black. The land had vanished, and was expressed only by the low and drear thunder of the surf.

"If I am going to be drowned—if I am going to be drowned—if I am going to be drowned, why, in the name of the seven mad gods who rule the sea, was I allowed to come thus far and contemplate sand and trees? Was I brought here merely to have my nose dragged away as I was about to nibble the sacred cheese of life?"

The patient captain, drooped over the water-jar, was sometimes obliged to speak to the oarsman.

"Keep her head up! Keep her head up!"

" 'Keep her head up,' sir." The voices were weary and low.

This was surely a quiet evening. All save the oarsman lay heavily and listlessly in the boat's bottom. As for him, his eyes were just capable of noting the tall black waves that swept forward in a most sinister silence, save for an occasional subdued growl of a crest.

The cook's head was on a thwart, and he looked without interest at the water under his nose. He was deep in other scenes. Finally he spoke. "Billie," he murmured, dreamfully, "what kind of pie do you like best?"

V

"Pie," said the oiler and the correspondent, agitatedly. "Don't talk about those things, blast you!"

"Well," said the cook, "I was just thinking about ham sandwiches, and——"

A night on the sea in an open boat is a long night. As darkness settled finally, the shine of the light, lifting from the sea in the south, changed to full gold. On the northern horizon a new light appeared, a small bluish gleam on the edge of the waters. These two lights were the furniture of the world. Otherwise there was nothing but waves.

Two men huddled in the stern, and distances were so magnificent in the dingey that the rower was enabled to keep his feet partly warmed by thrusting them under his companions. Their legs indeed extended far under the rowing-seat until they touched the feet of the captain forward. Sometimes, despite the efforts of the tired oarsman, a wave came piling into the boat, an icy wave of the night, and the chilling water soaked them anew. They would twist their bodies for a moment and groan, and sleep the dead sleep once more, while the water in the boat gurgled about them as the craft rocked.

The plan of the oiler and the correspondent was for one to row until he lost the ability, and then arouse the other from his sea-water couch in the bottom of the boat.

The oiler plied the oars until his head drooped forward, and the overpowering sleep blinded him. And he rowed yet afterward. Then he touched a man in the bottom of the boat, and called his name. "Will you spell me for a little while?" he said, meekly.

"Sure, Billie," said the correspondent, awakening and dragging himself to a sitting position. They exchanged places carefully, and the oiler, cuddling down in the sea-water at the cook's side, seemed to go to sleep instantly.

The particular violence of the sea had ceased. The waves came without snarling. The obligation of the man at the oars was to keep the boat headed so that the tilt of the rollers would not capsize her, and to preserve her from filling when the crests rushed past. The black waves were silent and hard to be seen in the darkness. Often one was almost upon the boat before the oarsman was aware.

In a low voice the correspondent addressed the captain. He was not sure that the captain was awake, although this iron man seemed to be always awake. "Captain, shall I keep her making for that light north, sir?"

The same steady voice answered him. "Yes. Keep it about two points off the port bow."

The cook had tied a life-belt around himself in order to get even the warmth which this clumsy cork contrivance could donate, and he seemed almost stove-like when a rower, whose teeth invariably chattered wildly as soon as he ceased his labor, dropped down to sleep.

The correspondent, as he rowed, looked down at the two men sleeping under foot. The cook's arm was around the oiler's shoulders, and, with their fragmentary clothing and haggard faces, they were the babes of the sea, a grotesque rendering of the old babes in the wood.

Later he must have grown stupid at his work, for suddenly there was a growling of water, and a crest came with a roar and a swash into the boat, and it was a wonder that it did not set the cook afloat in his life-belt. The cook continued to sleep, but the oiler sat up, blinking his eyes and shaking with the new cold.

"Oh, I'm awful sorry, Billie," said the correspondent, contritely.

"That's all right, old boy," said the oiler, and lay down again and was asleep.

Presently it seemed that even the captain dozed, and the correspondent thought that he was the one man afloat on all the oceans. The wind had a voice as it came over the waves, and it was sadder than the end.

There was a long, loud swishing astern of the boat, and a gleaming trail of phosphorescence, like blue flame, was furrowed on the black waters. It might have been made by a monstrous knife.

Then there came a stillness, while the correspondent breathed with the open mouth and looked at the sea.

Suddenly there was another swish and another long flash of bluish light, and this time it was alongside the boat, and might almost have been reached with an oar. The correspondent saw an enormous fin speed like a shadow through the water, hurling the crystalline spray and leaving the long glowing trail.

The correspondent looked over his shoulder at the captain. His face was hidden, and he seemed to be asleep. He looked at the babes of the sea. They certainly were asleep. So, being bereft of sympathy, he leaned a little way to one side and swore softly into the sea.

But the thing did not then leave the vicinity of the boat. Ahead or astern, on one side or the other, at intervals long or short, fled the long sparkling streak, and there was to be heard the whiroo of the dark fin. The speed and power of the thing was greatly to be admired. It cut the water like a gigantic and keen projectile.

The presence of this biding thing did not affect the man with the same horror that it would if he had been a picnicker. He simply looked at the sea dully and swore in an undertone.

Nevertheless, it is true that he did not wish to be alone with the thing. He wished one of his companions to awaken by chance and keep him company with it. But the captain hung motionless over the water-jar and the oiler and the cook in the bottom of the boat were plunged in slumber.

VI

"If I am going to be drowned—if I am going to be drowned—if I am going to be drowned, why, in the name of the seven mad gods who rule the sea, was I allowed to come thus far and contemplate sand and trees?"

During this dismal night, it may be remarked that a man would conclude that it was really the intention of the seven mad gods to drown him, despite the abominable injustice of it. For it was certainly an abominable injustice to drown a man who had worked so hard, so hard. The man felt it would be a crime most unnatural. Other people had drowned at sea since galleys swarmed with painted sails, but still——

When it occurs to a man that nature does not regard him as important, and that she feels she would not maim the universe by disposing of him, he at first wishes to throw bricks at the temple, and he hates deeply the fact that there are no bricks and no temples. Any visible expression of nature would surely be pelleted with his jeers.

Then, if there be no tangible thing to hoot he feels, perhaps, the desire to confront a personification and indulge in pleas, bowed to one knee, and with hands supplicant, saying: "Yes, but I love myself."

A high cold star on a winter's night is the word he feels that she says to him. Thereafter he knows the pathos of his situation.

The men in the dingey had not discussed these matters, but each had, no doubt, reflected upon them in silence and according to his mind. There was seldom any expression upon their faces save the general one of complete weariness. Speech was devoted to the business of the boat.

To chime the notes of his emotion, a verse mysteriously entered the correspondent's head. He had even forgotten that he had forgotten this verse, but it suddenly was in his mind.

A soldier of the Legion lay dying in Algiers,
There was lack of woman's nursing, there was dearth
    of woman's tears;
But a comrade stood beside him, and he took that
    comrade's hand,
And he said: "I never more shall see my own, my
    native land."

In his childhood, the correspondent had been made acquainted with the fact that a soldier of the Legion lay dying in Algiers, but he had never regarded it as important. Myriads of his school-fellows had informed him of the soldier's plight, but the dinning had naturally ended by making him perfectly indifferent. He had never considered it his affair that a soldier of the Legion lay dying in Algiers, nor had it appeared to him as a matter for sorrow. It was less to him than the breaking of a pencil's point.

Now, however, it quaintly came to him as a human, living thing. It was no longer merely a picture of a few throes in the breast of a poet, meanwhile drinking tea and warming his feet at the grate; it was an actuality—stern, mournful, and fine.

The correspondent plainly saw the soldier. He lay on the sand with his feet out straight and still. While his pale left hand was upon his chest in an attempt to thwart the going of his life, the blood came between his fingers. In the far Algerian distance, a city of low square forms was set against a sky that was faint with the last sunset hues. The correspondent, plying the oars and dreaming of the slow and slower movements of the lips of the soldier, was moved by a profound and perfectly impersonal comprehension. He was sorry for the soldier of the Legion who lay dying in Algiers.

The thing which had followed the boat and waited had evidently grown bored at the delay. There was no longer to be heard the slash of the cut-water, and there was no longer the flame of the long trail. The light in the north still glimmered, but it was apparently no nearer to the boat. Sometimes the boom of the surf rang in the correspondent's ears, and he turned the craft seaward then and rowed harder. Southward, some one had evidently built a watch-fire on the beach. It was too low and too far to be seen, but it made a shimmering, roseate reflection upon the bluff back of it, and this could be discerned from the boat. The wind came stronger, and sometimes a wave suddenly raged out like a mountain-cat and there was to be seen the sheen and sparkle of a broken crest.

The captain, in the bow, moved on his water-jar and sat erect. "Pretty long night," he observed to the correspondent. He looked at the shore. "Those life-saving people take their time."

"Did you see that shark playing around?"

"Yes, I saw him. He was a big fellow, all right."

"Wish I had known you were awake."

Later the correspondent spoke into the bottom of the boat.

"Billie!" There was a slow and gradual disentanglement. "Billie, will you spell me?"

"Sure," said the oiler.

As soon as the correspondent touched the cold comfortable sea-water in the bottom of the boat, and had huddled close to the cook's life-belt he was deep in sleep, despite the fact that his teeth played all the popular airs. This sleep was so good to him that it was but a moment before he heard a voice call his name in a tone that demonstrated the last stages of exhaustion. "Will you spell me?"

"Sure, Billie."

The light in the north had mysteriously vanished, but the correspondent took his course from the wide-awake captain.

Later in the night they took the boat farther out to sea, and the captain directed the cook to take one oar at the stern and keep the boat facing the seas. He was to call out if he should hear the thunder of the surf. This plan enabled the oiler and the correspondent to get respite together. "We'll give those boys a chance to get into shape again," said the captain. They curled down and, after a few preliminary chatterings and trembles, slept once more the dead sleep. Neither knew they had bequeathed to the cook the company of another shark, or perhaps the same shark.

As the boat caroused on the waves, spray occasionally bumped over the side and gave them a fresh soaking, but this had no power to break their repose. The ominous slash of the wind and the water affected them as it would have affected mummies.

"Boys," said the cook, with the notes of every reluctance in his voice, "she's drifted in pretty close. I guess one of you had better take her to sea again." The correspondent, aroused, heard the crash of the toppled crests.

As he was rowing, the captain gave him some whiskey and water, and this steadied the chills out of him. "If I ever get ashore and anybody shows me even a photograph of an oar——"

At last there was a short conversation.

"Billie. . . . Billie, will you spell me?"

"Sure," said the oiler.

VII

When the correspondent again opened his eyes, the sea and the sky were each of the gray hue of the dawning. Later, carmine and gold was painted upon the waters. The morning appeared finally, in its splendor, with a sky of pure blue, and the sunlight flamed on the tips of the waves.

On the distant dunes were set many little black cottages, and a tall white wind-mill reared above them. No man, nor dog, nor bicycle appeared on the beach. The cottages might have formed a deserted village.

The voyagers scanned the shore. A conference was held in the boat. "Well," said the captain, "if no help is coming, we might better try a run through the surf right away. If we stay out here much longer we will be too weak to do anything for ourselves at all." The others silently acquiesced in this reasoning. The boat was headed for the beach. The correspondent wondered if none ever ascended the tall wind-tower, and if then they never looked seaward. This tower was a giant, standing with its back to the plight of the ants. It represented in a degree, to the correspondent, the serenity of nature amid the struggles of the individual—nature in the wind, and nature in the vision of men. She did not seem cruel to him then, nor beneficent, nor treacherous, nor wise. But she was indifferent, flatly indifferent. It is, perhaps, plausible that a man in this situation, impressed with the unconcern of the universe, should see the innumerable flaws of his life and have them taste wickedly in his mind and wish for another chance. A distinction between right and wrong seems absurdly clear to him, then, in this new ignorance of the grave-edge, and he understands that if he were given another opportunity he would mend his conduct and his words, and be better and brighter during an introduction, or at a tea.

"Now, boys," said the captain, "she is going to swamp sure. All we can do is to work her in as far as possible, and then when she swamps, pile out and scramble for the beach. Keep cool now, and don't jump until she swamps sure."

The oiler took the oars. Over his shoulders he scanned the surf. "Captain," he said, "I think I'd better bring her about, and keep her head-on to the seas and back her in."

"All right, Billie," said the captain. "Back her in." The oiler swung the boat then and, seated in the stern, the cook and the correspondent were obliged to look over their shoulders to contemplate the lonely and indifferent shore.

The monstrous inshore rollers heaved the boat high until the men were again enabled to see the white sheets of water scudding up the slanted beach. "We won't get in very close," said the captain. Each time a man could wrest his attention from the rollers, he turned his glance toward the shore, and in the expression of the eyes during this contemplation there was a singular quality. The correspondent, observing the others, knew that they were not afraid, but the full meaning of their glances was shrouded.

As for himself, he was too tired to grapple fundamentally with the fact. He tried to coerce his mind into thinking of it, but the mind was dominated at this time by the muscles, and the muscles said they did not care. It merely occurred to him that if he should drown it would be a shame.

There were no hurried words, no pallor, no plain agitation. The men simply looked at the shore. "Now, remember to get well clear of the boat when you jump," said the captain.

Seaward the crest of a roller suddenly fell with a thunderous crash, and the long white comber came roaring down upon the boat.

"Steady now," said the captain. The men were silent. They turned their eyes from the shore to the comber and waited. The boat slid up the incline, leaped at the furious top, bounced over it, and swung down the long back of the wave. Some water had been shipped and the cook bailed it out.

But the next crest crashed also. The tumbling boiling flood of white water caught the boat and whirled it almost perpendicular. Water swarmed in from all sides. The correspondent had his hands on the gunwale at this time, and when the water entered at that place he swiftly withdrew his fingers, as if he objected to wetting them.

The little boat, drunken with this weight of water, reeled and snuggled deeper into the sea.

"Bail her out, cook! Bail her out," said the captain.

"All right, Captain," said the cook.

"Now, boys, the next one will do for us, sure," said the oiler. "Mind to jump clear of the boat."

The third wave moved forward, huge, furious, implacable. It fairly swallowed the dingey, and almost simultaneously the men tumbled into the sea. A piece of life-belt had lain in the bottom of the boat, and as the correspondent went overboard he held this to his chest with his left hand.

The January water was icy, and he reflected immediately that it was colder than he had expected to find it off the coast of Florida. This appeared to his dazed mind as a fact important enough to be noted at the time. The coldness of the water was sad; it was tragic. This fact was somehow so mixed and confused with his opinion of his own situation that it seemed almost a proper reason for tears. The water was cold.

When he came to the surface he was conscious of little but the noisy water. Afterward he saw his companions in the sea. The oiler was ahead in the race. He was swimming strongly and rapidly. Off to the correspondent's left, the cook's great white and corked back bulged out of the water, and in the rear the captain was hanging with his one good hand to the keel of the overturned dingey.

There is a certain immovable quality to a shore, and the correspondent wondered at it amid the confusion of the sea.

It seemed also very attractive, but the correspondent knew that it was a long journey, and he paddled leisurely. The piece of life-preserver lay under him, and sometimes he whirled down the incline of a wave as if he were on a hand-sled.

But finally he arrived at a place in the sea where travel was beset with difficulty. He did not pause swimming to inquire what manner of current had caught him, but there his progress ceased. The shore was set before him like a bit of scenery on a stage, and he looked at it and understood with his eyes each detail of it.

As the cook passed, much farther to the left, the captain was calling to him, "Turn over on your back, cook! Turn over on your back and use the oar."

"All right, sir." The cook turned on his back, and, paddling with an oar, went ahead as if he were a canoe.

Presently the boat also passed to the left of the correspondent with the captain clinging with one hand to the keel. He would have appeared like a man raising himself to look over a board fence, if it were not for the extraordinary gymnastics of the boat. The correspondent marvelled that the captain could still hold to it.

They passed on, nearer to shore—the oiler, the cook, the captain—and following them went the water-jar, bouncing gayly over the seas.

The correspondent remained in the grip of this strange new enemy—a current. The shore, with its white slope of sand and its green bluff, topped with little silent cottages, was spread like a picture before him. It was very near to him then, but he was impressed as one who in a gallery looks at a scene from Brittany or Holland.

He thought: "I am going to drown? Can it be possible? Can it be possible? Can it be possible?" Perhaps an individual must consider his own death to be the final phenomenon of nature.

But later a wave perhaps whirled him out of this small deadly current, for he found suddenly that he could again make progress toward the shore. Later still, he was aware that the captain, clinging with one hand to the keel of the dingey, had his face turned away from the shore and toward him, and was calling his name. "Come to the boat! Come to the boat!"

In his struggle to reach the captain and the boat, he reflected that when one gets properly wearied, drowning must really be a comfortable arrangement, a cessation of hostilities accompanied by a large degree of relief, and he was glad of it, for the main thing in his mind for some moments had been horror of the temporary agony. He did not wish to be hurt.

Presently he saw a man running along the shore. He was undressing with most remarkable speed. Coat, trousers, shirt, everything flew magically off him.

"Come to the boat," called the captain.

"All right, Captain." As the correspondent paddled, he saw the captain let himself down to bottom and leave the boat. Then the correspondent performed his one little marvel of the voyage. A large wave caught him and flung him with ease and supreme speed completely over the boat and far beyond it. It struck him even then as an event in gymnastics, and a true miracle of the sea. An overturned boat in the surf is not a plaything to a swimming man.

The correspondent arrived in water that reached only to his waist, but his condition did not enable him to stand for more than a moment. Each wave knocked him into a heap, and the under-tow pulled at him.

Then he saw the man who had been running and undressing, and undressing and running, come bounding into the water. He dragged ashore the cook, and then waded toward the captain, but the captain waved him away, and sent him to the correspondent. He was naked, naked as a tree in winter, but a halo was about his head, and he shone like a saint. He gave a strong pull, and a long drag, and a bully heave at the correspondent's hand. The correspondent, schooled in the minor formulæ, said: "Thanks, old man." But suddenly the man cried: "What's that?" He pointed a swift finger. The correspondent said: "Go."

In the shallows, face downward, lay the oiler. His forehead touched sand that was periodically, between each wave, clear of the sea.

The correspondent did not know all that transpired afterward. When he achieved safe ground he fell, striking the sand with each particular part of his body. It was as if he had dropped from a roof, but the thud was grateful to him.

It seems that instantly the beach was populated with men with blankets, clothes, and flasks, and women with coffeepots and all the remedies sacred to their minds. The welcome of the land to the men from the sea was warm and generous, but a still and dripping shape was carried slowly up the beach, and the land's welcome for it could only be the different and sinister hospitality of the grave.

When it came night, the white waves paced to and fro in the moonlight, and the wind brought the sound of the great sea's voice to the men on shore, and they felt that they could then be interpreters.

Richard Harding Davis

Richard Harding Davis (1864–1916), the son of the novelist Rebecca Harding Davis, began his journalistic career in 1886 and went on to become one of the most famous correspondents of his era. Over three decades Davis covered the Johnstown flood, the Cuban insurrection against Spain, the Greco-Turkish War of 1897, the Spanish-American War, the Boer War, the Russo-Japanese War, Belgian rule in the Congo, and World War I. These excerpts from his book The Cuban and Porto Rican Campaigns *describe the American invasion fleet that sailed from Florida to Cuba in June 1898. The Spanish garrison at Santiago surrendered on July 16 and Spain signed an armistice on August 12, 1898, less than four months after war was declared. Its rapid victory gained the United States a protectorate over Cuba, possession of Puerto Rico, Guam, and the Philippines, and new standing as a global naval power.*

from *The Voyage of the Transports*

The departure of the transports from Tampa Bay, when it came after many weary postponements and delays, was neither picturesque nor moving. The band did not play "The Girl I Left Behind Me," nor did crowds of weeping women cling to the bulkheads and wave their damp handkerchiefs; the men who were going to die for their country did not swarm in the rigging and cheer the last sight of land. They had done that on the morning of June 8th, and had been ingloriously towed back to the dock; they had done it again on the morning of June 10th, and had immediately dropped anchor a few hundred yards off shore. So they were suspicious and wary, and when the head-quarters ship, the *Segurança*, left the dock three colored women and a pathetic group of perspiring stevedores and three soldiers represented the popular interest in her departure. The largest number of United States troops that ever went down to the sea in ships to invade a foreign country were those that formed the Fifth Army Corps when it sailed for

Santiago. The thought of twelve thousand men on thirty-two troop ships and their escort of fourteen war-ships suggests the Spanish Armada.

It brings up a picture of a great flotilla, grim, sinister, and menacing, fighting its way through the waves on its errand of vengeance and conquest. But as a matter of fact the expedition bore a most distinct air of the commonplace. It moved through a succession of sparkling, sunlit days, over a sea as smooth as a lake, undisturbed by Spanish cruisers or by shells from Spanish forts. As far as the eye could see it had the ocean entirely to itself.

Scattered over a distance of seven miles the black passenger steamers and the mouse-colored war-ships steamed in three uneven columns and suggested a cluster of excursion steamers, and yachts and tugs as one sees them coming back from Sandy Hook after an international yacht-race.

The troop-ships were fitted up with pine cots and a small proportion of stalls for the horses; the first-class cabins were turned over to the officers. On some of them the men swarmed over every part of the ship, on others the officers held only the bridge to themselves.

Probably half of the men forming the expedition had never been to sea before. They probably will desire never to go again, but will say from the depth of their one experience that the dangers of the deep are vastly exaggerated. They will not wish to go again, because their first experience was more full of discomfort than any other trip they are likely to take could possibly be; on the other hand, they may sail the seas many times before they find it as smooth, or the rain as infrequent, the sun as beautiful, or the heavens as magnificent.

We travelled at the rate of seven miles an hour, with long pauses for thought and consultation. Sometimes we moved at the rate of four miles an hour, and frequently we did not move at all. Our delays were chiefly due to the fact that two of the steamers were each towing a great scow or lighter, on which the troops were to be conveyed to shore, and because another one was towing a schooner filled with water. The speed of the squadron was, of course, the speed of the slowest ship in it, so the water-boat set the pace.

The war-ships treated us with the most punctilious courtesy and concealed contempt. And we certainly deserved it. We could not keep in line and we lost ourselves and each other, and the gun-boats and torpedo-boats were kept busy rounding us up, and giving us sharp, precise orders in passing, through a megaphone, to which either nobody on board made any reply, or everyone did. The gun-boats were like swift, keen-eyed, intelligent collies rounding up a herd of bungling sheep. They looked so workmanlike and clean, and the men were so smart in their white duck, that the soldiers cheered them all along the line, as they dashed up and down it, waving their wigwags frantically.

The life on board the head-quarters ship was uneventful for those who were not in command. For these their tables and desks were spread in the "social hall," and all day long they worked busily and mysteriously on maps and lists and orders, and six typewriters banged on their machines until late at night. The ship was greatly overcrowded; it held all of General Shafter's staff, all of General Breckinridge's staff, the Cuban generals, the officers and five hundred men of the First Regiment, all the foreign *attachés*, and an army of stenographers, secretaries, clerks, servants, couriers, valets, and colored waiters.

All of these were jumbled together. There were three cane chairs with seats and two cane chairs without seats. If you were so unlucky as not to capture one of these, you clung sidewise to the bench around the ship's rail or sat on the deck. At no one moment were you alone. Your most intimate conversation was overheard by everyone, whether he wished to do so or not; the *attachés* could not compare notes on our deficiencies without being betrayed, nor could the staff discuss its plan of campaign without giving it to the whole ship. Seven different languages were in course of constant circulation, and the grievances of the servants and the badinage of the colored cooks mingled with the latest remarks on the war. At night you picked your way over prostrate forms of soldiers and of overworked stewards, who toiled eighteen hours a day in a temperature of 102 degrees.

The water on board the ship was so bad that it could not be used for purposes of shaving. It smelled like a frog-pond or a stable-yard, and it tasted as it smelt. Before we started from Tampa Bay the first time it was examined by the doctors, who declared that in spite of the bad smell and taste it was not unhealthy, but Colonel J. J. Astor offered to pay for fresh water, for which Plant charged two cents a gallon, if they would empty all of the bad-smelling water overboard. General Shafter said it was good enough for him, and Colonel Astor's very considerate offer was not accepted. So we all drank apollinaris water or tea. The soldiers, however, had to drink the water furnished them, except those who were able to pay five cents a glass to the ship's porter, who had a private supply of good water which he made into lemonade. The ship's crew and engineers used this water.

Before handing the ship over to the Government, the company removed all of her wine stock and table-linen, took out two of her dining-tables and generally stripped her, and then sent her South undermanned. Her steward hired and borrowed and bought linen and servants and table-waters at Tampa, but there was so little linen that it was seldom changed, and had it not been that the servants of the officers were willing to help wait at table, there would have been four stewards to look after the wants of fifty or sixty passengers. The food supplied by the line to which the ship belonged was villanous; the enlisted men forward were much better served by the Government with good beans, corned beef, and coffee. Apparently, no contract or agreement as to quantity or quality of food for the officers had been made by the Government with the owners.

The squadron at night, with the lights showing from every part of the horizon, made one think he was entering a harbor, or leaving one. But by day we seemed adrift on a sea as untravelled as it was when Columbus first crossed it. On the third day out we saw Romano Key. It was the first sight of land, and after that from time to time we made out a line of blue mountains on the starboard side. The squadron, though, had apparently been sighted from the shore, for the lighthouses along the coast were dark at night, which would seem to show that the lesson of the Armada has not been lost on the Spaniard.

Someone has said that "God takes care of drunken men, sailors, and the United States." This expedition apparently relied on the probability that that axiom would prove true. "The luck of the British Army," of which Mr. Kipling boasts, is the luck of Job in comparison to the good fortune that pursued that expedition. There was really nothing to prevent a Spanish torpedo-boat from running out and sinking four or five ships while they were drifting along, spread out over the sea at such distance that the vessels in the rear were lost to sight for fourteen hours at a time, and no one knew whether they had sunk or had been blown up, or had grown disgusted and gone back home. As one of the generals on board said, "This is God Almighty's war, and we are only His agents."

The foreign *attachés* regarded the fair weather that accompanied us, the brutal good health of the men, the small loss of horses and mules, and the entire freedom from interference on the part of the enemy with the same grudging envy that one watches a successful novice winning continuously at roulette. At night the fleet was as conspicuous as Brooklyn or New York, with the lights of the Bridge included, but the Spanish took no advantage of that fact; no torpedo-destroyers slipped out from Cardenas or Nuevitas, or waited for us in the old Bahama Channel, where for twelve miles the ships were crowded into a channel only seven miles across. Of course, our own escort would have finished them if they had, but not before they could have thrown torpedoes right and left into the helpless hulks of the transports, and given us a loss to remember even greater than that of the *Maine*.

But as it was, nothing happened. We rolled along at our own pace, with the lights the navy had told us to extinguish blazing defiantly to the stars, with bands banging out rag-time music, and with the foremost vessels separated sometimes for half a day at a time from the laggards in the rear.

It was a most happy-go-lucky expedition, run with real American optimism and readiness to take big chances, and with the spirit of a people who recklessly trust that it will come out all right in the end, and that the barely possible may not happen, that the joker may not turn up to spoil the hand, who risk grade crossings and all that they imply, who race transatlantic steamers through a fog for the sake of a record, and who on this occasion certainly "euchred God's almighty storm and bluffed the eternal sea."

No one complained and no one grumbled. The soldiers turned over to sleep on the bare decks, with final injunctions not to be awakened for anything under a Spanish battle-ship, and whenever the ships drew up alongside, the men bombarded each other with jokes on the cheerful fact that they were hungry and thirsty and sore for sleep. But, for all that, our army's greatest invasion of a foreign land was completely successful, but chiefly so, one cannot help thinking, because the Lord looks after his own.

There are three places in the West Indies where Columbus is said to have first landed; one of them is at Santiago. Some hundreds of years from now there will probably be as great a dispute as to where the American troops first landed when they came to drive the Spaniard across the sea and to establish the republic of Cuba. There were two "first landings" of the army of invasion; but before it came to Cuba soldiers of the Regular Army were put ashore at Arbolitas Point, when they acted as an escort to the *Gussie* expedition. On this occasion a Spanish lieutenant and several of his soldiers were killed, and on the American side a correspondent was shot through the arm. Still another landing was made before the Regulars came in force, this time by marines, at Guantanamo Bay; and as they established a camp there and remained on shore, the credit of first raising the American flag on Cuban soil, and of keeping it in its place, belongs to them, and through them to the navy. The first American flag raised temporarily was put up on a block-house near Cardenas by Lieutenant Willard, also of the navy.

When the army came at last, sixteen thousand strong, in thirty-one transports, and with an escort of fourteen war-ships, it made two landings: a preliminary one on June 20th, when only twenty people went ashore at Aserraderos, and on June 22d at Daiquiri, when all through the day there was a continuous going and coming of shore-boats from the transports, each carrying from twenty to thirty men, and following after each other as swiftly as cable-cars on Broadway.

* * *

It was delightful to see the fine scorn of the coxswains as the "dough-boys" fell and jumped and tumbled from the gangway ladder into the heaving boats, that dropped from beneath them like a descending elevator or rose suddenly and threw them on their knees. It was much more dangerous than anyone imagined, for later in the day when two men of the Twenty-fifth Regiment were upset at the pier, the weight of the heavy cartridge-belt and haversack and blanket-roll carried them to the bottom. Soon the sea was dotted with rows of white boats filled with men bound about with white blanket-rolls and with muskets at all angles, and as they rose and fell on the water and the newspaper yachts and transports crept in closer and closer, the scene was strangely suggestive of a boat-race, and one almost waited for the starting gun.

It came at last, though in a different spirit, from the *New Orleans*, and in an instant the *Detroit*, the *Castine*, and the little *Wasp* were enveloped in smoke. The valleys sent back the reports of the guns in long, thundering echoes that reverberated again and again, and the mountain-side began at once to spurt up geysers of earth and branches of broken bushes, as though someone had stabbed it with a knife and the blood had spurted from the wound. But there were no answering shots, and under the cover of the smoke the long-boats and launches began to scurry toward the shore. Meanwhile, the war-ships kept up their fierce search for hidden batteries, tearing off the tin roofs of the huts, dismantling the block-houses, and sending the thatched shacks into bonfires of flame. The men in the boats pulled harder at the oars, the steam-launches rolled and pitched, tugging at the weight behind them, and the first convoy of five hundred men were soon bunched together, racing bow by bow for the shore. A launch turned suddenly and steered for a long pier under the ore-docks, the waves lifted it to the level of the pier, and a half-dozen men leaped through the air and landed on the pier-head, waving their muskets above them. At the same moment two of the other boats were driven through the surf to the beach itself, and the men tumbled out and scrambled to their feet upon the shore of Cuba. In an instant a cheer rose faintly from the shore, and more loudly from the war-ships. It was caught up by every ship in the transport fleet, and was carried for miles over the ocean. Men waved their hats, and jumped up and down, and shrieked as though they themselves had been the first to land, and the combined cheering seemed as though it must surely reach to the walls of Santiago and tell the enemy that the end was near. But the cheers were whispers to what came later, when, outlined against the sky, we saw four tiny figures scaling the sheer face of the mountain up the narrow trail to the highest blockhouse. For a moment they were grouped together there at the side of the Spanish fort, and then thousands of feet above the shore the American flag was thrown out against the sky, and the sailors on the men-of-war, the Cubans, and our own soldiers in the village, the soldiers in the long-boats, and those still hanging to the sides and ratlines of the troop-ships, shouted and cheered again, and every steam-whistle on the ocean for miles about shrieked and tooted and roared in a pandemonium of delight and pride and triumph.

Joshua Slocum

On June 27, 1898, Joshua Slocum sailed the 37-foot Spray *into Newport harbor, completing the first solo circumnavigation of the globe, a voyage that lasted three years, two months, and two days, and took him 46,000 miles. Born in 1844, Slocum first went to sea at 14, as cook on a fishing schooner. After many merchant voyages he rose to the command of the tall-masted* Northern Light, *one of the finest ships of its time. In 1884, resisting the transition to cheaper steam-powered vessels that saw the* Northern Light *turned into a coal barge, Slocum bought a smaller ship, the 326-ton* Aquidneck, *and with his family began to carry freight between Baltimore and Pernambuco, Brazil. After three years in this trade, the* Aquidneck *was wrecked off the Brazilian coast. With no money for a passage home, Slocum built a 35-foot "canoe," the* Liberdade, *in which he and his family returned, destitute but alive, to the United States. Slocum tried without success to make money with his self-published* Voyage of the Liberdade *(1890). Finding his skills largely obsolete in the new era of steam, he took odd jobs in New England shipyards. In one of these, as "something of a joke," a retired whaling friend gave him an old sloop—the* Spray*—which he began quixotically to rebuild. Slocum's account of his adventures in this tiny ship,* Sailing Alone Around the World *(1900), has become a classic—the "nautical equivalent," as Van Wyck Brooks puts it, of Thoreau's* Walden. *Indeed, Slocum can make solo voyaging seem so pleasant as to downplay the magnitude of his daring. He made a second voyage aboard the* Spray *in 1909 but never returned, and is presumed to have died at sea.*

from *Sailing Alone Around the World*

One midwinter day of 1892, in Boston, where I had been cast up from old ocean, so to speak, a year or two before, I was cogitating whether I should apply for a command, and again eat my bread and butter on the sea, or go to work at the shipyard, when I met an old acquaintance, a whaling-captain, who said: "Come to Fairhaven and I'll give you a ship. But," he added, "she wants some repairs." The captain's terms, when fully explained, were more than satisfactory to me. They included all the assistance I would require to fit the craft for sea. I was only too glad to accept, for I had already found that I could not obtain work in the shipyard without first paying fifty dollars to a society, and as for a ship to command—there were not enough ships to go round. Nearly all our tall vessels had been cut down for coal-barges, and were being ignominiously towed by the nose from port to port, while many worthy captains addressed themselves to Sailors' Snug Harbor.

The next day I landed at Fairhaven, opposite New Bedford, and found that my friend had something of a joke on me. For seven years the joke had been on him. The "ship" proved to be a very antiquated sloop called the *Spray*, which the neighbors declared had been built in the year 1. She was affectionately propped up in a field, some distance from salt water, and was covered with canvas. The people of Fairhaven, I hardly need say, are thrifty and observant. For seven years they had asked, "I wonder what Captain Eben Pierce is going to do with the old *Spray*?" The day I appeared there was a buzz at the gossip exchange: at last some one had come and was actually at work on the old *Spray*. "Breaking her up, I s'pose?" "No; going to rebuild her." Great was the amazement. "Will it pay?" was the question which for a year or more I answered by declaring that I would make it pay.

My ax felled a stout oak-tree near by for a keel, and Farmer Howard, for a small sum of money, hauled in this and enough timbers for the frame of the new vessel. I rigged a steam-box and a pot for a boiler. The timbers for ribs, being straight saplings, were dressed and steamed till supple, and then bent over a log, where they were secured till set. Something tangible appeared every day to show for my labor, and the neighbors made the work sociable. It was a great day in the *Spray* shipyard when her new stern was set up and fastened to the new keel. Whaling-captains came from far to survey it. With one voice they pronounced it "A 1," and in their opinion "fit to smash ice." The oldest captain shook my hand warmly when the breast-hooks were put in, declaring that he could see no reason why the *Spray* should not "cut in bow-head" yet off the coast of Greenland. The much-esteemed stern-piece was from the butt of the smartest kind of a pasture oak. It afterward split a coral patch in two at the Keeling Islands, and did not receive a blemish. Better timber for a ship than pasture white oak never grew. The breast-hooks, as well as all the ribs, were of this wood, and were steamed and bent into shape as required. It was hard upon March when I began work in earnest; the weather was cold; still, there were plenty of inspectors to back me with advice. When a whaling-captain hove in sight I just rested on my adz awhile and "gammed" with him.

New Bedford, the home of whaling-captains, is connected with Fairhaven by a bridge, and the walking is good. They never "worked along up" to the shipyard too often for me. It was the charming tales about arctic whaling that inspired me to put a double set of breast-hooks in the *Spray*, that she might shunt ice.

The seasons came quickly while I worked. Hardly were the ribs of the sloop up before apple-trees were in bloom. Then the daisies and the cherries came soon after. Close by the place where the old *Spray* had now dissolved rested the ashes of John Cook, a revered Pilgrim father. So the new *Spray* rose from hallowed ground. From the deck of the new craft I could put out my hand and pick cherries that grew over the little grave. The planks for the new vessel, which I soon came to put on, were of Georgia pine an inch and a half thick. The operation of putting them on was tedious, but, when on, the calking was easy. The outward edges stood slightly open to receive the calking, but the inner edges were so close that I could not see daylight between them. All the butts were fastened by through bolts, with screw-nuts tightening them to the timbers, so that there would be no complaint from them. Many bolts with screw-nuts were used in other parts of the construction, in all about a thousand. It was my purpose to make my vessel stout and strong.

Now, it is a law in Lloyd's that the *Jane* repaired all out of the old until she is entirely new is still the *Jane*. The *Spray* changed her being so gradually that it was hard to say at what point the old died or the new took birth, and it was no matter. The bulwarks I built up of white-oak stanchions fourteen inches high, and covered with seven-eighth-inch white pine. These stanchions, mortised through a two-inch covering-board, I calked with thin cedar wedges. They have remained perfectly tight ever since. The deck I made of one-and-a-half-inch by three-inch white pine spiked to beams, six by six inches, of yellow or Georgia pine, placed three feet apart. The deck-inclosures were one over the aperture of the main hatch, six feet by six, for a cooking-galley, and a trunk farther aft, about ten feet by twelve, for a cabin. Both of these rose about three feet above the deck, and were sunk sufficiently into the hold to afford head-room. In the spaces along the sides of the cabin, under the deck, I arranged a berth to sleep in, and shelves for small storage, not forgetting a place for the medicine-chest. In the midship hold, that is, the space between cabin and galley, under the deck, was room for provision of water, salt beef, etc., ample for many months.

The hull of my vessel being now put together as strongly as wood and iron could make her, and the various rooms partitioned off, I set about "calking ship." Grave fears were entertained by some that at this point I should fail. I myself gave some thought to the advisability of a "professional calker." The very first blow I struck on the cotton with the calking-iron, which I thought was right, many others thought wrong. "It'll crawl!" cried a man from Marion, passing with a basket of clams on his back. "It'll crawl!" cried another from West Island, when he saw me driving cotton into the seams. Bruno simply wagged his tail. Even Mr. Ben J——, a noted authority on whaling-ships, whose mind, however, was said to totter, asked rather confidently if I did not think "it would crawl." "How fast will it crawl?" cried my old captain friend, who had been towed by many a lively sperm-whale. "Tell us how fast," cried he, "that we may get into port in time." However, I drove a thread of oakum on top of the cotton, as from the first

I had intended to do. And Bruno again wagged his tail. The cotton never "crawled." When the calking was finished, two coats of copper paint were slapped on the bottom, two of white lead on the topsides and bulwarks. The rudder was then shipped and painted, and on the following day the *Spray* was launched. As she rode at her ancient, rust-eaten anchor, she sat on the water like a swan.

The *Spray's* dimensions were, when finished, thirty-six feet nine inches long, over all, fourteen feet two inches wide, and four feet two inches deep in the hold, her tonnage being nine tons net and twelve and seventy-one hundredths tons gross.

Then the mast, a smart New Hampshire spruce, was fitted, and likewise all the small appurtenances necessary for a short cruise. Sails were bent, and away she flew with my friend Captain Pierce and me, across Buzzard's Bay on a trial-trip—all right. The only thing that now worried my friends along the beach was, "Will she pay?" The cost of my new vessel was $553.62 for materials, and thirteen months of my own labor. I was several months more than that at Fairhaven, for I got work now and then on an occasional whale-ship fitting farther down the harbor, and that kept me the overtime.

* * *

It was the 3d of March when the *Spray* sailed from Port Tamar direct for Cape Pillar, with the wind from the northeast, which I fervently hoped might hold till she cleared the land; but there was no such good luck in store. It soon began to rain and thicken in the northwest, boding no good. The *Spray* neared Cape Pillar rapidly, and, nothing loath, plunged into the Pacific Ocean at once, taking her first bath of it in the gathering storm. There was no turning back even had I wished to do so, for the land was now shut out by the darkness of night. The wind freshened, and I took in a third reef. The sea was confused and treacherous. In such a time as this the old fisherman prayed, "Remember, Lord, my ship is small and thy sea is so wide!" I saw now only the gleaming crests of the waves. They showed white teeth while the sloop balanced over them. "Everything for an offing," I cried, and to this end

I carried on all the sail she would bear. She ran all night with a free sheet, but on the morning of March 4 the wind shifted to southwest, then back suddenly to northwest, and blew with terrific force. The *Spray*, stripped of her sails, then bore off under bare poles. No ship in the world could have stood up against so violent a gale. Knowing that this storm might continue for many days, and that it would be impossible to work back to the westward along the coast outside of Tierra del Fuego, there seemed nothing to do but to keep on and go east about, after all. Anyhow, for my present safety the only course lay in keeping her before the wind. And so she drove southeast, as though about to round the Horn, while the waves rose and fell and bellowed their never-ending story of the sea; but the Hand that held these held also the *Spray*. She was running now with a reefed forestaysail, the sheets flat amidship. I paid out two long ropes to steady her course and to break combing seas astern, and I lashed the helm amidship. In this trim she ran before it, shipping never a sea. Even while the storm raged at its worst, my ship was wholesome and noble. My mind as to her seaworthiness was put at ease for aye.

When all had been done that I could do for the safety of the vessel, I got to the fore-scuttle, between seas, and prepared a pot of coffee over a wood fire, and made a good Irish stew. Then, as before and afterward on the *Spray*, I insisted on warm meals. In the tide-race off Cape Pillar, however, where the sea was marvelously high, uneven, and crooked, my appetite was slim, and for a time I postponed cooking. (Confidentially, I was seasick!)

The first day of the storm gave the *Spray* her actual test in the worst sea that Cape Horn or its wild regions could afford, and in no part of the world could a rougher sea be found than at this particular point, namely, off Cape Pillar, the grim sentinel of the Horn.

Farther offshore, while the sea was majestic, there was less apprehension of danger. There the *Spray* rode, now like a bird on the crest of a wave, and now like a waif deep down in the hollow between seas; and so she drove on. Whole days passed, counted as other days, but with always a thrill—yes, of delight.

On the fourth day of the gale, rapidly nearing the pitch of Cape Horn, I inspected my chart and pricked off the course and distance to Port Stanley, in the Falkland Islands, where I might find my way and refit, when I saw through a rift in the clouds a high mountain, about seven leagues away on the port beam. The fierce edge of the gale by this time had blown off, and I had already bent a squaresail on the boom in place of the mainsail, which was torn to rags. I hauled in the trailing ropes, hoisted this awkward sail reefed, the forestaysail being already set, and under this sail brought her at once on the wind heading for the land, which appeared as an island in the sea. So it turned out to be, though not the one I had supposed.

I was exultant over the prospect of once more entering the Strait of Magellan and beating through again into the Pacific, for it was more than rough on the outside coast of Tierra del Fuego. It was indeed a mountainous sea. When the sloop was in the fiercest squalls, with only the reefed forestaysail set, even that small sail shook her from keelson to truck when it shivered by the leech. Had I harbored the shadow of a doubt for her safety, it would have been that she might spring a leak in the garboard at the heel of the mast; but she never called me once to the pump. Under pressure of the smallest sail I could set she made for the land like a race-horse, and steering her over the crests of the waves so that she might not trip was nice work. I stood at the helm now and made the most of it.

Night closed in before the sloop reached the land, leaving her feeling the way in pitchy darkness. I saw breakers ahead before long. At this I wore ship and stood offshore, but was immediately startled by the tremendous roaring of breakers again ahead and on the lee bow. This puzzled me, for there should have been no broken water where I supposed myself to be. I kept off a good bit, then wore round, but finding broken water also there, threw her head again offshore. In this way, among dangers, I spent the rest of the night. Hail and sleet in the fierce squalls cut my flesh till the blood trickled over my face; but what of that? It was daylight, and the sloop was in the midst of the Milky Way of the sea, which is northwest of Cape Horn, and it was the white breakers of a huge sea over sunken rocks which had threatened to engulf her through the night. It was Fury Island I had sighted and steered for, and what a panorama was before me now and all around! It was not the time to complain of a broken skin. What could I do but fill away among the breakers and find a channel between them, now that it was day? Since she had escaped the rocks through the night, surely she would find her way by daylight. This was the greatest sea adventure of my life. God knows how my vessel escaped.

The sloop at last reached inside of small islands that sheltered her in smooth water. Then I climbed the mast to survey the wild scene astern. The great naturalist Darwin looked over this seascape from the deck of the *Beagle*, and wrote in his journal, "Any landsman seeing the Milky Way would have nightmare for a week." He might have added, "or seaman" as well.

The *Spray*'s good luck followed fast. I discovered, as she sailed along through a labyrinth of islands, that she was in the Cockburn Channel, which leads into the Strait of Magellan at a point opposite Cape Froward, and that she was already passing Thieves' Bay, suggestively named. And at night, March 8, behold, she was at anchor in a snug cove at the Turn! Every heart-beat on the *Spray* now counted thanks.

Here I pondered on the events of the last few days, and, strangely enough, instead of feeling rested from sitting or lying down, I now began to feel jaded and worn; but a hot meal of venison stew soon put me right, so that I could sleep. As drowsiness came on I sprinkled the deck with tacks, and then I turned in, bearing in mind the advice of my old friend Samblich that I was not to step on them myself. I saw to it that not a few of them stood "business end" up; for when the *Spray* passed Thieves' Bay two canoes had put out and followed in her wake, and there was no disguising the fact any longer that I was alone.

Now, it is well known that one cannot step on a tack without saying something about it. A pretty good Christian will whistle when he steps on the "commercial end" of a carpet-tack; a savage will howl and claw the air, and that was just what happened that night about twelve o'clock, while I was asleep in the cabin, where the savages thought they "had me," sloop and all, but changed their minds when they stepped on deck, for then they thought that I or somebody else had them. I had no need of a dog; they howled like a pack of hounds. I had hardly use for a gun. They jumped pell-mell, some into their canoes and some into the sea, to cool off, I suppose, and there was a deal of free language over it as they went. I fired several guns when I came on deck, to let the rascals know that I was home, and then I turned in again, feeling sure I should not be disturbed any more by people who left in so great a hurry.

The Fuegians, being cruel, are naturally cowards; they regard a rifle with superstitious fear. The only real danger one could see that might come from their quarter would be from allowing them to surround one within bow-shot, or to anchor within range where they might lie in ambush. As for their coming on deck at night, even had I not put tacks about, I could have cleared them off by shots from the cabin and hold. I always kept a quantity of ammunition within reach in the hold and in the cabin and in the forepeak, so that retreating to any of these places I could "hold the fort" simply by shooting up through the deck.

Perhaps the greatest danger to be apprehended was from the use of fire. Every canoe carries fire; nothing is thought of that, for it is their custom to communicate by smoke-signals. The harmless brand that lies smoldering in the bottom of one of their canoes might be ablaze in one's cabin if he were not on the alert. The port captain of Sandy Point warned me particularly of this danger. Only a short time before they had fired a Chilean gun-boat by throwing brands in through the stern windows of the cabin. The *Spray* had no openings in the cabin or deck, except two scuttles, and these were guarded by fastenings which could not be undone without waking me if I were asleep.

On the morning of the 9th, after a refreshing rest and a warm breakfast, and after I had swept the deck of tacks, I got out what spare canvas there was on board, and began to sew the pieces together in the shape of a peak for my square-mainsail, the tarpaulin. The day to all appearances promised fine weather and light winds, but appearances in Tierra del Fuego do not always count. While I was wondering why no trees grew on the slope abreast of the anchorage, half minded to lay by the sail-making and land with my gun for some game and to inspect a white boulder on the beach, near the brook, a williwaw came down with such terrific force as to carry the *Spray*, with two anchors down, like a feather out of the cove and away into deep water. No wonder trees did not grow on the side of that hill! Great Boreas! a tree would need to be all roots to hold on against such a furious wind.

From the cove to the nearest land to leeward was a long drift, however, and I had ample time to weigh both anchors before the sloop came near any danger, and so no harm came of it. I saw no more savages that day or the next; they probably had some sign by which they knew of the coming williwaws; at least, they were wise in not being afloat even on the second day, for I had no sooner gotten to work at sail-making again, after the anchor was down, than the wind, as on the day before, picked the sloop up and flung her seaward with a vengeance, anchor and all, as before. This fierce wind, usual to the Magellan country, continued on through the day, and swept the sloop by several miles of steep bluffs and precipices overhanging a bold shore of wild and uninviting appearance. I was not sorry to get away from it, though in doing so it was no Elysian shore to which I shaped my course. I kept on sailing in hope, since I had no choice but to go on, heading across for St. Nicholas Bay, where I had cast anchor February 19. It was now the 10th of March! Upon reaching the bay the second time I had circumnavigated the wildest part of desolate Tierra del Fuego. But the *Spray* had not yet arrived at St. Nicholas, and by the merest accident her bones were saved from resting there when she did arrive. The parting of a staysail-sheet in a williwaw, when the sea was turbulent and she was plunging into the storm, brought me forward to see instantly a dark cliff ahead and breakers so close under the bows that I felt surely lost, and in my thoughts cried, "Is the hand of fate against me, after all, leading me in the end to this dark spot?" I sprang aft again, unheeding the flapping sail, and threw the wheel over, expecting, as the sloop came down into the hollow of a wave, to feel her timbers smash under me on the rocks. But at the touch of her helm she swung clear of the danger, and in the next moment she was in the lee of the land.

It was the small island in the middle of the bay for which the sloop had been steering, and which she made with such unerring aim as nearly to run it down. Farther along in the bay was the anchorage, which I managed to reach, but before I could get the anchor down another squall caught the sloop and whirled her round like a top and carried her away, altogether to leeward of the bay. Still farther to leeward was a great headland, and I bore off for that. This was retracing my course toward Sandy Point, for the gale was from the southwest.

I had the sloop soon under good control, however, and in a short time rounded to under the lee of a mountain, where the sea was as smooth as a mill-pond, and the sails flapped and hung limp while she carried her way close in. Here I thought I would anchor and rest till morning, the depth being eight fathoms very close to the shore. But it was interesting to see, as I let go the anchor, that it did not reach the bottom before another williwaw struck down from this mountain and carried the sloop off faster than I could pay out cable. Instead of resting, I had to "man the windlass" and heave up the anchor and fifty fathoms of cable hanging up and down in deep water. This was in that part of the strait called Famine Reach. I could have wished it Jericho! On that little crab-windlass I worked the rest of the night, thinking how much easier it was for me when I could say, "Do that thing or the other," than to do it myself. But I hove away on the windlass and sang the old chants that I sang when I was a sailor, from "Blow, Boys, Blow for Californy, O" to "Sweet By and By."

It was daybreak when the anchor was at the hawse. By this time the wind had gone down, and cat's-paws took the place of williwaws. The sloop was then drifting slowly toward Sandy Point. She came within sight of ships at anchor in the roads, and I was more than half minded to put in for new sails, but the wind coming out from the northeast, which was fair for the other direction, I turned the prow of the *Spray* westward once more for the Pacific, to traverse a second time the second half of my first course through the strait.

Jack London

The brief but crowded life of Jack London (1876–1916) began in poverty in San Francisco, and by the age of 15 he was already making a precarious living with his own sloop as an oyster "pirate" in San Francisco Bay. Not long afterward he changed sides and went to work for the California Fish Patrol, helping to suppress the raiding of oyster beds. A seven-month voyage on the whaler Sophia Sutherland *in 1893 was followed by interludes as a hobo and a gold miner; he also ran twice for mayor of Oakland on the Socialist ticket, reported on the Russo-Japanese War for the Hearst syndicate, and studied social conditions in the East End of London, while maintaining a prolific output of novels, stories, memoirs, and social studies. In 1906 he began building his schooner, the* Snark, *on which he undertook a 27-month voyage to Hawaii, the Marquesas, Tahiti, the Solomons, and other ports of call, before illness forced him in 1909 to interrupt what was intended as a journey around the world.* The Cruise of the Snark *was published in 1911, and includes this account of London's initiation into surfing. Later voyages took him around Cape Horn, to Veracruz, and again to Hawaii.*

A Royal Sport

That is what it is, a royal sport for the natural kings of earth. The grass grows right down to the water at Waikiki Beach, and within fifty feet of the everlasting sea. The trees also grow down to the salty edge of things, and one sits in their shade and looks seaward at a majestic surf thundering in on the beach to one's very feet. Half a mile out, where is the reef, the white-headed combers thrust suddenly skyward out of the placid turquoise-blue and come rolling in to shore. One after another they come, a mile long, with smoking crests, the white battalions of the infinite army of the sea. And one sits and listens to the perpetual roar, and watches the unending procession, and feels tiny and fragile before this tremendous force expressing itself in fury and foam and sound. Indeed, one feels microscopically small, and the thought that one may wrestle with this sea raises in one's imagination a thrill of apprehension, almost of fear. Why, they are a mile long, these bull-mouthed monsters, and they weigh a thousand tons, and they charge in to shore faster than a man can run. What chance? No chance at all, is the verdict of the shrinking ego; and one sits, and looks, and listens, and thinks the grass and the shade are a pretty good place in which to be.

And suddenly, out there where a big smoker lifts skyward, rising like a sea-god from out of the welter of spume and churning white, on the giddy, toppling, overhanging and downfalling, precarious crest appears the dark head of a man. Swiftly he rises through the rushing white. His black shoulders, his chest, his loins, his limbs—all is abruptly projected on one's vision. Where but the moment before was only the wide desolation and invincible roar, is now a man, erect, full-statured, not struggling frantically in that wild movement, not buried and crushed and buffeted by those mighty monsters, but standing above them all, calm and superb, poised on the giddy summit, his feet buried in the churning foam, the salt smoke rising to his knees, and all the rest of him in the free air and flashing sunlight, and he is flying through the air, flying forward, flying fast as the surge on which he stands. He is a Mercury—a brown Mercury. His heels are winged, and in them is the swiftness of the sea. In truth, from out of the sea he has leaped upon the back of the sea, and he is riding the sea that roars and bellows and cannot shake him from its back. But no frantic outreaching and balancing is his. He is impassive, motionless as a statue carved suddenly by some miracle out of the sea's depth from which he rose. And straight on toward shore he flies on his winged heels and the white crest of the breaker. There is a wild burst of foam, a long tumultuous rushing sound as the breaker falls futile and spent on the beach at your feet; and there, at your feet steps calmly ashore a Kanaka, burnt golden and brown by the tropic sun. Several minutes ago he was a speck a quarter of a mile away. He has "bitted the bull-mouthed breaker" and ridden it in, and the pride in the feat shows in the carriage of his magnificent body as he glances for a moment carelessly at you who sit in the shade of the shore. He is a Kanaka—and more, he is a man, a member of the kingly species that has mastered matter and the brutes and lorded it over creation.

And one sits and thinks of Tristram's last wrestle with the sea on that fatal morning; and one thinks further, to the fact that that Kanaka has done what Tristram never did, and that he knows a joy of the sea that Tristram never knew. And still further one thinks. It is all very well, sitting here in cool shade of the beach, but you are a man, one of the kingly species, and what that Kanaka can do, you can do yourself. Go to. Strip off your clothes that are a nuisance in this mellow clime. Get in and wrestle with the sea; wing your heels with the skill and power that reside in you; bit the sea's breakers, master them, and ride upon their backs as a king should.

And that is how it came about that I tackled surf-riding. And now that I have tackled it, more than ever do I hold it to be a royal sport. But first let me explain the physics of it. A wave is a communicated agitation. The water that composes the body of a wave does not move. If it did, when a stone is thrown into a pond and the ripples spread away in an ever widening circle, there would appear at the centre an ever increasing hole. No, the water that composes the body of a wave is stationary. Thus, you may watch a particular portion of the ocean's surface and you will see the same water rise and fall a thousand times to the agitation communicated by a thousand successive waves. Now imagine this communicated agitation moving shoreward. As the bottom shoals, the lower portion of the wave strikes land first and is stopped. But water is fluid, and the upper portion has not struck anything, wherefore it keeps on communicating its agitation, keeps on going. And when the top of the wave keeps on going, while the bottom of it lags behind, something is bound to happen. The bottom of the wave drops out from under and the top of the wave falls over, forward, and down, curling and cresting and roaring as it does so. It is the bottom of a wave striking against the top of the land that is the cause of all surfs.

But the transformation from a smooth undulation to a breaker is not abrupt except where the bottom shoals abruptly.

Say the bottom shoals gradually for from quarter of a mile to a mile, then an equal distance will be occupied by the transformation. Such a bottom is that off the beach of Waikiki, and it produces a splendid surf-riding surf. One leaps upon the back of a breaker just as it begins to break, and stays on it as it continues to break all the way in to shore.

And now to the particular physics of surf-riding. Get out on a flat board, six feet long, two feet wide, and roughly oval in shape. Lie down upon it like a small boy on a coaster and paddle with your hands out to deep water, where the waves begin to crest. Lie out there quietly on the board. Sea after sea breaks before, behind, and under and over you, and rushes in to shore, leaving you behind. When a wave crests, it gets steeper. Imagine yourself, on your board, on the face of that steep slope. If it stood still, you would slide down just as a boy slides down a hill on his coaster. "But," you object, "the wave doesn't stand still." Very true, but the water composing the wave stands still, and there you have the secret. If ever you start sliding down the face of that wave, you'll keep on sliding and you'll never reach the bottom. Please don't laugh. The face of that wave may be only six feet, yet you can slide down it a quarter of a mile, or half a mile, and not reach the bottom. For, see, since a wave is only a communicated agitation or impetus, and since the water that composes a wave is changing every instant, new water is rising into the wave as fast as the wave travels. You slide down this new water, and yet remain in your old position on the wave, sliding down the still newer water that is rising and forming the wave. You slide precisely as fast as the wave travels. If it travels fifteen miles an hour, you slide fifteen miles an hour. Between you and shore stretches a quarter of mile of water. As the wave travels, this water obligingly heaps itself into the wave, gravity does the rest, and down you go, sliding the whole length of it. If you still cherish the notion, while sliding, that the water is moving with you, thrust your arms into it and attempt to paddle; you will find that you have to be remarkably quick to get a stroke, for that water is dropping astern just as fast as you are rushing ahead.

And now for another phase of the physics of surf-riding. All rules have their exceptions. It is true that the water in a wave does not travel forward. But there is what may be called the send of the sea. The water in the overtoppling crest does move forward, as you will speedily realize if you are slapped in the face by it, or if you are caught under it and are pounded by one mighty blow down under the surface panting and gasping for half a minute. The water in the top of a wave rests upon the water in the bottom of the wave. But when the bottom of the wave strikes the land, it stops, while the top goes on. It no longer has the bottom of the wave to hold it up. Where was solid water beneath it, is now air, and for the first time it feels the grip of gravity, and down it falls, at the same time being torn asunder from the lagging bottom of the wave and flung forward. And it is because of this that riding a surf-board is something more than a mere placid sliding down a hill. In truth, one is caught up and hurled shoreward as by some Titan's hand.

I deserted the cool shade, put on a swimming suit, and got hold of a surf-board. It was too small a board. But I didn't know, and nobody told me. I joined some little Kanaka boys in shallow water, where the breakers were well spent and small—a regular kindergarten school. I watched the little Kanaka boys. When a likely-looking breaker came along, they flopped upon their stomachs on their boards, kicked like mad with their feet, and rode the breaker in to the beach. I tried to emulate them. I watched them, tried to do everything that they did, and failed utterly. The breaker swept past, and I was not on it. I tried again and again. I kicked twice as madly as they did, and failed. Half a dozen would be around. We would all leap on our boards in front of a good breaker. Away our feet would churn like the stern-wheels of river steamboats, and away the little rascals would scoot while I remained in disgrace behind.

I tried for a solid hour, and not one wave could I persuade to boost me shoreward. And then arrived a friend, Alexander Hume Ford, a globe trotter by profession, bent ever on the pursuit of sensation. And he had found it at Waikiki. Heading for Australia, he had stopped off for a week to find out if there were any thrills in surf-riding, and he had become wedded to it. He had been at it every day for a month and could not yet see any symptoms of the fascination lessening on him. He spoke with authority.

"Get off that board," he said. "Chuck it away at once. Look at the way you're trying to ride it. If ever the nose of that board hits bottom, you'll be disembowelled. Here, take my board. It's a man's size."

I am always humble when confronted by knowledge. Ford knew. He showed me how properly to mount his board. Then he waited for a good breaker, gave me a shove at the right moment, and started me in. Ah, delicious moment when I felt that breaker grip and fling me. On I dashed, a hundred and fifty feet, and subsided with the breaker on the sand. From that moment I was lost. I waded back to Ford with his board. It was a large one, several inches thick, and weighed all of seventy-five pounds. He gave me advice, much of it. He had had no one to teach him, and all that he had laboriously learned in several weeks he communicated to me in half an hour. I really learned by proxy. And inside of half an hour I was able to start myself and ride in. I did it time after time, and Ford applauded and advised. For instance, he told me to get just so far forward on the board and no farther. But I must have got some farther, for as I came charging in to land, that miserable board poked its nose down to bottom, stopped abruptly, and turned a somersault, at the same time violently severing our relations. I was tossed through the air like a chip and buried ignominiously under the downfalling breaker. And I realized that if it hadn't been for Ford, I'd have been disembowelled. That particular risk is part of the sport, Ford says. Maybe he'll have it happen to him before he leaves Waikiki, and then, I feel confident, his yearning for sensation will be satisfied for a time.

When all is said and done, it is my steadfast belief that homicide is worse than suicide, especially if, in the former case, it is a woman. Ford saved me from being a homicide. "Imagine your legs are a rudder," he said. "Hold them close together, and steer with them." A few minutes later I came charging in on a comber. As I neared the beach, there, in the water, up to her waist, dead in front of me, appeared a woman. How was I to stop that comber on whose back I was? It looked like a dead woman. The board weighed seventy-five pounds, I weighed a hundred and sixty-five. The added weight had a velocity of fifteen miles per hour. The board and I constituted a projectile. I leave it to the physicists to figure out the force of the impact upon that poor, tender woman. And then I remembered my guardian angel, Ford. "Steer with your legs!" rang through my brain. I steered with my legs, I steered sharply, abruptly, with all my legs and with all my might. The board sheered around broadside on the crest. Many things happened simultaneously. The wave gave me a passing buffet, a light tap as the taps of waves go, but a tap sufficient to knock me off the board and smash me down through the rushing water to bottom, with which I came in violent collision and upon which I was rolled over and over. I got my head out for a breath of air and then gained my feet. There stood the woman before me. I felt like a hero. I had saved her life. And she laughed at me. It was not hysteria. She had never dreamed of her danger. Anyway, I solaced myself, it was not I but Ford that saved her, and I didn't have to feel like a hero. And besides, that leg-steering was great. In a few minutes more of practice I was able to thread my way in and out past several bathers and to remain on top my breaker instead of going under it.

"To-morrow," Ford said, "I am going to take you out into the blue water."

I looked seaward where he pointed, and saw the great smoking combers that made the breakers I had been riding look like ripples. I don't know what I might have said had I not recollected just then that I was one of a kingly species. So all that I did say was, "All right, I'll tackle them to-morrow."

The water that rolls in on Waikiki Beach is just the same as the water that laves the shores of all the Hawaiian Islands; and in ways, especially from the swimmer's standpoint, it is wonderful water. It is cool enough to be comfortable, while it is warm enough to permit a swimmer to stay in all day without experiencing a chill. Under the sun or the stars, at high noon or at midnight, in midwinter or in midsummer, it does not matter when, it is always the same temperature—not too warm, not too cold, just right. It is wonderful water, salt as old ocean itself, pure and crystal-clear. When the nature of the water is considered, it is not so remarkable after all that the Kanakas are one of the most expert of swimming races.

So it was, next morning, when Ford came along, that I plunged into the wonderful water for a swim of indeterminate length. Astride of our surf-boards, or, rather, flat down upon them on our stomachs, we paddled out through the kindergarten where the little Kanaka boys were at play. Soon we were out in deep water where the big smokers came roaring in. The mere struggle with them, facing them and paddling seaward over them and through them, was sport enough in itself. One had to have his wits about him, for it was a battle in which mighty blows were struck, on one side, and in which cunning was used on the other side—a struggle between insensate force and intelligence. I soon learned a bit. When a breaker curled over my head, for a swift instant I could see the light of day through its emerald body; then down would go my head, and I would clutch the board with all my strength. Then would come the blow, and to the onlooker on shore I would be blotted out. In reality the board and I have passed through the crest and emerged in the respite of the other side. I should not recommend those smashing blows to an invalid or delicate person. There is weight behind them, and the impact of the driven water is like a sand-blast. Sometimes one passes through half a dozen combers in quick succession, and it is just about that time that he is liable to discover new merits in the stable land and new reasons for being on shore.

Out there in the midst of such a succession of big smoky ones, a third man was added to our party, one Freeth. Shaking the water from my eyes as I emerged from one wave and peered ahead to see what the next one looked like, I saw him tearing in on the back of it, standing upright on his board, carelessly poised, a young god bronzed with sunburn. We went through the wave on the back of which he rode. Ford called to him. He turned an airspring from his wave, rescued his board from its maw, paddled over to us and joined Ford in showing me things. One thing in particular I learned from Freeth, namely, how to encounter the occasional breaker of exceptional size that rolled in. Such breakers were really ferocious, and it was unsafe to meet them on top of the board. But Freeth showed me, so that whenever I saw one of that caliber rolling down on me, I slid off the rear end of the board and dropped down beneath the surface, my arms over my head and holding the board. Thus, if the wave ripped the board out of my hands and tried to strike me with it (a common trick of such waves), there would be a cushion of water a foot or more in depth, between my head and the blow. When the wave passed, I climbed upon the board and paddled on. Many men have been terribly injured, I learn, by being struck by their boards.

The whole method of surf-riding and surf-fighting, I learned, is one of non-resistance. Dodge the blow that is struck at you. Dive through the wave that is trying to slap you in the face. Sink down, feet first, deep under the surface, and let the big smoker that is trying to smash you go by far overhead. Never be rigid. Relax. Yield yourself to the waters that are ripping and tearing at you. When the undertow catches you and drags you seaward along the bottom, don't struggle against it. If you do, you are liable to be drowned, for it is stronger than you. Yield yourself to that undertow. Swim with it, not against it, and you will find the pressure removed. And, swimming with it, fooling it so that it does not hold you, swim upward at the same time. It will be no trouble at all to reach the surface.

The man who wants to learn surf-riding must be a strong swimmer, and he must be used to going under the water. After that, fair strength and common-sense are all that is required. The force of the big comber is rather unexpected. There are mix-ups in which board and rider are torn apart and separated by several hundred feet. The surf-rider must take care of himself. No matter how many riders swim out with him, he cannot depend upon any of them for aid. The fancied security I had in the presence of Ford and Freeth made me forget that it was my first swim out in deep water among the big ones. I recollected, however, and rather suddenly, for a big wave came in, and away went the two men on its back all the way to shore. I could have been drowned a dozen different ways before they got back to me.

One slides down the face of a breaker on his surf-board, but he has to get started to sliding. Board and rider must be moving shoreward at a good rate before the wave overtakes them. When you see the wave coming that you want to ride in, you turn tail to it and paddle shoreward with all your strength, using what is called the windmill stroke. This is a sort of spurt performed immediately in front of the wave. If the board is going fast enough, the wave accelerates it, and the board begins its quarter-of-a-mile slide.

I shall never forget the first big wave I caught out there in the deep water. I saw it coming, turned my back on it and paddled for dear life. Faster and faster my board went, till it seemed my arms would drop off. What was happening behind me I could not tell. One cannot look behind and paddle the windmill stroke. I heard the crest of the wave hissing and churning, and then my board was lifted and flung forward. I scarcely knew what happened the first half-minute. Though I kept my eyes open, I could not see anything, for I was buried in the rushing white of the crest. But I did not mind. I was chiefly conscious of ecstatic bliss at having caught the wave. At the end of the half-minute, however, I began to see things, and to breathe. I saw that three feet of the nose of my board was clear out of water and riding on the air. I shifted my weight, forward, and made the nose come down. Then I lay, quite at rest in the midst of the wild movement, and watched the shore and the bathers on the beach grow distinct. I didn't cover quite a quarter of a mile on that wave, because, to prevent the board from diving, I shifted my weight back, but shifted it too far and fell down the rear slope of the wave.

It was my second day at surf-riding, and I was quite proud of myself. I stayed out there four hours, and when it was over,

I was resolved that on the morrow I'd come in standing up. But that resolution paved a distant place. On the morrow I was in bed. I was not sick, but I was very unhappy, and I was in bed. When describing the wonderful water of Hawaii I forgot to describe the wonderful sun of Hawaii. It is a tropic sun, and, furthermore, in the first part of June, it is an overhead sun. It is also an insidious, deceitful sun. For the first time in my life I was sunburned unawares. My arms, shoulders, and back had been burned many times in the past and were tough; but not so my legs. And for four hours I had exposed the tender backs of my legs, at right-angles, to that perpendicular Hawaiian sun. It was not until after I got ashore that I discovered the sun had touched me. Sunburn at first is merely warm; after that it grows intense and the blisters come out. Also, the joints, where the skin wrinkles, refuse to bend. That is why I spent the next day in bed. I couldn't walk. And that is why, to-day, I am writing this in bed. It is easier to than not to. But to-morrow, ah, to-morrow, I shall be out in that wonderful water, and I shall come in standing up, even as Ford and Freeth. And if I fail to-morrow, I shall do it the next day, or the next. Upon one thing I am resolved: the *Snark* shall not sail from Honolulu until I, too, wing my heels with the swiftness of the sea, and become a sunburned, skin-peeling Mercury.

Alfred Thayer Mahan

Alfred Thayer Mahan (1840–1914) graduated from the U.S. Naval Academy in 1859 and served on blockade duty with the Union navy during the Civil War. He was promoted to the rank of captain in 1885 and the following year became president of the newly founded Naval War College at Newport, Rhode Island. In 1890 he published The Influence of Sea Power upon History, 1660–1783, *based on his War College lectures; a sequel,* The Influence of Sea Power upon the French Revolution and Empire, 1789–1812, *appeared in 1892. Stressing the strategic importance of achieving control of maritime commerce through naval command of the open seas, Mahan's books rapidly reached a wide international audience and became the most influential studies of naval warfare ever written by an American. Mahan retired from the navy in 1896 and published a memoir,* From Sail to Steam: Recollections of a Naval Life, *in 1907. The excerpt printed here describes the small, insular world of the U.S. Navy on the eve of the profound transformation in maritime warfare wrought by steam, armor plate, and long-range gunnery.*

from *From Sail to Steam*

Naval Conditions Before The War Of Secession

THE OFFICERS AND SEAMEN

NAVAL officers who began their career in the fifties of the past century, as I did, and who survive till now, as very many do, have been observant, if inconspicuous, witnesses of one of the most rapid and revolutionary changes that naval science and warfare have ever undergone. It has been aptly said that a naval captain who fought the Invincible Armada would have been more at home in the typical war-ship of 1840, than the average captain of 1840 would have been in the advanced types of the American Civil War.* The twenty years

*J. R. Soley, *The Blockade and the Cruisers*, 1883. Scribner's, *Navy in the Civil War.*

here chosen for comparison cover the middle period of the century which has but recently expired. Since that time progress has gone on in accelerating ratio; and if the consequent changes have been less radical in kind, they have been more extensive in scope. It is interesting to observe that within the same two decades, in 1854, occurred the formal visit of Commodore Perry to Japan, and the negotiations of the treaty bringing her fairly within the movement of Western civilization; starting her upon the path which has resulted in the most striking illustration yet given of the powers of modern naval instruments, ships and weapons, diligently developed and elaborated during the period that has since elapsed.

When I received my appointment to the Naval School at Annapolis, in the early part of the year 1856, the United States navy was under the influence of one of those spasmodic awakenings which, so far as action is concerned, have been the chief characteristic of American statesmanship in the matter of naval policy up to twenty years ago. Since then there has been a more continuous practical recognition of the necessity for a sustained and consistent development of naval power. This wholesome change has been coincident with, and doubtless largely due to, a change in appreciation of the importance of naval power in the realm of international relations, which, within the same period, has passed over the world at large. The United States of America began its career under the Constitution of 1789 with no navy; but in 1794 the intolerable outrages of the Barbary pirates, and the humiliation of having to depend upon the armed ships of Portugal for the protection of American trade, aroused Congress to vote the building of a half-dozen frigates, with the provision, however, that the building should stop if an arrangement with Algiers were reached. Not till 1798 was the navy separated from the War Department. The President at that date, John Adams, was, through his New England origin, in profound sympathy with all naval questions; and, while minister to Great Britain, in 1785, had had continual opportunity to observe the beneficial effect of maritime activity and naval power upon that kingdom. He had also bitter experience of the insolence of its government towards our interests, based upon its conscious control of the sea. He thus came into office strongly biassed towards naval development. To the impulse given by him contributed also the outrageous course towards our commerce initiated by the French Directory, after Bonaparte's astounding campaigns in Italy had struck down all opposition to France save that of the mistress of the seas. The nation, as represented in Congress, woke up, rubbed its eyes, and built a small number of vessels which did exemplary service in the subsequent *quasi* war with France. Provision was made for a further increase; and it is not too much to say that this beginning, if maintained, might have averted the War of 1812. But within four years revulsion came. Adams gave place to Jefferson and Madison, the leaders of a party which frankly and avowedly rejected a navy as an element of national strength, and saw in it only a menace to liberty. Save for the irrepressible marauding of the Barbary corsairs, and the impressment of our seamen by British ships-of-war, the remnant of Adams' ships would not improbably have been swept out of existence. This result was feared by naval officers of the day; and with what good reason is shown by the fact that, within six months of the declaration of the War in 1812, and when the party in control was determined that war there should be, a proposition to increase the navy received but lukewarm support from the administration, and was voted down in Congress. The government, awed by the overwhelming numbers of the British fleet, proposed to save its vessels by keeping them at home; just as a few years before it had undertaken to save its commerce by forbidding its merchant-ships to go to sea.

Such policy with regard to a military service means to it not sleep, but death. The urgent remonstrances of three or four naval captains obtained a change of plan; and at the end of the year the President admitted that, for the very reasons advanced by them, the activity of a small squadron, skilfully directed, had insured the safe return of much the most part of our exposed merchant-shipping. It is not, however, such broad general results of sagacious management that bring conviction to nations and arouse them to action. Professionally, the cruise of Rodgers's squadron, unsuccessful in outward seeming, was a much more significant event, and much more productive, than the capture of the *Guerrière* by the *Constitution*; but it was this which woke up the people. The other probably would not have turned a vote in either House. As a military exploit the frigate victory was exaggerated, and not unnaturally; but no words can exaggerate its influence upon the future of the American navy. Here was something that men could see and understand, even though they might not correctly appreciate. Coinciding as the tidings did with the mortification of Hull's surrender at Detroit, they came at a moment which was truly psychological. Bowed down with shame at reverse where only triumph had been anticipated, the exultation over victory where disaster had been more naturally awaited produced a wild reaction. The effect was decisive. Inefficient and dilatory as was much of the subsequent administration of the navy, there was never any further question of its continuance. And yet, from the ship which thus played the most determining part in the history of her service, it has been proposed to take her name, and give it to another, of newer construction; as though with the name could go also the association. Could any other *Victory* be Nelson's *Victory* to Great Britain? Can calling a man George Washington help to perpetuate the services of the one Washington? The last much-vaunted addition to the British fleet, the *Dreadnaught*, bears a family name extending back over two centuries, or more. She is one of a series reasonably perpetuated, ship after ship, as son after sire; a line of succession honored in the traditions of the nation. So there were *Victorys*, before the one whose revered hulk still maintains a hallowed association; but her individual connection with one event has set her apart. The name might be transferred, but with it the association cannot be transmitted. But not even the *Victory*, with all her clinging memories, did for the British navy what the *Constitution* did for the American.

There was thenceforward no longer any question about votes for the navy. Ships of the line, frigates, and sloops, were ordered to be built, and the impulse thus received never wholly died out. Still, as with all motives which in origin are emotional rather than reasoned, there was lack of staying power. As the enthusiasm of the moment languished, there came languor of growth; or, more properly, of development. Continuance became routine in character, tending to reproduce contentedly the old types consecrated by the War of 1812. There was little conscious recognition of national exigencies, stimulating a demand that the navy, in types and numbers, should be kept abreast of the times. In most pursuits of life American intelligence has been persistently apt and quick in search of improvement; but, while such characteristics have not been absent from the naval service, they have been confined chiefly, and naturally, to the men engaged in the profession, and have lacked the outside support which immediate felt needs impart to movements in business or politics. Few men in civil life could have given an immediate reply to the question, Why do we need a navy? Besides, although the American people are aggressive, combative, even warlike, they are the reverse of military; out of sympathy with military tone and feeling. Consequently, the appearance of professional pride, the insistence upon the absolute necessity for professional training, which in the physician, lawyer, engineer, or other civil occupation is accepted as not only becoming, but conducive to uplifting the profession as a whole, is felt in the military man to be the obtrusion of an alien temperament, easily stigmatized as the arrogance of professional conceit and exclusiveness. The wise traditional jealousy of any invasion of the civil power by the military has no doubt played some part in this; but a healthy vigilance is one thing, and morbid distrust another. Morbid distrust and unreasoned prepossession were responsible for the feebleness of the navy in 1812, and these feelings long survived. An adverse atmosphere was created, with results unfortunate to the nation, so far as the navy was important to national welfare or national progress.

Indeed, between the day of my entrance into the service, fifty years ago, and the present, nowhere is change more notable than in the matter of atmosphere; of the national attitude towards the navy and comprehension of its office. Then it was accepted without much question as part of the necessary lumber that every adequately organized maritime state carried, along with the rest of a national establishment. Of what use it was, or might be, few cared much to inquire. There was not sufficient interest even to dispute the necessity of its existence; although, it is true, as late as 1875 an old-time Jeffersonian Democrat repeated to me with conviction the master's dictum, that the navy was a useless appendage; a statement which its work in the War of Secession, as well on the Confederate as on the Union side, might seem to have refuted sufficiently and with abundant illustration. To such doubters, before the war, there was always ready the routine reply that a navy protected commerce; and American shipping, then the second in the world, literally whitened every sea with its snowy cotton sails, a distinctive mark at that time of American merchant shipping. In my first long voyage, in 1859, from Philadelphia to Brazil, it was no rare occurrence to be becalmed in the doldrums in company with two or three of these beautiful semi-clipper vessels, their low black hulls contrasting vividly with the tall pyramids of dazzling canvas which rose above them. They needed no protection then, and none foresaw that within a decade, by the operations of a few small steam-cruisers, they would be swept from the seas, never to return. Everything was taken for granted, and not least that war was a barbarism of the past. From 1815 to 1850, the lifetime of a generation, international peace had prevailed substantially unbroken, despite numerous revolutionary movements internal to the states concerned; and it had been lightly assumed that these conditions would thenceforth continue, crowned as they had been by the great sacrament of peace, when the nations for the first time gathered under a common roof the fruits of their several industries in the World's Exposition of 1851. The shadows of disunion were indeed gathering over our own land, but for the most of us they carried with them no fear of war. American fight American? Never! Separation there might be, and with a common sorrow officers of both sections thought of it; but, brother shed the blood of brother? No! By

1859 the Crimean War had indeed intervened to shake these fond convictions; but, after all, rules have exceptions, and in the succeeding peace the British government, consistent with the prepossessions derived from the propaganda of Cobden, yielded perfectly gratuitously the principle that an enemy's commerce might be freely transported under a neutral flag, thereby wrenching away prematurely one of the prongs of Neptune's trident. Surely we were on the road to universal peace.

San Francisco before and after its recent earthquake—at this moment of writing ten days ago—scarcely presented a greater contrast of experience than that my day has known; and the political condition and balance of the world now is as different from that of the period of which I have been writing as the new city will be from the old one it will replace at the Golden Gate. Of this universal change and displacement the most significant factor—at least in our Western civilization—has been the establishment of the German Empire, with its ensuing commercial, maritime, and naval development. To it certainly we owe the military impulse which has been transmitted everywhere to the forces of sea and land—an impulse for which, in my judgment, too great gratitude cannot be felt. It has braced and organized Western civilization for an ordeal as yet dimly perceived. But between 1850 and 1860 long desuetude of war, and confident reliance upon the commercial progress which freedom of trade had brought in its train, especially to Great Britain, had induced the prevalent feeling that to-morrow would be as to-day, and much more abundant. This was too consonant to national temperament not to pervade America also; and it was promoted by a distance from Europe and her complications much greater than now exists, and by the consistent determination not to be implicated in her concerns. All these factors went to constitute the atmosphere of indifference to military affairs in general; and particularly to those external interests of which a navy is the outward and visible sign and champion.

I do not think there is error or exaggeration in this picture of the "environment" of the navy in popular appreciation at the time I entered. Under such conditions, which had obtained substantially since soon after the War of 1812, and which long disastrously affected even Great Britain, with all her proud naval traditions and maritime and colonial interests, a military service cannot thrive. Indifference and neglect tell on most individuals, and on all professions. The saving clauses were the high sense of duty and of professional integrity, which from first to last I have never known wanting in the service; while the beauty of the ships themselves, quick as a docile and intelligent animal to respond to the master's call, inspired affection and intensified professional enthusiasm. The exercises of sails and spars, under the varying exigencies of service, bewildering as they may have seemed to the uninitiated, to the appreciative possessed fascination, and were their own sufficient reward for the care lavished upon them. In their mute yet exact response was some compensation for external neglect; they were, so to say, the testimony of a good conscience; the assurance of professional merit, and of work well done, if scantily recognized. Poor and beloved sails and spars—*la joie de la manœuvre*, to use the sympathetic phrase of a French officer of that day—gone ye are with that past of which I have been speaking, and of which ye were a goodly symbol; but like other symptoms of the times, had we listened aright, we should have heard the stern rebuke: Up and depart hence; this is not the place of your rest.

The result of all this had been a body of officers, and of men-of-war seamen, strong in professional sentiment, and admirably qualified in the main for the duties of a calling which in many of its leading characteristics was rapidly becoming obsolete. There was the spirit of youth, but the body of age. As a class, officers and men were well up in the use of such instruments as the country gave them; but the profession did not wield the corporate influence necessary to extort better instruments, and impotence to remedy produced acquiescence in, perhaps, more properly, submission to, an arrest of progress, the evils of which were clearly seen. Yet the salt was still there, nor had it lost its savor. The military professions are discouraged, even enjoined, against that combined independent action for the remedy of grievances which is the safeguard of civil liberty, but tends to sap the unquestioning obedience essential to unity of action under a single will—at once the virtue and the menace of a standing army. Naval officers had neither the privilege nor the habits which would promote united effort for betterment; but when individuals among them are found, like Farragut, Dupont, Porter, Dahlgren—to mention only a few names that became conspicuous in the War of Secession—there will be found also in civil and political life men who will become the channels through which the needs of the service will receive expression and ultimately obtain relief. The process is overslow for perfect adequacy, but it exists. It may be asked, Was not the Navy Department constituted for this special purpose? Possibly; but experience has shown that sometimes it is effective, and sometimes it is not. There is in it no provision for a continuous policy. No administrative period of our naval history since 1812 has been more disastrously stagnant and inefficient than that which followed closely the War of Secession, with its extraordinary, and in the main well-directed, administrative energy. The deeds of Farragut, his compeers, and their followers, after exciting a moment's enthusiasm, were powerless to sustain popular interest. Reaction ruled, as after the War of 1812.

To whomsoever due, in the decade immediately preceding the War of Secession there were two notable attempts at regeneration which had a profound influence upon the fortunes of that contest. Of these, one affected the personnel of the navy, the other the material. It had for some time been recognized within the service that, owing partly to easy-going toleration of offenders, partly to the absence of authorized methods for dealing with the disabled, or the merely incompetent, partly also, doubtless, to the effect of general professional stagnation upon those naturally inclined to worthlessness, there had accumulated a very considerable percentage of officers who were useless; or, worse, unreliable. In measure, this was also due to habits of drinking, much more common in all classes of men then than now. Even within the ten years with which I am dealing, an officer not much my senior remarked to me on the great improvement in this respect in his own experience; and my contemporaries will bear me out in saying that since then the advance has been so sustained that the evil now is practically non-existent. But then the compassionate expression, "A first-rate officer when he is not drinking," was ominously frequent; and in the generation before too little attention had been paid to the equally significant remark, that with a fool you know what to count on, but with one who drank you never knew.

But drink was far from the only cause. There were regular examinations, after six years of service, for promotion from the warrant of midshipman to a lieutenant's commission; but, that successfully passed, there was no further review of an officer's qualifications, unless misconduct brought him before a court-martial. Nor was there any provision for removing the physically incompetent. Before I entered the navy I knew one such, who had been bedridden for nearly ten years. He had been a midshipman with Farragut under Porter in the old *Essex*, when captured by the *Phœbe* and *Cherub*. A gallant boy, specially named in the despatch, he had such aptitude that at sixteen, as he told me himself, he wore an epaulette on the left shoulder—the uniform of a lieutenant at that time; and a contemporary assured me that in handling a ship he was the smartest officer of the deck he had ever known. But in early middle life disease overtook him, and, though flat on his back, he had been borne on the active list because there was nothing else to do with him. In that plight he was even promoted. There was another who, as a midshipman, had lost a foot in the War of 1812, but had been carried on from grade to grade for forty years, until at the time I speak of he was a captain, then the highest rank in the navy. Possibly, probably, he never saw water bluer than that of the lakes, where he was wounded. The undeserving were not treated with quite the same indulgence. Those familiar with the *Navy Register* of those days will recall some half-dozen old die-hards, who figured from year to year at the head of the lieutenant's list; continuously "overslaughed," never promoted, but never dismissed. To deal in the same manner with such men as the two veterans first mentioned would have been insulting; the distinction of promotion had to be conceded.

But there were those also who, despite habits or inefficiency, slipped through even formal examination; commanders whose ships were run by their subordinates, lieutenants whose watch on deck kept their captains from sleeping, midshipmen whose unfitness made their retention unpardonable; for at their age to re-begin life was no hardship, much less injustice. Of one such the story ran that his captain, giving him the letter required by regulation, wrote, "Mr. So and So is a very excellent young gentleman, of perfectly correct habits, but nothing will make an officer of him." He answered his questions, however; and the board considered that they could not go beyond that fact. They passed him in the face of the opinion of a superior of tried efficiency who had had his professional conduct under prolonged observation. I never knew this particular man professionally, but the general estimate of the service confirmed his captain's opinion. Twenty or thirty years later, I was myself one of a board called to deal with a precisely similar case. The letter of the captain was explicitly condemnatory and strong; but the president of the board, a man of exemplary rectitude, was vehement even in refusing to act upon it, and his opinion prevailed. Some years afterwards the individual came under my command, and proved to be of so eccentric worthlessness that I thought him on the border-line of insanity. He afterwards disappeared, I do not know how.

Talking of examinations, a comical incident came under my notice immediately after the War of Secession, when there were still employed a large number of those volunteer officers who had honorably and usefully filled up the depleted ranks of the regular service—an accession of strength imperatively needed. There were among them, naturally, inefficients as well as efficients. One had applied for promotion, and a board of three, among them myself, was assembled to examine. Several commonplace questions in seamanship were put to him, of which I now remember only that he had no conception of the difference between a ship moored, and one lying at single anchor—a subject as pertinent to-day as a hundred years ago. After failing to explain this, he expressed his wish not to go further; whereupon one of the board asked why, if ignorant of these simple matters, he had applied for examination. His answer was, "I did not apply for examination, I applied for promotion." Even in this case, when the applicant had left the room, the president of the board, then a somewhat notorious survival of the unfittest, long since departed this life, asked whether we refused to pass him. The third member, himself a volunteer officer, and myself, said we did. "Well," he rejoined, "you know this man may get a chance at *you* some day." This prudent consideration, however, did not save him.

Such tolerance towards the unfit, the reluctance to strike the individual in the interests of the community, was but a special, and not very flagrant, instance of the sympathy evoked for much worse offenders—murderers, and defrauders—in civil life. In such cases, the average man, except when personally affected, sides unreasonably with the sufferer and against the public; witness the easily signed petitions for pardon which flow in. It can be understood that in a public employment, civil or military, there will usually be reluctance to punish, and especially to take the bread out of the mouths of a man and his family by ejection. Usually only immediate personal interest in efficiency can supply the needed hardness of heart. Speaking after a very extensive and varied inside experience of courts-martial, I can say most positively that their tendency is not towards the excessive severity which I have heard charged against them by an eminent lawyer. On the contrary, the difficulty is to keep the members up to the mark against their natural and professional sympathies. Their superiors in the civil government have more often to rebuke undue leniency. How much more hard when, instead of an evil-doer, one had only to deal with a good-tempered, kindly ignoramus, or one perhaps who drew near the borderline of slipshod adequacy; and especially when to do so was to initiate action, apparently invidious, and probably useless, as in cases I have cited. It was easier for a captain or first lieutenant to nurse such a one along through a cruise, and then dismiss him to his home, thanking

God, like Dogberry, that you are rid of a fool, and trusting you may see him no more. But this confidence may be misplaced; even his ghost may return to plague you, or your conscience. Basil Hall tells an interesting story in point. When himself about to pass for lieutenant, in 1808, while in an anteroom awaiting his summons, a candidate came out flushed and perturbed. Hall was called in, and one of the examining captains said to him, "Mr. ——, who has just gone out, could not answer a question which we will put to you." He naturally looked for a stunner, and was surprised at the extremely commonplace problem proposed to him. From the general incident he presumed his predecessor had been rejected, but when the list was published saw his name among the passed. Some years later he met one of the examiners, who in the conversation recalled to him the circumstances. "We hesitated," he said, "whether to let him go through: but we did, and I voted for him. A few weeks later I saw him gazetted second lieutenant of a sloop-of-war, and a twinge of compunction seized me. Not long afterwards I read also the loss of that ship, with all on board. I never have known how it happened, but I cannot rid myself of an uneasy feeling that it may have been in that young man's watch." He added, "Mr. Hall, if ever you are employed as I then was, do not take your duties as lightly as I did."

Sometimes retribution does not assume this ghastly form, but shows the humorous side of her countenance; for she has two faces, like the famous ship that was painted a different color on either side and always tacked at night, that the enemy might imagine two ships off their coast. I recall—many of us recall—a well-known character in the service, "Bobby," who was a synonyme for inefficiency. He is long since in his grave, where reminiscence cannot disturb him; and the Bobby can reveal him only to those who knew him as well and better than I, and not to an unsympathetic public. Well, Bobby after much indulgence had been retired from active service by that convulsive effort at re-establishment known as the Retiring Board of 1854–55, to which I am coming if ever I see daylight through this thicket of recollections that seems to close round me as I proceed, instead of getting clearer. The action of that board was afterwards extensively reviewed, and among the data brought before the reviewers was a letter from a commander, who presumably should have known better, warmly endorsing Bobby. In consequence of this, and perhaps other circumstances, Bobby was restored to an admiring service; but the Department, probably through some officer who appreciated the situation, sent him to his advocate as first lieutenant —that is, as general manager and right-hand man. The joke was somewhat grim, and grimly resented. It fell to me a little later to see the commander on a matter of duty. He received me in his cabin, his feet swathed on a chair, his hands gnarled and knotted with gout or rheumatism, from which he was a great sufferer. Business despatched, we drifted into talk, and got on the subject of Bobby. His face became distorted. "I suppose the Department thinks it has done a very funny thing in sending me him as first lieutenant; but I tell you, Mr. Mahan, every word I wrote was perfectly true. There is nothing about a ship from her hold to her trucks that Bobby don't know; but—" here fury took possession of him, and he vociferated—"put him on deck, handling men, he is the d——dest fool that ever man laid eyes on." How far his sense of injury biassed his judgments as to the acquirements of his protégé, I cannot say; but a cruise or two before I had happened to hear from eye-witnesses of Bobby's appearance in public after his restoration as first lieutenant in charge of the deck. On the occasion in question he was to exercise the whole crew at some particular manœuvre. Taking his stand on the hawse-block, he drew from his pocket a small note-book, cast upon it his eye and announced—doubtless through the trumpet—"Man the fore-royal braces!" A pause, and further reference. "Man the main-royal braces!" Again a pause: "Man the mizzen-royal braces—Man *all* the royal braces." It is quite true, however, that there may be plenty of knowledge with lack of power to apply it professionally—a fact observable in all callings, but one which examination alone will not elicit. I knew such a one who said of himself, "Before I take the trumpet I know what ought to be said and done, but with the trumpet in my hand everything goes away from me." This was doubtless partly stage-fright; but stage-fright does not last where there is real aptitude. This man, of very marked general ability, esteemed and liked by all, finally left the navy; and probably wisely. On the other hand, I remember a very excellent seaman—and officer—telling me that the poorest officer he had ever known tacked ship the best. So men differ.

Thus it happened, through the operation of a variety of causes, that by the early fifties there had accumulated on the lists of the navy, in every grade, a number of men who had been tried in the balance of professional judgment and found distinctly wanting. Not only was the public—the nation—being wronged by the continuance in positions of responsibility of men who could not meet an emergency, or even discharge common duties, but there was the further harm that they were occupying places which, if vacated, could be at once filled by capable men waiting behind them. Fortunately, this had come to constitute a body of individual grievance among the deserving, which counterbalanced the natural sympathy with the individual incompetent. The remedy adopted was drastic enough, although in fact only an application of the principle of selection in a very guarded form. Unhappily, previous neglect to apply selection through a long series of years had now occasioned conditions in which it had to be used on a huge scale, and in the most invidious manner—the selecting out of the unfit. It was therefore easy for cavillers to liken this process to a trial at law, in which unfavorable decision was a condemnation without the accused being heard; and, of course, once having received this coloring, the impression could not be removed, nor the method reconciled to a public having Anglo-Saxon traditions concerning the administration of justice. A board of fifteen was constituted—five captains, five commanders, and five lieutenants. These were then the only grades of commissioned officers, and representation from them all insured, as far as could be, an adequate acquaintance with the entire personnel of the navy. The board sat in secret, reaching its own conclusions by its own methods; deciding who were, and who were not, fit to be carried longer on the active list. Rejections were of three kinds: those wholly removed, and those retired on two different grades of pay, called "Retired," and "Furloughed." The report was accepted by the government and became operative.

This occurred a year or two before I entered the Naval School; and, as I was already expecting to do so, I read with an interest I well recall the lists of person unfavorably affected. Of course, neither then nor afterwards had I knowledge to form an independent opinion upon the merits of the cases; but as far as I could gather in the immediately succeeding years, from different officers, the general verdict was that in very few instances had injustice been done. Where I had the opportunity of verifying the mistakes cited to me, I found instead reason rather to corroborate than to impugn the action of the board; but, of course, in so large a review as it had to undertake, even a jury of fifteen experts can scarcely be expected never to err. In the navy it was a first, and doubtless somewhat crude, attempt to apply the method of selection which every business man or corporation uses in choosing employés; an arbitrary conclusion, based upon personal knowledge and observation, or upon adequate information. But in private affairs such decisions are not regarded as legal judgment, nor rejection as condemnation; and there is no appeal. The private interest of the employer is warrant that he will do the best he can for his business. This presumption does not lie in the case of public affairs, although after the most searching criticism the action of the board of fifteen might probably be quoted to prove that selection for promotion could safely be trusted at all times to similar means. I mean, that such a body would never recommend an unfit man for promotion, and in three cases out of five would choose very near the best man. But no such system can work unless a government have the courage of its findings; for private and public opinion will inevitably constitute itself a court of appeal. In Great Britain, where the principle of selection has never been abandoned, in the application the Admiralty is none the less constrained—browbeaten, I fancy, would hardly be too strong a word—by opinion outside. P. has been promoted, say the service journals;

but why was A. passed over, or F., or K.? Choice is difficult, indeed, in peace times; but years sap efficiency, and for the good of the nation it is imperative to get men along while in the vigor of life, which will never be effected by the slow routine in which each second stands heir to the first. P. possibly may not be better than A. or K., but the nation will profit more, and in a matter vital to it, than if P., whose equality may be conceded, has to wait for the whole alphabet to die out of his way. The injustice, if so it be, to the individual must not be allowed to impede the essential prosperity of the community.

In 1854–55, the results of a contrary system had reached proportions at once disheartening and comical. It then required fourteen years after entrance to reach a lieutenant's commission, the lowest of all. That is, coming in as a midshipman at fifteen, not till twenty-nine, after ten to twelve years probably on a sea-going vessel, was a man found fit, by official position, to take charge of a ship at sea, or to command a division of guns. True, the famous Billy Culmer, of the British navy, under a system of selection found himself a midshipman still at fifty-six, and then declined a commission on the ground that he preferred to continue senior midshipman rather than be the junior lieutenant;* but the injustice, if so it were, to Billy, and to many others, had put the ships into the hands of captains in the prime of life. Of the historic admirals of that navy, few had failed to reach a captaincy in their twenties. *Per contra*, I was told the following anecdote by an officer of our service whose name was—and is, for he still lives—a synonyme for personal activity and professional seamanship, but who waited his fourteen years for a lieutenancy. On one

*This statement when written rested on my childhood's memory only. A few months later there came into my hands a volume of the publications of the British Navy Records Society, containing the Recollections of Commander James Anthony Gardner, 1775–1814. Gardner was at one time shipmates with Culmer, who it appears eventually received a commission. By Gardner's reckoning he would have been far along in the forties in 1790. The following is the description of him. "Billy was about five feet eight or nine, and stooped; hard features, marked with the small-pox; blind in an eye, and a wen nearly the size of an egg under his cheek-bone. His dress on a Sunday was a mate's uniform coat, with brown velvet waistcoat and breeches; boots with black tops; a gold-laced hat, and a large hanger by his side like the sword of John-a-Gaunt. He was proud of being the oldest midshipman in the navy, and looked upon young captains and lieutenants with contempt."

occasion the ship in which he returned to Norfolk from a three-years' cruise was ordered from there to Portsmouth, New Hampshire, to go out of commission. For some cause almost all the lieutenants had been detached, the cruise being thought ended. It became necessary, therefore, to intrust the charge of the deck to him and other "passed" midshipmen, and great was the shaking of heads among old stagers over the danger that ship was to run. If this were exceptional, it would not be worth quoting, but it was not. A similar routine in the British navy, in a dry-rot period of a hundred years before, had induced a like head-wagging and exchange of views when one of its greatest admirals, Hawke, was first given charge of a squadron; being then already a man of mark, and four years older than Nelson at the Nile. But he was younger than the rule, and so distrusted.

The vacancies made by the wholesale action of 1854 remedied this for a while. The lieutenants who owed their rank to it became such after seven or eight years, or at twenty-three or four; and this meant really passing out of pupilage into manhood. The change being effected immediately, anticipated the reaction in public opinion and in Congress, which rejected the findings of the board and compelled a review of the whole procedure. Many restorations were made; and, as these swelled the lists beyond the number then authorized by law, there was established a reduced pay for those whose recent promotion made them in excess. For them was adopted, in naval colloquialism, the inelegant but suggestive term "jackass" lieutenants. It should be explained to the outsider, perhaps even many professional readers now may not know, that the word was formerly used for a class of so-called frigates which intervened between the frigate-class proper and the sloop-of-war proper, and like all hybrids, such as the armored cruiser, shared more in the defects than in the virtues of either. It was therefore not a new coinage, and its uncomplimentary suggestion applied rather to the grudging legislation than to the unlucky victims. Of course, promotion was stopped till this block was worked off; but the immediate gain was retained. Before the trouble came on afresh the War of

Secession, causing a large number of Southerners to leave the service, introduced a very different problem;—namely, how to find officers enough to meet the expansion of the navy caused by the vast demands of the contest. The men of my time became lieutenants between twenty and twenty-three. My own commission was dated a month before my twenty-first birthday, and with what good further prospects, even under the strict rule of seniority promotion, is evident, for before I was twenty-five I was made lieutenant-commander, corresponding to major in the army. Those were cheerful days in this respect for the men who struck the crest of the wave; but already the symptoms of inevitable reaction to old conditions of stagnancy were observable to those careful to heed.

It would be difficult to exaggerate the benefit of this measure to the nation, through the service, despite the subsequent reactionary legislation. By a single act a large number of officers were advanced from the most subordinate and irresponsible positions to those which called all their faculties into play. "Responsibility," said one of the most experienced admirals the world has known, "is the test of a man's courage"; and where the native fitness exists nothing so educates for responsibility as the having it. The responsibility of the lieutenant of the watch differs little from that of the captain in degree, and less in kind. To early bearing of responsibility Farragut attributed in great part his fearlessness in it, which was well known to the service before his hour of strain. It was much that the government found ready for the extreme demands of the war a number of officers, who, instead of supervising the washing of lower decks and stowing of holds during their best years, had been put betimes in charge of the ship. From there to the captain's berth was but a small step. "Passed midshipman," says one of Cooper's characters, "is a good grade to reach, but a bad one to stop in." From a fate little better than this a large and promising number of young officers were thus rescued for the commands and responsibilities of the War of Secession.

Eugene O'Neill

From his childhood summers in the port town of New London, Connecticut, Eugene O'Neill (1888–1953) had a close connection with the sea. Early voyages to Honduras (to prospect for gold) and to Buenos Aires (where he worked in a sewing-machine factory and as a stevedore) were followed by employment in 1911 as an ordinary seaman on the British freighter Ikala *and as an able-bodied seaman on the ocean liner* Philadelphia. *Many aspects of O'Neill's seagoing days filter into his early plays, especially in the one-acters collected as* The Moon of the Caribbees and Six Other Plays of the Sea *(1919), the waterfront drama* Anna Christie *(1921), and* The Hairy Ape *(1922), his portrait of an impassioned and inarticulate stoker.* Ile *was first produced by The Provincetown Players in Greenwich Village in 1917. Although its Arctic setting is remote from O'Neill's maritime experience, the domestic conflict at its core is a compressed and melodramatic foreshadowing of such later masterpieces as* Long Day's Journey into Night.

Ile

SCENE. *Captain Keeney's cabin on board the steam whaling ship* Atlantic Queen*—a small, square compartment about eight feet high with a skylight in the center looking out on the poop deck. On the left (the stern of the ship) a long bench with rough cushions is built in against the wall. In front of the bench, a table. Over the bench, several curtained portholes.*

In the rear, left, a door leading to the CAPTAIN'S *sleeping quarters. To the right of the door a small organ, looking as if it were brand-new, is placed against the wall.*

On the right, to the rear, a marble-topped sideboard. On the sideboard, a woman's sewing basket. Farther forward, a doorway leading to the companionway, and past the officers' quarters to the main deck.

In the center of the room, a stove. From the middle of the ceiling a hanging lamp is suspended. The walls of the cabin are painted white.

There is no rolling of the ship, and the light which comes through the skylight is sickly and faint, indicating one of those gray days of calm when ocean and sky are alike dead. The silence is unbroken except for the measured tread of someone walking up and down on the poop deck overhead.

It is nearing two bells—one o'clock—in the afternoon of a day in the year 1895.

At the rise of the curtain there is a moment of intense silence. Then the STEWARD *enters and commences to clear the table of the few dishes which still remain on it after the* CAPTAIN'S *dinner. He is an old, grizzled man dressed in dungaree pants, a sweater, and a woolen cap with ear-flaps. His manner is sullen and angry. He stops stacking up the plates and casts a quick glance upward at the skylight; then tiptoes over to the closed door in rear and listens with his ear pressed to the crack. What he hears makes his face darken and he mutters a furious curse. There is a noise from the doorway on the right and he darts back to the table.*

BEN *enters. He is an overgrown, gawky boy with a long, pinched face. He is dressed in sweater, fur cap, etc. His teeth are chattering with the cold and he hurries to the stove, where he stands for a moment shivering, blowing on his hands, slapping them against his sides, on the verge of crying.*

THE STEWARD. (*in relieved tones—seeing who it is*) Oh, 'tis you, is it? What're ye shiverin' 'bout? Stay by the stove where ye belong and ye'll find no need of chatterin'.

BEN. It's c-c-cold. (*Trying to control his chattering teeth—derisively*) Who d'ye think it were—the Old Man?

THE STEWARD. (*makes a threatening move*—BEN *shrinks away*) None o' your lip, young un, or I'll learn ye. (*More kindly*) Where was it ye've been all o' the time—the fo'c's'tle?

BEN. Yes.

THE STEWARD. Let the Old Man see ye up for'ard monkey-shinin' with the hands and ye'll get a hidin' ye'll not forget in a hurry.

BEN. Aw, he don't see nothin'. (*A trace of awe in his tones—he glances upward*) He just walks up and down like he didn't notice nobody—and stares at the ice to the no'the'ard.

THE STEWARD. (*the same tone of awe creeping into his voice*) He's always starin' at the ice. (*In a sudden rage, shaking his fist at the skylight*) Ice, ice, ice! Damn him and damn the ice! Holdin' us in for nigh on a year—nothin' to see but ice—stuck in it like a fly in molasses!

BEN. (*apprehensively*) Ssshh! He'll hear ye.

THE STEWARD. (*raging*) Aye, damn him, and damn the Arctic seas, and damn this stinkin' whalin' ship of his, and damn me for a fool to ever ship on it! (*Subsiding as if realizing the uselessness of this outburst—shaking his head—slowly, with deep conviction*) He's a hard man—as hard a man as ever sailed the seas.

BEN. (*solemnly*) Aye.

THE STEWARD. The two years we all signed up for are done this day. Blessed Christ! Two years o' this dog's life, and no luck in the fishin', and the hands half starved with the food runnin' low, rotten as it is; and not a sign of him turnin' back for home! (*Bitterly*) Home! I begin to doubt if ever I'll set foot on land again. (*Excitedly*) What is it he thinks he's goin' to do? Keep us all up here after our time is worked out till the last man of us is starved to death or frozen? We've grub enough hardly to last out the voyage back if we started now. What are the men goin' to do 'bout it? Did ye hear any talk in the fo'c's'tle?

BEN. (*going over to him—in a half-whisper*) They said if he don't put back south for home today they're goin' to mutiny.

THE STEWARD. (*with grim satisfaction*) Mutiny? Aye, 'tis the only thing they can do; and serve him right after the manner he's treated them—'s if they weren't no better nor dogs.

BEN. The ice is all broke up to s'uth'ard. They's clear water 's far 's you can see. He ain't got no excuse for not turnin' back for home, the men says.

THE STEWARD. (*bitterly*) He won't look nowheres but no'the'ard where they's only the ice to see. He don't want to see no clear water. All he thinks on is gittin' the ile—'s if it was our fault he ain't had good luck with the whales. (*Shaking his head*) I think the man's mighty nigh losin' his senses.

BEN. (*awed*) D'you really think he's crazy?

THE STEWARD. Aye, it's the punishment o' God on him. Did ye ever hear of a man who wasn't crazy do the things he does? (*Pointing to the door in rear*) Who but a man that's mad would take his woman—and as sweet a woman as ever was—on a stinkin' whalin' ship to the Arctic seas to be locked in by the rotten ice for nigh on a year, and maybe lose her senses forever—for it's sure she'll never be the same again.

BEN. (*sadly*) She useter be awful nice to me before— (*his eyes grow wide and frightened*) —she got—like she is.

THE STEWARD. Aye, she was good to all of us. 'Twould have been hell on board without her; for he's a hard man—a hard, hard man—a driver if there ever was one. (*With a grim laugh*) I hope he's satisfied now—drivin' her on till she's near lost her mind. And who could blame her? 'Tis a God's wonder we're not a ship full of crazed people—with the damned ice all the time, and the quiet so thick you're afraid to hear your own voice.

BEN. (*with a frightened glance toward the door on right*) She don't never speak to me no more—jest looks at me 's if she didn't know me.

THE STEWARD. She don't know no one—but him. She talks to him—when she does talk—right enough.

BEN. She does nothin' all day long now but sit and sew—and then she cries to herself without makin' no noise. I've seen her.

THE STEWARD. Aye, I could hear her through the door a while back.

BEN. (*tiptoes over to the door and listens*) She's cryin' now.

THE STEWARD. (*furiously—shaking his fist*) God send his soul to hell for the devil he is! (*There is the noise of someone coming slowly down the companionway stairs.* THE STEWARD *hurries to his stacked-up dishes. He is so nervous from fright that he knocks off the top one, which falls and breaks on the floor. He stands aghast, trembling with dread.* BEN *is violently rubbing off the organ with a piece of cloth which he has snatched from his pocket.* CAPTAIN KEENEY *appears in the doorway on right and comes into the cabin, removing his fur cap as he does so. He is a man of about forty, around five-ten in height but looking much shorter on account of the enormous proportions of his shoulders and chest. His face is massive and deeply lined, with gray-blue eyes of a bleak hardness, and a tightly clenched, thin-lipped mouth. His thick hair is long and gray. He is dressed in a heavy blue jacket and blue pants stuffed into his sea-boots.*

(*He is followed into the cabin by the* SECOND MATE, *a rangy six-footer with a lean weather-beaten face. The* MATE *is dressed about the same as the* CAPTAIN. *He is a man of thirty or so.*)

KEENEY. (*comes toward* THE STEWARD—*with a stern look on his face.* THE STEWARD *is visibly frightened and the stack of dishes rattles in his trembling hands.* KEENEY *draws back his fist and* THE STEWARD *shrinks away. The fist is gradually lowered and* KEENEY *speaks slowly*) 'Twould be like hitting a worm. It is nigh on two bells, Mr. Steward, and this truck not cleared yet.

THE STEWARD. (*stammering*) Y-y-yes, sir.

KEENEY. Instead of doin' your rightful work ye've been below here gossipin' old woman's talk with that boy. (*To* BEN, *fiercely*) Get out o' this, you! Clean up the chart-room. (BEN *darts past the* MATE *to the open doorway*) Pick up that dish, Mr. Steward!

THE STEWARD. (*doing so with difficulty*) Yes, sir.

KEENEY. The next dish you break, Mr. Steward, you take a bath in the Bering Sea at the end of a rope.

THE STEWARD. (*tremblingly*) Yes, sir. (*He hurries out. The* SECOND MATE *walks slowly over to the* CAPTAIN.)

MATE. I warn't 'specially anxious the man at the wheel should catch what I wanted to say to you, sir. That's why I asked you to come below.

KEENEY. (*impatiently*) Speak your say, Mr. Slocum.

MATE. (*unconsciously lowering his voice*) I'm afeard there'll be trouble with the hands by the look o' things. They'll likely turn ugly, every blessed one o' them, if you don't put back. The two years they signed up for is up today.

KEENEY. And d'you think you're tellin' me somethin' new, Mr. Slocum? I've felt it in the air this long time past. D'you think I've not seen their ugly looks and the grudgin' way they worked? (*The door in rear is opened and* MRS. KEENEY *stands in the doorway. She is a slight, sweet-faced little woman primly dressed in black. Her eyes are red from weeping and her face drawn and pale. She takes in the cabin with a frightened glance and stands as if fixed to the spot by some nameless dread, clasping and unclasping her hands nervously. The two men turn and look at her.*)

KEENEY. (*with rough tenderness*) Well, Annie?

MRS. KEENEY. (*as if awakening from a dream*) David, I— (*She is silent. The* MATE *starts for the doorway.*)

KEENEY. (*turning to him—sharply*) Wait!

MATE. Yes, sir.

KEENEY. D'you want anything, Annie?

MRS. KEENEY. (*after a pause, during which she seems to be endeavoring to collect her thoughts*) I thought maybe—I'd go on deck, David, to get a breath of fresh air. (*She stands humbly awaiting his permission. He and the* MATE *exchange a significant glance.*)

KEENEY. It's too cold, Annie. You'd best stay below today. There's nothing to look at on deck—but ice.

MRS. KEENEY. (*monotonously*) I know—ice, ice, ice! But there's nothing to see down here but these walls. (*She makes a gesture of loathing.*)

KEENEY. You can play the organ, Annie.

MRS. KEENEY. (*dully*) I hate the organ. It puts me in mind of home.

KEENEY. (*a touch of resentment in his voice*) I got it jest for you.

MRS. KEENEY. (*dully*) I know. (*She turns away from them and walks slowly to the bench on left. She lifts up one of the curtains and looks through a porthole; then utters an exclamation of joy*) Ah, water! Clear water! As far as I can see! How good it looks after all these months of ice! (*She turns round to them, her face transfigured with joy*) Ah, now I must go up on the deck and look at it, David.

KEENEY. (*frowning*) Best not today, Annie. Best wait for a day when the sun shines.

MRS. KEENEY. (*desperately*) But the sun never shines in this terrible place.

KEENEY. (*a tone of command in his voice*) Best not today, Annie.

MRS. KEENEY. (*crumbling before this command—abjectly*) Very well, David. (*She stands there staring straight before her as if in a daze. The two men look at her uneasily.*)

KEENEY. (*sharply*) Annie!

MRS. KEENEY. (*dully*) Yes, David.

KEENEY. Me and Mr. Slocum has business to talk about—ship's business.

MRS. KEENEY. Very well, David. (*She goes slowly out, rear, and leaves the door three-quarters shut behind her.*)

KEENEY. Best not have her on deck if they's goin' to be any trouble.

MATE. Yes, sir.

KEENEY. And trouble they's going to be. I feel it in my bones. (*Takes a revolver from the pocket of his coat and examines it*) Got your'n?

MATE. Yes, sir.

KEENEY. Not that we'll have to use 'em—not if I know their breed of dog—jest to frighten 'em up a bit. (*Grimly*) I ain't never been forced to use one yit; and trouble I've had by land and by sea 's long as I kin remember, and will have till my dyin' day, I reckon.

MATE. (*hesitatingly*) Then you ain't goin'—to turn back?

KEENEY. Turn back? Mr. Slocum, did you ever hear o' me pointin' s'uth for home with only a measly four hundred barrel of ile in the hold?

MATE. (*hastily*) No, sir—but the grub's gittin' low.

KEENEY. They's enough to last a long time yit, if they're careful with it; and they's plenty o' water.

MATE. They say it's not fit to eat—what's left; and the two years they signed on fur is up today. They might make trouble for you in the courts when we git home.

KEENEY. To hell with 'em! Let them make what law trouble they kin. I don't give a damn 'bout the money. I've got to git the ile! (*Glancing sharply at the* MATE) You ain't turnin' no damned sea-lawyer, be you, Mr. Slocum?

MATE. (*flushing*) Not by a hell of a sight, sir.

KEENEY. What do the fools want to go home fur now? Their share o' the four hundred barrel wouldn't keep 'em in chewin' terbacco.

MATE. (*slowly*) They wants to git back to their folks an' things, I s'pose.

KEENEY. (*looking at him searchingly*) 'N you want to turn back, too. (*The* MATE *looks down confusedly before his sharp gaze*) Don't lie, Mr. Slocum. It's writ down plain in your eyes. (*With grim sarcasm*) I hope, Mr. Slocum, you ain't agoin' to jine the men again me.

MATE. (*indignantly*) That ain't fair, sir, to say sich things.

KEENEY. (*with satisfaction*) I warn't much afeard o' that, Tom. You been with me nigh on ten year and I've learned ye whalin'. No man kin say I ain't a good master, if I be a hard one.

MATE. I warn't thinkin' of myself, sir—'bout turnin' home, I mean. (*Desperately*) But Mrs. Keeney, sir—seems like she ain't jest satisfied up here, ailin' like—what with the cold an' bad luck an' the ice an' all.

KEENEY. (*his face clouding—rebukingly but not severely*) That's my business, Mr. Slocum. I'll thank you to steer a clear course o' that. (*A pause*) The ice'll break up soon to no'th'ard. I could see it startin' today. And when it goes and we git some sun Annie'll perk up. (*Another pause—then he bursts forth*) It ain't the damned money what's keepin' me up in the Northern seas, Tom. But I can't go back to Homeport with a measly four hundred barrel of ile. I'd die fust. I ain't never come back home in all my days without a full ship. Ain't that truth?

MATE. Yes, sir; but this voyage you been icebound, an'—

KEENEY. (*scornfully*) And d'you s'pose any of 'em would believe that—any o' them skippers I've beaten voyage after voyage? Can't you hear 'em laughin' and sneerin'—Tibbots 'n' Harris 'n' Simms and the rest—and all o' Homeport makin' fun o' me? "Dave Keeney what boasts he's the best whalin' skipper out o' Homeport comin' back with a measly four hundred barrel of ile?" (*The thought of this drives him into a frenzy, and he smashes his fist down on the marble top of the sideboard*) Hell! I got to git the ile, I tell you. How could I figger on this ice? It's never been so bad before in the thirty year I been acomin' here. And now it's breakin' up. In a couple o' days it'll be all gone. And they's whale here, plenty of 'em. I know they is and I ain't never gone wrong yit. I got to git the ile! I got to git it in spite of all hell, and by God, I ain't agoin' home till I do git it! (*There is the sound of subdued sobbing from the door in the rear. The two men stand silent for a moment, listening. Then* KEENEY *goes over to the door and looks in. He hesitates for a moment as if he were going to enter—then closes the door softly.* JOE, *the harpooner, an enormous six-footer with a battered, ugly face, enters from right and stands waiting for the captain to notice him.*)

KEENEY. (*turning and seeing him*) Don't be standin' there like a gawk, Harpooner. Speak up!

JOE. (*confusedly*) We want—the men, sir—they wants to send a depitation aft to have a word with you.

KEENEY. (*furiously*) Tell 'em to go to— (*Checks himself and continues grimly*) Tell 'em to come. I'll see 'em.

JOE. Aye, aye, sir. (*He goes out.*)

KEENEY. (*with a grim smile*) Here it comes, the trouble you spoke of, Mr. Slocum, and we'll make short shift of it. It's better to crush such things at the start than let them make headway.

MATE. (*worriedly*) Shall I wake up the First and Fourth, sir? We might need their help.

KEENEY. No, let them sleep. I'm well able to handle this alone, Mr. Slocum. (*There is the shuffling of footsteps from outside and five of the crew crowd into the cabin, led by* JOE. *All are dressed alike—sweaters, sea-boots, etc. They glance uneasily at the* CAPTAIN, *twirling their fur caps in their hands.*)

KEENEY. (*after a pause*) Well? Who's to speak fur ye?

JOE. (*stepping forward with an air of bravado*) I be.

KEENEY. (*eyeing him up and down coldly*) So you be. Then speak your say and be quick about it.

JOE. (*trying not to wilt before the* CAPTAIN'S *glance and avoiding his eyes*) The time we signed up for is done today.

KEENEY. (*icily*) You're tellin' me nothin' I don't know.

JOE. You ain't pintin' fur home yit, far 's we kin see.

KEENEY. No, and I ain't agoin' to till this ship is full of ile.

JOE. You can't go no further no'the with the ice afore ye.

KEENEY. The ice is breaking up.

JOE. (*after a slight pause during which the others mumble angrily to one another*) The grub we're gittin' now is rotten.

KEENEY. It's good enough fur ye. Better men than ye are have eaten worse. (*There is a chorus of angry exclamations from the crowd.*)

JOE. (*encouraged by this support*) We ain't agoin' to work no more 'less you puts back for home.

KEENEY. (*fiercely*) You ain't, ain't you?

JOE. No; and the law courts'll say we was right.

KEENEY. To hell with your law courts! We're at sea now and I'm the law on this ship. (*Edging up toward the harpooner*) And every mother's son of you what don't obey orders goes in irons. (*There are more angry exclamations from the crew.* MRS. KEENEY *appears in the doorway in rear and looks on with startled eyes. None of the men notice her.*)

JOE. (*with bravado*) Then we're agoin' to mutiny and take the old hooker home ourselves. Ain't we, boys? (*As he turns his head to look at the others,* KEENEY'S *fist shoots out to the side of his jaw.* JOE *goes down in a heap and lies there.* MRS. KEENEY *gives a shriek and hides her face in her hands. The men pull out their sheath-knives and start a rush, but stop when they find themselves confronted by the revolvers of* KEENEY *and the* MATE.)

KEENEY. (*his eyes and voice snapping*) Hold still! (*The men stand huddled together in a sullen silence.* KEENEY'S *voice is full of mockery*) You've found out it ain't safe to mutiny on this ship, ain't you? And now git for'ard where ye belong, and— (*He gives* JOE'S *body a contemptuous kick*) Drag him with you. And remember the first man of ye I see shirkin' I'll shoot dead as sure as there's a sea under us, and you can tell the rest the same. Git for'ard now! Quick! (*The men leave in cowed silence, carrying* JOE *with them.* KEENEY *turns to the* MATE *with a short laugh and puts his revolver back in his pocket*) Best get up on deck, Mr. Slocum, and see to it they don't try none of their skulkin' tricks. We'll have to keep an eye peeled from now on. I know 'em.

MATE. Yes, sir. (*He goes out, right.* KEENEY *hears his wife's hysterical weeping and turns around in surprise—then walks slowly to her side.*)

KEENEY. (*putting an arm around her shoulder—with gruff tenderness*) There, there, Annie. Don't be afeard. It's all past and gone.

MRS. KEENEY. (*shrinking away from him*) Oh, I can't bear it! I can't bear it any longer!

KEENEY. (*gently*) Can't bear what, Annie?

MRS. KEENEY. (*hysterically*) All this horrible brutality, and these brutes of men, and this terrible ship, and this prison cell of a room, and the ice all around, and the silence. (*After this outburst she calms down and wipes her eyes with her handkerchief.*)

KEENEY. (*after a pause during which he looks down at her with a puzzled frown*) Remember, I warn't hankerin' to have you come on this voyage, Annie.

MRS. KEENEY. I wanted to be with you, David, don't you see? I didn't want to wait back there in the house all alone as I've been doing these last six years since we were married—waiting, and watching, and fearing—with nothing to keep my mind occupied—not able to go back teaching school on account of being Dave Keeney's wife. I used to dream of sailing on the great, wide, glorious ocean. I wanted to be by your side in the danger and vigorous life of it all. I wanted to see you the hero they make you out to be in Homeport. And instead—(*Her voice grows tremulous*) All I find is ice and cold—and brutality! (*Her voice breaks.*)

KEENEY. I warned you what it'd be, Annie. "Whalin' ain't no ladies' tea-party," I says to you, and "you better stay to home where you've got all your woman's comforts." (*Shaking his head*) But you was so set on it.

MRS. KEENEY. (*wearily*) Oh, I know it isn't your fault, David. You see, I didn't believe you. I guess I was dreaming about the old Vikings in the story-books and I thought you were one of them.

KEENEY. (*protestingly*) I done my best to make it as cozy and comfortable as could be. (MRS. KEENEY *looks around her in wild scorn*) I even sent to the city for that organ for ye, thinkin' it might be soothin' to ye to be playin' it times when they was calms and things was dull-like.

MRS. KEENEY. (*wearily*) Yes, you were very kind, David. I know that. (*She goes to left and lifts the curtains from the port-hole and looks out—then suddenly bursts forth*) I won't stand it—I can't stand it—pent up by these walls like a prisoner. (*She runs over to him and throws her arms around him, weeping. He puts his arm protectingly over her shoulders*) Take me away from here, David! If I don't get away from here, out of this terrible ship, I'll go mad! Take me home, David! I can't think any more. I feel as if the cold and the silence were crushing down on my brain. I'm afraid. Take me home!

KEENEY. (*holds her at arm's length and looks at her anxiously*) Best go to bed, Annie. You ain't yourself. You got fever. Your eyes look so strange-like. I ain't never seen you look this way before.

MRS. KEENEY. (*laughing hysterically*) It's the ice and the cold and the silence—they'd make anyone look strange.

KEENEY. (*soothingly*) In a month or two, with good luck, three at the most, I'll have her filled with ile and then we'll give her everything she'll stand and pint for home.

MRS. KEENEY. But we can't wait for that—I can't wait. I want to get home. And the men won't wait. They want to get home. It's cruel, it's brutal for you to keep them. You must sail back. You've got no excuse. There's clear water to the south now. If you've a heart at all you've got to turn back.

KEENEY. (*harshly*) I can't, Annie.

MRS. KEENEY. Why can't you?

KEENEY. A woman couldn't rightly understand my reason.

MRS. KEENEY. (*wildly*) Because it's a stupid, stubborn reason. Oh, I heard you talking with the second mate. You're afraid the other captains will sneer at you because you didn't come back with a full ship. You want to live up to your silly reputation even if you do have to beat and starve men and drive me mad to do it.

KEENEY. (*his jaw set stubbornly*) It ain't that, Annie. Them skippers would never dare sneer to my face. It ain't so much what anyone'd say—but— (*He hesitates, struggling to express his meaning*) You see—I've always done it—since my first voyage as skipper. I always come back—with a full ship—and —it don't seem right not to—somehow. I been always first whalin' skipper out o' Homeport, and— Don't you see my meanin', Annie? (*He glances at her. She is not looking at him but staring dully in front of her, not hearing a word he is saying*) Annie! (*She comes to herself with a start*) Best turn in, Annie, there's a good woman. You ain't well.

MRS. KEENEY. (*resisting his attempts to guide her to the door in rear*) David! Won't you please turn back?

KEENEY. (*gently*) I can't, Annie—not yet awhile. You don't see my meanin'. I got to git the ile.

MRS. KEENEY. It'd be different if you needed the money, but you don't. You've got more than plenty.

KEENEY. (*impatiently*) It ain't the money I'm thinkin' of. D'you think I'm as mean as that?

MRS. KEENEY. (*dully*) No—I don't know—I can't understand— (*Intensely*) Oh, I want to be home in the old house once more and see my own kitchen again, and hear a woman's voice talking to me and be able to talk to her. Two years! It seems so long ago—as if I'd been dead and could never go back.

KEENEY. (*worried by her strange tone and the far-away look in her eyes*) Best go to bed, Annie. You ain't well.

MRS. KEENEY. (*not appearing to hear him*) I used to be lonely when you were away. I used to think Homeport was a stupid, monotonous place. Then I used to go down on the beach, especially when it was windy and the breakers were rolling in, and I'd dream of the fine free life you must be leading. (*She gives a laugh which is half a sob*) I used to love the sea then. (*She pauses; then continues with slow intensity*) But now—I don't ever want to see the sea again.

KEENEY. (*thinking to humor her*) 'Tis no fit place for a woman, that's sure. I was a fool to bring ye.

MRS. KEENEY. (*after a pause—passing her hand over her eyes with a gesture of pathetic weariness*) How long would it take us to reach home—if we started now?

KEENEY. (*frowning*) 'Bout two months, I reckon, Annie, with fair luck.

MRS. KEENEY. (*counts on her fingers—then murmurs with a rapt smile*) That would be August, the latter part of August, wouldn't it? It was on the twenty-fifth of August we were married, David, wasn't it?

KEENEY. (*trying to conceal the fact that her memories have moved him—gruffly*) Don't *you* remember?

MRS. KEENEY. (*vaguely—again passes her hand over her eyes*) My memory is leaving me—up here in the ice. It was so long ago. (*A pause—then she smiles dreamily*) It's June now. The lilacs will be all in bloom in the front yard—and the climbing roses on the trellis to the side of the house—they're budding. (*She suddenly covers her face with her hands and commences to sob.*)

KEENEY. (*disturbed*) Go in and rest, Annie. You're all wore out cryin' over what can't be helped.

MRS. KEENEY. (*suddenly throwing her arms around his neck and clinging to him*) You love me, don't you, David?

KEENEY. (*in amazed embarrassment at this outburst*) Love you? Why d'you ask me such a question, Annie?

MRS. KEENEY. (*shaking him—fiercely*) But you do, don't you, David? Tell me!

KEENEY. I'm your husband, Annie, and you're my wife. Could there be aught but love between us after all these years?

MRS. KEENEY. (*shaking him again—still more fiercely*) Then you do love me. Say it!

KEENEY. (*simply*) I do, Annie!

MRS. KEENEY. (*gives a sigh of relief—her hands drop to her sides.* KEENEY *regards her anxiously. She passes her hand across her eyes and murmurs half to herself*) I sometimes think if we could only have had a child. (KEENEY *turns away from her, deeply moved. She grabs his arm and turns him around to face her—intensely*) And I've always been a good wife to you, haven't I, David?

KEENEY. (*his voice betraying his emotion*) No man has ever had a better, Annie.

MRS. KEENEY. And I've never asked for much from you, have I, David? Have I?

KEENEY. You know you could have all I got the power to give ye, Annie.

MRS. KEENEY. (*wildly*) Then do this this once for my sake, for God's sake—take me home! It's killing me, this life—the brutality and cold and horror of it. I'm going mad. I can feel the threat in the air. I can hear the silence threatening me—day after gray day and every day the same. I can't bear it. (*Sobbing*) I'll go mad, I know I will. Take me home, David, if you love me as you say. I'm afraid. For the love of God, take me home! (*She throws her arms around him, weeping against his shoulder. His face betrays the tremendous struggle going on within him. He holds her out at arm's length, his expression softening. For a moment his shoulders sag, he becomes old, his iron spirit weakens as he looks at her tear-stained face.*)

KEENEY. (*dragging out the words with an effort*) I'll do it, Annie—for your sake—if you say it's needful for ye.

MRS. KEENEY. (*with wild joy—kissing him*) God bless you for that, David! (*He turns away from her silently and walks toward the companionway. Just at that moment there is a clatter of footsteps on the stairs and the* SECOND MATE *enters the cabin.*)

MATE. (*excitedly*) The ice is breakin' up to no'the'ard, sir. There's a clear passage through the floe, and clear water beyond, the lookout says. (KEENEY *straightens himself like a man coming out of a trance.* MRS. KEENEY *looks at the* MATE *with terrified eyes.*)

KEENEY. (*dazedly—trying to collect his thoughts*) A clear passage? To no'the'ard?

MATE. Yes, sir.

KEENEY. (*his voice suddenly grim with determination*) Then get her ready and we'll drive her through.

MATE. Aye, aye, sir.

MRS. KEENEY. (*appealingly*) David!

KEENEY. (*not heeding her*) Will the men turn to willin' or must we drag 'em out?

MATE. They'll turn to willin' enough. You put the fear o' God into 'em, sir. They're meek as lambs.

KEENEY. Then drive 'em—both watches. (*With grim determination*) They's whale t'other side o' this floe and we're going to git 'em.

MATE. Aye, aye, sir. (*He goes out hurriedly. A moment later there is the sound of scuffling feet from the deck outside and the* MATE'S *voice shouting orders.*)

KEENEY (*speaking aloud to himself—derisively*) And I was agoin' home like a yaller dog!

MRS. KEENEY. (*imploringly*) David!

KEENEY. (*sternly*) Woman, you ain't adoin' right when you meddle in men's business and weaken 'em. You can't know my feelin's. I got to prove a man to be a good husband for ye to take pride in. I got to git the ile, I tell ye.

MRS. KEENEY. (*supplicatingly*) David! Aren't you going home?

KEENEY. (*ignoring this question—commandingly*) You ain't well. Go and lay down a mite. (*He starts for the door*) I got to git on deck. (*He goes out. She cries after him in anguish*) David! (*A pause. She passes her hand across her eyes—then commences to laugh hysterically and goes to the organ. She sits down and starts to play wildly an old hymn.* KEENEY *re-enters from the doorway to the deck and stands looking at her angrily. He comes over and grabs her roughly by the shoulder.*)

KEENEY. Woman, what foolish mockin' is this? (*She laughs wildly and he starts back from her in alarm*) Annie! What is it? (*She doesn't answer him.* KEENEY'S *voice trembles*) Don't you know me, Annie? (*He puts both hands on her shoulders and turns her around so that he can look into her eyes. She stares up at him with a stupid expression, a vague smile on her lips. He stumbles away from her, and she commences softly to play the organ again.*)

KEENEY. (*swallowing hard—in a hoarse whisper, as if he had difficulty in speaking*) You said—you was agoin' mad—God! (*A long wail is heard from the deck above*) Ah bl-o-o-o-ow! (*A moment later the* MATE'S *face appears through the skylight. He cannot see* MRS. KEENEY.)

MATE. (*in great excitement*) Whales, sir—a whole school of 'em—off the star'b'd quarter 'bout five miles away—big ones!

KEENEY. (*galvanized into action*) Are you lowerin' the boats?

MATE. Yes, sir.

KEENEY. (*with grim decision*) I'm acomin' with ye.

MATE. Aye, aye, sir. (*Jubilantly*) You'll git the ile now right enough, sir. (*His head is withdrawn and he can be heard shouting orders.*)

KEENEY. (*turning to his wife*) Annie! Did you hear him? I'll git the ile. (*She doesn't answer or seem to know he is there. He gives a hard laugh, which is almost a groan*) I know you're foolin' me, Annie. You ain't out of your mind— (*anxiously*) be you? I'll git the ile now right enough—jest a little while longer, Annie—then we'll turn hom'ard. I can't turn back now, you see that, don't ye? I've got to git the ile. (*In sudden terror*) Answer me! You ain't mad, be you? (*She keeps on playing the organ, but makes no reply. The* MATE'S *face appears again though the skylight.*)

MATE. All ready, sir. (KEENEY *turns his back on his wife and strides to the doorway, where he stands for a moment and looks back at her in anguish, fighting to control his feelings.*)

MATE. Comin', sir?

KEENEY. (*his face suddenly grown hard with determination*) Aye. (*He turns abruptly and goes out.* MRS. KEENEY *does not appear to notice his departure. Her whole attention seems centered in the organ. She sits with half-closed eyes, her body swaying a little from side to side to the rhythm of the hymn. Her fingers move faster and faster and she is playing wildly and discordantly as the curtain falls.*)

Langston Hughes

When Langston Hughes (1902–1967) traveled to Africa in 1923 on board the freighter West Hesseltine *(referred to in his memoir* The Big Sea *as the* Malone*), he felt exhilarated at the prospect of adventure in the merchant marine. Though not without excitement, the voyage soon tempered Hughes' youthful illusions with the realities of seagoing life. The crew was undisciplined and verged on mutiny from almost the moment the ship left New York; passengers and crew were in constant conflict. A seaman was left behind at Horta in the Azores, and on their first shore leave the men of the* West Hesseltine *were involved in a ferocious fight with British sailors of a rival freighter. The* West Hesseltine *traveled along the coast of West Africa, stopping at Dakar, Freetown, and Accra; in Lagos for a week, Hughes walked the streets with Hausa, Ibo, Fulani, and Yoruba tribesmen. When the ship cruised up the Congo, Hughes saw the brutality of Belgian colonial rule; the inland town of Matadi presented "the saddest lot of Negro workers seen in Africa." Hughes' experiences as a sailor were the basis for a series of poems in his first book,* The Weary Blues *(1926).*

from *The Big Sea*

from *Beyond Sandy Hook*

MELODRAMATIC maybe, it seems to me now. But then it was like throwing a million bricks out of my heart when I threw the books into the water. I leaned over the rail of the S.S. *Malone* and threw the books as far as I could out into the sea—all the books I had had at Columbia, and all the books I had lately bought to read.

The books went down into the moving water in the dark off Sandy Hook. Then I straightened up, turned my face to the wind, and took a deep breath. I was a seaman going to sea for the first time—a seaman on a big merchant ship. And I felt that nothing would ever happen to me again that I didn't want to happen. I felt grown, a man, inside and out. Twenty-one.

I was twenty-one.

Four bells sounded. As I stood there, whiffs of salt spray blew in my face. The afterdeck was deserted. The big hatches were covered with canvas. The booms were all tied up to the masts, and the winches silent. It was dark. The old freighter, smelling of crude oil and garbage, engines pounding, rolled through the pitch-black night. I looked down on deck and noticed that one of my books had fallen into the scupper. The last book. I picked it up and threw it far over the rail into the water below, that was too black to see. The wind caught the book and ruffled its pages quickly, then let it fall into the rolling darkness. I think it was a book by H. L. Mencken.

You see, books had been happening to me. Now the books were cast off back there somewhere in the churn of spray and night behind the propeller. I was glad they were gone.

I went up on the poop and looked over the railing toward New York. But New York was gone, too. There were no longer any lights to be seen. The wind smelt good. I was sleepy, so I went down a pair of narrow steps that ended just in front of our cabin—the mess boys' cabin.

Inside the hot cabin, George lay stark naked in a lower bunk, talking and laughing and gaily waving his various appendages around. Above him in the upper bunk, two chocolate-colored Puerto Rican feet stuck out from one end of a snow-white sheet, and a dark Puerto Rican head from the other. It was clear that Ramon in the upper bunk didn't understand more than every tenth word of George's Kentucky vernacular, but he kept on laughing every time George laughed—and that was often.

George was talking about women, of course. He said he didn't care if his Harlem landlady pawned all his clothes, the old witch! When he got back from Africa, he would get some more. He might even pay her the month's back rent he owed her, too. Maybe. Or else—and here he waved one of his appendages around—she could have what he had in his hand.

Puerto Rico, who understood all the bad words in every language, laughed loudly. We all laughed. You couldn't help it. George was so good-natured and comical you couldn't keep from laughing with him—or at him. He always made everybody laugh—even when the food ran out on the return trip and everybody was hungry and mad.

Then it was ten o'clock, on a June night, on the S.S. *Malone*, and we were going to Africa. At ten o'clock that morning I had never heard of the S.S. *Malone*, or George, or Ramon, or anybody else in its crew of forty-two men. Nor any of the six passengers. But now, here were the three of us laughing very loudly, going to Africa.

I had got my job at a New York shipping office. Ramon got his job at another shipping office. But George just simply walked on board about supper time. A Filipino pantry boy got mad and quit at the last moment. Naturally, the steward didn't want to sail short-handed. He saw George hanging around the entrance to the pier, watching the stevedores finish loading. The Filipino steward said: "Hey, colored boy! You, there! You want a job?" And George said: "Yes," so he walked on board, with nothing but a shirt and a pair of overalls to his back, and sailed.

Now, he lay there in his bunk, laughing about his landlady. He said she intended to put him out if he didn't find a job. And now that he had found a job, he wouldn't be able to tell her for six months. He wondered if she knew Africa was six months away from Harlem.

"*Largo viaje*," said Ramon.

George commented in pig-Latin—which was the only "foreign" language he knew.

I might as well tell you now what George and Ramon were like. Everybody knew all about George long before we reached the coast of Africa. But nobody ever knew much about Ramon.

George was from Kentucky. He had worked around race horses. And he spoke of several white gentlemen out of his past as "Colonel." We were all about the same age, George, Ramon, and I.

After Kentucky, George had worked in a scrap-iron yard in St. Louis. But he said the work wasn't good for his back, so he quit. He went and got a job in a restaurant near the station in

Springfield, Illinois, washing dishes. A female impersonator came through with a show and took George with him as his valet. George said he got tired of being maid to the female impersonator, so as soon as he got a new suit of clothes, he quit in Pittsburgh. He found a good job in a bowling alley, but had a fight with a man who hit him with one of the balls because he set the pins up wrong. George claimed he won the fight. But he lit out for South Street in Philadelphia to avoid arrest. And after that, Harlem.

George had a thousand tales to tell about every town he'd ever been in. And several versions of each tale. No doubt, some of the stories were true—and some of them not true at all, but they sounded true. Sometimes George said he had relatives down South. Then, again, he said he didn't have anybody in the whole world. Both versions concerning his relatives were probably correct. If he did have relatives they didn't matter—lying there as he was now, laughing and talking in his narrow bunk on a hot night, going to Africa.

But Ramon of the upper bunk didn't talk much, in English or Spanish. He simply did his work in the morning. Then he got in bed and slept all the afternoon till time to set up the sailors' mess hall for supper. After supper, he got in bed again and laughed at George until George went to sleep

Ramon told us once that his mother was a seamstress in Ponce. Ernesto, the Puerto Rican sailor aboard, said "seamstress" was just another name for something else. Anyhow, Ramon was decent enough as a cabin mate, and practically always asleep. He didn't gamble. I saw him drunk only once. He seldom drew any money, and when he did he spent it on sweets—seldom on a woman. The only thing that came out of his mouth in six months that I remember is that he said he didn't care much for women, anyway. He preferred silk stockings—so halfway down the African coast, he bought a pair of silk stockings and slept with them under his pillow.

George, however, was always saying things the like of which you never heard before or since, making up fabulous jokes, playing pranks, and getting in on all the card games or fights aboard. George and I became pretty good pals. He could tap dance a little, shuffle a lot, and knew plenty of blues. He said he could play a guitar, but no one on the *Malone* possessed a guitar, so we never knew.

I had the petty officers' mess to take care of and their staterooms to make up. There was nothing hard about a mess boy's work. You got up at six in the morning, with the mid-Atlantic calm as a sun-pool, served breakfast, made up the rooms, served luncheon, had all the afternoon off, served dinner, and that was all. The rest of the time you could lie on deck in the sun, play cards with the sailors, or sleep. When your clothes were dirty, you washed them in a bucket of soapsuds and lye. The lye made the washing easy because it took all of the dirt out quick.

When we got to Africa we took on a full African crew to supplement the regular crew who weren't supposed to be able to stand the sun. Then I had an African boy to do my washing, my cleaning, and almost all my work—as did everybody on board. The Africans stood both work and sun without difficulty, it seems.

Going over, it was a nice trip, warm, calm, the sea blue-green by day, gold-green at sunset. And at night phosphorescent stars in the water where the prow cut a rift of sparkling foam.

The S.S. *Malone* had been built during the war. It was a big, creaking, old freight boat, two or three years in the African trade now. It had cabins for a half dozen passengers. This trip the passengers were all Nordic missionaries—but one. That one was a colored tailor, a Garveyite who had long worshipped Africa from afar, and who had a theory of civilization all his own. He thought that if he could just teach the Africans to wear proper clothes, coats and pants, they would be brought forward a long way toward the standards of our world. To that end, he carried with him on his journey numberless bolts of cloth, shears, and tailoring tools, and a trunk full of smart patterns. The missionaries carried Bibles and hymnbooks. The Captain carried invoices and papers having to do with trade. We sailors carried nothing but ourselves.

At Horta, our only port of call in the Azores, we anchored at sea some distance from the rocky shore. Everybody went ashore in rowboats or motor launches. Some of the boys made straight for women, some for the wine shops. It depended on your temperament which you sought first. Nobody had much money, because the Captain didn't permit a draw. I had an American dollar, so George and I bought a big bottle of cognac, walked up a hill to the top of the town, and drank it. The sun was setting. The sea and the palm trees and the roofs of Horta were aglow. On the way down the hill in the amber dusk, George smashed the cognac bottle against the wall of a blue house and said: "I wants to holler."

"George, don't holler right here on the main street," I cautioned.

George said: "This town's too small to holler in, but I got to holler, anyhow." And he let out a tremendous "Yee-hoo-oo-o!" that sent children rushing to their mothers' arms and women scurrying into doorways. But a sleepy-looking cop, leaning against a wall with a lantern, must have been used to the ways of sailors, because he paid George no mind. In fact, he didn't even stir as we went on to the center of the village, where there were lots of people and lights.

We came across the bo'sun and some sailors in a bar, emptying their pockets, trying to get enough together to pay for a round of drinks that Slim—who didn't have a penny—had ordered for all. I had four cents to contribute. Chips had a quarter. But, all told, it didn't make enough to pay for the drinks, so the bartender said they should give him the rest when the S.S. *Malone* came back to Horta in five months. So everybody agreed they would settle then. Whereupon, the bartender set up another round of drinks for nothing.

The *Malone*'s whistle began to blow. The bo'sun said: "Come on, you bloody so-and-so's, the Old Man's calling you!" We went down to the wharf. Some other boys were there. An Irish kid from Brooklyn and his cousin had two girls on their arms, and the wireless man, Sparks, was in the middle between the two girls. Sparks said they were the best two girls in town and that he always traded with them. The Irish kid said his was the best girl he ever had.

His cousin said: "Aw, nuts! You never had one before!" (The Irish kid was just out of high school and this was his first trip to sea. He looked like a choirboy, except that he couldn't sing.) We waited for the launch that we had paid to take us back. Finally it came. At seven bells we went on toward Africa, the engines chugging soft and serene.

The next day was Sunday and the missionaries wanted everybody to come to prayers in the saloon, but nobody went except the Captain and the Chief Mate. The bo'sun said he'd go if the missionaries had any communion wine, but the missionaries didn't have any, so he didn't go.

When we got to Teneriffe, in the Canary Islands, it was mid-afternoon and very bright. The Canaries looked like fairy islands, all sharp peaks of red rock and bright sandy beaches and little green fields dropped like patchwork between the beaches and the rocks, with the sea making a blue-white fringe around.

The Captain let us draw money—so Las Palmas seemed a gay city indeed. Ashore, three or four of us, including Ernesto and a Norwegian boy named Sven, had supper at a place with very bright lights, where they served huge platters of delicious mixed fish with big bottles of cool, white wine. Then we all went to a white villa by the sea, called *El Palacio de Amor* and stayed all night. In the morning very early, when the sun was just coming up, we drove back to the wharf in an open carriage. We kept thinking about the girls, who were Spanish, and very young and pretty. And Sven said he would like to take one of them with him.

But all those days I was waiting anxiously to see Africa. And finally, when I saw the dust-green hills in the sunlight, something took hold of me inside. My Africa, Motherland of the Negro peoples! And me a Negro! Africa! The real thing, to be touched and seen, not merely read about in a book.

That first morning when we sighted the coast, I kept leaving my work to lean over the rail and look at Africa, dim and far away, off on the horizon in a haze of light, then gradually nearer and nearer, until you could see the color of the foliage on the trees.

We put in at the port of Dakar. There were lots of Frenchmen, and tall black Senegalese soldiers in red fezes, and Mohammedans in robes, so that at first you couldn't tell if the Mohammedans were men or women.

The next day we moved on. And farther down the coast it was more like the Africa I had dreamed about—wild and lovely, the people dark and beautiful, the palm trees tall, the sun bright, and the rivers deep. The great Africa of my dreams!

* * *

from *S. S. "Malone"*

The poor missionaries on our boat, the passengers, were in a state of continual distress. They declared the ship unsafe, and they were glad, when they came to their respective ports, to get off. Later, we learned, they wrote irate letters back to the New York office, disclosing in full the gaily mutinous state of things aboard the S.S. *Malone*. They said they would never sail on that line again. Some even threatened to sue the company. Others wrote their congressmen.

On the surface, the missionaries seemed to be nice, stout, white folks from places like Iowa and Vermont, but, naturally, they didn't like all the excitement of a drunken crew, oily decks, riotous nights, and a host of naked Africans—our extra helpers—bathing nude beneath a salt-water hose every evening on the afterdeck in plain sight of everybody. The Africans were very polite, however—more so than the Nordics—and, respecting the missionaries, they turned their backs and hid their sex between their legs, evidently not realizing it then stuck out behind.

They were of the Kru tribe, those Africans. And they proved very useful, working, loading, and cleaning all day long. They had one very dangerous job. They had to load the mahogany logs. These logs, some of them weighing tons, were dragged by human beings driven like mules, from the forests to the beaches. There they were floated out to our ship, at anchor offshore. Bouncing and bobbing in the waves, they had to be secured with great iron chains so that the cranes could lift them into the hold of the ship. To chain them was the job!

A dozen black Kru boys would dive into the water, swimming under and about the log until the chains were tight around the great bobbing hulk of wood. If a boy was caught between the floating black logs, or between a log and the ship, death would often result. Or if the sharks came, death would come, too. Watching them, I had somewhat the same feeling I had had in Mexico, watching Sanchez Mejias turning his red cape so gracefully before a bull's horns. It was beautiful and dangerous work, those black boys swimming there in the tossing waves among the iron chains and the great rolling logs, that would perhaps someday be somebody's grand piano or chest of drawers made of wood and life, energy and death out of Africa.

The colored tailor got off at Lagos, a largely Mohammedan city, peopled with Hausas in flowing robes and colored turbans, Fulani, and Yorubas. (Years later, by accident, I ran into that same tailor in Washington and he said he had had no luck at all selling suits to Africans.)

When we got to Loanda, we began to pick up passengers for the return trip. All the way up and down the coast, we carried deck passengers from one port to another, natives. Once, on a windy day when the surf was high off some French African Village, whose name I have forgotten, a rowboat came out for the debarking passengers, but no one landed. The boat went back empty. Our whistle sounded and we continued our voyage.

Two days later, down the coast, when we came to our next port of call, a little family of Africans who had been travelling on deck came to the gangplank to go ashore. But the English inspector found that their papers called for a French colony, not a British one. They should have got off at the last stop. The father said they couldn't have got off there because the surf was too high to go ashore, and he did not wish to risk his family in the rowboat that came out to get them. The African said they would get off here in the British colony and walk back.

The inspector would not let them off. He sent for the Captain, who came fuming down from the bridge, very wroth at all the trouble this barefooted little family of Africans was causing him. Angrily, he raised his cane to strike them, but they ran. The Captain, looking like the father of the Katzenjammer Kids, very fat and German in his white suit, chased them half-way around the deck. But the Africans were so fleet of foot that they did not feel a single blow of his cane, because they ran too fast, man, wife, and offspring, like deer.

It looked very funny—this chase—and I wanted to laugh, but somehow I couldn't laugh, because it is too much like today's Africa, real, beyond humor—the raised club, the commanding white man, and the frightened native.

Somehow, it was arranged with the officials for the little black family to get off in that strange English colony, where the surf was not so high, and to walk back the two or three hundred miles that they had come beyond their destination.

I never had a session with the Captain. In fact, he never said a word to me the whole trip except, when money was being issued, the customary: "How much?"

And all I ever said to him was: "A pound, sir," each time.

I had had no reason to be called before the Captain, because I never acted any worse than the rest of the crew. And, although it was a pretty tough crew, I got along fine with everybody but the Third Engineer.

The Third Engineer was from Arkansas, the same State, strangely enough, as the lady who had taken my English classes in Mexico. He was tall, sallow of complexion, and very dour. Nobody liked him. The Filipinos hated him. He frequently made unkind remarks about spicks and niggers, but he ate in my mess room, so I had to look at him three times a day, sitting at the table.

In my mess room, I had also to feed the customs inspectors, the cargo clerks, and whatever local harbor officials came aboard in the various ports. These persons were almost always Negroes, often Africans who had been to England or

France to school. They were usually very quiet, educated, and decent black fellows. When all my petty officers were fed, they would come in and eat at the second sitting. I enjoyed waiting on them, and talking to them, if they spoke English.

Deliberately, I think, the Third Engineer would often be late to meals when we were in port, since he knew I had to feed the clerks and port officials. One day, everyone had eaten on my mess list but the Third Engineer. I waited nearly an hour for him to come to luncheon. Then I asked the steward what to do. The steward said: "Call in the customs men and the clerks."

They were entirely Negroes that day, Africans in European clothes, four or five of them, very clean and courteous in their white duck suits. They were in the midst of their meal at the single long table, when the Third Engineer came in.

He ordered: "Get these niggers out of here. I haven't eaten yet."

I said: "You can eat with them if you like. Or I'll serve you afterwards."

"I don't eat with niggers," he said. "And you know damn well an officer don't have to wait for no coons to be fed." He turned on the startled Africans. "Get out of here!" he shouted.

"You get out of here yourself," I said, reaching for the big metal soup tureen on the steam table.

The Third Engineer was a big fellow, and I couldn't fight him barehanded, so I raised the tureen, ready to bring it down on his head.

"I'll report you to the Captain, you black—!"

"Go ahead, you —— and double—!" I said, raising the soup tureen. He went. The Africans finished their meal in peace.

That afternoon I visited the Chief Steward, a grave little Filipino, and told him I would not wait on the Third Engineer any more. No, sir, under no circumstances! But the steward, who had plenty of troubles on his mind, such as an impending meat shortage and sailors who threw whole containers of food into the sea when they didn't like it, and missionaries who complained that the cooking wasn't what they had been used to at home in Iowa, and a German Captain who wanted nothing but sauerkraut—the steward said, forlornly: "Mess boy, in this my life things is not always easible. Sometimes hard like hell! I wish you please help me out and feed the Third."

So, because I liked the steward, I continued to serve the Third Engineer for the rest of the trip, and he continued to come as late as he could for meals when we were in port and he knew that there were Negroes to follow him in the mess hall. But he kept quiet and never referred to the day of the soup tureen.

Marianne Moore

"The sea is a collector," wrote Marianne Moore (1887–1972) in her poem "A Grave." In "The Fish," first published in 1918, Moore renders the profusion of undersea life with her characteristic detachment and attentiveness. However precise, the poem is also alert to the less tangible presence of the ocean, its unseen essence of force and motion. Out of the immediacy of the aquatic world emerges a vision of the sea in all its battered, timeless grandeur.

The Fish

Wade
through black jade
Of the crow-blue mussel shells, one
keeps
adjusting the ash heaps;
opening and shutting itself like

an
injured fan.
The barnacles which encrust the
side
of the wave, cannot hide
there for the submerged shafts of the

sun,
split like spun
glass, move themselves with spotlight swiftness
into the crevices—
in and out, illuminating

the
turquoise sea
of bodies. The water drives a

wedge
of iron through the iron edge
of the cliff, whereupon the stars,

pink
rice grains, ink
bespattered jelly-fish, crabs like
green
lilies and submarine
toadstools, slide each on the other.

All
external
marks of abuse are present on
this
defiant edifice—
all the physical features of

ac-
cident—lack
of cornice, dynamite grooves, burns
and
hatchet strokes, these things stand
out on it; the chasm side is

dead.
Repeated
evidence has proved that it can
live
on what cannot revive
its youth. The sea grows old in it.

Henry Beston

In September 1926, Henry Beston (1888–1968) moved into a two-room cabin that he had built for himself the year before on Cape Cod's Great Beach. Although he had planned to stay for two weeks, Beston was so impressed by his surroundings that he remained in his solitary house for a full year, writing the journals that became The Outermost House *(1928), from which the following chapter is taken. Like those of his predecessor Thoreau, Beston's descriptions of nature are striking for their blend of attentive observation and reflection; later nature writers, most notably Rachel Carson and John Hay, have claimed him as an influence. Beston also wrote two books based on his experiences in World War I (which included a stint with the U.S. submarine service), numerous children's books, and a study of the St. Lawrence River. In 1964 his cabin was declared a National Literary Landmark, but it was destroyed by a hurricane in 1978.*

The Headlong Wave

I

This morning I am going to try my hand at something that I do not recall ever having encountered either in a periodical or in a book, namely, a chapter on the ways, the forms, and the sounds of ocean near a beach. Friends are forever asking me about the surf on the great beach and if I am not sometimes troubled or haunted by its sound. To this I reply that I have grown unconscious of the roar, and though it sounds all day long in my waking ears, and all night long in my sleeping ones, my ears seldom send on the long tumult to the mind. I hear the roar the instant I wake in the morning and return to consciousness, I listen to it a while consciously, and then accept and forget it; I hear it during the day only when I stop again to listen, or when some change in the nature of the sound breaks through my acceptance of it to my curiosity.

They say here that great waves reach this coast in threes. Three great waves, then an indeterminate run of lesser rhythms, then three great waves again. On Celtic coasts it is the seventh wave that is seen coming like a king out of the grey, cold sea. The Cape tradition, however, is no half-real, half-mystical fancy, but the truth itself. Great waves do indeed approach this beach by threes. Again and again have I watched three giants roll in one after the other out of the Atlantic, cross the outer bar, break, form again, and follow each other in to fulfilment and destruction on this solitary beach. Coast guard crews are all well aware of this triple rhythm and take advantage of the lull that follows the last wave to launch their boats.

It is true that there are single giants as well. I have been roused by them in the night. Waked by their tremendous and unexpected crash, I have sometimes heard the last of the heavy overspill, sometimes only the loud, withdrawing roar. After the roar came a briefest pause, and after the pause the return of ocean to the night's long cadences. Such solitary titans, flinging their green tons down upon a quiet world, shake beach and dune. Late one September night, as I sat reading, the very father of all waves must have flung himself down before the house, for the quiet of the night was suddenly overturned by a gigantic, tumbling crash and an earthquake rumbling; the beach trembled beneath the avalanche, the dune shook, and my house so shook in its dune that the flame of a lamp quivered and pictures jarred on the wall.

The three great elemental sounds in nature are the sound of rain, the sound of wind in a primeval wood, and the sound of outer ocean on a beach. I have heard them all, and of the three elemental voices, that of ocean is the most awesome, beautiful, and varied. For it is a mistake to talk of the monotone of ocean or of the monotonous nature of its sound. The sea has many voices. Listen to the surf, really lend it your ears, and you will hear in it a world of sounds: hollow boomings and heavy roarings, great watery tumblings and tramplings, long hissing seethes, sharp, rifle-shot reports, splashes, whispers, the grinding undertone of stones, and sometimes vocal sounds that might be the half-heard talk of people in the sea. And not only is the great sound varied in the manner of its making, it is also constantly changing its tempo, its pitch, its accent, and its rhythm, being now loud and thundering, now almost placid, now furious, now grave and solemn-slow, now a simple measure, now a rhythm monstrous with a sense of purpose and elemental will.

Every mood of the wind, every change in the day's weather, every phase of the tide—all these have subtle sea musics all their own. Surf of the ebb, for instance, is one music, surf of the flood another, the change in the two musics being most clearly marked during the first hour of a rising tide. With the renewal of the tidal energy, the sound of the surf grows louder, the fury of battle returns to it as it turns again on the land, and beat and sound change with the renewal of the war.

Sound of surf in these autumnal dunes—the continuousness of it, sound of endless charging, endless incoming and gathering, endless fulfilment and dissolution, endless fecundity, and endless death. I have been trying to study out the mechanics of that mighty resonance. The dominant note is the great spilling crash made by each arriving wave. It may be hollow and booming, it may be heavy and churning, it may be a tumbling roar. The second fundamental sound is the wild seething cataract roar of the wave's dissolution and the rush of its foaming waters up the beach—this second sound *diminuendo*. The third fundamental sound is the endless dissolving hiss of the inmost slides of foam. The first two sounds reach the ear as a unisonance—the booming impact of the tons of water and the wild roar of the up-rush blending—and this mingled sound dissolves into the foam-bubble hissing of the third. Above the tumult, like birds, fly wisps of watery noise, splashes and counter splashes, whispers, seethings, slaps, and chucklings. An overtone sound of other breakers, mingled with a general rumbling, fells earth and sea and air.

Here do I pause to warn my reader that although I have recounted the history of a breaker—an ideal breaker—the surf process must be understood as mingled and continuous, waves hurrying after waves, interrupting waves, washing back on waves, overwhelming waves. Moreover, I have described the sound of a high surf in fair weather. A storm surf is mechanically the same thing, but it *grinds*, and this same long, sepulchral grinding—sound of utter terror to all mariners—is a development of the second fundamental sound; it is the cry of the breaker water roaring its way ashore and dragging at the sand. A strange underbody of sound when heard through the high, wild screaming of a gale.

Breaking waves that have to run up a steep tilt of the beach are often followed by a dragging, grinding sound—the note of the baffled water running downhill again to the sea. It is loudest when the tide is low and breakers are rolling beach stones up and down a slope of the lower beach.

I am, perhaps, most conscious of the sound of surf just after I have gone to bed. Even here I read myself to drowsiness, and, reading, I hear the cadenced trampling roar filling all the dark. So close is the Fo'castle to the ocean's edge that the rhythm of sound I hear oftenest in fair weather is not so much a general tumult as an endless arrival, overspill, and dissolution of separate great seas. Through the dark, mathematic square of the screened half window, I listen to the rushes and the bursts, the tramplings, and the long, intermingled thunderings, never wearying of the sonorous and universal sound.

Away from the beach, the various sounds of the surf melt into one great thundering symphonic roar. Autumnal nights in Eastham village are full of this ocean sound. The "summer people" have gone, the village rests and prepares for winter, lamps shine from kitchen windows, and from across the moors, the great levels of the marsh, and the bulwark of the dunes resounds the long wintry roaring of the sea. Listen to it a while, and it will seem but one remote and formidable sound; listen still longer and you will discern in it a symphony of breaker thunderings, an endless, distant, elemental cannonade. There is beauty in it, and ancient terror. I heard it last as I walked through the village on a starry October night; there was no wind, the leafless trees were still, all the village was abed, and the whole sombre world was awesome with the sound.

II

The seas are the heart's blood of the earth. Plucked up and kneaded by the sun and the moon, the tides are systole and diastole of earth's veins.

The rhythm of waves beats in the sea like a pulse in living flesh. It is pure force, forever embodying itself in a succession of watery shapes which vanish on its passing.

I stand on my dune top watching a great wave coursing in from sea, and know that I am watching an illusion, that the distant water has not left its place in ocean to advance upon me, but only a force shaped in water, a bodiless pulse beat, a vibration.

Consider the marvel of what we see. Somewhere in ocean, perhaps a thousand miles and more from this beach, the pulse beat of earth liberates a vibration, an ocean wave. Is the original force circular, I wonder? and do ocean waves ring out from the creative beat as they do on a quiet surface broken by a stone? Are there, perhaps, ocean circles so great and so intricate that they are unperceived? Once created, the wave or the arc of a wave begins its journey through the sea. Countless vibrations precede it, countless vibrations follow after. It approaches the continent, swings into the coast line, courses ashore, breaks, dissolves, is gone. The innermost waters it last inhabited flow back in marbly foam to become a body to another beat, and to be again flung down. So it goes night and day, and will go till the secret heart of earth strikes out its last slow beat and the last wave dissolves upon the last forsaken shore.

As I stand on my dune top, however, I do not think of the illusion and the beat of earth, for I watch the waves with my outer rather than my inner eye. After all, the illusion is set off by an extraordinary, an almost miraculous thing—the embodiment of the wave beat in an almost constant shape. We see a wave a quarter of a mile off, then a few hundred yards nearer in, then just offshore; we seem to have been watching the same travelling mass of water—there has been no appreciable change in mass or in shape—yet all the while the original beat has taken on a flowing series of liquid bodies, bodies so alike, so much the same, that our eye will individualize them and follow them in—the third wave, we say, or the second wave behind the great wave. How strange it is that this beat of earth, this mysterious undulation of the seas, moving through and among the other forces stirring the waters close off the continent, should thus keep its constancy of form and mass, and how odd a blend of illusion and reality it all is! On the whole, the outer eye has the best of it.

Blowing all day long, a northwest wind yesterday swept the sky clear of every tatter and wisp of cloud. Clear it still is, though the wind has shifted to the east. The sky this afternoon is a harmony of universal blue, bordered with a surf rim of snowiest blue-white. Far out at sea, in the northeast and near the horizon, is a pool of the loveliest blue I have ever seen here —a light blue, a petal blue, blue of the emperor's gown in a Chinese fairy tale. If you would see waves at their best, come on such a day, when the ocean reflects a lovely sky, and the wind is light and onshore; plan to arrive in the afternoon so that you will have the sun facing the breakers. Come early, for the glints on the waves are most beautiful and interesting when the light is oblique and high. And come with a rising tide.

The surf is high, and on the far side of it, a wave greater than its fellows is shouldering out of the blue, glinting immensity of sea.

Friends tell me that there are certain tropic beaches where waves miles long break all at once in one cannonading crash: a little of this, I imagine, would be magnificent; a constancy of it, unbearable. The surf here is broken; it approaches the beach in long intercurrent parallels, some a few hundred feet long, some an eighth of a mile long, some, and the longest, attaining the quarter-mile length and perhaps just over. Thus, at all times and instants of the day, along the five miles of beach visible from the Fo'castle deck, waves are to be seen breaking, coursing in to break, seething up and sliding back.

But to return to the blue wave rolling in out of the blue spaciousness of sea. On the other side of the world, just opposite the Cape, lies the ancient Spanish province of Galicia, and the town of Pontevedra and St. James Compostella, renowned of pilgrims. (When I was there they offered me a silver cockle shell, but I would have none of it, and got myself a sea shell from some Galician fisherfolk.) Somewhere between this Spanish land and Cape Cod the pulse of earth has engendered this wave and sent it coursing westward through the seas. Far off the coast, the spray of its passing has, perhaps, risen on the windward bow of some rusty freighter and fallen in rainbow drops upon her plates; the great liners have felt it course beneath their keels.

A continent rises in the west, and the pulse beat approaches this bulwark of Cape Cod. Two thirds of a mile out, the wave is still a sea vibration, a billow. Slice it across, and its outline will be that of a slightly flattened semicircle; the pulse is shaped in a long, advancing mound. I watch it approach the beach. Closer and closer in, it is rising with the rise of the beach and the shoaling of the water; closer still, it is changing from a mound to a pyramid, a pyramid which swiftly distorts, the seaward side lengthening, the landward side incurving—the wave is now a breaker. Along the ridge of blue forms a rippling crest of clear, bright water; a little spray flies off. Under the racing foam churned up by the dissolution of other breakers the beach now catches at the last shape of sea inhabited by the pulse—the wave is *tripped* by the shoaling sand—the giant stumbles, crashes, and is pushed over and ahead by the sloping line of force behind. The fall of a breaker is never the work of gravity alone.

It is the last line of the wave that has captured the decorative imagination of the world—the long seaward slope, the curling crest, the incurved volute ahead.

Toppling over and hurled ahead, the wave crashes, its mass of glinting blue falling down in a confusion of seething, splendid white, the tumbling water rebounding from the sand to a height almost always a little above that of the original crest. Out of the wild, crumbling confusion born of the dissolution of the force and the last great shape, foamy fountains spurt, and ringlets of spray. The mass of water, still all furiously a-churn and seething white, now rushes for the rim of the beach as it might for an inconceivable cataract. Within thirty-five feet the water shoals from two feet to dry land. The edge of the rush thins, and the last impulse disappears in inch-deep slides of foam which reflect the sky in one last moment of energy and beauty and then vanish all at once into the sands.

Another thundering, and the water that has escaped and withdrawn is gathered up and swept forward again by another breaking wave. Night and day, age after age, so works the sea, with infinite variation obeying an unalterable rhythm moving through an intricacy of chance and law.

I can watch a fine surf for hours, taking pleasure in all its wild plays and variations. I like to stand on my beach, watching a long wave start breaking in many places, and see the curling water run north and south from the several beginnings, and collide in furious white pyramids built of the opposing energies. Splendid fountains often delight the eye. A towering and deep-bellied wave, toppling, encloses in its volute a quantity of air, and a few seconds after the spill this prisoned and compressed vapour bursts up through the boiling rush in feathery, foamy jets and geyser plumes. I have seen fountains here, on a September day, twenty and twenty-five and even thirty feet high. Sometimes a curious thing happens. Instead of escaping vertically, the rolled-up air escapes horizontally, and the breaker suddenly blows, as from a dragon's mouth, a great lateral puff of steamy spray. On sunny days, the toppling crest is often mirrored in the glassy volute as the wave is breaking. One lovely autumn afternoon, I saw a beautiful white gull sailing along the volute of a breaker accompanied by his reflection in the wave.

I add one curious effect of the wind. When the wind is directly offshore or well offshore, the waves approach fighting it; when the wind is offshore but so little off that its angle with the coast line is oblique—say an angle never greater than twenty-two degrees and never less than about twelve—the waves that approach the coast do not give battle, but run in with their long axis parallel to the wind. Sitting in the Fo'castle, I can often tell the exact quarter of an offshore wind simply by looking at this oblique alignment of the waves.

The long miles of beach are never more beautiful than when waves are rolling in fighting a strong breeze. Then do the breakers actually seem to charge the coast. As they approach, the wind meets them in a shock of war, the chargers rear but go on, and the wind blows back their manes. North and south, I watch them coursing in, the manes of white, sun brilliant spray streaming behind them for thirty and even forty feet. Sea horses do men call such waves on every coast of the world. If you would see them at their best, come to this beach on a bright October day when a northwest wind is billowing off to sea across the moors.

III

I will close my chapter with a few paragraphs about heavy surf.

It is best to be seen, I think, when the wind is not too high. A gale blows up a surf, but it also flattens out the incoming rollers, making monstrous, foamy travelling mounds of them much like those visible from a ship at sea. Not until the wind has dropped do the breakers gather form. The finest surf I have ever seen here—it was a Northern recoil of the great Florida hurricane—broke on three pleasant and almost windless autumn days. The storm itself had passed us, but our seas had been stirred to their deeps. Returning to the Cape at night from a trip to town, I heard the roar of the ocean in Orleans, and on arriving at Nauset, found the beach flooded to the dunes, and covered with a churn of surf and moonlight. Dragging a heavy suitcase and clad in my go-to-town clothes, I had an evil time getting to the Fo'castle over the dune tops and along the flooded marsh.

Many forces mingle in the surf of a storm—the great earth rhythm of the waves, the violence of wind, the struggle of water to obey its own elemental law. Out of the storm at sea come the giants and, being giants, trip far out, spilling first on the outer bar. Shoreward then they rush, breaking all the way. Touching the beach, they tumble in a roar lost in a general noise of storm. Trampled by the wind and everlastingly moved and lifted up and flung down by the incoming seas, the water offshore becomes a furious glassiness of marbly foam; wild, rushing sheets of seethe fifty feet wide border it; the water streams with sand.

Under all this move furious tidal currents, the longshore undertow of outer Cape Cod. Shore currents here move in a southerly direction; old wreckage and driftwood is forever being carried down here from the north. Coast guard friends often look at a box or stick I have retrieved, and say, "Saw that two weeks ago up by the light."

After an easterly, I find things on the beach which have been blown down from the Gulf of Maine—young, uprooted spruce trees, lobster buoys from Matinicus, and, after one storm, a great strewing of empty sea-urchin shells. Another easterly washed up a strewing of curious wooden pebbles shaped by the sea out of the ancient submerged forests which lie just off the present coast. They were brown-black, shaped like beach stones, and as smooth as such stones.

The last creature I found in the surf was a huge horseshoe crab, the only one I have ever chanced to find on the outside. Poor *Limulus polyphemus*! The surf having turned him upside down, he had as usual doubled up, and the surf had then filled with sand the angle of his doubling. When I discovered him, he was being bullied by a foam slide, and altogether in a desperate way. So I picked him up, rinsed the sand out of his waving gills, held him up all dripping by the tail, and flung him as far as I could to seaward of the breakers. A tiny splash, and I had seen the last of him, a moment more, and the surf had filled the hollow in which he had lain.

Autumnal easterlies and November tides having scoured from the beach its summer deeps of sand, the high seasonal tides now run clear across to the very foot of the dunes. Under this daily overflow of cold, the last of the tide-rim hoppers and foragers vanish from the beach. An icy wind blusters; I hear a dry tinkle of sand against my western wall; December nears, and winter closes in upon the coast.

HART CRANE

"'Cutty Sark,'" Hart Crane (1899–1932) explained to his patron Otto Kahn in a 1927 letter, "is a phantasy on the period of the whalers and clipper ships. . . . The form of the poem may seem erratic, but it is meant to present the hallucinations incident to rum-drinking in a South Street dive, as well as the lurch of a boat in heavy seas." The ships mentioned in the poem—which first appeared in the magazine Poetry *in 1927 and later became part of* The Bridge *(1930)—were real vessels in the China trade. ("Music still haunts their names," Crane wrote, "long after the wind has left their sails.") Crane did his share, too, of drinking in waterfront bars; he claimed to prefer the "society of vagabonds and sailors—who don't enjoy chit-chat" to that of his literary friends, and hoped to go to sea with Emil Opffer, a Danish merchant seaman with whom he had an intense live-in affair. On April 27, 1932, returning from a trip to Mexico aboard the* Orizaba, *Crane was drowned in the Caribbean, probably a suicide.*

Cutty Sark

O, the navies old and oaken,
O, the Temeraire no more!
—MELVILLE

I met a man in South Street, tall—
a nervous shark tooth swung on his chain.
His eyes pressed through green glass
—green glasses, or bar lights made them
so—
shine—
GREEN—
eyes—
stepped out—forgot to look at you
or left you several blocks away—

in the nickel-in-the-slot piano jogged
"Stamboul Nights"—weaving somebody's nickel—sang—

O Stamboul Rose—dreams weave the rose!

Murmurs of Leviathan he spoke,
and rum was Plato in our heads . . .

"It's S.S. *Ala*—Antwerp—now remember kid
to put me out at three she sails on time.
I'm not much good at time any more keep
weakeyed watches sometimes snooze—" his bony hands
got to beating time . . . "A whaler once—
I ought to keep time and get over it—I'm a
Democrat—I know what time it is—No
I don't want to know what time it is—that
damned white Arctic killed my time . . ."

O Stamboul Rose—drums weave—

"I ran a donkey engine down there on the Canal
in Panama—got tired of that—
then Yucatan selling kitchenware—beads—
have you seen Popocatepetl—birdless mouth
with ashes sifting down—?
and then the coast again . . ."

Rose of Stamboul O coral Queen—
teased remnants of the skeletons of cities—
and galleries, galleries of watergutted lava
snarling stone—green—drums—drown—

Sing!
"—that spiracle!" he shot a finger out the door . . .
"O life's a geyser—beautiful—my lungs—
No—I can't live on land—!"

I saw the frontiers gleaming of his mind;
or are there frontiers—running sands sometimes
running sands—somewhere—sands running . . .
Or they may start some white machine that sings.

Then you may laugh and dance the axletree—
steel—silver—kick the traces—and know—

ATLANTIS ROSE drums wreathe the rose,
the star floats burning in a gulf of tears
and sleep another thousand—
interminably
long since somebody's nickel—stopped—
playing—

A wind worried those wicker-neat lapels, the
swinging summer entrances to cooler hells . . .
Outside a wharf truck nearly ran him down
—he lunged up Bowery way while the dawn
was putting the Statue of Liberty out—that
torch of hers you know—

I started walking home across the Bridge . . .
. . . . .

Blithe Yankee vanities, turreted sprites, winged
British repartees, skil-
ful savage sea-girls
that bloomed in the spring—Heave, weave
those bright designs the trade winds drive . . .

Sweet opium and tea, Yo-ho!
Pennies for porpoises that bank the keel!
Fins whip the breeze around Japan!

Bright skysails ticketing the Line, wink round the Horn
to Frisco, Melbourne . . .
Pennants, parabolas—
clipper dreams indelible and ranging,
baronial white on lucky blue!

Perennial-*Cutty*-trophied-*Sark*!

Thermopylae, *Black Prince*, *Flying Cloud* through Sunda
—scarfed of foam, their bellies veered green esplanades,
locked in wind-humors, ran their eastings down;

at Java Head freshened the nip
(sweet opium and tea!)
and turned and left us on the lee . . .

Buntlines tusseling (91 days, 20 hours and anchored!)
Rainbow, *Leander*
(last trip a tragedy)—where can you be
Nimbus? and you rivals two—

a long tack keeping—

Taeping?
Ariel?

ERNEST HEMINGWAY

Ernest Hemingway (1899–1961) moved to Key West in early 1930, and discovered deep-sea fishing soon after. By 1934 he had bought his own boat—the 38-foot Pilar*—on board which he hosted dozens of friends both local and literary, and where he lived for a time. Hemingway's passion for the Keys and for his boat are recurrent themes in much of his writing, both journalism and fiction—most notably in* The Old Man and the Sea *(1952), "After the Storm" (first collected in* Winner Take Nothing *in 1933), and the unfinished novel* Islands in the Stream *(published posthumously in 1970).*

After the Storm

IT wasn't about anything, something about making punch, and then we started fighting and I slipped and he had me down kneeling on my chest and choking me with both hands like he was trying to kill me and all the time I was trying to get the knife out of my pocket to cut him loose. Everybody was too drunk to pull him off me. He was choking me and hammering my head on the floor and I got the knife out and opened it up; and I cut the muscle right across his arm and he let go of me. He couldn't have held on if he wanted to. Then he rolled and hung onto that arm and started to cry and I said:

"What the hell you want to choke me for?"

I'd have killed him. I couldn't swallow for a week. He hurt my throat bad.

Well, I went out of there and there were plenty of them with him and some came out after me and I made a turn and was down by the docks and I met a fellow and he said somebody killed a man up the street. I said "Who killed him?" and he said "I don't know who killed him but he's dead all right," and it was dark and there was water standing in the street and no lights and windows broke and boats all up in the town and trees blown down and everything all blown and I got a skiff and went out and found my boat where I had her inside of

Mango Key and she was all right only she was full of water. So I bailed her out and pumped her out and there was a moon but plenty of clouds and still plenty rough and I took it down along; and when it was daylight I was off Eastern Harbor.

Brother, that was some storm. I was the first boat out and you never saw water like that was. It was just as white as a lye barrel and coming from Eastern Harbor to Sou'west Key you couldn't recognize the shore. There was a big channel blown right out through the middle of the beach. Trees and all blown out and a channel cut through and all the water white as chalk and everything on it; branches and whole trees and dead birds, and all floating. Inside the keys were all the pelicans in the world and all kinds of birds flying. They must have gone inside there when they knew it was coming.

I lay at Sou'west Key a day and nobody came after me. I was the first boat out and I seen a spar floating and I knew there must be a wreck and I started out to look for her. I found her. She was a three-masted schooner and I could just see the stumps of her spars out of water. She was in too deep water and I didn't get anything off of her. So I went on looking for something else. I had the start on all of them and I knew I ought to get whatever there was. I went on down over the sand-bars from where I left that three-masted schooner and I didn't find anything and I went on a long way. I was way out toward the quicksands and I didn't find anything so I went on. Then when I was in sight of the Rebecca light I saw all kinds of birds making over something and I headed over for them to see what it was and there was a cloud of birds all right.

I could see something looked like a spar up out of the water and when I got over close the birds all went up in the air and stayed all around me. The water was clear out there and there was a spar of some kind sticking out just above the water and when I come up close to it I saw it was all dark under water like a long shadow and I came right over it and there under water was a liner; just lying there all under water as big as the whole world. I drifted over her in the boat. She lay on her side and the stern was deep down. The port holes were all shut tight and I could see the glass shine in the water and the whole of her; the biggest boat I ever saw in my life laying there and I went along the whole length of her and then I went over and anchored and I had the skiff on the deck forward and I shoved it down into the water and sculled over with the birds all around me.

I had a water glass like we use sponging and my hand shook so I could hardly hold it. All the port holes were shut that you could see going along over her but way down below near the bottom something must have been open because there were pieces of things floating out all the time. You couldn't tell what they were. Just pieces. That's what the birds were after. You never saw so many birds. They were all around me; crazy yelling.

I could see everything sharp and clear. I could see her rounded over and she looked a mile long under the water. She was lying on a clear white bank of sand and the spar was a sort of foremast or some sort of tackle that slanted out of water the way she was laying on her side. Her bow wasn't very far under. I could stand on the letters of her name on her bow and my head was just out of water. But the nearest port hole was twelve feet down. I could just reach it with the grains pole and I tried to break it with that but I couldn't. The glass was too stout. So I sculled back to the boat and got a wrench and lashed it to the end of the grains pole and I couldn't break it. There I was looking down through the glass at that liner with everything in her and I was the first one to her and I couldn't get into her. She must have had five million dollars worth in her.

It made me shaky to think how much she must have in her. Inside the port hole that was closest I could see something but I couldn't make it out through the water glass. I couldn't do any good with the grains pole and I took off my clothes and stood and took a couple of deep breaths and dove over off the stern with the wrench in my hand and swam down. I could hold on for a second to the edge of the port hole and I could see in and there was a woman inside with her hair floating all out. I could see her floating plain and I hit the glass twice with the wrench hard and I heard the noise clink in my ears but it wouldn't break and I had to come up.

I hung onto the dinghy and got my breath and then I climbed in and took a couple of breaths and dove again. I swam down and took hold of the edge of the port hole with my fingers and held it and hit the glass as hard as I could with the wrench. I could see the woman floated in the water through the glass. Her hair was tied once close to her head and it floated all out in the water. I could see the rings on one of her hands. She was right up close to the port hole and I hit the glass twice and I didn't even crack it. When I came up I thought I wouldn't make it to the top before I'd have to breathe.

I went down once more and I cracked the glass, only cracked it, and when I came up my nose was bleeding and I stood on the bow of the liner with my bare feet on the letters of her name and my head just out and rested there and then I swam over to the skiff and pulled up into it and sat there waiting for my head to stop aching and looking down into the water glass, but I bled so I had to wash out the water glass. Then I lay back in the skiff and held my hand under my nose to stop it and I lay there with my head back looking up and there was a million birds above and all around.

When I quit bleeding I took another look through the glass and then I sculled over to the boat to try and find something heavier than the wrench but I couldn't find a thing; not even a sponge hook. I went back and the water was clearer all the time and you could see everything that floated out over that white bank of sand. I looked for sharks but there weren't any. You could have seen a shark a long way away. The water was so clear and the sand white. There was a grapple for an anchor on the skiff and I cut it off and went overboard and down with it. It carried me right down and past the port hole and I grabbed and couldn't hold anything and went on down and down, sliding along the curved side of her. I had to let go of the grapple. I heard it bump once and it seemed like a year before I came up through to the top of the water. The skiff was floated away with the tide and I swam over to her with my nose bleeding in the water while I swam and I was plenty glad there weren't sharks; but I was tired.

My head felt cracked open and I lay in the skiff and rested and then I sculled back. It was getting along in the afternoon. I went down once more with the wrench and it didn't do any good. That wrench was too light. It wasn't any good diving unless you had a big hammer or something heavy enough to do good. Then I lashed the wrench to the grains pole again and I watched through the water glass and pounded on the glass and hammered until the wrench came off and I saw it in the glass, clear and sharp, go sliding down along her and then off and down to the quicksand and go in. Then I couldn't do a thing. The wrench was gone and I'd lost the grapple so I sculled back to the boat. I was too tired to get the skiff aboard and the sun was pretty low. The birds were all pulling out and leaving her and I headed for Sou'west Key towing the skiff and the birds going on ahead of me and behind me. I was plenty tired.

That night it came on to blow and it blew for a week. You couldn't get out to her. They come out from town and told me the fellow I'd had to cut was all right except for his arm and I went back to town and they put me under five hundred dollar bond. It came out all right because some of them, friends of mine, swore he was after me with an ax, but by the time we got back out to her the Greeks had blown her open and cleaned her out. They got the safe out with dynamite. Nobody ever knows how much they got. She carried gold and they got it all. They stripped her clean. I found her and I never got a nickel out of her.

It was a hell of a thing all right. They say she was just outside of Havana harbor when the hurricane hit and she couldn't get in or the owners wouldn't let the captain chance coming in; they say he wanted to try; so she had to go with it and in the dark they were running with it trying to go through the gulf between Rebecca and Tortugas when she struck on the quicksands. Maybe her rudder was carried away. Maybe they weren't even steering. But anyway they couldn't have known they were quicksands and when she struck the captain must have ordered them to open up the ballast tanks so she'd lay solid. But it was quicksand she'd hit and when they opened the tank she went in stern first and then over on her beam ends. There were four hundred and fifty passengers and the crew on board of her and they must all have been aboard of her when I found her. They must have opened the tanks as soon as she struck and the minute she settled on it the quicksands took her down. Then her boilers must have burst and that must have been what made those pieces that came out. It was funny there weren't any sharks though. There wasn't a fish. I could have seen them on that clear white sand.

Plenty of fish now though; jewfish, the biggest kind. The biggest part of her's under the sand now but they live inside of her; the biggest kind of jewfish. Some weigh three to four hundred pounds. Sometime we'll go out and get some. You can see the Rebecca light from where she is. They've got a buoy on her now. She's right at the end of the quicksand right at the edge of the gulf. She only missed going through by about a hundred yards. In the dark in the storm they just missed it; raining the way it was they couldn't have seen the Rebecca. Then they're not used to that sort of thing. The captain of a liner isn't used to scudding that way. They have a course and they tell me they set some sort of a compass and it steers itself. They probably didn't know where they were when they ran with that blow but they come close to making it. Maybe they'd lost the rudder though. Anyway there wasn't another thing for them to hit till they'd get to Mexico once they were in that gulf. Must have been something though when they struck in that rain and wind and he told them to open her tanks. Nobody could have been on deck in that blow and rain. Everybody must have been below. They couldn't have lived on deck. There must have been some scenes inside all right because you know she settled fast. I saw that wrench go into the sand. The captain couldn't have known it was quicksand when she struck unless he knew these waters. He just knew it wasn't rock. He must have seen it all up in the bridge. He must have known what it was about when she settled. I wonder how fast she made it. I wonder if the mate was there with him. Do you think they stayed inside the bridge or do you think they took it outside? They never found any bodies. Not a one. Nobody floating. They float a long way with life belts too. They must have took it inside. Well, the Greeks got it all. Everything. They must have come fast all right. They picked her clean. First there was the birds, then me, then the Greeks, and even the birds got more out of her than I did.

WILLIAM BEEBE

William Beebe (1877–1962) was already well-known as a tropical explorer and prolific travel writer when, in 1928, with support from the New York Zoological Society, he and Otis Barton began to develop a deep-sea exploration chamber they called a bathysphere. A hollow steel sphere about five feet wide and weighing over 4,000 pounds, the vessel was lowered into the sea on a single steel cable. Six years later, to much fanfare, Beebe made a record half-mile dive off the coast of Bermuda; his account of this experience, Half Mile Down, *from which this chapter is taken, was published in 1934. Beebe's descent began an era in deep-sea exploration that culminated in 1960, when the Belgian-designed U.S. Navy bathyscaphe* Trieste *touched the bottom of the Marianas Trench, at 35,800 feet.*

from *A Descent Into Perpetual Night*

AT 9:41 in the morning we splashed beneath the surface, and often as I have experienced it, the sudden shift from a golden yellow world to a green one was unexpected. After the foam and bubbles passed from the glass, we were bathed in green; our faces, the tanks, the trays, even the blackened walls were tinged. Yet seen from the deck, we apparently descended into sheer, deep ultramarine. The only hint of this change of color vouchsafed those above was the increasing turquoise of the bathysphere as it approached the vanishing point, about 100 feet.

We were dropped several fathoms and dangled there awhile, until all the apparatus on deck was readapted to the vertical cable close to the ship's side. I made the most of my last glimpse of the upper world. By peering up I could see the watery ceiling crinkling, and slowly lifting and settling, while here and there, pinned to this ceiling, were tufts of sargassum weed. I could see small dots moving just below the weed, and for the first time I tried, and successfully, to focus low power binoculars through the water. I had no trouble in recognizing a small ocean turbot and a flyingfish, trailing its half-spread wings as it swam. The bathysphere then revolved slightly and the hull of the *Ready* came into view. It was even more like a coral reef than it had appeared four years ago, great streamers of plant and animal life floating out from it. There is something wholly unreal and at the same time rather amusing about an upward view of the slow-rolling bottom of an unanchored boat, whose deck, a few minutes before, had seemed so solid and staunch.

The sun was blazing over the ocean, the surface was unusually quiet; conditions were perfect for whatever the eyes could carry to the brain. A question came over the phone, an answer went, and down we slipped through the water. As I have said, the first plunge erases, to the eye, all the comforting, warm rays of the spectrum. The red and the orange are as if they had never been, and soon the yellow is swallowed up in the green. We cherish all these on the surface of the earth and when they are winnowed out at 100 feet or more, although they are only one-sixth of the visible spectrum, yet, in our mind, all the rest belongs to chill and night and death. Even modern war bears this out; no more are red blood and scarlet flames its symbols, but the terrible grayness of gas, the ghastly blue of Very lights.

The green faded imperceptibly as we went down, and at 200 feet it was impossible to say whether the water was greenish-blue or bluish-green. At this depth I made my eyes focus in mid-water and saw small creatures clearly, copepods and others of the innumerable swarms which haunt the upper layers.

At 320 feet a lovely colony of siphonophores drifted past. At this level they appeared like spun glass. Others which I saw at far greater and blacker depths were illumined, but whether by their own or by reflected light I cannot say. These are colonial creatures like submerged Portuguese men-o'-war, and similar to those beautiful beings are composed of a colony of individuals, which perform separate functions, such as flotation, swimming, stinging, feeding, and breeding, all joined by the common bond of a food canal. Here in their own haunts they swept slowly along like an inverted spray of lilies-of-the-valley, alive and in constant motion. In our nets we find only the half-broken swimming bells, like cracked, crystal chalices, with all the wonderful loops and tendrils and animal flowers completely lost or contracted into a mass of tangled threads. Twenty feet lower a pilotfish looked in upon me—the companion of sharks and turtles, which we usually think of as a surface fish, but with only our pitiful, two-dimensional, human observation for proof.

When scores of bathyspheres are in use we shall know much more about the vertical distribution of fish than we do now. For example, my next visitors were good-sized yellowtails and two blue-banded jacks which examined me closely at 400 and 490 feet respectively. Here were so-called surface fish happy at 80 fathoms. Several silvery squid balanced for a moment, then shot past, and at 500 feet a pair of lanternfish with no lights showing looked at the bathysphere unafraid.

At 600 feet the color appeared to be a dark, luminous blue, and this contradiction of terms shows the difficulty of description. As in former dives, it seemed bright, but was so lacking in actual power that it was useless for reading and writing.

There are certain nodes of emotion in a descent such as this, the first of which is the initial flash. This came at 670 feet, and it seemed to close a door upon the upper world. Green, the world-wide color of plants, had long since disappeared from our new cosmos, just as the last plants of the sea themselves had been left behind far overhead.

At 700 feet the light beam from our bulb was still rather dim; the sun had not given up and was doing his best to assert his power. At 800 feet we passed through a swarm of small beings, copepods, sagitta or arrow worms and every now and then a worm which was not a worm but a fish, one of the innumerable round-mouths or *Cyclothones*. Eighty feet farther and a school of about 30 lanternfish passed, wheeled and returned; I could guess *Myctophum laternatum*, but I cannot be certain. The beam of light drove them away.

At 1000 feet we took stock of our surroundings. The stuffing box and the door were dry, the noise of the blower did not interfere with the telephone conversation, the humidity was so well taken care of that I did not need a handkerchief over nose and mouth when talking close to the glass. The steel was becoming very cold. I tried to name the water; blackish-blue, dark gray-blue. It is strange that as the blue goes, it is not replaced by violet—the end of the visible spectrum. That has apparently already been absorbed. The last hint of blue tapers into a nameless gray, and this finally into black, but from the present level down, the eye falters, and the mind refuses any articulate color distinction. The sun is defeated and color has gone forever, until a human at last penetrates and flashes a yellow electric ray into what has been jet black for two billion years.

I kept the light on for a while and at 1050 feet through a school of little flying snails there suddenly passed a "large dark body, over four feet long" (so I telephoned it). I shut off the light, but looked into empty gray space without a trace of lumination—the fish had dissolved. Later, with the light on again, ten feet lower, a pilotfish appeared, showing how easily his kind can adapt itself to a shift of more than 30 atmospheres and from 15 pounds an inch at the surface to 480 at this level.

Lights now brightened and increased, and at 1100 feet I saw more fish and other organisms than my prebathysphere experience had led me to hope to see on the entire dive. With the light on, several chunky little hatchet-fish approached and passed through; then a silver-eyed larval fish two inches long; a jelly; suddenly a vision to which I can give no name, although I saw others subsequently. It was a network of luminosity, delicate, with large meshes, all aglow and in motion, waving slowly as it drifted. Next a dim, very deeply built fish appeared and vanished; then a four-inch larval eel swimming obliquely upward; and so on. This ceaseless telephoning left me breathless and I was glad of a hundred feet of only blue-blackness and active sparks.

At 1200 feet an explosion occurred, not at the window but a few feet away, so baffling that I decided to watch intently for repetitions. The large fish came again, and a loose, open school of pteropods and small shrimps bobbed about. The snails were shield-shaped as I well knew from having handled thousands in the deep-sea nets. Their empty shells form most of the sea bottom hereabouts.

Suddenly in the distance a strong glow shot forth, covering a space of perhaps eight inches. Not even the wildest guess would help with such an occurrence. Then the law of compensation sent, close to the window, a clear-cut, three-inch, black anglerfish with a pale, lemon-colored light on a slender tentacle. All else my eye missed, so I can never give it a name.

One great source of trouble in this bathysphere work is the lag of mind behind instantaneous observation. For example, at 1300 feet a medium-sized, wide-mouthed angler came in sight, then vanished, and I was automatically describing an eight-inch larval eel looking like a transparent willow leaf, when my mind shot back to the angler and demanded how I had seen it. I had recorded no individual lights on body or tentacle, and now I realized that the teeth had glowed dully, the two rows of fangs were luminous. It is most baffling to gaze into outer darkness, suddenly see a vision, record the bare facies—the generality of the thing itself—and then, in the face of complete distraction by another spark or organism, to have to hark back and recall what special characters escaped the mind but were momentarily etched upon the retina. On this point I had thoroughly coached Miss Hollister at the other end of the telephone, so I constantly received a fire of questions, which served to focus my attention and flick my memory. Again and again when such a question came, I willfully shut my eyes or turned them into the bathysphere to avoid whatever bewilderment might come while I was searching my memory for details of what had barely faded from my eye. At a few stops on the descent, as I have said, I permitted myself a minute or two of emotional debauch, of reciting to myself the where and the what of locality, surroundings, time of day, pressure, temperature, and so on. But all the rest of the time I allowed myself no rest from direct observation and reporting. The unproductive Oh's! and Ah's! of my first few dives were all too vivid in my mind.

Just above 1400 feet two black eels, about eighteen inches in length, went through the beam—distinctly *Serrivomer*. At 1400 feet my recent studies came to mind, and told me that I saw a male golden-tailed sea-dragon with a big cheek light (*Idiacanthus*), but before it vanished I saw it was black, and considerably larger even than the giant female of the species. So it was wholly unknown.

At 1500 I swung for two and a half minutes, and here occurred the second memorable moment in these dives—opportunity for the deliberate, accurate record of a fish wholly new to science, seen by one or both of us, the proof of whose existence, other than our word, must await the luck of capture in nets far more effective than those we now use in our oceanographic work. First, a quartet of slender, elongate fish passed through the electric light literally like arrows, about twenty inches long, whether eels or not I shall never know; then a jelly, so close that it almost brushed the glass. Finally, without my seeing how it got there, a large fish swung suspended, half in, half out of the beam. It was poised with only a slow waving of fins. I saw it was something wholly unknown, and I did two things at once; I reached behind for Mr. Barton, to drag him away from his camera preparations to the windows, to see and corroborate, and I disregarded Miss Hollister's insistent questions in my ears. I had to grunt or say something in reply to her, for I had already exceeded the five seconds which was our danger duration of silence throughout all the dives. But all this time I sat absorbing the fish from head to tail through the wordless, short-circuiting of sight, later to be materialized into spoken and written words, and finally into a painting dictated by what I had seen through the clear quartz.

The strange fish was at least two feet in length, wholly without lights or luminosity, with a small eye and good-sized mouth. Later, when it shifted a little backwards I saw a long, rather wide, but evidently filamentous pectoral fin. The two most unusual things were first, the color, which, in the light, was an unpleasant pale, olive drab, the hue of water-soaked flesh, an unhealthy buff. It was a color worthy of these black depths, like the sickly sprouts of plants in a cellar. Another strange thing was its almost tailless condition, the caudal fin being reduced to a tiny knob or button, while the vertical fins, taking its place, rose high above and stretched far beneath the body, these fins also being colorless. I missed its pelvic fins and its teeth, if it had any, while such things as nostrils and ray counts were, of course, out of the question.

There is a small family of deep-sea fish known as *Cetomimidæ*, and somewhere in or close to this the strange apparition belongs. Only three species are known, and only twenty-four individuals have so far been captured, sixteen of which have been in our own deep nets drawn through these very waters. I have called the fish we saw the Pallid Sailfin, and am naming it *Bathyembryx istiophasma*, which is a Grecian way of saying that it comes from deep in the abyss and swims with ghostly sails.

Although I had already seen many deep-sea forms on this dive, yet here was one larger than any we had ever taken in nets. The Sailfin was alive, quiet, watching our strange machine, apparently oblivious that the hinder half of its body was bathed in a strange luminosity. Preëminently, however, it typified the justification of the money, time, trouble, and worry devoted to bringing the bathysphere to its present efficiency. Amid nameless sparks, unexplained luminous explosions, abortive glimpses of strange organisms, there came, now and then, adequate opportunity to add a definite new fish or other creature to our knowledge of the life of the deep sea. At the possible risk of cumbering taxonomy with a *nomen nudum*, I have chosen to give definite names to a very few of these clearly seen fish, the physical type of which must, for a time, be represented by a drawing, made under my direction, with only the characters of which I am certain. With no visible increase of fin vibration, my Pallid Sailfin moved into outer darkness, and when I had finished telephoning the last details I ordered a further descent. This entire volume would not contain the detailed recital of even a fraction of all the impressive sights and forms I saw, and nothing at these depths can be spoken of without superlatives.

At 1630 feet a light grew to twice its diameter before our eyes, until it was fully the diameter of a penny, appearing to emanate from some creature which bore irregular patches of dull luminosity on its body. The outline was too indistinct to tell whether it was with or without a backbone.

At 1900 feet, to my surprise, there was still the faintest hint of dead gray light, 200 feet deeper than usual, attesting the almost complete calm of the surface and the extreme brilliancy of the day far overhead. At 2000 feet the world was forever black. And this I count as the third great moment of descent, when the sun, source of all light and heat on the earth, has been left behind. It is only a psychological mile-post, but it is a very real one. We had no realization of the outside pressure but the blackness itself seemed to close in on us.

At 2000 feet I made careful count and found that there were never less than ten or more lights—pale yellow and pale bluish—in sight at any one time. Fifty feet below I saw another pyrotechnic network, this time, at a conservative estimate, covering an extent of two by three feet. I could trace mesh after mesh in the darkness, but could not even hazard a guess at the cause. It must be some invertebrate form of life, but so delicate and evanescent that its abyssal form is quite lost if ever we take it in our nets. Another hundred feet and Mr. Barton saw two lights blinking on and off, obviously under control of the fish.

At this level and again on the way up, I saw at the very end of our beam some large form swimming. On earlier dives I had observed this and had hesitated even to mention it, for it savored too much of imagination backed by imperfect observation. But here it was again. The surface did not seem black, and what outline came momentarily to view was wholly problematic. But that it was some very large creature or creatures of which we had glimpses five separate times on dives separated by years, we are certain. Whether fish or squid or other organism we cannot say.

At 2300 some exclamation of mine was interrupted by a request from above to listen to the tug's whistles saluting our new record, and my response was, "Thanks ever so much, but take this: two very large leptocephali have just passed through the light, close together, vibrating swiftly along; note—why should larval eels go in pairs?" And with this the inhabitants of our dimly remembered upper world gave up their kindly efforts to honor us. On down we went through a rich, light-filled 2400, and to rest at 2500 feet, for a long half hour.

A pair of large, coppery-sided scimitar-mouths (*Gonostoma elongatum*) swam past; *Sternoptyx*, the skeletonfish, appeared in a group of four; a fish as flat as a moonfish entered the beam, and banking steeply, fled in haste. One flying snail, from among the countless billions of his fellows, flapped back and forth across my glass. Three times, at different levels, creatures had struck against the glass and, utterly meaningless as it sounds, exploded there, so abruptly that we instinctively jerked back our heads.

We tried out the full power of the 1500-watt light, heating the bathysphere and window considerably, but not too dangerously. At 11:17 o'clock I turned the light on suddenly, and saw a strange quartet of fish to which I have not been able to fit genus or family. Shape, size, color, and one fin I saw clearly, but Abyssal Rainbow Gars is as far as I dare go, and they may be anything but gars. About four inches over all, they were slender and stiff with long, sharply pointed jaws. They were balanced in the center of the electric ray when it was first turned on, and the unheard-of glare affected them not at all. There they stood, for they were almost upright, and I could see only a slight fanning with a dorsal fin. Keeping equal distances apart, and maintaining their upright pose, they swam slowly into the uttermost dark. The amazing thing about them was their unexpected pattern and color. The jaws and head were brilliant scarlet, which, back of the gills, changed abruptly into a light but strong blue and this merged insensibly into clear yellow on the posterior body and tail. Unless in the light of some other fish, or in my electric path, their colors could never have been visible, and were assuredly useless by-products.

I alternated with Mr. Barton's camera at the window and there were hardly any seconds without lights or definite organisms coming into view. In one period of this duration, chosen at random, I counted 46 lights, ten of which were of unusual size, most of them pale yellow, but a few bluish. The sight I enjoyed most was a momentary glimpse of what I am certain was the same, or another, Pallid Sailfin. In all this vast extent in three dimensions, of black water, the chance of confirming at a wholly different depth a new observation made my satisfaction complete.

The change in the electric beam itself from 1000 feet downward was interesting. At the upper layers it was weak but decidedly yellow, with a turquoise cap at the farther end of the oblique luminous shaft. As we descended, the yellow changed to a luminous gray, and the turquoise crept down, until, at this extreme depth, it reached to the very window. Along each side of the sharply marked beam extended a broad border of rich, velvety, dark blue, and abruptly outside of this came the black pit itself. At two well-separated depths, I focused very carefully on the rain of small creatures passing and repassing through the farthest extreme end of the light. In both cases the focus was the same and I brought the glass to the surface without changing it. On deck, walking back from the bow until it was in perfect focus with the glass, I found that the visible end of the beam of electric light was 45 feet distant from the bathysphere window, five feet farther than I had been estimating.

The several nodes of high lights of which I have written occur on every descent, but there is in addition a compounding of sensations. At first we are quick to see every light, facile in sending up notes, but when we have used up most of our adjectives it is difficult to ring changes on sparks, lights, and darkness. More and more complete severance with the upper world follows, and a plunging into new strangenesses, unpredictable sights continually opening up, until our vocabularies are pauperized, and our minds drugged.

Over two hours had passed since we left the deck and I knew that the nerves both of my staff and myself were getting ragged with constant tenseness and strain. My eyes were weary with the flashing of eternal lights, each of which had to be watched so carefully, and my mind was surfeited with visions of the continual succession of fish and other organisms, and alternately encouraged and depressed by the successful or abortive attempts at identification. So I asked for our ascent.

One minute later, at 2470 feet, all my temporarily relaxed attention was aroused and focused on another splendid piece of luck. A tie rope had to be cut and in this brief interval of suspension, extended by my hurried order, a new anglerfish came out of all the ocean and hesitated long enough close to my window for me to make out its dominant characters. I am calling it the Three-starred Anglerfish, *Bathyceratias trilynchnus*. It was close in many respects to the well-known genera *Ceratias* and *Cryptosparas*, but the flattened angle of the mouth and the short, even teeth were quite different. It was six inches long, typically oval in outline, black, and with small eye. The fin rays were usual except that it had three tall tentacles or illicia, each tipped with a strong, pale yellow light organ. The light was clearly reflected on the upper side of the fish. In front of the dorsal fin were two pear-shaped organs exactly like those of the common *Cryptosparas*. The paired fins escaped me. No pioneer, peering at a Martian landscape, could ever have a greater thrill than did I at such an opportunity.

Once more I rearranged my aching limbs, stretched and twisted to make my muscles cease complaining, and watched the small fry slip downward through the beam, as the winch drew us steadily upward. Everything of interest was still relayed through the phone, but I was slumped down, relaxed. Suddenly I leaned forward, banging my head against the steel but not losing a second of observation. A small school of luminous fish had just passed, when, fortunately at a moment of suspension, came a new and gorgeous creature. I yelled for continuance of the stop, which was at 1900 feet, and began to absorb what I saw; a fish almost round, with long, moderately high, continuous, vertical fins; a big eye, medium mouth, and small pectoral fins. The skin was decidedly brownish. We swung around a few degrees to port, bringing the fish into the dark blue penumbra of the beam, and then I saw its real beauty. Along the sides of the body were five unbelievably beautiful lines of light, one equatorial, with two curved ones above and two below. Each line was composed of a series of large, pale yellow lights, and every one of these was surrounded by a semicircle of very small, but intensely purple photophores.

The fish turned slowly and, head on, showed a narrow profile. If it were at the surface and without lights I should, without question, have called it a butterflyfish (*Chætodon*) or a surgeonfish (*Acanthurus*). But this glowing creature was assuredly neither, unless a distant relation, adapted for life at three hundred fathoms. My name for it is *Bathysidus pentagrammus*, the Five-lined Constellationfish. In my memory it will live throughout the rest of my life as one of the loveliest things I have ever seen.

Cornelia Otis Skinner

A graduate of Bryn Mawr and the Sorbonne, Cornelia Otis Skinner (1901–1979) was the daughter of the famous actor Otis Skinner, in whose productions she began her acting career in the early 1920s. From 1926 to 1929 she toured the United States in a one-woman show. Skinner later displayed her gift for anecdote, caricature, and gentle social satire in a series of books including Tiny Garments *(1932),* Excuse It, Please! *(1936),* Dithers and Jitters *(1938),* Soap Behind the Ears *(1941),* Our Hearts Were Young and Gay *(1942), and* Elegant Wits and Grand Horizontals *(1962). In "The Captain's Table," originally printed in* Harper's Bazaar *in June 1932, Skinner looks at some of the discomforts of the modern Atlantic crossing. No longer routinely troubled by the elements, the traveler of her day still encountered the hazards of her fellow passengers' bad manners.*

The Captain's Table

An Impression of a Social Hardship Borne by Marine Commanders

THE distinction of coming on board a transatlantic liner armed with a letter to the captain is of doubtful advantage. To my mind these letters of marque from powers higher up in the steamship world only succeed in making things more complicated and tips more extensive. The passenger unhonored with a letter to the commander can slink unobtrusively ashore at Southampton without tipping the lift-boy; but he who wears this badge of favor is a marked man and will, before he lands, find himself distributing largess among the second class stewardesses, and the man in the crow's-nest, besides being given the plate to pass for the benefit of the orchestra, and a singularly hideous doll to auction off to whoever is tight enough to bid it in at the ship's concert.

He will find himself visiting the engine room, which (if he feels as I do, namely, that a stroll through the inner crater of Stromboli would be as agreeable) is a somewhat qualified treat. Just as he is in the midst of a good book he is summoned to inspect the bridge, where he is expected to stare with interest, if without comprehension, at the gyrocompass and the quartermaster as if they were rare bits of Limoges in the Cluny, and about the time he is contemplating a soothing draught of lager, he is invited to drink lukewarm tea with the chief officer. All because he has come on board with a letter and the captain and the crew feel they should do something about it. Often as not he finds himself at the captain's table. This is certainly a most pleasant honor and surely he must judge it as such. Sea captains are generally most charming and interesting individuals and a chance to converse with them cannot fail to be welcome to any one.

I am wondering, however, about the captain's point of view. For some time I have been observing the type of person one sees at his table and listening to excerpts from their conversation, and it seems to me this is one hardship of marine life that he might be spared. As if to command a ship's company of some five hundred and to convey a crowded liner safely across the Atlantic were not enough, he must sit at table with a certain favored group of disable-bodied seafarers, reply with tact to their questions, and listen without hitting them to their yarns of adventure on the *Priscilla* of the Fall River Line, or their hazards in a Cris-Craft on Lake Champlain. Just why they all feel they must limit their conversation with the commander to navigation, a topic about which they know nothing, and with which he must be considerably fed-up, is one of those strange quirks of human psychology such as prompted the young woman who, when meeting Amundsen remarked, "Oh, how do you do, Mr. Amundsen. You know we keep a Swedish cook."

Behold the captain's table. On his right sit a nautical trio from St. Louis: Papa, who owns the building in which the steamship line's offices are located; Mama, who resembles one of the emergency rafts on the boat deck; and Sister, aged eighteen, who has a beau at Princeton and is determined to hate everything in Europe and to make everybody's summer one long hell. Beyond them and almost beyond words is a lady now called "princess" and then "marchesa" and occasionally "you" who says she's Sicilian or Roumanian (it seems to depend on the weather). She makes up very heavily and seems to regard whatever food is set before her as if it were kennel ration. Papa from St. Louis, who steals a good many furtive glances at her, has a feeling she's fairly "hotsie-totsie"; but Mama, who has sniffed her perfume, entertains a similar impression, which spoils everything. Next her is a county magistrate from North Country—a pleasant soul who endeavors to regale any one who bears the semblance of listening to him with stories in Lancashire dialect. As no one understands Lancashire, his act is a complete flop though his optimism is unbounded. Next him and ending back next to the captain is a good old salt from Detroit who all but asks if the ship is equipped with a free-wheeling device. And amid these goodly yo-heave-ho'ers the commander must perforce sit, doubtless endeavoring to dismiss from his mind the insinuating thought that on the high seas he holds the power of life and death.

"What sort of weather you giving us, Cap'n?" shouts Papa from St. Louis in a voice he considers hearty, though the others consider it appalling. People have a habit of talking to sea captains as if they were in a gale. The captain, who wonders why he is accredited with the dispensing of the weather like the cook ladling out soup, replies noncommittally, and Papa sits back rubbing his hands vigorously to show what a bully-bully boy he is to be sure, though Sister is far from sure. Mama then, in a motherly tone, makes some inquiries about icebergs, and the marchesa, shuddering, draws a cloak about her and glares over her shoulder at the steward who, she implies, has suddenly turned into Boreas. Sister remarks that there was a lovely picture of an iceberg in Sunday's rotogravure entitled "the white terror of the Atlantic"—a speech that has a certain finality about it. The Michigan mariner pipes up, however. He's one of those men who know all there is to know about everything and then some. He manages to create the impression he is running the ship and the sea too. At one minute he is keeping score at deck tennis, quite uninvited, the next he is giving free advice to the sailor at work on a windlass. He is the self-appointed little brother of the seasick, informing them good-naturedly, "It's all imagination," a remark that is always welcome, and twice a day he musters out the occupants of the smoking-room to look at a school of porpoise, a sail-boat, or something on the horizon no one but he can see, but which he informs them is a whale.

"Well," he begins, "this is my eighteenth crossing. [He fails to explain that six of these were to and from Bermuda] . . . and let me tell you. . . ."

They do let him, for some reason. His yarn seems to be a list of the liners he has patronized and the dates of his voyages —a form of dramatic narration employed by Homer in his list of ships but strangely ineffective on the lips of this million-dollar bard. The captain echoes the names politely and says, "Yes, indeed." The county magistrate speaks for the first time.

"I am minded of the story of the North Country man," he says, "who was going from Manchester to Liverpool . . ." But this bit of rustic humor is cut short by the Detroit Hakluyt who begins: "I remember a little incident, Captain, in 1909 on the old *Adriatic*! Let's see now, was it in 1909 or 1910? It must have been in 1909 because 1910 was the year of the Passion Play. Of course, it might have been 1911, but I'm pretty darn certain it was 1909. Yes. Well, we'll say 1909." The county magistrate is the only one to comply. He croaks a hollow "1909." This exactitude in the matter of dates has nothing whatever to do with the anecdote, which might have occurred in 1931 or in 1066 for that matter. It is something about the Gulf Stream and a school of white seal.

Nobody listens and at the end the marchesa remarks: "I see you have traveled a lot. Always you American men are so adventuresome." If the narrator's appearance seems adventuresome to this imaginative lady, then Papa across the table must be the incarnation of Marco Polo. He, meanwhile, has temporarily fallen from grace with his wife and child, as he has been persistently calling the Chief Steward "Captain" and his table-steward "George" and the female side of his family is pretending not to know him. Sister bridges the gap by pointing to the Commander's ribbons and asking what "all those cute little colors are for." On being informed by the county magistrate that they are decorations, she exclaims, "Well forever more!" and wonders if she couldn't make a hit with this distinguished officer and induce him to give her this pretty strip to wear in place of a frat pin.

Papa then pipes up in his best hurricane voice. "Chief," he begins (his sense of the forms of address is enthusiastic if inaccurate), "have you ever been in a canoe on a Wisconsin lake and had a squall hit ya?"

The Commander, whose adventures include a number of West Indian cyclones and a water-spout in the China Sea, not to mention submarine encounters during the War, is forced to admit this maritime hazard has been denied him, and Papa, whose vocabulary fails him, merely shakes a wise and grinning head and says, "Oh, boy!"

The Detroit Magellan then starts an interesting recital of the tonnage of the various ships he has honored with his patronage. "Let's see," he begins, "this boat is 20,000. Last time I crossed was in 1929 on the *Majestic*. She's 56,622 or rather 56,621, if I remember correctly. Then there was the *President Harding* . . . she's 13,500. Yes, sir, she's 13,500." No one listens to him except the *femme fatale*, who has decided any one so dull must be fabulously wealthy and hangs onto his every word with the poetic rapture of a medieval lady listening to the *Chanson de Roland*. Encouraged by such appreciation the Michigan minstrel goes on to express himself regarding the tendency to roll, vibrate, or list some of the dozen or more vessels to the edification of no one but himself. In the interval that follows this interesting catalogue Mama asks politely if the captain expects to be using the fog-horn much during this trip.

And so it continues . . . every meal for six, seven, or eight days across the Atlantic. My sympathies are all with the commander. How he must long to change the subject! The passenger who discusses any topic other than the sea and seafaring must be as welcome as a first view of land to the man set adrift on a dory. Sea captains generally have pet hobbies utterly unconnected with ships or even water. Often as not they live in an attractive house in the country near Liverpool or Southampton where their main interest is a garden or terriers or some specie of bird. Their wives are usually comfortable, intelligent, and quite terra-firma persons, and to suppose the house reverberates to the thunder of maritime oaths or that family repasts are enlivened with the roaring of sea chanteys is about as intelligent as to believe the poor gentleman when at sea must be conversed with in a "Fifteen men on a dead man's chest" manner. The British understand these things better than we. They know a man can be capable of collecting Wedgwood and still navigate a ship, or that his interest in politics will in no way interfere with his knowledge of winds and currents, and they converse with him accordingly. But we are more simple-minded. We expect our captains to smack of the sea just as we expect all Russian taxi-drivers to be princes, and all Chinamen to be named Sam.

It is all very naïve and refreshing, I daresay, to everybody save the captain. He, smiling, continues to bear these American gems of the ocean with the courtesy of the gentleman that he is, doubtless looking forward to an after-dinner chat with the chief of staff, when he can relax and discuss the winner for the Derby or a problem in the cultivation of Darwin tulips.

James Thurber

At the end of his comic memoir My Life and Hard Times, *James Thurber (1894–1961) writes: "The mistaken exits and entrances of my thirties have moved me several times to some thought of spending the rest of my days wandering aimlessly around the South Seas, like a character out of Conrad, silent and inscrutable. But the necessity for frequent visits to my oculist and dentist has prevented this." Thurber's real-life island experiences were pretty much restricted to frequent visits to Bermuda, beginning in 1936, where he became a regular contributor to the local magazine* The Bermudian. *One of his first articles was "The Story of Sailing," a wry meditation on the technical difficulties of maritime vocabulary; it was later collected in* My World—And Welcome To It *(1942).*

The Story of Sailing

PEOPLE who visit you in Bermuda are likely to notice, even before they notice the flowers of the island, the scores of sailing craft which fleck the harbors and the ocean round about. Furthermore, they are likely to ask you about the ships before they ask you about the flowers and this, at least in my own case, is unfortunate, because although I know practically nothing about flowers I know ten times as much about flowers as I know about ships. Or at any rate I did before I began to study up on the subject. Now I feel that I am pretty well qualified to hold my own in any average discussion of rigging.

I began to brush up on the mysteries of sailing a boat after an unfortunate evening when a lady who sat next to me at dinner turned to me and said, "Do you reef in your gaff-topsails when you are close-hauled or do you let go the mizzen-top-bowlines and cross-jack-braces?" She took me for a sailor and not a landlubber and of course I hadn't the slightest idea what she was talking about.

One reason for this was that none of the principal words (except "reef") used in the sentence I have quoted is pronounced the way it is spelled: "gaff-topsails" is pronounced "gassles," "close-hauled" is pronounced "cold," "mizzen-top-bowlines" is pronounced "mittens," and "cross-jack-braces" is pronounced "crabapples" or something that sounds a whole lot like that. Thus what the lady really said to me was, "Do you reef in your gassles when you are cold or do you let go the mittens and crabapples?" Many a visitor who is asked such a question takes the first ship back home, and it is for these embarrassed gentlemen that I am going to explain briefly the history and terminology of sailing.

In the first place, there is no doubt but that the rigging of the modern sailing ship has become complicated beyond all necessity. If you want proof of this you have only to look up the word "rigging" in the Encyclopædia Britannica. You will find a drawing of a full-rigged modern ship and under it an explanation of its various spars, masts, sails, etc. There are forty-five different major parts, beginning with "bowsprit" and going on up to "davit topping-lifts." Included in between are, among others, these items: the fore-top-mast staysail halliards (pron. "fazzles"), the topgallant mast-yard-and-lift (pron. "toft"), the mizzen-topgallant-braces (pron. "maces"), and the fore-topmast backstays and top-sail tye (pron. "frassantossle"). The tendency of the average landlubber who studies this diagram for five minutes is to turn to "Sanscrit" in the encyclopedia and study up on that instead, but only a coward would do that. It is possible to get something out of the article on rigging if you keep at it long enough.

Let us creep up on the formidable modern sailing ship in our stocking feet, beginning with one of the simplest of all known sailing craft, the Norse Herring Boat. Now when the Norse built their sailing boats they had only one idea in mind: to catch herring. They were pretty busy men, always a trifle chilly, and they had neither the time nor the inclination to sit around on the cold decks of their ships trying to figure out all the different kinds of ropes, spars, and sails that might be hung on their masts. Each ship had, as a matter of fact, only one mast. Near the top of it was a crosspiece of wood and on that was hung one simple square sail, no more complicated than the awning of a cigar store. A rope was attached to each end of the crosspiece and the other ends of these ropes were held by the helmsman. By manipulating the ropes he could make the ship go ahead, turn right, or turn left. It was practically impossible to make it turn around, to be sure, and that is the reason the Norsemen went straight on and discovered America, thus proving that it isn't really necessary to turn around.

As the years went on and the younger generations of Norsemen became, like all younger generations, less hard-working and more restless than their forebears, they began to think less about catching herring and more about monkeying with the sails of their ships. One of these restless young Norsemen one day lengthened the mast of his ship, put up another crosspiece about six feet above the first one, and hung another but smaller sail on this new crosspiece, or spar (pronounced, strange as it may seem, "spar"). Thus was the main topsail born.

After that, innovations in sails followed so fast that the herring boat became a veritable shambles of canvas. A Norseman named Leif the Sailmaker added a second mast to his ship, just in front of the first one, and thus the foremast came into being and with it the fore mainsail and the fore topsail. A Turk named Skvar added a third mast and called it the mizzen. Not to be outdone, a Muscovite named Amir put up a third spar on each of his masts; Skvar put up a fourth; Amir replied with a fifth; Skvar came back with a sixth, and so it went, resulting in the topgallant foresail, the top-topgallant mizzen sail, the top-top-topgallant main topsail, and the tip-top-topgallant-gallant mainsail (pron. "twee twee twee twa twa").

Practically nobody today sails a full-rigged seven-masted ship, so that it would not be especially helpful to describe in detail all the thousands of different gaffs, sprits, queeps, weems, lugs, miggets, loords (spelled "leewards"), gessels, grommets, etc., on such a ship. I shall therefore devote what space I have left to a discussion of how to come back alive from a pleasant sail in the ordinary 20- or 30-foot sailing craft such as you are likely to be "taken for a ride" in down in

Bermuda. This type of so-called pleasure ship is not only given to riding on its side, due to coming about without the helmsman's volition (spelled "jibe" and pronounced "look out, here we go again!"), but it is made extremely perilous by what is known as the flying jib, or boom.

The boom is worse than the gaff for some people can stand the gaff (hence the common expression "he can stand the gaff") but nobody can stand the boom when it aims one at him from the floor. With the disappearance of the Norse herring fisherman and the advent of the modern pleasure craft sailor, the boom became longer and heavier and faster. Helmsmen will tell you that they keep swinging the boom across the deck of the ship in order to take advantage of the wind but after weeks of observation it is my opinion that they do it to take advantage of the passengers. The only way to avoid the boom and have any safety at all while sailing is to lie flat on your stomach in the bottom of the ship. This is very uncomfortable on account of the hard boards and because you can't see a thing, but it is the one sure way I know of to go sailing and come back in the boat and not be washed up in the surf. I recommend the posture highly, but not as highly as I recommend the bicycle. My sailing adventures in Bermuda have made me appreciate for the first time the essential wonder of the simple, boomless bicycle.

James Agee

After graduating from Harvard in 1932, James Agee (1909–1955) joined the staff of Fortune *magazine, where "Havana Cruise" appeared in June 1937. More than six decades later the cruise ship industry still flourishes and continues to draw the attention of young writers—David Foster Wallace, for example, in his essay "A Supposedly Fun Thing I'll Never Do Again"—but it is unlikely that anyone will ever capture as well as Agee the melancholy nexus between the pursuit of pleasure at sea and the "inestimable pressures of loneliness and spiritual fear" experienced in modern life ashore.*

Havana Cruise

Force of habit awakened elderly Mr. and Mrs. B. early and they were strolling the long decks hand in hand a half-hour before the dining saloon opened at eight. Two heavy women in new house dresses helped each other up the stairs, their lungs laboring. They were Mrs. C. and her feeble sister. They and the B.'s nodded and smiled and said what a lovely morning it was and moved on in opposite directions. Mr. B. replaced his alpaca cap and told his gentle, pretty wife how fine the sea air was and what an appetite it gave a fellow. The sun stood bright on the clean, already warm decks, the blue water enlarged quietly without whitening, and sang along the flanks of the ship like seltzer.

Miss Cox appeared with her aunt Miss Box, a frugal and sweet-smiling spinster. Miss Box wore a simple print and a shining black straw garlanded with cloth flowers; Miss Cox was in severely informal new sports attire. Like most of the other young women, low-salaried office workers upon whom the self-sufficiency, the independence of city work and city living had narrowed their inestimable pressures of loneliness and of spiritual fear, she set a greater value of anticipation upon this cruise than she could dare tell herself. For this short leisure among new faces she had invested heavily in costume, in fear, in hope; and like her colleagues she searched among the men as for steamer smoke from an uncharted atoll.

Small and very lonesome in a great space of glassed-in deck, an aging Jew in a light flannel suit gazed sorrowfully at the Atlantic Ocean. A blond young man who resembled an airedale sufficiently intelligent to count to ten, dance fox trots, and graduate from a gentleman's university came briskly to the dining room in sharply pressed slacks and a navy blue sports shirt, read the sign, dashed away, and soon reappeared plus a checkered coat and a plaid tie. The dining saloon opened. Among big white tables glistening with institutional silverware all the white-coated stewards stood in sunlight with nothing yet to do. They were polite, but by no means obsequious; like the room stewards and the rank and file of the crew they had had a good stiff draught of the C.I.O. The headwaiter, a prim Arthur Treacher type, convoyed his guests to their tables with the gestures of an Eton-trained sand-hill crane in flight. His snobbishness rather flattered a number of the passengers.

Mr. and Mrs. B. studied the pretentious menu with admiration and ordered a whale of a breakfast. They may charge you aplenty, but they certainly do give you your money's worth. Mr. L., a bearish Jew, and his wife, the hard, glassy sort of blonde who should even sleep in jodhpurs, tinkered at their fruit and exchanged monosyllables as if they were forced bargains. The airedale pricked up his ears as two girls came in and as quickly drooped them and worried his Krispies, hoping that to two girls already seated he had appeared to establish no relationship with the newcomers, who were not at all his meat. Mr. and Mrs. L., in the manner of the average happily married couple, brightened immediately and genuinely as friends entered. The cool china noise and the chattering thickened in the cheerful room while, with the casualness of concealed excitement, studiously dressed and sharply anticipatory, singly and by twos and threes the shining breakfast faces assembled, looking each other over. The appraisals of clothes, of class, of race, of temperament, and of the opposed sexes met and crossed and flickered in a texture of glances as swift and keen as the leaping closures of electric arcs, and essentially as irrelevant to mercy. These people had come aboard in New York late the evening before, and this was their first real glimpse of each other.

All told, there were a hundred and thirty-two of them aboard. Perhaps twenty of them, mostly Cubans, were using the ship for the normal purpose of getting where they were going, namely, Havana. The others were creatures of a different order. They were representatives of the lower to middle brackets of the American urban middle class and they were on a cruise. Forty of them would stop over a week in Havana; they were on the thirteen-day cruise. Sixty eight of them would spend only eighteen hours in that city. They were on the six-day cruise. Most of them were from the cities of the eastern seaboard; many were from the New York City area. Roughly one in three of them was married, one in three was Jewish, one in three was middle-aged. Most of the middle-aged and married were aboard for a rest; most of the others were aboard for one degree or another of a hell of a big time. The unattached women and girls, who were aboard partly for a good time and partly for the more serious, not to say desperate, purpose of finding a husband, outnumbered the unattached men about four to one going down and about six to one coming back. There were few children. It wasn't a very expensive outing they were taking: most of them spent between $85 and $110 for passage, but $70 was enough to cover every expense except tips for six days, including two conducted tours of Havana. Besides that there were bar expenses; and plenty of the passengers, particularly the younger ones, had invested pretty heavily in new clothes they could feel self-assured in; for most of them had never been on a cruise before, and had rather glamorous ideas of what it would be like. Few of them could swing this expense lightly, and plenty of them knew they should never have afforded it at all. But they were of that vast race whose freedom falls in summer and is short. Leisure, being no part of their natural lives, was precious to them; and they were aboard this ship because they were convinced that this was going to be as pleasurable a way of spending that leisure as they could afford or imagine. What they made of it, of course, and what they failed to make, they made in a beautifully logical image of themselves: of their lifelong environment, of their social and economic class, of their mother, of their civilization. And that includes their strongest and most sorrowful trait: their talent for self-deceit. Already, as their eyes darted and reflexed above the grapefruit and the coffee, they were beginning to find out a little about all that.

The ship these passengers were aboard was the turbo-electric liner *Oriente*, the property of the New York & Cuba Mail Steamship Co., which is more tersely and less gently known as the Ward Line. The T.E.L. *Oriente* is fashioned in the image of her clientele: a sound, young, pleasant, and somehow invincibly comic vessel, the seafaring analogy to a second-string summer resort, a low-priced sedan, or the newest and best hotel in a provincial city. She can accommodate some 400 passengers, and frequently enough carries less than half that many. She makes fifty voyages a year, New York—Havana—New York, carrying freight, mail, and passengers, of whom a strong preponderance are cruising.

All the big lines and plenty of the minor ones run cruises any distance from round-the-world on down and at any toll from $5 to $25 or better per day. Of the passenger traffic of all flags sailing from U.S. ports in 1935 the cruising passengers accounted for 10 per cent. In the same year, according to the Department of Commerce, 83,000 passengers left U.S. ports on cruises. Of these 72,000 were U.S. citizens and 69,000 sailed from New York. Not more than one in four of them shipped on U.S. vessels, and U.S. shipping took only $1,000,000 of the $15,000,000 U.S. citizens spent on cruising. The cruising trade on the whole is sharply on the upswing. For 1936 the Department of Labor estimates a 25 per cent increase in cruising population. For the first half of 1937 as against the first half of the previous year the Italian Line reports an increase of 50 per cent; Cook's an increase of 38.2; Canadian Pacific's *Empress of Britain* an increase of 25 per cent in advance bookings (she was booked solid for 1936). The *Empress* does the biggest world-cruise business; the Italian Line has the Mediterranean trade pretty well sewed up; in 1935 Cunard handled about as many cruise passengers as all U.S. ships lumped together.

The popularity of cruising in general and of the particular cruise naturally depends respectively upon economic and local political conditions. In times answering to the names of peace and prosperity the Mediterranean and the world cruises take the class; and Canada, the Atlantic coastal islands, and the Caribbean the mass trade. During those years when prohibition and depression overlapped, the short cheap cruises "to nowhere" and to Bermuda did a howling business in more senses than one. Bermuda is still the strongest draw for short cruises. Just now people in the cruise business see a future brightening over the coastal cities of South America as it fades over Europe. Both the *Normandie* and the *Rex* will cruise to Rio de Janeiro this winter; by middle July, 500 of the 700 planned for had already booked passage on the *Rex*, though American Express travel service had made no promotive gesture beyond publication of an announcement.

By the time the *Rex* and the *Normandie* are cutting south with their carriage trade the *Oriente* too will once again be carrying what one officer, speaking in summer, described as "a better class of people." Winter is always best; late summer is the low. In July and August the unattached women, most of them schoolteachers, outnumber the unattached men ten and even twelve to one. On the trip we are talking about, which occurred in early summer, she carried what was in every respect just a good average crowd; and their cruise, accordingly, was going to be a good average cruise. It was that from the moment when the first pair of strangers nodded and shyly smiled; it was that all through breakfast; it kept right on being that as they changed to sneakers and took their sun-tan oil and moved up to the sports deck. It continued to same straight through the trip.

Up on the sports deck in bright sun a gay plump woman in white shied rubber rings at a numbered board and chattered at her somber female companion. The gay lady was from Washington and had friends at the Embassy in Havana. She admired

Noel Coward almost fatuously and sat at the Captain's table. She was the godsend-of-the-week to the Captain, a dickensian-built Swede who enjoyed gallantry and wit and whom even the stewards liked. A slender Jew made a few listless passes at shuffleboard and then settled down to obstacle putting. The airedale and a duplicate appeared in naughty trunks, laid towels aside from their pretty shoulders, oiled themselves, and, after a brief warm-up, began to play deck tennis furiously before the gradually assembling girls. Some of the girls wore brand-new sports clothes, others wore brand-new slacks or beach combinations. Some of them traveled in teams, most of the others teamed up as quickly as they could. They strolled against the wind, they stood at the white rail with wind in their waved hair, they swung their new shoes from primly crossed knees, they lay back with shaded eyes, their crisp white skirts tucked beneath them in the flippant air, they somewhat shyly laid their slacks back from their pale thighs, they lay supine, skull-eyed in goggles; their cruel vermilion nails caught at the sunlight. They examined each other quietly but sharply, and from behind dark white-rimmed lenses affected to read drug-store fiction and watched those beautiful bouncing blond boys' bodies and indulged the long, long thoughts of youth. The airedales were fast and skillful, and explosive with such Anglo-Saxonisms as Sorry, Tough, Nice Work, Too Bad, Nice Going. Later they were joined by a couple of other bipeds who had the same somehow suspect unself-consciousness about their torsos, and the exclamations of good sportsmanship came to resemble an endless string of firecrackers set off under a dishpan and the innocent childlike abandon of the exhibitionism acquired almost Polynesian proportions in everything except perhaps sincerity and results. To come to the quick of the ulcer, it is generously estimated that the sexual adventures of the entire cruise did not exceed two dozen in number and most nearly approached their crises not in staterooms but aboveboard; that in no case was the farthest north more extreme than a rumpling hand or teeth industriously forced open; that in 70 per cent of these cases the gentleman felt it obligatory to fake or even to feel true love and the lady murmured either "please" or "please don't" or "yes I like you very much but I don't feel That Way about you," or all three; and that the man, in every case, took it bravely on the chin, sincerely adopted the attitude of a Big Brother, and went to his own bunk tired but happy.

Mr. and Mrs. L. sat quietly in the heightening sun. Mr. L. leaned far forward to let the sun fight its way through the black hair on his back and swapped business anecdotes with a man with epaulets of red hair; Mrs. L. incisively read *I Can Get It For You Wholesale* until the strong sun slowed her and she slept. Miss Cox, conversing with two young men, tried with her eyes to sharpen competition between them and to indicate that she was whichever they might prefer: good fun or an incipient good wife. Each of the men tried to establish excitement in her and jotted her on his mental cuff as useful if worst came to worst. Miss Box sat in the shade and read *Lost Ecstasy*. In the writing room Mrs. C. wrote a lot of postcards for herself and her sister who hadn't the energy. She wrote all morning and then wondered how to mail them back to Connecticut. On the promenade deck Mr. B. was saying, "When I retire my wife and I just want to travel from one end of the United States to the other." Mrs. B. was telling of an adventure her nephew had had in Yellowstone National Park when his car broke down. A stocky smiling blonde in an alarming cobalt bathing suit sank into her chair and disposed all that was lawful of her body before the sun. The airedales wagged their tails and did their gentlemanly best to lose themselves in good clean exercise. In the cool shadow of the empty lounge a tall nurse with an extraordinarily pure forehead lazily laid out self-taught breaks on the shallow-toned grand piano. On the shady side of the ship a torpid husband sat under five fathom of the Sunday *Times* and stuffed in the state of the world without appetite while wife caught a beauty sleep with her nostrils inverted, her goggles cockeyed, and her mouth open. People went past him and then more people and he knew something must be going on. He shoveled his way out and followed, in his new, brilliantly white sneakers, into the glassed-in dance floor.

Nearly everyone was on hand in folding chairs and the place was rustling, curiously subdued under one voice, with occasional pigeon-like rushes of shy and uncertain laughter. The Cruise Director, whose name was Earle M. Wilkens, was staging the Get-Together. He gave out information about landing cards and shopping and the good times ahead, introduced the deck steward, a professionally Cute Character whose popularity is significant of the whole nature of the cruise, and spent his best efforts trying as tactfully as possible to tell his charges not to be utter fools, not to be afraid of each other, that it was perfectly sound etiquette to speak to whom you pleased here without introduction. The audience remained amiable and embarrassed. Nine out of ten of them, much against their wishes, retained their onshore inhibitions to the somewhat bitter end; few individuals got to know more than four or five others better than faintly well.

The lunch bugle ended the meeting. A few men and fewer girls sloped into the modernistic bar; the rest went below to dope out some more costumes they could feel secure in. The drinks were cheap, a quarter for cocktails and thirty cents for highballs, and were weak out of all proportion even to that price. Though plenty of the passengers had anticipated Drinking quite as much as Sex, few of them drank much during cruise; apparently because few others drank much. Not even the trip's topers spent more than $20 or so.

There were a number of shifts of table assignments at lunch as new acquaintances got together. It was standard, sterile, turgid, summer-hotel type food, turkey, duck, the sort of stuffing that tastes like kitchen soap, fancy U.S. salads, and so on, and served with a pomp and circumstance that would have sufficed for the body and blood of Brillat-Savarin. The average passenger behaved a little as if this were his regular Thursday evening at the Tour d'Argent, and staggered upstairs to digest at the horse racing.

The horse racing was done with dice and varied with handicaps and gag races. The betting unit was a quarter. Two-thirds of the passengers were on hand; about half of them bet steadily. On the outskirts a small neatly made girl in blue slacks who had operated a horse race in a summer hotel was wondering how profitably the ship jockeyed the odds in its favor. It broke up in about an hour: and the sports deck filled, and the passengers disposed themselves once again among the diversions and facilities of the morning.

Mrs. C., her sister, and a pleasant younger woman sat and passed the time of day. Mrs. C. said: "The water in the thermos bottle in our stateroom is not as cool as the water in the cooler in the corridor." The younger woman said that hers seemed to be. Mrs. C. said to her sister: "She says the water in the thermos bottle in *her* stateroom *is* as cool as the water in the cooler in the corridor." A mean-eyed freckled young woman whose mahogany hair shone with black lights spoke to a new male acquaintance in the remarkable language of Arthur Kober: "I hate mountains; somehow they don't cope with my life." Mr. B. was saying that he and his wife both loved to see new places and try out new drinks, not really getting drunk of course but just seeing what they tasted like. It certainly was a lot of fun. Having Wonderful Time was saying "I don't mind my freckles any more but I used to be terribly sentimental about them; used to cry all the time when people teased me." Mr. B., whose wife was below resting, struck the ash from his popular-priced cigar and said, secure and happy: "Well if I should die tonight I'd leave my wife fourteen hundred dollars, but matter of fact I hope to make that more before I'm done." The younger woman said to Mrs. C., "I noticed you were reading *News-Week* this morning. How do you like it?" Mrs. C. replied that she thought it was awful cute.

There was a fire drill, with everyone looking sheepish in life belts and a few cracks about the *Morro Castle* and for that sinking feeling, travel on the Ward Line, and after the drill a rather pompous tea, with dancing, to the spiritless commercial rhythms of a hard-working four-man band, and then the dinner horn, at whose command dressing was for the third to fifth time that day unanimously resumed.

The redressing for the evening ran the whole range—formal, semiformal, informal, with every variant that open insecurity or pretended sophistication could give it. There was a good deal of glancing around and checking up during dinner and quite a few made immediate revisions. After dinner *John Meade's Woman* was shown, with breaks between reels, to a packed house that received it with polite apathy. The floor was cleared of chairs, the tables filled, blue and green bulbs went on among the leaves of the dwarf tubbed trees, the weak drinks were ordered, and the band redistributed the platitudes of the afternoon among warmer colors in a warmer light.

Some of the married couples sat alone; others had found each one other married couple. The latter swapped among their foursome, the former danced together all evening. The four airedales scampered about with two pink girls who looked like George Washington, the cobalt bathing suit and a couple of other blondes, and once in a while, with a face-saving air gracefully combined of wild oats and democracy, swung the more attractive Jewesses around the floor. The inevitable Ship's Card, a roguish fellow of forty, did burlesque rumbas and under protection of parody achieved unusual physical contacts amid squeals of laughter. An earnest and charming young Jew, brows bent, did better dancing than the music would support. The seconds among the girls fell to the elder of the unattached men and most of them (along with the men) got stuck there. The third run sat and smiled and smiled until their mouths ached and their cheeks went numb, while the men passed them with suddenly unfocused eyes. Six Cuban college boys sat at a ringside table drinking and looking very young and not dancing at all. The wow of the evening was a blonde who was born out of her time: her glad and perpetually surprised face was that which appears in eighteenth-century pornographic engravings wherein the chore boy tumbles the milkmaid in an explosion of hens and alfalfa. Her dress was cut with considerable extra *élan* to set off her uncommonly beautiful breasts, which in the more extreme centrifuges of the dance swung almost entirely free of ambush. She had a howling rush and a grand time. The six Cuban boys watched her constantly and chattered among themselves. Whenever she approached their corner their plum-jelly eyes bugged out with love. Twice, without a trace of anything save naive admiration too great to be restrained, they broke into applause.

The dancing stopped and the bar closed at the ungodly hour of 1:00 a.m. A few couples talked quietly in dark parts of the overlighted decks, but by two they were all in bed and a gang moved up the darkness grooming the decks and then went below; and the wet decks yielded a tarnish of light and the ship, with a steady throe like that of blood, poured strongly through the shaded water. After a while the morning opened upon the mild stare, the insane musical comedy blue of the Gulf Stream, whereon the *Oriente* crept like a jazzy little toy; the decks dried and brightened in the lifted sun; in those hierarchic depths of a ship that passengers scarcely suspect, the crew and the service crews were waking, like rain-chilled insects that fair weather warms; the passengers were assembling themselves toward consciousness; the breakfast horn laced the ship with its bluff brightness; and another day had begun.

It had precisely the same shape and rhythm. Breakfast brought the passengers together, and cast them forth upon their own resources: sports, flirting, bathing, reading, sleeping, talking, tanning. The lunch horn gave them something to do, they dressed; they ate; they played the wooden ponies; more sports, flirting, bathing, reading, sleeping, talking, tanning; tea dancing brought them together with something to do; they dressed for dinner; they ate it; they played Bingo; they danced; they went to bed; they slept. There were certain variants and certain developments. Mr. L. showed his tremendous sunburn to a young woman but it was all right, his wife was there reading *I Can Get It For You Wholesale*. Two Cubans nearly beat two airedales at deck tennis. Miss Box no longer enjoyed *Lost Ecstasy*, which is a piece of housewives' problem fiction about the troubles of a sophisticated deb who marries a big clean cowboy; it was too serious. The head deck steward found still some more passengers to fascinate with his modest account of the *Morro Castle*. A steward and a passenger talked enthusiastically about Spain and the C.I.O. A girl won three straight pots at Bingo. Earle Wilkens skillfully disposed of a heckler. There were gag dances with inexpensive prizes, an elimination number dance, a musical-chair dance. Two contest dances were announced but were not staged; there weren't many good dancers. The high point of gayety for the cruise was reached at the rough climax of the musical-chairs game. After the dancing was over quite a crowd lingered on deck in the obscenely ticklish darkness and drank stiff Scotches and rums. One of the Cuban boys played a trumpet very softly; another played the guitar and with extreme quietness, their faces softened, they sang. First they sang popular Havana tunes whose very banality made their beauty manifold, then they sang sorrowful romantic ballads, lyrics of fighting and of homesickness, and dirty songs. The guitarist kept singing straight at a blonde who sat directly in front of him, her knees withdrawn from touching his. Her partner touched her shoulder and murmured Let's take a walk around the deck. She said In a minute, not looking at him. After a little he leaned above her and murmured When you're ready, let me know. She did not answer. Her knees relaxed. He poured himself a steep Scotch and kept his nose in it. The peculiar quality of the night had everyone as shaky as a well-determined kiss. Far out to starboard, small, frail, and infrequent, lights walked past. They denominated the low and bone-white coast of pre-Columbian unimagined Florida, and of that dilapidated playground where wasps whine in hot voids of disheveling stucco, and Townsendites sit in squealing rockers under the slow fall of their ashes, and high-school girls are excused from civics class to snap into their one-piece bathing suits and demonstrate the teasing amenities of their hot, trite little bodies for the good of the community; and the trumpet sprang agile gold on the darkness, and the guitar spoke in the Spanish language, and the eloquent songs continued, and the remote lights thickened and were Miami; and Miami spread, and sank into the north; and the lights thinned, and just at this time there was a new feeling through the body of the ship that could not at first be analyzed; then a couple guessed that the ship was changing her course, and silently detaching themselves from their companions, strolled back to the stern. The faint wake, spuming with phosphorus, trailed abruptly bent behind them, and straightened even as they watched, and their guess had been right. The ship had left the shelf of the continent behind and had directed herself upon the world's deep water. Not very far ahead now, beyond a bulge and world shape of this water, tumescent beneath the shade of the summer planet, her whole sleep stirred and streamed in music such as this, Havana lay.

The passengers saw their best of Havana before they set foot in it. The instant they landed they submitted themselves to the guidance of a spectacled brown-uniformed hog with a loud retching voice who stuffed them into a noisy flotilla of open cars and took them on two tours, called the City Tour and the Night Tour. On the City Tour they saw the Church of Our Lady of Mercy, a cigar factory, the Maine Monument, and a cemetery. On the Night Tour they saw a game of jai alai, Sloppy Joe's, the Sans Souci, and the Casino. Between tours the *Oriente* served a goose dinner for those who mistrusted the dirty foreign food.

At the church they saw a number of bruiselike Italianate paintings, an assortment of wax martyrs under glass among shriveled real and fresh wax flowers, and the high altar with all the electric lights on. A collection was taken as they went out. At the cigar factory they saw a dozen men with bad eyesight working overtime for their benefit in bad light, handmaking highgrade cigars for British clubmen. Cigars were on sale as they went out. At the Maine Monument, which is capstoned by the quaint word Liberty, the hog reminded his little charges how the U.S. gave Cuba Hobson's (not by any chance Iscariot's) Kiss and made our little brown boy friend safe for the canebrake, the sugar mill, and the riding boss, and his island a safe place for decent American citizens to do business in. At the cemetery he pointed out the $197,000 black marble modernistic mausoleum of a lady in high society who had died in Paris; a monument to certain students who had desecrated a general's grave and been shot for it; and the monument to the American Legion.

Some of the men liked the jai alai and placed bets but a lot of the girls were bored and the general impression was it was a queer sort of a game. At Sloppy Joe's, the Grant's Tomb of bars, at which no self-respecting Cuban would be caught dead, the tourists themselves seemed a little embarrassed. They huddled rather silent at the bar and few of them ordered more than one drink. Night life in one of the whoriest cities of the Western Hemisphere was represented by the Sans Souci, meaning Care Free, and the Casino, meaning Casino. Lowing gently, the tourists stepped out of their vans. The marble floors were absolutely beautiful. The trees were just exquisite. The music was every bit as smooth as Wayne King and even the native Cubans that went there seemed an awfully nice, refined class of people. Everyone had such a good time they didn't get back to the ship till nearly four o'clock in the morning.

An heroic majority wrenched themselves up from four hours' sleep and spent the morning buying cigars, perfumes, rum, and souvenirs. Later they hung at the rail and talked of Havana, and watched men and boys dive for coins in the foul olive water. Of those who liked Havana the elder spoke of it as quaint, the more youthful as cute. Most of the passengers disliked Havana and were glad to be leaving it. One man raised his voice among a group and, in one of those mental dialects that are perpetually surprising by virtue of their genuine existence, summed up: "Well, I'm telling you. When you see the Statue of Liberty you're going to say this is the country for me." The group nodded as one. Someone threw another Cuban penny in the sewage.

Slowly, regretted by few, Havana shrank in the lunchtime sun and faded. All afternoon the exhausted passengers slept; and awakening, came slowly to realize that somehow the best of their cruise was over. Only a few of the middle-aged, those who desired and demanded least, those who feared each other least, those innocent and gentle and guileless whom little can harm, seemed to escape the blight that, as the next two days dragged on, fastened upon the others more and more pitilessly. All novelty was gone out of the ship, her facilities, her entertainments. Married couples, used to spending their long days apart, were wearing on each other. New acquaintances had run out of small talk and had no other and did not know how to get rid of each other. The girls knew now that none of them was going to find a husband or even any excitement to speak of. There were even fewer men coming back than had gone down. Only one airedale was left and his nose was hot all the way home. The new passengers were no help. Most of them were families of Cuban bourgeois on their way north for the summer. One new American, a brutal spinster whose life seemed to have been spent on cruises for the sole satisfaction of snotting everything she saw, was soon left to her own cruelly lonely devices. Two moderately but genuinely smart couples, one German, one American, caused some excitement at first. They talked like Frederick Lonsdale first acts and looked like a page out of the late *Vanity Fair*, and accordingly represented the average passenger's most cherished dream of a cruise and of what he himself would be on one. But they turned out to be worse than useless for they kept hermetically to themselves and made visible wit about the passengers.

Friday was worst of all. The Gulf Stream was gone, the water was cold and gray, the weather was cold and gray and rather windy, and by afternoon the ship was traveling very slowly in a deathening absence of engine pulsation, for it had been decided to delay docking until Saturday morning. The passengers were depressed beyond even appetite, and a majority of them stayed below. The tea dancing was notably gelid and when the dressing horn flared through the corridors everyone got stiffly and gratefully from his rumpled bunk and took a very hot bath and put on what crowning creation, if any, he or she had managed to hold in reserve for the last evening aboard.

At the last supper, with its tasseled menus, its signal flags, hats, and noisemakers, things picked up. As each latecomer entered everyone made noises, yelled Yaaay, and applauded. There was a sudden blast of music and everyone took up Happy Birthday To You (slurring the name) dear Whosis, We're Glad to See You, and peering around to make out who it was they were glad to see. A waiter brought in a large cake flaming like a Catholic shrine and set it before an old woman, who was totally astonished. Everyone cheered and her tablemates urged her to get up. Reluctantly and with difficulty she helped her aged body half erect and sat quickly down again blushing and swallowing back tears. The lights went out and a baby spot went on and balloons fell from the balcony in a slow bouncing shower while the band played Bubbles.

Customs thickened around the bar that evening stronger than ever before. This was the last night now, the last few hours. Nobody had anything to lose and something, perhaps, to gain. Inhibitions began to drop off like the clothes at a Norman Rockwell swimming hole. Several of the girls to whom a good time meant most and who were in that proportion the most cruelly disappointed members of the cruise, began to get pretty drunk and pretty loud. People who had thus far only nodded and smiled began to order each other drinks and to put hands on each other's shoulders. An amateur photographer got busy with flash bulbs. He made friends with three drunken girls and sat them on the bar and made a picture. A ripe redhead with hot warlike eyes came up and stood very close to him and asked him would he make a pitcher at her table. One of the girls said, "Would you mind going away from here?" She replied yes, she certainly would mind. Another of the girls said, "Would you kindly move off our territory before I break your jaw?" The amateur, who had probably never before overheard himself described as territory, became very careful. The girl moved away. One of the girls said in a narrowed murderous voice: *"If you take a picture of that bitch I'll never speak to you again."* He overheard another say to her friend, glaring at him meanwhile, "Let him go ahead. Let him take her pitcher. *She'll* sleep with him." He put up his camera.

By now the band was playing and somewhat lit couples were making use of it. Many more than usual of the middle-aged sat smiling on the sidelines, indirectly lighted by the good fun the young people seemed to be having, and very cautiously trying to learn from each other how much to tip whom. A hitherto shy young man volubly told a girl who had at no time been shy that like all American girls she was disgracefully inhibited about her dancing and that there were a number of other things he could teach her and would be delighted to. He showed her how the knee is used in pivoting and she cried: "That's it! Pivot! Pivot! Pivot!" After a great deal too much persuasive applause one of the Vanity Fair couples took the floor alone and executed a 3.2 rumba. A bald, heavy man palmed coins and did handkerchief tricks at the bar. A lot of people became fond of him and he set them up to drinks and they set him and his girl up to drinks. The more amorous of the ship's officers were working four and five girls each, in a somewhat nerve-racking synchronization of duty and pleasure.* The Vanity Fair foursome, in a mood for scornful parody, ordered champagne—a thing no one else had thought of doing. They drank a toast and smashed their glasses. A wife and husband sat in a dark corner talking intensely: two phrases kept re-emerging with almost liturgical monotony: keep your voice down, and god damn you. And god damn you too you god damned. Quite suddenly she struck her full glass of planter's punch into his lap and they left the table walking stiffly, their whole bodies fists. The International Smart Set broke some more glasses. A waiter asked them please not to break glasses and set them down some more. They broke them immediately and ordered that a bottle from the next table, whose occupants were dancing, be put on their table. The waiter refused as politely as possible. They ordered it again as if they had not heard him. He slammed it down in front of them as hard as he could. Everyone craned at the noise. In an icy rage they told him they would take this matter up with the Line, and left their table. The pleasant young Jew who danced well went around getting names signed on a petition stating that the service had been excellent and that the waiter had been provoked beyond

*The officer's duty: cheering up disappointed girls. His pleasure: flirtation, one way out of his boredom, which in time becomes titanic. The operation is nerve-racking because no better than any steward can he afford to provoke the least conceivable complaint from a passenger on any sexual ground.

human endurance. The husband came back with his suit nearly dry and drank two Scotches rapidly and danced unskillfully but viciously with a blonde girl. The band played Good Night Sweetheart and packed up their instruments. He quickly ordered four more Scotches and retired to a dark corner. The bar shut down. It was one o'clock. Everyone was troubled and frozen in the sudden silence. Life had warmed up a good deal during the evening but not enough to get on under its own steam. Tentative pacts had been hinted at but not strongly enough. The bafflement sank into embarrassment, the embarrassment into straight tiredness, and very soon nearly everyone, muted and obscurely disappointed, drained off to bed. At one table around a diminishing bottle several girls, two male passengers, and two officers hung on. They were determined, they kept telling each other, to stay up till four, when the passengers would be called and breakfast would be served. Their talk and sidelong looks, their flirtation and their frustration, ground along like a crankcase without oil. The damp husband finished the last of his whiskeys, wove over, hung above the table like a lame dirigible, with thanks refused an invitation to sit in, and went to bed. They cherished their liquor but it was running low. Each of the girls wanted a man but had to abide his leisure. Each of the men wanted a girl but they were concentrated on two girls and on the others only as second-best stopgaps. Each of the prettier girls had developed loyalties toward a homelier girl. Everyone was playing the hopeless game of waiting everyone else out. About two-thirty, half nauseated with liquor and fatigue and frustration, they all gave it up at once and went alone to their respective bunks.

At four the cornetist blasted up and down the corridors. He played The Sidewalks of New York and Home, Sweet Home. A Spanish steward knocked on a friendly door, leaned in, and said, "Better wake op: see Statch."

The passenger was too tired to care to catch the toastmistress of Bedloe Island, but after a little he went to his porthole and looked out. The ship was riding in silence softly past the foot of the island. The water lifted and relaxed in one slow floor of glass. The city lifted, it seemed, a mile above it, and very near; and smokeless behind the city, morning, the mutilation of honey. The city stood appareled in the sober purple and silver of supreme glory, no foal of nature, nor intention of man, but one sublime organism, singular and uncreated; and it stretched upward from its stone roots in the water as if it were lifted on a dream. Nor yet was it soft, nor immaterial. Every window, every wheatlike stone, was distinct in the eye as a razor and serenely, lost, somnambulists, the buildings turned one past another upon the bias of the ship's ghostly movement, not unlike those apostolic figures who parade with the clock's noon in Strasbourg.

John Steinbeck

*A year after he published his first novel (*Cup of Gold, *1929), John Steinbeck (1902–1968) met Edward Ricketts, a young marine scientist who ran a biological supply house on Monterey's Cannery Row. The two became close friends, and Steinbeck began to accompany Ricketts on collecting trips along the California and Baja California coasts. He eventually became part-owner in Ricketts' company, Pacific Biological Laboratory, whose often colorful operations are featured in* Cannery Row *(1945). In March 1940 the pair embarked on their most ambitious expedition, a two-month collecting and research trip in the Gulf of California aboard the 76-foot* Western Flyer. *The results were published the next year in* Sea of Cortez, *for which Ricketts supplied a 300-page scientific appendix, and Steinbeck the keen-eyed, funny, and casually philosophical narrative, from which the excerpt below is taken.*

from *Sea of Cortez*

COSTUME on the *Western Flyer* had degenerated completely. Shirts were no longer worn, but the big straw hats were necessary. On board we went barefoot, clad only in hats and trunks. It was easy then to jump over the side to freshen up. Our clothes never got dry; the salt deposited in the fibers made them hygroscopic, always drawing the humidity. We washed the dishes in hot salt water, so that little crystals stuck to the plates. It seemed to us that the little salt adhering to the coffee pot made the coffee delicious. We ate fish nearly every day: bonito, dolphin, sierra, red snappers. We made thousands of big fat biscuits, hot and unhealthful. Twice a week Sparky created his magnificent spaghetti. Unbelievable amounts of coffee were consumed. One of our party made some lemon pies, but the quarreling grew bitter over them; the thievery, the suspicion of favoritism, the vulgar traits of selfishness and perfidy those pies brought out saddened all of us. And when one of us who, from being the most learned should have been the most self-controlled, took to hiding pie in his bed and munching it secretly when the lights were out, we decided there must be no more lemon pie. Character was crumbling, and the law of the fang was too close to us.

One thing had impressed us deeply on this little voyage: the great world dropped away very quickly. We lost the fear and fierceness and contagion of war and economic uncertainty. The matters of great importance we had left were not important. There must be an infective quality in these things. We had lost the virus, or it had been eaten by the anti-bodies of quiet. Our pace had slowed greatly; the hundred thousand small reactions of our daily world were reduced to very few. When the boat was moving we sat by the hour watching the pale, burned mountains slip by. A playful swordfish, jumping and spinning, absorbed us completely. There was time to observe the tremendous minutiae of the sea. When a school of fish went by, the gulls followed closely. Then the water was littered with feathers and the scum of oil. These fish were much too large for the gulls to kill and eat, but there is much more to a school of fish than the fish themselves. There is constant vomiting; there are the hurt and weak and old to cut out; the smaller prey on which the school feeds sometimes escape and die; a moving school is like a moving camp, and it leaves a camp-like debris behind it on which the gulls feed. The sloughing skins coat the surface of the water with oil.

At six P.M. we made anchorage at San Francisquito Bay. This cove-like bay is about one mile wide and points to the north. In the southern part of the bay there is a pretty little cove with a narrow entrance between two rocky points. A beach of white sand edges this cove, and on the edge of the beach there was a poor Indian house, and in front of it a blue canoe. No one came out of the house. Perhaps the inhabitants were away or sick or dead. We did not go near; indeed, we had a strong feeling of intruding, a feeling sharp enough even to prevent us from collecting on that little inner bay. The country hereabouts was stony and barren, and even the brush had thinned out. We anchored in four fathoms of water on the westerly side of the bay, then went ashore immediately and set up our tide stake at the water's edge, with a bandanna on it so we could see it from the boat. The wind was blowing and the water was painfully cold. The tide had dropped two feet below the highest line of barnacles. Three types of crabs were common here. There were many barnacles and great limpets and two species of snails, *Tegula* and a small *Purpura*. There were many large smooth brown chitons, and a few bristle-chitons. Farther down under the rocks were great anastomosing masses of a tube-worm with rusty red gills, some tunicates, *Astrometis*, and the usual holothurians.

Tiny found the shell of a fine big lobster, newly cleaned by isopods. The isopods and amphipods in their millions do a beautiful job. It is common to let them clean skeletons designed for study. A dead fish is placed in a jar having a cap pierced with holes just large enough to permit the entrance of the isopods. This is lowered to the bottom of a tide pool, and in a very short time the skeleton is clean of every particle of flesh, and yet is articulated and perfect.

The wind blew so and the water was so cold and ruffled that we did not stay ashore for very long. On board, we put down the baited bottom nets as usual to see what manner of creatures were crawling about there. When we pulled up one of the nets, it seemed to be very heavy. Hanging to the bottom of it on the outside was a large horned shark. He was not caught, but had gripped the bait through the net with a bulldog hold and he would not let go. We lifted him unstruggling out of the water and up onto the deck, and still he would not let go. This was at about eight o'clock in the evening. Wishing to preserve him, we did not kill him, thinking he would die quickly. His eyes were barred, rather like goat's eyes. He did not struggle at all, but lay quietly on the deck, seeming to look at us with a baleful, hating eye. The horn, by the dorsal fin, was clean and white. At long intervals his gill-slits opened and closed but he did not move. He lay there all night, not moving, only opening his gill-slits at great intervals. The next morning he was still alive, but all over his body spots of blood had appeared. By this time Sparky and Tiny were horrified by him. Fish out of water should die, and he didn't die. His eyes were wide and for some reason had not dried out, and he seemed to regard us with hatred. And still at intervals his gill-slits opened and closed. His sluggish tenacity had begun to affect all of us by this time. He was a baleful personality on the boat, a sluggish, gray length of hatred, and the blood spots on him did not make him more pleasant. At noon we put him into the formaldehyde tank, and only then did he struggle for a moment before he died. He had been out of the water for sixteen or seventeen hours, had never fought or flopped a bit. The fast and delicate fishes like the tunas and mackerels waste their lives out in a complete and sudden flurry and die quickly. But about this shark there was a frightful quality of stolid, sluggish endurance. He had come aboard because he had grimly fastened on the bait and would not release it, and he lived because he would not release life. In some earlier time he might have been the basis for one of those horrible myths which abound in the spoken literature of the sea. He had a definite and terrible personality which bothered all of us, and, as with the sea-turtle, Tiny was shocked and sick that he did not die. This fish, and all the family of the Heterodontidae, ordinarily live in shallow, warm lagoons, and, although we do not know it, the thought occurred to us that sometimes, perhaps fairly often, these fish may be left stranded by a receding tide so that they may have developed the ability to live through until the flowing tide comes back. The very sluggishness in that case would be a conservation of vital energy, whereas the beautiful and fragile tuna make one frantic rush to escape, conserving nothing and dying immediately.

ALVIN KERNAN

When the Japanese struck Pearl Harbor on December 7, 1941, they destroyed or damaged eight American battleships, but failed to hit their most important targets, the three aircraft carriers assigned to the U.S. Pacific fleet, all of which were at sea during the attack. Alvin Kernan (b. 1923) was then a young sailor serving on one of the carriers, the Enterprise, *and this chapter from his 1994 memoir* Crossing the Line: A Bluejacket's World War II Odyssey *describes his experiences during the early months of the Pacific war, the first—and so far, only—naval conflict in history to be fought primarily between opposing carrier forces. The* Enterprise *fought at Midway and in the Solomons and served in the Pacific until the Japanese surrender. Kernan went on to become a professor of English at Yale and Princeton and to publish several books of literary criticism, including* The Death of Literature *(1990) and* In Plato's Cave *(1999).*

Cruising

To a young man war is exciting, and there can have been few wars as exciting, at least at the start, as the naval war between the United States and Japan from December 1941 to September 1945. The ocean itself was vast and filled with mysterious places whose exotic names now became as familiar as the little towns in Wyoming where I had grown up had once been: Medicine Bow, Saratoga, Rawlins, Encampment, and Laramie. Now the names were Truk (the major Japanese base in the Marianas), Cavite and Bataan, the Java Sea and the Coral Sea, Guam and Wake Island, Mindanao and Balikpapan, New Caledonia and Guadalcanal.

Great fleets steamed across vast spaces of ocean at high speed, surprising the enemy with sudden raids and then disappearing into the emptiness of blue ocean extending from the Aleutians and the Bering Strait in the north to Port Moresby and New Zealand in the south, from the California coast to the Indian Ocean. The ships were fast, heavily armed, and technically considerably advanced, never before tried in combat, but now about to develop by trial and error a new kind of war of aircraft carriers, ship-based aircraft fighting with other ship-based aircraft for control of the air and the sea.

The crews on both sides at that point in the war were professional and volunteer; everyone was there because he had wanted, or at least agreed, to be there, and as a consequence the morale was high, as were the skills of the combatants. Few civilians were caught in the middle until we came to east Asia. It was a war both navies wanted, and, tired of messing with one another, they went at it with a lot of energy. We despised the Japanese at first, and it took a long time and a lot of pain to realize that, at least at the beginning of the war, theirs was a better navy than ours: better ships and aircraft, better-trained personnel, better tactics and fighting ability. We improved rapidly, but in the end we only overcame them by the sheer weight of equipment and men. They remained to the end a worthy foe—courageous, skilled, tenacious, gallant in their strange way—whom we had seriously underestimated. Never after the first days of the war did the fleet look down on "the Japs" or speak contemptuously, like the yellow press, of the cowardice of the enemy.

All of us on the *Enterprise* assumed after Pearl Harbor that she and the other carriers in the Pacific would be sent at once to relieve the Philippines, or at least to break up the attack on Wake Island. Our admiral, William F. "Bull" Halsey, a real fire-eater, thought so too. His quarters were just down the passageway, beneath the flight deck and the island, from our ordnance shack, and when we went down to try to wheedle fresh fruit from his mess attendants, we could hear him thundering away, cursing Washington and the shore-based admirals for their cowardice. The only reason we could think of for not being sent to sink the Japanese fleet forthwith—this is how we thought in our innocence—was that nearly all our battleships were lying broken and burned on the mud bottom of the anchorages alongside Ford Island.

But Adm. Chester Nimitz, soon to be the commander of the Pacific Fleet, must have had some understanding of what had happened at Pearl Harbor, for, as I learned many years later, when he was assembling the fleet to fight the Battle of Midway, he did not include the several seaworthy battleships that had at that time been assembled in San Francisco.

Wisely, no one ordered us to fight our way to Manila, Truk, or Yokosuka, and we were kept on patrols during December and early January, guarding the approaches to the Hawaiian Islands, going back and forth across the 180th meridian, the International Date Line. On December 24, 1941, with a kind of black humor, we crossed the dateline to the west at midnight, so that it became December 25, and then crossed back on the twenty-sixth, getting two Christmases that way, neither very joyful.

The American carriers—there were still only three, *Lexington*, *Yorktown*, and *Enterprise*, after the *Saratoga* was hit by a torpedo in early January—operated separately, each the center of a task force. Cruising the ocean with one carrier in the middle of a task force of a few heavy cruisers and destroyers soon became routine. Standard watches were Condition Three—four hours on duty and eight off—and Condition Two—four hours on and four off—with most watertight doors and hatches dogged closed. It was difficult to move about the ship under these conditions, and everyone was always tired. Reveille came before sunrise so that general quarters could be sounded in time for everyone to be at their battle stations at sunrise. Sunrise and sunset were considered the two most dangerous moments when submarine or airplane attacks could be made out of the sun without being seen. Six fighter planes would be launched just before sunup to fly combat air patrol over the task force, and soon after, a number of dive-bombers and torpedo planes armed with aerial depth charges would be sent up to fly searches out a hundred miles or more looking for submarines or surface vessels. After the planes were off the deck and general quarters secured, the smoking lamp was lit, and breakfast was served. Coffee and beans, sometimes Spam, occasionally dried eggs, dry cereal with powdered milk, prunes or some other kind of dried or canned fruit. Oranges or apples if you had been in port recently.

Then the day's work began, cleaning and polishing, repairing the equipment for which you were responsible, belting ammunition, providing working parties for one job after another, shifting ammunition in the magazines, restowing the heavy towing cable, and the dreaded chipping detail. Peacetime navy ships were beautifully painted inside and out, and the lower decks were covered with a heavy red linoleum kept at a high shine. The Pearl Harbor attack, however, had taught the terrible lesson that paint and linoleum burn fiercely, giving off a heavy toxic smoke, and so after December 7 all ships were ordered to get rid of all the interior paint, except in the light green officers' quarters, and all the linoleum.

The interior of a carrier, like other warships, is a maze of hatches, welded supports, air ducts, cables, pipes, and tangled metal, all covered generously with several coats of white or gray paint, and to chip it all off, flake by flake, with a flat scraping tool—bent at a right angle and sharpened on one end—was a labor of the damned. It was hot inside the ship, and the men stripped to their skivvies, rags around their heads, and chipped away—clink, clink, clink, damn!—hour after hour. It was maddening work, as I found after I got off the flight deck crew, difficult, endless, seemingly pointless, and when it was finished after many months in which it took up every spare hour, the linoleum ripped off the rusty decks, the compartments with their raw steel plates and rusting, pitted, paint-flecked bulkheads were depressing, as if the ship had already been burned out.

Everyone stayed on deck as much as possible, watching the task force spread out over the ocean, which never ceased to be interesting, even after months of steaming. The carrier was in the center, and two or three cruisers—the *Salt Lake City*, *Northampton*, *Chester*, or *Pensacola*—were usually with us, plunging steadily along on both sides. The destroyers, ten or twelve, raced about on the flanks, ahead and to the stern, listening for submarines, transferring material and personnel, and serving as plane guards to pick up the crews of crashed planes.

We fueled at sea, and occasionally a big tanker, named after a faraway American river—the Platte or the Cimarron—

would come alongside, some twenty-five to fifty feet away, and with both ships still under way, pitching and rolling toward each other, riggings sometimes fouled, these thousands of tons of mass would send rubber hoses across and pump fuel and aviation gas out of the tanker into the carrier. Sometimes, as we became more adept, a cruiser or destroyer would get fuel at the same time on the other side of the tanker, or would take fuel from the carrier herself on the side away from the tanker. The waves between the ships in this operation were huge, and standing on the flight deck of the carrier, you could watch the great bulk of the tanker rise up above you, and then crash down. It was blue-water seamanship at its best, always pleasant to watch how smartly it was done. It permitted our ships to stay at sea much longer and to operate while there without having to run at slow speeds to conserve fuel. It also meant that, keeping radio silence, you could disappear for months at a time in the distances of the ocean, to appear, suddenly, somewhere where you weren't expected or wanted.

This is what the *Enterprise* did at the beginning of February 1942, on the first major American carrier raid of the war, the attack on the Marshall Islands—Roi, Wotje, Kwajalein—where atomic bombs would be tested many years later. We had been down to Samoa escorting troop ships and looking longingly at the green tropical islands off in the far distance. The *Yorktown* had come around from the Atlantic, and after we joined with her, we moved to the north together. The run in to the islands began in the evening and continued at thirty-three knots all night long. Here for the first time I sweated through the night before the battle in one of the great carriers.

The crew's compartments were aft, where, lying in your bunk with the whole stern of the ship vibrating, jumping up and down, really, the propeller shafts turning at near maximum rpms, sleep was fitful. Restless with the noise and rattle, the quiet shush of the air ducts bringing fresh air to compartments where all portholes had long been welded shut, there was general uneasiness, communicated by endless nervous shifting in the bunks and constant movement back and forth to the head in the dim red glare of the night-lights. During battle conditions the red lights went out, and the blue battle lamps here and there created an eerie, never-to-be-forgotten, spooky feeling, sweat dripping down into your eyes from under your gray steel World War I helmet, the stale chemical smell of the fireproofed canvas covers of the bulky gray kapok-filled life jackets tied tightly up under your chin.

Reveille was a relief. A rush to get up to the deck, hoping to see the islands we were attacking, but there were only the familiar blue water and the escort vessels. The Marshalls were still many miles away, islands attacked but never seen. The strike force went off about 0500—a few torpedo planes carrying bombs for a high-level bombing attack, some dive-bombers with a yellow five-hundred-pound bomb under the fuselage, a handful of fighters to provide air cover—and the cruisers moved in to shell the landing fields on some of the islands. It seemed a mighty air armada to us then, who had not yet seen the sky filled from horizon to horizon with carrier planes at the end of the war on their way to the Japanese mainland. Now, for the attack, I was released from plane-pushing duties to help load bombs on the torpedo planes, hoisting them up and locking them into the bomb rack, inserting the fuses and threading the long copper arming wire through the holes in the fuse vanes, tightening up the sway brackets. Off in the distance the strike group was no bigger than a fist held up in the sky.

The *Enterprise* was still after her strike had been launched. Work stopped, and everyone waited nervously to see if we had been spotted by the enemy. Ship's radar was primitive in those days, but we did have it, and the Japanese did not—one of our few advantages—and this morning it kept telling us that the skies were clear, that the Japanese planes had been caught on the ground and their ships in the great anchorage inside the circular atoll. Then the wait began for the return of our own planes, and about mid-morning a few fighters arrived, then some dive-bombers, and at last the torpedo planes. All eyes tried to count to see how many planes from the air group had been lost. A few, it turned out; not more than three or four.

The *Enterprise* turned into the wind, picked up maximum speed, cleared the flight deck, and raised the arresting cables to catch the planes' tailhooks. The hydraulic crash barriers three-quarters of the way up the deck came up with a swoosh, and the carrier began to take her air group aboard. The planes roared by in loose formation on the starboard side, a few hundred feet up, and as they passed the ship, began to peel off, one by one, to their port, flying around the ship and coming in low and aft, following the wake, onto the deck. The landing signal officer stood at the rear on the port side, facing aft, with two yellow paddles, one in each hand, giving visual signals to the incoming plane. Up a little, a bit to port, less power, cut.

The plane hit the deck heavily, its hook grabbed one of the elevated tailhook wires and pulled it out until the plane came to a stop. Men raced out to release the arresting wire, the tailhook retracted, the crash barriers went down, the plane taxied forward at high speed, slammed on the brakes, and the barrier came up just as the next plane was landing. A tricky and a dangerous business, but everything depended on doing it fast and doing it well. In peacetime the navy was miserly about every piece of equipment, but in wartime a badly wrecked plane went over the side instantly to clear room for the following plane.

How effective the strike had been no one seemed to know, and if they did, no one bothered to tell the crew, who filled what later times would call an information gap with scuttlebutt about monstrous battleships sunk in the channel, hundreds of planes exploding from direct hits while taxiing out to take off, disgraced and distraught Japanese admirals committing hara-kiri on the control tower to apologize to the emperor. Quite satisfying stuff, which made the morning seem extremely worthwhile, though in fact the few planes with their light bomb loads had done little harm.

After another small follow-up strike was launched, we were told to rearm all the torpedo planes with torpedoes, which were considered, as the Japanese had demonstrated at Pearl Harbor, the right weapons with which to sink warships. I was moving one of the stubby 21-inch aerial torpedoes that weighed two thousand pounds on a hydraulic lift across the oily, slippery hangar deck. Suddenly the 5-inch antiaircraft guns on the after starboard sponson above began firing, and the deck heeled sharply up fifteen degrees on that side as the ship turned abruptly to port to evade an attack.

My first real experience of a shooting war! The steep angle of the deck caused the heavy torpedo to slide down toward the port side, carrying me and the other man I was working with, with it. We lowered the hydraulic skid to the deck, but the torpedo still slid on the oily steel until we at last got some lashings on it and secured it to the rings in the deck used for tying down planes. There we stood, two sailors with a lashed-down torpedo, in the middle of the vast empty hangar deck, which was shifting rapidly from one crazy angle to another. We wanted to get the hell out of there but couldn't leave the torpedo with its live warhead for fear it would break loose and smash into a bulkhead and explode. We stayed, even though by then the smaller guns (.50-caliber machine guns) along the catwalk were firing.

You could measure the progress of an attack by the number and caliber of guns firing. As long as the five-inchers were booming, the enemy was still high and far away, but when the small-caliber guns (first the four-barreled deliberate one-point-ones—bang, bang, bang, bang—and then the fifties) began rattling away, it was time to put your head down. When someone ran out on the deck and began firing a pistol, which frequently happened, the attack was really closing in.

Water splashed in one of the openings in the hangar deck from a near miss. In a few minutes it was all over, and the *Enterprise*, undamaged, was on her way back to Pearl Harbor.

One of our torpedo planes flying a search vector did not return one bright blue day. We waited for it and the three men aboard hour after hour until we knew that it had surely run out of gas in an ocean where there was no place to land except on the deck of the *Enterprise*. Search planes were sent out, and destroyers patrolled for miles in all directions, but no trace of the plane was found and the men were assumed lost. When they turned up in Pearl Harbor about two months later, looking a bit thin but fit, we were all astounded. They had spent thirty days on their small yellow rubber raft, all three of them, with no rations or water at all, having lost everything when they ditched with engine failure. Rainwater, seabirds, and fish kept them going until purely by accident, in all that vastness, they washed ashore on a small island, losing their raft getting across the coral reef, and then, exhausted, flung up on the beach by a wave.

The March 23, 1942, issue of *Time* magazine referred to the pilot, an enlisted chief named Harold Dixon, as "a man that Bligh would fancy," and encouraged by this kind of doubtful praise, he published a book (with help from a ghostwriter) later in 1942 about the journey, making, so we heard, a fortune from it. The book made its way out to the squadron where everyone hooted and traded foolish quotes because Dixon was by no means a writer. The book reported him as saying to his crew when they lay exhausted, emaciated and totally dehydrated on the beach of the island, "If there are Japs on this island, they'll not see an American sailor crawl. We'll stand, and march, and make them shoot us down like men-o'-warsmen." The squadron wits amused us for weeks with aping the way that men-o'-warsmen, a term most of us had never heard, would march to the center of the island and be shot down.

Entering Pearl Harbor after the Marshall raid was the most moving moment of the war for me; far more than Nagasaki, which was hard to take in, or Tokyo Bay. We were in whites, lined up at quarters on the flight deck, and as we came down the channel, the sunken and burned battleships along Ford Island in plain sight, the crews of the anchored ships, at quarters themselves, their white uniforms showing up against their gray ships, cheered us, one after another, again and again. The frustration of defeat and helplessness after Pearl Harbor, while the Japanese overran the entire western Pacific and sank our ships wherever they found them, in the Philippines or in Indonesia, was enormous. The raid by the *Enterprise* on the Marshalls was the first successful action by an American ship; small, yes, but it was enough to give the fleet a lift.

Exultation was brief for me. I had already been a plane-handler, but that was a noble occupation compared to mess cooking: three months in the galleys, literally, peeling and slicing potatoes in enormous machines, washing huge pots and pans for days at a time, carrying out garbage pails filled to the brim with slops to be dumped over the side at night, serving food to the endless lines of sailors coming through to be fed and making nasty remarks about what you gave them.

Everyone did it, but mess cooking was real exile. You had to move to the mess halls with your bedding, stow your hammock in the nets there, and sleep in it at night, one of the few places in the modern navy where hammocks were used. The food-serving operation ran night and day, with watches coming on and going off duty every four hours, and only the exhaustion of eighteen-hour days of heavy labor made sleep possible in compartments where the lights were never out and people came and went constantly.

Good luck sent me after a month of work in the vegetable locker (peeling potatoes) to the galley of the chief petty officers' quarters, where the work was lighter, the nights uninterrupted, and a tip given by the chiefs every month for satisfactory service.

One of the most disagreeable jobs was handling the huge galvanized garbage cans filled with slop. It took two men to get them up the slippery narrow ship's ladders, step by painful step, with some inevitable spillage on you, and the deck, along the way to where they could be emptied over the side, to leeward, of course, not always an easy place to find in the dark if the ship was maneuvering and the wind was shifting. This was done at night to avoid leaving a trail of our presence in the ocean.

One night my fellow garbage handler and I fell on a steep ladder. In a failed attempt to keep the can from spilling, Whitey slipped and hit his mouth on the edge of the can, knocking out one of his upper-front teeth. The ship's dentist did only fillings and extractions, no cosmetic work, and so Whitey spent the next eight hours of the liberty we got every month or two when we came into Pearl going to a Honolulu dentist to get a false tooth installed. This was both a painful and an expensive way to spend what little liberty and money he had—even though we were by that time seamen first class making all of fifty-four dollars a month—and I used to argue with him long and earnestly, in the way that only a young man who knows nothing could, that it was pointless to waste his time and money in this fashion. Better to wait until the war was over and you knew whether you would survive to use a false tooth, ran my foolish and boring refrain.

But Whitey was not only stubborn, he was, it turned out to my vast surprise, hugely vain, and though small and nondescript physically, like the rest of us—we did not look at all like the sailors we saw dancing their lives away in the movies!—he could not bear the thought of being what he considered mutilated. I know now that he was right, but then so was I, without really knowing anything, for, having taken up the trade of a cook, he was killed along with Dallas, the head cook, by an armor-piercing bomb that exploded in the chiefs' galley the following October at the Battle of Santa Cruz.

A month at sea, cruising back and forth across the International Date Line, up and down over the equator, inducted with some strenuous naval horseplay into "The Ancient and Honorable Order of Shellbacks," a quick air attack on some little island, Wake or Marcus, and then back to Pearl for supplies and a brief liberty.

Honolulu in those days was more out of Somerset Maugham than Gauguin, but it seemed the proper setting for the heroes we felt we were, dressed in fresh white uniforms, rushing onto the buses and roaring down to Canal Street. A few minutes were spent in the New Congress Hotel, where the "French line" went up the long wooden stairs on the right, and the "old-fashioned line" ascended the left staircase. (Such sophistication! What could the *Old* Congress have been like?) Going once through each line—take your choice of the order—was considered a sign of true manhood, and the really virile went right back into the line rather than getting a few drinks before returning to the service of Venus.

On to the honky-tonks with the jukeboxes, the fights between sailors from different ships, and several bottles of the unspeakable local brew, Primo Beer, no hard liquor being sold. Dirty, bedraggled, and obscenely noisy we made our way back to the navy yard by late afternoon, ran the gauntlet of the marine guards at the gate who took out their frustrations with clubs on sailors looking for a fight, and then crowded into the fifty-foot motor launches that took us at last back to ships with names as epic—*Enterprise*, *Yorktown*, *Salt Lake City*, *Pensacola*—as those at Trafalgar or Jutland. Weighed soberly, Honolulu liberty was not much, but it had the effect of making us glad to be, as sailors always are, aboard ship again.

I fancied myself quite a dancer at the time, though the hornpipe had passed, and I found my way in time to the servicemen's club—the USO that had just been opened—to dance with the local Portuguese girls who volunteered to mingle with the sailors. Honolulu was an old liberty port, long familiar with naval antics ashore, and while nothing we did could any longer surprise the outrage-hardened citizenry, they wanted as little to do with us as possible. Most especially, they did not want us even to look at their daughters. Unaware of what it meant to be a sailor in Honolulu, I thought I cut quite a fine nautical figure and was crestfallen when I tried to make a date with one of the beautiful Portuguese girls, only to learn that her father would rather see her date one of the lepers from Molokai than a sailor. But my heart was not broken.

In April we put to sea and to our surprise went north for a change. Morale dropped conspicuously low with the news that Bataan had surrendered. As it became cold and colder, woolen gloves and winter uniforms long stowed away in seabags in storage lockers appeared. White water broke over the flight deck as the ship rose and fell in heavy green seas. One morning there was another carrier, the USS *Hornet* (CV 8), sister ship of the *Enterprise*, running alongside, about a hundred yards away. Instead of the usual pale blue-and-white naval aircraft, her deck was loaded with khaki-colored twin-engine army light bombers, B-25s, from a point forward of the island, in two rows, all the way to the stern. We assumed that they were intended for delivery somewhere in the Aleutians, but the public address system soon announced, there being no need for secrecy since there was no one we could tell and no way we could tell them, that this was an army squadron commanded by Col. James Doolittle, to be launched for an attack on Tokyo after we carried it to a point five hundred miles off the Japanese mainland. The *Enterprise* was to provide combat air patrols and antisubmarine patrols for the *Hornet* since she could launch none of her own planes stowed away on the hangar deck.

We were tremendously excited, not only at the idea of hitting Tokyo itself but also at the danger of going so close to Japan. But we were technicians, and it was the technical problem that really intrigued us. Could the heavy planes with a bomb load of two thousand pounds, even when stripped of guns and armor, get to Japan and then make it to the nearest safe landing point in China? Even before that, could such heavy planes designed for long landing strips get off a short carrier deck? The B-25s spotted farthest forward had a run of only about three hundred feet before dropping off the bow, which was about the minimum run needed for even the much smaller carrier planes designed for this work. Sailors, like stockbrokers, work everything out by betting, and there was soon heavy money down on both sides: would they make it, would they not? The odds were that the B-25s wouldn't have been on the *Hornet* if there had not been tests somewhere, but with all the skepticism of an old salt about anything the services did, I put down ten dollars at even money that less than half of them would get off.

April 18 was a cold and windy morning: near gale-force winds, gray and blue everywhere, with high dark green waves and the real taste and smell of the northern ocean. We were spotted some six hundred miles off the Japanese coast by fishing boats serving as pickets and patrol craft. The light cruiser *Nashville*, with fifteen 6-inch guns in five turrets, three forward and two aft, looked the picture of naval warfare in the age of steam as she came up to flank speed—about thirty-five knots—turned sharply to port, and began firing. Signal flags crackled as they ran up and down on the halyards, black smoke blew in the wind, yellow flashes came out of the gun barrels, and salvo after salvo missed the little boats bobbing on the waves, now in sight, now hidden. They were not easy targets, but the *Nashville*'s gunnery was disgraceful, and she was afterwards dispatched back to the States with those ominous orders, "For Further Training," that every unit that fails to meet standards dreads. The *Enterprise*'s fighters, the stubby little bee-like Grumman F4Fs, swarmed on the Japanese boats instantly and sank them with machine-gun fire.

Everyone assumed, however, that the *Nashville*'s failure had given the Japanese time to radio warnings. After the war it became known that, screwed up themselves, they had not transmitted a warning, but the assumption on the American ships had to be that the Japanese now knew that two carriers were close to their shores and that we had better get out of there if we wanted to save the ships on which the Pacific war depended. The range was a hundred miles or so too long for the B-25s, but the decision was made to risk it and launch anyway. So, turning into the gale, over forty knots by now, which helped the launch, the *Hornet* began to send the bombers off. The first plane, Doolittle's, didn't even use up the deck available. So powerful was the wind added to the full speed of the ship—about seventy-five knots combined—that the B-25s needed only to get up about thirty knots' speed to float off the deck like some great kites, only slowly moving ahead of the ship, which seemed to remain almost stationary below them. One after another the entire squadron went off, and we all cheered loudly, choked down a few patriotic tears, and I thought my ten dollars well lost in a good cause, as if I had actually contributed the money to success in the war.

We turned back at once to get out of range of the Japanese aircraft, and though we were told that Doolittle had bombed Tokyo, we heard no details about how most but not all of the planes made it to China until years afterward, when the entire story of the minor damage, but heavy blow to Japanese pride, became public.

Within a few days it was warm again, and after another brief stop at Pearl we departed, still with the *Hornet*, for the southwest Pacific, where the battle to contain the Japanese drive to the south and the east—Australia, New Guinea, and the Solomon Islands—was shaping up. By now the surface ships in Indonesia, that is, the cruisers *Houston* and *Marblehead*, having been annihilated, and the *Prince of Wales* and *Repulse* having been sunk off Malaya, the war on both sides was being fought by task forces centered on aircraft carriers, which maneuvered to locate the enemy and get in the first strike, sinking or damaging his carriers. Two of our four active carriers in the Pacific, the *Lexington* and *Yorktown*, were already in the Coral Sea, off the eastern end of New Guinea, trying to block two Japanese fleets coming at them from opposing directions. We were being sent to equal the odds and to come in from the east to surprise the Japanese two-carrier task force coming south from Truk.

Wartime cruising had settled down to a routine in which boredom and tiredness ate away at life at sea. Stripped of paint and linoleum, rusting everywhere, constantly hot from cruising near the equator, with few air blowers open below deck, shuddering with high-speed maneuvers in a way that knocked over anything set on shelf or table, the ships and life aboard them began to get to us. Fresh food lasted only a few days after we had been in port; we had only salt water to wash and shave in, with the irritation of sandy saltwater soap; there was no entertainment of any kind, only work and sleep. Men began to get irritable.

Dungarees and blue work shirts, the standard uniform of the day, were never ironed, only washed and dried together in a great bag that had to be rummaged through to find those with your name stenciled on them. Put on clean and dry, they were soaking wet from the heat in a few minutes. White hats were dyed an anemic purple, and white socks were forbidden in order to avoid the flashes of white on the flight deck that would betray the presence of the ship to a snooper aircraft. Heat rash tormented everyone, particularly around the waist where several layers of wet clothing twisted and pulled inside the belt. A story circulated that when the heat rash—a quarter of an inch high and several inches wide, red and angry—girdled your waist, you died. No one believed it, but everyone kept a careful eye on the progress of the rash around his middle.

No one died, but every free moment was spent somewhere where the cooling breeze could blow over the rash and the sun could dry it out. Lacking any movies and music to entertain us, we gambled. It became the only relief from the tedium of what now was becoming not weeks but months at sea without even seeing land in the distance. I was a more enthusiastic than skillful poker player, but I loved the game, as I did bridge, and even though I regularly lost my money in games in one small compartment or another about the ship, the first glimpse of the five cards in draw poker or the hole card in stud poker were the high moments, ironically, of days that were routinely filled with the real adventure of accidents and frequent death.

Death lived on an aircraft carrier operating in wartime conditions. One day a plane would crash taking off, and the lucky pilot lost no more than an eye on his telescopic sight mounted in front of him. The next day a plane landing on deck would drop a wheel strut into the catwalk and run screeching up it for a hundred feet. A mangled crewman would be carried away. A thoughtless step backward on the flight and hangar decks where the planes were turning up led to decapitation and gory dismemberment by propeller. Planes went out on patrol and were never heard of again. Death took many forms, but I think I first really came to know him on a day when I was standing on the flight deck and a Dauntless dive-bomber flew across the ship to drop a message about something seen on a patrol.

Once ships had put to sea, strict radio silence was maintained except for certain high-frequency VHF short-range transmissions used to direct the CAP (Combat Air Patrol) of fighters, close by the ship. Beanbags trailing long red streamers were used for message drops in order to preserve radio silence. As the dive-bomber came across the ship at about 120 knots, with the starboard wing sharply down to give the radioman an open field to throw the message bag on the flight deck, the down wing caught, ever so slightly, just a tick, the railing on the catwalk at the very edge of the ship. Just a flicker, but it was enough. In an instant the plane was in the water off the starboard side, broken in half between the radioman and the pilot, neither of whom, knocked out by the crash, heads hanging limply forward, moved. Then in an instant both pieces were gone, the water was unruffled, and the ship sailed on. The quickness with which active life, so much energy and skill in the banking plane, disappeared as if it had never been stunned me.

It was the instantaneous contrast of something and nothing that caught my attention, and like some eighteen-year-old ancient mariner, I went around for days trying to tell people what had *really* happened, how astounding it was. The response was polite; death was a grave matter to everyone and never lightly dismissed. But no one, quite rightly, wanted to philosophize or make too much of what was common and likely to be the end of all of us, much sooner than later.

Edward V. Rickenbacker

Edward "Eddie" Rickenbacker (1890–1973) first gained fame as a driver in the earliest Indianapolis 500 races. He then became the leading American fighter pilot of World War I, credited with the destruction of 22 German planes and four observation balloons in 1918. Rickenbacker became president of Eastern Airlines in 1938 and was asked in 1942 to report on the readiness of American air force units overseas. On October 21, 1942, he left Hawaii on board a B-17 bomber to begin an inspection tour in the southwestern Pacific. Navigational error caused the aircraft to miss its refueling stop and ditch in the ocean 600 miles north of Samoa. After drifting for 22 days, Rickenbacker and six other survivors were rescued by U.S. Navy seaplanes and ships. He describes their struggle in Seven Came Through *(1943), from which this chapter is taken.*

The Death of Sergeant Alex

The line around my waist was now put to good use. Because the wind and seas were fast sweeping the rafts apart, I called the others in and, fastening the rope to the hand lines around the rafts, we formed a line astern, twenty feet or so apart. Cherry being captain, his raft was first, mine was second, and the two-man raft brought up the rear. The arrangement had its drawbacks. In the heavy swell, as the rafts rose and fell at their different intervals, the interminable, uneven shocks on the line made rest impossible. But I shall always believe that had we separated, few if any of us would now be alive. A strong man may last a long time alone but men together somehow manage to last longer.

My memory of that first afternoon is not wholly clear. The spray and the green water coming over the roll of the raft kept us soaked, and I bailed for hours with my hat—my wonderful old hat. This gave me exercise, besides keeping me from thinking too much.

Some time during the afternoon we totted up our possessions. The only food was four oranges that Cherry had stuffed in his pocket just before the crash, together with the chocolate bar that I had and half a dozen more that Alex had, which an Army doctor had given him the day before. The chocolate was never eaten. Alex' was ruined by his thrashing around in the water and he had to throw it away. Next day, when I felt in the pocket for mine, it had become a green mush, which neither I nor my companions would touch.

So, except for the oranges, we started with nothing. But knowing that a man can live a long time without food or water, I was more worried over the shortage of clothing. Only Adamson and I were fully dressed. He had his uniform and cap and I had on a blue summer-weight business suit, complete with necktie, pocket handkerchief, and refillable pencil. The others, expecting to swim, had taken off their shoes and hats before abandoning ship. None had hats or sweaters, but the two pilots had their leather jackets. Several had even thrown their socks away. Bartek, in fact, was naked except for a one-piece jumper.

I may have forgotten an item or two, but these were our total possessions: a first-aid kit, eighteen flares, and one Very pistol for firing them; two hand pumps for both bailing and renewing the air in the rafts; two service sheath knives; a pair of pliers; a small pocket compass; two revolvers belonging to Cherry and Adamson; two collapsible rubber bailing buckets; three sets of patching gear, one for each raft; several pencils; and my map of the Pacific. We all had cigarettes, but the salt water got to these immediately, and they were thrown away. And, finally, Reynolds produced two fish lines, with hooks attached, which he had snatched from a parachute bag after the crash. But there was no bait, and unless we managed to shoot down a gull, our chances of "living off the country" were decidedly thin.

But that first afternoon no one was conscious of our poverty; we were too exhausted to care. Three or four of the boys were violently seasick and I didn't feel any too comfortable myself, although I never reached the point of vomiting. Adamson was in agony from his wrenched back; every jerk of the boat, he said, felt as if someone was kicking him in the kidneys. But I was more worried about Sergeant Alex, in the little raft astern. Long after the others had stopped, he continued to retch. "What's the matter with him?" I called to De Angelis. "I don't know," answered De Angelis, "he must have swallowed a lot of salt water when we tipped over."

The sun went down swiftly, a cold mist gathering on the sea, and the moon came up—a three-quarter moon—beautiful to see. The wisecracks and the small talk, which sounded pretty silly in the immensity of the night, petered out and we were beginning to realize that we were in for hard times.

Naturally, one of the first things we had to do was to work out some organization of habits. Keeping a continuous watch—what we called an alert—was an obvious necessity. That first night we arranged to stand two-hour watches, relieving each other in turn. It seems pretty silly now, but I offered $100 to the first man to see land, a ship, or an airplane. But nobody slept that night. We were wet and miserable. Although the swell moderated just before midnight, the waves kept slopping into the rafts. Both air and water were warm, yet with each splash I felt as if I was being doused with buckets of ice water. Bartek and I changed positions every hour or so, to share the comfort of the other's lee. But I was never warm, and put in most of the night bailing. Sharks followed us from the plane; the water seemed full of them.

The second day came on slowly, first a gray mist and then the sun breaking through clear. It took hours to get warm, for the night mist penetrated to the bone. As I have said, we had those four oranges, but we decided to save them against the future. By popular vote I was made their custodian, and Cherry generously handed them over. We agreed to divide the first that morning, and the others on alternate days. That way, they would last eight days.

I cut the orange in half, then halved the halves, then halved the quarters, giving each man one eighth. With seven men watching, you can be sure I made an exact division. In fact, I studied the fruit a full minute before I cut. Some sucked and ate the peel, but Cherry and I saved ours for bait.

Men have been lost at sea before; others have spent more days on rafts than we did. A good deal of what we went through was what you might expect—hunger, thirst, heat, cold, and a slow rotting away. In some respects, the period from the second to the eighth day was the worst. A glassy calm fell upon the sea; the sun beat down fiercely all day; the rafts stood still, with the lines slack between; I even imagined I smelled flesh burning, and the sweet stink of hot rubber.

Face, neck, hands, wrists, legs, and ankles burned, blistered, turned raw, and burned again. In time De Angelis and Whittaker, having darker skins, developed a protecting tan, but the rest of us cooked day after day. My hands swelled and blistered; when the salt water got into the flesh, it burned and cracked and dried and burned again. Three months later the scars still show on the knuckles. Our mouths became covered with ugly running sores. Reynolds, having no covering for his legs, turned into a sodden red mass of hurt. Even the soles of his feet were burned raw.

These first five or six days were the worst I have ever known. The night I lay in a wrecked plane near Atlanta, with a dead man half crushed under my chest, had produced its own kind of suffering. But then the pain had been dulled by delirium, and after a while I knew help was near because I could hear people moving around in the dark. But on the Pacific I was something being turned on a spit. Without my hat, I would have been badly off. I would fill it with water, then jam it down over my ears. Before our rescue, the brim was half torn away from the crown.

Some of the others, to escape the terrible heat, paddled for hours in the water. But they paid a stiff price for the relief because their flesh burned again as it dried, and the salt brine stung. Without my handkerchiefs we would have had a much harder time. I passed them around and, folded bandit-fashion across the nose, they protected the lower part of the face. But there was no sparing the eyes. The sea sent back billions of sharp splinters of light; no matter where one looked it was painful. A stupor descended upon the rafts. Men simply sat or sprawled, heads rolling on the chest, mouths half open, gasping. Reynolds, from the cut on his nose, was a horrible sight. The sun would not let the wound heal. He washed the blood off with salt water, but it soon oozed again, spreading over his face, drying in a red crust. Bartek, too, was in agony from his cut fingers. He splashed them with iodine from the first-aid kit, but the salt water ate it away.

Daytimes we prayed for the coolness of the nights; nights we craved the sun. But I really came to hate the nights. Daytimes, I could see my fellow men, the play of the water, the gulls, all the signs of life. But the night brought us all close to fear. A cold, dense mist always rose around us. The damp soaked our clothes and we pressed together for warmth. Sometimes, when the mist was very heavy, the other rafts would be hidden. If the sea was calm and the line had fallen slack, I would sometimes come out of a nightmare, and pull in the towlines until they fetched up hard, and I knew the others were still there. Other times, I would hear moans or groans, or a cry and often a prayer. Or I would see a shadow move and twist as a man tried to ease his torture.

I know I can never hope to describe the awful loneliness of the night. Perhaps it affected me more than the others. I seldom slept more than an hour or so at a time, and even then, it seemed, with one eye open and one ear cocked. That was because I was always worried that the man who was supposed to be on watch might doze off and let a ship go by. I have gotten along most of my life with a good deal less sleep than most men are accustomed to have. This habit stood me in good stead on the Pacific. But the younger men had trouble staying awake. The stupor induced by the terrific heat of the day, together with the lulling motion of the raft as it listed and fell on the swell—a motion that at times was not unlike that of a hammock—seemed to put them quickly to sleep.

What also made the night hard for me was that I could never stretch out. Someday I shall meet the man who decided these rafts could hold two men and five men each. When I do, he is either going to revise his opinions or prove them on a long voyage, under conditions I shall be happy to suggest. Adamson weighed over two hundred pounds and I was not much lighter. On our five-man raft, he and Bartek and I shared an inside room measuring six feet nine inches by two feet four inches. Counting the narrow inflated roll, on which a man could stretch out for an hour or so with his feet dangling in the water, the dimensions were nine feet by five.

Because Adamson was in such pain, Bartek and I gave him one end to himself. He lay with his bumpus on the bottom, his head against the carbon-dioxide bottle, his feet across the roll. Bartek and I lay facing each other, or back to back, with our legs crooked over the roll. This was the way it was in Cherry's boat. But Alex and De Angelis in the two-man raft, although the smallest men, were much worse off. They had to sit facing each other, one with his legs over the other man's shoulders, while he took the legs of the other under his armpits, or they sat back to back, dangling their legs in the water. And sometimes De Angelis lay sprawled out, with Alex on his chest. Imagine two men in a small, shallow bathtub, and you will have a reasonably good idea of how much room they had.

Whenever you turned or twisted, you forced the others to turn or twist. It took days to learn how to make the most of the space, at an incalculable price in misery. A foot or hand or shoulder, moved in sleep or restlessness, was bound to rake the raw flesh of a companion. With the flesh, tempers turned raw and many things said in the night had best be forgotten.

The moon was turning into full. I was awake a good part of the time, hoping to catch the loom of a ship. In those first nights of utter calm the clouds would form the most unusual pictures, beautiful women, elephants, birds. It sounds fantastic. I remember seeing one shaped like a wild boar. I saw trees, completely formed.

The first two or three nights I thought I was seeing things. Finally I mentioned it to Adamson and he agreed with me that they were there. There was some reason for them because you could see them night in and night out, particularly during the first ten days. The moonlight helped to make these forms seem more vivid. I suppose there is a scientific explanation but I don't know what it is.

The forms were so vivid, so concise, so positive that they fascinated me. This helped some; it gave me something to think about during the long hours of the night.

The stars helped also to keep our minds occupied. We were on the equator and so all the familiar stars were in different positions, the Big Dipper, the Little Dipper, the North Star. We used to talk about them. Colonel Adamson had been in charge of the Planetarium in New York for a number of years and he was able to tell us a great deal about the different constellations and the movements of the stars. I kept promoting these discussions because of the good it did all of us.

What bothered us most of all was not knowing where we were. Every member of the party had his own ideas about this. I was under the impression—and later events confirmed it—that we were somewhere west or northwest of our island destination. Captain Cherry agreed with me in this.

The next day a terrible calm settled down which made the sea just like a glassy mirror. There were very little swells only and the sun was intensely hot. The glare was terrible on the eyes and most of the boys fell into a doze or sort of stupor. Most of them had injuries of one kind or another to add to their plight. I was afraid that Sergeant Reynolds had a broken nose. In getting out he had struck his head against the radio and the blood had dried on his face. He had no hat and the sun was beginning to burn him badly, and the combination made him an awesome-looking spectacle. Bartek had had all his fingers cut on the inside of the hand, two of them to the bone, and they had bled very badly. We had hauled out the iodine from the first-aid kit as soon as we settled down on the rafts and had done what we could to dress the fingers. The effect did not last long because the salt water would take it off. It would get into the little cuts and so kept him in agony for the first two or three nights. Finally, of course, it dried out and started to heal.

On the fourth morning the second orange was divided. Except for the orange on the second morning, we had then been seventy-two hours without food or liquid. Fish were all around; I could see hundreds swimming idly just below the raft. Cherry and I fished for hours with pieces of orange peel. I even borrowed Adamson's keyring, which was shiny, and tried to manipulate it as a spinner. The fish would nose the hook, fan their tails in curiosity, but they never struck.

For six days on that glassy, sizzling sea, the rafts did not seem to move. But by our watches we knew we were drifting; each morning the sun rose just a little bit later. This meant the rafts were inching west and south. We argued interminably over where we were, but it turned out only Cherry and I were right. We were positive of having overshot our island and, if our guess was true, we could count on no land nearer than certain Japanese-held islands four hundred to five hundred miles away. I studied the map two or three times a day, always returning it to my inside coat pocket, to protect it against the water. But the colors were already beginning to run.

Commencing the second night, Cherry sent up a flare every night. Having eighteen, we first decided to use three a night, the first after sundown, the second around midnight, the last before dawn. But of the first three sent aloft, one was a complete dud and the second flickered for only a few seconds. The third, swinging on its parachute, gave a scary, blinding red light, lasting perhaps a minute and a half. Next night, cutting down the expenditure to two good ones, we had another dud; this decided us to reduce the nightly allotment to a single good one.

Always, after the light had exhausted itself, my eyes strained into the darkness, hoping to catch a responding gleam—a gleam which would not settle into the steadiness of a star. It was plain that unless we soon had food or water or the terrible hot calm relented, some of us were bound to die. Adamson, being portly, felt the heat worse than the rest. Reynolds, thin anyway, was fading to skin and bones. Alex, though, was really in a bad way. His mouth was dry and frothing; he cried continually for water. He was only a boy—barely twenty-two—and thinking he was quitting, I pulled his raft in close and asked why the hell he couldn't take it? It was a brutal thing to do, yet I was determined to shock him back to his senses. I found out then what was wrong. He was only three weeks out of the hospital. In addition, he had contracted a lip disease, something like trench mouth, with a scientific name I do not remember. All this had left him with less strength than the rest from the start, and the salt water he swallowed when his raft capsized had helped to do him in.

Unfortunately for him that wasn't the only salt water Alex had had. De Angelis woke one night to find him half out of the raft, gulping salt water. Now I had admonished everybody the first afternoon out not to drink salt water, knowing that it would drive them wild with thirst. Alex admitted he had been doing this persistently. It explained the cries for water we didn't have. "I tried not to," Alex said, "but I had to. I just had to have water."

So it was only a question of time for poor Alex. He sank deeper into delirium, murmuring his "Hail Mary" and other Catholic prayers. In his wallet was a photograph of a young girl to whom he was engaged: he talked to it, prayed over it. Finally he could neither sleep nor lie down. De Angelis tried to keep the sun off him, but there was no shadow anywhere. So he burned and burned. At night in the moonlight I could see him sitting on the raft shaking as if with ague. He literally vibrated, he was so horribly cold. Yet, except to cry for water, he never really complained.

Bartek had a New Testament in his jumper pocket. Watching him read it, the thought came to me that we might all profit by his example. I am not a religious man, but I was taught the Lord's Prayer at my mother's knee and I had gone to Sunday school. If I had any religion in my later life, it was based on the Golden Rule. Yet I have always been conscious of God.

With the New Testament as an inspiration, we held morning and evening prayers. The rafts were pulled together, making a rough triangle. Then, each in turn, one of us would read a passage. None of us, I must confess, showed himself to be very familiar with them, but thumbing the book we found a number that one way or another bespoke our needs. The Twenty-third Psalm was, of course, a favorite. I have always been stirred by it, but out on the Pacific I found a beauty in it that I had never appreciated. Yet there was another that we never failed to read, because it so clearly set forth what was in our minds:

Therefore take no thought, saying, What shall we eat? or, What shall we drink? or, Wherewithal shall we be clothed?

. . . For your heavenly Father knoweth that ye have need of all these things. But seek ye first the kingdom of God, and his righteousness; and all these things shall be added unto you.

Take therefore no thought for the morrow: for the morrow shall take thought for the things of itself. Sufficient unto the day is the evil thereof. (Matthew 6:31–34.)

One or two turned scornful and bitter because the answer was slow in coming, but the rest went on praying with deep-felt hope. Yet we did not neglect anything that might help us to help ourselves. Whittaker tried to make a spear from one of the aluminum oars, tearing the flat corners away with the pliers. He drove it into the back of a shark which rubbed alongside, but the hide was tougher than the point. After several tries it was so blunted as to be useless. Whittaker threw it angrily into the bottom of the raft. He had gained nothing and wasted an oar.

Also, Cherry sat all day long with a loaded revolver in his lap, hoping to knock down a gull. But none came close enough for a shot. He broke the revolver open two or three times a day and rubbed the moving parts with oil from his nose and the back of his ears, but he could not halt the sea-water corrosion. When the parts froze solid he threw the gun into the Pacific. Adamson's gun rusted in the same way and I dropped it over the side.

To keep the sick men alive, we finished the oranges faster than we had intended. We had the third on the morning of the fifth day, the last on the sixth. The last two were shrunken, much of the juice appeared to have evaporated, and the last one was beginning to rot. So long as there was that sliver of orange to anticipate, no one complained of hunger. Now, memories of food and drink began to haunt us. We tried to catch the sharks that cruised near the rafts with our hands. I actually had several small ones by the back but the hide was too slippery for a firm grip.

The desire for food in several men became almost violent. They agonized over their hunger pains and talked constantly about food, and whether they could go on much longer without it.

Reynolds talked about how much soda pop he was going to drink the rest of his life. Cherry couldn't think about anything but chocolate ice cream. As I listened to the thirsty talk between the rafts, my own mind slowly filled with visions of chocolate malted milk. I could actually taste it, to the point where my tongue worked convulsively. The strange part is that I hadn't had a chocolate malted milk in nearly twenty-five years.

From the start I had advised against talk as I realized how necessary it was going to be for all of us to conserve our strength in every way possible; but looking back now I am rather amazed at the little talking that we did.

During the first few days, while we suffered from the shock of the fall and our minds were filled with speculation as to the chances of rescue, there was much more than later. This was particularly noticeable after several days had passed and the prospect of escape was becoming dimmer. It was then we began to sing hymns after prayer meetings. The singing seemed to release something in the minds of most of us and the talk for the first time became intensely personal. As I have already stated, there was no time that I lost faith in our ultimate rescue, but the others did not seem to share this state of mind fully with me. My companions clearly began to think of what lay beyond death and to think of it in terms of their own lives.

They began to tell of what they had experienced in life: their hopes, fears, ambitions, their achievements, their mistakes. I suppose it takes the imminence of death to release one completely from inhibitions. The talk was entirely honest and, I am sure, entirely frank. What was said will always be locked up in our minds. As far as I am concerned, no hint of those long, man-to-man conversations will ever be revealed. I am sure of one thing, that it did us a great deal of good.

As the days wore on and our strength left us, we talked less and less. A drowsiness, which in the later stages amounted almost to coma, had taken possession of us. We would lie for hours in the intense heat of the sun without a single word being spoken. What I seem to remember most about the last days was the almost complete silence. If one man spoke there would be no response. We were so completely divorced from living that we had nothing to talk about, even if we had had the strength for it.

I recall no mention of the war. It was continually in my own mind because of my conviction of survival. I was sure I would live to see the struggle through, and consequently did not get away from the speculations that I would have engaged in under normal conditions. I never put them into words, however. If my companions were thinking along the same line, they observed the same reticence that I did.

All conversation during the last stages had to do with the changes of position we found necessary in the rafts and the negative results of the Very lights we set off. Sometimes our hopes would kindle when one of us mistook a low star for the light of a ship. There would be eager discussion then, dwindling off into hopeless silences when it became certain that it had been nothing more than a delusion.

Twenty-one days of it, and during all that time, I am inclined to believe, we talked less than we would have done in the course of one normal day.

The eighth day was another hot, flat calm. It did not help our stomachs any to look down and see dolphin and mackerel, sleek and fat and twelve to eighteen inches long, and thousands of smaller fish swimming in the depths. That afternoon Cherry read the service, with the usual quotation from Matthew. About an hour later, when I was dozing with my hat pulled down over my eyes, a gull appeared from nowhere and landed on my hat.

I don't remember how it happened or how I knew he was there. But I knew it instantly, and I knew that if I missed this one, I'd never find another to sit on my hat. I reached up for him with my right hand—gradually. The whole Pacific seemed to be shaking from the agitation in my body, but I could tell he was still there from the hungry, famished, almost insane eyes in the other rafts. Slowly and surely my hand got up there; I didn't clutch, but just closed my fingers, sensing his nearness, then closing my fingers hard.

I wrung his neck, defeathered him, carved up the body, divided the meat into equal shares, holding back only the intestines for bait. Even the bones were chewed and swallowed. No one hesitated because the meat was raw and stringy and fishy. It tasted fine. After Cherry had finished his piece, I baited a hook and passed it over to him. The hook, weighted with Whittaker's ring, had hardly got wet before a small mackerel hit it, and was jerked into the raft. I dropped the other line, with the same miraculous result, except that mine was a small sea bass.

All this food in the space of a few minutes bolstered us beyond words. We ate one of the fish before dark and put the other aside for the next day. Even the craving for water seemed to abate, perhaps from chewing the cool, wet flesh while grinding the bones to a pulp. Alex and Adamson ate their shares, and I was optimistic enough to believe they were immediately better. I say in all truth that at no time did I ever doubt we would be saved, but as that eighth night rose around us I was sure we could last forever. The ocean was full of fish, and we could catch them.

As the sun went down, the sky clouded over, the air turned cool, a soft, uncertain wind made cat's-paws on the water—all portents of rain. I tried to stay awake to have everything in readiness if it came, but I finally dozed off with my head across Adamson's knees.

My next recollection is of being jolted awake, as if from a blow. The raft was slamming up and down on a heavy, irregular swell. It was pitch black—so black that I could scarcely make out the other rafts, except when they were thrown up on a swell. Gusts of wind came at us from every quarter. And I knew, if I ever knew anything, that rain was near.

From midnight we were on the watch for the rushing shadows of rain squalls. About three o'clock in the morning I heard the cry, "Rain." Drops splattered against my face and mouth, clean and sweet to taste. After the first few drops there was nothing more, but far off I could see the squall. The wind had a new sound, as if it were no longer empty. We paddled toward the squall and I prayed to God to put us in its path. We had a plan all worked out—bailing buckets ready and the empty canvas covers for the Very light cartridges. We took our shirts and socks off to spread over our heads and shoulders. The handkerchiefs were to be laid on the inflated roll until they became soaked. Adamson had even taken off his shorts to wring.

It was one hell of a night—all wind, waves, noise, lightning, and big black shadows. We paddled into it, shouting at the tops of our lungs. Out of that uproar came a cry for help. The little raft, with De Angelis and Alex, had broken loose. Bartek and I, with an oar to the side, set out after them, Cherry's raft following in our wake. I was afraid we'd lost them, but we sighted the raft against the white rush of a breaking wave, overtook it, and made it fast. A moment later the squall enveloped us.

Rain fell as from a waterfall. I spread the handkerchiefs on the roll of the raft, where they would catch the water, and fluffed my shirt over my head. Adamson, roused by the cool water on his body, draped his underpants over his chest to catch more water. I appointed myself wringer, and as fast as the others passed over the soaked pieces of cloth, I would twist them hard, forcing the water out, to rid the cloth of salt rime. I had done this several times with each piece, always tasting the last drippings for salt. I had finished rinsing out the bucket and cartridge covers, and was ready to collect the first water, when a sharp pull came on the bow line, twisting the raft around. Out of the corner of my eye I saw Cherry's raft being rolled over on its beam ends by a wave.

All three men were thrown out, and with Reynolds so weak I was sure he was going to drown. But in the next flash of lightning I counted three heads bobbing around the sides. While they clung to the hand line around the sides, we pulled in the line, bringing them in on our lee side, holding the raft steady while they helped each other in. Reynolds, gasping, mustered the strength to haul himself back. I shall never stop marveling at the hidden resources of men whose minds never give up. Cherry and Whittaker saved the oars, but they saved little else. The Very pistol and the last of the cartridges were lost. So were the bailing bucket and the little water they had collected.

All this—from the breaking away of the little raft to the righting of Cherry's—took no more than ten minutes, perhaps as little as five. But rather than wearing us down the exertions seemed to fill us with strength. I passed Cherry the bailing bucket, and while he bailed I watched anxiously for any letup in the rain. Adamson and Bartek sucked at the wet cloths, filling their mouths with the first water in eight days. To make up for his lost bucket, we gave Cherry the cartridge cover.

When they finally pulled away, I fell to wringing the sopping garments Bartek and Adamson had ready for me. Lightning flashed, the sea rumbled, the raft tossed wildly, but I was not really aware of them. My hands were terribly burned and blistered, and the flesh cracked and the blood spurted out, but I never felt it. As fast as I could wring out the cloths I handed them back to the others, who spread them out to soak again. I was gauging matters by just one thing—the water level in the bailing bucket.

Quite suddenly the wind died down and the rain stopped. The squall could not have lasted more than twenty minutes. But I had nearly a quart and a half of water in the bucket. Cherry, in his boat, had about a quart, but De Angelis and Alex, who had nothing to catch water in, had none. They had simply sucked their shirts.

In the calm that followed, the rafts were pulled in close. The round-table decision was that we'd better try to go on with as little water as possible—a half jigger per man per day. In the dark I poured what I guessed to be that much into one of the empty Very cartridge cases, and passed it seven times down the line of hands. It was the sweetest water I ever tasted. And the rain that had drenched our bodies, washing away the salt rime and cleansing the sores, had refreshed us quite as much.

On the ninth morning we shared the second fish and another half jigger of water. From this point on my memory may be hazy. Alex got no better, and on the tenth day, for his safety and Adamson's, we increased the water ration to two jiggers a day, one in the morning and one at sundown. On the following day we added another at noon.

The weather now took a change, and the sea turned rougher. The three of us in the middle boat had the worst of it, due to the yawing action from the pulls of the raft ahead and the raft behind. As each raft rose to a swell at a different interval, a shock would come on the lines and then would twist our raft first one way, then another. The little raft, being lighter, would coast down a swell and smack us, drenching us with salt water.

This was terribly hard on Adamson, and I insisted that the front raft exchange position with us for a few hours. This was done. It was much smoother. After Adamson had had a few hours' comfort, we returned to our original position in the middle of the line.

It was on the tenth evening, I think, that I asked Bartek to change rafts with Sergeant Alex, thinking that Alex might rest better. It took the combined strength of Bartek, De Angelis, and myself to move him. I stretched him on the lee side on the bottom of the boat and put my arm around him, as a mother cuddles a child, hoping in that way to transfer the heat of my body to him during the night. In an hour or so his shivering stopped and sleep came—a shallow sleep in which Alex mumbled intermittently in Polish—phrases about his mother and his girl "Snooks."

I kept Alex there all night, the next day and night, and the twelfth day. He was weaker, although more rational. When evening came, after the customary prayer, he asked to be put back in the little boat with De Angelis. I knew he couldn't last many hours longer, and so we pulled the other boat up and changed around again. We had to lift him like a baby. A strong wind came up and I slept fitfully that night, worrying about that little raft bouncing on the rough sea. Yet I must have dozed off, because my next recollection is of the sound of a long sigh.

I called to De Angelis: "Has he died?"

De Angelis said, after a pause, "I think so."

It was about 3:00 A.M. and very dark, and although it was hard on De Angelis to wait for dawn with a dead man across his body, I did not want to make a decision until there was light to see by. The other men stirred, woke up, and understood, almost without being told, what had happened. I remember someone saying, "Well, his sufferings are over." I think we were all a little frightened, with the wind blowing and clouds rushing across the sky, and Alex dead in that plunging raft. Somewhere I have read that sharks can sense the coming of death. That night there seemed twice as many as we had seen before.

At daybreak Bartek hauled Alex' little raft alongside, and Cherry paddled up in his. The body was already stiff, but I checked the heart, the pulse, checked in every way I knew. And I asked Cherry and Whittaker to do so, not wishing to accept the responsibility alone. We agreed Alex was dead. We removed his wallet and identification disc, which Captain Cherry has since returned to the family, and we saved the jacket. De Angelis murmured what he remembered of the Catholic burial service. Then we rolled the body over the side. It did not sink at once but rather floated off face down a little while.

This was the thirteenth morning.

Robert Lowell

Descended on both sides from prominent New England families, Robert Lowell (1917–1977) attended elite schools and studied poetry with some of the leading literary figures of his time: Richard Eberhart, Allen Tate, Robert Penn Warren, Cleanth Brooks. He served a prison sentence during World War II for conscientious objection; in 1944, soon after his release, he published his first book of poetry, Land of Unlikeness. *As his career progressed, Lowell's poetry adopted a markedly confessional voice and began to explore, among other subjects, his history of psychotic breakdowns. "The Quaker Graveyard in Nantucket"—an elegy, first collected in* Lord Weary's Castle *(1946), for a cousin lost at sea during the war—offers a distinctively bitter and self-lacerating portrait of the turbulent Atlantic and the violence of Nantucket's whaling past.*

The Quaker Graveyard in Nantucket

(for Warren Winslow, Dead at Sea)

Let man have dominion over the fishes of the sea and the fowls of the air and the beasts and the whole earth, and every creeping creature that moveth upon the earth.

I

A brackish reach of shoal off Madaket,—
The sea was still breaking violently and night
Had steamed into our North Atlantic Fleet,
When the drowned sailor clutched the drag-net. Light
Flashed from his matted head and marble feet,
He grappled at the net
With the coiled, hurdling muscles of his thighs:
The corpse was bloodless, a botch of reds and whites,
Its open, staring eyes
Were lustreless dead-lights
Or cabin-windows on a stranded hulk
Heavy with sand. We weight the body, close

Its eyes and heave it seaward whence it came,
Where the heel-headed dogfish barks its nose
On Ahab's void and forehead; and the name
Is blocked in yellow chalk.
Sailors, who pitch this portent at the sea
Where dreadnaughts shall confess
Its hell-bent deity,
When you are powerless
To sand-bag this Atlantic bulwark, faced
By the earth-shaker, green, unwearied, chaste
In his steel scales: ask for no Orphean lute
To pluck life back. The guns of the steeled fleet
Recoil and then repeat
The hoarse salute.

II

Whenever winds are moving and their breath
Heaves at the roped-in bulwarks of this pier,
The terns and sea-gulls tremble at your death
In these home waters. Sailor, can you hear
The Pequod's sea wings, beating landward, fall
Headlong and break on our Atlantic wall
Off 'Sconset, where the yawing S-boats splash
The bellbuoy, with ballooning spinnakers,
As the entangled, screeching mainsheet clears
The blocks: off Madaket, where lubbers lash
The heavy surf and throw their long lead squids
For blue-fish? Sea-gulls blink their heavy lids
Seaward. The winds' wings beat upon the stones,
Cousin, and scream for you and the claws rush
At the sea's throat and wring it in the slush
Of this old Quaker graveyard where the bones
Cry out in the long night for the hurt beast
Bobbing by Ahab's whaleboats in the East.

III

All you recovered from Poseidon died
With you, my cousin, and the harrowed brine

Is fruitless on the blue beard of the god,
Stretching beyond us to the castles in Spain,
Nantucket's westward haven. To Cape Cod
Guns, cradled on the tide,
Blast the eelgrass about a waterclock
Of bilge and backwash, roil the salt and sand
Lashing earth's scaffold, rock
Our warships in the hand
Of the great God, where time's contrition blues
Whatever it was these Quaker sailors lost
In the mad scramble of their lives. They died
When time was open-eyed,
Wooden and childish; only bones abide
There, in the nowhere, where their boats were tossed
Sky-high, where mariners had fabled news
Of IS, the whited monster. What it cost
Them is their secret. In the sperm-whale's slick
I see the Quakers drown and hear their cry:
"If God himself had not been on our side,
If God himself had not been on our side,
When the Atlantic rose against us, why,
Then it had swallowed us up quick."

IV

This is the end of the whaleroad and the whale
Who spewed Nantucket bones on the thrashed swell
And stirred the troubled waters to whirlpools
To send the Pequod packing off to hell:
This is the end of them, three-quarters fools,
Snatching at straws to sail
Seaward and seaward on the turntail whale,
Spouting out blood and water as it rolls,
Sick as a dog to these Atlantic shoals:
Clamavimus, O depths. Let the sea-gulls wail

For water, for the deep where the high tide
Mutters to its hurt self, mutters and ebbs.
Waves wallow in their wash, go out and out,

Leave only the death-rattle of the crabs,
The beach increasing, its enormous snout
Sucking the ocean's side.
This is the end of running on the waves;
We are poured out like water. Who will dance
The mast-lashed master of the Leviathans
Up from this field of Quakers in their unstoned graves?

V

When the whale's viscera go and the roll
Of its corruption overruns this world
Beyond tree-swept Nantucket and Wood's Hole
And Martha's Vineyard, Sailor, will your sword
Whistle and fall and sink into the fat?
In the great ash-pit of Jehoshaphat
The bones cry for the blood of the white whale,
The fat flukes arch and whack about its ears,
The death-lance churns into the sanctuary, tears
The gun-blue swingle, heaving like a flail,
And hacks the coiling life out: it works and drags
And rips the sperm-whale's midriff into rags,
Gobbets of blubber spill to wind and weather,
Sailor, and gulls go round the stoven timbers
Where the morning stars sing out together
And thunder shakes the white surf and dismembers
The red flag hammered in the mast-head. Hide
Our steel, Jonas Messias, in Thy side.

VI

Our Lady of Walsingham

There once the penitents took off their shoes
And then walked barefoot the remaining mile;
And the small trees, a stream and hedgerows file
Slowly along the munching English lane,
Like cows to the old shrine, until you lose
Track of your dragging pain.
The stream flows down under the druid tree,
Shiloah's whirlpools gurgle and make glad

The castle of God. Sailor, you were glad
And whistled Sion by that stream. But see:

Our Lady, too small for her canopy,
Sits near the altar. There's no comeliness
At all or charm in that expressionless
Face with its heavy eyelids. As before,
This face, for centuries a memory,
Non est species, neque decor,
Expressionless, expresses God: it goes
Past castled Sion. She knows what God knows,
Not Calvary's Cross nor crib at Bethlehem
Now, and the world shall come to Walsingham.

VII

The empty winds are creaking and the oak
Splatters and splatters on the cenotaph,
The boughs are trembling and a gaff
Bobs on the untimely stroke
Of the greased wash exploding on a shoal-bell
In the old mouth of the Atlantic. It's well;
Atlantic, you are fouled with the blue sailors,
Sea-monsters, upward angel, downward fish:
Unmarried and corroding, spare of flesh
Mart once of supercilious, wing'd clippers,
Atlantic, where your bell-trap guts its spoil
You could cut the brackish winds with a knife
Here in Nantucket, and cast up the time
When the Lord God formed man from the sea's slime
And breathed into his face the breath of life,
And blue-lung'd combers lumbered to the kill.
The Lord survives the rainbow of His will.

ELIZABETH BISHOP

"I've always had a day dream," Elizabeth Bishop (1911–1979) wrote Robert Lowell in the summer of 1960, "of being a lighthouse keeper, absolutely alone . . . I now see a wonderful cold rocky shore in the Falklands, or a house in Nova Scotia on the bay, exactly *like my grandmother's." Perhaps in order to satisfy this longing, Bishop lived on islands or near the shore as often as she could—on Cuttyhunk off the Massachusetts coast, North Haven off Maine, Nova Scotia, Nantucket, Newfoundland, Key West. "At the Fishhouses," published in* The New Yorker *in 1947 but begun as early as 1934 when she jotted some of its lines in her Cuttyhunk notebook, distills many years of seaside meditation.*

At the Fishhouses

Although it is a cold evening,
down by one of the fishhouses
an old man sits netting,
his net, in the gloaming almost invisible,
a dark purple-brown,
and his shuttle worn and polished.
The air smells so strong of codfish
it makes one's nose run and one's eyes water.
The five fishhouses have steeply peaked roofs
and narrow, cleated gangplanks slant up
to storerooms in the gables
for the wheelbarrows to be pushed up and down on.
All is silver: the heavy surface of the sea,
swelling slowly as if considering spilling over,
is opaque, but the silver of the benches,
the lobster pots, and masts, scattered
among the wild jagged rocks,
is of an apparent translucence
like the small old buildings with an emerald moss
growing on their shoreward walls.
The big fish tubs are completely lined

with layers of beautiful herring scales
and the wheelbarrows are similarly plastered
with creamy iridescent coats of mail,
with small iridescent flies crawling on them.
Up on the little slope behind the houses,
set in the sparse bright sprinkle of grass,
is an ancient wooden capstan,
cracked, with two long bleached handles
and some melancholy stains, like dried blood,
where the ironwork has rusted.
The old man accepts a Lucky Strike.
He was a friend of my grandfather.
We talk of the decline in the population
and of codfish and herring
while he waits for a herring boat to come in.
There are sequins on his vest and on his thumb.
He has scraped the scales, the principal beauty,
from unnumbered fish with that black old knife,
the blade of which is almost worn away.

Down at the water's edge, at the place
where they haul up the boats, up the long ramp
descending into the water, thin silver
tree trunks are laid horizontally
across the gray stones, down and down
at intervals of four or five feet.

Cold dark deep and absolutely clear,
element bearable to no mortal,
to fish and to seals . . . One seal particularly
I have seen here evening after evening.
He was curious about me. He was interested in music;
like me a believer in total immersion,
so I used to sing him Baptist hymns.
I also sang "A Mighty Fortress Is Our God."
He stood up in the water and regarded me
steadily, moving his head a little.
Then he would disappear, then suddenly emerge

almost in the same spot, with a sort of shrug
as if it were against his better judgment.
Cold dark deep and absolutely clear,
the clear gray icy water . . . Back, behind us,
the dignified tall firs begin.
Bluish, associating with their shadows,
a million Christmas trees stand
waiting for Christmas. The water seems suspended
above the rounded gray and blue-gray stones.
I have seen it over and over, the same sea, the same,
slightly, indifferently swinging above the stones,
icily free above the stones,
above the stones and then the world.
If you should dip your hand in,
your wrist would ache immediately,
your bones would begin to ache and your hand would burn
as if the water were a transmutation of fire
that feeds on stones and burns with a dark gray flame.
If you tasted it, it would first taste bitter,
then briny, then surely burn your tongue.
It is like what we imagine knowledge to be:
dark, salt, clear, moving, utterly free,
drawn from the cold hard mouth
of the world, derived from the rocky breasts
forever, flowing and drawn, and since
our knowledge is historical, flowing, and flown.

Rachel Carson

Rachel Carson (1907–1964) is best remembered today for her book Silent Spring *(1962), which dramatically exposed the dangers, both to the environment and to human health, of agricultural pesticides. She was also throughout her career a passionate observer and defender of the oceans. Born in Springdale, Pennsylvania, she first saw the sea as a college senior. Becoming a specialist in marine biology, she spent her summers at the Woods Hole Oceanographic Institute and took her first job as an aquatic biologist with the federal Bureau of Fisheries. Five years later she published the first of three eloquent and popular works on marine science,* Under the Sea Wind *(1941); it was followed by* The Sea Around Us *(1951), winner of the National Book Award, and* The Edge of the Sea *(1956), from which this excerpt has been taken.*

The Marginal World

THE edge of the sea is a strange and beautiful place. All through the long history of Earth it has been an area of unrest where waves have broken heavily against the land, where the tides have pressed forward over the continents, receded, and then returned. For no two successive days is the shore line precisely the same. Not only do the tides advance and retreat in their eternal rhythms, but the level of the sea itself is never at rest. It rises or falls as the glaciers melt or grow, as the floor of the deep ocean basins shifts under its increasing load of sediments, or as the earth's crust along the continental margins warps up or down in adjustment to strain and tension. Today a little more land may belong to the sea, tomorrow a little less. Always the edge of the sea remains an elusive and indefinable boundary.

The shore has a dual nature, changing with the swing of the tides, belonging now to the land, now to the sea. On the ebb tide it knows the harsh extremes of the land world, being exposed to heat and cold, to wind, to rain and drying sun. On the flood tide it is a water world, returning briefly to the relative stability of the open sea.

Only the most hardy and adaptable can survive in a region so mutable, yet the area between the tide lines is crowded with plants and animals. In this difficult world of the shore, life displays its enormous toughness and vitality by occupying almost every conceivable niche. Visibly, it carpets the intertidal rocks; or half hidden, it descends into fissures and crevices, or hides under boulders, or lurks in the wet gloom of sea caves. Invisibly, where the casual observer would say there is no life, it lies deep in the sand, in burrows and tubes and passageways. It tunnels into solid rock and bores into peat and clay. It encrusts weeds or drifting spars or the hard, chitinous shell of a lobster. It exists minutely, as the film of bacteria that spreads over a rock surface or a wharf piling; as spheres of protozoa, small as pinpricks, sparkling at the surface of the sea; and as Lilliputian beings swimming through dark pools that lie between the grains of sand.

The shore is an ancient world, for as long as there has been an earth and sea there has been this place of the meeting of land and water. Yet it is a world that keeps alive the sense of continuing creation and of the relentless drive of life. Each time that I enter it, I gain some new awareness of its beauty and its deeper meanings, sensing that intricate fabric of life by which one creature is linked with another, and each with its surroundings.

In my thoughts of the shore, one place stands apart for its revelation of exquisite beauty. It is a pool hidden within a cave that one can visit only rarely and briefly when the lowest of the year's low tides fall below it, and perhaps from that very fact it acquires some of its special beauty. Choosing such a tide, I hoped for a glimpse of the pool. The ebb was to fall early in the morning. I knew that if the wind held from the northwest and no interfering swell ran in from a distant storm the level of the sea should drop below the entrance to the pool. There had been sudden ominous showers in the night, with rain like handfuls of gravel flung on the roof. When I looked out into the early morning the sky was full of a gray dawn light but the sun had not yet risen. Water and air were pallid. Across the bay the moon was a luminous disc in the western sky, suspended above the dim line of distant shore—the full August moon, drawing the tide to the low, low levels of the threshold of the alien sea world. As I watched, a gull flew by, above the spruces. Its breast was rosy with the light of the unrisen sun. The day was, after all, to be fair.

Later, as I stood above the tide near the entrance to the pool, the promise of that rosy light was sustained. From the base of the steep wall of rock on which I stood, a moss-covered ledge jutted seaward into deep water. In the surge at the rim of the ledge the dark fronds of oarweeds swayed, smooth and gleaming as leather. The projecting ledge was the path to the small hidden cave and its pool. Occasionally a swell, stronger than the rest, rolled smoothly over the rim and broke in foam against the cliff. But the intervals between such swells were long enough to admit me to the ledge and long enough for a glimpse of that fairy pool, so seldom and so briefly exposed.

And so I knelt on the wet carpet of sea moss and looked back into the dark cavern that held the pool in a shallow basin. The floor of the cave was only a few inches below the roof, and a mirror had been created in which all that grew on the ceiling was reflected in the still water below.

Under water that was clear as glass the pool was carpeted with green sponge. Gray patches of sea squirts glistened on the ceiling and colonies of soft coral were a pale apricot color. In the moment when I looked into the cave a little elfin starfish hung down, suspended by the merest thread, perhaps by only a single tube foot. It reached down to touch its own reflection, so perfectly delineated that there might have been, not one starfish, but two. The beauty of the reflected images and of the limpid pool itself was the poignant beauty of things that are ephemeral, existing only until the sea should return to fill the little cave.

Whenever I go down into this magical zone of the low water of the spring tides, I look for the most delicately beautiful of all the shore's inhabitants—flowers that are not plant but animal, blooming on the threshold of the deeper sea. In that fairy cave I was not disappointed. Hanging from its roof were the pendent flowers of the hydroid. Tubularia, pale pink, fringed and delicate as the wind flower. Here were creatures so exquisitely fashioned that they seemed unreal, their beauty too fragile to exist in a world of crushing force. Yet every detail was functionally useful, every stalk and hydranth and petal-like tentacle fashioned for dealing with the realities of existence. I knew that they were merely waiting, in that moment of the tide's ebbing, for the return of the sea. Then in the rush of water, in the surge of surf and the pressure of the incoming tide, the delicate flower heads would stir with life. They would sway on their slender stalks, and their long tentacles would sweep the returning water, finding in it all that they needed for life.

And so in that enchanted place on the threshold of the sea the realities that possessed my mind were far from those of the land world I had left an hour before. In a different way the same sense of remoteness and of a world apart came to me in a twilight hour on a great beach on the coast of Georgia. I had come down after sunset and walked far out over sands that lay wet and gleaming, to the very edge of the retreating sea. Looking back across that immense flat, crossed by winding, water-filled gullies and here and there holding shallow pools left by the tide, I was filled with awareness that this intertidal area, although abandoned briefly and rhythmically by the sea, is always reclaimed by the rising tide. There at the edge of low water the beach with its reminders of the land seemed far away. The only sounds were those of the wind and the sea and the birds. There was one sound of wind moving over water, and another of water sliding over the sand and tumbling down the faces of its own wave forms. The flats were astir with birds, and the voice of the willet rang insistently. One of them stood at the edge of the water and gave its loud, urgent cry; an answer came from far up the beach and the two birds flew to join each other.

The flats took on a mysterious quality as dusk approached and the last evening light was reflected from the scattered pools and creeks. Then birds became only dark shadows, with no color discernible. Sanderlings scurried across the beach like little ghosts, and here and there the darker forms of the willets stood out. Often I could come very close to them before they would start up in alarm—the sanderlings running, the willets flying up, crying. Black skimmers flew along the ocean's edge silhouetted against the dull, metallic gleam, or they went flitting above the sand like large, dimly seen moths. Sometimes they "skimmed" the winding creeks of tidal water, where little spreading surface ripples marked the presence of small fish.

The shore at night is a different world, in which the very darkness that hides the distractions of daylight brings into sharper focus the elemental realities. Once, exploring the night beach, I surprised a small ghost crab in the searching beam of my torch. He was lying in a pit he had dug just above the surf, as though watching the sea and waiting. The blackness of the night possessed water, air, and beach. It was the darkness of an older world, before Man. There was no sound but the all-enveloping, primeval sounds of wind blowing over water and sand, and of waves crashing on the beach. There was no other visible life—just one small crab near the sea. I have seen hundreds of ghost crabs in other settings, but suddenly I was filled with the odd sensation that for the first time I knew the creature in its own world—that I understood, as never before, the essence of its being. In that moment time was suspended; the world to which I belonged did not exist and I might have been an onlooker from outer space. The little crab alone with the sea became a symbol that stood for life itself—for the delicate, destructible, yet incredibly vital force that somehow holds its place amid the harsh realities of the inorganic world.

The sense of creation comes with memories of a southern coast, where the sea and the mangroves, working together, are building a wilderness of thousands of small islands off the southwestern coast of Florida, separated from each other by a tortuous pattern of bays, lagoons, and narrow waterways. I remember a winter day when the sky was blue and drenched with sunlight; though there was no wind one was conscious of flowing air like cold clear crystal. I had landed on the surf-washed tip of one of those islands, and then worked my way around to the sheltered bay side. There I found the tide far out, exposing the broad mud flat of a cove bordered by the mangroves with their twisted branches, their glossy leaves, and their long prop roots reaching down, grasping and holding the mud, building the land out a little more, then again a little more.

The mud flats were strewn with the shells of that small, exquisitely colored mollusk, the rose tellin, looking like scattered petals of pink roses. There must have been a colony nearby, living buried just under the surface of the mud. At first the only creature visible was a small heron in gray and rusty plumage—a reddish egret that waded across the flat with the stealthy, hesitant movements of its kind. But other land creatures had been there, for a line of fresh tracks wound in and out among the mangrove roots, marking the path of a raccoon feeding on the oysters that gripped the supporting roots with projections from their shells. Soon I found the tracks of a shore bird, probably a sanderling, and followed them a little; then they turned toward the water and were lost, for the tide had erased them and made them as though they had never been.

Looking out over the cove I felt a strong sense of the interchangeability of land and sea in this marginal world of the shore, and of the links between the life of the two. There was also an awareness of the past and of the continuing flow of time, obliterating much that had gone before, as the sea had that morning washed away the tracks of the bird.

The sequence and meaning of the drift of time were quietly summarized in the existence of hundreds of small snails—the mangrove periwinkles—browsing on the branches and roots of the trees. Once their ancestors had been sea dwellers, bound to the salt waters by every tie of their life processes. Little by little over the thousands and millions of years the ties had been broken, the snails had adjusted themselves to life out of water, and now today they were living many feet above the tide to which they only occasionally returned. And perhaps, who could say how many ages hence, there would be in their descendants not even this gesture of remembrance for the sea.

The spiral shells of other snails—these quite minute—left winding tracks on the mud as they moved about in search of food. They were horn shells, and when I saw them I had a nostalgic moment when I wished I might see what Audubon saw, a century and more ago. For such little horn shells were the food of the flamingo, once so numerous on this coast, and when I half closed my eyes I could almost imagine a flock of these magnificent flame birds feeding in that cove, filling it with their color. It was a mere yesterday in the life of the earth that they were there; in nature, time and space are relative matters, perhaps most truly perceived subjectively in occasional flashes of insight, sparked by such a magical hour and place.

There is a common thread that links these scenes and memories—the spectacle of life in all its varied manifestations as it has appeared, evolved, and sometimes died out. Underlying the beauty of the spectacle there is meaning and significance. It is the elusiveness of that meaning that haunts us, that sends us again and again into the natural world where the key to the riddle is hidden. It sends us back to the edge of the sea, where the drama of life played its first scene on earth and perhaps even its prelude; where the forces of evolution are at work today, as they have been since the appearance of what we know as life; and where the spectacle of living creatures faced by the cosmic realities of their world is crystal clear.

PETER MATTHIESSEN

The sea has been central to the life and work of Peter Matthiessen (b. 1927). While serving in the navy in 1945, Matthiessen was caught in a terrifying storm and experienced an epiphany he later described in The Snow Leopard *(1978): "Overwhelmed, exhausted, all thought and emotion beaten out of me, I lost my sense of self, the heartbeat I heard was the heart of the world, I breathed with the mighty risings and declines of earth, and this evanescence seemed less frightening than exalting. Afterward, there was pain of loss—loss of what, I wondered, understanding nothing." Matthiessen's sense of awe before the sea is part of the imaginative intensity of such novels as* Far Tortuga *(1975), set in the Cayman Islands. His novels are complemented by his essays and travel books, including* Oomingmak: The Expedition to the Musk Ox Island in the Bering Sea *(1967) and* Blue Meridian: The Search for the Great White Shark *(1971).* Men's Lives: The Surfmen and Baymen of the South Fork *(1986), from which this chapter is taken, mixes memoir, social history, and reportage. Matthiessen moved with his family to Long Island in August 1953 and spent the next three years working as a commercial fisherman for most of the year. "Doing hard labor with my hands," Matthiessen has said of the experience, "I felt more free, less malcontent than at any time in my life."*

Under Montauk Light

IN the early summer of 1954, a power boat with the most beautiful lines I had ever seen was riding at anchor in the harbor of Rockport, Massachusetts. Her designer turned out to be a local sailmaker who had built her as a tuna harpoon boat; she was the only one of her kind, and she was for sale. The following day I took the helm on a run around Cape Ann, as the owner ran forward to the pulpit and harpooned a small harbor seal (bountied in Massachusetts) with an astonishing throw of the clumsy pole. In Ipswich Bay, giant bluefin tuna were carving circles on the surface, and the sailmaker showed me how to approach them, how much to lead the swift fish on the throw, how important it was that everyone aboard stay well clear of the line tub when the fish was struck, but because he was selling his beautiful boat, he seemed too disheartened to pursue them.

With her high bow and deep hull forward, her long low cockpit and flat stern, the thirty-two foot boat looked like a trim and elegant Maine lobsterman, and she handled well in any kind of sea. Powered by a 120-horsepower Buick engine adapted to marine use (automobile engines, readily and cheaply acquired at wrecked-car yards, are often adapted by commercial fishermen), she came equipped with spotting tower, outriggers, harpoon stand, harpoons and line, a heavy tuna rod and reel and fighting chair, boat rods, shark hooks, and miscellaneous gear of all descriptions. At five thousand dollars, she was a bargain even in those days, and I knew from the first that she was my boat, though I had to borrow to obtain her; she was the most compulsive purchase of my life.

Signing the papers, the sailmaker was close to tears. He had designed and built this lovely craft with his own hands, he was losing her for an unworthy purpose (his wife desired a breezeway for their house), and throwing in all the fishing gear was an acknowledgment that a vital aspect of his life was at an end.

A few days later I ran the boat southward down the coast off Salem and Boston and on through the Cape Cod Canal and Buzzards Bay, putting in at Block Island late that evening, and continuing on to Three Mile Harbor the next day. By that time it had come to me, a little late, that writing and commercial fishing were barely paying my household expenses, that there was nothing left over for boat insurance, berth fees, maintenance, or even gas for a boat this size (the one-cylinder engine on my scallop boat ran mostly on air, and the rude hull could be berthed on a mud bank, invulnerable to theft or serious damage). And so, within a few days of her arrival, the beautiful boat I had rechristened *Merlin*—after the small swift falcon of that name as well as the celebrated magician—was sailing out of Montauk as a charter boat, with John Cole as mate. For the next two summers, often twice a day, we headed east along Gin Beach, rounding Shagwong Point and running south to join the fishing fleet off Montauk Point, or continuing offshore to the tuna grounds at the eighty-fathom line, where one misty morning of long and oily swells, many years before, I had seen the first whales of my life, the silver steam rising from the silver surface, the great dark shapes breaking the emptiness of ocean sky.

For many years as a boy in the late thirties, I had gone deep-sea fishing off Montauk with my father, and to this day I cannot see that high promontory of land with its historic lighthouse without a stirring of excitement and affection. Montauk is essentially a high rock island, cut off from the glacial moraines of the South Fork by a strait four miles wide. This strait, now filled with ocean sand, was known to the Indians as Napeague, or "water land"—old-timers speak of going "on" and "off" Montauk as if it were still an island—and the headland at Montauk's eastern end was known to the Indians as Wompanon. A lighthouse fired by sperm whale oil was constructed at Wompanon in 1795 by order of President George Washington, who proposed that it should stand for two hundred years.

Montauk's access to swift rips and deep ledges, to the wandering Gulf Stream, forty to seventy miles off to the south, has made it a legendary fishing place since Indian times. It was the fishing that attracted the developer Arthur Benson in 1879, when New York sportsmen were establishing striped bass fishing clubs in New York and Rhode Island. In 1880 some visionary anglers caused the construction of an iron fishing pier over seven hundred feet long on the ocean beach at Napeague, only to see it torn away in its first winter.

Meanwhile, a small camp had been established at Fort Pond Bay by commercial fishermen from the North Fork. In the early 1880s, fishing was poor, and most of them transferred their operations to Rhode Island. Three years later, when the Rhode Island fishery declined, they returned to Montauk, finding the fish "more plentiful than was ever known before."

Then, at the turn of the century, a William J. Morgan, surfcasting under the Light, landed a seventy-six-pound striped bass that made Montauk famous. Wherever this hero went thereafter, it was said, people would point and say, "That's Morgan!" But Morgan was no doubt well aware of the 101-pound specimen taken off East Hampton in this period by Nathaniel Dominy's haul-seine crew. Cap'n Dominy laid the monster out in style in a farm wagon and trundled it around East Hampton and Sag Harbor, charging the villagers ten cents each for a good look before selling it for five dollars to a Sag Harbor hotel; no doubt people draw breath today whose forebears dined on that historic fish. The obsessed Morgan, who tried for the rest of his life to catch one larger, built a house on Montauk overlooking a surfcasting site that was known as "Morgan's" for decades thereafter.

Within a few years of the arrival of the railroad in 1895—and despite Montauk's meager population and facilities—the fishing community at Fort Pond Bay became the principal fish shipping port on the East End, with hundreds of tons of black sea bass and other species shipped every day. Tracks were built onto the dock for a special fish train that was loaded directly from the boats. It left Montauk at 4:30 P.M., picked up boxes of fish at the depot platform known as Fanny Bartlett's, or Napeague Station, as well as at Amagansett and East Hampton, and arrived in the New York markets before daylight.

For years to come there was no paved road across the sands of Napeague, and Montauk's shantytown of fishermen and fish packers remained clustered on the eastern shore of Fort Pond Bay, with four or five pioneer summer cottages on the dunes opposite. Mrs. Agnew's Tea Room was the only building on the wagon road between the settlement and Montauk Light. The fishing community, notably the Parsons, Edwards, and Hulse families from Amagansett and the large Tuthill clan from Orient and East Marion on the North Fork, in addition to some people from Connecticut, would usually arrive in early May and go home in fall; most of them lived in simple shacks constructed from "fish box boards"—the big sugar boxes, made from sugar pine, that would carry ten bushels of skimmers or six hundred pounds of fish. Since Fort Pond Bay was relatively unprotected, the fishing boats were moored to spiles, or stakes, offshore that were limber enough to bend with the strong winds. The Parsonses and Tuthills ran their own boats and kept their own fish houses on the east shore of the bay; the fishing company on the south shore belonged to J. C. Wells.

The Edwards Brothers, running ocean traps off Amagansett, unloaded their catch at the Tuthill dock. In early April, four to ten ocean traps, or barrel traps—a leader or wing turned fish offshore into a series of funnels and pens—were set up to a mile offshore in about seven fathoms of water, to catch whatever came along in the strong spring run. The ocean trap was similar in design to a large pound trap but used anchors instead of stakes. A crew of forty, in four seine boats, was required to lift these traps, from which twelve tons or more of edible fish might be harvested each day. When the ocean traps were taken up, about June 1, the crews were switched to the big bunker steamers, which sailed from the Edwards Brothers docks near the menhaden factories (called Bunker City) now concentrated in the vicinity of Promised Land, west of Napeague Harbor. In the twenties, the Tuthills and Jake Wells hired summer help from Nova Scotia to work in the packing houses and on the docks, and some of these men moved down to Promised Land to crew on the Edwards Brothers boats. A Montauk colony of Nova Scotia families—including such fishing clans as the Pittses and Beckwiths—are part of the Montauk community to this day.

Most of the early Montauk fishermen were trappers, and the Tuthills lifted their fish pounds, or traps, on Gardiners Island as well as in the environs of Fort Pond Bay. On a map made early in the century, nearly three hundred traps are shown between North Bar at Montauk Point and Eastern Plains Point on Gardiners Island, a far denser concentration than exists today. Captain Nat Edwards, son of Cap'n Gabe, ran a dozen pound traps between Shagwong Point and Water Fence; Captain Sam Edwards and other fishermen ran small low-powered draggers, thirty to thirty-five feet long, or set lobster pots, or hand-lined for pollock, sea bass, and bluefish.

Throughout the Hamptons, small scallop boats and other craft had been catering to summer fishing parties since the turn of the century. Montauk draggermen did well with swordfish (by August 7 in the summer of 1925, Captain George Beckwith had harpooned thirty-seven) and in the late twenties and early thirties, when Montauk was developed as a resort, many draggers joined the early charter fleet. In 1927 the first swordfish ever taken on rod and reel was brought into Fort Pond Bay by one of the Florida fishing guides drawn to the area. The following year the former Great Pond, rechristened Lake Montauk, was permanently opened to the bay, creating an all-weather harbor.

In the mid-twenties, when agitation to restrict the activities of commercial men had already started, a federal hatchery for production of lobster, codfish, flounder, and pollock was proposed for Fort Pond Bay, and a freezing plant designed to market prepacked fish was already under construction. But these enterprises were abandoned with the opening and development of Great Pond. Although certain old-timers stuck to Fort Pond Bay for another twenty years, the construction of additional docks, and the protected anchorage, had drawn most of the fleet to the new harbor. The Napeague road was long since paved, and the fish train was now replaced by truckers. Commercial men such as Gus and Fred Pitts (of the Nova Scotia colony), draggermen Dan Grimshaw and Harry Conklin (who took out President Herbert Hoover), and the Beckwith, Erickson, and Tuma brothers soon adapted their work boats for chartering; even Captains Sam and Bert Edwards, and later Sam's sons Kenneth and Dick, took time off from bunkering to join the fleet. Before long, big bottom-fishing boats were developed that would attract thousands of people to Montauk every year. Over five thousand customers were recorded in 1932, and this number tripled the following year and doubled again in 1934, when the Long Island Rail Road established daily excursion trains from New York and Brooklyn. S. Kip Farrington of East Hampton (ignoring the surfmen) described the pioneer fish guides of the thirties as the rightful heirs of Captain Josh Edwards and the shore whalers; as a big game fisherman and sport-fishing writer, he did more to advertise the new craze for deep-sea fishing than anyone else before or since. By the mid-thirties, special deep-sea fishing boats with twin screw engines and flying bridges had been designed for working the Gulf Stream, sometimes as far as seventy miles offshore; the fish prized most were swordfish, marlin, and the giant bluefin tuna, moving north and south from its summer grounds off Wedgeport, Nova Scotia.

The 1938 hurricane created the Shinnecock Inlet, now a fishing station, but it mostly destroyed the Montauk fishing village at Fort Pond Bay. The railroad depot is still there, however, and so is the fish company founded by E. D. Tuthill and owned today by Perry Duryea, Jr., whose father married Captain Ed Tuthill's daughter. The hundreds of boats that once littered the bay are now in Montauk Harbor, which by the time of my arrival in the early fifties was already home port for one of the largest sport-fishing fleets on the East Coast.

That summer of 1954, the charter season was well under way when the *Merlin* arrived. There was one slip left at the town dock, right across from one of the pioneer charter men, John Messbauer, and we soon found out why nobody had wanted it; the current was strong and the approach narrow, and the one way to back a single-engine boat into this berth was a sequence of swirling maneuvers at full throttle. Unless executed with precision, these maneuvers would strand the boat across the bows of neighboring boats, held fast by the current, while the customers wondered how their lives had been consigned to such lubberly hands. Before I got the hang of it, there was more than one humiliating episode, not helped by the embarassment of my trusty mate, who would shrug, wince, and roll his eyes, pretending to the old salts along the dock that if only this greenhorn would let him take the helm, he could do much better.

At thirty-two feet, the *Merlin* was small by Montauk standards, and she lacked the customary flying bridge, not to mention upholstered fighting chairs, teak decks, and chrome. We had no old customers to depend on, and no big shiny cockpit to attract new ones, and Captain Al Ceslow on the *Skip II*, for whom John had worked as mate the previous summer, was the only man in the whole fleet of forty-five-odd boats who would offer advice or help of any kind. However, it was soon July, and fish and fishing parties both abounded (and were biting hard, said cynical Jimmy Reutershan, who was bluefishing out of Montauk in his Jersey skiff, and who believed strongly in lunar tide tables as a guide to the feeding habits of fish and man; he had noticed, he said, that *Homo sapiens*, wandering the docks with a glazed countenance, would suddenly stir into feeding frenzy, signing up boats with the same ferocity—and at the same stage of the tide—that *Pomatomus saltatrix* would strike into the lures around the Point).

And so, from the first, the *Merlin* did pretty well. We made up in eagerness and love of fishing what we lacked in experience of our new trade, we worked hard to find fish for our clients, and except on week-ends, when we ran two six-hour trips each day, we sailed overtime without extra charge whenever the morning had been unproductive. Also, unlike many of the charter men, who seemed to feel that anglers of other races belonged on "barf barges"—the party or bottom-fishing boats—we welcomed anyone who came along. One day we sailed a party of Chinese laundrymen from up-Island, each one equipped with a full-sized galvanized garbage can. Their one recognizable utterance was "Babylon." Conveying to us through their Irish-American interpreter that trolling for hard-fighting and abundant bluefish did not interest them, they said that they wished to be taken to the three coal barges sunk southwest of the Point in a nor'easter, a well-known haunt of the black sea bass so highly esteemed in Chinese cookery. Once the hulks were located, they set out garbage cans along the cockpit and pin-hooked sea bass with such skill (to cries of "Bobby-lon!") that every man topped off his garbage can. The half ton of sea bass that they took home more than paid the cost of the whole charter, while gladdening every Oriental heart in western Suffolk.

Another day, three Shinnecock Indian chiefs in quest of "giants" (they were soon off to Alaska, they declared, to shoot giant brown bear) took us all the way to Rosie's Hole off the coast of Rhode Island in vain pursuit of giant bluefin. Because of the fuel, the barrel of bunker chum bought at Ted's freezer, and the installation of the *Merlin*'s heavy tuna chair, the trip was expensive even for car dealers from Washington, D.C., where the three chiefs spent most of the year, passing themselves off as black men. The chiefs liked us because the other boats had refused their trade, and we liked them because they spent their money cheerfully, though they saw neither hide nor hair of giants.

No other boat got a bluefin that day either, and John and I were relieved as well as disappointed; in theory, we knew what to do once the huge fish took the mackerel bait that we drifted down the current (crank up the engine, cast off the buoy on the anchor, and chase after the exhilarated fish before it stripped the last line off the reel), but being inexperienced with giant tuna, we foresaw all sorts of possibilities for dangerous error. Big bluefin may be ten feet long, and nearly a half ton in weight, and the speed and power of these fish are awesome. (In the *Merlin*'s former life in Ipswich Bay, a passenger had come too close to the blur of green line leaving the tub after a horse mackerel had been harpooned. The line whipped around his leg and snapped him overboard and down thirty feet under the sea before someone grabbed a hatchet and whacked the line where it sizzled across the brass strip on the combing. Had that hatchet not been handy, and wits quick, the nosy passenger would have lost his life.)

Toward the end of the homeward journey across Block Island Sound, I encouraged the chiefs to stop on Shagwong Reef and pick up a few bluefish to take home for supper. The thwarted giant-killers had consoled themselves with gin on the long voyage, and one man agreed to fish for blues if we would strap him into the big fighting chair and give him that thick tuna rod to work with, so that he could imagine what it must be like to deal masterfully with one of those monsters back at Rosie's Hole. When the strike came, it failed to bend even the rod tip, but the angler, cheered on by his friends, set the hook with a mighty backward heave into the fighting chair. "It's charging the boat!" his assistants yelled as something broke the surface; the only porgy in the *Merlin*'s history that ever went for a trolled bluefish lure had been snapped clear out of the water by that heave and came skimming through the air over the wake in a graceful flight that a flying fish might well have envied.

So much did all three chiefs enjoy this exciting fishing experience that they felt obliged to lie down in the cockpit, collapsed with laughter. "No mo' bluefishin," they cried helplessly, waving us on. "Giant pogie's good enough!" Once ashore, they gave both of us giant tips, thanked us as "scholars and gentlemen" for a splendid outing, and went off merrily down the dock with their souvenir porgy. Next time they visited these parts, they said, they would bring their girlfriends down to meet us (which they did).

Not all our clients were such good sports as the three chiefs. A charter demands six hours at close quarters with company that is rarely of one's choice, and often there are two charters each day. While most of our people were cooperative and pleasant, others felt that their money entitled them to treat captain and mate as servants, and one ugly customer advised me even before the *Merlin* cleared the breakwater that he knew all about the charter men's tricks and cheating ways. I turned the boat around, intending to put him on the dock, but his upset friends made him apologize.

Another day the motor broke down on Shagwong Reef in clear, rough weather of a northwest wind. A cockpit full of queasy passengers wanted to know why I did not call the Coast Guard. The truth was that their captain, having had no time to go to New York and apply to the Coast Guard for a captain's license, was running a renegade boat, and was stalling for time until Al Ceslow on the *Skip II* could finish his morning charter and tow us in. One of the men, under the horrified gaze of his newlywed wife, actually panicked, shrieking at the other passengers that the captain's plan was to put this death craft on the rocks; I had to grab him by the shirtfront and bang him up against the cabinside to calm him down. (On another charter boat one morning—we could hear the shouts and crashing right over the radio-telephone—a disgruntled client had to be slugged into submission, with the skipper bellowing for police assistance at the dock.)

The *Merlin* was plagued by persistent hazing from two charter boats that now and then would turn across our wake, out on the Elbow, and cut off all four of our wire lines; no doubt other new boats were welcomed in this way as well. Wire line, lures, and leaders are expensive, and because wire line is balky stuff, it often took most of an hour of good fishing tide to re-rig the lines for the unhappy customers. The two big captains of these big boats (both of them sons of earlier big captains who now ran big enterprises on the docks) were successful charter men who had nothing to fear from the small *Merlin*; often this pair trolled side by side, chatting on radio-telephones from their flying bridges. One day off Great Eastern Rock, heart pounding with mixed fear and glee, and deaf to all oaths and shouts of warning, I spun my wheel and cut across both of their fat sterns, taking all eight of their wire lines at a single blow.

In the long stunned silence on all three boats, John Cole said quietly, "Oh boy," and suggested a long detour to Connecticut. "Those guys are going to be waiting for us on the dock," he said, "and they are BIG." But there was no reception party, and our lines were never cut again. Not long thereafter one of these skippers called the *Merlin* on "the blower," passing terse word in the charter man's way that he was into fish: "See where we are, Cap, down to the east'rd? Better come this way."

One day on the ocean side, working in close to the rocks west of the Light, we picked up a striped bass on the inshore line and a bluefish on the outside; we did this on three straight passes, and probably could have done it again if we had not been late for our afternoon charter and had to head in. So far as we knew, those three bass, and three more the next day from the same place, were the only stripers taken out of Montauk for nearly a fortnight in the bass dog days of late July.

From that day on, we had to wait to fish this spot until the fleet went in at noon, because other boats began to tail us with binoculars, in the same way that the *Merlin* sometimes tailed Gus Pitts when the *Marie II* worked the striper holes along the beach, watching his mate strip out the wire to guess the depth at which Cap'n Gus was trolling, or glimpse what lure he was rigging to his rods.

On days when we had no charter, we went out hand-lining for blues, heading west past Culloden Point and Fort Pond Bay to Water Fence, at the western boundary of the land acquired by the Proprietors of Montauk, where the cattle fence that once kept East Hampton's livestock on the Montauk pastures during the summer had extended out into the water; past the walking dunes, a sand flow at the old forest edge on the north side of Hither Hills; past Goff Point and the fallen chimney of the abandoned bunker factory at Hicks Island. East of Cartwright Shoal, the shallow waters teemed with small three-pound "tailor" bluefish that bit as fast as the hand lines were tossed overboard, and brought a good price on the market.

The *Merlin* was no longer a renegade boat (I got my license in late summer), and no one ignored her radio queries or disdained to call her; she had already built up a list of clients who wished to charter her again the following year. The bluefishing was strong and steady, and offshore the school tuna were so thick that by leaving one fish on the line while boating the other three, we could keep all four lines loaded almost continually until the box had overflowed. On some days, poor John, skidding around on the bloody deck, exhausted from pumping the strong tuna off the bottom for the weary customers, would send me wild-eyed signals to get the boat away from the goddamn fish, maybe show the clients a nice shark or ocean sunfish.

But there were days in that first summer when the *Merlin* sat idle at the dock, and in August the price of bluefish was so low that hand-lining would not make us a day's pay. Bass remained scarce in the dead of summer, and one morning when his boat was hauled out for repairs, we decided to show our friend Al Ceslow our secret striper spot on the ocean shore west of the Light.

In the days before, there had been offshore storms, and the big smooth swells collapsing on the coast would make it difficult to work close to the rocks. We also knew that Cap'n Gus, widely regarded as the best striped bass fisherman ever to sail under the Light, had put three boats on those rocks in his twenty years of hard experience. And so we rode in as close as we dared on the backs of the broad waves, letting the lures coast in on the white wash. We were not close enough, and tried to edge in closer, keeping an eye out for the big freak sea that would break offshore and wash us onto the rock shore under the cliffs. Unlike the established boats, we were not booked solid a full year in advance, and the loss of the *Merlin*—we could not yet afford insurance—would mean the end of our careers as charter boatmen, apart from endangering our lives.

The wave we feared rose up behind us, sucking the water off the inshore rocks, and as Al or John shouted, I spun the wheel and gave the *Merlin* her full throttle. With a heavy thud, our trusty boat struck into the midsection of a high, clear, cresting wave, and for one sickening moment, seemed to lose headway. Then the wave parted, two walls of green water rushed past the cockpit, over our heads, and the boat sprang up and outward, popping free. If we ever fished that spot again, I do not recall it.

Hurricane Carol, on the last day of August 1954, blew so hard at Montauk that I ran the *Merlin* at eight knots in her slip in order to ease the pressure on her lines. At high water, only the spile tops on the town dock were visible above the flood, which carried loose boats and capsized hulks down toward the breakwater. In leaping from the stern to fetch more lines or lend a hand with another boat, one could only pray that the town dock was still there.

The hurricane's eye passed over about noon, in an eerie silver light and sulfureous pall. Then the winds struck in again, subsiding only as our fuel ran low in midafternoon. By evening we felt free to leave for home, but could not get there; the storm seas, surging through the dunes, had reopened the old strait in a new channel into Napeague Harbor, knocking down one of the radio towers that transmitted to the ships at sea. Until late that night, when the tide turned and the sea subsided, we were stranded on Montauk, which was once again an island.

I was not sorry when the season was over and I ran my boat back west to Three Mile Harbor. To judge from the sour, contemptuous remarks that were traded back and forth on the radio-telephones, a lot of charter men were opportunists, out for an easy dollar that was not forthcoming. Almost all of us made good money between July 4 and Labor Day, but only the best boats in the fleet, with the longest lists of faithful customers (these were the charter captains we admired, the skilled and happy ones who loved to fish) could make it in the colder days of spring and autumn. The *Merlin* was not yet one of those boats, and we quit right after Labor Day, to make the most of the first weeks of the scallop season. It was a poor season that year, with so many scallops destroyed by Hurricane Carol.

The Merlin's summer in 1955 was busy and successful, but I ended my second year of chartering with the same feeling. I chartered because it paid for my boat and I made a living out of doors in the season between haul-seining and scalloping; I scalloped and hauled seine because I liked the work, and liked the company of the commercial fishermen, the baymen.

Gary Snyder

The poetry of Gary Snyder (b. 1930) uniquely fuses the worlds of spiritual exploration, literary scholarship, and hard physical work. In books such as Riprap *(1959),* Myths and Texts *(1960),* Turtle Island *(1974), and* Axe Handles *(1983), he has sought a sharp-edged, sensually exact language in which to distill his knowledge of a wide range of American and Asian landscapes and cultures and his concerns for wilderness and community. "Oil" was first collected in* The Back Country *(1968) and reflects his experience as a seaman on Pacific tankers in the 1950s.*

Oil

soft rainsqualls on the swells
south of the Bonins, late at night. Light
from the empty mess-hall
throws back bulky shadows
of winch and fairlead
over the slanting fantail where I stand.

but for men on watch in the engine room,
the man at the wheel, the lookout in the bow,
the crew sleeps. in cots on deck
or narrow iron bunks down drumming
passageways below.

the ship burns with a furnace heart
steam veins and copper nerves
quivers and slightly twists and always goes—
easy roll of the hull and deep
vibration of the turbine underfoot.

bearing what all these
crazed, hooked nations need:
steel plates and
long injections of pure oil.

JOSEPH MITCHELL

Born in North Carolina to a well-to-do cotton and tobacco merchant, Joseph Mitchell (1908–1996) came to New York City to take a job at the World, *arriving one day after the beginning of the 1929 stock market crash. Through the Depression, at the* Herald Tribune, *the* World-Telegram, *and eventually at* The New Yorker, *he became known for his funny yet poignant profiles of raffish urban characters: underworld figures, gypsies, saloonkeepers, street-corner revivalists, and especially the harbormen, fishmongers, and other denizens of New York's old docks. Mitchell reworked his seaport material, first as fiction (*Old Mr. Flood, *1948), then in literary nonfiction reportage that stands comparison with the best American writing in any genre.* The Bottom of the Harbor *(1960), which collected the title piece and five others, is at once history, urban archaeology, and an elegy for a fading maritime world.*

The Bottom of the Harbor

THE bulk of the water in New York Harbor is oily, dirty, and germy. Men on the mud suckers, the big harbor dredges, like to say that you could bottle it and sell it for poison. The bottom of the harbor is dirtier than the water. In most places, it is covered with a blanket of sludge that is composed of silt, sewage, industrial wastes, and clotted oil. The sludge is thickest in the slips along the Hudson, in the flats on the Jersey side of the Upper Bay, and in backwaters such as Newtown Creek, Wallabout Bay, and the Gowanus Canal. In such areas, where it isn't exposed to the full sweep of the tides, it accumulates rapidly. In Wallabout Bay, a nook in the East River that is part of the Brooklyn Navy Yard, it accumulates at the rate of a foot and a half a year. The sludge rots in warm weather and from it gas-filled bubbles as big as basketballs continually surge to the surface. Dredgemen call them "sludge bubbles." Occasionally, a bubble upsurges so furiously that it brings a mass of sludge along with it. In midsummer, here and there in the harbor, the rising and breaking of sludge bubbles makes the water seethe and spit. People sometimes stand on the coal and lumber quays that line the Gowanus Canal and stare at the black, bubbly water.

Nevertheless, there is considerable marine life in the harbor water and on the harbor bottom. Under the paths of liners and tankers and ferries and tugs, fish school and oysters spawn and lobsters nest. There are clams on the sludgy bottom, and mussels and mud shrimp and conchs and crabs and sea worms and sea plants. Bedloe's Island, the Statue of Liberty island, is in a part of the harbor that is grossly polluted, but there is a sprinkling of soft-shell clams in the mud beneath the shallow water that surrounds it. The ebb of a spring tide always draws the water off a broad strip of this mud, and then flocks of gulls appear from all over the Upper Bay and light on it and thrash around and scratch for clams. They fly up with clams in their beaks and drop them on the concrete walk that runs along the top of the island's sea wall, and then they swoop down and pluck the meats out of the broken shells. Even in the Gowanus Canal, there are a few fish; the water is dead up at the head of it—only germs can live there—but from the crook at the Sixth Street Basin on down to the mouth there are cunners and tomcods and eels. The cunners nibble on the acorn barnacles on the piles under the old quays.

In the spring, summer, and fall, during the great coastwise and inshore and offshore migrations of fishes along the Middle Atlantic Coast, at least three dozen species enter the harbor. Only a few members of some species show up. Every spring, a few long, jaggy-backed sea sturgeon show up. Every summer, in the Lower Bay, dragger nets bring up a few small, weird, brightly colored strays from Southern waters, such as porcupine fish, scorpion fish, triggerfish, lookdowns, halfbeaks, hairtails, and goggle-eyed scad. Every fall, a few tuna show up. Other species show up in the hundreds of thousands or in the millions. Among these are shad, cod, whiting, porgy, blackback flounder, summer herring, alewife, sea bass, ling, mackerel, butterfish, and blackfish. Some years, one species, the mossbunker, shows up in the hundreds of millions. The mossbunker is a kind of herring that weighs around a pound when full-grown. It migrates in enormous schools and is caught in greater quantity than any other fish on the Atlantic Coast, but it is unfamiliar to the general public because it isn't a good table fish; it is too oily and bony. It is a factory fish; it is converted into an oil that is used in making soaps, paints, and printing inks (which is why some newspapers have a fishy smell on damp days), and into a meal that is fed to pigs and poultry. In the summer and fall, scores of schools of mossbunkers are hemmed in and caught in the Lower Bay, Sandy Hook Bay, and Raritan Bay by fleets of purse seiners with Negro crews that work out of little fishing ports in North Carolina, Virginia, Delaware, New Jersey, and Long Island and rove up and down the coast, following the schools.

The migratory fishes enter the harbor to spawn or to feed. Some mill around in the bays and river mouths for a few days and leave; some stay for months. Only one fish, the eel, is present in great numbers in all seasons. Eels are nocturnal scavengers, and they thrive in the harbor. They live on the bottom, and it makes no difference to them how deep or dirty it is. They live in ninety feet of water in the cable area of the Narrows and they live in a foot of water in tide ditches in the Staten Island marshes; they live in clean blue water in Sandy Hook Bay and they live around the outfalls of sewers in the East River. There are eight or nine hundred old hulks in the harbor. A few are out in the bays, deeply submerged, but most of them lie half sunk behind the pierhead line in the Jersey Flats and the flats along the Arthur Kill and the Kill van Kull—old scows and barges, old boxcar floats, old tugs, old ferryboats, old side-wheel excursion steamers, old sailing ships. They were towed into the flats and left to rot. They are full of holes; the water in the hulls of many of them rises and falls with the tides. Some are choked with sea lettuce and sea slime. In the summer, multitudes of eels lay up in the hulks during the day and wriggle out at night to feed. In the winter, they bed down in the hulks and hibernate. When they begin to hibernate, usually around the middle of December, they are at their best; they are fleshy then, and tender and sweet. At that time, Italian-Americans and German-Americans from every part of Staten Island go to certain old scows in the flats along the kills and spear so many eels that they bring them home in washtubs and potato sacks. The harbor eels—that is, the eels that live in the harbor the year round—are all males, or bucks. The females, or roes, until they become mature, live in rivers and creeks and ponds, up in fresh water. They become mature after they have spent from seven to thirteen years in fresh water. Every fall, thousands upon thousands of mature females run down the rivers that empty into the harbor—the Hudson, the Hackensack, the Passaic, the Elizabeth, the Rahway, and the Raritan. When they reach salt water, they lie still awhile and rest. They may rest for a few hours or a few days. Divers say that some days in October and November it is impossible to move about anywhere on the harbor bottom without stirring up throngs of big, fat, silver-bellied female eels. After resting, the females congregate with the mature harbor males, and they go out to sea together to spawn.

Hard-shell clams, or quahogs, the kind that appear on menus as littlenecks and cherrystones, are extraordinarily abundant in the harbor. Sanitary engineers classify the water in a number of stretches of the Lower Bay and Jamaica Bay as "moderately polluted." In these stretches, on thinly sludge-coated bottoms, under water that ranges in depth from one to thirty-five feet, are several vast, pullulating, mazy networks of hard-shell-clam beds. On some beds, the clams are crowded as tightly together as cobblestones. They are lovely clams—the inner lips of their shells have a lustrous violet border, and their meats are as pink and plump as rosebuds—but they are unsafe; they sometimes contain the germs of a variety of human diseases, among them bacillary and protozoal dysentery and typhoid fever, that they collect in their systems while straining nourishment out of the dirty water. The polluted beds have been condemned for over thirty years, and are guarded against poachers by the city Department of Health and the state Conservation Department. Quite a few people in waterfront neighborhoods in Staten Island, Brooklyn, and Queens have never been fully convinced that the clams are unsafe. On moonless nights and foggy days, they slip out, usually in rowboats, and raid the beds. In the course of a year, they take tons of clams. They eat them in chowders and stews, and they eat them raw. Every once in a while, whole families get horribly sick.

Just west of the mouth of the harbor, between Sandy Hook and the south shore of Staten Island, there is an area so out-of-the-way that anchorage grounds have long been set aside in it for ships and barges loaded with dynamite and other explosives. In this area, there are three small tracts of clean, sparkling, steel-blue water, about fifteen square miles in all. This is the only unpolluted water in the harbor. One tract of about five square miles, in Raritan Bay, belongs to the State of New York; the others, partly in Raritan Bay and partly in Sandy Hook Bay, belong to New Jersey. The bottoms of these tracts are free of sludge, and there are some uncontaminated hard-shell-clam beds on them. They are public beds; after taking out a license, residents of the state in whose waters they lie may harvest and sell clams from them. The New York beds are clammed by about a hundred and fifty Staten Islanders, most of whom live in or near the sleepy little south-shore ports of Prince's Bay and Great Kills. Some do seasonal work in shipyards, on fishing boats, or on truck farms, and clam in slack times, and some—thirty or so, mostly older men—clam steadily. They go out at dawn in sea skiffs and in rowboats equipped with outboard motors. When they reach the beds, they scatter widely and anchor. They lean over the sides of their boats and rake the bottom with clumsy rakes, called Shinnecock rakes, that have twenty-four-foot handles and long, inturned teeth. Last year, they raked up eighteen thousand bushels. A soup factory in New Jersey bought about half of these, and the rest went to fish stores and hotels and restaurants, mainly in New York City. Every New Yorker who frequently eats clams on the half shell has most likely eaten at least a few that came out of the harbor.

In Dutch and English days, immense beds of oysters grew in the harbor. They bordered the shores of Brooklyn and

Queens, and they encircled Manhattan, Staten Island, and the islands in the Upper Bay; to the Dutch, Ellis Island was Oyster Island and Bedloe's Island was Great Oyster Island. One chain of beds extended from Sandy Hook straight across the harbor and up the Hudson to Ossining. The Dutch and the English were, as they still are, gluttonous oyster eaters. By the end of the eighteenth century, all but the deepest of the beds had been stripped. Oysters, until then among the cheapest of foods, gradually became expensive. In the eighteen-twenties, a group of Staten Island shipowners began to buy immature oysters by the schooner-load in other localities and bring them to New York and bed them in the harbor until they got their growth, when they were tonged up and shipped to the wholesale oyster market in Manhattan, to cities in the Middle West, and to London, where they were prized. This business was known as bedding. The bedders obtained most of their seed stock in Chesapeake Bay and in several New Jersey and Long Island bays. Some bought three-year-olds and put them down for only six or seven months, and some bought younger oysters and put them down for longer periods. At first, the bedders used the shoals in the Kill van Kull, but by and by they found that the best bottoms lay along the seaward side of Staten Island, in the Lower Bay and Raritan Bay. Back then, the inshore water in these bays was rich in diatoms and protozoa, the tiny plants and animals on which oysters feed. Spread out in this water, on clean bottoms, at depths averaging around thirteen feet, oysters matured and fattened much faster than they did crowded together on their shell-cluttered spawning grounds; a thousand bushels of three-year-olds from Chesapeake Bay, put down in April in a favorable season, might amount to fourteen hundred bushels when taken up in October. Bedding was highly profitable in good years and many fortunes were made in it. It was dominated by old-settler Staten Island families—the Tottens, the Winants, the De Harts, the Deckers, the Manees, the Mersereaus, the Van Wyks, the Van Duzers, the Latourettes, the Housmans, the Bedells, and the Depews. It lasted for almost a century, during which, at one time or another, five Staten Island ports—

Mariner's Harbor, Port Richmond, Great Kills, Prince's Bay, and Tottenville—had oyster docks and fleets of schooners, sloops, and tonging skiffs. Prince's Bay had the biggest fleet and the longest period of prosperity; on menus in New York and London, harbor oysters were often called Prince's Bays. Approximately nine thousand acres of harbor bottom, split up into plots varying from a fraction of an acre to four hundred acres, were used for beds. The plots were leased from the state and were staked with a forest of hemlock poles; nowadays, in deepening and widening Ambrose Channel, Chapel Hill Channel, Swash Channel, and other ship channels in the Lower Bay, dredges occasionally dig up the tube-worm-incrusted stumps of old boundary poles. Bedding was most prosperous in the thirty years between 1860 and 1890. In good years in that period, as many as fifteen hundred men were employed on the beds and as many as five hundred thousand bushels of oysters were marketed. Some years, as much as a third of the crop was shipped to Billingsgate, the London fish market. For a while, the principal bedders were the richest men on Staten Island. They put their money in waterfront real estate, they named streets after themselves, and they built big, showy wooden mansions. A half dozen of these mansions still stand in a blighted neighborhood in Mariner's Harbor, in among refineries and coal tipples and junk yards. One has a widow's walk, two have tall fluted columns, all have oddly shaped gables, and all are decorated with scroll-saw work. They overlook one of the oiliest and gummiest stretches of the Kill van Kull. On the south shore, in the sassafras barrens west of Prince's Bay, there are three more of these mansions, all empty. Their fanlights are broken, their shutters swag, and their yards are a tangle of weeds and vines and overturned birdbaths and dead pear trees.

After 1900, as more and more of the harbor became polluted, people began to grow suspicious of harbor oysters, and the bedding business declined. In the summer of 1916, a number of cases of typhoid fever were traced beyond all doubt to the eating of oysters that had been bedded on West Bank Shoal, in the Lower Bay, and it was found that sewage from a huge New Jersey trunk sewer whose outfall is at the confluence of the Kill van Kull and the Upper Bay was being swept through the Narrows and over the beds by the tides. The Department of Health thereupon condemned the beds and banned the business. The bedders were allowed to take up the oysters they had down and rebed them in clean water in various Long Island bays. They didn't get them all, of course. A few were missed and left behind on every bed. Some of these propagated, and now their descendants are sprinkled over shoaly areas in all the bays below the Narrows. They are found on West Bank Shoal, East Bank Shoal, Old Orchard Shoal, Round Shoal, Flynns Knoll, and Romer Shoal. They live in clumps and patches; a clump may have several dozen oysters in it and a patch may have several hundred. Divers and dredgemen call them wild oysters. It is against state and city laws to "dig, rake, tong, or otherwise remove" these oysters from the water. A few elderly men who once were bedders are still living in the old Staten Island oyster ports, and many sons and grandsons of bedders. They have a proprietary feeling about harbor oysters, and every so often, in cold weather, despite the laws, some of them go out to the old, ruined beds and poach a mess. They know what they are doing; they watch the temperature of the water to make sure that the oysters are "sleeping," or hibernating, before they eat any. Oysters shut their shells and quit feeding and begin to hibernate when the temperature of the water in which they lie goes down to forty-one degrees; in three or four days, they free themselves of whatever germs they may have taken in, and then they are clean and safe.

There is a physician in his late fifties in St. George whose father and grandfather were bedders. On a wall of his waiting room hangs an heirloom, a chart of oyster plots on West Bank Shoal that was made in 1886 by a marine surveyor for the state; it is wrinkled and finger-smudged and salt-water-spotted, and his grandfather's plot, which later became his father's—a hundred and two acres on the outer rim of the shoal, down below Swinburne Island—is bounded on it in red ink. The physician keeps a sea skiff in one of the south-shore ports and goes fishing every decent Sunday. He stores a pair of pole-handled tongs in the skiff and sometimes spends a couple of hours hunting for clumps of harbor oysters. One foggy Sunday afternoon last March, he got in his skiff, with a companion, and remarked to the people on the dock that he was going codfishing on the Scallop Ridge, off Rockaway Beach. Instead, picking his way through the fog, he went up to the West Bank and dropped anchor on one of his father's old beds and began tonging. He made over two dozen grabs and moved the skiff four times before he located a clump. It was a big clump, and he tonged up all the oysters in it; there were exactly sixty. All were mature, all were speckled with little holes made by boring sponges, and all were wedge-shaped. Sea hair, a marine weed, grew thickly on their shells. One was much bigger than the others, and the physician picked it up and smoothed aside its mat of coarse, black, curly sea hair and counted the ridges on its upper shell and said that it was at least fourteen years old. "It's too big to eat on the half shell," he told his companion. He bent over the gunnel of the skiff and gently put it back in the water. Then he selected a dozen that ranged in age from four to seven years and opened them. Their meats were well developed and gray-green and glossy. He ate one with relish. "Every time I eat harbor oysters," he said, "my childhood comes floating up from the bottom of my mind." He reflected for a few moments. "They have a high iodine content," he continued, "and they have a characteristic taste. When I was a boy in Prince's Bay, the old bedders used to say that they tasted like almonds. Since the water went bad, that taste has become more pronounced. It's become coppery and bitter. If you've ever tasted the little nut that's inside the pit of a peach, the kernel, that's how they taste."

The fish and shellfish in the harbor and in the ocean just outside provide all or part of a living for about fifteen hundred men who call themselves baymen. They work out of bays and inlets and inlets within inlets along the coasts of Staten Island, Brooklyn, and Queens. Some baymen clam on the public beds. Some baymen set eelpots. Some baymen set pound nets, or fish traps. Pound nets are strung from labyrinths of stakes in shoal areas, out of the way of the harbor traffic. Last year, during the shad, summer herring, and mossbunker migrations, forty-one of them were set off the Staten Island coast, between Midland Beach and Great Kills, in an old oyster-bedding area. Some baymen go out in draggers, or small trawlers, of which there are two fleets in the harbor. One fleet has sixteen boats, and ties up at two shaky piers on Plumb Beach Channel, an inlet just east of Sheepshead Bay, on the Brooklyn coast. The other has nine boats, and ties up alongside a quay on the west branch of Mill Basin, a three-branched inlet in the bulrush marshes in the Flatlands neighborhood of Brooklyn. The majority of the men in both fleets are Italian-Americans, a few of whom in their youth fished out of the Sicilian ports of Palermo and Castellammare del Golfo. Some of them tack saints' pictures and miraculous medals and scapular medals and little evil-eye amulets on the walls of their pilothouses. The amulets are in the shape of hunchbacks, goat horns, fists with two fingers upraised, and opened scissors; they come from stores on Mulberry Street and are made of plastic. The harbor draggers range from thirty to fifty feet and carry two to five men. According to the weather and the season, they drag their baglike nets in the Lower Bay or in a fishing ground called the Mud Hole, which lies south of Scotland and Ambrose Lightships and is about fifteen miles long and five to ten miles wide. The Mud Hole is the upper part of the Old Hudson River Canyon, which was the bed of the river twenty thousand years ago, when the river flowed a hundred and twenty-five miles past what is now Sandy Hook before it reached the ocean. The draggers catch lower-depth and bottom feeders, chiefly whiting, butterfish, ling, cod, porgy, fluke, and flounder. They go out around 4 A.M. and return around 4 P.M., and their catches are picked up by trucks and taken to Fulton Market.

Some baymen set lines of lobster pots. In days gone by, there was a bountiful stock of lobsters in the harbor. Between 1915 and 1920, owing to pollution and overfishing and the bootlegging of berries, which are egg-carrying lobsters, and shorts and crickets, which are undersized lobsters, the stock began dwindling at a rapid rate. As late as 1920, forty-five lobstermen were still working the Upper Bay, the Narrows, and the Lower Bay. They ran out of seven inlets in Brooklyn and Staten Island, and their buoys dipped and danced all the way from the Statue of Liberty to the Hook. Every year in the twenties, a few of them either dropped out for good or bought bigger boats and forsook the bays and started setting pots out beyond the three-mile limit, in the harbor approaches. By 1930, only one lobsterman of any importance, Sandy Cuthbert, of Prince's Bay, continued to work the bays. In the fall of that year, at the close of the season, Mr. Cuthbert took up his pots—he had two hundred and fifty—and stacked them on the bank of Lemon Creek, an inlet of Prince's Bay, and went into the rowboat-renting and fish-bait business. His pots are still there, rotting; generations of morning-glory and wild-hop vines are raveled in their slats and hold them together. During the thirties and forties, the lobsters began coming back, and divers say that now there are quite a few nests in the Upper Bay and many nests in the Lower Bay. However, they are still too scarce and scattered to be profitable. Sometimes, while repairing cables or pipelines on the bottom in parts of the Lower Bay where the water is clear and the visibility is good, divers turn over rocks and pieces of waterlogged driftwood and lobsters scuttle out and the divers pick them up and put them in the tool sacks hooked to their belts.

At present, there are nine lobster boats working out of the harbor—six out of Plumb Beach; two out of Ulmer Park, on Gravesend Bay; and one out of Coney Island Creek. They are of the sea-skiff type. They range from twenty-six to twenty-eight feet, they are equipped with gasoline engines that are strong enough for much bigger boats, and, except for canvas spray hoods, they are open to the weather. The men on these boats are Scandinavians and Italians. They set their pots in a section of the Mud Hole southeast of Ambrose Lightship where the water in most places is over a hundred feet deep. They use the trawl method, in which the pots are hung at intervals from thick, tarred lines half a mile long; as a rule, thirty-five pots are hung from each line. The lines are buoyed at both ends with bundles of old, discarded ferryboat life preservers, which the lobstermen buy from a ship chandler in Fulton Market, who buys them from the Department of Marine and Aviation. Once a day, the lines are lifted, and each pot is pulled up and emptied of lobsters and chewed-up bait and stray crabs and fish, and rebaited with three or four dead mossbunkers. The coastwise and South American shipping lanes cross the lobster grounds in the Mud Hole, and every now and then a ship plows into a line and tears it loose from its buoys. Dump scows with rubbish from the city sometimes unload on the grounds and foul the lines and bury the pots. Mud Hole lobsters are as good as Maine lobsters; they can't be told apart. Some are sold to knowledgeable Brooklyn housewives who drive down to the piers in the middle of the afternoon, when the boats come in, and take their pick, but most are sold to Brooklyn restaurants. A boat working seven lines, which is the average, often comes in with around two hundred and fifty pounds.

A good many baymen work on public fishing boats that take sports fishermen out to fishing grounds in the harbor, in the harbor approaches, and along the Jersey coast. These boats are of two types—charter and party. Charter boats are cabin cruisers that may be hired on a daily or weekly basis. They are used for going after roaming surface feeders, big and small. Most of them are equipped with fighting chairs, fish hoists, and other contrivances for big-game fishing. They go out in the Lower Bay, Sandy Hook Bay, and Raritan Bay for striped bass, bluefish, and mackerel, and they go out to the Mud Hole and the Jersey grounds for tuna, albacore, bonito, and skipjack. They carry a captain and a mate, who baits and gaffs. Great Kills, which has fifteen boats, and Prince's Bay, which has eight, are the principal charter-boat ports in the harbor.

Party boats, also called open boats, are bigger boats, which operate on regular schedules and are open to anyone who has the fare; it varies from three and a half to five dollars a day. Sheepshead Bay is the principal party-boat port. It has over fifty boats. All of them leave from Emmons Avenue, which many people consider the most attractive waterfront street in the city. Emmons is a wide street, with a row of fluttery-leaved plane trees down the middle of it, that runs along the north shore of the bay. It smells of the sea, and of beer and broiled fish. On one side of it, for a dozen blocks, are bar-and-grills, seafood restaurants, clam stands, diners, pizza parlors, tackle and boat-gear stores, and fish markets, one of which has a cynical sign in its show window that says, "CATCH YOUR FISH ON THE NEVER-FAIL BANKS. USE A SILVER HOOK." The party-boat piers—there are ten of them, and they are long and roomy—jut out diagonally from the other side. Retired men from all over Brooklyn come down to the piers by bus and subway on sunny days and sit on the stringpieces and watch the boats go out, and rejuvenate their lungs with the brine in the air, and fish for blue-claw crabs with collapsible wirework traps, and quarrel with each other over the gulls; some bring paper bags of table scraps from home and feed the gulls and coo at them, and some despise the gulls and shoo them away and would wring their necks if they could get their hands on them. Among the boats in the Sheepshead Bay fleet are stripped-down draggers, converted yachts, and converted subchasers from both World Wars. The majority carry a captain and a mate and take around thirty passengers; the old subchasers carry a captain, a mate, an engineer, a cook, and a deckhand and take up to a hundred and ten passengers. Some have battered iceboxes on their decks and sell beer and pop and sandwiches, and some have galleys and sell hot meals. Some have conventional fishing-boat names, such as the *Sea Pigeon*, the *Dorothy B*, and the *Carrie D II*, and some have strutty names, such as the *Atomic*, the *Rocket*, and the *Glory*. Most of them leave at 5, 6, 7, 8, 9, or 10 A.M. and stay out the better part of the day. The passengers bring their own tackle, and fish over the rails. Bait is supplied by the boats; it is included in the fare. In most seasons, for most species, shucked and cut-up skimmer clams are used. These are big, coarse, golden-meated ocean clams. Cut-up fish, live fish, fiddler crabs, calico crabs, sand worms, and blood worms are also used.

There are two dozen baymen in Sheepshead Bay who dig, dredge, net, and trap bait. They deliver it to three bait barges moored in the bay, and the bargekeepers put it into shape and sell it to the party boats by the tubful. For five weeks or so in the spring and for five weeks or so in the fall, during the mackerel migrations, the party boats go out and find schools of mackerel and anchor in the midst of them. The rest of the year, they go out and anchor over wrecks, reefs, scow dumps, and shellfish beds, where cod, ling, porgy, fluke, flounder, sea bass, blackfish, and other bottom feeders congregate.

There are many wrecks—maybe a hundred, maybe twice that; no one knows how many—lying on the bottom in the harbor approaches. Some are intact and some are broken up. Some are out in the Old Hudson River Canyon, with over two hundred feet of water on top of them. Some are close to shore, in depths of only twenty to thirty feet; around noon, on unusually clear, sunny fall days, when there is not much plankton in the water and the turbidity is low, it is possible to see these and see schools of sea bass streaming in and out of holes in their hulls. The wrecks furnish shelter for fish. Furthermore, they are coated, inside and out, with a lush, furry growth made up of algae, sea moss, tube worms, barnacles, horse mussels, sea anemones, sea squirts, sea mice, sea snails, and scores of other organisms, all of which are food for fish. The most popular party boats are those whose captains can locate the fishiest wrecks and bridle them. Bridling is a maneuver in which, say the wreck lies north and south, the party boat goes in athwart it and drops one anchor to the east of it and another to the west of it, so that party boat and wreck lie crisscross. Held thus, the party boat can't be skewed about by the wind and tide, and the passengers fishing over both rails can always be sure that they are dropping their bait on the wreck, or inside it. Good party-boat captains, by taking bearings on landmarks and lightships and buoys, can locate and bridle anywhere from ten to thirty wrecks. A number of the wrecks are quite old; they disintegrate slowly. Three old ones, all sailing ships, lie close to each other near the riprap jetty at Rockaway Point, in the mouth of the harbor. The oldest of the three, the *Black Warrior* Wreck, which shelters tons of sea bass from June until November, went down in 1859. The name of the next oldest has been forgotten and she is called the Snow Wreck; a snow is a kind of square-rigged ship similar to a brig; she sank in 1886 or 1887. The third one is an Italian ship that sank in 1890 with a cargo of marble slabs; her name has also been forgotten and she is called the Tombstone Wreck, the Granite Wreck, or the Italian Wreck. Over to the east, off the Rockaways, there is another group of old ones. In this group, all within five miles of shore, are the steamship *Iberia*, which sank in a snowstorm in 1889, after colliding with the steamship *Umbria*; the Wire Wreck, a sailing ship that sank around 1895 while outbound with a cargo of bedsprings and other wire products; the *Boyle* Wreck, a tug that sank around 1900; and the East Wreck, three coal barges that snapped their tow in a storm in 1917 and settled on the bottom in an equilateral triangle. Several of these wrecks have been fished steadily for generations, and party-boat captains like to say that they would be worth salvaging just to get the metal in the hooks and sinkers that have been snagged on them.

There are stretches of reefy bottom in the harbor approaches that are almost as productive of fish as the wrecks, and for the same reasons. These stretches are easier to locate than the wrecks, and much easier to fish. All have been named. Some are natural rock ledges, and among these are the Shrewsbury Rocks, the Buoy Four Grounds, the Cholera Bank, the Klondike Banks, the Seventeen Fathoms, and the Farms. Some are artificial ledges, consisting of debris from excavations and torn-down buildings that was transported from the city in scows and dumped. One such is the Subway Rocks, a ridge of underwater hills beginning four miles south of Ambrose Lightship and running south for several miles, that was made of rocks, bricks, concrete, asphalt, and earth excavated during the construction of the Eighth Avenue Subway. Another such is the New Grounds, or Doorknob Grounds, a stretch of bottom in the northwest corner of the Mud Hole that is used as a dump for slum-clearance projects. There are bricks and brownstone blocks and plaster and broken glass from hundreds upon hundreds of condemned tenements in the New Grounds. The ruins of the somber old red-brick houses in the Lung Block, which were torn down to make way for Knickerbocker Village, lie there. In the first half of the nineteenth century, these houses were occupied by well-to-do families; from around 1890 until around 1905, most of them were brothels for sailors; from around 1905 until they were torn down, in 1933, they were rented to the poorest of the poor, and the tuberculosis death rate was higher in that block than in any other block in the city. All the organisms that grow on wrecks grow on the hills of rubble and rubbish in the Subway Rocks and the New Grounds.

The comings and goings of the baymen are watched by a member of the staff of the Bureau of Marine Fisheries of the State Conservation Department. His name is Andrew E. Zimmer, his title is Shellfish Protector, and his job is to enforce the conservation laws relating to marine shellfish and finfish. Mr. Zimmer is a Staten Islander of German descent. He is muscular and barrel-chested and a bit above medium height. He is bald and he is getting jowly. The department issues him a uniform that closely resembles a state trooper's uniform, but he seldom wears it. On duty, he wears old, knockabout clothes, the same as a bayman. He carries a pair of binoculars and a .38 revolver. He is called Happy Zimmer by the baymen, some of whom grew up with him. He is a serious man, a good many things puzzle him, and he usually has a preoccupied look on his face; his nickname dates from boyhood and he has outgrown it. He was born in 1901 on a farm in New Springville, a truck-farming community on the inland edge of the tide marshes that lie along the Arthur Kill, on the western side of Staten Island. In the front yard of the farmhouse, his father ran a combined saloon and German-home-cooking restaurant, named Zimmer's, that attracted people from the villages around and about and from some of the Jersey towns across the kill. Picnics and clambakes and lodge outings were held in a willow grove on the farm. His father had been a vaudeville ventriloquist, and often performed at these affairs.

Specialties of the restaurant were jellied eels, clam broth with butter in it, and pear conchs from the Lower Bay boiled and then pickled in a mixture of vinegar and spices and herbs. As a boy, Mr. Zimmer supplied the restaurant with eels he speared in eel holes in the marshes and with soft-shell clams that he dug in the flats along the kill. Until 1916, when the harbor beds were condemned, Prince's Bay oysters were sold from the barrel in the saloon side of the restaurant. Friday afternoons, he and his father would drive down to the Oyster Dock in Prince's Bay in the farm wagon and bring back three or four barrels of selects for the week-end trade. In 1915, after completing the eighth grade, Mr. Zimmer quit school to help his father in the restaurant. In 1924, he took charge of it. In his spare time, mainly by observation in the marshes, he became a good amateur naturalist. In 1930, he gave up the restaurant and went to work for the Conservation Department.

Mr. Zimmer patrols the harbor in a lumbering, rumbly old twenty-eight-foot sea skiff. It has no flag or markings and looks like any old lobster boat, but the baymen can spot it from a distance; they call it the State Boat. Some of Mr. Zimmer's duties are seasonal. From March 15th to June 15th, when pound-netting is allowed, he makes frequent visits to the nets at pull-up time and sees to it that the fishermen are keeping only the species they are licensed for. When the mossbunker seiners come into the harbor, he boards them and looks into their holds and satisfies himself that they are not taking food fishes along with the mossbunkers. Now and then during the lobstering season, he draws up alongside the lobster boats inbound from the grounds and inspects their catches for shorts. Several times a year, he bottles samples of the water in various parts of the harbor and sends them to the department's laboratory. His principal year-round duty is to patrol the shellfish beds. He runs down and arrests poachers on the polluted beds, and he keeps an eye on the clammers who work the legal beds in Raritan Bay. It is against the law to do any kind of clamming between sundown and sunup, and he spends many nights out on the beds. He is a self-sufficient man. He can anchor his skiff in the shadow of a cattail hassock in Jamaica Bay and, without ever getting especially bored, sit there the whole night through with an old blanket over his shoulders, listening and watching for poachers and looking at the stars and the off-and-on lights on airplanes and drinking coffee out of a thermos jug. The legal beds in New Jersey territory in the harbor have been overworked and are not as fertile as the legal beds in New York territory. In recent years, allured by high clam prices, some of the Jersey clammers have become pirates. They tantalize Mr. Zimmer. On dark nights, using Chris Craft cruisers, they cross the state line, which bisects Raritan Bay, and poach on the New York beds. When they hear the rumble of Mr. Zimmer's skiff, they flee for Jersey. Mr. Zimmer opens his throttle and goes after them, shouting at them to halt and sometimes firing his revolver over their heads, but their cruisers draw less water than his skiff and at the end of the chase they are usually able to shoot up into one of the shallow tide creeks between South Amboy and the Hook and lose him. Mr. Zimmer keeps his skiff in Prince's Bay. Prince's Bay has gone down as a port since his boyhood. Not a trace of the oyster-bedding business is left there. It has a clam dock, a charter-boat pier, and two boatyards, and it has Sandy Cuthbert's rowboat livery and bait station, but its chief source of income is a factory that makes tools for dentists; the factory is on Dental Avenue. The old Prince's Bay Lighthouse still stands on a bluff above the village, but it is now a part of Mount Loretto, a Catholic home for children; it is used as a residence by the Monsignor and priests who run the home. The light has been taken down and supplanted by a life-size statue of the Virgin Mary. The Virgin's back is to the sea.

Once in a while, Mr. Zimmer spends a day patrolling the Staten Island tide marshes on foot. He feels drawn to the marshes and enjoys this part of his job most of all. A good many people wander about in the marshes and in the meadows and little woods with which they are studded. He is acquainted with scores of marsh wanderers. In the fall, old Italians come and get down on all fours and scrabble in the leaves and rot beneath the blackjack oaks, hunting for mushrooms. In the spring, they come again and pick dandelion sprouts for salads. In midsummer, they come again, this time with scap nets, and scoop tiny mud shrimp out of the tide ditches; they use them in a fried fish-and-shellfish dish called *frittura di pesce*. On summer afternoons, old women from the south-shore villages come to the fringes of the marshes. They pick herbs, they pick wild flowers, they pick wild grapes for jelly, and in the fresh-water creeks that empty into the salt-water creeks they pick watercress. In the fall, truck farmers come with scythes and cut salt hay. When the hay dries, they pack it around their cold frames to keep the frost out. Bird watchers and Indian-relic collectors come in all seasons. The relic collectors sift the mud on the banks of the tide ditches. Mr. Zimmer himself sometimes finds arrowheads and stone net-sinkers on the ditchbanks. Once, he found several old English coins. In September or October, the rabbis and elders come. On Hoshanna Rabbah, the seventh day of the Festival of Succoth, an ancient fertility rite is still observed in a number of orthodox synagogues in the city. The worshipers who take part in the rite are given bunches of willow twigs; each bunch has seven twigs and each twig has seven leaves. After marching in procession seven times around the altar, chanting a litany, the worshipers shake the bunches or strike them against the altar until the leaves fall to the floor. The twigs must be cut from willows that grow beside water, the buds on the ends of the twigs must be unblemished, and the leaves must be green and flawless. For generations, most of the willow bunches have come from black willows and weeping willows in the Staten Island tide marshes. In the two or three days preceding Hoshanna Rabbah—it usually falls in the last week of September or the first or second week of October—rabbis and trusted elders go up and down the ditchbanks, most often in pairs, the rabbi scrutinizing twigs and cutting those that pass the test, and the elder trimming and bunching them and stowing them gently in brown-paper shopping bags.

There is much resident and migratory wildlife in the marshes. The most plentiful resident species are pheasants, crows, marsh hawks, black snakes, muskrats, opossums, rabbits, rats, and field mice. There is no open season on the pheasants, and they have become so bold that the truck farmers look upon them as pests. One can walk through the pokeweed and sumac and blue-bent grass on any of the meadow islands at any time and put up pair after pair of pheasants. At the head of a snaky creek in one of the loneliest of the marshes, there is an old rickamarack of a dock that was built by rumrunners during prohibition. One morning, hiding behind this dock, waiting for some softshell-clam poachers to appear, Mr. Zimmer saw a hen pheasant walk across a strip of tide flat, followed by a brood of seventeen. At times, out in the marshes, Mr. Zimmer becomes depressed. The marshes are doomed. The city has begun to dump garbage on them. It has already filled in hundreds of acres with garbage. Eventually, it will fill in the whole area, and then the Department of Parks will undoubtedly build some proper parks out there, and put in some concrete highways and scatter some concrete benches about. The old south-shore secessionists—they want Staten Island to secede from New York and join New Jersey, and there are many of them—can sit on these benches and meditate and store up bile.

Mr. Zimmer is a friend of mine, and I sometimes go out on patrols with him. One cold, windy, spitty morning, we made a patrol of the polluted skimmer-clam beds in the ocean off Rockaway Beach. On the way back to Staten Island, he suggested that we stop in Sheepshead Bay and get some oyster stew to warm us up. We turned in to the bay and tied the skiff to the Harbor Police float and went across the street to Lundy's, the biggest and best of the Emmons Avenue seafood restaurants. We went into the oyster-bar side and took a table, and each of us ordered a double stew. Mr. Zimmer caught sight of a bayman named Leroy Poole, who was standing at the bar, bent over some oysters on the half shell. Mr. Poole is captain and owner of the party boat *Chinquapin*. Mr. Zimmer went over to the bar, and he and Mr. Poole shook hands and talked for a minute or two. When he returned, he said that Mr. Poole would join us as soon as he'd finished his oysters. He told the waiter to set another place and add another double stew to the order. "Do you know Roy?" Mr. Zimmer asked me. I said that I had often seen him around the party-boat piers but that I knew him only to speak to.

"Roy's a south-shore boy," Mr. Zimmer said. "His father was one of the biggest oyster-bedders in Prince's Bay—lost everything when they condemned the beds, and took a bookkeeping job in Fulton Market and died of a stroke in less than a year; died on the Staten Island ferry, on the way to work. After Roy finished grade school, one of his father's friends got him a job in the market, and he became a fish butcher. When the carcass of a three- or four-hundred-pound swordfish is cut into pieces that the retail trade can handle, it's about the same as dressing a steer, and Roy had a knack for that type of work. He got to be an expert. When he cut up a swordfish, or a tuna, or a sturgeon, or a big West Coast halibut, he didn't waste a pound. Also, he was a good fillet man, and he could bone a shad quicker and cleaner than any man in the market. He made good money, but he wasn't happy. Every now and then, he'd quit the market for a year or so and work on one of the government dredges that dredge the sludge out of the ship channels in the harbor. He generally worked on a dredge named the *Goethals*. He made better pay in the market, but he liked to be out in the harbor. He switched back and forth between the market and the *Goethals* for years and years. Somewhere along the line, he got himself tattooed. He's got an oyster tattooed on the muscle of his right arm. That is, an oyster shell. On his left arm, he's got one of those tombstone tattoos—a tombstone with his initials on it and under his initials the date of his birth and under that a big blue question mark. Six or seven years ago, he turned up in Sheepshead Bay and bought the *Chinquapin*. Roy's a good captain, and a good man, but he's a little odd. He says so himself. He's a harbor nut. Most of the baymen, when they're standing around talking, they often talk about the bottom of the harbor, what's down there, but that's *all* Roy talks about. He's got the bottom of the harbor on the brain."

The waiter brought in the stews, and a moment later Mr. Poole came over and sat down. He is a paunchy, red-haired, freckled man. His hair is thinning and the freckles on his scalp show through. He has drooping eyelids; they make his eyes look sleepy and sad. He remarked on the weather; he said he expected snow. Then he tasted his stew. It was too hot for him, and he put his spoon down. "I didn't rest so good last night," he said. "I had a dream. In this dream, a great earthquake had shook the world and had upset the sea level, and New York Harbor had been drained as dry as a bathtub when the plug is pulled. I was down on the bottom, poking around, looking things over. There were hundreds of ships of all kinds lying on their sides in the mud, and among them were some wormy old wrecks that went down long years ago, and there were rusty anchors down there and dunnage and driftwood and old hawsers and tugboat bumpers and baling wire and tin cans and bottles and stranded eels and a skeleton standing waist-deep in a barrel of cement that the barrel had rotted off of. The rats had left the piers and were down on the bottom, eating the eels, and the gulls were flopping about, jerking eels away from the rats. I came across an old wooden wreck all grown over with seaweed, an old, old Dutch wreck. She had a hole in her, and I pulled the seaweed away and looked in and I saw some chests in there that had money spilling out of them, and I tried my best to crawl in. The dream was so strong that I crawled up under the headboard of the bed, trying to get my hands on the Dutch money, and I damn near scraped an ear off."

"Eat your stew, Roy," Mr. Zimmer said, "before it gets cold."

"Pass me the salt," said Mr. Poole. We ate in silence. It isn't easy to carry on a conversation while eating oyster stew. Mr. Poole finished first. He tilted his bowl and worked the last spoonful of the stew into his spoon. He swallowed it, and then he said, "Happy, you've studied the harbor charts a lot in your time. Where would you say is the deepest spot in the harbor?"

"Offhand," said Mr. Zimmer, "I just don't know."

"One of the deepest spots I know is a hole in the bed of the Hudson a little bit south of the George Washington Bridge," said Mr. Poole. "On the dredges, we called it the Gut. It's half full of miscellaneous junk. The city used to dump bargeloads of boulders in there, and any kind of heavy junk that wasn't worth salvaging. Private concerns dumped in there, too, years back, but it's against the harbor regulations now. During the worst part of the last war, when the dredges cleaned sludge out of the ship channel in the Hudson, they had the right to dump it in the Gut—save them from taking it out to sea. The old-timers say the Gut used to go down a hundred and eighty feet. The last sounding I heard, it was around ninety feet. I know where the shallowest spot in the harbor is. I've sounded it myself with a boat hook. It's a spot on Romer Shoal, out in the middle of the Lower Bay, that's only four feet deep at low tide."

"Oh, yes," said Mr. Zimmer. "I've seen it on the charts. It's called a lump."

"It's right on the edge of Ambrose Channel, the channel that the big liners use," continued Mr. Poole. "I told my mate I want him to take me out there someday when the *Queen Mary* is due to come upchannel, and leave me standing there with a flag in my hand."

"What in hell would you do that for?" asked Mr. Zimmer.

"I'd just like to," said Mr. Poole. "I'd like to wave the flag and make the people on the *Queen Mary* wonder what I was standing on—shoulder-deep, out there in the middle of the Lower Bay. I'd wear a top hat, and I'd smoke a big cigar. I'd like to see what would happen."

"I'll tell you what would happen," said Mr. Zimmer. "The wash from the *Queen Mary* would drown you. Did you think of that?"

"I thought of it," said Mr. Poole. "I didn't do it, did I?" He crumpled up his napkin and tossed it on the table. "Another queer spot in the harbor," he said, "is Potter's Field. It's in the East River, in between Williamsburg Bridge and Manhattan Bridge. The river makes a sharp bend there, an elbow. On an ebb tide, there's an eddy in the elbow that picks up anything loose coming downriver, afloat or submerged, and sweeps it into a stretch of backwater on the Brooklyn side. This backwater is called Wallabout Bay on charts; the men on the dredges call it Potter's Field. The eddy sweeps driftwood into the backwater. Also, it sweeps drownded bodies into there. As a rule, people that drown in the harbor in winter stay down until spring. When the water begins to get warm, gas forms in them and that makes them buoyant and they rise to the surface. Every year, without fail, on or about the fifteenth of April, bodies start showing up, and more of them show up in Potter's Field than any other place. In a couple of weeks or so, the Harbor Police always finds ten to two dozen over there—suicides, bastard babies, old barge captains that lost their balance out on a sleety night attending to towropes, now and then some gangster or other. The police launch that runs out of Pier A on the Battery—Launch One—goes over and takes them out of the water with a kind of dip-net contraption that the Police Department blacksmith made out of tire chains. I ride the Staten Island ferry a good deal, and I'm forever hearing the tourists remark how beautiful the harbor is, and I always wish they could see Potter's Field some mornings in April—either that or the Gowanus Canal in August, when the sludge bubbles are popping like whips; they'd get a brand-new idea how beautiful the harbor is."

"Oh, I don't know, Roy," said Mr. Zimmer. "They've stopped dumping garbage out in the harbor approaches, where the tide washes it right back, and they're putting in a lot of sewage-disposal plants. The water's getting cleaner every year."

"I've read that," said Mr. Poole, "and I've heard it. Only I don't believe it. Did you eat any shad last spring—Staten Island shad *or* Hudson River shad? They've still got that kerosene taste. It was worse last spring than it ever was. Also, have you been up the Gowanus Canal lately? On the dredges, they used to say that the smell in the Gowanus would make the flag on a mast hang limp in a high wind. They used to tell about a tug that was freshly painted yellow and made a run up the Gowanus and came out painted green. I was up there last summer, and I didn't notice any change."

"Seriously, Roy," said Mr. Zimmer, "don't you think the water's getting cleaner?"

"Of course it isn't," said Mr. Poole. "It's getting worse and worse. *Every*thing is getting worse *every*where. When I was young, I used to dream the time would come when we could bed oysters in the harbor again. Now I'm satisfied that that time will never come. I don't even worry about the pollution any more. My only hope, I hope they don't pollute the harbor with something a million times worse than pollution."

"Let's don't get on that subject," said Mr. Zimmer.

"Sometimes I'm walking along the street," continued Mr. Poole, "and I wonder why the people don't just stand still and throw their heads back and open their mouths and howl."

"Why?" asked Mr. Zimmer.

"I'll tell you why," said Mr. Poole. "On account of the God-damned craziness of everything."

"Oh, well," said Mr. Zimmer, glancing at the empty stew bowls, "we can still eat."

Mr. Poole grunted. He looked at his wristwatch. "Well," he said, "this ain't making me any money." He got up and put on his hat. "Thanks for the stew," he said. "I enjoyed it. My treat next time. Take care, all."

"That's right, Roy," said Mr. Zimmer. "You take care of yourself."

"Thanks again," said Mr. Poole. "Give my regards home. Take care. Take care. Take care."

George Oppen

"I lived in a house on the water, near the harbor, in a small village," said George Oppen (1908–1984) of his childhood on Long Island Sound in New Rochelle, New York. In the late 1920s, with his wife, Mary, Oppen sailed a catboat through the Great Lakes, the Erie Canal, and the Hudson River to New York City. Years later—after a career that involved political activism as a communist in the 1930s, combat service in World War II, and a triumphant return to poetry, after a hiatus of three decades, in the early 1960s—he spent much time off the coast of Maine, where he and his wife returned to their earlier involvement with sailing: "Since 1963 we have come to Little Deer Isle every summer . . . to sail through every passage and into every inlet and around every island in Penobscot Bay in a very small and very fast sailboat, sleeping on the boat in a boom tent . . . Pound said: 'What a man loves, is his heritage.'" Oppen's book Of Being Numerous *won the Pulitzer Prize in 1968. In his later years he lived in San Francisco. "Product" was first collected in* The Materials *(1962).*

Product

There is no beauty in New England like the boats.
Each itself, even the paint white
Dipping to each wave each time
At anchor, mast
And rigging tightly part of it
Fresh from the dry tools
And the dry New England hands.
The bow soars, finds the waves
The hull accepts. Once someone
Put a bowl afloat
And there for all to see, for all the children,
Even the New Englander
Was boatness. What I've seen
Is all I've found: myself.

E. B. White

E. B. White (1899–1985)—the celebrated humorist, essayist, and children's writer, author of One Man's Meat *(1942),* Stuart Little *(1945),* Charlotte's Web *(1952),* The Points of My Compass *(1962), and a revised version (1979) of William Strunk Jr.'s* Elements of Style*—was a self-described "salt-water man." In his twenties he had worked as a mess boy on a 40-day voyage to Alaska. Later in life he owned a succession of small boats. In "The Sea and the Wind That Blows," first published in 1963, White looks with a characteristic wry elegance at his own enthusiasm for the nautical life.*

The Sea and the Wind That Blows

WAKING or sleeping, I dream of boats—usually of rather small boats under a slight press of sail. When I think how great a part of my life has been spent dreaming the hours away and how much of this total dream life has concerned small craft, I wonder about the state of my health, for I am told that it is not a good sign to be always voyaging into unreality, driven by imaginary breezes.

I have noticed that most men, when they enter a barber shop and must wait their turn, drop into a chair and pick up a magazine. I simply sit down and pick up the thread of my sea wandering, which began more than fifty years ago and is not quite ended. There is hardly a waiting room in the east that has not served as my cockpit, whether I was waiting to board a train or to see a dentist. And I am usually still trimming sheets when the train starts or the drill begins to whine.

If a man must be obsessed by something, I suppose a boat is as good as anything, perhaps a bit better than most. A small sailing craft is not only beautiful, it is seductive and full of strange promise and the hint of trouble. If it happens to be an auxiliary cruising boat, it is without question the most compact and ingenious arrangement for living ever devised by the restless mind of man—a home that is stable without being stationary, shaped less like a box than like a fish or a bird or a girl, and in which the homeowner can remove his daily affairs as far from shore as he has the nerve to take them, close-hauled or running free—parlor, bedroom, and bath, suspended and alive.

Men who ache all over for tidiness and compactness in their lives often find relief for their pain in the cabin of a thirty-foot sailboat at anchor in a sheltered cove. Here the sprawling panoply of The Home is compressed in orderly miniature and liquid delirium, suspended between the bottom of the sea and the top of the sky, ready to move on in the morning by the miracle of canvas and the witchcraft of rope. It is small wonder that men hold boats in the secret place of their mind, almost from the cradle to the grave.

Along with my dream of boats has gone the ownership of boats, a long succession of them upon the surface of the sea, many of them makeshift and crank. Since childhood I have managed to have some sort of sailing craft and to raise a sail in fear. Now, in my sixties, I still own a boat, still raise my sail in fear in answer to the summons of the unforgiving sea. Why does the sea attract me in the way it does? Whence comes this compulsion to hoist a sail, actually or in dream? My first encounter with the sea was a case of hate at first sight. I was taken, at the age of four, to a bathing beach in New Rochelle. Everything about the experience frightened and repelled me: the taste of salt in my mouth, the foul chill of the wooden bathhouse, the littered sand, the stench of the tide flats. I came away hating and fearing the sea. Later, I found that what I had feared and hated, I now feared and loved.

I returned to the sea of necessity, because it would support a boat; and although I knew little of boats, I could not get them out of my thoughts. I became a pelagic boy. The sea became my unspoken challenge: the wind, the tide, the fog, the ledge, the bell, the gull that cried help, the never-ending threat and bluff of weather. Once having permitted the wind to enter the belly of my sail, I was not able to quit the helm; it was as though I had seized hold of a high-tension wire and could not let go.

I liked to sail alone. The sea was the same as a girl to me—I did not want anyone else along. Lacking instruction, I invented ways of getting things done, and usually ended by doing them in a rather queer fashion, and so did not learn to sail properly, and still cannot sail well, although I have been at it all my life. I was twenty before I discovered that charts existed; all my navigating up to that time was done with the wariness and the ignorance of the early explorers. I was thirty before I learned to hang a coiled halyard on its cleat as it should be done. Until then I simply coiled it down on deck and dumped the coil. I was always in trouble and always returned, seeking more trouble. Sailing became a compulsion: there lay the boat, swinging to her mooring, there blew the wind; I had no choice but to go. My earliest boats were so small that when the wind failed, or when I failed, I could switch to manual control—I could paddle or row home. But then I graduated to boats that only the wind was strong enough to move. When I first dropped off my mooring in such a boat, I was an hour getting up the nerve to cast off the pennant. Even now, with a thousand little voyages notched in my belt, I still feel a memorial chill on casting off, as the gulls jeer and the empty mainsail claps.

Of late years, I have noticed that my sailing has increasingly become a compulsive activity rather than a source of pleasure. There lies the boat, there blows the morning breeze—it is a point of honor, now, to go. I am like an alcoholic who cannot put his bottle out of his life. With me, I cannot not sail. Yet I know well enough that I have lost touch with the wind and, in fact, do not like the wind any more. It jiggles me up, the wind does, and what I really love are windless days, when all is peace. There is a great question in my mind whether a man who is against wind should longer try to sail a boat. But this is an intellectual response—the old yearning is still in me, belonging to the past, to youth, and so I am torn between past and present, a common disease of later life.

When does a man quit the sea? How dizzy, how bumbling must he be? Does he quit while he's ahead, or wait till he makes some major mistake, like falling overboard or being flattened by an accidental jibe? This past winter I spent hours arguing the question with myself. Finally, deciding that I had come to the end of the road, I wrote a note to the boatyard, putting my boat up for sale. I said I was "coming off the water." But as I typed the sentence, I doubted that I meant a word of it.

If no buyer turns up, I know what will happen: I will instruct the yard to put her in again—"just till somebody comes along." And then there will be the old uneasiness, the old uncertainty, as the mild southeast breeze ruffles the cove, a gentle, steady, morning breeze, bringing the taint of the distant wet world, the smell that takes a man back to the very beginning of time, linking him to all that has gone before. There will lie the sloop, there will blow the wind, once more I will get under way. And as I reach across to the red nun off the Torry Islands, dodging the trap buoys and toggles, the shags gathered on the ledge will note my passage. "There goes the old boy again," they will say. "One more rounding of his little Horn, one more conquest of his Roaring Forties." And with the tiller in my hand, I'll feel again the wind imparting life to a boat, will smell again the old menace, the one that imparts life to me: the cruel beauty of the salt world, the barnacle's tiny knives, the sharp spine of the urchin, the stinger of the sun jelly, the claw of the crab.

Samuel Eliot Morison

Samuel Eliot Morison (1887–1976) was one of America's foremost maritime historians—author, among many other works, of The Maritime History of Massachusetts *(1921),* Admiral of the Ocean Sea: A Life of Christopher Columbus *(1942), the official, 15-volume* History of United States Naval Operations in World War II *(1947–62), and* John Paul Jones: A Sailor's Biography *(1955). Throughout his life Morison was also a passionate amateur sailor: "My feeling for the sea is such," he claimed, "that writing about it is almost as embarrassing as making a confession of religious faith." "An August Day's Sail" is taken from* Spring Tides, *his 1965 memoir of his lifelong affair with the sea.*

An August Day's Sail

A LIGHT, caressing southerly breeze is blowing; just enough to heel the yawl and give her momentum. The boy and I get under way from the mooring by the usual ritual. I take in the ensign, hoist the mizzen, cast off main sheet and slack the backstays; he helps me hoist the mainsail, sway the halyards and neatly coil them. I take the wheel and the main sheet in hand, the boy casts off the mooring rode and hoists the jib, and off she goes like a lively dog let off the leash.

We make a long, leisurely beat to windward out of the Western Way, with tide almost dead low; the reefs, sprayed with brown rockweed, show up clearly. We pass the bell buoy and leave to starboard the naked reef known to proper chart makers as South Bunkers Ledge, but to Mount Deserters as "Bunker's Whore."

Now we are in the open sea, nothing between us and Nova Scotia. The day is pleasantly cool and bright, with gathering cirrus clouds that sometimes obscure the sun. Old ocean today is green, heaving with a surge farflung from a blow somewhere between us and Europe. Visibility is so high that the horizon is a clean-cut line over which one can see the masts of fishing draggers whose hulls are concealed by the earth's bulge. Seaward, the Duck Islands seem to float on the emerald waters. Landward, the rocky shores of Great Cranberry Island are misty with the spray from a line of white breakers. One thinks of Heredia's line about Britanny: "Du Raz jusqu'à Penmarc'h la côte entière fume"—the entire coast is smoky. Ocean swell makes the yawl roll and pitch, not unpleasantly but in harmonious cadence with the sea, the motion starting little snaps and whistles among the cordage, and the tapping of reef-points on the mainsail.

This is the time for the lunch that Priscilla prepared for us—jellied eggs and baby carrots as hors d'oeuvres; mushroom soup in a thermos; succulent ham sandwiches freshly made with lettuce and mayonnaise; chilled beer from the icebox; homemade doughnuts, crisp outside and flaky-soft inside, as you find them only when made by a master hand in Maine.

Now we are off Bakers Island where the long, flat granite ledges, washed clean by winter gales, hang over a reddish-brown apron of kelp and dulse, whirling in the breakers that roar in past the Thumper ledge. We round the groaner, the perpetually whistling buoy, haul our wind and turn northward.

Here we face the superb panorama of Mount Desert Island and Frenchmans Bay. The westering sun kindles the granite summits of Sargent, Green and Newport mountains to rose color; and the ocean between us and them is cobalt blue. Spruce-dark Otter Cliff and bare, brown Great Head thrust out into Frenchmans Bay. Under this luminous northern sky, distant Schoodic stands out bold and clear; miles beyond, the summit of Pigeon Hill appears, and Petit Manan lighthouse tower, entrance post to the Bay of Fundy, pricks the eastern horizon.

We close-haul our sails, round the black can buoy and glide out of the ocean swell into the smooth, sheltered anchorage of Bakers Island. Flood tide is only one hour old; and my quest is for fresh mussels in that clear, unpolluted water. We shoot into the wind, avoiding the numerous lobster-pot buoys, hand the jib and mainsail, drop the anchor and pay out scope on the cable. I pull the skiff alongside and row ashore. Spicy late summer fragrance wells out from the sundrenched island—sweet grasses, goldenrod, aster; even some of the white and pink *Rosa rugosa* for which this place is famous are still in bloom. The colorful sea bottom appears; gray sand studded with big smooth pebbles tumbled and polished by millennia of winter gales, when the great combers at high water rip over the reef barrier that now makes this spot a sheltered harbor. Two more strokes of the oars, and the skiff grounds on a rock; bucket in one hand and boat painter in the other, I make a wobbly landing, unlike the fishermen who splash boldly ashore in their rubber boots. Mussels are there in great plenty, their dark blue shells with brown "beards" clinging in clusters to barnacled rocks and to the wooden ways laid years ago for the lighthouse keeper's skiff. In ten minutes' time I have gathered a pailful, then shove the skiff off the rock where she grounded, and row back to the yawl, facing forward to admire her perfect proportions, and the backdrop of mountains.

We make sail once more, weigh anchor, and the yawl pirouettes on her keel to head toward home. My young sailor, blond and lithe as one imagines ancient Greek sailors to have been in the Ægean, gazes, speechless, at sea and mountains. What is he, at nineteen, thinking of it all? Does the beauty of sunwashed shore and granite mountains mean the same to him as to me, four times his age? I respect the youth's right to his own thoughts and do not ask, fearing perhaps to break the spell by some offhand or discordant reply.

Now we close-haul the sails again to pass between Suttons Island and the two Cranberries. I turn my back on the Islesford shore where the summer houses are pretentiously inappropriate, but linger lovingly on the south shore of Suttons, its little cottages built in the good simple taste of a century ago, when Maine men knew how to create as beautiful a house as a ship. Suttons, with its memories of John Gilley and Mary Wheelwright, of picnics long ago, of clumps of blue harebell growing like weeds from the wild grass. In this bight of the Bay we encounter the inevitable spell of calm. The yawl holds her headway for two or three hundred yards, her sails full although the surface of the sea has become a wavy mirror; the ripples from her bows making sweet music. Finally her headway ceases, the sails gently flap, the booms swing from side to side, and the reef points play a tattoo on the mainsail.

What makes this particular day so memorable is its freedom from the mutter of motors. All power yachts are following the annual race in Blue Hill Bay, no snarling outboards are about. The lobstermen have finished hauling their traps and are at home eating supper. There is no sound but the lapping of waves on the shore, the lazy clang of Spurlings Ledge bell buoy, and the distant bark of a dog.

After a breathless calm of a quarter hour, the breeze returns, limp sheets stretch out taut with a clatter of blocks, sails fill, and the yawl heels to the last of the west wind.

Around the western point of Suttons, Bear Island makes out. Its white lighthouse tower and pyramidical bell house seem to look down like benign parents on three tiny sloops that flutter past, having a little race of their own as they did not rate the big cruise. How many thousands of sailing craft have passed that sea mark since 1839 when, at the suggestion of a naval captain, the government built the light station? How many seamen have blessed that winking white eye guiding them through Eastern or Western Way to the snug harbors within, or strained their ears to catch the deep-throated note of the fog bell?

Leaving the cliffs of Bear Island astern on the starboard quarter, we enter Northeast Harbor with the dying breeze, avoiding the ever present "Kimball's Calms" on the port hand. My boy lowers and neatly furls the jib, then stands with boat hook, poised like a classic harpooner, to spear the mooring buoy. Main and mizzen sheets are hauled flat to give the yawl one last graceful curvet before her way is checked in the wind's eye. Then the mooring rode is secured to the forward bitts, and the yacht's white wings are folded for the night.

BARRY LOPEZ

Barry Lopez (b. 1945) established himself as one of the foremost contemporary American nature writers with works such as Of Wolves and Men *(1978) and* Arctic Dreams *(1986). "A Presentation of Whales" examines human reactions to an especially dramatic instance of the still-unexplained phenomenon of mass whale stranding. Perhaps no more striking example of changing American attitudes toward marine mammal life can be found than in the contrast between the grief evoked by dying sperm whales in 1979 and the ruthlessness with which the same species was hunted in the 19th century. Whether in the era of Melville or Lopez, the sperm whale remains a profoundly mysterious presence in the human realm.*

A Presentation of Whales

On that section of the central Oregon coast on the evening of June 16, 1979, gentle winds were blowing onshore from the southwest. It was fifty-eight degrees. Under partly cloudy skies the sea was running with four-foot swells at eight-second intervals. Moderately rough. State police cadets Jim Clark and Steve Bennett stood at the precipitous edge of a foredune a few miles south of the town of Florence, peering skeptically into the dimness over a flat, gently sloping beach. Near the water's edge they could make out a line of dark shapes, and what they had taken for a practical joke, the exaggeration a few moments before of a man and a woman in a brown Dodge van with a broken headlight, now sank in for the truth.

Clark made a hasty, inaccurate count and plunged with Bennett down the back of the dune to their four-wheel-drive. Minutes before, they had heard the voice of Corporal Terry Crawford over the radio; they knew he was patrolling in Florence. Rather than call him, they drove the six miles into town and parked across the street from where he was issuing a citation to someone for excessive noise. When Crawford had finished, Clark went over and told him what they had seen. Crawford drove straight to the Florence State Police office and phoned his superiors in Newport, forty-eight miles up the coast. At that point the news went out over police radios: thirty-six large whales, stranded and apparently still alive, were on the beach a mile south of the mouth of the Siuslaw River.

There were, in fact, forty-one whales—twenty-eight females and thirteen males, at least one of them dying or already dead. There had never been a stranding quite like it. It was first assumed that they were gray whales, common along the coast, but they were sperm whales: *Physeter catodon*. Deep-ocean dwellers. They ranged in age from ten to fifty-six and in length from thirty to thirty-eight feet. They were apparently headed north when they beached around 7:30 P.M. on an ebbing high tide.

The information shot inland by phone, crossing the Coast Range to radio and television stations in the more-populous interior of Oregon, in a highly charged form: giant whales stranded on a public beach accessible by paved road on a Saturday night, still alive. Radio announcers urged listeners to head for the coast to "save the whales." In Eugene and Portland, Greenpeace volunteers, already alerted by the police, were busy throwing sheets and blankets into their cars. They would soak them in the ocean, to cool the whales.

The news moved as quickly through private homes and taverns on the central Oregon coast, passed by people monitoring the police bands. In addition to phoning Greenpeace—an international organization with a special interest in protecting marine mammals—the police contacted the Oregon State University Marine Science Center in South Beach near Newport, and the Oregon Institute of Marine Biology in Charleston, fifty-eight miles south of Florence. Bruce Mate, a marine mammalogist at the OSU Center, phoned members of the Northwest Regional [Stranding] Alert Network and people in Washington, D.C.

By midnight, the curious and the awed were crowded on the beach, cutting the night with flashlights. Drunks, ignoring the whales' sudden thrashing, were trying to walk up and down on their backs. A collie barked incessantly; flash cubes burst at the huge, dark forms. Two men inquired about reserving some of the teeth, for scrimshaw. A federal agent asked police to move people back, and the first mention of disease was in the air. Scientists arrived with specimen bags and rubber gloves and fishing knives. Greenpeace members, one dressed in a bright orange flight suit, came with a large banner. A man burdened with a television camera labored over the foredune after them. They wished to tie a rope to one whale's flukes, to drag it back into the ocean. The police began to congregate with the scientists, looking for a rationale to control the incident.

In the intensifying confusion, as troopers motioned onlookers back (to "restrain the common herd of unqualified mankind," wrote one man later in an angry letter-to-the-editor), the thinking was that, somehow, the whales might be saved. Neal Langbehn, a federal protection officer with the National Marine Fisheries Service, denied permission to one scientist to begin removing teeth and taking blood samples. In his report later he would write: "It was my feeling that the whales should be given their best chance to survive."

This hope was soon deemed futile, as it had appeared to most of the scientists from the beginning—the animals were hemorrhaging under the crushing weight of their own flesh and were beginning to suffer irreversible damage from heat exhaustion. The scientific task became one of securing as much data as possible.

As dawn bloomed along the eastern sky, people who had driven recreational vehicles illegally over the dunes and onto the beach were issued citations and turned back. Troopers continued to warn people over bullhorns to please stand away from the whales. The Oregon Parks Department, whose responsibility the beach was, wanted no part of the growing confusion. The U.S. Forest Service, with jurisdiction over land in the Oregon Dunes National Recreation Area down to the foredune, was willing to help, but among all the agencies there was concern over limited budgets; there were questions, gently essayed, about the conflict of state and federal enforcement powers over the body parts of an endangered species. A belligerent few in the crowd shouted objections as the first syringes appeared, and yelled to scientists to produce permits that allowed them to interfere in the death of an endangered species.

Amid this chaos, the whales, sealed in their slick black neoprene skins, mewed and clicked. They slammed glistening flukes on the beach, jarring the muscles of human thighs like Jell-O at a distance of a hundred yards. They rolled their dark, purple-brown eyes at the scene and blinked.

They lay on the western shore of North America like forty-one derailed boxcars at dawn on a Sunday morning, and in the days that followed, the worst and the best of human behavior was shown among them.

The sperm whale, for many, is the most awesome creature of the open seas. Imagine a forty-five-year-old male fifty feet long, a slim, shiny black animal with a white jaw and marbled belly cutting the surface of green ocean water at twenty knots. Its flat forehead protects a sealed chamber of exceedingly fine oil; sunlight sparkles in rivulets running off folds in its corrugated back. At fifty tons it is the largest carnivore on earth. Its massive head, a third of its body length, is scarred with the beak, sucker, and claw marks of giant squid, snatched out of subterranean canyons a mile below, in a region without light, and brought writhing to the surface. Imagine a four-hundred-pound heart the size of a chest of drawers driving five gallons of blood at a stroke through its aorta: a meal of forty salmon moving slowly down twelve-hundred feet of intestine; the blinding, acrid fragrance of a two-hundred-pound wad of gray ambergris lodged somewhere along the way; producing sounds more shrill than we can hear—like children shouting on a distant playground—and able to sort a cacophony of noise: electric crackling of shrimp, groaning of undersea quakes, roar of upwellings, whining of porpoise, hum of oceanic cables. With skin as sensitive as the inside of your wrist.

What makes them awesome is not so much these things, which are discoverable, but the mysteries that shroud them. They live at a remarkable distance from us and we have no *Pioneer II* to penetrate their world. Virtually all we know of sperm whales we have learned on the slaughter decks of oceangoing whalers and on the ways at shore stations. We do not even know how many there are; in December 1978, the Scientific Committee of the International Whaling Commission said it could not set a quota for a worldwide sperm whale kill—so little was known that any number written down would be ridiculous.*

The sperm whale, in all its range of behaviors—from the enraged white bull called Mocha Dick that stove whaling ships off the coast of Peru in 1810, to a nameless female giving birth to a fourteen-foot, one-ton calf in equatorial waters in the Pacific—remains distant. The general mystery is enhanced by specific mysteries: the sperm whale's brain is larger than the brain of any other creature that ever lived. Beyond the storage of incomprehensible amounts of information, we do not know what purpose such size serves. And we do not know what to make of its most distinctive anatomical feature, the spermaceti organ. An article in *Scientific American*, published several months before the stranding, suggests that the whale can control the density of its spermaceti oil, thereby altering its specific gravity to assist it in diving. It is argued also that the huge organ, located in the head, serves as a means of generating and focusing sound, but there is not yet any agreement on these speculations.

Of the many sperm whale strandings in recorded history, only three have been larger than the one in Oregon. The most recent was of fifty-six on the eastern Baja coast near Playa San Rafael on January 6, 1979. But the Florence stranding is perhaps the most remarkable. Trained scientists arrived almost immediately; the site was easily accessible, with even an

*A quota of 5000 was nevertheless set. In June 1979, within days of the Florence stranding but apparently unrelated to it, the IWC dropped the 1980 world sperm whale quota to 2203 and set aside the Indian Ocean as a sanctuary. (By 1987 the quota was 0, though special exemptions permit some 200 sperm whales still to be taken worldwide.)

airstrip close by. It was within an hour's drive of two major West Coast marine-science centers. And the stranding seemed to be of a whole social unit. That the animals were still alive meant live blood specimens could be taken. And by an uncanny coincidence, a convention of the American Society of Mammalogists was scheduled to convene June 18 at Oregon State University in Corvallis, less than a two-hour drive away. Marine experts from all over the country would be there. (As it turned out, some of them would not bother to come over; others would secure access to the beach only to take photographs; still others would show up in sports clothes—all they had—and plunge into the gore that by the afternoon of June 18 littered the beach.)

The state police calls to Greenpeace on the night of June 16 were attempts to reach informed people to direct a rescue. Michael Piper of Greenpeace, in Eugene, was the first to arrive with a small group at about 1:30 A.M., just after a low tide at 12:59 A.M.

"I ran right out of my shoes," Piper says. The thought that they would still be alive—clicking and murmuring, their eyes tracking human movement, lifting their flukes, whooshing warm air from their blowholes—had not penetrated. But as he ran into the surf to fill a bucket to splash water over their heads, the proportions of the stranding and the impending tragedy overwhelmed him.

"I knew, almost from the beginning, that we were not going to get them out of there, and that even if we did, their chances of survival were a million to one," Piper said.

Just before dawn, a second contingent of Greenpeace volunteers arrived from Portland. A Canadian, Michael Bailey, took charge and announced there was a chance with the incoming tide that one of the smaller animals could be floated off the beach and towed to sea (weights ranged from an estimated three and a half to twenty-five tons). Bruce Mate, who would become both scientific and press coordinator on the beach (the latter to his regret), phoned the Port of Coos Bay to see if an oceangoing tug or fishing vessel would be available to anchor offshore and help—Bailey's crew would ferry lines through the surf with a Zodiac boat. No one in Coos Bay was interested. A commercial helicopter service with a Skycrane capable of lifting nine tons also begged off. A call to the Coast Guard produced a helicopter, but people there pronounced any attempt to sky-tow a whale too dangerous.

The refusal of help combined with the apparent futility of the effort precipitated a genuinely compassionate gesture: Bailey strode resolutely into the freezing water and, with twenty-five or thirty others, amid flailing flukes, got a rope around the tail of an animal that weighed perhaps three or four tons. The waves knocked them down and the whale yanked them over, but they came up sputtering, to pull again. With the buoyancy provided by the incoming tide they moved the animal about thirty feet. The effort was heroic and ludicrous. As the rope began to cut into the whale's flesh, as television cameramen and press photographers crowded in, Michael Piper gave up his place on the rope in frustration and waded ashore. Later he would remark that, for some, the whale was only the means to a political end—a dramatization of the plight of whales as a species. The distinction between the suffering individual, its internal organs hemorrhaging, its flukes sliced by the rope, and the larger issue, to save the species, confounded Piper.

A photograph of the Greenpeace volunteers pulling the whale showed up nationally in newspapers the next day. A week later, a marine mammalogist wondered if any more damaging picture could have been circulated. It would convince people something could have been done, when in fact, he said, the whales were doomed as soon as they came ashore.

For many, transfixed on the beach by their own helplessness, the value of the gesture transcended the fact.

By midmorning Piper was so disturbed, so embarrassed by the drunks and by people wrangling to get up on the whales or in front of photographers, that he left. As he drove off through the crowds (arriving now by the hundreds, many in campers and motor homes), gray whales were seen offshore, with several circling sperm whales. "The best thing we could have done," Piper said, alluding to this, "was offer our presence, to be with them while they were alive, to show some compassion."

Irritated by a callous (to him) press that seemed to have only one question—Why did they come ashore?—Piper had blurted out that the whales may have come ashore "because they were tired of running" from commercial whalers. Scientists scoffed at the remark, but Piper, recalling it a week later, would not take it back. He said it was as logical as any other explanation offered in those first few hours.

Uneasy philosophical disagreement divided people on the beach from the beginning. Those for whom the stranding was a numinous event were estranged by the clowning of those who regarded it as principally entertainment. A few scientists irritated everyone with their preemptive, self-important air. When they put chain saws to the lower jaws of dead sperm whales lying only a few feet from whales not yet dead, there were angry shouts of condemnation. When townspeople kept at bay—"This is history, dammit," one man screamed at a state trooper, "and I want my kids to see it!"—saw twenty reporters, each claiming an affiliation with the same weekly newspaper, gain the closeness to the whales denied them, there were shouts of cynical derision.

"The effect of all this," said Michael Gannon, director of a national group called Oregonians Cooperating to Protect Whales, of the undercurrent of elitism and outrage, "was that it interfered with the spiritual and emotional ability of people to deal with the phenomenon. It was like being at a funeral where you were not allowed to mourn."

Bob Warren, a patrolman with the U.S. Forest Service, said he was nearly brought to tears by what faced him Sunday morning. "I had no conception of what a whale beaching would be like. I was apprehensive about it, about all the tourists and the law-enforcement atmosphere. When I drove up, the whole thing hit me in the stomach: I saw these *numbers*, these damn orange numbers—41, 40, 39—spray-painted on these dying animals. The media were coming on like the marines, in taxicabs, helicopters, low-flying aircraft. Biologists were saying, 'We've got to *euthanize* them.' It made me sick."

By this time Sunday morning, perhaps five hundred people had gathered; the crowd would swell to more than two thousand before evening, in spite of a drizzling rain. The state trooper who briefed Warren outlined the major problems: traffic was backing up on the South Jetty Road almost five miles to U.S. 101; the whales' teeth were "as valuable as gold" and individuals with hammers and saws had been warned away already; people were sticking their hands in the whales' mouths and were in danger of being killed by the pounding flukes; and there was a public-health problem—the whales might have come ashore with a communicable disease. (According to several experts, the danger to public health was minor, but in the early confusion it served as an excuse to keep the crowd back so scientists could work. Ironically, the threat would assume a life of its own two days later and scientists would find themselves working frantically ahead of single-minded state burial crews.)

One of the first things Warren and others did was to rope off the whales with orange ribbon and lath stakes, establishing a line beyond which the public was no longer permitted. Someone thoughtful among them ran the ribbon close enough to one whale to allow people to peer into the dark eyes, to see scars left by struggling squid, lamprey eels, and sharp boulders on the ocean floor, the patches of diatoms growing on the skin, the marbling streaking back symmetrically from the genital slit, the startlingly gentle white mouth ("What a really beautiful and chaste-looking mouth!" Melville wrote. "From floor to ceiling lined, or rather papered with a glistening white membrane, glossy as bridal satins"), to see the teeth, gleaming in the long, almost absurdly narrow jaw. In *The Year of the Whale*, Victor Scheffer describes the tooth as "creamy white, a cylinder lightly curved, a thing of art which fits delightfully in the palm of my hand."

The temptation to possess—a Polaroid of oneself standing over a whale, a plug of flesh removed with a penknife, a souvenir squid beak plucked deftly from an exposed intestine by a scientist—was almost palpable in the air.

"From the beginning," Warren continued, "I was operating on two levels: as a law-enforcement officer with a job, and as a person." He escorted people away from the whales, explaining as well as he could the threat of disease, wishing himself to reach out with them, to touch the animals. He recalls his rage watching people poke at a sensitive area under the whales' eyes to make them react, and calmly directing people to step back, to let the animals die in peace. Nothing could be done, he would say. How do you know? they would ask. He didn't.

Warren was awed by the sudden, whooshing breath that broke the silence around an animal perhaps once every fifteen minutes, and saddened by the pitiable way some of them were mired with their asymmetrical blowhole sanded in, dead. Near those still breathing he drove in lath stakes with the word live written on them. The hopelessness of it, he said, and the rarity of the event were rendered absurd by his having to yell into a bullhorn, by the blood on the beach, the whales' blinking, the taunters hoisting beer cans to the police.

One of the things about being human, Warren reflected, is learning to see beyond the vulgar. Along with the jocose in the crowd, he said, there were hundreds who whispered to each other, as if in a grove of enormous trees. And faces that looked as though they were awaiting word of relatives presumed dead in an air crash. He remembers in particular a man in his forties, "dressed in polyesters," who stood with his daughter in a tidal pool inside the barrier, splashing cool water on a whale. Warren asked them to please step back. "Why?" the man asked. Someone in the crowd yelled an obscenity at Warren. Warren thought to himself: Why is there no room for the decency of this gesture?

The least understood and perhaps most disruptive incident on the beach on that first day was the attempt of veterinarians to kill the whales, first by injecting M-99, a morphine-based drug, then by ramming pipes into their pleural cavities to collapse their lungs, and finally by severing major arteries and letting them bleed to death. The techniques were crude, but no one knew enough sperm whale anatomy or physiology to make a clean job of it, and no one wanted to try some of the alternatives—from curare to dynamite—that would have made the job quicker. The ineptitude of the veterinarians caused them a private embarrassment to which they gave little public expression. Their frustration at their own inability to do anything to "help" the whales was exacerbated by nonscientists demanding from the sidelines that the animals be "put out of their misery." (The reasons for attempting euthanasia were poorly understood, philosophically and medically, and the issue nagged people long after the beach bore not a trace of the incident itself.)

As events unfolded on the beach, the first whale died shortly after the stranding, the last almost thirty-six hours later; suffocation and overheating were the primary causes. By waiting as long as they did to try to kill some of the animals and by allowing others to die in their own time, pathologists, toxicologists, parasitologists, geneticists, and others got tissues of poor quality to work with.* The disappointment was all the deeper because never had so many scientists been in a position to gather so much information. (Even with this loss and an initial lack of suitable equipment—chemicals to preserve tissues, blood-analysis kits, bone saws, flensing knives—the small core of twenty or so scientists "increased human knowledge about sperm whales several hundred percent," according to Mate.)

The fact that almost anything learned was likely to be valuable was meager consolation to scientists hurt by charges that they were cold and brutal people, irreverently jerking fetuses

*A subsequent report, presented at a marine-mammals conference in Seattle in October 1979, made it clear that the whales began to suffer the effects of heat stress almost immediately. The breakdown of protein structures in their tissues made discovery of a cause of death difficult; from the beginning, edema, capillary dilation, and hemorrhaging made their recovery unlikely. Ice, seawater pumps, and tents for shade rather than Zodiac boats and towlines were suggested if useful tissue was to be salvaged in the future from large whales.

from the dead. Among these scientists were people who sat alone in silence, who departed in anger, and who broke down and cried.

No one knows why whales strand. It is almost always toothed whales that do, rather than baleen whales, most commonly pilot whales, Atlantic white-sided dolphins, false killer whales, and sperm whales—none of which are ordinarily found close to shore. Frequently they strand on gently sloping beaches. Among the more tenable explanations: 1) extreme social cohesion, where one sick animal is relentlessly followed ashore by many healthy animals; 2) disease or parasitic infection that affects the animals' ability to navigate; 3) harassment, by predators and, deliberate or inadvertent, by humans; 4) a reversion to phylogentically primitive escape behavior—get out of the water—precipitated by stress.

At a public meeting in Florence—arranged by the local librarian to explain to a public kept off the beach what had happened, and to which invited scientists did not come—other explanations were offered. Someone had noticed whales splashing in apparent confusion near a river dredge and thought the sound of its engines might have driven the whales crazy. Local fishermen said there had been an unusual, near-shore warm current on June 16, with a concentration of plankton so thick they had trouble penetrating it with their depth finders. Another suggestion was that the whales might have been temporarily deranged by poisons in diatoms concentrated in fish they were eating.

The seventy-five or so people at the meeting seemed irritated that there was no answer, as did local reporters looking for an end to the story. Had scientists been there it is unlikely they could have suggested one. The beach was a gently sloping one, but the Florence whales showed no evidence of parasitism or disease, and modern research makes it clear that no single explanation will suffice. For those who would blame the machinations of modern man, scientists would have pointed out that strandings have been recorded since the time of Aristotle's *Historia animalium*.

The first marine biologist to arrive on the beach, at 3:30 A.M. Sunday, was Michael Graybill, a young instructor from the Oregon Institute of Marine Biology. He was not as perplexed as other scientists would be; a few months before he had dismantled the rotting carcass of a fifty-six-foot sperm whale that had washed ashore thirty miles south of Florence.

Graybill counted the animals, identified them as sperm whales, noted that, oddly, there were no nursing calves or obviously young animals, and that they all seemed "undersized." He examined their skin and eyes, smelled their breath, looked for signs of oral and anal discharge, and began the task of sexing and measuring the animals.

Driving to the site, Graybill worried most about someone "bashing their teeth out" before he got there. He wasn't worried about communicable disease; he was "willing to gamble" on that. He regarded efforts to save the whales, however, as unnatural interference in their death. Later, he cynically observed "how much 'science' took place at the heads of sperm whales" where people were removing teeth; and he complained that if they really cared about the worldwide fate of whales, Greenpeace volunteers would have stayed to help scientists with postmortems. (Some did. Others left because they could not stand to watch the animals die.)

Beginning Sunday morning, scientists had their first chance to draw blood from live, unwounded sperm whales (they used comparatively tiny one-and-a-half-inch, 18-gauge hypodermic needles stuck in vessels near the surface of the skin on the flukes). With the help of a blue, organic tracer they estimated blood volume at five hundred gallons. In subsequent stages, blubber, eyes, teeth, testicles, ovaries, stomach contents, and specific tissues were removed—the teeth for aging, the eyes for corneal cells to discover genetic relationships within the group. Postmortems were performed on ten females; three near-term fetuses were removed. An attempt was made to photograph the animals systematically.

The atmosphere on the beach shifted perceptibly over the next six days. On Sunday, a cool, cloudy day during which it rained, as many as three thousand people may have been on the beach. Police finally closed the access road to the area to discourage more from coming. Attempts to euthanize the animals continued, the jaws of the dead were being sawed off, and, in the words of one observer, "there was a television crew with a backdrop of stranded whales every twenty feet on the foredune."

By Monday the crowds were larger, but, in the estimation of a Forest Service employee, "of a higher quality. The type of people who show up at an automobile accident were gone; these were people who really wanted to see the whales. It was a four-and-a-half-mile walk in from the highway, and I talked with a woman who was seven months pregnant who made it and a man in a business suit and dress shoes who drove all the way down from Seattle."

Monday afternoon the crowds thinned. The beach had become a scene of postmortem gore sufficient to turn most people away. The outgoing tide had carried off gallons of blood and offal, drawing spiny dogfish sharks and smoothhound sharks into the breakers. As the animals died, scientists cut into them to relieve gaseous pressure—the resultant explosions could be heard half a mile away. A forty-pound chunk of liver whizzed by someone's back-turned shoulders; sixty feet of pearly-gray intestine unfurled with a snap against the sky. By evening the beach was covered with more than a hundred tons of intestines. Having to open the abdominal cavities so precipitately precluded, to the scientists' dismay, any chance of an uncontaminated examination.

By Tuesday the beach was closed to the public. The whale carcasses were being prepared for burning and burial, a task that would take four days, and reporters had given up asking why the stranding had happened, to comment on the stench.

The man responsible for coordinating scientific work at the stranding, thirty-three-year-old Bruce Mate, is well regarded by his colleagues. Deborah Duffield, a geneticist from Portland State University, reiterated the feelings of several when she said of him: "The most unusual thing was that he got all of us with our different, sometimes competing, interests to work together. You can't comprehend what an extraordinary achievement that is in a situation like this."

On the beach Mate was also the principal source of information for the press. Though he was courteous to interviewers and careful not to criticize a sometimes impatient approach, one suspected he was disturbed by the role and uncertain what, if anything, he owed the nonscientific community.

In his small, cramped office at the Marine Science Center in South Beach, Mate agreed that everyone involved—scientists, environmentalists, the police, the state agencies, the public—took views that were occasionally in opposition and that these views were often proprietary. He thought it was the business of science to obtain data and physical specimens on the beach, thereby acquiring rights of "ownership," and yet he acknowledged misgivings about this because he and others involved are to some extent publicly funded scientists.

The task that faced him was deceptively simple: get as much information as possible off the beach before the burning crews, nervous about a public-health hazard and eager to end the incident, destroyed the animals. But what about the way science dominated the scene, getting the police, for example, to keep the crowd away so science could exercise its proprietary interest? "I don't know how to cope with the public's desire to come and see. Letting those few people onto the beach would have precluded our getting that much more information to give to a much larger, national audience."

What about charges that science operated in a cold-blooded and, in the case of trying to collapse the whales' lungs, ignorant way? "Coming among these whales, watching them die and in some cases helping them to die—needless suffering is almost incomprehensible to me . . ." Mate paused, studied the papers on his desk, unsatisfied, it seemed, with his tack; ". . . there are moral and ethical questions here. It's like dealing with terminal cancer."

No one, he seemed to suggest, liked how fast it had all happened.

Had he been worried about anything on the beach? "Yes! I was appalled at the way professional people were going about [postmortems] without gloves. I was afraid for the Greenpeace people in a potentially life-threatening situation in the surf." He was also afraid that it would all get away from him because of the unknowns. What, in fact, *did* one save when faced with such an enormous amount of bone and tissue? But he came away happy. "This was the greatest scientific shot anyone ever had with large whales." After a moment he added, "If it happened tomorrow, we would be four times better."

Sitting at his desk, nursing a pinched nerve in his back, surrounded by phone messages from the press, he seemed seasoned.

Mate's twenty-seven-year-old graduate assistant, Jim Harvey, arrived on the beach at dawn on Sunday. At the first sight of the whales from the top of the dunes, strung out nose to flukes in a line five or six hundred yards long, the waves of a high tide breaking over them, Harvey simply sat down, awestruck at their size and number. He felt deeply sad, too, but as he drew near he felt "a rush of exhilaration, because there was so much information to be gathered." He could not get over the feeling, as he worked, of the size of them. (One afternoon a scientist stood confounded in a whale's abdomen, asking a colleague next to him, "Where's the liver?")

Deborah Duffield said of her experience on the beach: "It hurt me more than watching human beings die. I couldn't cope with the pain, the futility. . . . I just turned into myself. It brought out the scientist in me." Another scientist spoke of his hostility toward the sullen crowd, of directing that anger at himself, of becoming cold and going to work.

For Harvey and others, there was one incident that broke scientific concentration and brought with it a feeling of impropriety. Several scientists had started to strip blubber from a dead whale. Suddenly the whale next to it began pounding the beach with its flukes. The pounding continued for fifteen minutes—lifting and slamming the flukes to the left, lifting and slamming the flukes to the right.

When the animal quieted, they resumed work.

"Scientists rarely get a chance to express their feelings," Harvey said. "I was interested in other people's views, and I wanted to share mine, which are biological. I noticed some people who sat quietly for a long time behind the barriers in religious stances. I very much wanted to know their views. So many of the people who came down here were so sympathetic and full of concern—I wished I had the time to talk to them all." Harvey remembered something vividly. On the first day he put his face near the blowhole of one of the whales: a cylinder of clean, warm, humid air almost a foot in diameter blew back his hair.

"My view on it," said Joe Davis of the Oregon Parks Department, "wasn't the scientific part. My thought on it now is how nice it would have been to have been somewhere else." His smile falls between wryness and regret.

When something remarkable happens and bureaucrats take it for only a nuisance, it is often stripped of whatever mystery it may hold. The awesome becomes common. Joe Davis, park manager at Honeyman Dunes State Park, adjacent to the stranding, was charged by the state with getting rid of the whales. He said he didn't take a moment to wonder at the mystery of it.

If ethical problems beset scientists, and mystical considerations occupied other onlookers, a set of concerns more prosaic confronted the police and the Oregon Parks Department. On Sunday night, June 17, police arrested a man in a camouflage suit caught breaking teeth out of a whale's jaw with a hammer and chisel. That night (and the next, and the next) people continued to play games with the police. The Parks Department, for its part, was faced with the disposal of five hundred tons of whale flesh that county environmental and health authorities said they couldn't burn—the solution to the problem at Playa San Rafael—and scientists said couldn't be buried. If buried, the carcasses would become hard envelopes of rotting flesh, the internal organs would liquefy and leach out onto the beach, and winter storms would uncover the whole mess.

This controversy, the public-health question, what to do about excessive numbers of press people, and concern over who was going to pay the bill (the Forest Service had donated tools, vehicles, and labor, but two bulldozers had had to be hired, at a hundred dollars and sixty dollars an hour) precipitated a meeting in Florence on Tuesday morning, June 19. A Forest Service employee, who asked not to be identified, thought the pressures that led to the meeting marked a difference between those who came to the beach out of compassion and genuine interest and those for whom it was "only a headache."

The principal issue, after an agreement was reached to burn the whales, then bury them, was who was going to pay. The state was reluctant; the scientists were impoverished. (It would be months before Mate would begin to recover $5,000 of his own money advanced to pay for equipment, transportation, and bulldozer time. "No one wants to fund work that's finished," Mate observed sardonically.) Commercial firms were averse to donating burning materials, or even transportation for them; G. P. Excavating of Florence did reduce rental fees on its bulldozers by about one-third and "broke even" after paying its operators.

The state finally took responsibility for the disposal and assumed the $25,000 cleanup bill, but it wanted to hear nothing about science's wish to salvage skeletons—it wanted the job finished.* Arrangements were made to bring in a crew of boys from the Young Adult Conservation Corps, and the Forest Service, always, it seemed, amenable, agreed to donate several barrels of Alumagel, a napalmlike substance.

It was further decided to ban the public from the beach during the burning, for health and safety reasons. Only the

*Three months later on September 6, 1979, an eighty-five-foot female blue whale washed ashore in Northern California. Ensuing argument over responsibility for disposal prevented scientists from going near the whale until September 13, by which time it had been severely battered on the rocks and vandalized.

disposal crews, scientists, police, and selected press would be admitted. The criterion for press admittance was possession of "a legitimate press card."

The role of the press at such events is somewhat predictable. They will repeatedly ask the same, obvious questions; they will often know little of the science involved; occasionally they will intimidate and harass in order to ascertain (or assign) blame. An upper-level Forest Service employee accused the press of asking "the most uninteresting and intimidating kinds of questions." A State Parks employee felt the press fostered dissension over who was going to pay for the disposal. He was also angry with newspaper people for ignoring "the human side," the fact that many state police troopers worked long hours of overtime, and that Forest Service employees performed a number of menial tasks in an emotionally charged environment of rotting flesh. "After a week of sixteen-hour days, your nerves are raw, you stink, you just want to get away from these continual questions."

In the press's defense, the people who objected most were those worried about criticism of their own performance and those deeply frustrated by the trivialization of the event. The press—probing, perhaps inexpertly—made people feel no more than their own misgivings.

The publisher of the local *Siuslaw News*, Paul Holman, said before it was over that the whale stranding had become a nuisance. When police closed the road to the beach a man in a stateside truck began ferrying people the four and a half miles to the whales for a dollar each. And a dollar back. The local airport, as well as tourist centers offering seaplane rides, were doing a "land-office business" in flyovers. Gas station operators got tired of telling tourists how to get to the beach. The Florence City Hall was swamped with calls about the burning, one from a man who was afraid his horses would be killed by the fallout on his pasture. Dune-buggy enthusiasts were angry at whale people who for two days blocked access to their hill-climbing area.

Whatever its interest, the press was largely gone by Monday afternoon. As the burning and burying commenced, the number of interested scientists also thinned. By Wednesday there were only about thirty people left on the beach. Bob Adams, acting director of the Lane Regional Air Pollution Authority, was monitoring the smoke. Neal Langbehn of the National Marine Fisheries Service stood guard over a pile of plastic-wrapped sperm whale jaws. Michael Graybill led a team flensing out skulls. The state fretted over a way to keep the carcasses burning. (It would finally be done with thousands of automobile and truck tires, cordwood, diesel fuel, and Alumagel.) As Mate watched he considered the threshold of boredom in people, and mourned the loss, among other things, of forty-one sperm whale skeletons.

A journalist, one of the last two or three, asked somebody to take her picture while she stood with a small poodle in her arms in front of the burning pits.

As is often the case with such events, what is salvaged is as much due to goodwill as it is to expertise. The Forest Service was widely complimented for helping, and Stafford Owen, the acting area ranger at the agency's Oregon Dunes National Recreation Area during the incident, tried to say why: "Most of us aren't highly educated people. We have had to work at a variety of things all our lives—operating a chain saw, repairing a truck engine, running a farm. We had the skills these doctors and scientists needed."

A soft-spoken colleague, Gene Large, trying to elaborate but not to make too much of himself, said, "I don't think the scientists had as much knowledge [of large mammalian anatomy] as I did. When it came to it, I had to show some of them where the ribs were." After a moment, Large said, "Trying to cut those whales open with a chain saw was like trying to slaughter a beef with a pen knife. I didn't enjoy any part of it," Large said of the dismembering with chain saws and winches. "I think the older you get, the more sensitive you get." He mentioned an older friend who walked away from a dead, fifteen-foot, near-term fetus being lifted out of a gutted whale, and for a time wouldn't speak.

On Wednesday afternoon the whales were ignited in pits at the foot of the foredune. As they burned they were rendered, and when their oil caught fire they began to boil in it. The seething roar was muffled by a steady onshore breeze; the oily black smoke drifted southeast over the dunes, over English beach grass and pearly everlasting, sand verbena, and the purple flowers of beach pea, green leaves of sweet clover, and the bright yellow blooms of the monkey flower. It thinned until it disappeared against a weak-blue sky.

While fire cracked the blubber of one-eyed, jawless carcasses, a bulldozer the size of a two-car garage grunted in a trench being dug to the north for the last of them. These were still sprawled at the water's edge. Up close, the black, blistered skin, bearing scars of knives and gouging fingernails, looked like the shriveled surface of a pond evaporated beneath a summer sun. Their gray-blue innards lay about on the sand like bags of discarded laundry. Their purple tongues were wedged in retreat in their throats. Spermaceti oil dripped from holes in their heads, solidifying in the wind to stand in translucent stalagmites twenty inches high. Around them were tidal pools opaque with coagulated blood and, beyond, a pink surf.

As far as I know, no novelist, no historian, no moral philosopher, no scholar of Melville, no rabbi, no painter, no theologian had been on the beach. No one had thought to call them or to fly them in. At the end they would not have been allowed past the barricades.

The whales made a sound, someone had said, like the sound a big fir makes breaking off the stump just as the saw is pulled away. A thin screech.

SYLVIA A. EARLE

A marine biologist and veteran diver, Sylvia Earle (b. 1935) served as chief scientist of the National Oceanic and Atmospheric Administration from 1990 to 1992. This excerpt from her book Sea Change: A Message of the Oceans *(1995) describes a dive she made six miles off the coast of Oahu in October 1979. Using* Jim, *an articulated armored diving suit named after Jim Jarrett, a deep-sea diver of the 1920s, Earle was able to descend 1,250 feet and walk along the ocean floor while breathing air at surface pressure, thus avoiding the serious risks involved in breathing highly pressurized gases. Her dive vividly illustrates the advances made in deep-sea exploration technology since the pioneering bathysphere descents of William Beebe in the 1930s.*

from *Sea Change: A Message of the Oceans*

STANDING at the upper edge of the great, sparkling cold darkness, I looked up to a full spectrum of light dancing from the waves overhead, each photon newly arrived, most having traveled from the sun through 93 million miles of space, a far lesser amount arriving from distant stars. When light reaches Earth's blue atmospheric "cocoon," it encounters its first significant obstacles. Some is reflected back into space or is absorbed by gases, clouds, water vapor, dust, pollen, and other ingredients that make up "air." But the barriers to free passage of light through the atmosphere are slight compared to the swift changes wrought the moment light enters the sea.

First, the quantity of light drops exponentially, so effectively absorbed by water that only one percent travels to a depth of 325 feet (100 meters), even in the clearest freshwater lakes or most transparent expanse of open ocean. The intensity diminishes tenfold with every 227 feet, yielding at midday a moonlightlike ambiance where I stood in *Jim*. At 1,950 feet (600 meters), illumination is equivalent to starlight; at 2,275 feet, the intensity is approximately one ten billionth of that at the surface, and at 2,925 feet and beyond—there is total blackness. It is not simple to determine the exact point in the sea where light fades and darkness begins, because there are numerous complicating factors: the place, the time of day, season of the year, the weather. Where the air and sea meet, light is further modified by reflection and refraction, both affected by surface roughness—waves and ripples—or the presence of ice and, in modern times, perhaps floating debris or a slick of oil. Water itself appears clear when viewed in a glass, but every drop contains organic and inorganic bits, including living creatures that scatter, diffuse, reflect, and absorb light, each in its small way altering the amount and kind of light that passes downward.

Plankton, silt, and the undefinable mix of substances that flow into the sea from most urban areas cause light in many coastal waters to diminish rapidly a few feet under the surface. One sunny October afternoon, I jumped overboard in San Francisco Bay to retrieve an outboard motor that had fallen off a dock next to a boat slip. I found the motor 13 feet down, by touch—not sight—half imbedded in silty mud. Only the slightest suggestion of a dark greenish-brown glow gave me a clue about which way was up as I turned to ascend. In harbors at San Francisco, Boston, Hong Kong, Bombay, and Tokyo—to name but a few—less than half of the light striking the surface makes it to as much as 6.5 feet; by 25 feet, more than 90 percent is gone.

Photosynthesis is light driven. In the sea, this process, fundamental to oxygen generation and food production, and thus to the vital functioning of the biosphere, occurs in the illuminated "photic zone," mostly in the uppermost 60 to 100 feet, but extending downward to the gray limits of where enough light can be effectively absorbed by plants to spark photosynthesis.

There is a level of illumination in the ocean where food production precisely balances the amount of energy required for cell maintenance and growth, a pivotal place in the sea known to oceanographers as the "compensation point." In less light (at greater depths), photosynthesis may still go on, but not fast enough to keep pace with energy needed for organisms to stay alive. For many years, textbooks suggested that one percent of surface illumination, or, in ideally clear water, a maximum of 325 feet (100 meters) framed the limits where photosynthesis could not only maintain a kind of cellular status quo, but also yield a dividend in terms of growth. At greater depths—anyplace with less than one percent of surface illumination—the need for energy for respiration and other activities would outstrip food production and the plants would not long survive.

Alas for the authors of the texts, a number of deep-dwelling algae did not get the news. Some plants, including various remarkable bottom-dwelling algae, prosper in depths greater than 650 feet, where the quantity of light is but a fraction of one percent of surface illumination. In murky coastal waters, where the one percent level of surface illumination may be reached about 30 feet underwater, and in polar seas, under several feet of ice, the photic zone is considerably more narrow. In the Arctic and Antarctic, light is also seasonal, with darkness prevailing for four months of the year and a state of twilight for another four months. Nonetheless, plants abound in polar seas, from jewel-like microscopic plankton and ice-hugging diatoms to large, slippery brown kelp fronds many feet long.

How deep *do* plants grow in the sea? The deepest-growing plant species thus far discovered is a kind of crustose red alga found growing in profusion on a sea mount in waters 871 feet deep, where the light is calculated to be about .0005 percent of full surface sunlight. I am confident that plants will someday be found growing just a little bit deeper than the most recently published pronouncement of the absolute maximum depth where they can occur. Below the depth where plants can grow, plant eaters live a catch-as-catch-can existence, relying on an occasional drifting banquet followed by a long period of fasting or, if omnivorous, munching on their fellow citizens while awaiting the next salad.

While the most dramatic impact water has on light is in reducing its quantity, it also strikingly modifies light's quality:

the portions of the spectrum it permits to pass. Light filtering through a dense canopy of rainforest plants may be of low intensity at ground level, but the full range of light visible to human eyes is all there in gloriously colorful hues of red, yellow, blue, and many shades between. At the moment light enters water, however, changes are swiftly wrought in the character and color transmitted downward. The long red and yellow wavelengths are quickly absorbed in the first few feet; shorter wavelengths—green and blue—penetrate the deepest. The effect is startling. In the prevailing blue atmosphere, brightly flowered swim trunks undergo a strange metamorphosis to conservative shades of Wall Street gray.

The all-encompassing blueness beyond 81 feet (25 meters) transforms even brilliantly colored creatures into monotonous tones of blue-gray or black, much as blue lights of a theater marquee can cause rosy cheeks and red lips to appear sickly bluish gray. I was horrified the first time I noticed wisps of a greenish-black substance oozing from a nick on my knee while diving, even though I knew from reading Jacques Cousteau's adventures that blood is supposed to look that way in deep blue light. In this sapphire world, red fish, like scarlet swim trunks, appear dowdy, blending well with the darkness below, and seeming to merge with the surrounding sea, blue on blue. At 162 feet (50 meters), coral and sponge-encrusted reefs appear to be painted from a palette featuring only shades of blue and gray, but their vibrant red, yellow, and orange secrets are readily revealed by the full-spectrum beam of a flashlight. Residents from hundreds of feet below are shown to be brightly colored when dragged to the surface in a net and exposed to sunlight, or when viewed in place using the incandescent lights of deep-diving submersibles.

In the small area I explored using *Jim* I noted dozens of red galatheid crabs clinging to shrubs of pink coral, several bright red shrimp, and a purplish-red jellyfish. There were no obvious plants, other than a few strands of drifting sea lettuce, a kind of bright, papery green algae that normally attaches to rocks in shallow water.

Because light in the deep sea is characteristically blue—whether from sun, moon, or starlight penetrating from the surface or from the predominantly blue light of bioluminescence—it is not such a bad idea for inhabitants of the deep to be red. In general, red pigments absorb and do not reflect blue light and red fish thus appear dark. It probably should not be surprising that many oceanic animals living in the deep sea are scarlet to purplish red, or black, because they appear black-on-black, and thus, in effect, invisible.

Peter Herring, an eloquent expert on bioluminescence, goes further with his explanation for the success of scarlet shrimp in the deep sea. He suggests that most deep-sea animals do not see color; since they have only blue light by which to view their surroundings, many have eyes tuned to see *only* blue light. Since blue light is perfectly absorbed by the scarlet shrimp's red pigment, the shrimp appear black and are simply not visible to predators with the ability to register only blue. A few fish provide a notable exception to the general rule of blue; they are among a small, elite number of creatures capable of producing—and seeing—red bioluminescence. A headlight on these fish emits deep red light, and they also have a red-sensitive visual pigment. According to Herring, it is:

> . . . in effect, a private channel of communication. In addition, this personal sniperscope enables its possessor to observe potential prey without their realizing that they are under surveillance; unlike most other inhabitants of the deep, it will be able to see, for instance, the unwary scarlet shrimp, oblivious to the fatal beam focused on it.

Some fish, sheathed in silver scales or highly reflective skin, employ a quite different slight-of-fin disappearing technique. Their bodies, like mirrors, reflect light coming from the surface—or the searching beam of one of the ingenious light-generating devices of predators.

Other creatures escape notice by being transparent, a fine strategy for survival adopted by various jellies, squids, octopuses, certain fish, and the larval stages of many creatures. A plankton net drawn through an apparently lifeless ocean typically yields a catch resembling minute fragments of broken glass mixed with quivering iridescent lumps of jelly creatures. Some of the glistening bits are minuscule but fully grown plants and animals, but many of the near-invisible dwellers of the open sea are the offspring of lobsters, crabs, eels, urchins, and a wide range of others. All are trying to avoid being eaten while they capture and eat as much as possible to prepare for the next phase of life on a reef or craggy rock crevice hundreds or thousands of miles from where they began life as seafarers on the open ocean.

The transparency trick is useful for many, but a full gullet or stuffed stomach is a glaring giveaway to an otherwise effective disappearing act. Also, for many organisms eyes, hearts, livers, and other organs are hard to conceal, and these creatures have developed other methods to survive in a realm where nearly everybody, even fellow hatchlings, may regard you as a tasty morsel—and there are no hiding places. Counter-shading, a dark upperside and pale or silvery belly, is a useful approach for avoiding detection, one that is commonly employed even in shallow water. Halfbeaks, needlefish, flying fish, mackerel, and many other fish seem to disappear when viewed from above because their dark topsides blend with the surrounding dark water, while from below, their silvery-white undersides merge with the surface light.

Peering out of one of *Jim*'s acrylic ports, I glimpsed a small, metallic-silver hatchetfish, a creature equipped with a suite of strategies to avoid being munched upon while seeking sustenance for itself. At first glance, hatchetfish, like camels, appear to have been designed by a committee, in this case, a drunken committee with a twisted sense of humor. Large tubular eyes are directed upward, while an impressive array of gleaming light organs, photophores, shine blue light downward. I laughed incredulously when, many years before I saw one of these wondrously puzzling creatures snagged in a midwater trawl and brought into the midst of a dozen eager oceanographers. I asked who could answer the question,

"Why would any creature in its right mind point a flashlight in one direction—down—while looking in another—up—meanwhile moving resolutely straight ahead?" There was much speculation, and no one knew for sure, but the best guesses were that the downward-pointing light provided countershading. Some beam-producing predators with a taste for hatchetfish might be fooled by the reflecting light striking the fish's silvery sides, but an attacker looking from below would see the distinctive silhouette of a favorite meal. By turning on its photophores, a hatchetfish can illuminate its body with a glow to match light from above, and thus reduce the risk of its silhouette being seen.

Cleverly controlled laboratory experiments with various deep-sea fish and observations from submersibles have confirmed the validity of this strategy. A similar technique was tested successfully during World War II by torpedo bombers who used lights against a bright sky to avoid detection by subs as they swooped in on their target, surfaced submarines. Many species of fish, squid, and shrimps inhabiting the ocean's upper 2,600 feet have developed an assortment of lights on their underbellies. Some, such as the not-so-crazy hatchetfish, the appropriately-named lanternfishes, and certain squids have an enhanced ability to fine-tune the angle and level of blueness to that of the changing levels of illumination from above.

As a child, I had puzzled about the value of bioluminescence while watching fireflies magically flashing brilliant yellow signals against dark evening skies. It was so easy to catch them! I often held them briefly cupped in my hand, eerie glints of light seeping through the cracks between my fingers as they blinked on, then off, delicate antennae and slender legs softly probing possible avenues of escape. Predators with a taste for fireflies would have an easy time of it, I thought, and I wondered how any of the enchanting, glowing creatures survived long enough to get together and do whatever it is fireflies do to produce the next generation. Much later, I learned that the advantages in terms of finding and signaling mates significantly outweigh the predation liabilities. The same is true for many spark-in-the-dark creatures in the sea.

More than a century ago, Charles Wyville Thomson, the distinguished biologist mentioned earlier, who spent many months exploring the depths of the North Sea with nets and trawls and other instruments, speculated about the mixed blessings bioluminescence might bestow. Describing one evening's catch of starfish, snared in deep water off the coast of Scotland, he noted, in *Depths of the Sea:*

> The tangles were sprinkled over with stars of the most brilliant uranium green. The light was not constant, nor continuous over all the star, but sometimes it struck out a line of fire all around the disk, flashing . . . up to the centre . . . or the whole five rays would light up at the ends and spread the fire inwards. . . . It is difficult to doubt that in a sea swarming with predaceous crustaceans . . . phosphorescence must be a fatal gift.

Fatal for some, perhaps, but advantageous enough that about 80 percent of the animals in the dimly illuminated midocean depths, at 650 to 3,900 feet (200 to 1,200 meters), have the ability to produce light, sometimes to locate food or use as a lure, sometimes to signal a prospective mate, and perhaps sometimes to frighten, distract, or decoy a determined pursuer. Nearer the surface and in deeper water, the percentage of light bearers appears to be less, but clearly, bioluminescence is a widespread, fundamental phenomenon of profound importance to life in most of the biosphere.

With *Jim*, I stood in a place where it is more normal for the local residents to have some kind of bioluminescence than to be without it. Of those that do not, many are equipped with eyes more exquisitely light-sensitive than those of cats and owls, able to register clear images in illumination that to me appears nonexistent. To them, *Jim* and the *Star II* submersible must have been a blindingly dazzling sight, aliens with "photophores" more powerfully brilliant than those of the largest squid, fish, or crustacean ever to venture into their domain. One such creature, a sinuously lovely cat shark with glowing green eyes, seemed disoriented by the sub's lights, bumping into a sponge as it careened away into the dark sea beyond.

With the sub's light turned off, I willed my eyes to adjust quickly to the barely visible seascape, wishing that I could enjoy even for a while the enhanced light-gathering skills of a hatchetfish, and longing to catch a glimpse of one of the deep-sea squids that emits clouds of glowing ink when frightened. Various deep-sea creatures employ a similar "squirt and run" strategy, using a burst of luminescence as a decoy while they make good their escape. Tiny crustaceans known to afficionados as ostracods use a dash of luminescence for other purposes. These tiny creatures manufacture in a special gland one of the critical chemicals needed for light production, luciferin, and in another, an enzyme, luciferase, that is required to activate the light-producing process. When the ostracod is excited (usually a male seeking to impress a nonluminous female, or outshine several rivals), both glands empty their contents into the water, where they react to form a miniature puff of astonishingly brilliant blue light.

In vain I looked for evidence of ostracods and squid, but minute sparks of light from disturbed microorganisms flashed as I moved *Jim*'s arm, and then a startling burst of blue fire erupted from a surprising source. I had brushed against a spiraling bamboo coral taller than *Jim*, initiating a light show that would have impressed even the most discriminating female ostracod.

I had landed with the sub in the midst of at least a hundred coral colonies, miraculously managing not to crush any, although several were within easy reach. Named for their resemblance to jointed stalks of bamboo, the stately formation appeared pale and unobtrusive until touched. The most gentle nudge of my "claw" provoked ring after ring of blue light to pulse from the point of contact down the full length of the coral, small bright circles cascading in neatly spaced sequences, fading to darkness after nearly a minute. Curious, I touched one of the spires at the base and near the tip and watched, anxious to see what would happen when descending rings collided with those racing upward. Would they cancel each other out, or what? Serenely, the miniature fiery blue doughnuts merged, then each passed through the other and continued onward, apparently unperturbed by what appeared to me to be a setup for a truly scintillating encounter.

I have to wonder about the usefulness of such powerful light-generating capability for a colony of animals that is firmly rooted in place. Is touch required to turn on the lights? If so, is it useful as a means of signaling clumsy fish to be more careful about where they swim? Might those venturing a bite of the coral's clusters of soft, delectable white tentacles be deterred by the equivalent of a deep-sea burglar alarm? Are there times, perhaps at the moment of spawning, when the lights come on for reasons obscure to human observers but of vital significance to the hundreds of interconnected polyps that make up a single coral colony? Or, I ask myself, is it possible that there is no special, serious function requiring a practical explanation of the sort that will satisfy rational human inquiry? Maybe bamboo coral just is that way. Period.

Stephen J. Pyne

The Ice: A Journey to Antarctica (1986) may seem an anomaly at first among the works of environmental historian Stephen J. Pyne (b. 1949). He is best known for his "Cycle of Fire," a series of books, beginning with Fire in America: A Cultural History of Wildland and Rural Fire *(1982), that investigates the interaction between humankind, fire, and the earth across epochs and continents.* The Ice, *based on Pyne's three-month residence in Antarctica, paradoxically forms part of that cycle. In Pyne's words: "Could the land without fire have a place in a suite of fire histories? It could, if fire was considered a kind of culture hero, and if a Cycle of Fire was conceived in mythic terms. Antarctica could conclude the grand narrative: here fire died." Here, as in all of his works, Pyne demonstrates his gift for revealing the dynamic complexity of elemental forces.*

from *The Ice: A Journey to Antarctica*

THE great berg spins in a slow, counterclockwise gyre.

It is only another of a series of rotations that have characterized the berg's fantastic journey. The continental plates that comprise the land form a lithospheric mosaic and spin with the infinitesimal patience of geologic time; the Southern Ocean courses around them, the gyre of the circumpolar current; storm cells swirl over the ocean, epicycles of the polar vortex; sea ice floes, like a belt of asteroids, circle endlessly, a life cycle of freezing and melting; icebergs, large and small, circle like comets around their peculiar icy sun. Superimposed over all these motions, the Earth itself rotates around its pole and revolves around the Sun. The ice terranes ring the core like concentric crystalline spheres. The ice mass that became the berg has passed from ice dome to sheet ice to glacier ice to shelf ice to pack ice to the diminutions of the bergs, cycle by cycle, like the gears of an ice orrery. The large bergs fragment into smaller bergs, the small bergs into bergy bits, the bits into growlers, the growlers into brash ice, the brash into chips and meltwater. With each outward frontier the pace of activity quickens.

Ice informs the geophysics and geography of Antarctica. It connects land to land, land to sea, sea to air, air to land, ice to ice. The Antarctic atmosphere consists of ice clouds and ice vapor. The hydrosphere exists as ice rivers and ice seas. The lithosphere is composed of ice plateaus and ice mountains. Even those features not completely saturated with ice are vastly reduced. The atmosphere is much thinner at the poles than elsewhere, in part because of the great height of the polar ice sheet. The hydrosphere is charged with bergs and coated with ice floes; during the polar night, its cover of sea ice effectively doubles the total ice field of Antarctica. The lithosphere is little more than a matrix for ice. Less than 3 percent of Antarctica consists of exposed rock, and the rock is profoundly influenced by periglacial processes, an indirect manifestation of ice.

Out of simple ice crystals is constructed a vast hierarchy of ice masses, ice terranes, and ice structures. These higher-order ice forms collectively compose the entire continent: *the icebergs*: tabular bergs, glacier bergs, ice islands, bergy bits, growlers, brash ice, white ice, blue ice, green ice, dirty ice; *the sea ices*: pack ice, ice floes, ice rinds, ice hummocks, ice ridges, ice flowers, ice stalactites, pancake ice, frazil ice, grease ice, congelation ice, infiltration ice, undersea ice, vuggy ice, new ice, old ice, brown ice, rotten ice; *the coastal ices*: fast ice, shore ice, glacial-ice tongues, ice piedmonts, ice fringes, ice cakes, ice foots, ice fronts, ice walls, floating ice, grounded ice, anchor ice, rime ice, ice ports, ice shelves, ice rises, ice bastions, ice haycocks, ice lobes, ice streams; *the mountain ices*: glacial ice, valley glaciers, cirque glaciers, piedmont glaciers, ice fjords, ice layers, ice pipes, ice falls, ice folds, ice faults, ice pinnacles, ice lenses, ice aprons, ice falls, ice fronts, ice slush; *the ground ices*: ice wedges, ice veins, permafrost; *the polar plateau ices*: ice sheets, ice caps, ice domes, ice streams, ice divides, ice saddles, ice rumples; *the atmospheric ices*: ice grains, ice crystals, ice dust, pencil ice, plate ice, bullet ice. The ice field is organized into a series of roughly concentric ice terranes, like the ordered rings comprising the hierarchy of Dante's cosmology.

It is not merely the variety of ice that is overwhelming: the magnitude of ice is no less staggering. The Earth, the fabled water planet, is also an ice planet. More than 10 percent of the terrestrial Earth now lies under ice, with another 14 percent affected by periglacial environments and permafrost. Some 7 percent of the world ocean is covered by sea ice, and at any minute nearly 25 percent of the world ocean is affected by ice, especially icebergs. The vast proportion of the bergs inhabit the Southern Ocean, corralled by the Antarctic convergence. Of the Earth's cryosphere, 99 percent is glacial ice, and 96 percent of that—over 60 percent of the world's freshwater reserves—is in Antarctica. Within past geologic eras, the proportion of ice on the Earth has grown enormously. During the last glaciation in the Pleistocene, ice extended over 30 percent of the planet's land surface and affected 50 percent of the world ocean. The immensity of the ice sheet even today is sufficient to deform the entire planet, so depressing the south polar region as to make the globe slightly pear-shaped.

The Ice is, in turn, a constituent of an ice regime broadcast throughout the solar system. Pluto is an entire ice planet; the satellites of the outer planets are ice moons. On Mars and Earth, there are polar ice sheets; on some asteroids and amid the rings of Saturn, ice debris; and in the form of comets, interplanetary icebergs from the Oort cloud. The Earth's cryosphere joins it to other worlds and other times—to the outer solar system and to vanished geologic pasts. It is a white warp in space and time. That the Earth's ice consists not of ammonia or carbon dioxide or methane but of water, that it is crystalline rather than amorphous, and that the planet's temperature range falls within the triple point of water account for the Earth's uniqueness, and dynamism, as a member of the ice cosmos.

The berg contains a record of all this. Its travels have a mythic quality, a retrograde journey out of an underworld. It is a voyage that joins microcosm to macrocosm, that builds from a single substance—ice crystals—a vast, almost unbounded continent. Yet a descent to this underworld—from the ice-induced fog that shrouds the continent to the unblinking emptiness that commands its center—does not lead to more splendid scenes, as a trip through the gorge of the Grand Canyon does, or to richer displays of life, as a voyage to the interior of the Amazon does, or to more opulent civilizations, living or dead, as the excavation of Egypt's Valley of the Kings or the cities of Troy does, or to greater knowledge, as the ultimately moral journeys of Odysseus, Aeneas, Dante, even Marlowe do. It leads only to more ice. Almost everything is there because almost nothing is there.

Antarctica is the Earth's great sink, not only for water and heat but for information. Between core and margin there exist powerful gradients of energy and information. These gradients measure the alienness of The Ice as a geographic and cultural entity. The Ice is profoundly passive: it does not give, it takes. The Ice is a study in reductionism. Toward the interior everything is simplifed. The Ice absorbs and, an imperfect mirror, its ineffable whiteness reflects back what remains. Toward the perimeter, ice becomes more complex, its shapes multiply, and its motions accelerate. The ephemeral sample, the berg, is more interesting than the invariant whole, the plateau. The extraordinary isolation of Antarctica is not merely geophysical but metaphysical. Cultural understanding and assimilation demand more than the power to overcome the energy gradient that surrounds The Ice: they demand the capacity and desire to overcome the information gradient. Of all the ice masses in Greater Antarctica the berg is the most varied, the most informative, and the most accessible. The assimilation of The Ice begins with the assimilation of the iceberg.

The great berg hesitates.

A cloud passes before the sun. The berg glows blue amid a tar-black sea. Then almost imperceptibly it retreats, drawn back into the fog and pack ice, back into the first of the great veils of The Ice.

John McPhee

Few contemporary American writers have shown the wide-ranging curiosity of John McPhee (b. 1931). In more than 20 books he has explored basketball, the environmental movement, the New Jersey Pine Barrens, nuclear weapons design, bark canoes, and recent discoveries in geology. The excerpt printed here from Looking for a Ship *(1990) examines the dangers of contemporary seafaring, and reminds us how little protection modern technology can offer ultimately against the immense elemental forces of wind and water.*

from *Looking for a Ship*

BELOW the bridge deck is the boat deck, and on the boat deck is Captain Washburn's office. Nine A.M. I often sit here in the morning drinking coffee, reading manifests, and listening to him. "My house is your house," he says, and the remark is especially amiable in this eight-deck tower called the house. During the night, a planned avalanche occurred in the office. From seaport to seaport, papers accumulate on the captain's desk. "Paperwork has become the bane of this job," he says. "If a ship doesn't have a good copying machine, it isn't seaworthy. The more ports, the more papers. South American paperwork is worse than the paperwork anywhere else in the world but the Arab countries and Indonesia." Deliberately, he allows the pile on his desk to rise until a deep roll on a Pacific swell throws it to the deck and scatters it from bulkhead to bulkhead. This he interprets as a signal that the time has come to do paperwork. The paper carpet may be an inch deep, but he leaves it where it fell. Bending over, he picks up one sheet. He deals with it: makes an entry, writes a letter—does whatever it requires him to do. Then he bends over and picks up another sheet. This goes on for a few days until, literally, he has cleared his deck.

The roll that set off last night's avalanche was probably close to thirty degrees. In a roll that is about the same, my tape recorder shoots across the office and picks up the captain with Doppler effect. Retrieving it, I ask him, "How many degrees will Stella roll?"

"She'll roll as much as she has to. She'd roll fifty degrees if you'd let her—if she was loaded wrong—but normally she'll roll in the twenty-to-thirty-degree range. That's average for ships. It doesn't slow her down or hurt her. She is a deep-sea vessel, built for rough weather. We don't see much rough weather down here. We used to run this coast with the hatches open. That would be suicidal anywhere else. Every day, somewhere someone is getting it from weather. They're running around. They're hitting each other. They're disappearing without a trace." Once, in a great storm, Terrible Terry Harmon said to Washburn, "Do you know how to pray?" When Washburn nodded, Harmon said, "Then try that. That's the only thing that's going to save us now."

Straightening up with a sheet of paper in his hand, Captain Washburn looks out a window past a lifeboat in its davits and over the blue sea. After a moment, he says, "I love going to sea. I do not love that sea out there. That is not my friend. That is my absolute twenty-four-hour-a-day sworn enemy." He shows me a map of maritime casualties. He also has back issues of the *Mariners Weather Log*, a publication of the National Oceanic and Atmospheric Administration that chronicles marine disasters throughout the world and features among its reported storms a "Monster of the Month." Nautical charts, such as the ones in use in our chartroom, include a surprising number of symbols denoting partially submerged wrecks and completely submerged wrecks. Nearly all the ships that appear on modern charts have been wrecked in the past fifty years. "Here's a handsome ship went down," the captain continues, with a finger on his map. "She just went out and was never heard from again. So it isn't just these little nondescript ships like In God We Trust that disappear. Almost every hour of every day someone is getting it. Right now someone is getting it somewhere."

A likely place is a foul sea about eight hundred miles north of Hawaii that is known to merchant seamen as the Graveyard of the North Pacific. "You can pick it up on the shortwave," Washburn says. "You hear, 'SOS. We're taking on water. SOS. We're taking on water.' Then you don't hear the SOS anymore." There are weather-routing services that help merchant ships figure out where to go. Washburn suggests that they are in business not to provide maximum safety or comfort but to shave as close as they dare to vicious weather and thus save time and fuel. He happened to be visiting the home office of one of these services when it had a client in the Graveyard of the North Pacific and was guiding it between two storm systems. He wondered what might happen if the storms coalesced. He asked why such ships did not go past Hawaii on a route that has proved safe for four hundred years. The weather-routers said, "Then who would need *us*?"

When Washburn was a teen-age ordinary seaman, he sailed with a master who had written what Washburn describes as "a big sign inside the logbook":

TAKE CARE OF THE SHIP AND
THE SHIP WILL TAKE CARE OF YOU

The sign now hangs in Washburn's head. In his unending dialogue with the ship, the ship tells him things that its instruments do not. There is no Weatherfax map on the Stella Lykes—only the barometer, the barographs, the teletypes from NOAA. The radar can see a storm, but that is like seeing a fist just before it hits you. When a storm is out there, somewhere, beyond the visible sky, the ship will let him know.

"When you get close to a big storm, you can feel it. For some reason, the ship takes on almost a little uncertainty. She's almost like a live thing—like they say animals can sense bad weather coming. Sometimes I almost believe a ship can. I know that doesn't make sense, because she's steel and wood and metal, but she picks up a little uncertainty, probably something that is being transmitted through the water. It's hard to define. It's just a tiny little different motion, a little hesitancy, a little tremble from time to time."

Off Hatteras, things can be really hesitant. A lashed-down crane will pull a pad eye out of the deck. A pad eye is a D ring made of steel two inches thick. "This ship is very strongly built," Washburn says. "She's sturdy and reliable. There's lots of horsepower down there. She will answer the rudder. She will respond. She's a capable and trustworthy ship. You know what she'll do and you know her limitations. They aren't crucial, but you can't expect her to do things where you know she's a little short. You can't suddenly demand that of her and expect to get it. It isn't there. She's American-built. There's good steel in the hull. Those frames are close together. She'll roll on a following sea, but she's got a high-raised fo'c'sle head and a sharp bow. She's built for rough weather. She's built for rough handling. She's built to take seas and fight back. You cannot overpower seas. But she can deal with what's out there. She was built to go to Scandinavia in the middle of winter."

To make the North Europe run in winter is something that many American sailors do everything they can to avoid and others just refuse to do. No matter how straitened they may be and hungry for work, they will pass up the winter North Atlantic. Having grown up near this ocean and knowing no other, I was surprised to learn this. Years ago, when I was a student for a time in Europe and went back and forth on ships in winter, I thought it was normal for the keel to come out of water as the hull prepared to smash the sea. I didn't know anything about load lines—Plimsoll marks—or classification societies. For a ship to thud like a ton of bricks and roll at least forty degrees seemed a basic and expectable standard condition. I had no idea that this ocean in winter was in a category of its own. On various ships on the North Europe run, Captain Washburn has stayed awake for as much as seventy-two hours, catnapping in a chair on the bridge. "You're tacking into weather," he explains. "Winds and seas can become so strong that you can't always go in the direction you want to." For more than four years, he was the skipper of the Ro/Ro Cygnus and most of its runs were to North Europe. In the early weeks of 1983, he was trying to make his way north into the English Channel, but the Cygnus's big diesels were overmatched, overwhelmed. Washburn tacked back and forth almost helplessly, and the ship—five hundred and sixty feet, fourteen thousand deadweight tons—was blown sideways into the Bay of Biscay. "We couldn't get out. We ended up near Bilbao."

On the side of a merchant ship is a painted circle, a foot in diameter, with a horizontal line running through it marking the depth to which the ship can be safely loaded in summer. Near it are shorter horizontal lines, more or less like the rungs of a ladder. They indicate the depth to which the ship can be safely loaded in various seasons and places. The highest line, representing the heaviest permissible load, is marked "TF." Tropical fresh. This means that you can go up a river in the tropics to a place like Guayaquil, load yourself down to the TF line, and go back to the ocean, where the density of the water will lift the ship to another line, marked "T." That is as deeply loaded as you are permitted to be in a tropical ocean. These levels, worked out specifically for each ship, "take into consideration the details of length, breadth, depth, structural strength and design, extent of superstructure, sheer, and round of beam," and are collectively called the Plimsoll mark, after Samuel Plimsoll, a member of Parliament who, in the eighteen-seventies, wrote the act creating them in order to outlaw the greed-driven excessive loading that was the primary factor in the sinking of ships. When British people call rubber-soled deck and tennis shoes plimsolls, they are referring to him. The United States adopted the Plimsoll mark more than fifty years later. Load lines are set by classification societies, which are private companies that play a checking, testing, and supervisory role in ship construction—services that are optional in the sense that if you don't sign up for them no one will insure your ship. Society initials appear on the hull of a ship as a part of the Plimsoll mark: the American Bureau of Shipping (AB), Lloyd's Register (LR), Bureau Veritas (BV), Germanischer Lloyd (GL), Norske Veritas (NV). Below the summer load line is a line marked "W." It marks the depth to which the ship can be safely loaded in winter. Some distance below that is the lowest line of all. It is marked "WNA." To burden a ship only to that line is to give it the lightest load in the whole Plimsoll series. The WNA line marks the maximum depth to which the ship can be safely loaded in the winter North Atlantic. Andy has remarked about a company that runs to Iceland, "If you get a ship on that line in the winter, you're going to get creamed and you know it." The North Sea, the Cape of Good Hope, Cape Horn, and the Gulf of Alaska are the stormiest waters in the shipping world after the winter North Atlantic.

The great-circle route between North Europe and New York bucks the storms of the upper latitudes. Captain Washburn likes to say that if you were to take two new ships and run one to North Europe via the Azores and the other to North Europe on the great circle, after a year you would have one new ship and one "damaged, beat-up ship." He continues, "If you go south and the weather comes after you, you can go on going south. If you go north and the weather comes after you, you have containers over the side and the crew in the hold chasing loose cargo. You—you are going nowhere."

While Vernon McLaughlin was on the American Legacy, her skipper tried to run to the north of a storm and ended up against Newfoundland in a Force 12 gale.

"For two days, the ship pounded as it pitched, and rolled forty; you looked out the sides in a trough, and it looked as if you were underwater. There was a great crack in the superstructure in front of the house. Containers were lost over the side. Others were stood against each other like swords when a marine gets married. One that broke open—shoes fell out of it for the rest of the voyage. On other ships, I have seen seamen fall on their knees and pray, they were so afraid."

While Andy was night-mating the Sea-Land Performance in Charleston, Captain Crook told me about a January crossing he had made years before on the great-circle route from the Virginia capes to the Strait of Gibraltar. "We hit the worst sea storm to hit the North Atlantic ocean in two hundred years," he said. "For fifty-two hours, the captain was on the bridge trying to save the ship. Speeding up in the trough to maintain control, slowing up just before the crest so he wouldn't pound the ship too hard. Waves tore the mast off. The bridge was a hundred and fifteen feet off the water. Waves went over us. The decks were solid ice. Whole tractor-trailers were washed over the side. A forty-five-ton truck-crane was loose on the deck like a battering ram. House trailers on the second deck were completely demolished. I was truly afraid." An ordinary seaman was on lookout on the bridge when the ship lurched and hurled him through the wheelhouse door onto the port-side bridge wing, where he slid on his back across ice and went through the railing. He grabbed the railing, hung on, and dangled above the monstrous sea. Crook went out and pulled him back.

Andy once said to me, "I love being up on the bridge when it's rough. I enjoy being on watch in rough weather. It's so impressive. It's spectacular. Huge seas. Strong winds. At some point, you cross from awe to terror. I haven't been at that point yet—the ultimate storm. It could change my attitude." Andy hasn't seen anything worse than a fifty-five-foot sea breaking over him when he was running coastwise on the Spray in the winter North Atlantic. "My height of eye was fifty-two feet off the water, and the water broke over the bridge and hit the radar mast. Water went down stacks into the engine room." Not enough water to change his attitude.

That wave was what the *Mariners Weather Log* calls an ESW, or Extreme Storm Wave—a rogue wave, an overhanging freak wave. Coincidence tends to produce such waves—for example, when the waters of colliding currents are enhanced by tidal effects in the presence of a continental shelf. Often described as "a wall of water," an Extreme Storm Wave will appear in a photograph to be a sheer cliff of much greater height than the ship from which the picture was taken. Captain Washburn calls it "a convex wave." He goes on to say, "You don't get up it before it's down on your foredeck. The center is above sixty feet high. You can't ride over the center. You *can* ride over the edge. A ship has no chance if the wave hits just right. It will break a ship in two in one lick. Because of the trough in front of it, mariners used to say that they fell into a hole in the ocean."

In the winter North Atlantic, the demac David Carter has oftentimes tied himself in his bunk after propping his mattress up and wedging himself against the bulkhead—to avoid getting thrown out and injured by a forty-five- or fifty-degree roll. He got his first ship after nearly everyone aboard had been injured. On one voyage, Carter had a big chair in his cabin that was "bouncing off the bulkhead like a *tennis* ball." In his unusually emphatic, italic way of speaking, he goes on, "Pots won't stay on a *stove*. After a night of no *sleep*, a full day of work, you get nothing but a *baloney* sandwich if you're lucky. They soak the tablecloth so nothing will *slide*. I hope you won't get to see that. If you wonder why we *party* and get *drunk* when we're in port, that's why."

On February 11, 1983, a collier called Marine Electric went out of the Chesapeake Bay in a winter storm with a million dollars' worth of coal. She was a ship only about ten per cent shorter than the Stella Lykes and with the same beam and displacement. Our chief mate, J. Peter Fritz, wished he were aboard her. She was headed for Narragansett Bay, her regular run, and his home is on Narragansett Bay. He grew up there. As a kid, he used to go around on his bike visiting ships. He took photographs aboard the ships, developed and printed them at home, and went back with the pictures to show the crews. They invited him to stay aboard for dinner. ("Some guys liked airplanes. To me it was just the ships.") He watched the shipping card in the Providence *Journal*—the column that reports arrivals and departures. Working on a tug and barge, he learned basic seamanship from the harbormaster of Pawtuxet Cove—knots, splicing, "how to lay around boats the right way." As a Christmas present an aunt gave him a picture book of merchant ships. As a birthday present she gave him the "American Merchant Seamans Manual."

Peter grew up, graduated from the Massachusetts Maritime Academy, and went to sea. It was his calling, and he loved it. He also loved, seriatim, half the young women in Rhode Island. He was a tall, blond warrior out of "The Twilight of the Gods" with an attractively staccato manner of speech. Not even his physical attractions, however, could secure his romantic hatches. "Dear Peter" letters poured in after he left his women and went off for months at sea. Eventually, he married, had a son, and left the Merchant Marine. For several years, he worked for an electronic-alarm company and miserably longed for the ocean. ("I will not admit how much I love this job. The simple life. Having one boss. Not standing still, not being stagnant; the idea of moving, the constant change.") Eventually, he couldn't stand it any longer, and went off to circle the world on the container ship President Harrison. ("I had *the* killer card. I had planned it.") He made more money in eighty-seven days than he could make in a year ashore. After a family conference, he decided to ship out again. Like his lifelong friend Clayton Babineau, he coveted a job that would take him on short runs from his home port. Every ten days, the Marine Electric went out of Providence for Hampton Roads, and nine days later she came back. She went right past Peter's house. He night-mated her. His wife, Nancy, said to him, "Hey, wouldn't it be great if you got a job on that one? You could be home with your family." He tried repeatedly, without success. His friend Clay Babineau, sailing as second mate, died of hypothermia that night off Chincoteague in the winter storm. The Marine Electric was thirty-nine years old in the bow and stern, younger in the middle, where she had been stretched for bulk cargo. In the language of the Coast Guard's Marine Casualty Report, her forward hatch covers were "wasted, holed, deteriorated, epoxy patched." Winds were gusting at sixty miles an hour, and the crests of waves were forty feet high. As the Marine Electric plowed the sea, water fell through the hatch covers as if they were colanders. By 1 A.M., the bow was sluggish. Green seas began pouring over it. A list developed. The captain notified the Coast Guard that he had decided to abandon ship. The crew of thirty-four was collecting on the starboard boat deck, but before a lifeboat could be lowered the ship capsized, and the men, in their life jackets, were in the frigid water. In two predawn hours, all but three of them died, while their ship went to rest on the bottom, a hundred and twenty feet below, destroyed by what the Coast Guard called "the dynamic effects of the striking sea."

Peter Fritz, who gives the routine lectures on survival suits to the successive crews of the Stella Lykes, carries in his wallet a shipping card clipped from the February 13, 1983, Providence *Journal*: "ARRIVING TODAY, MARINE ELECTRIC, 8 P.M."

She is remembered as "a rotten ship." So is the Panoceanic Faith, which went out of San Francisco bound for India with a load of fertilizer about six months after Fritz graduated from Massachusetts Maritime. Five of his classmates were aboard, and all of them died, including his friend John McPhee. Getting to know Fritz has not been easy. There have been times when I have felt that he regarded me as a black cat that walked under a ladder and up the gangway, a shipmate in a white sheet, a G.A.C. (Ghost in Addition to Crew). The Panoceanic Faith developed a leak, its dampened cargo expanded, its plates cracked. It sank in daytime. "People tried to make it to the life rafts but the cold water got them first."

Plaques at the maritime academies list graduates who have been lost at sea. A schoolmate of Andy Chase was on a ship called Poet that went out of Cape Henlopen in the fall of 1980 with a load of corn. She was never heard from again. Nothing is known. In Captain Washburn's words, "Never found a life jacket, never found a stick."

On the Spray, Andy went through one hurricane three times. A thousand-pound piece of steel pipe broke its lashings and "became the proverbial loose cannon." Ten crewmen—five on a side—held on to a line and eventually managed to control it, but they had almost no sleep for two days. The Spray once carried forty men. Reduced manning had cut the number to twenty. "Companies are trying to get it down to eleven or twelve by automating most functions," he says. "When everything's going right, four people can run a ship, but all the automation in the world can't handle emergencies like that."

A small ship can be destroyed by icing. Ocean spray freezes and thickens on her decks and superstructure. Freezing rain may add to the accumulation. The amount of ice becomes so heavy that the ship almost disappears within it before the toppling weight rolls her over and sinks her. Ships carry baseball bats. Crewmen club the ice, which can thicken an inch an hour.

To riffle through a stack of the *Mariners Weather Log*—a dozen or so quarterly issues—is to develop a stop-action picture of casualties on the sea, of which there are so many hundreds that the eye skips. The story can be taken up and dropped anywhere, with differing names and the same situation unending. You see the Arctic Viking hit an iceberg off Labrador, the Panbali Kamara capsize off Sierra Leone, the Maria Ramos sink off southern Brazil. A ferry with a thousand passengers hits a freighter with a radioactive cargo and sinks her in a Channel fog. A cargo shifts in high winds and the Islamar Tercero goes down with twenty-six, somewhere south of the Canaries. Within a few days of one another, the Dawn Warbler goes aground, the Neyland goes aground, the Lubeca goes aground, the Transporter II throws twenty-six containers, and the Heather Valley—hit by three waves—sinks off western Scotland. The Chien Chung sinks with twenty-one in high seas east of Brazil, and after two ships collide off Argentina suddenly there is one. A tanker runs ashore in Palm Beach, goes right up on the sand. The bow noses into someone's villa and ends up in the swimming pool. The Nomada, hit by lightning, sinks, off Indonesia. The Australian Highway rescues the Nomada's crew. The Blue Angel, with a crew of twenty, sinks in the Philippine Sea. The Golden Pine, with a shifting cargo of logs (what else?) sinks in the Philippine Sea. A hundred and fifteen people on the Asunción drown as she sinks in the South China Sea. The Glenda capsizes off Mindanao, and seven of twenty-seven are rescued. The Sofia sinks in rough water near Crete, abandoned by her crew. The Arco Anchorage grounds in fog. On the Arco Prudhoe Bay, bound for Valdez, a spare propeller gets loose on the deck and hurtles around smashing pipes. The Vennas, with sixty-nine passengers and crew, sinks in the Celebes Sea. The Castillo de Salas, a bulk carrier with a hundred thousand tons of coal, breaks in two in the Bay of Biscay. The container ship Tuxpan disappears at noon in the middle of the North Atlantic with twenty-seven Mexicans aboard. A container from *inside* the hold is found on the surface. Apparently, the ship was crushed by a wave. In the same storm in the same sea, a wave hits the Export Patriot hard enough to buckle her doors. Water pours into the wheelhouse. The quartermaster is lashed to a bulkhead so that he can steer the ship. In the same storm, the Balsa 24 capsizes with a crew of nineteen. In the Gulf of Mexico, off the mouth of the Rio Grande, fifteen Mexican shark-fishing vessels sink in one squall. In a fog near the entrance to the Baltic Sea, the Swedish freighter Syderfjord is cut in two in a collision and sinks in forty seconds. About a hundred miles off South Africa, the Arctic Career leaves an oil slick, some scattered debris, and no other clues. The Icelandic freighter Sudurland goes down in the Norwegian Sea. The Cathy Sea Trade, with twenty-seven, is last heard from off the Canary Islands. Off Portugal, the Testarossa sinks with thirty. Off eastern Spain, in the same storm, the cargo shifts on the Kyretha Star, and she sinks with eighteen or twenty. The Tina, a bulk carrier under the Cypriot flag, vanishes without a trace somewhere in the Sulu Sea. In a fog in the Formosa Strait, the Quatsino Sound goes down after colliding with the Ever Linking. In the English Channel, the Herald of Free Enterprise overturns with a loss of two hundred. The Soviet freighter Komsomolets Kirgizzii sinks off New Jersey. In the North Sea, the bridge of the St. Sunnivar is smashed by a hundred-foot wave. After a shift of cargo, the Haitian freighter Aristeo capsizes off Florida. On the Queen Elizabeth 2, Captain Lawrence Portet ties himself to a chair on the bridge. Among the eighteen hundred passengers, many bones are broken. Seas approach forty feet. After a series of deep rolls, there are crewmen who admit to fearing she would not come up. Off the Kentish coast with a hundred and thirty-seven thousand tons of crude, the tanker Skyron, of Liberian registry, plows a Polish freighter. The tanker bursts into flames. The fire is put out before it can reach the crude. Fifty-seven crewmen abandon two bulk carriers in the Indian Ocean. The Hybur Trader loses seventeen containers in a storm off Miami Beach. On the same day, off Fort Lauderdale, a Venezuelan crew of twenty-five abandons the container ship Alma Llanera. The Frio, out of Miami for Colombia, sinks off Yucatan. In the Gulf of Alaska, the Stuyvesant spills fifteen thousand barrels of Alaska crude. The Rolandia —twenty-seven hundred tons—capsizes off France. The Ro/Ro Vinca Gordon capsizes off the Netherlands. The Vishra Anurag, a cargo ship under the Indian flag, capsizes off Japan. A Philippine freighter capsizes, too, with forty thousand cases of beer. Somewhere, any time, someone is getting it.

Not every ship that goes down is destroyed by time or nature. Or by collision or navigational error. Crews have been rescued from lifeboats with packed suitcases and box lunches. Say South Africa needs oil desperately as the result of an embargo and is willing to pay at ransom rates. You disguise your supertanker by painting a false name, take it into a South African port to discharge the Persian crude, leave South Africa, open your skin valves to replace the oil with water, pack your suitcase, make your sandwiches, leave the valves open until the ship sinks. If you follow this scenario, you will win no awards for originality. Possibly you will collect insurance payments for the ship, and possibly for the "oil" that went down inside her. You may have to explain why there was no slick.

There is a lot of pentimento on the bows of the Stella Lykes. Former names are visible, even in fading light. The ship was built in 1964 and stretched in 1982. When she belonged to Moore-McCormack, she was called the Mormacargo. After Moore-McCormack died and United States Lines bought her, she became the American Argo. After United States Lines died, Lykes Brothers chartered her from financial receivers. Phil Begin, our chief engineer, has said, "We're operating someone else's ship. It's like a rental car. You don't want to come on here and spend a lot of money for one or two years. You want it to be safe and efficient but no more. You put up with irritations. You can't afford to scrimp and save, though. When you read about ships going down, that's what happens."

In Peter Fritz's letters home he avoids mentioning storms. He doesn't want to worry Nancy. On his long vacations, as he leans back, stretches his legs, and watches the evening news, a remark by a television reporter will sometimes cause him to sit straight up. To Peter it is the sort of remark that underscores the separateness of the American people from their Merchant Marine, and it makes him feel outcast and lonely. After describing the havoc brought by some weather system to the towns and cities of New England—the number of people left dead—the reporter announces that the danger has passed, for "the storm went safely out to sea."

Sources & Acknowledgments

William Strachey. *from* A True Reportory of the Wrack and Redemption of Sir Thomas Gates, Knight. Samuel Purchas, *Hakluytus Posthumus; or Purchas His Pilgrimes*, book 9. (London: Samuel Purchas, 1625).

William Bradford. *from* History of Plymouth Plantation. *History of Plymouth Plantation, 1620–1647*. (Boston: Houghton, Mifflin for the Massachusetts Historical Society, 1912).

Roger Williams. Of the Sea. *A Key into the Language of America* (London: G. Dexter, 1643).

Cotton Mather. *from* Magnalia Christi Americana. *Magnalia Christi Americana, or, The Ecclesiastical History of New-England* (London: Thomas Parkhurst, 1702).

William Walling. The Wonderful Providence of God Exemplified in the Preservation of William Walling. *The Wonderful Providence of God Exemplified in the Preservation of William Walling, Who Was Drove out to Sea from Sandy Hook near New-York, in a Leaky Boat and Taken Up by a Whaling Sloop and Brought into Nantucket, after He Had Floated on the Sea Eight Days without Victuals or Drink* (Boston: Francis Skinner, 1730).

Olaudah Equiano. *from* The Interesting Narrative of the Life of Olaudah Equiano. *Slave Narratives* (New York: The Library of America, 2000).

Hector St. John Crèvecoeur. *from* Peculiar Customs at Nantucket. *Letters from an American Farmer* (New York: Fox, Duffield, 1904).

John Ledyard. *from* A Journal of Captain Cook's Last Voyage. *A Journal of Captain Cook's Last Voyage to the Pacific Ocean, and in Quest of a North-West Passage, between Asia and America; Performed in the Years 1776, 1777, 1778, and 1779* (Hartford: N. Patten, 1783).

William Clark. *from* Journals of the Lewis & Clark Expedition. Gary E. Moulton, ed. *The Journals of the Lewis & Clark Expedition. Vol. 6: November 2, 1805–March 22, 1806* (Lincoln: University of Nebraska Press), pages 182–184. Reprinted by permission of the University of Nebraska Press. Copyright © 1990 by the University of Nebraska Press.

David Porter. *from* Journal of a Cruise Made to the Pacific Ocean. *Journal of a Cruise Made to the Pacific Ocean, by Captain David Porter, in the United States Frigate Essex, in the Years 1812, 1813, and 1814* (New York: Wiley and Halsted, 1822).

Washington Irving. The Voyage. *The Sketch Book of Geoffrey Crayon, Gent.* (New York: G. P. Putnam, 1848).

Amasa Delano. *from* A Narrative of Voyages and Travels in the Northern and Southern Hemispheres. *A Narrative of Voyages and Travels in the Northern and Southern Hemispheres, Comprising Three Voyages Round the World, together with a Voyage of Survey and Discovery in the Pacific Ocean and Oriental Islands* (Boston: For the author, 1817).

Owen Chase. *from* Narrative of the Most Extraordinary and Distressing Shipwreck of the Whale-Ship Essex, of Nantucket. *Narrative of the Most Extraordinary and Distressing Shipwreck of the Whale-Ship Essex, of Nantucket* (New York: W. B. Gilley, 1821).

William Lay and Cyrus M. Hussey. *from* A Narrative of the Mutiny On Board the Ship Globe. *A Narrative of the Mutiny on Board the Ship Globe, of Nantucket, in the Pacific Ocean, Jan. 1824* (New London: Wm. Lay and C. M. Hussey, 1828).

James Fenimore Cooper. *from* The Pilot. *The Pilot: A Tale of the Sea* (New York: D. Appleton, 1880).

Oliver Wendell Holmes. Old Ironsides. *American Poetry: The Nineteenth Century Vol. 1: Freneau to Whitman* (New York: The Library of America, 1993).

Fanny Kemble. *from* Journal of a Young Actress. Monica Gough, ed. *Fanny Kemble: Journal of a Young Actress* (New York: Columbia University Press, 1990), pages 1–11. Copyright © 1990 Monica Gough. Reprinted by permission of the publisher.

Nathaniel Parker Willis. *from* A Summer Cruise in the Mediterranean. *A Summer Cruise in the Mediterranean on Board an American Frigate* (New York: Charles Scribner, 1859).

Ralph Waldo Emerson. *from* Journals. Albert R. Ferguson, ed. *The Journals and Miscellaneous Notebooks of Ralph Waldo Emerson. Vol. IV: 1832–1843* (Cambridge, Mass: The Belknap Press of Harvard University Press, 1964), pages 102–116, 121–123. Copyright © 1964 by the President and Fellows of Harvard College. Reprinted by permission of the publishers.

Edgar Allan Poe. MS. Found in a Bottle. *Edgar Allan Poe: Poetry and Tales* (New York: The Library of America, 1984).

Richard Henry Dana Jr. *from* Two Years Before the Mast. *Two Years Before the Mast* (New York: Harper and Bros., 1840).

Nathaniel Hawthorne. Foot-prints on the Sea-shore. *Nathaniel Hawthorne: Tales and Sketches* (New York: The Library of America, 1982).

Henry Wadsworth Longfellow. The Wreck of the Hesperus. *American Poetry: The Nineteenth Century*, Vol. 1 (New York: The Library of America, 1993).

William Reynolds. *from* Voyage to the Southern Ocean. Anne Hoffman Cleaver and E. Jeffrey Stann, eds. *Voyage to the Southern Ocean: The Letters of Lieutenant William Reynolds from the U.S. Exploring Expedition, 1838–1842* (Annapolis: Naval Institute Press, 1988), pages 127–142. Copyright © 1988, Naval Institute Press. Reprinted by permission of Naval Institute Press.

Henry David Thoreau. *from* Cape Cod. *Henry David Thoreau: A Week, Walden, Maine Woods, Cape Cod* (New York: The Library of America, 1985), pages 852–858.

Herman Melville. *from* Mardi: "A Calm." (Evanston: Northwestern University Press / Newberry Library, 1970), pages 9–10; *from* White-Jacket: "The last of the Jacket." (Evanston: Northwestern University Press / Newberry Library, 1970), pages 391–394; *from* Moby-Dick: "Midnight, Forecastle," "Brit," "The Grand Armada." (Evanston: Northwestern University Press / Newberry Library, 1988), pages 173–178, 272–274, 380–390; *from* Israel Potter: "They Fight the Serapis" (Evanston: Northwestern University Press / Newberry Library, 1982), pages 120–130; "The Tuft of Kelp." *American Poetry: The Nineteenth Century*, vol. 2 (New York: The Library of America, 1993), from an unpublished Northwestern-Newberry edition. All texts taken from series The Writings of Herman Melville, Northwestern-Newberry, individual volumes (Harrison Hayford, Hershel Parker, G. Thomas Tanselle, eds.) copyright © 1970, 1970, 1988, 1993 by Northwestern University Press. All rights reserved. Reprinted by permission.

George Henry Preble. *from* The Opening of Japan. Boleslaw Szczesniak, ed. *The Opening of Japan: A Diary of Discovery in the Far East, 1853–1856* (Norman: University of Oklahoma Press), pages 150–153, 155–157. Reprinted by permission of the University of Oklahoma Press.

Walt Whitman. As I Ebb'd with the Ocean of Life; The World below the Brine; A Paumanok Picture; A Winter Day on the Sea-Beach; Sea-Shore Fancies. *Walt Whitman: Poetry and Prose* (New York: The Library of America, 1982).

Mary Rowland. *from* Remarks on Board Brig Thomas W. Roland. Previously unpublished transcription by Joan Druett of a diary. Reprinted by permission of the Three Village Historical Society, Long Island, New York.

Samuel Dana Greene. *from* In the Monitor's Turret. *Battles and Leaders of the Civil War. Vol. 1: The Opening Battles* (New York: Century, 1883), pages 719–729.

Raphael Semmes. *from* Memoirs of Service Afloat During the War Between the States. *Memoirs of Service Afloat, during the War between the States* (Baltimore: Kelly, Piet & Co., 1869), pages 453–456.

Charles Warren Stoddard. Pearl-Hunting in the Pomotous. *South-Sea Idyls* (NewYork: Charles Scribner's Sons, 1897).

Celia Thaxter. *from* Among the Isles of the Shoals. *Among the Isles of Shoals* (Boston: Houghton Mifflin, 1915), pages 20–23, 62–66, 84–91, 114–117.

James H. Williams. Betrayed. "Betrayed," *The Independent* 65 (August 20, 1908): 407–413; (August 27, 1908): 470–475.

Lafcadio Hearn. *from* Chita: A Memory of Last Island. *Chita: A Memory of Last Island* (New York: Harper and Brothers, 1917), pages 14–27.

Mark Twain. *from* About All Kinds of Ships. *Mark Twain: Collected Tales, Sketches, Speeches, and Essays, 1891–1910* (New York: The Library of America, 1992), pages 81–86, 94–97.

Stephen Crane. The Open Boat. *The Open Boat, and Other Tales of Adventure* (New York: Doubleday & McClure, 1898).

Richard Harding Davis. *from* The Voyage of the Transports. *The Cuban and Porto Rican Campaigns* (New York: Charles Scribner's Sons, 1898).

Joshua Slocum. *from* Sailing Alone around the World. *Sailing Alone around the World* (New York: Century, 1900), pages 4–10, 98–109.

Jack London. A Royal Sport. *The Cruise of the Snark* (New York: Macmillan, 1911).

Alfred Thayer Mahan. *from* From Sail to Steam. *From Sail to Steam: Recollections of Naval Life* (New York: Harper and Brothers, 1907), pages 3–24.

Eugene O'Neill. Ile. *Eugene O'Neill: Complete Plays, 1913–1920* (New York: The Library of America, 1988).

Langston Hughes. *from* The Big Sea. *The Big Sea* (New York: Alfred A. Knopf, 1940), pages 3–11, 111–117. Copyright © 1940 by Langston Hughes. Copyright renewed © 1968 by Arna Bontemps and George Houston Bass. Reprinted by permission of Hill and Wang, a division of Farrar, Straus and Giroux, LLC.

Marianne Moore. The Fish. *Observations* (New York: The Dial Press, 1924). Reprinted with the permission of Scribner, a division of Simon & Schuster, from *The Collected Poems of Marianne Moore*. Copyright © 1935 by Marianne Moore; copyright renewed © 1963 by Marianne Moore and T. S. Eliot.

Henry Beston. The Headlong Wave. *The Outermost House: A Year of Life on the Great Beach of Cape Cod* (Garden City: Doubleday, Doran, 1928). Copyright © 1928, 1949, 1956 by Henry Beston, © 1977 by Elizabeth C. Beston. Reprinted by permission of Henry Holt and Company, LLC.

Hart Crane. Cutty Sark. Marc Simon, ed. *Complete Poems of Hart Crane* (New York: Liveright, 1986). Copyright © 1933, 1958, 1966 by Liveright Publishing Corporation. Copyright © 1986 by Marc Simon. Used by permission of Liveright Publishing Corporation.

Ernest Hemingway. After the Storm. *The Short Stories of Ernest Hemingway* (New York: Charles Scribner's Sons, 1987). Copyright © 1932 by Ernest Hemingway. Copyright renewed © 1960 by Ernest Hemingway. Reprinted with permission of Scribner, a division of Simon & Schuster.

William Beebe. *from* A Descent into Perpetual Night. *Half-Mile Down* (New York: Harcourt Brace, 1934), pages 197–212. Copyright © 1934 by William Beebe.

Cornelia Otis Skinner. The Captain's Table. *Harper's Bazaar* 66 (June 1932): 72–73, 90. Courtesy of *Harper's Bazaar*.

James Thurber. The Story of Sailing. *My World–And Welcome to It.* (New York: Harcourt Brace, 1942). Copyright © 1942 by James Thurber. Copyright ©

renewed 1970 by Helen Thurber and Rosemary A. Thurber. Reprinted by arrangement with Rosemary A. Thurber and The Barbara Hogenson Agency. All rights reserved.

James Agee. Havana Cruise. Paul Ashdown, ed. *James Agee: Selected Journalism* (Knoxville: University of Tennessee Press, 1985). Copyright © 1937 by Time, Inc. Reprinted by permission of Time Inc

John Steinbeck. *from* Sea of Cortez. John Steinbeck and Edward Ricketts, *The Log from the Sea of Cortez: A Leisurely Journal of Travel and Research*. (New York: Viking, 1941), pages 210–213. Copyright © 1941 by John Steinbeck and Edward F. Ricketts. Copyright renewed © 1969 by John Steinbeck and Edward F. Ricketts, Jr. Used by permission of Viking Penguin, a division of Penguin Putnam Inc.

Alvin Kernan. Cruising. *Crossing the Line: A Bluejacket's World War II Odyssey*. (Annapolis: Naval Institute Press, 1994), pages 31–46. Copyright © 1994, Naval Institute Press. Reprinted by permission of Naval Institute Press.

Edward V. Rickenbacker. The Death of Sergeant Alex. *Seven Came Through* (Garden City: Doubleday, Doran, 1943). Copyright © 1943 by Doubleday, a division of Bantam Doubleday Dell Publishing Group, Inc. Used by permission of Doubleday, a division of Random House, Inc.

Robert Lowell. The Quaker Graveyard in Nantucket. *Lord Weary's Castle* (New York: Harcourt, Brace & Co., 1946). Copyright © 1946 and renewed 1974 by Robert Lowell, reprinted by permission of Harcourt, Inc.

Elizabeth Bishop. At the Fishhouses. *The Complete Poems, 1927–1979*. (New York: Farrar, Straus and Giroux, 1980). Copyright © 1979, 1983 by Alice Helen Methfessel. Reprinted by permission of Farrar, Straus and Giroux, LLC.

Rachel Carson. The Marginal World. *The Edge of the Sea* (Boston: Houghton Mifflin, 1955). Copyright © 1955 by Rachel L. Carson. Copyright renewed © 1983 by Roger Christie. Reprinted by permission of Houghton Mifflin Co. All rights reserved.

Peter Matthiessen. Under Montauk Light. *Men's Lives* (New York: Random House, 1986). Copyright © 1986 by Peter Matthiessen. Reprinted by permission of Peter Matthiessen. All rights reserved.

Gary Snyder. Oil. *The Back Country* (New York: New Directions, 1968). Copyright © 1968 by Gary Snyder. Reprinted by permission of New Directions Publishing Corp.

Joseph Mitchell. *from* The Bottom of the Harbor. *The Bottom of the Harbor* (Boston: Little, Brown, 1959), pages 37–68. Later reprinted in *Up in the Old Hotel*. Copyright © 1992 by Joseph Mitchell. Reprinted by permission of Pantheon Books, a division of Random House, Inc., and Sheila McGrath.

George Oppen. Product. *Collected Poems* (New York: New Directions, 1975). Copyright © 1975 by George Oppen. Reprinted by permission of New Directions Publishing Corp.

E. B. White. The Sea and the Wind That Blows. *Essays of E. B. White* (New York: Harper and Row, 1977). Copyright © 1977 by E. B. White. Reprinted by permission of International Creative Management, Inc.

Samuel Eliot Morison. An August Day's Sail. *Spring Tides* (Boston: Houghton Mifflin, 1965). Copyright © 1965 by Samuel Eliot Morison. Reprinted by permission of Curtis Brown, Ltd.

Barry Lopez. A Presentation of Whales. *Crossing Open Ground* (New York: Charles Scribner's Sons, 1988). Reprinted by permission of Sterling Lord Literistic, Inc. Copyright © 1988 by Barry Holstun Lopez.

Sylvia A. Earle. *from* Sea Change: A Message of the Oceans. *Sea Change: A Message of the Oceans* (New York: Fawcett Columbine, 1988), pages 112–121. Copyright ©

1995 by Sylvia Alice Earle. Used by permission of G. P. Putnam's Sons, a division of Penguin Putnam Inc. and Sylvia A. Earle.

Stephen J. Pyne. *from* The Ice: A Journey to Antarctica. *The Ice: A Journey to Antarctica* (Seattle: University of Washington Press, 1998), pages 2–7. Copyright © 1986 by University of Iowa. Reprinted by permission of University of Washington Press.

John McPhee. *from* Looking for a Ship. *Looking for a Ship* (New York: Farrar, Straus and Giroux, 1990), pages 126–144. Copyright © 1990 by John McPhee. Reprinted by permission of Farrar, Straus and Giroux, LLC.

Great care has been taken to trace all owners of copyrighted material included in this book; if any have been inadvertently omitted or overlooked, acknowledgment will gladly be made in future printings.

This book was set in Fournier by The Clarinda Company.
The paper is acid-free 50 lb. Westminster Tradebook.
The binding material is Brillianta, a woven rayon cloth
made by Van Heek-Scholco Textielfabrieken, Holland.
Printing and binding by R. R. Donnelley & Sons Co.
Design by Bruce Campbell.